The Routledge History of Literature in English

'Wide-ranging, very accessible . . . highly attentive to cultural and social change and, above all, to the changing history of the language. . . . An expansive, generous and varied textbook of British literary history . . . addressed equally to the British and the foreign reader.'

MALCOLM BRADBURY, *novelist and critic*

'The writing is lucid and eminently accessible while still allowing for a substantial degree of sophistication. . . . The book wears its learning lightly, conveying a wealth of information without visible effort.'

HANS BERTENS, *University of Utrecht*

This new guide to the main developments in the history of British and Irish literature uniquely charts some of the principal features of literary language development and highlights key language topics. Clearly structured and highly readable, it spans over a thousand years of literary history from AD 600 to the present day. It emphasises the growth of literary writing, its traditions, conventions and changing characteristics, and also includes literature from the margins, both geographical and cultural.

Key features of the book are:
• An up-to-date guide to the major periods of literature in English in Britain and Ireland
• Extensive coverage of post-1945 literature
• Language notes spanning AD 600 to the present
• Extensive quotations from poetry, prose and drama
• A timeline of important historical, political and cultural events
• A foreword by novelist and critic Malcolm Bradbury

RONALD CARTER is Professor of Modern English Language in the Department of English Studies at the University of Nottingham. He is editor of the Routledge *Interface* series in language and literary studies.

JOHN McRAE is Special Professor of Language in Literature Studies at the University of Nottingham and has been Visiting Professor and Lecturer in more than twenty countries.

The Routledge History of Literature in English

Britain and Ireland

Ronald Carter and John McRae

with a foreword by
Malcolm Bradbury

London and New York

First published 1997
by Routledge
11 New Fetter Lane, London EC4P 4EE

Simultaneously published in the USA and Canada
by Routledge
29 West 35th Street, New York, NY 10001

Typeset in Monotype Garamond by
RefineCatch Ltd, Bungay, Suffolk

Printed and bound in Great Britain by
TJ International Ltd, Padstow, Cornwall

British Library Cataloguing in Publication Data
A catalogue record for this book is available from the
British Library

Library of Congress Cataloguing in Publication Data
Carter, Ronald.
    The Routledge history of literature in English:
Britain and Ireland / Ronald Carter and John
McRae: with a foreword by Malcolm Bradbury.
        p.   cm.
    Includes index.
    1. English literature—History and criticism.
2. Great Britain—Intellectual life.
3. Ireland—Intellectual life.
4. English language—History.
I. McRae, John.   II. Title.
PR83.C28   1997
820.9—dc20   96-41221

ISBN 0-415-12342-9 (hbk)
ISBN 0-415-12343-7 (pbk)

Dedicated to Alex and Jean McRae
and Lilian and Kenneth Carter

What he wanted was not his accumulation of notes but an absence of notes: what he wanted was transparency. He was aware that scholarship – the acquisition of knowledge – brought with it a terrible anxiety. How much was enough? How much more was there? Was there any end to it? If one did not possess enough knowledge how could one be sure of possessing more? And if one called a halt to the process how could one not die of shame? Thus with his love for his books went a certain obscure desire to have done with them, or rather not to have been an officious midwife to small thoughts about great masterpieces.

Anita Brookner, *Lewis Percy* (1989)

Contents

List of illustrations   xiii
Foreword by Malcolm Bradbury   xv

THE BEGINNINGS OF ENGLISH:
OLD AND MIDDLE ENGLISH 600–1485
  Contexts and conditions   3
  Personal and religious voices   7
    Language note: The earliest figurative language   11
  Long poems   12
  French influence and English affirmation   15
  Language and dialect   20
    Language note: The expanding lexicon – Chaucer and Middle
      English   23
  From anonymity to individualism   25
  Women's voices   28
  Fantasy   30
  Travel   31
  Geoffrey Chaucer   32
  Langland, Gower and Lydgate   39
  The Scottish Chaucerians   44
  Mediaeval drama   46
  Malory and Skelton   49
    Language note: Prose and sentence structure   51

THE RENAISSANCE: 1485–1660
  Contexts and conditions   57
    Language note: Expanding world: expanding lexicon 62
  Renaissance poetry   64

Drama before Shakespeare   69
From the street to a building – the Elizabethan theatre   75
   Language note: The further expanding lexicon   77
Renaissance prose   78
Translations of the Bible   85
   Language note: The language of the Bible   87
Shakespeare   89
The plays   90
The sonnets   101
   Language note: Changing patterns of 'thou' and 'you'   103
The Metaphysical poets   105
The Cavalier poets   111
Jacobean drama – to the closure of the theatres, 1642   113
Ben Jonson   113
Masques   115
Other dramatists of the early seventeenth century   116
City comedy   123
The end of the Renaissance theatre   126

RESTORATION TO ROMANTICISM: 1660–1789

Contexts and conditions   129
Early Milton   133
Restoration drama   139
Rochester   150
Dryden   152
Pope   157
Journalism   159
Scottish Enlightenment, diarists and Gibbon   161
The novel   166
Criticism   181
   Language note: The expanding lexicon – 'standards of English'   182
Johnson   183
Sterne, Smollett and Scottish voices   186
Drama after 1737   194
Poetry after Pope   196
   Language note: Metrical patterns   202
Melancholy, madness and nature   203

The Gothic and the sublime   208
Language note: Point of view   211

THE ROMANTIC PERIOD: 1789–1832
Contexts and conditions   217
Language note: William Cobbett, grammar and politics   223
Blake, Wordsworth and Coleridge   224
Language note: The 'real' language of men   232
Keats   234
Shelley   239
Byron   243
Clare   248
Romantic prose   249
The novel in the Romantic period   253
Jane Austen   255
Language note: Jane Austen's English   259
Scott   260
From Gothic to *Frankenstein*   265
The Scottish regional novel   266

THE NINETEENTH CENTURY
Contexts and conditions   271
Dickens   273
Victorian thought and Victorian novels   279
The Brontës and Eliot   289
Other lady novelists   294
Late Victorian novels   296
Wilde and Aestheticism   307
Hardy and James   310
Language note: Dialect and character in Hardy   313
Victorian poetry   319
Language note: The developing uses of dialects in literature   338
Victorian drama   340

THE TWENTIETH CENTURY: 1900–45
Contexts and conditions   347
Modern poetry to 1945   351

Later Hardy   352
Language note: The fragmenting lexicon   355
Georgian and Imagist poetry   357
First World War poetry   359
Irish writing   363
W.B. Yeats   364
T.S. Eliot   366
Language note: Modernist poetic syntax   371
Popular poets   373
Thirties poets   374
Scottish and Welsh poetry   379
Modern drama to 1945   382
Irish drama   384
D.H. Lawrence   386
Popular and poetic drama   388
Language note: Literature about language   390
The novel to 1945   392
Subjectivity: the popular tradition   392
The Kailyard School   394
Provincial novels   395
Social concerns   396
Light novels   397
Genre fiction   398
Modernism and the novel   400
Forster, Conrad and Ford   401
Language note: Metaphor and metonymy   404
D.H. Lawrence   411
Woolf and Joyce   419
Language note: Irish English, nationality and literature   429
Novels of the First World War   431
Aldous Huxley   433
Women writers   434
Ireland   436
Early Greene and Waugh   438
Thirties novelists   440

THE TWENTIETH CENTURY:
1945 TO THE PRESENT

Contexts and conditions 447
Drama since 1945 451
   Language note: Drama and everyday language 451
Poetry of the Second World War 469
Poetry since 1945 471
Martians and gorgons 483
Towards the twenty-first century 487
The novel since 1945 489
   Language note: Discourse, titles and dialogism 490
Later Greene 492
Post-war Waugh 493
Orwell 495
Dialogue novels 499
The mid-century novel 502
Amis, father and son 505
   Language note: City slang 507
Golding 509
Fowles and Frayn 511
Novel sequences 512
The campus novel 513
Excellent women 515
Muriel Spark and others 519
Margaret Drabble 521
Lessing, Hill and Weldon 522
Iris Murdoch 523
Internationalism 525
'Insiders' from 'outside' 526
   Language note: English, Scots and Scotland 532
The contemporary Scottish novel 534
The contemporary Irish novel 538
Endings and beginnings 539

TIMELINES

Old and Middle English 543
The Renaissance 549

Contents

Restoration to Romanticism   553
The Romantic period   555
The nineteenth century   556
The twentieth century: 1900–45   559
The twentieth century: 1945 to the present   561

British and Irish winners of the Nobel Prize for Literature   565
Acknowledgements   566
Index   571

Illustrations

Figure 1   Linguistic boundaries and external influences   4

Figure 2   English possessions in France   22

Figure 3   An Elizabethan playhouse. De Witt's drawing of
the Swan, *c.*1596   91

Figure 4   Illustration from *Tristram Shandy*   188

Foreword

Malcolm Bradbury

In our own time the writing of literary history has famously become a difficult activity. In a global age, we have moved away from the nineteenth-century notion that literature is chiefly the product of a nation, place and people. We have also begun to challenge those 'great traditions' in literature that assumed that the history of writing led effortlessly onward from one great genius to another: Chaucer handed the torch to Shakespeare, Shakespeare to Milton, Milton to Words-worth, and so onward to the Olympic stadium of the present day. At the start of the twentieth century, the international 'Modern Move-ment', with its new forms, and its confident spirit of innovation, shook the foundations of the literary heritage. Now more recently 'post-modern' literary theory and cultural analysis have again questioned many of the traditional, monumental notions of author, genre. Litera-ture has increasingly been seen as a text in a context: a product not just of genius but of culture, society and that elusive medium, language.

The fact remains that literary histories still need to be written. The past of literature – what used to be called 'the tradition' – is not simply a random affair. And though international perspectives on literature, and even challenges to its dependence on the written word, are ever more important in a much more accessible, open, internetted, globally communicating world, there really are native traditions or heritages of literature. Their story needs to be properly told. Whether we ourselves are native speakers of English or foreign readers, to understand a literature – whether the literature of our own time or the past – we still need informed, appreciative textbooks that present the nature of that history and clearly show it in its context.

The Routledge History of Literature in English is designed to meet that need. It is an up-to-date enterprise, graphically and clearly presented, with good visual support, telling the story plainly, and without the weight of critical jargon that surrounds so much modern academic discussion. This book explores the long, jagged history of writing in the British Isles, from the Anglo-Saxon and the early Christian period up to the present day. It emphasises the growth and development of the English language, and how changing understanding of the nature of language has affected the growth of writing. It looks in detail at the social and cultural history of the centuries in which the British literary tradition has grown, and explores the historical experience as well as the literary importance of the writers it considers. It gives a sensible and up-to-date record of English writing – poetry, drama and fiction, including genre fiction – in the various regions, emphasising that the British Isles have always been a multilingual landscape, and the language or rather languages have always been in constant change. The Celtic heritage, the Viking invasion, the Norman invasion, the deep penetration of Latin as the lingua franca – all are part of the great word-stock we call English. And that has led to no less profound changes in language's most developed form of expression – that is, in its oral and, above all, its written literature.

Today, for a variety of different historical reasons English has become the world's first language, the modern lingua franca. It is used in all six continents as first, second or third language. Over 300 million people today speak it as a mother tongue; another 300 million use it regularly as a second language. All over the world, writers write in English, to describe worlds, landscapes, cultures for which the language itself was not originally devised. This has led to an extraordinary expansion not just in the spread but also in the vocabulary, structure and power of the language, which contemporary writers ignore at their peril. Writing written in English – whether written in the British Isles or not, and much of it is not – is read everywhere. This vivid, expanding, difficult language is one of the world's richest. Part of that richness comes from the remarkable history of its literary use. This is a language that has constantly recreated itself. The Anglo-Saxon of the *Beowulf* poet is a quite different English from that of the travelled and educated Geoffrey Chaucer, writing under the influence of court French, even while he was recreating the contemporary vernacular. The rich Elizabethan English is something else again – and different from the more formalised, Latinate language of John Milton. Dickens's English carries the noise of the Victorian streets of London when it was the world's biggest city. The language of writers today is shaped by contemporary multi-culturalism, by streets that are noisy with different sounds and by the universal spread of travel and contact.

So there is still a tradition to be remembered: a sequence of forms, myths, preoccupations, cultural debates, literary and artistic trends, great and influential literary movements. The flowering of verse in Anglo-Saxon times and again in the Middle Ages constructed a poetic tradition that still has influence on the most experimental poets of today. The flowering of drama in the Elizabethan age has, despite many transformations, founded a lineage that still has its impact on the theatricality of Samuel Beckett, Harold Pinter, Tom Stoppard, Caryl Churchill, Vaclav Havel or Athol Fugard. The remarkable emergence of the novel as a popular form in Britain in the early eighteenth century not only composed a form in which some of the essential stories of national life have been told, but helped create what is now one of our most important and popular of literary genres, practised right across the world.

As a writer, I can attest to the power of the tradition over what I do. Any writer draws in many ways on the previous heritage of the form he or she uses, the devices and artifices it has developed, the cultural energies it has acquired, the themes and experiences it has explored. The same is true of the history of the language, that elegant instrument of expression which has taken on such a complicated shape over time. A literary language goes through a great range of adventures and experiments. Forms and genres take shape: the comedy and the tragedy, the ode and the epic, the novel and the dramatic poem, blank verse, vers libre, stream of consciousness. Literary language moves between high formality and vernacular ease; common speech frequently transforms conventions when they grow fixed, so creating – as with the Romantic movement – a major literary and emotional revolution. Tradition deposits a vast stock of words and meanings, complex grammatical and artistic devices: simile and metaphor, irony and burlesque and satire. Literature is our link with great humane and moral ideas; it is part of the advancement of learning and the imaginative understanding of other people's lived experience. Literature is always an experiment, as significant and innovative as any in medicine and science – as well as an eternal story of the power of the human imagination.

The true tradition of literature is never simply national; it never has been. Writers constantly venture out of their own landscapes, borrow from other traditions and other tongues, welcome in travellers or influences from elsewhere. This book rightly emphasises the relationships among the different traditions within the British Isles, and their relation with other traditions beyond. T.S. Eliot, himself an expatriate from the United States to the British Isles, probably best expressed the relationship between the tradition and the individual talent. The tradition, he said, is necessary, so we do well to learn it by great labour. But every new writer of significance shifts the tradition slightly, adding something of his or her own, extending, sometimes totally upturning, what has gone before. At the end of the twentieth century, a time with its own conviction of deep and fundamental change in political, gender and global relations, as well as in science and the technologies, that extending and upturning is visibly happening again, as it did at the start of the twentieth century when Eliot was writing. Yet writing still needs the past and the tradition – if only as a help in discovering the present, and prospecting the future.

Speaking as someone who has written several literary histories (of the modern British and American novel, of American literature, and the Modern movement itself), I can welcome the form of the book Ron Carter and John McRae, two well-experienced authors and teachers, have constructed. Wide-ranging, very accessible, it puts literature into a context, while taking its reader through the major writers, the broad trends and movements, the changing eras through to the present. They have been highly attentive to cultural and social change, above all to the changing history of the language and what writers have constructed with it. They have seen that what today's reader is most likely to need is not a narrow, judgemental study, but an expansive, generous and varied textbook of British literary history, based on a wide reading and a firm sense of cultural history. They have addressed their book equally to the British and the foreign reader, and given it a strong apparatus. Each chapter opens with an introductory section giving historical background, and there are good plot summaries and plentiful quotations. There are glossaries of literary terms, useful summaries of the main points of a period. The work also recognises the importance of popular genres – detective stories, science fiction – and deals with a wide range of writers. It explores the transformation of language and literary forms that came with the Modern movement, and is especially strong on contemporary literature. The aim of a good literary history is to take readers – well informed, with an enlarged understanding of its variety and significance – back to the most important books and writers, to signal their value, and place them in useful relation to each other. So, as here, it should lead the way as effectively as possible to the works of past and present that show us British writing does have a long and fascinating history.

Norwich, 1996

From the earliest stages, Malcolm Bradbury and Richard Walker have been generous and constructive in their help and advice; at the later stages, Alan Durant and Helen Phillips provided painstaking and detailed suggestions. Carole Hough, Miquel Berga, Werner Delanoy, Hans Bertens, and Kathryn Sutherland gave invaluable insights and comments. All of these have helped to shape the book, but the authors alone are responsible for howlers which may have slipped through and for opinions which not all of these colleagues and friends might share.

Julia Hall supported the project enthusiastically; Louisa Semlyen and Moira Taylor saw it through with equal dedication. As ever, Jeremy Hunter was in many ways almost a co-author. To all we offer our thanks.

Ronald Carter and John McRae
Nottingham
December 1996

The beginnings of English

Old and Middle English
600–1485

Beowulf, the Dane, dear king of his people
(Beowulf)

CONTEXTS AND CONDITIONS

Literature is as old as human language, and as new as tomorrow's sunrise. And literature is everywhere, not only in books, but in videos, television, radio, CDs, computers, newspapers, in all the media of communication where a story is told or an image created.

It starts with words, and with speech. The first literature in any culture is oral. The classical Greek epics of Homer, the Asian narratives of Gilgamesh and the Bhagavad Gita, the earliest versions of the Bible and the Koran were all communicated orally, and passed on from generation to generation – with variations, additions, omissions and embellishments until they were set down in written form, in versions which have come down to us. In English, the first signs of oral literature tend to have three kinds of subject matter – religion, war, and the trials of daily life – all of which continue as themes of a great deal of writing.

There is a vast expanse of time *before* the Norman Conquest in 1066, from which fragments of literary texts remain, although these fragments make quite a substantial body of work. If we consider that the same expanse of time has passed between Shakespeare's time and now as passed between the earliest extant text and 1066, we can begin to imagine just how much literary expression there must have been. But these centuries remain largely dark to us, apart from a few illuminating flashes and fragments, since almost all of it was never written down,

Fifth-century England

Figure 1 Linguistic boundaries and external influences. Varieties of Old English largely correspond to the borders of the seven kingdoms, as shown on the map above, although the Mercian dialect was widespread in Essex, and the West Saxon dialect dominated in Sussex and south-western parts of Kent

Ninth to tenth centuries

United England 802
Ninth century: Danish invasions
Danish states (to north-east of heavy line) : E. Anglia and Danelaw
   (Five Boroughs) 870
    Northumbria 876
Partition 885
E. Anglia/Danelaw subj. 917
Northumbria subj. 926
Danish Conquest 1013

IONA
795

**NORWEGIAN
VIKINGS**

**DANISH VIKINGS
793/4**

ANGLO-
SAXON
INFLUENCE

NORWEGIAN
INFLUENCE,
10th c.

York

Dublin
839

Nottingham   Lincoln
Chester
Derby Leicester

Stamford

MERCIA

**DANES
868**

London

WESSEX

NORMANDY 911

and since most of what was preserved in writing was destroyed later, particularly during the 1530s.

The fragments that remain confirm that the motivations and inspirations for producing literature, and for listening to it, or later, reading it, are the same all through history: literature can give comfort and consolation (as religious literature often does), can illuminate and mirror our problems, and can affirm and reinforce social, political and ideological standpoints.

The spread of Anglo-Saxon, then English, as a language was one of the most significant elements, over several centuries, in moulding a national identity out of all the cultural and linguistic influences which the country underwent. Icelandic and Viking, Latin and French, Germanic and Celtic – as well as many local linguistic, cultural, and social forces – were all part of the Anglo-Saxon melting pot which would eventually become English: the language of England, then of Britain.

*c.*410	Withdrawal of the Roman legions from Britain
*c.*450	Anglo-Saxon and Jutish invasions from North-West Germany
Early sixth century	Reign of King Arthur (in Wessex; to 537)
597	Establishment of Saint Augustine's Christian mission at Canterbury
793–95	Viking invasions (Danish and Norwegian) in Scotland, northern and eastern England
802	England united, under King Egbert of Wessex
Ninth century	Danish invasions; occupation of eastern England
885	Partition of England (under King Alfred the Great)
917–26	England reoccupied Danish-held territories
1013	Danish Conquest (monarchy, 1016–42)
1066	Death of English King Edward (the Confessor); election of Harold, son of Godwin, as king. Norwegian forces defeated at Stamford Bridge (near York)
	NORMAN CONQUEST: Harold defeated by William of Normandy at Hastings

PERSONAL AND RELIGIOUS VOICES

That evil ended. So also may this!
(Deor's Lament)

The first fragment of literature is known as *Caedmon's Hymn*. It dates from the late seventh century (around 670). The story goes that Caedmon was a lay worker on the estate of the monastery of Whitby, in Northumbria, and the voice of God came to him. His hymn is therefore the first song of praise in English culture, and the first Christian religious poem in English, although many Latin hymns were known at the time. It was preserved by the monks of Whitby, and it is not certain whether the few lines which have survived through the ages are the complete hymn or not.

Christian monks and nuns were, in effect, the guardians of culture, as they were virtually the only people who could read and write before the fourteenth century. It is interesting therefore that most of the native English culture they preserved is not in Latin, the language of the church, but in Old English, the language of the Angles, Saxons, and Jutes.

It is the voice of everyday people, rather than of a self-conscious 'artist', that we hear in *Caedmon's Hymn*, and in such texts as *Deor's Lament* (also known simply as *Deor*) or *The Seafarer*. These reflect ordinary human experience and are told in the first person. They make the reader or hearer relate directly with the narratorial 'I', and frequently contain intertextual references to religious texts. Although they express a faith in God, only *Caedmon's Hymn* is an overtly religious piece. Already we can notice one or two conventions creeping in; ways of writing which will be found again and again in later works. One of these is the use of the first-person speaker who narrates his experience, inviting the reader or listener to identify with him and sympathise with his feelings. The frame of reference of these texts is to the Latin exegetical commentaries and liturgical texts. *The Seafarer*, for instance, while describing much of the day-to-day life of the seafarer, also reflects a close familiarity with contemporary interpretations of the Psalms.

The speaker in *Deor's Lament* recounts the day-to-day trials of life, naming several heroes of Germanic origin and their sufferings, with the repeated chorus, 'That evil ended. So also may this!' Having gone through the heroic names, he arrives at his own troubles: he was a successful bard, or minstrel, who sang for an important family, but now another bard has taken his place. This is the first poem in history about unemployment, but with a refrain that the bad times will pass!

> And so I can sing   of my own sad plight
> Who long stood high   as the Heodenings' bard
> Deor my name,   dear to my lord.
> Mild was my service   for many a winter,
> Kingly my king   till Heorrenda came
> Skilful in song   and usurping the land-right
> Which once my gracious lord   granted to me.
>
> That evil ended.   So also may this!

The Seafarer and *The Wanderer*, along with various other texts, were preserved in *The Exeter Book*, a manuscript containing only poetry, which dates from the end of the tenth century and is still kept in Exeter Cathedral library in Devon. Like *Deor's Lament*, these are two elegiac poems of solitude, exile, and suffering. The theme of the solitary outcast, with no help or protection from a noble lord, is found again here, and memory plays a significant part in the speaker's thoughts. He recalls 'old legends of battle and bloodshed' and wonders 'Where now is the warrior? Where is the war-horse?' This reflects the biblical tradition of questioning epitomised in the famous 'Ubi sunt?' (Where are they?). The only reply he can give in his own context is 'In the night of the past, as if they never had been.'

> He who has wisely mused   on these mouldering ruins,
> And deeply ponder   this darkling life,
> Must brood on old legends   of battle and bloodshed,
> And heavy the mood   that troubles his heart:
> Where now is the warrior?   Where is the war-horse?
> Bestowal of treasure,   and sharing of feast?
> Alas! the bright ale-cup,   the byrny-clad warrior,
> The prince in his splendour   – those days are long sped
> In the night of the past,   as if they never had been.
>
> *(The Wanderer)*

So there is a clash between past and present, between remembered glory and the despair of the moment. But there is always some consolation, some hope for the future, usually ending with a hope of heaven. The speaker – the 'I' of the poem – is a figure who will return again and again in literature through the ages, described here as 'the sage, in solitude, pondering'.

Lo! I will tell the dearest of dreams
(The Dream of the Rood)

It would seem that the church, in preserving texts in Old English, was aware of a particularly English linguistic and cultural identity which, over the centuries, it would nurture in its own written works in different genres, as the language moves towards Early Middle English in the thirteenth century.

The genres include: history, such as the Venerable Bede's Latin *Ecclesiastical History of the English People* and *The Anglo-Saxon Chronicle*; devotional works for those dedicated to a life of religious observance, such as the twelfth-century *Ancrene Rewle*; philosophy, by Alcuin and Saint Anselm, and so on. Translations of parts of the Christian Bible were made, such as *The Book of Genesis*, a version of which was for a long time believed to be the work of Caedmon. This was translated from Saxon into Old English. In its use of the local language, it is a conscious attempt to strengthen the position of the Christian faith throughout the island.

Perhaps the most clearly Christian of Old English texts is *The Dream of the Rood* (the 'Rood' is the Cross), one version of which is found on the Ruthwell Cross, a standing stone in Dumfriesshire (Galloway), in what is now southern Scotland, quite close to Northumbria where the original was written, perhaps as early as the end of the seventh century.

One fascinating feature of *The Dream of the Rood* is the large number of words, phrases and images used for the figure of Christ and his cross: a tree, a glorious gold cross, a simple bare cross, and a cross which speaks of its own transformation from tree to bearer of Christ. As with many texts of the time there are many references to Latin hymns and liturgy embedded in the text. It is a highly visual text, full of joy and suffering, light and darkness, earthly reality and heavenly bliss.

> Lo! I will tell   the dearest of dreams
> That I dreamed in the midnight   when mortal men
> Were sunk in slumber.   Me-seemed I saw
> A wondrous Tree   towering in air,
> Most shining of crosses   compassed with light.

This indicates a certain complexity of expression. It shows an ability in the receiver who hears or reads the story to identify on more than one level the meanings and references the text contains. This is an important feature of all literature, in that it is *representational* more than simply *referential*: it shows, illustrates and exemplifies, often in very refined and sophisticated ways. Anglo-Saxon literature is full of images. The speaker in *The Seafarer*, despite his sufferings as 'my bark was beaten by the breaking seas', rejects land, and the town, because his 'heart is haunted by love of the sea'. 'Bark', meaning the wood from which the ship was made, stands for the whole ship; 'haunted' takes the idea of a supernatural presence and places it in the speaker's heart.

As *The Dream of the Rood* gives us images of suffering and redemption, *The Seafarer* gives us images of ships and the sea. Each provides images of human life, using the tree, the cross, the sea, to stand for aspects of human experience, including, again in *The Dream of the Rood*, the sense of being alone – without human protection and in need of spiritual support from the cross.

> This is my heart's desire,   and all my hope
> Waits on the Cross.   In this world now
> I have few powerful friends.

All the texts in the oral tradition in Anglo-Saxon literature are poetry: they were written down probably many years after they were first performed. Most are short; *Beowulf* is the only long epic poem. What they have in common is their verse form, a double line with a break in the middle (called the caesura, from the Latin). This gives the verse its distinctive rhythm, which the minstrel or scop would use in performing the text for his audience. The use of alliteration, repeated sounds, is another characteristic of Old English verse.

LANGUAGE NOTE
The earliest figurative language

Old English poetry is characterised by a number of poetic tropes which enable a writer to describe things indirectly and which require a reader imaginatively to construct their meaning. The most widespread of these figurative descriptions are what are known as *kennings*. Kennings often occur in compounds: for example, *hronrad* (whale-road) or *swanrad* (swan–road) meaning 'the sea'; *banhus* (bone-house) meaning the 'human body'. Some kennings involve borrowing or inventing words; others appear to be chosen to meet the alliterative requirement of a poetic line, and as a result some kennings are difficult to decode, leading to disputes in critical interpretation. But kennings do allow more abstract concepts to be communicated by using more familiar words: for example, God is often described as *moncynnes weard* ('guardian of mankind').

Old English poetry also contained a wide range of conventional poetic diction, many of the words being created to allow alliterative patterns to be made. There are therefore numerous alternatives for key words like battle, warrior, horse, ship, the sea, prince, and so on. Some are decorative periphrases: a king can be a 'giver of rings' or a 'giver of treasure' (literally, a king was expected to provide his warriors with gifts after they had fought for him).

Beowulf stands out as a poem which makes extensive use of this kind of figurative language. There are over one thousand compounds in the poem, totalling one-third of all the words in the text. Many of these compounds are kennings. The word 'to ken' is still used in many Scottish and Northern English dialects, meaning 'to know'. Such language is a way of knowing and of expressing meanings in striking and memorable ways; it has continuities with the kinds of poetic compounding found in nearly all later poetry but especially in the Modernist texts of Gerard Manley Hopkins and James Joyce.

The only other poet whose name has come down to us is also probably Northumbrian: Cynewulf, who probably lived in the eighth or ninth century. He has been credited with writing many poems (at one time *The Dream of the Rood* was thought to have been his work) but he is only definitely known to have written two poems in *The Exeter Book* and two in another collection, now in the chapter of Vercelli in Italy, known as *The Vercelli Book*. This is a collection of prose as well as poetry on exclusively religious themes. Cynewulf's poems are all on religious themes, such as stories of saints, *The Fates of the Apostles*, and Christ's Ascension.

LONG POEMS

The ruinous deeds of the ravaging foe
(*Beowulf*)

The best-known long text in Old English is the epic poem *Beowulf*. Beowulf himself is a classic hero, who comes from afar. He has defeated the mortal enemy of the area – the monster Grendel – and has thus made the territory safe for its people. The people and the setting are both Germanic. The poem recalls a shared heroic past, somewhere in the general consciousness of the audience who would hear it.

It starts with a mention of 'olden days', looking back, as many stories do, to an indefinite past ('once upon a time'), in which fact blends with fiction to make the tale. But the hero is a mortal man, and images of foreboding and doom prepare the way for a tragic outcome. He will be betrayed, and civil war will follow. Contrasts between splendour and destruction, success and failure, honour and betrayal, emerge in a story which contains a great many of the elements of future literature. Power, and the battles to achieve and hold on to power, are a main theme of literature in every culture – as is the theme of transience and mortality.

The language of *Beowulf* is extremely rich and inventive, full of imposing tones and rhythms: there are a great many near synonyms for 'warrior'; many compound adjectives denoting hardness; many images of light, colour, and blood; many superlatives and exaggerations to underline the heroic, legendary aspects of the tale.

It is, at the same time, a poem of praise for 'valour and venturous deeds', a tragedy, since the hero inevitably dies, and an elegy, since it recalls heroic deeds and times now past. Beowulf dies at the moment of his greatest triumph – 'Beowulf, dauntless, pressed on to his doom' – fifty years on from the killing of Grendel, but then has to face the newest threat: a second monster, a dragon – 'the hideous foe in a horror of flame'. But the poem looks to the future as well, as power passes to 'Wiglaf, the lad', the kinsman who fought at Beowulf's side. The old hero dies; long live the young hero:

> That was the last fight Beowulf fought
> That was the end of his work in the world.

When the battles are lost and won, the world is for the young, and the next generation must take on the responsibilities of the warrior king.

Beowulf can be read in many ways: as myth; as territorial history of the Baltic kingdoms in which it is set; as forward-looking reassurance. Questions of history, time and humanity are at the heart of it: it moves between past, present, and hope for the future, and shows its origins in oral tradition. It is full of human speech and sonorous images, and of the need to resolve and bring to fruition a proper human order, against the enemy – whatever it be – here symbolised by a monster and a dragon, literature's earliest 'outsiders'.

> Beowulf spoke,   the son of Ecgtheow:
> 'My dear lord Hygelac,   many have heard
> Of that famous grapple   'twixt Grendel and me,
> The bitter struggle   and strife in the hall
> Where he formerly wrought   such ruin and wrong,
> Such lasting sorrow   for Scylding men!
> All that I avenged! . . .'

With such a repeated concern for time past, time future and time present, it is perhaps understandable that the date of composition of *Beowulf* cannot be accurately pinned down. Opinions among critics and scholars vary from the sixth to the eleventh century. Recent scholars have challenged the general opinion that it dates from the middle of the eighth century, around the year 750, making it as much as three hundred years later. This is an area of study where there is much controversy and debate – and no consensus.

Beowulf is the beginning of a heroic tradition, emphasising strength and the territorial imperative. But *Beowulf* is also, in a way, a text that comes close to its listeners when performed in the hall of a castle, using spoken language – words which everyone can understand and remember. The structure of *Beowulf* involves a main plot featuring animals and monsters with only the sub-plot involving human beings. The two narratives are interlaced with conflicts between the two groups and even a sermon on human behaviour. *Beowulf* suggests what a hero is, and how important the hero is as a focus of public attention and admiration.

> For he was of all men   the worthiest warrior
> In all the earth,   while he still might rule
> And wield the wealth   of his lordly land.

Bold in battle   fighters fell
Weary with wounds. Death covered earth
(*The Battle of Maldon*)

By way of contrast, another text whose subject is war, *The Battle of Maldon,* is less fanciful. It is again a poem, but more a documentary of the battle than a glorification of warlike values. It recounts a defeat, stressing bloodshed and loss, commemorating a battle in the year 991. As against most of the texts of the time, *The Battle of Maldon* may have been written down fairly close to the time of the events it describes, and this may contribute to its more factual, less 'fictional' tone. This can be read as a rather more realistic depiction of the necessity of victory, and therefore the need for a hero. However, yet again, there is an ongoing debate about whether *The Battle of Maldon* is to be seen as a more distanced work of literature than a more or less contemporary 'semi-documentary' account, with a celebration of honour, fidelity and bravery in the face of defeat. Like all Old English verse, *The Battle of Maldon* uses the divided line to create the rhythm, the sound of battle.

> Then fighting was near,
> Honour in battle.   The hour was come
>
> Doomed men must fall.   A din arose.
> Raven and eagle   were eager for carnage;
> There was uproar on earth.

Perhaps *Beowulf,* in having three generations of mythical monsters as the principal enemy (Grendel's mother, Grendel and the son), is more suited to the myth-making hero it extols. It is fascinating, however, that two such different approaches to war – which is a constant theme in literature – should emerge at almost the same time, in a world which was constantly at war. We do not know who the authors of *Beowulf* and *The Battle of Maldon* were, but the texts clearly show different authorial points of view. Even an anonymous text almost always has something of an author's personality in it, although texts in the oral tradition probably underwent many changes at the hands of individual scops, or bards.

The concept of an author, the single creative person who gives the text 'authority', only comes later in this period. Most Old English poetry is anonymous, even though names which are in no way comparable, such as Caedmon and Deor, are used to identify single texts. Caedmon and Deor might indeed be as mythical as Grendel, might be the originators of the texts which bear their names, or, in Deor's case only, the persona whose first-person voice narrates the poem. Only Cynewulf 'signed' his works, anticipating the role of the 'author' by some four hundred years.

Alfred the Great, king of the West Saxons at the end of the ninth century, was known as the translator of *Cura Pastoralis*, a guide to living and spiritual education. Alfred launched a significant programme of translations into the vernacular, and had a major impact on the shift from Latin to English as a language of learning. He commissioned several more translations, of history, geography, and even of *Caedmon's Hymn* into West Saxon, which became the dominant language in the tenth and eleventh centuries. *The Anglo-Saxon Chronicle*, begun in the last decade of his reign, was probably inspired if not partly written by him. Alfred's influence on translation into idiomatic accessible language took England ahead of the rest of Europe in beginning a tradition of language and literacy in the vernacular which in many ways marks the beginning of the long traditions of literature in English.

FRENCH INFLUENCE AND ENGLISH AFFIRMATION

The world of Old English literature is a world of warriors and battles, a world where the individual, if not under the protection of his local lord, is a solitary outsider in a harsh and difficult society.

The world was to change, slowly but radically, as a result of the most famous single event in English history – the Norman Conquest of 1066. The Normans (originally 'North Men') crossed the Channel from France, won the Battle of Hastings, and took over the kingdom of England, which legitimately belonged to the family of the new king, William the Conqueror.

The Normans brought with them the French language and culture. The two centuries after the Conquest were a period of consolidation, as the two languages struggled to integrate: bilingualism was widespread, with French being widely read and written in England from the twelfth century to the late fourteenth century. It was, however, only after 1204, when King John's losses of French lands led the aristocracy to opt for England or France, that the Norman conquerors themselves began to develop a fuller English identity and a desire to use the English language. Subsequently, more and more French words entered the English language. Lay literacy developed widely at this time and books were commercially produced as English established itself as the language of writing for a growing readership who bought and lent books.

At this time, London established itself as the capital city. The characteristics of the dialect which came to be recognised as the London dialect show that its main influences came from the north: from the university cities of Oxford and Cambridge and from the Midlands, rather than from the south. It now began its rise to prominence as the dominant spoken English – although local dialects remained throughout the land, and are found again and again in the literature of the next hundred and fifty years. Anglo-Latin was different from Paris Latin, and Chancery English developed away from French in many ways. French was finally rejected only in 1415, when King Henry V affirmed English domination, territorial and linguistic, over what had by then become the nation's oldest enemy.

Lenten is come with love to town
(Spring, c. 1330)

The idea of an author comes into English literature significantly with Layamon, in the early thirteenth century. He wrote *Brut*, the first national epic in English, taking material from many sources and recounting tales of the Dark Ages, the two centuries between the departure of the Romans at the beginning of the fifth century and the first traces of the culture of the Britons. He takes the story up to the arrival of Saint Augustine, the first Archbishop of Canterbury, in 597, telling the story of King Arthur and the Knights of the Round Table – which will feature time and again in English literature as a mixture of history, legend, myth and magic.

Layamon's immediate source was a twelfth-century work by Wace, written in French, from Celtic sources, based on the history of Geoffrey of Monmouth. This traced the foundation of Britain back to Brutus, a great-grandson of Aeneas – hero of Virgil's Latin epic, *The Aeneid*, and hero of the Trojan wars described in the Greek epics of Homer, in particular *The Iliad*. This search for classical (not Christian) roots is interesting, as it shows a wish for historical continuity, for heroic antecedents, and for an element of political myth-making.

There had been earlier versions of the history of the country, but this was a conscious attempt to emulate classical epics. There will be many more 'national epics' throughout the centuries, as authors go back in history in order to reinterpret the past in relation to the present. Often, these epics are manifestations of a time of crisis and transition in terms of national identity. Layamon is a case in point. He, in his own words, 'put the book together' as England was seeking to establish its 'Englishness'; absorbing the immensely formative French influences which had come in with the Norman Conquest, but subordinating them to the dominant English culture.

Among the French influences, in literary terms, was a new subject for minstrels, singers and poets. The warrior hero began to settle down, his territories now rather more secure, and to think of other things. He hung up his sword, took up a musical instrument, and began to sing of love. Until the Norman Conquest, there is hardly any love poetry in English literature. Clearly, land was more important than love. However, Old English poems such as *The Wife's Lament* and *Wulf and Eadwacer* could be said to belong to this genre: very probably some of the lost works of Old English will have been love poems.

The new love theme comes from Provence in the south-east of France, where poets known as troubadours gave voice to the concept of courtly love. (The term was only coined several centuries later.) Love was an almost religious passion, and the greatest love was unfulfilled. This is the beginning of the concept of ideal love, chaste but passionate, which will give rise to a huge amount and variety of lyric poetry over the centuries. Very often, the focus of love takes on a religious note: it is no coincidence that worship of the Virgin Mary begins to spread in the twelfth century in Europe. This example dates from the fifteenth century:

> I sing of a maiden
> That is makeles; . . .
> As dew in Aprille
> That falleth on the spray.
> Moder and maiden
> Was never none but she;
> Wel may swich a lady
> Godes moder be.

At almost the same time, around 1100, the good soldier was beginning to go off on the Holy Crusades, all the way across Europe to the Christian holy shrines of Jerusalem. While the menfolk went on Crusades, women were expected to wait at home – embodying patience, beauty and ideal virtue. Like many of the 'roots' of British history, this concept has classical origins. Penelope, the wife of Odysseus in Homer's *The Odyssey*, waited twenty years, we are told, rejecting all suitors in the meantime.

This romantic notion of fidelity, with its feminine imagery – such as the rose, from *Le Roman de la Rose* (The Romance of the Rose), possibly the most influential imported text of the Early Middle English period – establishes a code of behaviour, sets a value on chastity, and orders a subordinate role for women. The rose symbolises the lady's love; the god of love is seen inside a walled garden, with the harsh realities of life, and the masculine world outside. From this image, a whole allegorical and philosophical concept of love developed, although it would be mistaken to see *Le Roman* as a treatise on chaste love: it is full of sexuality, a multi-faceted examination of the nature of love in all its forms from the idealised to the earthy. The work had two authors, and gave rise to the 'Question of the Rose' in a controversy about its intentions: it ranges from misogyny to worship of the beloved, from immorality to chastity, so these contrasting philosophies have made the text both ambiguous and controversial. However, it is perhaps best seen as covering a great range, albeit from a male point of view and starting off a wide-ranging new tradition of love literature which can be both pure and earthy. The love literature of the next few centuries will do its best to uphold this new tradition, despite frequent temptations to bring love to a more realistic and earthly expression.

It is interesting that the two strands of war literature and religious literature united to foster this new theme. Love is thus romanticised, instead of being allowed to become dangerous, anarchic, and subvert the order of things. It has its own emblems, symbols and patterns, but largely without the realistic elements of daily life. Realism, we will find, often has to be kept down if literature is to affirm the accepted dominant values of its time.

As we have seen, French culture and language interacted with native English culture for several generations after the Norman Conquest. A common word such as 'castle' is a French loan word, for example; and the whole romance tradition comes from the French. But this sensibility, culture, and language becomes integrated with native culture.

As well as the beginnings of what came to be called a courtly love tradition, we can find in Early Middle English (around the time that Layamon was writing *Brut*) the growth of a local tradition of songs and ballads. The song lyric might celebrate the changing of the seasons, like 'Lenten is come with love to town' (from *Spring*), it might praise the glories of nature, it might even sing of love in a more direct way than the courtly poem. *Summer is i-cumen in* – welcoming the arrival of summer – is one of the first such songs, and is usually dated around 1250.

> Summer is i-cumen in,
> Lude sing, cuccu!
> Groweth seed and bloweth med
> And springth the wode nu.

The ballad traditionally told a story, based on a character (like Robin Hood, unfortunate Lord Randal, or the Wife of Usher's Well), in memorable rhythmic verses. The ending was generally unhappy, in contrast with the simple, positive assertions of the song lyrics. The ballad *Lord Randal* is a question/answer dialogue, ending in his death:

> 'What d'ye leave to your true-love, Lord Randal my son?
> What d'ye leave to your true-love, my handsome young man?'
> 'I leave her hell and fire; mother, make my bed soon,
> For I'm sick at the heart and fain wad lie down.'

It is difficult to put dates to most ballads, since they were collected for publication centuries after they first appeared in the oral tradition. Some scholars date the earliest ballads to the thirteenth century, others trace them back to the fifteenth century. Whatever the case, this is the beginning of a popular tradition of song, story, and ballad, which will run through every century. It is sometimes quite close in style and subject matter to the more 'literary' writings, but is often a quite separate, distinct and more unrestrained voice of popular dissent and dissatisfaction.

LANGUAGE AND DIALECT

Writers in what we now call the Middle English period (late twelfth century to 1485) did not necessarily always write in English. The language was in a state of flux: attempts were made to assert the French language, to keep down the local language, English, and to make the language of the church (Latin) the language of writing. The major growth of literature comes more than a century after Layamon's *Brut*, and confirms the range of potential languages for literature. Robert Mannyng based his lively *Handling Synne*, a verse treatise on the Ten Commandments and the Seven Deadly Sins, on a French source. John Gower wrote his best-known work *Confessio Amantis* in English (despite its Latin title), but wrote others in Latin (*Vox Clamantis*) and French (*Mirour de l'Omme*). Geoffrey Chaucer wrote wholly in English and gave most of his works English titles, but derived his inspiration and found his forms in a wide range of European sources, including Latin and Italian.

These European influences were largely channelled through London, now the capital city of the kingdom of England. The kingdom was quite different geographically from present-day Britain: it extended into several regions of France, and (from 1284) included Wales, but did not include Scotland.

Writing gave London language the beginning of its predominance as a means of artistic expression. The university cities of Oxford and Cambridge, where centres of learning were established in the thirteenth century, were also part of this cultural and linguistic affirmation, which had London – base of the court, law, and trade – as its focus. The writers we know of lived in the city of London, but they did not write only about city life. Although the poet lived part of his life in London, William Langland's *Piers Plowman* is largely based in the countryside; his origins are believed to have been in the west of England. *Piers Plowman* brings together English traditions and French romance influences.

Many English dialects besides the language of London are found in the literature of the time. The texts are usually anonymous, unlike the London group's works, but some can be identified as probably by the same hand: *Sir Gawain and the Green Knight, Patience, Pearl* and *Cleanness* are examples. However, the provincial 'Gawain poet' cannot be definitively named. The fact that the four texts are found together in a manuscript dating from 1400 may be no more than coincidence, but linguistic and stylistic affinities suggest that they may be by the same poet.

Texts such as *Winner and Waster, Pearl*, and *Patience* also form part of what is known as the Alliterative Revival, dating from about 1350 to the early fifteenth century. This growth of a distinctively English poetic voice recalls the Anglo-Saxon use of alliteration in verse several centuries earlier. In fact, although alliteration is seen as a distinctive feature of Anglo-Saxon texts, there is a greater body of alliterative verse from the time of this 'revival'; and although it is usually called a 'revival', it is perhaps more correctly a flourishing of the form, since it had continued largely uninterrupted since Old English times. Most of the texts originate from an area of the country to the north and west of a line between the Wash and the Severn estuary – very far from London in terms of distance, culture and values.

Layamon, in the early 1200s, was, as we have seen, a figure who linked older historical traditions with modern Englishness. His is the

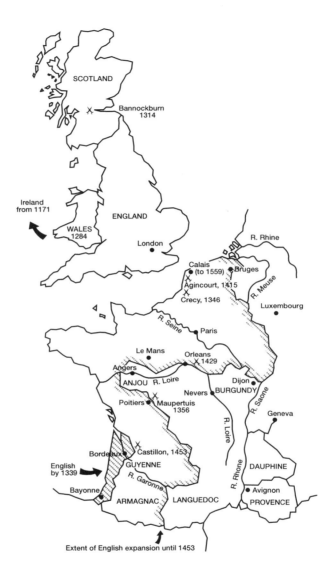

Figure 2 The greatest extent of English possessions in France was reached during the Hundred Years' War (1339–1453). After Scotland was liberated at the Battle of Bannockburn in 1314, it was not until the Union of the Crowns in 1603 that it became part of the United Kingdom. By then England had long since lost its possessions in France – Calais being the last in 1559

first voice in Middle English. As the use of English becomes less self-conscious, writers develop a more colloquial and familiar style, using idioms and proverbs to bring their writing closer to the reader. Since Latin (the language of religion) and French (the language of the conquerors) dominated the nation and its culture for almost two centuries, such writings are a valuable indication of the assertion of a national linguistic identity, despite the considerable diversity of dialects in use.

LANGUAGE NOTE
The expanding lexicon: Chaucer and Middle English

A distinctive stylistic feature of the Middle English period was a rapid expansion in the number of words. These words often entered the language from Latin but by far the majority of imports were French (and, indeed, some of the Latin words may have arrived through the vehicle of French). Middle English vocabulary thus often has sets of words each with a different origin and each conveying more or less the same meaning but with different patterns of use. For example, some modern equivalents are:

Old English	*French*	*Latin*
ask	question	interrogate
kingly	royal	regal
holy	sacred	consecrated
fire	flame	conflagration
clothes	attire	
house	mansion	domicile
sheep	mutton	
calf	veal	

In each case, the Old English-derived lexical items are generally more frequent in English and more colloquial and are more central and core to the language; the words of Latin origin are more formal, learned and bookish in their use; the French words are considered to be more literary in function. It can also be noted that the French words confer a more elevated style on words used in domestic and culinary domains.

French words also penetrated into the law and administration, heraldry, the arts, fashion, and hunting – areas of cultural and political dominance. The French words tended to spread from London and the court as well as locally from the lord's castle. Many of these words came down from a higher social and cultural level and had no equivalent in English. By contrast, English and Scandinavian-derived words are more homely and much more part of a 'ground-level' daily life.

After the Norman Conquest, the language of the Norman ruling class was Northern French. The language of the English court in the twelfth century was Parisian French, which carried more prestige than Anglo-Norman or other varieties. Until the second half of the fourteenth century the language of instruction in English schools was French. The following extract from the *Prologue* of Chaucer's *The Prioress's Tale*, illustrates the extent to which Chaucer made use of words of French or Latin via French origin, particularly for the expression of elevated praise:

> Lady, thy bountee, thy magnificence,
> Thy vertu, and thy grete humylitee,
> Ther may no tonge expresse in no science.

Yet Chaucer also makes extensive use of everyday colloquial speech which contains more Old English-derived words as in, for example, the following brief extract from *The Summoner's Tale*:

> 'Ey, Goddess mooder', quod she, 'Blissful mayde!
> Is ther ought elles? tell me feithfully.'
> 'Madame,' quod he,'how thynke ye herby?'
> 'How that me thynketh?' quod she, 'so God me speede,
> I seye, a cherl hath doon a cherles deede.'

The range and variety of Chaucer's English did much to establish English as a national language. Chaucer also contributed much to the formation of a standard English based on the dialect of the East Midlands region which was basically the dialect of London which Chaucer himself spoke. Indeed, by the end of the fourteenth century the educated language of London, bolstered by the economic power of London itself, was beginning to become the standard form of written language throughout the country, although the process was not to be completed for several centuries. The cultural, commercial, administrative and intellectual importance of the East Midlands (one of the two main universities, Cambridge, was also in this region), the agricultural richness of the region and the presence of major cities, Norwich and

London, contributed much to the increasing standardisation of the dialect. (See also Language notes, pages 62 and 77.)

FROM ANONYMITY TO INDIVIDUALISM

These are the ground of all my bliss
(Pearl)

Many texts from this period are described as 'anonymous', but it often happens that 'anon' has a distinctive voice or style, even though no actual name can be given to the author: 'unknown' might sometimes be a more precise term than 'anonymous', especially in the case of the troubadours.

The anonymous verse characteristic of the beginning of the period shows some of the concerns which will preoccupy the later 'named' writers. The theme of nature becomes important in *The Owl and the Nightingale*, which dates from around 1225. This poem uses the Latin genre of debate (*conflictus*) between two sides in a comic way, to show differing attitudes and values, and uses the English countryside as a setting. The nightingale is described in a rhyme – which no longer works today – as she

> sat upon a fair bough
> and there were around blossoms enough [enow]

This kind of debate, between the serious (the owl) and the light-hearted (the nightingale), can be seen to reflect the period's concerns; torn, as it was, between religious issues and the new thoughts of love.

Winner and Waster, from about 1360, uses the debate form in a more serious way, contrasting the man who wants wealth in society with the carefree person who spends all his money. This is one of the first allusions in literature to the importance of money, and contains a strong element of social criticism: the Pope and his greedy priests are contrasted with the noble lords and their followers. But, like *The Owl and the Nightingale*, no final judgement is given. The reader does not know who wins the debate, and must decide independently.

There is a growing awareness, in the texts of this time, of an audience – a readership – and, consequently, a widening range of effects is used. The audience would probably not have been limited to the dialect where the texts were written, but would have had a wide range of cultural reference – Latin, French and European. The audience was, however, limited to educated court and aristocratic circles: although the production of literature was growing, mass literacy did not happen until more than five hundred years later. At this time there was sufficiently widespread literacy among lay people for there to be a wide circulation of books lent and borrowed, the beginnings of a commercial readership more than a century before Caxton printed the first books in English.

King Horn, dating from about 1225, is the earliest surviving verse romance in English. It is a tale of love, betrayal, and adventure, showing how English has assimilated the characteristics of French courtly stories, and adapted them to a local setting. The range of poems is now expanding rapidly: religious, secular, moral, and political themes are becoming the subjects for writing and reading.

The Alliterative Revival, in the second half of the fourteenth century, and a growing literate readership, expands this range, and many more manuscript copies of texts are found, showing that writing and reading were spreading, and were not limited either to the capital city, London, or to highly educated readers.

Story telling is a fundamental part of Middle English literature. Bible stories had been retold in the Anglo-Saxon period (versions of *Genesis* and *Exodus* in particular). Now, for example, *Patience* (from the late fourteenth century) retells the biblical story of Jonah and the whale, making it both comic and instructive (reinforcing the virtue of patience). Man's smallness in relation to God is stressed, with Jonah compared to

> a mote of dust at a munster door/ so big the whale's jaws were.

The word 'munster' is interesting: interpreted as 'minster' or 'cathedral', it is clearly linked to 'monastery' and – if only in sound – to 'monster'. But the intention is humorous as well as moral, and this is an important step in the handling of religious subject matter. Irreverence, alongside devotion, will become more and more frequent as a feature of writing about religion.

Pearl introduces an original story, in a form which was to become one of the most frequent in mediaeval literature, the dream-vision. Authors like Chaucer and Langland use this form, in which the narrator describes another world – usually a heavenly paradise – which is compared with the earthly human world. In *Pearl*, the narrator sees his daughter who died in infancy, 'the ground of all my bliss'. She now has a kind of perfect knowledge, which her father can never comprehend. The whole poem underlines the divide between human comprehension and perfection; these lines show the gap between possible perfection and fallen humanity which, thematically, anticipate many literary examinations of man's fall, the most well known being Milton's late Renaissance epic, *Paradise Lost*.

Inoghe is knawen that mankyn grete	It is well-known that great mankind
Fyrste was wroght to blysse parfyt;	Was first created in perfect bliss;
Oure forme fader hit con forfete	Our first father then suddenly lost it
Thurgh an apple that he upon con byte.	Through an apple which he went and bit.
Al wer we dampned for that mete	All were damned for that meat/food
To dyye in doel, out of delyt . . .	To die in pain, out of delight . . .

In a sense, *Pearl* is a forerunner not only of utopian writing about a perfect world, but it is also an examination of human limitations and knowledge; a theme which will recur in the Renaissance – in Marlowe's *Doctor Faustus,* Milton's *Paradise Lost* and a host of other texts. It is more humanly direct and personal than these later works, giving the reader a sense of involvement in the narrator's loss and incomprehension. The reader, in a sense, identifies with the personal feelings expressed, and can share the emotions described.

The most significant anonymous text of the period is *Sir Gawain and the Green Knight*, described as a 'lay' by the minstrel who tells it:

> If you will list to this lay just a little while
> I shall tell it straight away, as I heard it in the town.

As with the opening line of *Beowulf* – 'Lo! we have listened to many a lay' – there is an implied listening audience and an explicit, personal voice of the bard. The lay derives from Brittany, and was a kind of French romance of the twelfth century, intended to be sung. There were several imitations of French lays in English. The lay was used to recount imaginative or legendary tales, fiction, rather than historical tales based on fact. *Sir Orfeo*, for example, transposes the classical Greek legend of Orpheus and Eurydice into this form in an English setting.

WOMEN'S VOICES

Marie de France, who was English, wrote in the late twelfth century twelve *Lais*, a series of short romances based on unwritten Breton songs. Marie's was not by any means the only female voice of her time. Hrotsvitha, a tenth-century abbess from Saxony, is generally seen as the first woman writer in Europe; *Ancrene Wisse*, also known as *Ancrene Rewle*, a book of advice on how to live, directed first at nuns but clearly also to a wider readership of women, became one of the main texts of the thirteenth century – it dates from about 1225.

In the following century, Christine de Pisan in France was the first woman to be a full-time, 'professional' writer – and one of the first to question the authority of men's writing. In her *Book of the City of Ladies* she comments on a work by Matheolus:

> the sight of this book, even though it was of no authority, made me wonder how it happened that so many different men . . . all concur in one conclusion: that the behaviour of women is inclined to and full of every vice.

A text by Christine de Pisan, translated by Anthony Woodville, her *Moral Proverbs of Christine*, was the first written by a woman to be printed in England by Caxton in 1478. It is here that the word 'authoress' first appears in English.

Long before Caxton, however, there was a growing readership for Marie's *Lais*, for books of instruction and devotion, and for 'visionary' writing. Julian of Norwich experienced such visions at the age of 30 on her deathbed, but made a miraculous recovery, became a nun and set down her visions in a probing, analytical discussion of such difficult themes as faith, sin, and the motherhood of God. This is the conclusion of her challenging writing, given here in the original Middle English:

> Thus was I lerid that love was Our Lords mening. And I saw full sekirly in this and in all, that ere God made us, he lovid us: which

love was never slakid no never shall. And in this love he hath don all his werke, and in this love he hath made all things profitable to us. And in this love our life is everstand. In our making we had beginning. But the love wherin he made us, was in him fro withoute begynning, in which love we have our beginning. And this shall be seen in God without end, which Jhesus mot grant us. Amen.

[*lerid*: taught; *sekirly*: surely; *ere*: before; *slakid*: diminished; *no*: nor; *everstand*: everlasting; *making*: creation; *which* i.e. that endless vision of God; *mot*: may]

Margery Kempe is quite a different kind of visionary writer but just as original in her way as Christine de Pisan, though less assured than Julian. She dictated her work *The Book of Margery Kempe* (to two men) as she could neither read nor write, but her woman's voice speaks loud and clear down the centuries in her revelations of her psychological state of mind through the dramas of childbirth and intense sexual desires, towards her maturity and a life of contemplation. She speaks of herself in the third person as 'this creature', although she gives the book her own name. Moll Flanders in Daniel Defoe's novel which bears her name is perhaps the nearest later self-castigating heroine of her own moral tale (again given in the original):

> Ower mercyful lord Crist Jhesu, seyng this creaturys presumpcyon, sent hire, as is wrete before, thre yere of greet temptacyon. Of the whech on of the hardest I purpos to wrytyn for exampyl of hem that com aftyr, that thei schuld not trostyn on here owyn self, ne have no joy in hemself as this creature had. Fore no drede, owyr gostly enmy slepeth not, but he ful besyly sergyth our complexions and owyre dysposycionys, and where that he fyndeth us most freel, ther be Owyr Lordys sufferawns he leyth hys snare, whech may no man skape be hys owyn powere.
>
> And so he leyd befom this creature the snare of letchery, whan sche wend that alle fleschly lust had al hol ben qwenchyd in hire. And so long sche was temptyd with the syn of letchory, for owt that sche cowd do: and yet sche was oftyn schrevyn, sche weryd the hayr and dede gret bodyly penawns and wept many a bytter teere and preyd ful oftyn to Owrye Lord that he schuld preserve hire and kepe hire that sche schuld not fallyn into temptacyon. For sche thowt sche had lever ben deed than consentyn therto. And in al this tyme sche had

no lust to comown wyth hire husbond, but it was very peynful and horrybyl unto hire.

[*seyng*: seeing; *Of . . . hardest*; one of the hardest of which; *purpos to wrytyn*: intend to write down; *for . . . hem*: as an example for them; *trostyn on*: trust in; *here*: their; *hemself*: themselves; *no drede*: doubtless; *owyr . . . enmy*: our spiritual enemy (i.e. the Devil); *ful besyly*: very industriously; *sergyth*: searches, investigates; *complexions*: temperaments; *dysposycionys*: characters; *freel*: frail, vulnerable; *skape*: escape; *wend*: thought; *al hol*: completely; *owt*: aught, anything; *cowd*: could; *schrevyn*: confessed and absolved; *weryd the hayr*: wore a hair shirt; *lever*: rather; *deed*; dead; *comown*: have intercourse; *peynful*: painful].

FANTASY

The fairy or fantastic world replaces the classical Hades (or Hell) in *Sir Orfeo*, and *Sir Gawain and the Green Knight* takes this fantasy element to new heights. Sir Gawain is one of the Knights of the Round Table, the followers of King Arthur, who is so much of a presence in English history, myth and literature. Arthur is always seen, as in *Brut*, as the greatest of the English kings, all of whom are linear descendants of the Roman hero Brutus. The poem concentrates on one episode rather than on the whole story, and opens up an ambiguous treatment of the chivalric code of truth and honour. This code is part of the courtly love ideal, with a chevalier being the ideal knight whose behaviour is a model to all. But the chivalric tradition in *Sir Gawain and the Green Knight* is subverted and made impossible by the Green Knight's offering that his head be struck off as long as he can strike a return blow one year later.

> . . . he truthfully told them of his tribulations –
> What chanced at the chapel, the good cheer of the knight,
> The lady's love-making, and lastly, the girdle.
> He displayed the scar of the snick on his neck
> Where the bold man's blow had hit, his bad faith to
> > Proclaim;
> > He groaned at his disgrace,
> > Unfolding his ill-fame,
> > And blood suffused his face
> > When he showed his mark of shame.

The lay is used here to question the value of heroism and the value of historical myths. It brings human weakness to the fore, but at the end ironically reinforces belief in human capacities. Gawain, who knows that deep down he has traits of cowardice and treason and was only protected by a magic belt, the symbol of his contrition, which redeems him and makes him a human hero, returns in triumph to Camelot.

The 101 stanzas of *Sir Gawain and the Green Knight* all end with this four-and-a-half line conclusion, in shorter lines, giving a rhythmic and narrative variation to the regular four-stress line of many earlier works.

In these later Middle English texts, i.e. from the fourteenth century, there is generally a sense of optimism and high spirits which contrasts with the later questioning and doubt that will be found in much literature of the Renaissance.

TRAVEL

One of the first books of travel, giving European readers some insight into the unfamiliar world of the Orient, was published in 1356–67 in Anglo-Norman French. Called simply *Travels*, it was said to be by Sir John Mandeville, but a French historian, Jean d'Outremeuse, may well have written the book. It is a highly entertaining guide for pilgrims to the Holy Land, but goes beyond, taking the reader as far as Tartary, Persia, India and Egypt, recounting more fantasy than fact, but containing geographical details to give the work credence.

Mandeville's book whetted the Western European reader's appetite for the travel book as a journal of marvels: dry scientific detail was not what these readers wanted. Rather it was imagination plus information. Thus, myths of 'the fountain of youth' and of gold-dust lying around 'like ant-hills' caught the Western imagination, and, when the voyagers of the late fifteenth and sixteenth centuries found 'new worlds' in the Americas, these myths were enlarged and expanded, as Eldorado joined the Golden Road to Samarkand in the imagination of readers concerning distant lands.

Mandeville begins a long tradition of writings about faraway places which created the idea now called 'Orientalism'. He talks of rivers such as the Ganges, the Nile, the Tigris and Euphrates, which are, of course, all real. He suggests that Paradise may be somewhere beyond, but:

> Of Paradise ne can I not speak properly, for I was not there. It is far beyond . . . Paradise is enclosed all about with a wall, and men wit not whereof it is, for the walls be covered all over with moss, as it seemeth. And it seemeth not that the wall is stone of nature nor of no other thing that the wall is. And that wall stretcheth from the south to the north, and it hath not but one entry that is closed with fire burning, so that no man that is mortal ne dare not enter.

Not being able to describe Paradise, Mandeville, in attempting to give his writings credibility, concludes:

> . . . of that place I can say you no more. And therefore I shall hold me still and return to that I have seen.

Such writings emphasise cultural strangeness and difference, and for many centuries they have conditioned Western perceptions of the societies they purport to describe.

GEOFFREY CHAUCER

If no love is, O God, what fele I so?
(Troilus and Criseyde)

As we have mentioned, Geoffrey Chaucer used a wide range of cultural references from throughout Europe in his writing, but he wrote almost exclusively in English. This is highly significant, not only in giving him his place as the first of the major English writers, but in placing him as a pivotal figure who encompasses many of the earlier traditions, genres and subjects of literature, applying them in the context of a new, highly active and developing society.

Chaucer was a professional courtier, a kind of civil servant. His writing was a sideline rather than a vocation: the full-time English writer was still a couple of centuries in the future. Chaucer was born into a family of wine traders; he was thus from the class of the new wealthy city gentleman. His work took him to Kent (which he represented in Parliament from 1386), to France, and twice to Italy, where he made the acquaintance of the works of writers such as Dante, Petrarch, and Boccaccio.

Chaucer's first work, *The Book of the Duchess*, is a dream-poem on the death in 1368 of Blanche, Duchess of Lancaster, the wife of John of Gaunt (third son of King Edward III). It is a poem of consolation, modelled on French examples:

'She is dead!' 'Nay!' 'Yes, by my troth!'
'Is that your loss?' 'By God, that is routhe!' [*routhe*: pity]

The simplicity and directness of the emotion, and the handling of dialogue, show Chaucer's capacity to bring language, situation, and emotion together effectively.

The House of Fame (*c.*1374–85) is another dream-poem, this time influenced by the Italian of Dante. It is the first time that Dante's epic of a journey to Paradise, Purgatory, and Hell – *The Divine Comedy* (*c.*1310–20) – is echoed in English. Here Chaucer becomes a participant in his own writing. He is the ingenuous poet who visits the Latin poet Ovid's 'house of fame' to learn about love. He brings together aspects of love which will become the frequent subject matter of poets throughout the ages. Cupid and Venus, passion and desire, innocence and knowledge, are all invoked, using the new verse form of the rhyme-royal stanza. (The name derives from its later use by Scottish King James I in his *Kingis Quair*, *c.*1424.)

The subject of love is taken up again in Chaucer's two greatest poems before *The Canterbury Tales*: *Troilus and Criseyde* and *The Legend of Good Women*. The first takes the Italian writer Boccaccio as its source. It brings together the classical Trojan war story, the Italian poetic version of that story, and the sixth-century philosophical work of Boethius, *The Consolation of Philosophy*. Like Layamon, Chaucer consciously uses other writers' books, and deliberately gives himself the role of intermediary, relating, revisiting and refining old stories.

If Chaucer had never gone on to write *The Canterbury Tales*, *Troilus and Criseyde* would remain as one of the outstanding poems in European literature of the mediaeval period. It has even been called 'the first modern novel'. Although this is an exaggeration, it serves to remind us of Chaucer's considerable descriptive capacity both in terms of character and scene. Chaucer uses, as part of his authorial technique, the reader's ability to *recognise* and *identify with* what is being described. These are the words of Troilus on the joys and pains of love; the first line is a direct use of intertextual reference quoting Petrarch:

> If no love is, O God, what fele I so?
> And if love is, what thing and whiche is he?
> If love be good, from whennes comth my wo?
> If it be wikke, a wonder thinketh me,
> When every torment and adversitee
> That cometh of him, may to me savory thinke;
> For ay thurst I, the more that I it drinke.
>
> And if that at myn owene lust I brenne,
> Fro whennes cometh my wailing and my pleynte?

This theme of the joys and pain of love becomes more and more important through Chaucer's writing. In *The Legend of Good Women*, for example, he takes up an awareness that Criseyde, who is the symbol of inconstancy, has followed the wishes of men, and attempts to redress the balance in women's favour. It is interesting that the views of a female audience are considered, although the stories of women who died for love are not necessarily standard romantic fare! Incidentally, this is the first English poem to use heroic couplets, as it describes some of the famous classical women who sacrificed themselves for love:

> And Cleopatre, with all thy passioun,
> Hide ye your trouthe of love and your renoun;
> And thou, Tisbe, that hast for love swich peine:
> My lady comth, that al this may disteine.

'Tee hee!' she cried and clapped the window to
(The Miller's Tale)

All Chaucer's earlier writing can be seen to lead to his masterpiece, *The Canterbury Tales*. He probably began writing it around 1387 and the work was uncompleted at his death in 1400. The idea of using a series of linked stories appears in *The Legend of Good Women*, but the greatest innovation is to use the 'here and now': the London area and English society of the time. Originally, 120 tales were planned, with each of thirty pilgrims from Southwark to Canterbury telling two tales on the way there and two on the way back. Rather less than a quarter of the project was realised, but the whole range of genres, styles, and subjects which history and tradition, England and Europe offered Chaucer were exploited in these tales.

Why Canterbury? Why Southwark? Why, indeed, April, in the famous opening lines of the prologue?

> When that April with his showers sote [*sote*: sweet]
> The drought of March hath pierced to the root . . .

Canterbury and Southwark bring together the religious and the secular. Canterbury Cathedral was the site of the martyrdom of Saint Thomas à Becket in 1170, during the reign of Henry II. As such, it became a shrine, the object of pilgrimage in a British sense, reflecting the duty of pilgrimage to Jerusalem which was the inspiration for the Crusades in the twelfth and thirteenth centuries. Some critics see a literal 'falling off', or decadence, in this jolly jaunt. Compared to the high but conventional ideals of the Crusades and the noble intentions of the heroes of earlier literature, there is certainly a 'decline' to more day-to-day concerns. This is all part of an underlying reflection on religion and the individual in the modern world, reflected in many texts, from *Winner and Waster* to *Patience* and beyond.

The starting point of the journey, the Tabard Inn at Southwark, represents the city, the new focal institution in society. The inn's role as meeting place and hostelry affirms the importance of drinking and conviviality in this society. It is not new: the scops sang of the deeds of Beowulf at feasts in castle halls, and convivial celebration is important in that society too. But there is a new social order here, with people of all levels of modern society apart from the aristocracy and the lowest peasants – the very highest and the very lowest in the land – sharing an undertaking which combines duty and pleasure.

> In Southwark, at The Tabard, as I lay
> Ready to go on pilgrimage and start
> For Canterbury, most devout at heart,
> At night there came into that hostelry

> Some nine and twenty in a company
> Of sundry folk happening then to fall
> In fellowship, and they were pilgrims all
> That towards Canterbury meant to ride.
> (*The General Prologue* – in modern English)

Pleasure had been noticeably lacking in literary expression until this time. Duty, war, reconciliation, consolation, love (and the pains of love), honour, suffering, history, religious doubt; all of these and more had been familiar subjects. But, just as authors became more individualistic, so did the members of this society.

The knight, the miller, the wife of Bath, the prioress, the cleric, and others are all identified by their occupation or marital status, but the narrator's descriptions of them as individuals – and their tales and the telling of them – not only bring out individual differences and characteristics, but invite the reader to recognise and identify the pilgrims as stereotypical characters.

Chaucer himself (or his narratorial persona) prefers not to take sides and does not overtly judge the characters he presents, but he allows the reader a new degree of interpretative freedom, based on the recognition of an ironic gap between how the characters see themselves and how others see them. This is new to English literature.

Why April? we asked. April is the spring month when the showers bring new fertility to the earth, when there is a reawakening, a rebirth, and the rigours of winter are overcome. This is, together with the Christian pilgrimage, an almost pagan element of ritual spiritual renewal, which finds echoes throughout literature from the Dark Ages as far as the 'wastelands' of twentieth-century writing. A land, a kingdom, awaits rebirth, and then gives thanks for that rebirth, for the continuity of life that it inspires.

So there is a great deal going on in the seemingly simple framework of *The Canterbury Tales*. It absorbs literary, historical, religious, social, and moral concerns, and transcends them all. It gives a wide-ranging view of the late fourteenth-century world and its people. The specific people and places described become emblems of their period and the text becomes an image of its time.

Critics are still divided over to what extent Chaucer treats his characters seriously or ironically. One recent trend suggested that Chaucer's irony permits the reader to see the knight, 'a very perfect gentle knight', not as the true model of courtly perfection (as these words suggest) but as a mercenary soldier who will fight for anyone who pays him. This reading has the knight always on the losing side, making him an out-of-date hero figure, ill at ease in the modern world. However, the knight is more traditionally viewed as a genuine 'gentle knight'. Whatever the case, his tale is an old-fashioned philosophical story of rivalry in love, set in classical Greece.

A similar gentle irony may surround the nun, a prioress, Madame Eglantyne. She is a sensual woman, one who enjoys the pleasures of the senses. Hanging from the bracelet around her wrist, there is not a cross (as the reader might expect) but a 'brooch' with the motto in Latin, 'Love conquers all'. Again critics have shown that this is ambiguous, to say the least. Love of Christ and sensual love are brought together in one very vivacious female character. Her tale is a fairly traditional, uncritical story of murder and religion, which is surprisingly open in its conclusions.

The Miller's Tale is an old-fashioned fable, a story of deception in love, in almost complete contrast to *The Knight's Tale*, and full of earthy humour. As the lover Absalon kisses Alison on quite the opposite end of her anatomy to where he expected, the whole idea of illicit love is suddenly made comic:

> Dark was the night as pitch, as black as coal,
> And at the window out she put her hole,
> And Absalon, so fortune framed the farce,
> Put up his mouth and kissed her naked arse
> Most savourously before he knew of this.

The wife of Bath gives a staunch defence of having had five husbands, and her tale, set at the time of King Arthur, opens up the question of what women really 'most desire' – again a challenge to courtly values.

> Some said that women wanted wealth and treasure,
> 'Honour,' said some, some 'Jollity and pleasure,'
> Some 'Gorgeous clothes' and others 'Fun in bed,'
> 'To be oft widowed and remarried,' said

Others again, and some that what most mattered
Was that we should be cossetted and flattered.

The friar is described not as a holy figure, but as 'wanton and merry'. He tells a teasing tale about an extortionate religious figure, a summoner, who is carried off to Hell by the devil.

Ponder my words, reflect upon my story.
The lion's always on the watch for prey
To kill the innocent, if so he may . . .

The summoner then answers this with a comic story of a greedy friar, again using low humour to mock religious attitudes:

Fat as a whale and waddling like a swan,
They stink of wine like bottles in a bar;
How reverent their supplications are!
When they say prayers for souls their psalm of David
Is just a 'Burp! *Cor meum eructavit!*'

This gentle mocking of heroic courtly values reveals that Chaucer's intention is more than just to describe the world in which he lived. Although himself conservative, he examines, and wants the reader to see, the changes that society is undergoing. There is a sense of shifting emphasis as older values are questioned and new values affirmed. Throughout the *Tales* there is also a joyful sense of humour, of enjoyment of sensual pleasures, and of popular, earthy fun. Serious and comic intentions go hand in hand, and give a new vision of a fast-developing and richly textured world. Above all, individual self-interest is more important than social, shared interests. Many of the characters are seen to be set in their ways. They are old-fashioned and unwilling to change. But, again, Chaucer does not judge – it is the reader who must enjoy, evaluate, and decide.

The tales may have the 'storial thing that toucheth gentleness': that is, they tell of noble deeds in days gone by, like *The Wife of Bath's Tale* which talks of 'the old days of the King Arthur'; or they may be popular stories – 'churls' tales' – which tend to be told by the tradesmen. These – deriving from a French tradition of *fabliaux*, or comic tales – allow for descriptions of everyday life, rather than romanticised tales of the past. They also give Chaucer the opportunity to have his characters speak of areas outside London: Oxford (the miller); Cambridge (the reeve); Yorkshire (the summoner). This is the beginning of a provincial voice in London-based literature.

There are also holy tales of 'morality and holyness', as told by the prioress, the second nun, and the other religious figures. The host, Harry Bailey, is in charge of this early package tour, and it is he who keeps harmony among the diverse characters, classes and professions, and who, incidentally, underlines the need for drink to keep the group from dissension.

Chaucer's world in *The Canterbury Tales* brings together, for the first time, a diversity of characters, social levels, attitudes, and ways of life. The tales themselves make use of a similarly wide range of forms and styles, which show the diversity of cultural influences which the author had at his disposal. Literature, with Chaucer, has taken on a new role: as well as affirming a developing language, it is a mirror of its times – but a mirror which teases as it reveals, which questions while it narrates, and which opens up a range of issues and questions, instead of providing simple, easy answers.

It is from Chaucer that later writers began to trace the history of English poetry, beginning with George Puttenham's *The Arte of English Poesie*, published in 1589. This account, two hundred years after Chaucer was writing *The Canterbury Tales*, finds 'little or nothing worth commendation' in poetry before Chaucer. However, it must be remembered how many manuscripts were destroyed in the Reformation of the 1530s and how few copies of any earlier writing remained extant.

LANGLAND, GOWER AND LYDGATE

On a May morning, on Malvern Hills
(*Piers Plowman*)

It is interesting that George Puttenham, the author of the first critical treatise on English Literature *The Arte of English Poesie* (1589), describes the major work of William Langland, *Piers Plowman*, as a 'satire'. The origin of English satire, looking back to the Latin of Juvenal, is usually credited to Joseph Hall (1574–1656) who, in *Virgidemiarum Sex Libris*

(*Six Books of Rods*) (1598), staked his claim to be the first English satirist. But, if satire is the mocking observation of human behaviour, Langland can, with Chaucer, be considered a worthy forerunner of what was to become a notable tradition.

Piers Plowman is an alliterative poem recounting a series of dreams, with waking interludes to connect them. Long Will, the dreamer, is the unifying character and main speaker. Piers enters the narrative now and then as a kind of *alter ego* of Will; by the end he becomes semi-divine. The dreams tell of how England might be reformed, and of truth in justice and behaviour. A credo or 'Do Well' leads to a disillusioned view of human nature, in which the church, which should exemplify salvation, is shown as corrupt. As in *The Canterbury Tales*, the friar is seen as weak and corrupt, and Piers is seen, in his own dream, as the honest man:

> 'Contrition is on his back, asleep and dreaming,' said Peace, 'and most of the others are in the same state. The Friar has bewitched them with his cures; his plasters are so mild that they have lost all fear of sin.'
> 'Then by Christ!' cried Conscience, 'I will become a pilgrim, and walk to the ends of the earth in search of Piers the Ploughman. For he can destroy Pride, and find an honest livelihood for these Friars who live by flattery and set themselves against me. Now may Nature avenge me, and send me His help and healing, until I have found Piers the Ploughman!'
> Then he cried aloud for Grace, and I awoke.
> (Prose translation of *Piers Plowman* into modern English)

Langland gives us a worldview, in which the church and man should be as one; but the individual is imperfect, and society always lacking. The poem is allegorical, but does not force a moral, or lead to an ideal solution. Rather it exposes a problem, which could very roughly be summed up as human fallibility in relation to religious idealism, a problem which was to concern writers more and more down the centuries.

The poem is, at the same time, realistic and transcendent: it rises above reality but, inevitably, it is the real world which wins. For this was not a time of social harmony, despite Harry Bailey's staunch efforts in

Southwark! In 1381, Wat Tyler led the Peasants' Revolt, an uprising of agricultural workers against excessive taxation and enforced poverty. This was the same period when John Ball, one of the first social agitators in history, claimed:

> . . . matters cannot go well in England and never will until all things be in common, and there shall be neither serfs nor gentlemen, but we shall all be equal.

There are three versions of Langland's *Piers Plowman*, of various dates. Critics tend to place the main text some three or four years earlier than the Peasants' Revolt, and Chaucer's *Troilus and Criseyde* some four years later. Less than two hundred years after the Magna Carta, agreed in 1215 between King John and the landowners, the stability of the nation was threatened. The kind of problems examined in *Patience* and *Piers Plowman* were perhaps rather more intellectual than the concerns of the peasants, for whom life was clearly very hard. The leaders of the Revolt, including John Ball, are known to have cited *Piers Plowman*, though they were not necessarily peasants themselves.

A popular voice is heard in the continuing oral tradition of the ballad. That popular voice is always English. (When King Richard II spoke to the peasants' representatives at the time of the Revolt, it is recorded that he used English.) Ballads almost always told a story, perhaps of a popular hero like Robin Hood, but usually they represent a coming to terms with harsh realities of life and death, in a situation – like Long Will's – far removed from the centres of power.

A lusty life with her he had
(*Confessio Amantis*)

There is a remarkable degree of consistency in the way mediaeval literature affirms humanity. With all its faults, humanity emerges as more realistic than heavenly ideals. John Gower uses this human element in *Confessio Amantis* (A Lover's Confession).

Sin is a moral offence in the eyes of the church, and confession was the Roman Catholic church's way of holding its believers in a moral tie to the church, which could forgive or absolve sins as long as the believers paid due penance. An emphasis on the confession of sins, and thus of the personal responsibility for the naming of sins, is stressed especially after Pope Innocent III's Fourth Lateran Council of 1215.

Gower's 'confession' uses the concept with a degree of irony. He uses stories to recount the seven deadly sins of love (*Amans*), deriving considerable inspiration from the Latin poet Ovid, in a mock-religious dream-vision. At the end, when the speaker has confessed all his sins, he announces that he will renounce love – but only because he is old, and nature has overtaken his capacity to love. A farewell to love rather than a vow of chastity is the ironic outcome.

The most natural of human fears, and the most potent symbol of the transitory nature of human life, is fear of death. A great deal of mediaeval and earlier writing – from *Beowulf* to Chaucer and Gower – is, in this sense, life-affirming. Gower ends his *Confessio Amantis* with one eye on heaven and the everlasting:

> Wher resteth love and alle pes
> Our joie mai ben endeles.

It is a feature we find less noticeably in Gower's and Chaucer's two main fifteenth-century English successors, John Lydgate (the most prolific of all pre-Renaissance writers) and Thomas Hoccleve.

Because the mediaeval period is seen from our own times as historically distant, 'behind' the Renaissance with all the changes which that period brought, it has been undervalued for its own debates, developments and changes. The fact that mediaeval times have been revisited, re-imagined and rewritten, especially in the Romantic period, has tended to compound the ideas of difference and distance between this age and what came after. But in many ways the mediaeval period presages the issues and concerns of the Renaissance period and prepares the way for what was to come.

John Lydgate is a key figure in this connection. He achieved immense success and influence in his own lifetime and was regarded as just as important and influential as Chaucer. With the invention of printing in the late fifteenth century, Caxton and later Wynkyn de Worde turned to Lydgate's works for several of their early bestsellers, often reprinting them. His position is as a man of letters rather than as a major poet. He consolidates rather than extends the multiplicity of language sources and styles. He does not push the bounds of literature forward towards the Renaissance. His voice is, however, central to his times; and his writings touch on a vast range of themes and interests, from epic to politics, from love to court concerns.

Lydgate's works are largely historical subjects in translation, the best known of which was *The Fall of Princes* (1431–38). This work enjoyed more than a century of considerable popularity. His *Troy Book* (1412–20), much longer than Chaucer's *Troilus and Criseyde*, is seen by many as Lydgate's main achievement: a major contribution to the rendering of classical myth into English. Perhaps his greatest fame lies, ironically, in his praise of Chaucer, to whom he was among the first to give credit as the first great English poet:

> That made firste to distille and rayne
> The golde dewe dropes of speche and eloquence
> Into our tunge, thurgh his excellence
>
> And fonde the floures first of Retoryke
> Our rude speche, only to enlumyne
> That in our tunge was never noon hym like.

Hoccleve's writing is semi-autobiographical, and contains the first description in literature of a mental breakdown. He also praises Chaucer, in *The Regiment of Princes* (1411–12):

> O maister deere and fadir reverent
> Mi maister Chaucer, flour of eloquence . . .

These two writers, quoted here in the original Middle English, although usually classed as followers or imitators of Chaucer, have a great deal of individuality; they are writers of considerable range, and of great importance in the fifteenth century. They perhaps lack the breadth of vision and empathy which gives Chaucer his place in history, but it is their misfortune that they come between two richly productive periods in English literature, and thus have not maintained their original popularity.

THE SCOTTISH CHAUCERIANS

Timor mortis conturbat me
(William Dunbar, *Lament for the Makers*)

The group known as the Scottish Chaucerians gives us the most memorable writing between Chaucer's death in 1400 and the Renaissance, begun in England about a hundred years later. These Scottish poets are quite different in style, tone, and subject matter from their English contemporaries.

King James I of Scotland, who reigned from 1394 to 1437, was influenced by English writing while a prisoner of the English, and his *Kingis Quair* (The King's Book) owes a lot to Chaucer. It is a love poem, one of the first of what was to become a popular form. The verse form used is called 'rhyme-royal' because of King James's use of it, but it was already known, and had, indeed, been used by Chaucer. English (or Inglis as it was spelled and pronounced) was by now the language of Scots who lived south of the Highlands. In the north, the dominant language of the Celts was Gaelic.

One of the earliest Scottish texts in English was a celebration of the hero, Robert the Bruce. This was *The Bruce* (1375–76), a chronicle usually attributed to John Barbour and written in octosyllabic couplets, intended to keep Bruce's exploits and memory alive:

> To put in writ a steadfast story
> That it last aye furth in memorye [*aye furth*: for ever after]

The Bruce is the first text to celebrate Scottish nationalism, with such sentiments as 'A! freedom is a noble thing!'

About a hundred years later, towards the end of the fifteenth century, Robert Henryson and William Dunbar take mediaeval traditions to new heights. Henryson's *Testament of Cresseid* treats Chaucer's heroine most unromantically, indeed violently, as her life of promiscuity leads to leprosy, beggary, and death. It is almost misogynistic in its tracing of the fall of the flower of womanhood. The sense of punishment was to pervade Scottish writing through the centuries, especially after the severe and highly influential Protestant theology of the Swiss-based reformer Jean Calvin (1509–64) took hold. Henryson gives us a neat early example of this 'binary' of joy and pain.

Yit efter joy oftymes cummis cair
And troubill efter grit prosperitie . . .

Henryson's *The Moral Fables of Aesop the Phrygian*, from which these lines come, are moralities in the Aesop vein, but show a great sympathy for the animals, like this mouse who was dancing for joy:

The sweet season provoked us to dance
And make such mirth as nature to us learned.

Again, as in Chaucer, the reader is left to judge. Human roles are examined and questioned as the reader recognises and identifies with the characters of the fable.

William Dunbar's *Lament for the Makers* is about poets ('makers') — including Chaucer, Gower, and Henryson — and the fact that they die. This intimation of his own mortality troubles Dunbar, and he makes it into a Latin line, one of the most resonant of repeated lines in poetry. The last line of each stanza goes:

Timor mortis conturbat me. [The fear of death does trouble me.]

This is the first great work which concentrates on death as the ultimate leveller, which brings 'all estates' to the same end. Dunbar, conscious in his writings of the immortality of his own work, anticipates one of the major concerns of Renaissance poetry: the transitory nature of all human achievement.

The stait of man dois change and vary,
Now sound, now seik, now blith, now sary,
Now dansand, mery, now like to dee;
Timor mortis conturbat me.

We have come a long way from the Anglo-Saxon celebration of heroic valour, and are heading rapidly towards the new world of the Renaissance, where Protestant and Humanist values will dominate.

MEDIAEVAL DRAMA

He playeth Herod on a scaffold high
(Geoffrey Chaucer, *The Miller's Tale*)

From classical Greek times, and in many other cultures, theatre has maintained strong religious connections. The origins of English theatre are religious too.

Literary representation was, as we have seen, in the hands of monasteries as the guardians and propagators of the written word. From Caedmon onwards, the local language appears in literature and history, although Latin, the language of the English church, whose base in Rome was accepted in England until the 1530s, was the language of documentation. Even the source which contains the account of Caedmon (Bede's *Ecclesiastical History*) was written in Latin. King Alfred encouraged the use of the vernacular in the late ninth century, but he made it clear that this was very much second best, necessitated by the deplorably low standards of Latin learning in his kingdom. The growing use of English may also reflect the church's constant concern over several centuries to reach out to people in the vernacular, which led to a wide number of translations of the Bible, or parts of it.

The earliest and simplest church drama was a similarly motivated attempt to bring Bible stories to a wider audience, to make liturgical stories more widely accessible. Initially, the scenes represented were the miracles performed by Christ, or the 'mysteries' of the nativity and the resurrection, Heaven and Hell. The genre of miracle and mystery plays evolves during the fourteenth and fifteenth centuries from the representation of these scenes inside the church, and later outside.

The move to bring the mysteries outside the church is highly significant. It opens up the performance to all the citizens of the growing cities and allows the festivals at which they were presented to develop into full holy-days, or holidays. The presentation of the plays became the civic responsibility of the guilds, the associations of tradesmen. Each guild would present its play, often on a mobile wagon which would then be moved to various points around the city. Thus the audience, staying in one place, could watch a whole cycle of mystery plays covering episodes in the Bible from *Genesis* to the resurrection, and on to the last judgement.

The best-known cycles of miracle or mystery plays come from York, Wakefield, and Chester, and a composite manuscript from an anonymous 'N-town'. Although these probably date from the fifteenth century, guild performances were certainly taking place long before Chaucer's time. Indeed, Chaucer's miller tells in his tale of the parish clerk who, 'to show his lightness', played 'Herod on a scaffold high'.

In the play of *The Marshals* in the York cycle, Mary and Joseph talk about the angel's warning to them to flee Herod:

> JOSEPH And for thy dear son's sake
>   Will he destroy all here.
>   May that traitor him take!
> MARY Love Joseph, who told you this?
>   How had you witting of this deed?
> JOSEPH An angel bright that came from bliss
>   This tiding told for sure indeed . . .

All the cycles are anonymous, but some of the episodes in the Wakefield cycle are of such quality that their putative author has been called The Wakefield Master.

Where mystery or miracle plays are based on the Bible and religious stories, morality plays are allegorical representations of human life. However, they differ from *Piers Plowman* in that they take their hero to his heavenly reward, transcending humanity's limitations and frustrations, to point up religious values in a way the other literary genres of the time tended to avoid.

Everyman, dating from the early sixteenth century, is one of the most lasting of this kind of work, and is found in several other countries, the English version originally having been adapted from the Dutch. God (seen as the Holy Trinity with the voice of Jovus) is one of the first 'characters' to speak in the play, but most of the characters are personifications. The hero, Everyman, towards the end of his life, meets such personifications as Fellowship, Kindred, Cousin, and Good Deeds. They cannot accompany him on his final journey; so it is Good Deeds (neglected until late in the drama) who must be his strongest support. Knowledge offers to 'go with thee and be thy guide', but he can only be Everyman's companion for a limited distance on his earthly journey. God recognises that mankind has forgotten him:

> I could do no more than I did, truly;
> And now I see the people do clean forsake me.
> They use the seven deadly sins damnable . . .

But, after his journey through life, Everyman points up the moral: the word 'forsake' takes on new resonances.

> EVERYMAN Take example, all ye that this do hear or see,
> How they that I loved best do forsake me,
> Except my Good Deeds that bideth truly.
> GOOD DEEDS All earthly things is but vanity:
> Beauty, Strength, and Discretion do man forsake,
> Foolish friends and kinsmen, that fair spake –
> All fleeth save Good Deeds, and that am I.

The earliest complete morality play is one of a series from the early fifteenth century, containing such titles as *Mankind* and *Wisdom*, called *The Castle of Perseverance*. Its title indicates the virtue the play will extol. Life is seen as a struggle, a series of challenges and disappointments. Sin and repentance, twice over, are the lot of Humanum Genus, the main character, as his lifetime relates to historical time and the everlasting time of mankind's salvation, as death and judgement are enacted in a setting which anticipates the modern 'theatre in the round'.

In the Scottish literary canon, *A Satire of the Three Estates* (1540) offers a contribution to late mediaeval drama which exemplifies and goes beyond the limitations of its English counterparts. Written by Sir David Lindsay, it presents class conflict between upper, middle and lower classes ('estates') with humour and an absence of the sanctimoniousness which sometimes tends to dominate the genre. Theft, Deceit, and Falset (Untruth) – personifications again – are hanged at the end of the play, but their reactions are human and lively. Theft would like to name all the thieves he knows:

> THEFT I have na time to tell your names.
> With King Correctioun and ye be fangit,
> Believe richt weill ye will be hangit!
> [THEFT *is hanged to a roll of drums. Then the* SERGEANTS *take* DECEIT

and FALSET *from the stocks and lead them to the gallows, where each makes his*
speech and is hanged with the same ceremony.]

FIRST SERGEANT Come here, Deceit, my companyoun!
    Saw ever man liker a loon
    To hing upon a gallows!
DECEIT This is eneuch to mak me mangit!
    Dule fell me that I mon be hangit!

All these plays use allegorical characters – vices and virtues, and easily identifiable human traits – to make their points. The style is didactic and unsubtle. The moral is made as explicit as possible. However, only fifty years after Lindsay's *Three Estates* was performed at the Scottish court, a whole new era of dramatic literature had begun in England.

MALORY AND SKELTON

'Alas!' said Sir Bedevere,
'that was my lord King Arthur.'
(Sir Thomas Malory, *Le Morte D'Arthur*)

Two literary figures bridge the gap between the mediaeval age and the Renaissance. They are Sir Thomas Malory, the author of *Le Morte D'Arthur*, and the first 'poet-laureate', John Skelton. In their entirely separate ways, they made distinctive contributions to the history of literature and to the growth of English as a literary language.

Malory's prose version of the story of King Arthur and the Knights of the Round Table unites, under one title, eight romances which had been a mainstay of English writing, both historical and imaginative, since the earliest times. It was completed in 1470, and its importance lies principally in the fact that it was published in 1485 by William Caxton. It was the first imaginative work to achieve the wide circulation that the newly invented techniques of printing allowed. Caxton's work as a publisher was continued into the sixteenth century by his long-term assistant, Jan van Wynkyn, known as Wynkyn de Worde. He moved the business from Westminster to Fleet Street, which remained a centre for publishing – chiefly newspapers – until the 1980s.

Le Morte D'Arthur is, in a way, the climax of a tradition of writing, bringing together myth and history, with an emphasis on chivalry as a kind of moral code of honour. The supernatural and fantastic aspects of the story, as in *Sir Gawain and the Green Knight*, are played down, and the more political aspects, of firm government and virtue, emphasised. It was a book for the times. The Wars of the Roses ended in the same year as *Le Morte D'Arthur* was published. Its values were to influence a wide readership for many years to come. There is sadness, rather than heroism, in Arthur's final battle, quoted in the original:

> Kynge Arthur toke hys horse and seyde, 'Alas, this unhappy day!' and so rode to hys party, and Sir Mordred in lyke wyse. And never syns was there even seyne a more dolefuller batayle in no Crytsen londe, for there was but russhynge and rydynge, foynynge and strykynge, and many a grym worde was there spokyn of aythir to othir, and many a dedely stroke. But ever Kynge Arthur rode thorowoute the batayle of Sir Mordred and ded full nobly, as a noble kynge shulde do, and at all tymes he faynted never. And Sir Mordred ded hys devoure that day and put hymselffe in grete perell.
> And thus they fought all the longe day, and never stynted tylle the noble knyghtes were layde to the colde erthe. And ever they fought stylle tylle hit was nere nyght, and by than was there an hondred thousand leyde dede uppon the erthe. Than was Kynge Arthur wode wrothe oute of mesure, whan he saw hys people so slayne from him.

John Skelton was a court poet, but he also wrote of low life and drinking; he was an outspoken satirist who also wrote, in *Philip Sparrow*, one of the most unusual elegies in English to a pet bird. It is almost comic in its grief:

> I wept and I wailed,
> The teares down hailed,
> But nothing it availed
> To call Philip again,
> Whom Gib, our cat, hath slain.

Gib, incidentally, was short for Gilbert; and was a very common name for a cat in England in the fifteenth and sixteenth centuries. Another feline of the same name is found in the anonymous play *Gammer Gurton's Needle*, dating from about 1566; this was one of the earliest theatrical comedies during the early Renaissance period.

Skelton's morality play, *Magnificence*, probably from the 1520s, is the only late mediaeval drama whose author is known. His range and inventiveness have rather ironically counted against him, in that he cannot be categorised with any other writer, or seen as a part of any particular movement or trend.

Skelton's individuality led him to invent his own style of poetic writing – in short, rapid lines:

> Tell you I chyll [*chyll*: shall]
> If that ye will
> A while be still
> Of a comely gyll [*gyll*: girl]
> That dwelt on a hill.

This helter-skelter verse form, close to the rhythms of speech and to the spirit of the ordinary people's lives it describes, was later called Skeltonics, and remains unique. For, with the coming of the Renaissance, poetry was to move towards a new self-consciousness and refinement, with new forms, genres, and linguistic devices depicting the rhythms of life.

John Skelton was dismissed by George Puttenham in a parenthesis. Although Skelton was 'surnamed the poet laureate', the author of *The Arte of English Poesie* says, 'I wot [know] not for what great worthiness'. Puttenham prefers the subsequent 'courtly makers', and later critics have tended to follow him. Skelton makes critics uncomfortable. He remains a unique poet, one who links court life and low life as no other writer of his time was able to do.

LANGUAGE NOTE
Prose and sentence structure

Two of the commonest methods used for linking clauses in English are *co-ordination* and *parataxis*. In Old English this kind of intersentential structure is the principal mode of ordering statements. Co-ordination involves sentences which are linked by co-ordinating conjunctions such as *and, then* or a comparable linking word; in the case of parataxis, linking words are absent and the clauses are arranged in a sequence which is understood to be connected. For example:

Ic arise, ond ic fare to minum faeder, ond ic secge him.
I will arise, and go to my father, and will say unto him.

(CO-ORDINATION)

Drihten, haele us: we mote forwurthan.
Lord, save us; we perish.

(PARATAXIS)

Much of the prose of the Authorised Version of the Bible involves essentially uncomplicated, co-ordinating structures:

> And his disciples came to him, and awoke him, saying, Lord, save us; we perish.

The style has come to be known as Alfredian (after the writings of King Alfred) and the 'Alfredian' sentence certainly abounds in works such as the following preface to Alfred's translation of Pope Gregory I's *Cura Pastoralis*:

> . . . and I cause you to know that it often comes into my mind what learned men there once were throughout England, both religious and laymen; and how blessed a time it was then throughout England; and how the kings who had rule over the people obeyed God and his messengers; and how they maintained both their peace, morality and control within, and also expanded their realm externally.

It is a distinctive style which forms the backbone of much English prose through to the present day. It achieves its communicative effects with syntactic compactness and coherence and it is a style particularly suited to a plain recounting of narrative events, as the following extract from Malory's *Le Morte D'Arthur* indicates (even though it was a self-conscious choice by Malory to fashion a deliberately Anglo-Saxon style for his Arthurian material):

> And then Sir Marhaus rode unto his shield, and saw how it was defouled, and said, 'Of this despite I am a part avenged, but for her love that gave me this white shield I shall wear thee and hang mine where thou was;' and so he hanged it about his neck. Then he rode straight unto Sir Uwain, and asked what they did there. They answered him that they came from King Arthur's court for to see adventures.

The influence on the development of English of French and Latin syntactic styles had become more marked by the sixteenth century when, in particular, the Latinate syntactic structures (and more ornate vocabulary) of Cicero were much imitated. One main consequence of this influence was that writers explored more complex structures of *subordination* and *hypotaxis*. The use of subordinating conjunctions such as *because* and *so that* enabled more explicit description of reasons and of cause and effect. Such a style was regarded as the proper style for serious expository prose. The following extract from Francis Bacon's *The Advancement of Learning* illustrates the length and complexity of sentence structure which resulted:

> And so to Seneca, after he had consecrated that *Quinquennium Neronis* to the eternall glorie of learned governors, held on his honest and loyall course of good and free counsell, after his maister grew extreamly corrupt in his government; neither can this point otherwise be: for learning endueth mens minds with a true sence of the frailtie of their persons . . . so that it is impossible for them to esteeme that any greatnesse of their owne fortune can bee, a true or worthy end of their being and ordainment; and therefore are desirous to give their account to God . . .

Other equally complex structures are to be found in Milton's writings, both poetry and prose. The opening sixteen lines of Milton's *Paradise Lost* comprise just one sentence. However, it would be inaccurate to suggest that one stylistic pole implies the absence of another; for example, Bacon and Milton both exhibit a simultaneous command of everyday, speech-based rhythms, plain vocabulary and paratactic concision where they judged that the subject matter required it.

By the end of the sixteenth century a general reaction against elaborate prose structures began to be felt. The Royal Society, founded in 1660, gave final authority to the rejection of more elaborate syntax and associated rhetorical patterns and encouraged a return to essentially Anglo-Saxon sentence structure. Further related stylistic issues are discussed in the Language note on page 182.

(It will be seen that in this section quotations have been given sometimes in the original and sometimes in modern translation, and sometimes words and phrases have been glossed. The aim is to offer both accessibility and contact with the original text.)

The Renaissance

1485–1660

CONTEXTS AND CONDITIONS

At the end of the 1400s, the world changed. Two key dates can mark the beginning of modern times. In 1485, the Wars of the Roses came to an end, and, following the invention of printing, William Caxton issued the first imaginative book to be published in England – Sir Thomas Malory's retelling of the Arthurian legends as *Le Morte D'Arthur*. In 1492, Christopher Columbus's voyage to the Americas opened European eyes to the existence of the New World. New worlds, both geographical and spiritual, are the key to the Renaissance, the 'rebirth' of learning and culture, which reached its peak in Italy in the early sixteenth century and in Britain during the reign of Queen Elizabeth I, from 1558 to 1603.

England emerged from the Wars of the Roses (1453–85) with a new dynasty in power, the Tudors. As with all powerful leaders, the question of succession became crucial to the continuation of power (like Beowulf with Wiglaf; like Shakespeare's Henry IV and his son, Prince Hal, later Henry V). So it was with the greatest of the Tudor monarchs, Henry VIII, whose reign lasted from 1509 to 1547. In his continued attempts to father a son and heir to the line, Henry married six times. But his six wives gave him only one son and two daughters, who became King Edward VI, Queen Mary I, and Queen Elizabeth I.

The need for the annulment of his first marriage, to Catherine of Aragon, brought Henry into direct conflict with the Catholic church, and with Pope Clement VII (1521–32) in particular. In reaction to the Catholic church's rulings, Henry took a decisive step which was to influence every aspect of English, then British, life and culture from that time onwards. He ended the rule of the Catholic church in England, closed (and largely destroyed) the monasteries – which had for centuries been the repository of learning, history, and culture – and established himself as both the head of the church and head of state.

The importance of this move, known as the Reformation, is huge. In a very short period of time, centuries of religious faith, attitudes and beliefs were replaced by a new way of thinking. Now, for example, the King as 'Defender of the Faith' was the closest human being to God – a role previously given to the Pope in Rome. Now, England became Protestant, and the nation's political and religious identity had to be redefined. Protestantism, which had originated with Martin Luther's *95 Theses* in Wittenberg in 1517, became the official national religion, and the King rather than the Pope became head of the church. Although King Henry himself remained nominally Catholic, despite being excommunicated by the Pope, all the Catholic tenets, from confession to heaven and hell, were questioned. It was, quite simply, the most radical revolution in beliefs ever to affect the nation. The closest equivalent shock to the nation's religious and moral identity is Charles Darwin's *On the Origin of Species* (1859), whose theories undermined the religious and biblical beliefs of Victorian society and led to a colossal crisis of identity and faith.

The Reformation in the reign of Henry VIII provoked a similarly overwhelming crisis in England in the sixteenth century. England's identity began to be separate and distinct from Europe. The nation was to affirm its inviduality historically in two ways: in the conquest of Empire, and in the domination of the seas, achieved during the reign of Henry's daughter Elizabeth I.

Henry VIII's break with Rome was not carried out as an isolated rebellion. Two European thinkers, in particular, established the climate which made it possible. The first of these was the Dutch scholar Erasmus whose enthusiasm for classical literature was a major source for the revival in classical learning. His contempt for the narrowness of Catholic monasticism (expressed in *The Praise of Folly*) was not an attempt to deny the authority of the Pope, but a challenge to the corruption of the Catholic church. Erasmus had no time for unnecessary ritual, the sale of pardons and religious relics. He wished to return to the values of the early Christian church and in order to do so, produced a Greek edition (1516) of the Scriptures in place of the existing Latin one. Through his visits to England, Erasmus became a friend of Sir Thomas More, who was later beheaded for refusing to support Henry VIII's divorce from Catherine of Aragon. Although much of Erasmus's work prepared the ground for Protestant reforms, his aim was to purify and remodel the Catholic church, not to break away from it. He represented the voice of learning and knowledge, of liberal culture and tolerance.

It was a quite different temperament, the German Martin Luther's, which marked the decisive break with Rome. Luther agreed with much of what Erasmus said about the corruption of the Catholic church but they disagreed on their responses and Luther refused to submit to the Pope's authority. Many historians regard 1517, when Luther pinned to a chapel door his *95 Theses Against the Sale of Papal Indulgences*, as the start of the Reformation and the birth of Protestantism. Luther's continuing opposition to the Pope led to his excommunication (1521) and the further spread of religious individualism in Northern Europe. It is against this background that we should place Henry VIII's adoption of the role of the head of the English church and the church's own quite separate style of Anglicanism.

Luther's mission in developing the church outside Catholicism was taken up by the Frenchman, Jean Calvin. Like Luther, Calvin saw the Bible as the literal word of God and the very foundation for his ideas. For the last twenty years of Calvin's life, Geneva became the powerhouse of Protestantism. It functioned as a model of civic organisation and behaviour and included a much stricter morality – for example, dress was austere, patriarchy took a stronger grip, drama was censored, women were drowned and men beheaded for adultery. This was significant because the ideas developed in Geneva spread to regions of Northern Europe, including Scotland and the non-conformist tradition in England and Wales. This influential movement culminated a century later in the triumph of Cromwell's Puritan Commonwealth.

After the Reformation, the relationship between man and God, and consequently the place of man in the world, had to be re-examined. This was a world which was expanding. In 1492, Christopher Columbus travelled in search of the Indies, landing first in the Caribbean island of Hispaniola. For many years he was credited with having 'discovered' the Americas. Over the next century or so, Copernicus and Galileo would establish scientifically that the Earth was not the centre of the universe. This expansion was reflected in the mental explorations of the time. The figure of the Dutch philosopher Erasmus also takes on considerable importance here. His humanist thinking had a great influence on generations of writers whose work placed man at the centre of the universe.

It was not by accident that neo-Platonic philosophy, from the great age of classical Greece, became dominant in the Renaissance. Its ideals of the harmony of the universe and the perfectibility of mankind, formulated before the birth of Christianity, opened up the humanist ways of thinking that pervaded much European and English Renaissance writing.

Literature before the Renaissance had frequently offered ideal patterns for living which were dominated by the ethos of the church, but after the Reformation the search for individual expression and meaning took over. Institutions were questioned and re-evaluated, often while being praised at the same time. But where there had been conventional modes of expression, reflecting ideal modes of behaviour – religious, heroic, or social – Renaissance writing explored the geography of the human soul, redefining its relationship with authority, history, science, and the future. This involved experimentation with form and genre, and an enormous variety of linguistic and literary innovations in a short period of time.

Reason, rather than religion, was the driving force in this search for rules to govern human behaviour in the Renaissance world. The power and mystique of religion had been overthrown in one bold stroke: where the marvellous no longer holds sway, real life has to provide explanations. Man, and the use he makes of his powers, capabilities, and free will, is thus the subject matter of Renaissance literature, from the early sonnets modelled on Petrarch to the English epic which closes the period, *Paradise Lost*, published after the Restoration, when the Renaissance had long finished.

The Reformation gave cultural, philosophical, and ideological impetus to English Renaissance writing. The writers in the century following the Reformation had to explore and redefine all the concerns of humanity. In a world where old assumptions were no longer valid, where scientific discoveries questioned age-old hypotheses, and where man rather than God was the central interest, it was the writers who reflected and attempted to respond to the disintegration of former certainties. For it is when the universe is out of control that it is at its most frightening – and its most stimulating. There would never again be such an atmosphere of creative tension in the country. What was created was a language, a literature, and a national and international identity.

At the same time there occurred the growth, some historians would say the birth, of modern science, mathematics and astronomy. In the fourth decade of the sixteenth century Copernicus replaced Aristotle's system with the sun, rather than the Earth, at the centre of the universe. In anatomy, Harvey discovered (1628) the circulation of the blood, building on sixteenth-century work in Italy. There was a similar explosion from the start of the seventeenth century in the discovery, development and use of clocks, telescopes, thermometers, compasses, microscopes – all instruments designed to measure and investigate more closely the visible and invisible world.

The writing of the era was the most extensive exploration of human freedom since the classical period. This led English literature to a new religious, social and moral identity which it maintained until the mid-nineteenth century. English became one of the richest and most varied of world literatures, and is still the object of interest and study in places and times distant from its origin. The Reformation and the century of cultural adjustment and conflict which followed are crucial keys in understanding English literature's many identities.

The literature of the English Renaissance contains some of the greatest names in all world literature: Shakespeare, Marlowe, Webster, and Jonson, among the dramatists; Sidney, Spenser, Donne, and Milton among the poets; Bacon, Nashe, Raleigh, Browne, and Hooker in prose; and, at the centre of them all, the Authorised Version of the Bible, published in 1611.

So many great names and texts are involved because so many questions were under debate: what is man, what is life for, why is life so short, what is good and bad (and who is to judge), what is a king, what is love . . . ? These are questions which have been the stuff of literature and of philosophy since the beginning of time, but they were never so actively and thoroughly made a part of everyday discussion as in the Elizabethan and Jacobean ages.

Politically, it was an unsettled time. Although Elizabeth reigned for some forty-five years, there were constant threats, plots, and potential rebellions against her. Protestant extremists (Puritans) were a constant presence; many people left the country for religious reasons, in order to set up the first colonies in Virginia and Pennsylvania, the beginnings of another New World. Catholic dissent (the Counter-Reformation) reached its most noted expression in Guy Fawkes's Gunpowder Plot of 5 November 1605, still remembered on that date every year. And Elizabeth's one-time favourite, the Earl of Essex, led a plot against his monarch which considerably unsettled the political climate of the end of the century.

Elizabeth's reign did, however, give the nation some sense of stability, and a considerable sense of national and religious triumph when, in 1588, the Spanish Armada, the fleet of the Catholic King Philip of Spain, was defeated. England had sovereignty over the seas, and her seamen (pirates or heroes, depending on one's point of view) plundered the gold of the Spanish Empire to make their own Queen the richest and most powerful monarch in the world.

With this growth in the wealth and political importance of the nation, London developed in size and importance as the nation's capital. The increasing population could not normally read or write, but did go to the theatre. Hence, from the foundation of the first public theatre in 1576, the stage became the forum for debate, spectacle, and entertainment. It was the place where the writer took his work to an audience which might include the Queen herself and the lowliest of her subjects. Hand in hand with the growth in theatrical expression goes the growth of modern English as a national language.

LANGUAGE NOTE
Expanding world: expanding lexicon

The sixteenth century witnessed not only geographical and intellectual expansion but also a rapid growth in the number of foreign words which became English words. English as a language had always been open to lexical invasions and by the time of the Renaissance had absorbed innumerable words with Latin and Greek origins but had also borrowed many words from French, Italian, Spanish and Portuguese – other countries similarly involved in an expansion of their usual territorial boundaries. During the sixteenth century, however, and in a time of worldwide exploration and expansion, new words came into English from over fifty other languages, including the languages of Africa, Asia, and North America.

The lexicon of English expanded to meet the need to talk about the new concepts, especially scientific concepts, inventions, materials and descriptive terms which accompanied the rapidly developing fields of medicine, technology, science and the arts. The expansion provoked much discussion and argument and led to the 'Inkhorn Controversy' (see Language note, page 77).

The influx of foreign words was only one aspect of an expanding lexicon during this period. Many new formations of words were made by adding prefixes and suffixes and by creating new compounds. The following words entered English at this time and in these ways:

PREFIXES: *non*sense; *un*civilised; *un*comfortable; *dis*robe; *en*dear.
SUFFIXES: laugh*able*; immatur*ity*; frequent*er*.
COMPOUNDING: Frenchwoman; heaven-sent; laughing-stock.

Also common was word-class conversion, a process whereby one class of words is changed into another: for example, a noun ('an invite') is formed from the verb 'to invite'; or the verb 'to gossip' is formed from the noun ('gossip'). The use of one word class with the function of another was a common feature of Shakespeare's English. In the following two examples verbs are made from nouns:

Julius Caesar/ Who at Philippi the good Brutus *ghosted*

It out-herods Herod

The expansion of the lexicon of English owes much to the linguistic creativity of Shakespeare whose inventions have become a part of modern English idiom, although the same meanings are not necessarily preserved. Here are examples from Shakespeare's *Hamlet*, all of which occur in the modern English lexicon:

'To the manner born'   (Act I, scene iv)
'Brevity is the soul of wit'   (Act II, scene ii)
'I must be cruel only to be kind'   (Act III, scene iv)

SHAKESPEARE, LATIN AND A DOUBLE VOICE

Here is an example of the way Shakespeare exploits tensions between formal,

Latin-derived vocabulary and more informal English vocabulary for purposes of dramatic effect. The extract is taken from *Macbeth*'s soliloquy in the last scene of Act I:

> If it were done when 'tis done, then 'twere well
> It were done quickly. If the assassination
> Could trammel up the consequence, and catch
> With his surcease success – that but this blow
> Might be the be-all and end-all – here
> But here, upon this bank and shoal of time,
> We'd jump the life to come.

The soliloquy contains two voices: the lexicon of Latin and the lexicon of English. The Latin words are deployed almost as if Macbeth cannot find an ordinary word for the act of murder he is considering. 'Assassination' and 'consequence' are uncommon, unspoken words for uncommon, unspoken acts. Macbeth is caught between surface appearance and sordid reality and the two alternatives are expressed by two kinds of diction.

Shakespeare satirised the over-use of formal, Latinate diction in the character of Holofernes in *Love's Labour's Lost*, but his main purpose is not satirical, nor is it simply to use Latinisms and new poetic compounds because they were fashionable. Throughout *Macbeth* the double voice is an essential element in the characterisation of Macbeth.

RENAISSANCE POETRY

They flee from me that sometime did me seek
(Sir Thomas Wyatt, *They flee from me*)

The Renaissance did not break completely with mediaeval history and values. Sir Philip Sidney is often considered the model of the perfect Renaissance gentleman. He embodied the mediaeval virtues of the knight (the noble warrior), the lover (the man of passion), and the scholar (the man of learning). His death in 1586, after the Battle of Zutphen, sacrificing the last of his water supply to a wounded soldier, made him a hero. His great sonnet sequence *Astrophel and Stella* is one of the key texts of the time, distilling the author's virtues and beliefs into the first of the Renaissance love masterpieces. His other great work, *Arcadia*, is a prose romance interspersed with many poems and songs. Its own history is complicated: Sidney finished what is known as *The Old Arcadia* by about 1580. He then started rewriting it. *The New Arcadia*, unfinished, was published in 1590, and later versions added parts of *The Old Arcadia*, thereby creating textual problems for generations of Sidney scholars. *Arcadia* is a complex and still controversial mixture of pastoral romance, narrative intrigue, and evocative poetry of love and nature. It is a work which has no equivalent in English literature.

The direct literary influence on the English Renaissance love sonnet was the Italian Francesco Petrarca – known in English as Petrarch – who wrote sonnets to his ideal woman, Laura. This idealisation is very much a feature of early Renaissance verse. Classical allusions, Italian Renaissance references, and contemporary concerns make the poetry of the sixteenth century noticeably different in tone and content from the poetry of the early seventeenth century, when Elizabeth was no longer the monarch. There is a universalisation of personal feeling and a concern with praise in the earlier verse. This becomes more directly personal and more anguished as the sixteenth century comes to a close.

The earliest sonnets of the period are found in an anthology, *Tottel's Miscellany*, published in 1557. Sir Thomas Wyatt and Henry Howard, Earl of Surrey (who both died in the 1540s), transposed Petrarch directly into English, finding a formal expressiveness which native English poetry had not enjoyed for two centuries. The native rhythms of the Skeltonics of the turn of the century gave way almost completely to the upper-class, courtly, highly formal, imported form. Poetry became the pastime of educated high society. It is poetry of love and of loss, of solitude and change. The theme of transience, which was to feature strongly in all Shakespeare's work, began to appear with greater frequency through the 1570s and 1580s.

A number of contrasts, or binaries, begin to emerge; these, from the Renaissance onwards, will be found again and again to express the contrasts, the extremes, and the ambiguities of the modern world.

> I find no peace and all my war is done;
> I fear and hope, I burn and freeze like ice;
> I fly above the wind, yet can I not arise,

And naught I have and all the world I seize on . . .
(Sir Thomas Wyatt, *I find no peace*)

Time past and time present will be a constant source of contrast in literature: change, mutability, infidelity, and transience will be found in many texts from Wyatt onwards:

They flee from me that sometime did me seek,
With naked foot stalking in my chamber.
I have seen them, gentle, tame, and meek,
That now are wild, and do not remember
That sometime they put themselves in danger
To take bread at my hand, and now they range,
Busily seeking with a continual change.
(Sir Thomas Wyatt, *They flee from me*)

The self-conscious awareness that they were producing a new English literature gave some Elizabethan poets their true ambition. Edmund Spenser, in *The Faerie Queene* (1590–96), brings together English myth and topical adulation of the monarch to make a poem of praise and critique – the most ambitious single contribution to Elizabethan poetry and the single most important work in the history of English poetry since *The Canterbury Tales*. Indeed, Chaucer was Spenser's favourite English poet and, in constructing his 'allegory, or darke conceit', Spenser was acutely alive to the traditions on which he was building. Following Malory, he chose the 'hystorye of king Arthure, as most fitte for the excellency of his person', and it was the imaginative freedom of King Arthur's adventures which provided Spenser with the narrative licence of the poem.

Yet beyond these two Englishmen, Chaucer and Malory, Spenser was looking back to the 'antique Poets historicall', by which he chiefly meant Homer, Virgil and Ariosto. In particular, he modelled much of his poetic career on Virgil's pastoral. This enabled Spenser in *The Faerie Queene* to look back to a golden age of pastoral harmony but also to celebrate the court of Elizabeth I, through drawing a parallel with King Arthur's legendary court. The poem absorbs and reflects a vast range of myth, legend, superstition and magic, and explores both history and contemporary politics. The section entitled 'Justice', for instance, features the suppression of the Irish rebellion in which

Spenser himself was implicated as a civil servant as well as covering religion and philosophy, and attitudes to women and sexuality.

The Faerie Queene is Elizabeth, seen abstractly as Glory, and appearing in various guises. In a deliberate echo of the Arthurian legends, twelve of her knights undertake a series of adventures. The work is highly symbolic, and allusive, and is inevitably episodic in its effects. 'A Gentle Knight' (recalling Chaucer's Knight; see page 37), with a red cross on his breast, is on a quest. He is Saint George, the symbolic saint of England. He had seen Gloriana (the Faerie Queene) in a vision, and would go in search of her.

> Upon a great adventure he was bond,
> That greatest Gloriana to him gave,
> That greatest Glorious Queene of Faerie lond,
> To winne him worship, and her grace to have,
> Which of all earthly things he most did crave;
> And ever as he rode, his hart did earne
> To prove his puissance in battell brave
> Upon his foe, and his new force to learne;
> Upon his foe, a Dragon horrible and stearne.

His adventures in trying to find her would form the poem's story. The Faerie Queene has an annual twelve-day feast, on each day of which one of her courtiers leaves the court to set right a wrong. Each journey would involve a different virtue and the hero would be involved in each, while still seeking Gloriana.

Spenser only completed just over half of the planned twelve books of *The Faerie Queene*, but some of his writings – notably the early *The Shepheardes Calender* (1579) and the marriage hymn *Epithalamion* (1595–96) – are particularly interesting for their relation of poetry to time: twelve eclogues representing the twelve months of the year in the former, and the twenty-four stanzas representing the hours of Midsummer's Day in the latter. The last line of *Epithalamion* embodies the transience that we have seen emerging: one day becomes eternity.

> And for short time an endlesse monument.

Spenser has divided critical opinion more than any other major poet. He is seen variously as the great poet of the Renaissance, as 'a penpusher in the service of imperialism', as following and enlarging upon the tradition of Chaucer, or as 'a colonial administrator' who 'had difficulty making ends meet'. He wrote a male adventure for a male readership, celebrating a female virgin, affirming an ideal, in order, like most Renaissance writers, to shore himself up against the flawed realities of economic and colonial power and rule. He wanted to make himself the laureate of a generation, and in his formal, linguistic and imaginative invention he is generally considered to have surpassed all earlier poetic achievements.

Spenser made a radical attempt to relocate and reintroduce the epic form for England and the Elizabethan age by inventing the Spenserian stanza as the new form for his poem. The epic, as in *Beowulf*, celebrates the achievements of heroes or heroines of history and myth, affirming nation and values. Perfection of the virtues, and the affirmation of truth (and true religion) are expressed through the adventures of the queen's Knights: Truth, Temperance, Chastity, Friendship, Justice and Courtesy are the themes of the six completed books.

The poet actively sought advancement from the monarch he eulogised but, in fact, his career was spent largely away from the court, in Dublin, where most of *The Faerie Queene* was written. Despite his qualities of formal invention and his concern with some of the deepest preoccupations of the time – notably in the *Mutabilitie Cantos* fragment – for some critics he stands somewhat outside the era's main intellectual and emotional debate. In Canto 56, for example – which is far from the narrative romance of most of Spenser's writing – Mutability, which reigns over all the elements, is the speaker:

> Then since within this great wide Universe
> Nothing doth firme and permanent appeare,
> But all things tost and turned by transverse:
> What then should let, but I aloft should reare
> My Trophee, and from all, the triumph beare?

Other critics might argue that his reflections on history, Puritanism, poetry and colonial development make him central. It is perhaps Spenser's historical misfortune that it was the dramatists who brought the issues of the age into clearest focus.

DRAMA BEFORE SHAKESPEARE

All the world's a stage
And all the men and women merely players
(Shakespeare, *As You Like It*)

The move from self-conscious literary awareness to a broader-based popular appeal is in part due to the work of the 'university wits': Christopher Marlowe, Robert Greene, George Peele, Thomas Nashe and Thomas Lodge, the generation educated at Oxford and Cambridge universities who used their poetry to make theatre, breathed life into dead classical models and brought a new audience to the issues and conflicts which the stage could dramatise.

The earliest plays of the period, in the 1550s and 1560s, establish comedy and tragedy as the types of drama. Both were derived from Latin sources: comedies from the works of Terence and Plautus, tragedies largely from Seneca, with echoes from Greek antecedents in both cases. The mediaeval miracle and mystery plays, and the kind of court 'interludes' played for the monarch, also contributed to the development of Renaissance drama. Its broad humour, its use of ballad, poetry, dance and music, its tendency towards allegory and symbolism flow from this native English source. Thus, although drama went through rapid changes in the period, its historical credentials were rich and varied as indeed were its range and impact. It was an age when the need for a social demonstration of an English nationalism and Protestantism climaxed in the public arena of a diverse and energetic theatre. This was the golden age of English drama.

One clear link between late mediaeval morality plays and sixteenth-century theatre is *The Four PP*, by John Heywood, which dates from the early 1540s. The four speakers are a palmer, a pardoner, a 'pothecary, and a pedlar; their 'drama' is little more than a debate, but it is a significant precursor of the realistic comedies of later in the century. Heywood's other works include *The Play of the Weather* (1533) in which the main character is Jupiter. Again a debate drama (*Winner and Waster* (see page 25) is a poetic equivalent from two centuries before), this has been seen as a precursor of the Jacobean masque (see page 115), but it is quite different in purpose: an entertainment with some appeal to the audience's intelligence rather than a celebration of the monarchy with an underlying moral purpose, which is what the masque became. The language of this speech by Jupiter provides a useful link between mediaeval English and the more modern language found little more than fifty years later in the early plays of William Shakespeare.

> And so in all thynges, wyth one voyce agreable,
> We have clerely fynyshed our foresayd parleament,
> To your great welth, whyche shall be fyrme and stable,
> And to our honour farre inestymable.
> For syns theyr powers, as ours, addyd to our owne,
> Who can, we say, know us as we shulde be knowne?
>
> *(The Play of the Weather)*

Henry Medwall's comic interlude *Fulgens and Lucrece* (1497) is generally held to be the most successful of such early Tudor dramas.

Ralph Roister Doister (about 1552) by Nicholas Udall, and *Gorboduc* (1561) by Thomas Norton and Thomas Sackville are generally taken to be the first comedy and tragedy respectively. *Gammer Gurton's Needle* (acted at Cambridge in 1566; author unknown) introduced a farcical element within a local domestic scenario more closely related to the daily life of the audience. What is fundamentally important in these first plays, as opposed to many direct translations from the classics, is that the early models were rapidly superseded. What emerges is the essential Englishness of the characters and settings, despite continuing adherence to classical models in the works of some major playwrights. *Gorboduc*, for instance, replaced the awkward distancing of the characters speaking in rhymed verse with the blank verse which became the standard form of Elizabethan and Jacobean drama.

Classical writers, from Greek and Latin, are somewhere in the background of *all* English literature, from Chaucer up until the twentieth century. Their presence cannot be ignored, and their influence – direct or indirect – cannot be overvalued. Drama was in fact moving away from these models and establishing its own style and form. Classical influences reached a threefold climax around 1590 with the great tragedies of Christopher Marlowe, the major Senecan-influenced play *The Spanish Tragedy* by Thomas Kyd, and the best reworking of a Plautus comedy in *The Comedy of Errors* by a new young dramatist, William Shakespeare.

In *The Spanish Tragedy* (1592), Hieronimo makes many long speeches, questioning and justifying his actions. At the end of the play, he memorably 'bites out his tongue' as part of a climax of bloodshed which will come to be typical of the tragedy of revenge. Shortly before the end, he proclaims his grief to his on-stage listeners:

> No, princes, know I am Hieronimo,
> The hopeless father of a hapless son,
> Whose tongue is tun'd to tell his latest tale,
> Not to excuse gross errors in the play.
> I see your looks urge instance of these words,
> Behold the reason urging me to this:
>
> > [*Shows his dead son.*]
>
> See here my show, look on this spectacle:
> Here lay my hope, and here my hope hath end:
> Here lay my heart, and here my heart was slain:
> Here lay my treasure, here my treasure lost:
> Here lay my bliss, and here my bliss bereft:
> But hope, heart, treasure, joy and bliss,
> All fled, fail'd, died, yea, all decay'd with this.

This repeated bewailing of loss is also used by Shakespeare in *Richard the Third*, one of his early tragedies (*c.*1592), when the queens bemoan their loss:

> QUEEN MARGARET Tell o'er your woes again by viewing mine.
> I had an Edward, till a Richard kill'd him;
> I had a husband, till a Richard kill'd him:
> Thou hadst an Edward, till a Richard kill'd him;
> Thou hadst a Richard, till a Richard kill'd him.
> DUCHESS OF YORK I had a Richard too, and thou didst kill him;
> I had a Rutland too: thou holpst to kill him.
> QUEEN MARGARET Thou hadst a Clarence too, and Richard kill'd him.

This contrasts with the lighter language of comedy, full of sexual play and even geography, as Dromio of Syracuse describes a woman to

Antipholus in Shakespeare's *The Comedy of Errors* (*c.*1589) as 'One that claims me, one that haunts me, one that will have me':

ANTIPHOLUS OF SYRACUSE Then she bears some breadth?
DROMIO OF SYRACUSE No longer from head to foot than from hip to hip. She is spherical, like a globe. I could find out countries in her.
ANTIPHOLUS OF SYRACUSE In what part of her body stands Ireland?
DROMIO OF SYRACUSE Marry, sir, in her buttocks. I found it out by the bogs.
ANTIPHOLUS OF SYRACUSE Where Scotland?
DROMIO OF SYRACUSE I found it by the barrenness, hard in the palm of her hand.

As this shows, Shakespeare's audience was quite happy to laugh at fat ladies, lavatorial humour and legendary Scottish meanness!

William Shakespeare moves rapidly on from his classical models. Christopher Marlowe, however, who was to achieve great success as a playwright, used his classical background to create rich, rolling, heroic verses whose heightened rhetoric matched the hugely spectacular dramatic intentions of the writing. *Hero and Leander*, a long poem on a classical subject, contains the famous line:

Whoever loved who loved not at first sight?

This is indicative of Marlowe. Romantic, rhetorical, subversive, radical and powerfully memorable, all his writing is exciting, stretching the bounds of language and imagination to new limits, making his heroes overreach themselves and suffer the consequences. Critics have, at different times, stressed the tragic end of Marlowe's heroes or, conversely, the spectacular subversiveness of their aims: like all great writers, Christopher Marlowe can be interpreted and reinterpreted by readers and audiences of every age.

Every age, sometimes every decade, has different heroes. It is instructive to compare the Marlovian dramatic hero of the late 1580s and early 1590s with the Shakespearean hero that evolved after Marlowe's early death (in a pub brawl; some say because he was a spy). Marlowe's heroes are larger than life, exaggerated both in their faults and their qualities. They want to conquer the whole world (Tamburlaine), to attain limitless wealth (Barabas, the Jew of Malta), to possess all knowledge (Doctor Faustus). The verse they speak is correspondingly powerful, rhetorical, rich in metaphor and effect.

Continuing with geographical references, Tamburlaine, victorious over his enemies, rejoices in the 'divine' Zenocrate, and tells her how he would redraw the map of the world:

> Zenocrate, were Egypt Jove's own land,
> Yet would I with my sword make Jove to stoop.
> I will confute those blind geographers
> That make a triple region in the world,
> Excluding regions which I mean to trace,
> And with this pen reduce them to a map,
> Calling the provinces, cities, and towns,
> After my name and thine, Zenocrate:
> Here at Damascus will I make the point
> That shall begin the perpendicular. . . .
> > (*Tamburlaine the Great*, Part One)

Barabas, similarly, is quite explicit about his role, his greed, and his religion:

> Thus, loving neither, will I live with both,
> Making a profit of my policy;
> And he from whom my most advantage comes,
> Shall be my friend.
> This is the life we Jews are us'd to lead;
> And reason too, for Christians do the like.
> > (*The Jew of Malta*)

Faustus sells his soul to the devil, Mephistopheles. But, all through the play, Faustus is torn by doubts and fears; he is one of the first tragic heroes to go through such intellectual torment. Here, he speaks to himself:

> Now, Faustus, must thou needs be damn'd,
> And canst thou not be sav'd:
> What boots it, then, to think of God or heaven?
> Away with such vain fancies, and despair;
> Despair in God, and trust in Belzebub:
> Now go not backward; no, Faustus, be resolute:
> Why waverest thou? Oh, something soundeth in mine ears,
> 'Abjure this magic, turn to God again!'

Ay, and Faustus will turn to God again.
To God? he loves thee not;
The god thou servest is thine own appetite,
Wherein is fix'd the love of Belzebub:
To him I'll build an altar and a church,
And offer lukewarm blood of new-born babes.

(*Doctor Faustus*)

Marlowe was one of the first major writers to affirm what can be identified as a clearly homosexual sensibility, and his historical tragedy *Edward the Second* examines sexual choice and preference in relation to the questioning of authority, power, and love in a way which few other writers were able to do until the twentieth century. Marlowe has been described as a 'sexual political thinker' whose writings successfully question and reveal, through a process of estrangement, the terms of the contemporary debate. Here King Edward asserts his role as king, against the threats of his nobles, in honouring his beloved Gaveston:

KING EDWARD I cannot brook these haughty menaces:
    Am I a king, and must be over-rul'd?
    Brother, display my ensigns in the field;
    I'll bandy with the barons and the earls,
    And either die or live with Gaveston.
GAVESTON I can no longer keep me from my lord.
KING EDWARD What, Gaveston! welcome! Kiss not my hand:
    Embrace me, Gaveston, as I do thee: . . .

(*Edward the Second*)

It is King Edward's love for Gaveston which brings about his downfall. In his imprisonment, Edward reaches a tragic dignity in the face of humiliation and disgrace:

Immortal powers, that know the painful cares
That waits upon my poor distressed soul,
Oh, level all your looks upon these daring men
That wrongs their liege and sovereign, England's king!
O Gaveston, it is for thee that I am wrong'd,
For me both thou and both the Spencers died;
And for your sakes a thousand wrongs I'll take.

The Spencers' ghosts, wherever they remain,
Wish well to mine; then, tush, for them I'll die.

Marlowe's plays explore the boundaries of the new world and the risks that mankind will run in the quest for power, for knowledge, for love. His plays are full of spectacular action, bloodshed, and passion, to match the language he uses. When Doctor Faustus must yield his soul to the Devil, Mephistopheles, at the end of the tragedy, it can be interpreted as a moment of self-knowledge – an epiphany of how weak, how transient, how empty is man's life on earth, especially in relation to the eternal and the powerful. This transience of human life is echoed again and again in Elizabethan writing, and the 'two hours' traffic of our stage' becomes the symbol and emblem of man's role in the world. The Chorus proclaims:

Cut is the branch that might have grown full straight,

with the warning not

To practise more than heavenly power permits.
(*Doctor Faustus*)

FROM THE STREET TO A BUILDING – THE ELIZABETHAN THEATRE

By the time Marlowe was writing, a new type of audience had been created for a different kind of theatrical performance. Earlier in the century, the mystery and morality plays had been performed almost anywhere, outside, often moved from location to location by wagon. In contrast, 'interludes' – little more than dramatic verse – were performed for the elite at court or in manor houses. In the latter part of Elizabeth's reign, these two groups came together to form an audience mixed across the classes, professions and trades.

Fixed theatres were established in London and while most, like the Globe, were open to the sky, a small number, such as the later Blackfriars, were completely enclosed. This entailed daytime performances without lights or a stage curtain and very few, if any, props, though the actors were dressed in rich costumes. There were no scene changes in the modern sense and the action moved fluidly from one scene to the next without an apparent break. The platform stage – known as a thrust stage – was pushed out into the audience who stood around it on three sides with a few privileged persons seated on the edge of the stage. This entailed a much closer intimacy between the actors and their audience and made more sense, for instance, of the soliloquy as an aside to the dramatic action. It also required a greater imaginative effort by the audience compared with the modern theatre, but this was perhaps not so difficult for spectators who had previously watched performances on wagons.

Alongside the development of theatres came the growth of an acting culture; in essence it was the birth of the acting profession. Plays had generally been performed by amateurs – often men from craft guilds. Towards the end of the sixteenth century there developed companies of actors usually under the patronage of a powerful or wealthy individual. These companies offered some protection against the threat of Puritan intervention, censorship, or closure on account of the plague. They encouraged playwrights to write drama which relied on ensemble playing rather than the more static set pieces associated with the classical tradition. They employed boys to play the parts of women and contributed to the development of individual performers. Audiences began to attend the theatre to see favourite actors, such as Richard Burbage or Will Kempe, as much as to see a particular play.

Although the companies brought some stability and professionalism to the business of acting – for instance, Shakespeare's company, the Lord Chamberlain's, subsequently the King's, Men, continued until the theatres closed (1642) – they offered little security for the playwright. Shakespeare was in this respect, as in others, the exception to the rule that even the best-known and most successful dramatists of the period often remained financially insecure.

In the humanist world following Erasmus, man is at the centre of the universe. Man becomes largely responsible for his own destiny, behaviour and future. This is the new current of thought which finds its manifestation in the writing of the 1590s and the decades which follow. The euphoria of Elizabeth's global affirmation of authority was undermined in these years by intimations of mortality: in 1590 she was 57 years old. No one could tell how much longer her golden age would last; hence, in part, Spenser's attempts to analyse and encapsulate that glory in an epic of the age. This concern about the death of a monarch who – as Gloriana, the Virgin Queen – was both symbol and totem, underscores the deeper realisation that mortality is central to life. After the Reformation, the certainties of heaven and hell were less clear, more debatable, more uncertain.

LANGUAGE NOTE
The further expanding lexicon

> Among all other lessons this should first be learned, that wee never affect any straunge ynkehorne termes, but to speke as is commonly received. . . . Some seeke so far for outlandish English that they forget altogether their mothers language.
>
> (Thomas Wilson, *Arte of Rhetorique*, 1553)

During the period of the Renaissance, the English language changed very swiftly in keeping with rapid social, economic and political changes. However, writers in particular soon came to realise that the vocabulary of the English language did not always allow them to talk and write accurately about the new concepts, techniques and inventions which were emerging in Europe. At the same time a period of increasing exploration and trade across the whole world introduced new words, many of which had their origin in other languages. Historians of the language have suggested that between 1500 and 1650 around 12,000 new words were introduced into English. As noted in the related Language note (The expanding lexicon, page 62), words came into English from over fifty different languages, although by far the majority were derived from Latin. Here are one or two further examples of words which entered the English language during the Renaissance: banana, embargo, tobacco (Spanish and Portuguese); balcony, design, stanza (Italian); bizarre, detail, vogue, volunteer (French); yacht (Dutch); caravan (Persian); coffee (Turkish); appropriate, contradictory, utopia, vacuum (Latin and Greek). Many of the Latin and Greek words provided a more formal alternative to existing native English words: for example, cheap: inexpensive; mean: parsimonious; dig: excavate. In many cases, however, no suitable English word existed.

A number of controversies were provoked by such changes, one example being the 'Inkhorn Controversy'. This controversy involved issues of Latin and Greek words in English. On the one hand, some writers argued that Latin and Greek were superior resources and that words derived from these languages had to be 'Englished', that is, made into English words, if a whole range of new ideas and concepts were to be expressed. On the other hand, it was argued that such words corrupted the native vernacular by displacing it with 'inkhorn' terms, that is, words coming from the scholar's horn of ink and therefore wholly scholarly, frequently polysyllabic and often pedantic.

The arguments were complicated further, however, by a desire to replace Latin with English as the national language, yet at the same time to continue to recognise Latin as a repository of cultural values and literary models.

Such paradoxes and tensions continue to influence language choices, particularly choices in vocabulary in English, and have affected debates about the nature of literature and of literary language since the sixteenth century. The resulting lexicon of English is certainly one which is rich in synonyms and alternative phrasings, allowing switches in formality between the more written and elevated character of classical vocabulary and the more spoken, everyday and 'natural' English which has grown from more distinctly Anglo-Saxon roots. Other language notes which deal with 'standards' of language (page 182), Wordsworth's 'real' language of men (page 232), and 'the fragmenting lexicon (page 355) also deal with issues raised by the 'Inkhorn Controversy' and by the fundamental lexical divisions brought about by the history of language change and variation in English.

RENAISSANCE PROSE

What is Truth; said jesting Pilate; and would not stay for an answer

(Sir Francis Bacon, *Of Truth*)

In prose, the classical influences found in poetry and drama are reflected in different ways. There is the flowery style of John Lyly's *Euphues* (1578–80). This work gives its name to an over-elaborate style, which is well exemplified in Euphues's speech to his beloved:

> Gentlewoman, my acquaintance being so little I am afraid my credit will be less, for that they commonly are soonest believed that are best beloved, and they liked best whom we have known longest. Nevertheless, the noble mind suspecteth no guile without cause, neither condemneth any wight without proof. Having therefore notice of your heroical heart I am the better persuaded of my good hap. So it

is, Lucilla, that coming to Naples but to fetch fire, as the byword is, not to make my place of abode, I have found such flames that I can neither quench them with the water of free will neither cool them with wisdom. For as the hop, the pole being never so high, groweth to the end, or as the dry beech, kindled at the root, never leaveth until it come to the top, or as one drop of poison disperseth itself into every vein, so affection having caught hold of my heart, and the sparkles of love kindled my liver, will suddenly though secretly flame up into my head and spread itself into every sinew.

This elaboration contrasts with the much more economical, yet rhetorical, style of Sir Francis Bacon.

What is Truth; said jesting Pilate; and would not stay for an answer. . . . The knowledge of truth, which is the presence of it; and the belief of truth, which is the enjoying of it; is the sovereign good of human nature.

Bacon, who perfected the essay form in English on the French model of Montaigne, used his writing to ask questions and initiate discussion with witty provocation as in *The Advancement of Learning*: 'If a man will begin with certainties, he shall end in doubts, but if he will be content to begin with doubts, he shall end in certainties.'

The range of his interests was vast. No single English intellectual symbolises the idea of Renaissance man more than Bacon. He wrote on aspects of law, science, history, government, politics, ethics, religion and colonialism, as well as gardens, parents, children and health. The key work for appreciating the width of his interests is his *Essays*, originally published in 1597, and enlarged twice before his death. These meditations, often only a page long, give a remarkable insight into the thought of the period. On occasion this coincides with late twentieth-century sensibilities, as when he advises that negotiation is generally better conducted face to face than by letter (Essay 47); at other times one might not agree with the assumptions on which his judgements are made but within the constraints of the period they are sensibly tolerant – when establishing a 'plantation' or colony, for instance, he suggests treating the 'savages' with justice (Essay 33). *Of Death* is a good example of how Bacon handles a vast subject in an accessible way:

Men fear death, as children fear to go in the dark: and, as that natural fear in children is increased with tales, so is the other. Certainly, the contemplation of death, as the *wages of sin*, and passage to another world, is holy, and religious; but the fear of it, as a tribute due unto nature, is weak.

Many of Bacon's essays raise issues fundamental to the era. For example, *Of Revenge* explores the notion of revenge which frequently featured in the period and is dominant in Elizabethan and Jacobean drama. 'Revenge is a kind of wild justice', he begins. The Old Testament had apparently sanctioned revenge but, as Bacon shows, if justice is to be redefined, the wildness of revenge becomes dangerous. Kyd's *The Spanish Tragedy* (1592), the pre-eminent revenge tragedy before Shakespeare's *Hamlet* (1600), uses the personification of revenge as a 'Chorus in this Tragedy', a visible presence motivating character and action. Where Kyd's play uses revenge as a motif for passion and bloodshed, *Hamlet* uses it as a starting point for a new kind of hero.

Rather like the character Hamlet, Bacon was at the forefront of an endless questioning and 'perpetual renovation' which characterised the Renaissance. Bacon, incidentally, has been seen by a few literary historians as the author of the plays attributed to Shakespeare. While this is highly unlikely, it is a reminder of how much the two writers share the concerns of the age. Bacon regarded the pursuit of knowledge, irrespective of politics or religion, as useful to the individual and beneficial to society. He recognised the need for laws and rules to proceed from the observation of the human and natural world rather than attempting to fit these phenomena into preconceived, abstract structures. In many respects he can thus be regarded as one of the leading figures in the development of English thinking.

The issues of the time are also reflected in the writings of Richard Hooker, who wrote one of the first major prose classics in modern English, *Of the Laws of Ecclesiastical Politie*, published in 1593 and 1597, with posthumous additions more than half a century later. The work is a broadminded and tolerant defence of Anglicanism against Puritan attacks, advocating intellectual liberty as opposed to the dogma of extremists. Hooker's prose affirms a new outlook, where Bacon's writing questions traditional concepts and assumptions in order to stimulate discussion and reflection.

> To think we may pray unto God for nothing but what he hath promised in Holy Scripture we shall obtain, is perhaps an error. For of Prayer there are two uses. It serveth as a mean to procure those things which God hath promised to grant when we ask, and it serveth as a mean to express our lawful desires also towards that, which, whether we shall have or no, we know not till we see the event.
>
> (Richard Hooker, *Of the Laws of Ecclesiastical Politie*)

The period also exhibits a fascination with books of manners such as *The Courtyer* (1561) translated from Castiglione's Italian and describing how the young gentleman of style should behave. Numerous such 'how-to' books were published to cater for all levels of society, from statesmen, as in *The Book Named the Governour* (1531) by Sir Thomas Elyot, to confidence tricksters with *The Gull's Hornbook* (1609) by Thomas Dekker. Elyot affirms, for example, the qualities which dancing brings:

> In every dance of a most ancient custom there danceth together a man and a woman holding each other by the hand or the arm: which betokeneth concord. Now it behoveth the dancers and also the beholders of them to know all qualities incident to a man and also all qualities to a woman likewise appertaining. . . . These qualities . . . being knit together, and signified in the personages of the man and woman dancing, do express or set out the figure of very nobility: which in the higher estate it is contained, the more excellent is the virtue in estimation.

By contrast, Dekker's work confirms that books about low life in London – known as 'cony-catching' pamphlets – were a lively manifestation of the city's subculture around the time when the theatre began to produce 'city comedies', in which Dekker's satirical voice was also prominent.

The effectiveness of prose as both an argumentative and a descriptive genre is reflected in a growing range of writing during the Renaissance: sermons, religious tracts, and versions of the Bible were among the most frequently found texts. John Donne, better known as a poet, left many fascinating sermons from his time as Dean of St Paul's in the 1620s. His sermon on death – the last enemy – makes a useful counterpoint to his poetry:

> Death is the last, and in that respect the worst enemy. In an enemy, that appears at first, when we are or may be provided against him, there is some of that, which we call Honour: but in the enemy that reserves himself unto the last, and attends our weak estate, there is more danger. Keep it, where I intend it, in that which is my sphere, the Conscience: . . .
>
> *(Sermon Preached Upon Easter Day 1622)*

The period also saw a growth in travel writing, with the more exotic and imaginative texts heir to the tradition established by the earlier appearance of Sir Thomas More's *Utopia* (1516), written in Latin. This fantastical account of an imaginary society offered enough points of reference to the known world to leave its status as fact or fiction ambiguous. Its pretence of second-hand reporting ('my job was simply to write down what I'd heard') and its throwaway humour – More claims to have missed the location of Utopia (Greek for 'Noplace') because a servant had coughed – suggested a technique and tone adopted by many later English writers of fiction. Critics debate how far More's *Utopia* is a model for a real society or a satire on the contemporary – 'anyone who committed a really shameful crime is forced to go about with gold rings on his ears and fingers'. In either case, *Utopia* is an account of a journey which had enormous influence on subsequent fiction – *Robinson Crusoe, Gulliver's Travels, Brave New World, Nineteen Eighty-four*, and *Lord of the Flies* to name a few – as well as on the strange mixture of fact and fantasy in Renaissance travel writing.

The leading exponent of this genre was Richard Hakluyt (pronounced Haklit), chaplain to the Embassy in Paris and later archdeacon of Westminster. He spent much of his life collecting and publishing accounts of English explorations including Drake's voyage round the world. Yet he also brought to public attention the discoveries of lesser known English navigators, such as the voyage of Hawkins to the West Indies, and he supported Raleigh's plan to colonise Virginia in *A Discourse Concerning the Western Planting* (1584). He was friendly with many leading figures of the day and his travel publications helped shape and encourage the expanding role of English exploration and colonisation – a topic which was dramatised in what was probably Shakespeare's last play, *The Tempest*. Hakluyt's work and influence was continued by the man who had become his assistant, Samuel Purchas, who in turn published accounts of voyages to countries as distant as China and Japan. The Romantic poet Coleridge said he was reading Purchas when he became inspired to write of Xanadu in *Kubla Khan*.

The description of Eldorado, as a kind of new world Eden, appears in *The Discovery of Guiana* by Sir Walter Raleigh, published in 1596.

> On both sides of this river, we passed the most beautiful country that ever mine eyes beheld: and whereas all that we had seen before was nothing but woods, prickles, bushes, and thorns, here we beheld plains of twenty miles in length, the grass short and green, and in divers parts groves of trees by themselves, as if they had been by all the art and labour in the world so made of purpose: and still as we rowed, the Deer came down feeding by the water's side, as if they had been used to a keeper's call. Upon this river there were great store of fowl, and of many sorts: we saw in it divers sorts of strange fishes, and of marvellous bigness.

Raleigh was one of the central figures of the age, a Renaissance man who was a traveller, a courtier, a notable poet, and later a political prisoner. During his imprisonment, he embarked on an ambitious *History of the World* (1614). The discovery of the Americas by Columbus in 1492 had naturally made a huge impact on the European imagination. Symbols of discovery, themes of geography and visions of utopia are found throughout Renaissance literature, from *The Tempest* to Donne's praise of his mistress – 'my America, my New-found-land'.

The name of Shakespeare is found in a prose work by Robert Greene, who was, like Marlowe, one of the 'university wits' – the generation of young writers of the 1580s and 1590s who had been educated at Oxford and Cambridge universities. Greene was a prolific writer of plays, romances, and cony-catching pamphlets. It is in an autobiographical piece, *A Groat's-Worth of Wit* (1592), that we find the slighting reference to Shakespeare, the first time his name is mentioned by another writer. Greene describes him as an 'upstart Crow, beautified with Our Feathers', who 'is in his own conceit the only Shake-scene in a country'. There is probably a touch of envy here: unlike the 'university wits', Shakespeare had not been to university, but was already a more successful playwright than his rivals. However, about twenty years later, Shakespeare returned to Greene, using his popular prose romance *Pandosto, or The Triumph of Time* (1588) as the basis for *The Winter's Tale*.

The figure of Thomas Nashe is of major importance in the history of narrative. Indeed, he is credited by some as having 'invented' modern narrative, particularly with *The Unfortunate Traveller* (1594), which the author himself described as 'being a clean different vein from other my former courses of writing'. These former courses of writing were criticisms of contemporary fashions in writing, such as *The Anatomie of Absurditie* (1589) and *Pierce Penniless* (1592), which engaged in the religious controversy of the time, in a satirical low-life complaint to the Devil. It is one of the few works in English to celebrate eating and drinking in the style of the French writer Rabelais.

The Unfortunate Traveller does something quite different: it is a mixture of genres and styles from picaresque to mock-historical, from parody to character comedy. Nashe is much more than the journalist he is often described as. He is an entertainer, an experimenter, a committed social commentator.

> This was one of my famous achievements, insomuch as I never light upon the like famous fool – but I have done a thousand better jests if they had been booked in order as they were begotten. It is pity posterity should be deprived of such precious records, and yet there is no remedy – and yet there is too, for when all fails well fare a good memory. Gentle readers (look you be gentle now, since I have called you so), as freely as my knavery was mine own, it shall be yours to use in the way of honesty.

Not afraid to be controversial, Nashe, like Ben Jonson, ended up in prison for offending authority. He collaborated with Marlowe, Greene and Jonson, although most of his dramatic writing has not survived. *The Terrors of the Night* (1594) is surprisingly modern, part Gothic fantasy, part treatise on dreams, nightmares, and apparitions: an early exploration of a theme which would become a mainstay of fiction and the cinema in future centuries.

Robert Burton's *The Anatomy of Melancholy* (1621) was a profoundly important analysis of human states of mind – a kind of early philosophical/psychological study. He sees 'melancholy' as part of the human condition, especially love melancholy and religious melancholy. His concerns are remarkably close to those which Shakespeare explores in his plays. Ambition, for example, Burton describes as 'a proud covetousness or a dry thirst of Honour, a great torture of the mind, composed of envy, pride and covetousness, a gallant madness' – words which could well be applied to Macbeth.

Burton's work had a medical thrust to it, as, later, did Sir Thomas Browne's *Religio Medici* (1642). This is a self-analytical work, studying, as the Latin title says, 'the religion of doctors'. It is witty as well as pious, tolerant and wide-ranging in its sympathy, and had a constant readership throughout Europe for centuries. Browne's *Urn Burial* (also known as *Hydriotaphia*, 1658) is an early work of archaeology, using the idea of the fragility of monuments to underscore the affirmation of faith. In many ways, Browne's Christian humanism is very modern:

> Opinions do find, after certain Revolutions, men and minds like those that first begat them. To see ourselves again, we need not look for Plato's year: every man is not only himself; there hath been many Diogenes, and as many Timons, though but few of that name: men are lived over again, the world is now as it was in Ages past; there was none then, but there hath been some one since that parallels him, and is, as it were, his revived self.
>
> (*Religio Medici*)

TRANSLATIONS OF THE BIBLE

The increasing variety of texts which were written in English throughout the sixteenth and early seventeenth centuries marks a watershed in the development and establishment of the national language. In many respects, the Authorised or King James Version of the Bible, commissioned in 1604 by King James I shortly after his accession and published in 1611, signals the final victory of English, not Latin, prose as the medium for the affirmation of Anglicanism. A few writers as late as Milton continued to use Latin on occasions but generally the English language had won an unchallenged dominance.

The King James Version was the culmination of a long series of translations of the Bible into English which had begun with Aelfric in the Anglo-Saxon era and continued with Wycliff's late fourteenth-century translation known as the Lollard Bible. Both these translations had been made from a fourth-century Latin version of the Bible termed the Vulgate.

Renaissance scholarship, however, had a decisive impact on sixteenth-century biblical translations into English. William Tyndale, in the 1520s and 1530s, used a Greek text established by Erasmus for a translation of the New Testament, and a Hebrew text for translations from the Old Testament. Tyndale was regarded as a religious subversive and, mainly on account of these translations, was burnt at the stake near Brussels. Nevertheless, his work formed the basis of future versions of the Bible in English. Once Henry VIII had broken with Rome in 1534, the Anglican church ordered an English version of the Bible to be made in 1539. This did not appear until 1560 when it was presented to Elizabeth I by Miles Coverdale, who had spent much of the intervening period in Geneva working on a translation based on Tyndale's version. Coverdale's version became known as the Geneva Bible and it is this text which was familiar to most readers, including Shakespeare, until well into the seventeenth century. Meanwhile, in 1568, a rival version appeared known as the Bishop's Bible. This was a return to translating from the Latin Vulgate and published as a counterbalance to the Calvinist Geneva Bible.

The King James Version, which was the product of fifty-four scholars, was largely based on the Bishop's and Geneva Bibles. Before the end of the seventeenth century it had effectively replaced the Geneva Bible in popularity. The King James Version, which can be seen as the affirmation of Protestant England and a celebration of its freedom from Rome, is arguably the single most influential work in the English language. It is a repository rich in poetry as well as parable, so that its cadences have not only been heard in church confirming the religious direction of the nation; but its language has contributed immensely to English cultural identity through the innumerable writers who for almost four centuries have echoed its phrasing.

LANGUAGE NOTE
The language of the Bible

The Bible has been one of the major shaping influences in the development of the English language. However, the history of the relationship between the Bible and the English language has been a long and at times controversial one. For example, in 1382 John Wycliff translated the Vulgate edition of the Bible, published in Latin, into Middle English but caused controversy because many people believed that English was not a language worthy of conveying the profound moral sentiments of the Bible. Over one hundred and fifty years later, William Tyndale translated the New Testament into English from the original Greek, seeking in the process to produce a version of the Bible which could be accessible to anyone who could read, and to ordinary working people in particular. He was a strong proponent of the view that people should be able to read the Bible in their own language and, accordingly, contributed much to the development of a plain, colloquial English style. Yet Tyndale had to work abroad and was eventually put to death by burning as a result of his work. Here is an example from Tyndale's Bible, extracted from *Genesis*, which illustrates the main features of his vernacular style:

> And the woman sawe that it was a good tree to eate of and lustie unto the eyes and a plesant tre for to make wyse. And toke of the frute of it and ate and gave unto hir husband also with her. . . . And the eyes of both of them were opened.

In many ways Tyndale's English is the first popular expression of modern English. Many of his phrases have entered the language:

> The powers that be
> The signs of the times
> A law unto themselves
> Eat, drink and be merry

having eventually established themselves in the Authorised Version.

Other influential Bibles in English were the Coverdale Bible (1535), which was a translation from German and the first complete Bible to be published in English and the Bishop's Bible (1568) which was a revised version of the Great Bible (1568). The most important and influential Bible was, however, the King James Bible, published in 1611, and also known as the Authorised Version. In 1604 the new king, King James I, wanted to have a version of the Bible which would become the single standardised version for use in all churches and throughout the country and ordered a panel of scholars and translators to produce a version on which there could be general agreement and which would be acceptable to the bishops of the country.

The translators aimed for a formal rather than a vernacular style and tended to look to the past for inspiration both in terms of previous Bibles, relying especially on the Tyndale and Coverdale Bibles, and in terms of forms of the English language. The language of the King James Bible is not, therefore, wholly the language of the beginning of the seventeenth century but its idiom has entered the modern English language as a whole pervasively and in a variety of ways.

In terms of grammar, the Authorised Version of the Bible maintains an older word order: for example, *they knew him not* (for 'they did not know him') and *things eternal* (for 'eternal things'); the -eth/th third-person singular form of present tense verbs is common: for example, *God doth know* (for 'God does know') and *your cup runneth over* (for 'your cup runs over'); several irregular verbs appear in older forms: for example, *spake* (for 'spoke'), *wist* (for 'knew'), and *gat* (for 'got'); and several prepositions have a marked usage: for example, the preposition 'of' in *tempted of* ('by') *Satan*; and the use of 'his' as a possessive form: *if the salt have lost* his *savour, wherewith shall it be salted* (for 'if the salt has lost its savour'). Above all, however, phrases, proverbial expressions and sayings which occur in the Authorised Version are now so much part of everyday English that their origins are hardly ever recognised. For example, *money is the root of all evil* (1 Tim. 6), *all things to all men* (1 Cor. 9), *the blind lead/leading the blind* (Matt. 15), *at their wit's end* (Psalm 107).

Comparisons between the King James Bible and the Modern English Bible (1961) illustrate the extent to which modern English had already been substantially formed by the beginning of the seventeenth century:

> Now Peter sate without in the palace: and a damosell came unto him saying, Thou also wast with Iesus of Galilee. But hee denied before them all saying, I know not what thou saiest . . . And after a while came unto him they that stood by, and saide to Peter, Surely thou also art one of them, for thy speech bewrayeth thee.

> Meanwhile Peter was sitting outside in the courtyard when a serving–maid accosted him and said, 'You were there too with Jesus the Galilean'. Peter denied it in face of them all. 'I do not know what you mean', he said. . . . Shortly afterwards the bystanders came up and said to Peter, 'Surely you are another of them; your accent gives you away!'

The language of the Bible was primarily *heard* by churchgoers and the rhythms and music of its cadences exerted a major influence on the development of spoken and written English. It reached a vast number of people, as the King James Bible was used in every church in the land over the next three centuries.

The Book of Common Prayer exerted a similar influence and many of its phrases have also become conventionalised in the English language. For example:

> Those whom God hath joined together let no man
> put asunder.

> Read, mark, learn and inwardly digest.

> Earth to earth, ashes to ashes, dust to dust.

SHAKESPEARE

> *What is a man,*
> *If his chief good and market of his time*
> *Be but to sleep and feed? A beast, no more.*
> (*Hamlet*)

There is no one kind of Shakespearean hero, although in many ways Hamlet is the epitome of the Renaissance tragic hero, who reaches his perfection only to die. In Shakespeare's early plays, his heroes are mainly historical figures, kings of England, as he traces some of the historical background to the nation's glory. But character and motive are more vital to his work than praise for the dynasty, and Shakespeare's range expands considerably during the 1590s, as he and his company became the stars of London theatre. Although he never went to university, as Marlowe and Kyd had done, Shakespeare had a wider range of reference and allusion, theme and content than any of his contemporaries. His plays, written for performance rather than publication, were not only highly successful as entertainment, they were also at the cutting edge of the debate on a great many of the moral and philosophical issues of the time.

Shakespeare's earliest concern was with kingship and history, with how 'this sceptr'd isle' came to its present glory. As his career progressed, the horizons of the world widened, and his explorations encompassed the geography of the human soul, just as the voyages of such travellers as Richard Hakluyt, Sir Walter Raleigh, and Sir Francis Drake expanded the horizons of the real world.

Shakespeare wrote thirty-seven plays over a period of some twenty-four years, as well as the most famous sonnet collection in English and a number of longer poems: he wrote all these while working with his theatre company and frequently performing with them. His was *a working life in the theatre*, and his subsequent fame as the greatest writer in English should not blind us to this fact. He was a constant experimenter with dramatic form and content, and with the possibilities that the open thrust stage gave him to relate to his audience (Figure 3).

THE PLAYS

The plays of Shakespeare, in approximate order of composition:

Early plays from 1589 to 1593

1	KING HENRY VI, PART ONE
2	KING HENRY VI, PART TWO
3	KING HENRY VI, PART THREE
4	TITUS ANDRONICUS
5	THE COMEDY OF ERRORS
6	THE TWO GENTLEMEN OF VERONA
7	THE TAMING OF THE SHREW
8	KING RICHARD III

Plays from 1593 to 1598

9	KING JOHN
10	LOVE'S LABOUR'S LOST
11	ROMEO AND JULIET
12	A MIDSUMMER NIGHT'S DREAM
13	THE MERCHANT OF VENICE
14	KING RICHARD II
15	KING HENRY IV, PART ONE
16	KING HENRY IV, PART TWO
17	THE MERRY WIVES OF WINDSOR

Figure 3 An Elizabethan playhouse. De Witt's drawing of the Swan, *c.*1596
Source: University Library, Utrecht

Plays from 1598, with likely dates of composition

1598	18	MUCH ADO ABOUT NOTHING
1599	19	KING HENRY V
1599	20	JULIUS CAESAR
1600	21	AS YOU LIKE IT
1600	22	HAMLET
1601	23	TWELFTH NIGHT
1602	24	TROILUS AND CRESSIDA
1603	25	ALL'S WELL THAT ENDS WELL
1604	26	MEASURE FOR MEASURE
1604	27	OTHELLO
1605	28	KING LEAR
1606	29	MACBETH
1607	30	ANTONY AND CLEOPATRA
1607	31	TIMON OF ATHENS
1608	32	CORIOLANUS

'Late' plays

1608	33	PERICLES
1610	34	CYMBELINE
1611	35	THE WINTER'S TALE
1611	36	THE TEMPEST
1613	37	KING HENRY VIII

The starting point of Shakespeare's writing career was English history. The year 1588 had been the high point of Elizabeth's reign. The defeat of the Spanish Armada signalled England's supremacy of the seas. Shakespeare, beginning to write for the theatre in 1589, turns to the recent history of England in order to trace the human elements behind this conquest of power. From the three parts of *Henry VI* (1589–92) to the tragedy of *Richard II* (1595) and the historical pageant of *Henry V* (1599), Shakespeare examines the personalities who were the monarchs of England between 1377 and 1485. Generally called the history plays, these works are, on one level, a glorification of the nation and its past, but, on another level, they examine the qualities which make a man a hero, a leader, and a king. This is a process not of hero-worship, but of humanising the hero. The king is brought close to his people. His virtues and faults are brought to life before the audience's eyes. Literature is no longer distant, no longer the preserve only of those who can read. It is familiar history enacted close to the real life of the people it concerns.

All Renaissance drama, especially the works of Marlowe and Shakespeare, is profoundly concerned with shifting power relations within society. The individual was a new force in relation to the state. The threat of rebellion, of the overturning of established order, was forcefully brought home to the Elizabethan public by the revolt of the Earl of Essex, once the Queen's favourite. The contemporary debate questioned the relationship between individual life, the power and authority of the state, and the establishing of moral absolutes. Where mediaeval drama was largely used as a means of showing God's designs, drama in Renaissance England focuses on man, and becomes a way of exploring his weaknesses, depravities, flaws – and qualities.

Henry VI is portrayed as weak, indecisive, in complete contrast to the heroic young Henry V. The audience can follow this prince in his progress from the rumbustious, carefree Prince Hal (in the two parts of *Henry IV*) to the more mature, responsible hero who wins the Battle of Agincourt, but who becomes tongue-tied when he tries to woo the princess of France.

This balance between the role of king and the role of man becomes one of Shakespeare's main concerns. Richard III is portrayed as a complete villain: the epitome of 'Machiavellian' evil, the enemy whom the Tudor dynasty had to destroy. But, as a theatrical character, this villain becomes a fascinating hero. Like Marlowe's heroes, he overreaches himself, and his fall becomes a moral lesson in the singleminded pursuit of power. He famously introduces himself in his opening soliloquy:

> Now is the winter of our discontent
> Made glorious summer by this son of York;

and goes on, later in the same speech, to announce his evil intentions:

> I am determined to prove a villain.

The idea that the king, the nearest man to God, could be evil, and a negative influence on the nation, was a new and dangerous idea in the political context of England in the 1590s. It raises the frightening possibility that the people might want or, indeed, have the right to remove and replace their ruler. This idea comes to the fore in several of Shakespeare's tragedies, from *Richard III* to *Julius Caesar* and *Coriolanus*, and is a major theme in *Hamlet, Macbeth* and *King Lear*.

Shakespeare was conscious that he was engaging in his plays with the struggle between past, present, and future; between history and the new, expanding universe of the Renaissance. In *Hamlet*, Shakespeare gives the hero these words when he addresses a troupe of actors:

> The purpose of playing . . . both at the first and now, was and is to hold as 'twere the mirror up to nature; to show . . . the very age and body of the time his form and pressure.

The form of the time, and the pressures shaping the move into a new century, meant the re-evaluation of many fundamental concepts. Time and again, Shakespeare's characters ask, 'What is a man?'

> What is a man,
> If his chief good and market of his time
> Be but to sleep and feed? A beast, no more.
> (*Hamlet*)

Time and again, aspects of human vulnerability are exposed, examined, and exploited for their theatrical possibilities. Love in *Romeo and Juliet* and *Antony and Cleopatra*, and the same subject, in a comic vein, in *Love's Labour's Lost, Twelfth Night*, and *As You Like It*; the theme of revenge and family duty in *Hamlet*; jealousy in *Othello*; sexual corruption and the bounds of justice in *Measure for Measure*; misanthropy, or rejection of the world, in *Timon of Athens*; family rejection and madness in *King Lear*; the power of money and the vulnerability of the minority in *The Merchant of Venice*; the healing effects of the passage of time, and hope in the new generation, in the late plays – with a final return to historical pageantry in *Henry VIII*, the monarch with whose Reformation it all began.

Shakespeare's themes are frequently the great abstract, universal themes, seen both on the social level and the individual level: ambition, power, love, death, and so on. The theatre permitted him to create characters who embody the themes directly, and who speak to the audience in language that is recognisably the same language as they speak. From kings to ordinary soldiers, from young lovers to old bawds, Shakespeare's characters speak modern English. The language of Shakespeare is the first and lasting affirmation of the great changes that took place in the sixteenth century, leaving the Middle English of Chaucer far behind. In many ways, the language has changed less in the 400 years since Shakespeare wrote than it did in the 150 years before he wrote.

The theatre was therefore the vehicle for poetry, action, and debate. In formal terms, Shakespeare used many kinds of play. His first tragedy, *Titus Andronicus*, uses the 'blood tragedy' model of the Latin writer, Seneca, which was very much to the taste of the late 1580s audiences. *The Comedy of Errors* similarly uses the model of the Roman comic dramatist Plautus; but Shakespeare soon goes beyond these classical forms in *The Comedy of Errors*. Plautus's plot of the confusion of identical twins is *doubled* – with two sets of twins, and twice the complicity of plot. In the next twenty or so years of his career he will constantly experiment with dramatic forms and techniques.

All Shakespeare's plays have come down to us in a standard form: five acts. But this division into acts and scenes is not always Shakespeare's own. He wrote the plays for performance, and there are many differences and variations between the various editions published in his own lifetime (usually called Quartos) and the First Folio, put together by John Heminge and Henry Condell in 1623. The division into acts and scenes of most of the plays belongs to almost a century later. In 1709, one of the first editors of Shakespeare's works, Nicholas Rowe, imposed a pattern of structural order on the works. This confirms his own age's concern with order and propriety rather than stressing Shakespeare's formal innovations and experiments. It was also Rowe who, for the first time, added many stage directions, and gave some indication of the location of scenes.

Shakespeare both affirms and challenges accepted values. He upholds, in general, the necessity of strong central power in the hands of a monarch, but he challenges any automatic right to power; worthiness is vital. He asserts the importance of history, but is quite prepared to bend historical 'truth' to make the play more viable – as in *Richard III* and *Macbeth*. (The original Macbeth was a good king who had no particular problems with his wife or with witches!) Where Shakespeare is perhaps most innovative is in his exploration of human defects, and the necessary acceptance of them as part of what makes humanity valuable.

> . . . this blow
> Might be the be-all and the end-all here,
> But here, upon this bank and shoal of time,
> We'd jump the life to come.
>
> *(Macbeth)*

Shakespeare's plays can be read as showing that imperfectibility has not only to be understood, but has also to be enjoyed in all its individual variety. This is what leads to the 'wisdom' of a long line of clowns and fools; comic characters with a serious purpose.

> When we are born, we cry that we are come
> To this great stage of fools.
>
> *(King Lear)*

Many of Shakespeare's characters have become so well known that they have almost taken on a life of their own. Queen Elizabeth I's own favourite was Falstaff (in *Henry IV, Parts One and Two*) and it was at her command that a comedy, *The Merry Wives of Windsor*, was created around this jovial, cynical, humorous, fat, pleasure-loving adventurer. Romeo and Juliet are the embodiment of young love which triumphs over everything, even death; Lady Macbeth is often seen as the strong, scheming woman behind an indecisive husband – and sometimes as the fourth witch, in a play where the witches represent demonic power; Othello and Desdemona are the perfect union of warrior and virgin (the classical Mars and Diana), whose union is ruined by the devil-figure, Iago; Shylock is almost the traditional stage Jew, but as human as any other character: as he says,

> Hath not a Jew eyes? Hath not a Jew hands, organs, dimensions, senses, affections, passions, fed with the same food, hurt with the same weapons, subject to the same diseases, healed by the same means, warmed and cooled by the same winter and summer, as a Christian is? If you prick us, do we not bleed? If you tickle us, do we not laugh? If you poison us, do we not die? And if you wrong us,

shall we not revenge? If we are like you in the rest, we will resemble you in that.

(The Merchant of Venice)

The list is endless, and, indeed, some of the major Shakespearean critics have been accused of treating the characters too much as if they were real people. This has been widely regarded as testimony to the timeless universality of their preoccupations, desires, fears, and basic humanity. Although the concerns are Renaissance and Western European, they strike a chord in many other cultures and times.

The character and the play of *Hamlet* are central to any discussion of Shakespeare's work. Hamlet has been described as melancholic and neurotic, as having an Oedipus complex, as being a failure and indecisive, as well as being a hero, and a perfect Renaissance prince. These judgements serve perhaps only to show how many interpretations of one character may be put forward. 'To be or not to be' is the centre of Hamlet's questioning. Reasons *not* to go on living outnumber reasons *for* living. But he goes on living, until he completes his revenge for his father's murder, and becomes 'most royal', the true 'Prince of Denmark' (which is the play's subtitle), in many ways the perfection of Renaissance man.

Hamlet's progress is a 'struggle of becoming' – of coming to terms with life, and learning to accept it, with all its drawbacks and challenges. He discusses the problems he faces directly with the audience, in a series of seven soliloquies – of which 'To be or not to be' is the fourth and central one. These seven steps, from the zero-point of a desire not to live, to complete awareness and acceptance (as he says, 'the readiness is all'), give a structure to the play, making the progress all the more tragic, as Hamlet reaches his aim, the perfection of his life, only to die.

> . . . we defy augury: there is a special providence in the fall of a sparrow. If it be now, 'tis not to come; if it be not to come, it will be now; if it be not now, yet it will come – the readiness is all. Since no man owes of aught he leaves, what is't to leave betimes?
>
> (Hamlet)

The play can thus be seen as a universal image of life and of the necessity of individual choice and action. No matter how tortured or successful a life will be, the end is death, and, to quote Hamlet's final words, 'the rest is silence'.

Shakespeare's plays became 'darker' or, according to some critical views, are 'problem' plays, in the years immediately before and after Queen Elizabeth's death and the accession of James VI of Scotland as King James I of the United Kingdom in 1603. But when viewed in theatrical terms – of character and action, discussion and debate – the 'problem' areas can be seen as examinations of serious social and moral concerns. The balance between justice and authority in *Measure for Measure* is set against a society filled with sexual corruption and amorality. The extremes of Puritanism and Catholicism meet in the characters of Angelo and Isabella. The justice figure of the Duke is, for most of the play, disguised as a priest. A false priest, giving false advice to an innocent man who is condemned to death, in a play which is basically a comedy, is an indication of the complexity of Shakespeare's experimentation with form and content at this stage of his career.

When the false priest/humanist Duke says 'Be absolute for death', it is almost exactly the reverse of Hamlet's decision 'to be' – and is rendered the more ambiguous by the Catholic friar's costume. The reply of the condemned Claudio must catch the sympathy of the audience, making them side with young love *against* hypocritical justice:

> Ay, but to die, and go we know not where;
> . . . 'tis too horrible.

Shakespeare's plays do not present easy solutions. The audience has to decide for itself. *King Lear* is perhaps the most disturbing in this respect. One of the key words of the whole play is 'Nothing'. When King Lear's daughter Cordelia announces that she can say 'Nothing' about her love for her father, the ties of family love fall apart, taking the king from the height of power to the limits of endurance, reduced to 'nothing' but 'a poor bare forked animal'. Here, instead of 'readiness' to accept any challenge, the young Edgar says 'Ripeness is all'. This is a maturity that comes of learning from experience. But, just as the audience begins to see hope in a desperate and violent situation, it learns that things can always get worse:

Who is't can say 'I am at the worst?'
　　. . . The worst is not
So long as we can say 'This is the worst.'

Shakespeare is exploring and redefining the geography of the human soul, taking his characters and his audience further than any other writer into the depths of human behaviour. The range of his plays covers all the 'form and pressure' of mankind in the modern world. They move from politics to family, from social to personal, from public to private. He imposed no fixed moral, no unalterable code of behaviour. That would come to English society many years after Shakespeare's death, and after the tragic hypothesis of *Hamlet* was fulfilled in 1649, when the people killed the King and replaced his rule with the Commonwealth. Some critics argue that Shakespeare supported the monarchy and set himself against any revolutionary tendencies. Certainly he is on the side of order and harmony, and his writing reflects a monarchic context rather than the more republican context which replaced the monarchy after 1649.

It would be fanciful to see Shakespeare as foretelling the decline of the Stuart monarchy. He was not a political commentator. Rather, he was a psychologically acute observer of humanity who had a unique ability to portray his observations, explorations, and insights in dramatic form, in the richest and most exciting language ever used in the English theatre. His works are still quoted endlessly, performed in every language and culture in the world, rewritten and reinterpreted by every new generation.

Shakespeare's final plays move against the tide of most Jacobean theatre, which was concentrating on blood tragedy or social comedy. After the tragedies of *Coriolanus* and *Antony and Cleopatra*, and the sheer misanthropy of *Timon of Athens*, there is a change of tone, a new optimism. Prose writing about voyages across the sea and faraway places had created a vogue for romances. The late plays, from *Pericles* to *The Tempest*, have been variously described as pastorals, romances, and even tragi-comedies. They all end in harmony, and use the passage of time (usually a whole generation) to heal the disharmony with which the plays open. They echo the structure of the masque form which was now popular at court: 'anti-masque' or negative elements being defeated by positive elements, and a final harmony achieved. A 'brave new world', as Miranda describes it in *The Tempest*, is created out of the turbulence of the old.

Prospero's domination of the native Caliban has been interpreted by some critics as having overtones of colonialism, which reflect the period's interest in voyages and in the new colonial experiments in Virginia and elsewhere.

> CALIBAN This island's mine, by Sycorax my mother,
>   Which thou tak'st from me. When thou camest first,
>   Thou strok'st me, and made much of me; wouldst give me
>   Water with berries in it; and teach me how
>   To name the bigger light, and how the less,
>   That burn by day and night: and then I loved thee,
>   And showed thee all the qualities o' the isle,
>   The fresh springs, brine-pits, barren place and fertile:
>   Cursed be I that did so! All the charms
>   Of Sycorax, toads, beetles, bats, light on you!
>   For I am all the subjects that you have,
>   Which first was mine own King: and here you sty me
>   In this hard rock, whiles you do keep from me
>   The rest o' the island.
>
> (*The Tempest*)

This is the beginning of a theme which will grow considerably in importance in literature from *The Tempest* to Aphra Behn's *Oroonoko* at the end of the century, and on to the international recognition of colonial voices in literature in modern times.

It is fashionable to see *The Tempest* as Shakespeare's farewell to his art. However, as with the early comedy *A Midsummer Night's Dream*, the audience is left with a sense of magic, of transience, of awareness of the potential of humanity and the expressive potential of the theatre as a form.

The idea of transience, of the brevity of human life, is important in Renaissance writing. Before the Reformation, there was an emphasis on eternity and eternal life which implied security and optimism. Now the life of man is seen as 'nasty, brutish, and short', and there are many images which underline this theme. In *Measure for Measure*, man is seen 'like an angry ape' who is 'dressed in a little brief authority'; Macbeth describes life as 'but a walking shadow, a poor player, / That struts and frets his hour upon the stage, / And then is heard no more'. The stage becomes an image, a metaphor of the world and human action. The stage can encompass the huge range of emotions, from magic and joy to tragedy and despair, which mankind experiences. The audience is invited to *share* the experience rather than simply watch it from a distance, and to identify with the characters in their joys and sufferings.

> When we are born, we cry that we are come
> To this great stage of fools.
>
> (*King Lear*)

THE SONNETS

If Shakespeare had not become the best-known dramatist in English, he would still be remembered as a poet. His longer poems, such as *Venus and Adonis* (1593) and *The Rape of Lucrece* (1594) are classically inspired narratives. *Venus and Adonis*, in *sesta rima*, was one of Shakespeare's most immediately popular works, being reprinted at least fifteen times before 1640.

His sonnets, probably written in the mid-1590s, use the Elizabethan form – rhyming a b a b c d c d e f e f g g – rather than the Petrarchan form which had been popular earlier. They are poems of love and of time; of love outlasting time, and poetry outlasting all. Critics have tried to identify the mysterious young man and dark lady to whom the sonnets are addressed, but it is more realistic to see the poems not as having particular addressees but rather as examining the masculine/feminine elements in all humanity and in all love relationships. Power, as in the plays, is another major concern of the sonnets. The power of the beloved to command is a microcosm of all power. The suffering of a lover is a symbol of all suffering.

For some critics, the Elizabethan sonnet sequence is largely to be regarded as 'a long poem in fourteen-line stanzas'. Such collections as Sidney's *Astrophel and Stella* and Shakespeare's *Sonnets* have been much analysed in terms of their formal organisation, especially in relation to numerology. In this reading, Shakespeare's 154 sonnets are based on a triangle: 17 times 3, times 3, plus 1. No definitive explanation for the order in which the sonnets are numbered has ever been put forward convincingly. This only serves to add to the pleasantly enigmatic nature of the collection.

Indeed, ambiguity is at the heart of Shakespeare's sonnets. Whether the 'I' loves or is loved by a man or a woman:

> Two loves I have, of comfort and despair,
> Which like two spirits do suggest me still;
> The better angel is a man right fair,
> The worser spirit a woman colour'd ill . . .
>
> (Sonnet 144)

Whether, in the 1590s, he considers himself a success or a failure, together with the constant preoccupation with time and transience, all serve to underline the lack of certainty in the poems. 'I' very often presents himself as rejected, some kind of outcast:

> When in disgrace with Fortune and men's eyes,
> I all alone beweep my outcast state,
> And trouble deaf heaven with my bootless cries,
> And look upon myself, and curse my fate . . .
>
> (Sonnet 29)

There is a truth of emotion and of constancy in the affections of the poetic 'I'. Homoerotic the attraction to his male love certainly is:

> . . . my state
> Like to the lark at break of day arising
> From sullen earth, sings hymns at heaven's gate;
> For thy sweet love remember'd such wealth brings
> That then I scorn to change my state with kings.
>
> (Sonnet 29)

The more modern word 'homosexual' does not really apply, as Sonnet 20 makes clear in its final, sexually punning lines:

> But since she prick'd thee out for women's pleasure,
> Mine be thy love, and thy love's use their treasure.

Shakespeare has been staged, adapted, studied and adopted throughout the centuries. It is a mark of his universality that his plays have survived all the appropriations, attacks, uses and interpretations made of them. They are used institutionally in education to show what is best in high-cultural ideology; they have been read as nihilistically modern, incorrigibly reactionary, and as 'a cultural creation which has no intrinsic authority and whose validity is wide open to dispute'. It is true that Shakespeare has been made into something he was not in his own lifetime, a cultural institution and an emblem, whose quality and artistry are not in doubt. So he will no doubt survive radical and systematic counter–interpretation just as he has survived institutional appropriation from Victorian times to the present. He can be, as critics have described him, 'our contemporary', 'alternative', 'radical', 'historicist', 'subversive', 'traditional' and 'conservative'. But his plays continue to speak to audiences and readers, as 'imagination bodies forth / The forms of things unknown', and he explores the known and the unknown in human experience. Reinterpretation, on a wide scale of opinions from radical to hegemonic, will always be a vital part of Shakespearean study. As long as the critics never take on more importance than the texts, Shakespeare's plays and poems will survive as 'eternal lines to time'.

LANGUAGE NOTE
Changing patterns of 'thou' and 'you'

> TOBY Go, write it in a martial hand. Be curst and brief; it is no matter how witty, so it be eloquent and full of invention. Taunt him with the license of ink. If thou thoust him thrice, it shall not be amiss. . . .
>
> *(Twelfth Night)*

By the time of the Elizabethan period, a distinction had developed in the language between the singular pronouns YOU and THOU and their related pronoun forms (ye, your, yours, yourself / thee, thine, thyself, thy, etc.). In general, the differences can be explained by analogy with the ways in which in modern English names are used as terms of address between individuals. Thus, THOU is similar to the use of a personal name such as John or Mary, whereas YOU is rather more formal and compares with the use of titles such as Mr Jones, Dr Davies.

THOU and YOU thus marked different personal relations, the former pronoun being more intimate and informal and the latter more polite and respectful. However, uses at this time were becoming more varied and increasingly indicative of particular social relationships. These changing patterns of pronouns were noticeable in the writing of the time, particularly in Elizabethan drama.

For example, in the extract from *Twelfth Night* above, the use of THOU to a stranger (Cesario – who is to be challenged to a fight) is encouraged by Sir Toby as an unambiguous insult. In Ben Jonson's *Volpone*, Celia, somewhat submissively, addresses Corvino as YOU, but is in turn frequently addressed by him as THOU, most markedly when he is being playful and affectionate with her but also when he is angry with her, as in the scene where he takes her to Volpone's bedroom and has difficulty in persuading her to comply with their wishes. In the scene from *King Lear* in which Edgar, disguised as a madman, meets with his father, the blinded Gloucester, the pronoun YOU maintains the deliberately polite distance of the encounter. The Steward, however, who believes Edgar to be a beggar, uses the THOU form to him as a clear marker of social inferiority. In much of the drama of the time there are similar swift fluctuations in usage, allowing dramatists to chart the ebb and flow of personal, emotional and social relationships with considerable subtlety.

During the seventeenth century, YOU becomes the preferred form and THOU begins to disappear, although THOU is preserved in the Bible and in many religious uses, as a deliberately informal use in Quaker writings and to refer to inanimate or abstract objects (for example, nature is frequently directly addressed by poets as 'THOU'). The retention of THOU for reference to God indicates that the personal and intimate take precedence over the perception of God as a superior being.

The social pressures on YOU are considerable at this time, with YOU being increasingly identified with 'polite' society in and around the court and with the City of London, which was now growing even more rapidly to become the economic and political power base of the country. People wished to be associated with the social power of the people of London and gradually language use changed in accordance with economic and social reality. YOU thus became the standard form it is today – in both singular and plural forms – as it was used increasingly between and across all social classes and language groups and for the wide range of functions which had previously been served by YOU and THOU together.

THE METAPHYSICAL POETS

Had we but world enough, and time,
This coyness, lady, were no crime
(Andrew Marvell, *To His Coy Mistress*)

While theatre was the most public literary form of the period, poetry tended to be more personal, more private. Indeed, it was often published for only a limited circle of readers. This was true of Shakespeare's sonnets, as we have seen, and even more so for the Metaphysical poets, whose works were published mostly after their deaths. John Donne and George Herbert are the most significant of these poets.

The term 'Metaphysical' was used to describe their work by the eighteenth-century critic, Samuel Johnson. He intended the adjective to be pejorative. He attacked the poets' lack of feeling, their learning, and the surprising range of images and comparisons they used. Donne and Herbert were certainly very innovative poets, but the term 'Metaphysical' is only a label, which is now used to describe the modern impact of their writing. After three centuries of neglect and disdain, the Metaphysical poets have come to be very highly regarded and have been influential in twentieth-century British poetry and criticism. They used contemporary scientific discoveries and theories, the topical debates on humanism, faith, and eternity, colloquial speech-based rhythms, and innovative verse forms, to examine the relationship between the individual, his God, and the universe. Their 'conceits', metaphors and images, paradoxes and intellectual complexity make the poems a constant challenge to the reader.

Among the contrasts which the works of Donne and Herbert present is their emphasis on sensuality and pleasure, which seems to conflict with their profoundly religious concerns and experiences. Both became men of the church after varied careers in public affairs and Parliament and before their involvement with official religion. So the balance, and conflict, between religion, doubt and secular reality is no more nor less than a reflection of their own experiences.

As university-educated men, living at the centre of public life in a time of intellectual and spiritual change, it is hardly surprising that their interests should include the new discoveries of science, geography and astronomy. Even in one of his later Divine Poems (*Hymn to God my God, in my Sickness*), Donne compares his doctors to 'cosmographers' and himself to 'their map'. What is perhaps surprising is the humour which is employed in the conceits. For example, Donne describes his mistress as his 'New-found-land'. He imagines the sun going round the earth but finding no greater joy than he and his lover find in their small room. In *The Flea*, for instance, he tries to persuade his lover that sleeping with him would be no worse a sin than a flea sucking her blood. Early on in his poetic career Donne constantly challenges death with the eternity of love; later he challenges it with spiritual salvation as in his sonnet, *Death be not proud*.

Donne's prolific poetic career – his Songs and Sonnets, Elegies, Epigrams, Satires, Verse Letters, Divine Poems – span a remarkable range from his first celebrations of the sensual to his final spiritual humility before God, but this is still phrased in erotic terms, as shown in his Holy Sonnets: *Batter my heart, three person'd God*. The poet compares himself to a town under siege and closes with the paradoxical couplet addressing God:

> For I
> Except you enthral me, never shall be free
> Nor ever chaste, except you ravish me.

Certainly, of all the Metaphysical poets, and perhaps of all poets writing before the Romantic period, Donne's scope and depth both in form and emotion is the poetic achievement which has found most recognition and sympathy in the latter part of the twentieth century. Direct address – to God, to the sun:

> Busy old fool, unruly Sun,
> Why dost thou thus,
> Through windows, and through curtains call on us?
>
> (*The Sun Rising*)

to death, to a lover:

> I wonder by my troth, what thou and I
> Did till we lov'd? were we not wean'd till then?
>
> (*The Good Morrow*)

and to the reader – is characteristically part of the Metaphysical poets' challenge to their own positions in relation to society, to their self-perceptions, to love and religion. George Herbert's interlocutor is most often his God. His work, whether filled with doubt or praise, is a chronicle of feelings and thoughts mostly in relation to God, and is set down in forms which are often striking.

Although his poems can appear simple, sometimes taking the pictorial form of their subject such as an altar or wings, Herbert's arguments with his God can be tortuous and complex. He moves between faith and doubt, acceptance and rejection, in a way which echoes the struggle in his own life to abandon the possibility of civil advancement in favour of a quiet life as a country parson. One of his best-known poems, *The Collar* – itself a significant metaphor – opens with an outraged shout of defiance in which the poet refuses to submit to God's will but closes with a humble acceptance:

> I struck the board, and cry'd, No more.
> > I will abroad.
> > What? shall I ever sign and pine?
>
> . . .
>
> But as I rav'd and grew more fierce and wild
> > At every word
> > Me thoughts I heard one calling, *Child!*
> > And I reply'd, *My Lord.*

The twentieth-century critic T.S. Eliot, whose influence was considerable in recovering the works of Donne and Herbert to critical acceptance, makes an important point about how they differ from the poets of the Restoration and after. 'Something,' he suggests, 'happened to the mind of England between the time of Donne and Herbert and the time of Tennyson and Browning; it is the difference between the intellectual poet and the reflective poet.' Thought, according to Eliot, becomes separate from feeling, whereas 'a thought to Donne was an experience; it modified his sensibility'.

John Donne and George Herbert can be seen as experimenters both in poetic form and the subject matter they used. They were also innovators in linguistic directness of expression. They reflect in poetry the intellectual and spiritual challenges of an age which wanted to expand human horizons. When the mood of the age altered, and safety and stability came to be preferred over exploration and excitement, their poetry met with less approval. It had to wait for the atmosphere of the twentieth century to find acclaim.

> Lord, who createst man in wealth and store,
>   Though foolishly he lost the same,
>   Decaying more and more,
>   Till he became
>   Most poor;
>   With thee
>   O let me rise
>   As larks, harmoniously,
>   And sing this day thy victories:
> Then shall the fall further the flight in me.
>
> My tender age in sorrow did begin:
>   And still with sicknesses and shame
>   Thou didst so punish sin:
>   That I became
>   Most thin.
>   With thee
>   Let me combine
>   And feel this day thy victory:
>   For, if I imp my wing on thine
> Affliction shall advance the flight in me.
>   (George Herbert, *Easter Wings*)

Henry Vaughan described himself as a 'convert' to Herbert, one of many 'of whom I am the least'. In Vaughan's poetry there is less of the anguished struggle and negotiation found in Herbert. Rather he presents a world of innocence, bordering on the mystical, which in some ways anticipates the concerns of the Romantic poets. It is important to consider him as Welsh rather than English, and his visions are of the countryside – he is a poet of flowers and clouds, of childhood innocence and 'shadows of eternity'. As such, he has always appealed to writers concerned with childhood, notably the twentieth-century novelist Forrest Reid, who used the title of one of Vaughan's best-known poems *The Retreat* for the central novel of a trilogy on childhood and the loss of innocence (1936). The innocence in Vaughan is an ethereal and marvelling spirit of enchantment which could produce such lines as 'I saw Eternity the other night'.

> O how I long to travel back,
> And tread again that ancient track!
> That I might once more reach that plain
> Where first I left my glorious train;
> From whence the enlightened spirit sees
> That shady City of Palm-trees.

Deep emotion can enter this world of wonder, as when he laments the loss of his friends in 'They are all gone into the world of light'. *Silex Scintillans* (1650) is the first major volume of his poems, and an enlarged second edition appeared in 1655. He also wrote secular poems, love poems, and devotional works, and in 1678 published a volume containing poems by himself and his twin brother, Thomas, who was one of the most important writers in the field of alchemy, magic and Rosicrucianism of his time.

Thomas Carew (pronounced Carey) wrote many lyrics and songs, though with a rather more cynical tone than those of his friend, Sir John Suckling. He is first noted for an elegy to John Donne and for one of the best-known masques of the 1630s, *Coelum Britannicum*, performed with settings by Inigo Jones in 1634. Carew's *Poems* of 1640, the year of his death, range from the erotic to the satirical, and express passion vividly, as in *Mediocrity in Love Rejected*:

> Give me more love, or more disdain;
> The torrid, or the frozen zone,
> Bring equal ease unto my pain;
> The temperate affords me none:
> Either extreme, of love, or hate,
> Is sweeter than a calm estate.

The poetry of Thomas Traherne is, more than any other poetry of the seventeenth century, poetry of joy. He anticipates Christopher Smart in his celebration of creation, and has even been compared to the nineteenth-century American poet Walt Whitman for his unconventional, exuberant verse forms. Traherne was, however, more moderate in his life than these comparisons might suggest. He was a devout man who worked in the sphere of antiquities, publishing *Roman Forgeries* in 1673, which documented the falsification of church documents by the church of Rome in the ninth century. His poems were not published until after his death, some in *Christian Ethics* (1675), more in *Centuries* in 1699 and, through the good luck of his notebook being found in the 1890s, *Poetical Works* in 1903 and *Select Meditations* in 1908. Like Henry Vaughan, he gives a highly original depiction of childhood experience, and stresses the need for the adult to return to an appreciation of childhood simplicity. But what perhaps sets him apart is his expression of notions of the infinite.

> Look how far off those lower Skies
> Extend themselves! scarce with mine Eyes
> I can them reach. O ye my Friends,
> What Secret borders on those Ends?
> (*Shadows in the Water* from *Poems of Felicity*)

Traherne explores the infinite possibilities of the human mind and spirit, finding, in a way, a concept of God in this vastness of human potentiality: 'Life: life is all!'

Richard Crashaw is an unusual case. The son of a Puritan clergyman, he converted to Catholicism at around the age of 33 in the mid-1640s, and had to flee the country. His poetry is religious, and is exaggerated in style and expression, making him perhaps the most baroque of English religious writers. His main themes are ecstasy and martyrdom, although his secular poems touch on the more usual themes of love and the search for 'That not impossible she'.

> Who ere she be,
> That not impossible she
> That shall command my heart and me . . .
> (*Wishes to His Supposed Mistress* from *Delights of the Muses*)

Steps to the Temple (1646) and *Carmen Deo Nostro* (1652) contain most of his poems, the best known of which is probably *The Flaming Heart*. Like all the poets classified as 'Metaphysical', Crashaw has a mastery of verse form, and an ability to match natural language and heightened emotion with vivid imagery and a highly personalised view of religion and suffering. Not until Swinburne, at the end of the nineteenth century, was there to be a poet who so extravagantly celebrated the bliss of suffering.

The only Metaphysical poet who spans the early and later parts of the seventeenth century is Andrew Marvell. His poetry ranged from political to passionate. *An Horatian Ode upon Cromwell's Return from Ireland* was written in 1650 to celebrate the triumph of the Commonwealth, and is one of the few important political poems in English.

> And now the Irish are asham'd
> To see themselves in one Year tam'd:
>   So much one Man can do,
>   That does both act and know.
> They can affirm his Praises best,
> And have, though overcome, confest
>   How good he is, how just,
>   And fit for the highest Trust:
> Nor yet grown stiffer with Command,
> But still in the Republick's hand:
>   How fit he is to sway
>   That can so well obey.

The praise of Cromwell may, with hindsight, seem exaggerated; but 'one Man' (i.e. not the King) was regarded as the new hope of the nation. Marvell has been accused of being a time-server; but, in the climate of the seventeenth century, almost every poet changed sides, wrote flattering verses, and satirical works criticising public figures.

Marvell's seductive address *To His Coy Mistress* brings together the favourite Renaissance themes of love and transience, with one of the most memorable images of time passing in all English poetry:

> Had we but world enough, and time,
> This coyness, lady, were no crime, . . .
> But at my back I always hear
> Time's wingèd chariot hurrying near.

THE CAVALIER POETS

One sign that England was changing in the 1630s and 1640s was the polarisation of political opinions between those who supported the

King, Charles I, and the Puritan Parliament led by Oliver Cromwell. A group of monarchists collectively known as the Cavalier poets – Carew, Herrick, Lovelace and Suckling were the most prominent – provided a last flourish of lyricism before the Revolution brought in a different intellectual climate after the execution of the King in 1649. The Cavaliers' poetry is simpler than that of the Metaphysicals. It recalls the writings of Sir Philip Sidney, in early Renaissance writing, rather than the more deeply engaged writing of Shakespeare and his contemporaries. Formally, the Cavaliers' poetic master was Ben Jonson, whose combination of classical distance and elegance in his poetry was the main model for their verse.

'Gather ye rosebuds while ye may' echoes the theme of transience so common in the Renaissance, but the poet Robert Herrick (in this exhortation *To the Virgins, to Make Much of Time*, 1648) deliberately avoids either the seductiveness of Marvell or the depths of Donne.

> Gather ye rosebuds while ye may,
> Old Time is still a-flying;
> And this same flower that smiles today,
> Tomorrow will be dying.

The intention is deliberately lyrical, aiming at the delicacy of a miniature rather than engaging in debate or polemic. But Herrick, like his contemporary Richard Lovelace, was very much concerned with the political upheavals of the time; and the refinement of the lyric forms may often contain serious reflections, as in Lovelace's impassioned lines on freedom, *To Althea, From Prison*:

> Stone walls do not a prison make,
> Nor iron bars a cage.

These lines were written as the somewhat authoritarian Puritan rule took command under Oliver Cromwell, who remains one of the most ambiguous of English heroes. John Milton hailed him in a sonnet as 'our chief of men', and praised his defence of liberty and conscience. Cromwell seemed the embodiment of Renaissance values: Marvell wrote, 'If these the times, then this must be the man'. Yet two years after his death the monarchy was restored, and for many years the Commonwealth was seen as a black period of Puritan extremism, austerity and restraint. Many writers such as Milton and Dryden found themselves changing allegiance as they saw the Revolution lose its impact and decline into a return to older forms and ways.

JACOBEAN DRAMA – TO THE CLOSURE OF THE THEATRES, 1642

> *Come, violent death,*
> *Serve for mandragora to make me sleep!*
> (John Webster, *The Duchess of Malfi*)

BEN JONSON

Ben Jonson, who wrote an Ode (*To the Memory of my Beloved, the Author Mr William Shakespeare: And What He Hath Left Us*) for the First Folio of Shakespeare's collected plays (1623), is the Bard's greatest contemporary. It is difficult to sum Jonson up briefly because, as a writer, he was a master of many styles and genres, and, as a character, achieved high recognition. He was also imprisoned more than once.

Two comedies – *The Alchemist* (1610) and *Volpone* (1605) – are Jonson's lasting masterpieces. They depict characters in the grip of obsessions (usually for love or for money), and the farcical build-up of the plays reaches a climax of deceit and trickery that is unique in the theatre. The wonderfully named Sir Epicure Mammon is the target in *The Alchemist* of the crooks; among them, Subtle and Face. Here is the moment when he discovers they have gone, taking his money with them.

MAMMON   The whole nest are fled!
LOVEWIT What sort of birds were they?
MAMMON   A kind of choughs,
  Or thievish daws, sir, that have pick'd my purse
  Of eight score and ten pounds, within these five weeks,
  Beside my first materials; and my goods
  That lie i' the cellar; which I am glad they ha' left;
  I may have home yet.

These plays have been defined, inaccurately, as 'the comedy of humours'; where the 'humour' is the principal characteristic of an individual. The balance of the humours was considered to be a determining factor of human nature, and the exaggeration of any one of them (blood, phlegm, choler, and melancholy; corresponding to the physical 'elements' of earth, air, fire, and water) gave rise to the kind of comic obsession Jonson portrayed.

Two early plays are significant for their handling of 'humours'. 'Humours' are a character's main emotional driving force, such as jealousy, anger, over-protectiveness, or similar obsessive behavioural traits. *Every Man In his Humour,* performed in 1598 (tradition has it that Shakespeare was one of its actors), and *Every Man Out Of his Humour* (1599), give Jonson the opportunity to expound his theories of drama, and of how humours govern character.

Jonson offers us, in *Every Man In his Humour*, his own variations on the suspicious father (Knowell), the errant son (Edward), the wily servant (Brainworm), the braggart soldier (Bobadill), the would-be poet (Matthew), and the gull (Stephen). This play, and *Every Man Out Of his Humour*, are comedies of correction, in which a resolution of misunderstandings is accompanied by a degree of moral comment: Jonson, unlike Shakespeare, often did not resist the chance to point up a didactic moral in his plays. For some critics, too, Jonson's comedy of humours was a polemical weapon, to answer increasing attacks against the theatre and plays by the Puritans of the early seventeenth century.

Jonson also uses contemporary characters from London life in many of his works, notably *Bartholomew Fair* (1614), helping to establish a genre which came to be known as 'city comedy'. But Jonson's background was classical, and his tragedies are severely Roman, closely following Latin models in their subject matter and style. The styles of his poetry vary greatly too, and this has led perhaps to an undervaluing of his poetic achievement. They are a high point of English 'classical' writing, with a wholly English exuberance in the exploration of rhetoric and language.

The poetic form and language in Jonson's *My Picture Left in Scotland* (1618–19) portray as richly the sense of love and loss as works by the poets more usually considered the major poetic voices of the time.

I now think, Love is rather deaf, than blind,
    For else it could not be,
        That she,
Whom I adore so much, should so slight me,
    And cast my love behind:
I'm sure my language to her, was as sweet,
      And every close did meet
    In sentence, as of subtle feet,
          As hath the the youngest He,
      That sits in shadow of Apollo's tree.

MASQUES

The masque became an important theatrical form during the reigns of James I and Charles I. It was a court entertainment, performed for the King and others of the court on special occasions. Masque performances were quite different from the public theatre performances at the Globe, the Blackfriars, and the other London theatres. They were held in private royal halls (such as the Banqueting Hall in Whitehall), and were vastly expensive to mount: lavish costumes, elaborate stage designs and machinery, spectacular effects, laid on usually for one single performance. The designer of the most successful masques was Inigo Jones, who had studied architecture in Italy. He is credited with bringing a new architectural style to English theatre: the proscenium arch, a sort of picture frame behind which the stage action happens. It was this kind of stage which was gradually to replace Shakespeare's open thrust stage later in the seventeenth century, and was to put a distance between actors and audiences for the next three hundred years.

This theatrical distancing effect reflects the moral intention of the masque. Discussion and debate, common in the public drama, are reduced to simplified moralising – good defeating evil, light triumphing over darkness – always with the figure of the monarch (rather than a recognisably human individual) at the centre of the universe. Almost inevitably, the words of the text of the masque became less important than the spectacular scenic effects, the music and dance, and the celebratory atmosphere of the event.

Jonson himself described, in *The Masque of Beautie*, in the second decade of the seventeenth century, how his work was intended 'to glorify the Court', and to give the courtiers some roles to perform: negroes in *The Masque of Blackness*; classical figures very often, symbolic figures (of Good and Evil) almost always. We can see something of the spectacle involved, in this moment from *Oberon*:

SILENUS See, the rock begins to ope.
> Now you shall enjoy your hope;
> 'Tis about the hour, I know.
> [*There the whole scene opened, and within was discover'd the* Frontispiece *of a bright and glorious* Palace, *whose gates and walls were transparent.*]

Ben Jonson wrote the texts of many of the masques of James I's reign (1603–25), but became increasingly disillusioned that Inigo Jones's contribution was achieving greater recognition than his own words. This had led to an undervaluing of much of Jonson's court writing, and has contributed to the uncertain level of his critical stature as a playwright – with only *Volpone* and *The Alchemist* being generally regarded as masterpieces. In his own day, however, Jonson was the leading light of the literary world, Poet Laureate from 1616 to his death in 1637, and had a great influence on a generation of writers: 'the sons . . .' or 'the tribe of Ben'.

OTHER DRAMATISTS OF THE EARLY SEVENTEENTH CENTURY

The great flourishing of drama as a popular form in the 1590s left an enormous number of plays, and a generation of playwrights who are major writers but who have been overshadowed by the ever-present figure of William Shakespeare.

The distinction between tragedy and comedy, in writers other than Shakespeare, becomes more and more distinct during the first twenty-five years of the seventeenth century. The world of Jacobean tragedy is a dark world of corruption, perversion, blood and passion. The world of comedy is more localised, 'city comedy', based on the city of London and its people, with their obsessions, above all, with money and sex.

The major figures in Jacobean drama (Shakespeare and Ben Jonson aside) are Thomas Middleton, John Webster, Thomas Dekker, Francis Beaumont and John Fletcher (usually in collaboration), Thomas Heywood, and Philip Massinger. In the Caroline period (after the accession of Charles I in 1625) – although Jonson was still writing – the most significant (tragic) dramatist was John Ford.

Almost all playwrights in this period wrote some of their works in collaboration with other writers: such was the demand for new plays that collaboration was one means of keeping up with demand. Shakespeare is thought to have had collaborators on *Pericles* (not included in the First Folio, but in the second issue (1664) of the Third Folio) and on *Henry VIII*, and there are several apocryphal plays in which he might have had a hand. *Sir Thomas More* is the best known of these. *The Two Noble Kinsmen* is sometimes included in the Shakespeare canon, sometimes not. It is not included in any of the folio editions of Shakespeare's plays, but has now more or less been accepted as a collaboration between Shakespeare and John Fletcher.

Fletcher's name is usually associated with Francis Beaumont, and *The Maid's Tragedy* (1610–11) is among the most notable of their joint works. Both wrote plays individually, Beaumont's *The Knight of the Burning Pestle* (1607–8) being one of the most adventurous experiments in comedy of the time. As Ralph, an apprentice, sets himself up as the 'Knight' with a pestle (a kitchen implement used for grinding herbs) rather than a sword, there are comments from 'the audience' which create different levels of performance, as stage and 'audience' interact. There are also some neat jokes against the old-fashioned language of knights.

> RALPH My elder prentice Tim shall be my trusty squire, and little George my dwarf. Hence, my blue apron! Yet, in remembrance of my former trade, upon my shield shall be portrayed a Burning Pestle, and I will be called the Knight of the Burning Pestle.
> WIFE Nay, I dare swear thou wilt not forget thy old trade; thou wert ever meek.
> RALPH Tim!
> TIM Anon.
> RALPH My beloved squire, and George my dwarf, I charge you that from henceforth you never call me by any other name but 'the right courteous and valiant Knight of the Burning Pestle'; and that you

never call any female by the name of a woman or wench; but 'fair lady', if she have her desires, if not, 'distressed damsel'; that you call all forests and heaths 'deserts', and all horses 'palfreys'.

WIFE This is very fine, faith. – Do the gentlemen like Ralph, think you, husband?

CITIZEN Aye, I warrant thee; the players would give all the shoes in their shop for him.

RALPH My beloved squire Tim, stand out. Admit this were a desert, and over it a knight-errant pricking, and I should bid you inquire of his intents, what would you say?

TIM Sir, my master sent me to know whither you are riding?

RALPH No, thus: 'Fair sir, the right courteous and valiant Knight of the Burning Pestle commanded me to inquire upon what adventure you are bound, whether to relieve some distressed damsel, or otherwise.'

Jonson, Nashe, Middleton and many others worked on theatrical collaborations. One result of all this is that it can be difficult to attribute authorship to some texts.

The tragedy of revenge, which had been highly successful in the 1590s, reaches a kind of climax in *The Revenger's Tragedy*, published in 1607. In this scene, the revenger, Vindice, is pleased with his murderous work: *pleasure* in killing is something of a new development in Jacobean tragedy.

LUSSURIOSO Be witnesses of a strange spectacle:
  Choosing for private conference that sad room,
  We found the Duke my father geal'd in blood.

1ST SERVANT My Lord the Duke! – run, hie thee Nencio,
  Startle the court by signifying so much.

                                          [*Exit* NENCIO]

VINDICE [*aside*] Thus much by wit a deep revenger can,
  When murder's known, to be the clearest man.
  We're fordest off, and with as bold an eye,
  Survey his body as the standers-by.

LUSSURIOSO My royal father, too basely let blood,
  By a malevolent slave.

HIPPOLITO [*aside*]   Hark,
  He calls thee slave again.

VINDICE [*aside*]   H' 'as lost, he may.

LUSSURIOSO Oh sight, look hither, see, his lips are gnawn
  With poison.
VINDICE   How – his lips? by th' mass they be.
LUSSURIOSO O villain – O rogue – O slave – O rascal!
HIPPOLITO [*aside*] O good deceit, he quits him with like terms.

For many years, the author's name associated with this black farce, a chilling parody of the genre which reached its highest point in Shakespeare's *Hamlet*, was Cyril Tourneur. Recent research has suggested that the work is more probably by Thomas Middleton. He was an author of considerable range, writing many of the pageants for London's Lord Mayor's Shows, as well as two of the major tragedies of the time, both from the 1620s – *The Changeling* (in collaboration with William Rowley) and *Women Beware Women*. *The Changeling* uses the setting of a madhouse to bring out some of the contrasts between reason and madness. Here, Isabella speaks to Antonio – the changeling of the title – who pretends to be mad; Lollio is the keeper of the madhouse.

ISABELLA How long hast thou been a fool?
ANTONIO Ever since I came hither, Cousin.
ISABELLA Cousin? I'm none of thy cousins, fool.
ANTONIO Oh Mistress, fools have always so much wit as to claim their
  kindred.
                                        [*Madman within*]
  Bounce, bounce, he falls, he falls.
ISABELLA Hark you, your scholars in the upper room
  Are out of order.
LOLLIO Must I come amongst you there? Keep you the fool, Mistress,
  I'll go up, and play left-handed Orlando amongst the madmen.

In the final scene, murder is revealed as the final result of sexual corruption, when the heroine confesses to her husband; just before she and her corruptor, De Flores, die:

BEATRICE Beneath the stars, upon yon meteor
  Ever hung my fate, 'mongst things corruptible,
  I ne'er could pluck it from him, my loathing
  Was prophet to the rest, but ne'er believ'd;
  Mine honour fell with him, and now my life.
  Alsemero, I am a stranger to your bed,

> Your bed was coz'ned on the nuptial night,
> For which your false bride died.
> ALSEMERO   Diaphanta!
> DE FLORES Yes, and the while I coupled with your mate
> At barley-brake; now we are left in hell.
> VERMANDERO We are all there, it circumscribes here.
> DE FLORES I lov'd this woman in spite of her heart,
> Her love I earn'd out of Piracquo's murder.
> TOMAZO Ha, my brother's murtherer.

This atmosphere of corruption – sexual and moral – is central to Jacobean tragedy, and will explore even further the depths of human weakness in the two decades which follow *The Changeling*. It was partly this content and partly the political undertones wich gave the Puritans considerable grounds for opposing the theatre, and, indeed, censoring it on occasion.

Middleton's *A Game at Chess* (1624), an allegorical comedy on political themes, putting on stage the figures of the kings of England and Spain, as well as other recognisable aristocratic and political characters, was suppressed by the authorities – after an immensely successful run of nine performances: this was one of the earliest manifestations of political censorship. Jonson had had trouble earlier in the century, when some of his writing was considered treasonous, pro-Catholic and anti-Scottish; but the strongest complaint against *A Game at Chess* came from the Spanish Ambassador.

Censorship, at this time, generally reflected anxieties for the stability of the state at a time of considerable political uncertainty. Internal politics in the late 1590s were concerned with the possibility of revolt; with foreign powers, such as the Spanish in the 1620s, it was felt necessary to maintain diplomatic harmony: a play like *A Game at Chess* risked causing offence because of the way it satirised the Spanish in a religious and political context.

Some reason for the Puritans' objections to the 'immorality' of the stage can be found in the highly charged passions displayed, for instance, in John Webster's *The White Devil* and *The Duchess of Malfi* (both between 1609 and 1613), tragedies which raise the themes of blood, lust and intrigue to new heights of poetry and violence. It is this rich mixture of shocking themes and vivid language which characterises Jacobean tragedy, and gives it an intensity which no other age has repeated in English drama. In the scene of her death at the hands of Bosola, the Duchess of Malfi accepts her fate: but her servant, Cariola, is less amenable.

DUCHESS   Come, violent death,
    Serve for mandragora to make me sleep! –
    Go tell my brothers, when I am laid out,
    They then may feed in quiet.
                               [*They strangle her*]
BOSOLA   Where's the waiting-woman?
    Fetch her: some other strangle the children.
                     [*Enter* Executioners *with* CARIOLA]
    Look you, there sleeps your mistress.
CARIOLA   Oh, you are damn'd
    Perpetually for this! My turn is next;
    Is't not so order'd?
BOSOLA   Yes, and I am glad
    You are so well prepar'd for 't.
CARIOLA   You are deceiv'd, sir,
    I am not prepar'd for 't, I will not die,
    I will first come to my answer; and know
    How I have offended.
BOSOLA   Come, despatch her. –
    You kept her counsel, now you shall keep ours.

Bosola is one of the most corrupt figures in Jacobean tragedy. He says, 'my corruption stems from horse manure' (he is an ostler). He also memorably describes the negative aspect of politics, in the words:

    A politician is the devil's quilted anvil;
    He fashions all sins on him, and the blows
    Are never heard: . . .

John Ford's *'Tis Pity She's a Whore* dates from the early 1630s. The young love theme of *Romeo and Juliet* of almost forty years before is transformed into an incestuous love between a brother and sister, Giovanni and Annabella. In a corrupt world, their love is the only pure element; and the tragedy follows their inevitable destiny in an increasingly negative universe. The play is a deliberate challenge to moral values and the decline of virtue; but, equally, it was seen by Puritans as representative of the decadent influence of the Caroline theatre. In their final scene, Giovanni and Annabella's love recalls Romeo and Juliet's:

GIOVANNI Kiss me. If ever after-times should hear
    Of our fast-knit affections, though perhaps
    The laws of conscience and of civil use
    May justly blame us, yet when they but know
    Our loves, that love will wipe away that rigour
    Which would in other incests be abhorr'd.
    Give me your hand; how sweetly life doth run
    In these well-coloured veins! how constantly
    These palms do promise health! but I could chide
    With Nature for this cunning flattery.
    Kiss me again – forgive me.
ANNABELLA   With my heart.
GIOVANNI Farewell!
ANNABELLA   Will you be gone?
GIOVANNI   Be dark, bright sun,
    And make this mid-day night, that thy gilt rays
    May not behold a deed will turn their splendour
    More sooty than the poets feign their Styx!
    One other kiss, my sister.
ANNABELLA   What means this?
GIOVANNI To save thy fame, and kill thee in a kiss.

                                                     [Stabs her]

    Thus die, and die by me, and by my hand!
    Revenge is mine; honour doth love command.

A vein of domestic tragedy, set not in the 'exotic' locales used by Webster and Ford (usually Italy), is seen in plays like Thomas Heywood's *A Woman Killed with Kindness* (1603), and two anonymous plays of approximately the same period – *Arden of Faversham* (published 1592), and *A Yorkshire Tragedy* (published 1608). These are very English family plays, with a dominant sense of doom and helplessness as the characters try to escape from the amorous and financial problems which beset them.

    Something of the simplicity of domestic tragedy can be seen in the

final act of *Arden of Faversham*, when Mistress Alice Arden acknowledges her own fault in the death of her husband:

> MAYOR See, Mistress Arden, where your husband lies;
>   Confess this foul fault and be penitent.
> ALICE Arden, sweet husband, what shall I say?
>   The more I sound his name, the more he bleeds;
>   This blood condemns me, and in gushing forth
>   Speaks as it falls, and asks why I did it.
>   Forgive me, Arden: I repent me now,
>   And, would my death save thine, thou shouldst not die.
>   Rise up, sweet Arden, and enjoy thy love,
>   And frown not on me when we meet in heaven:
>   In heaven I love thee, though on earth I did not.
> MAYOR Say, Mosby, what made thee murther him?
> FRANKLIN Study not for an answer; look not down:
>   His purse and girdle found at thy bed's head
>   Witness sufficiently thou didst the deed;
>   It bootless is to swear thou didst it not.
> MOSBY I hired Black Will and Shakebagge, Ruffians both,
>   And they and I have done this murthrous deed.

Between the Arden family tragedy and the plays of John Ford, there
is a world of difference: from an English setting to the very frequent
Italian setting; from simple language to highly figurative poetic language; from stark, almost documentary, drama to highly complex
interaction of character and motive.

There is an increasing use of violence and corruption to illustrate the playwrights' concerns: but where an early Shakespearean
tragedy such as *Titus Andronicus* revelled in blood and violence (under
the influence of Seneca) to thrill the audience, the Jacobean and
Caroline tragedies have a deeper purpose: humanity's weaknesses and
corruptibility have seldom found more vivid illustration.

CITY COMEDY

Jacobean city comedy contains several of the themes of domestic
tragedy – unhappy marriages, debts, adultery, and so on. Such comedy
makes the audience laugh at these themes and at the characters who

enact them. Thomas Dekker's *The Shoemaker's Holiday* (1599) is one of the earliest of city comedies; Thomas Middleton's *A Mad World, My Masters*, from the first decade of the new century, and *A Chaste Maid in Cheapside* (1613) are among the most successful of the genre.

At the climax of *A Mad World, My Masters*, Sir Bounteous finds the goods which had been stolen from him by his nephew Follywit and his friends, who presented a play as a pretext for their theft. A stolen watch, with an alarm, rings in Follywit's pocket:

> SIR BOUNTEOUS Faith, son, would you had come sooner with these gentlemen.
>
> FOLLYWIT Why, grandsire?
>
> SIR BOUNTEOUS We had a play here.
>
> FOLLYWIT A play, sir? No.
>
> SIR BOUNTEOUS Yes, faith, a pox o' th' author!
>
> FOLLYWIT [*aside*] Bless us all! – Why, were they such vild ones, sir?
>
> SIR BOUNTEOUS I am sure villainous ones, sir.
>
> FOLLYWIT Some raw, simple fools?
>
> SIR BOUNTEOUS Nay, by th' mass, these were enough for thievish knaves.
>
> FOLLYWIT What, sir?
>
> SIR BOUNTEOUS Which way came you, gentlemen? You could not choose but meet 'em.
>
> FOLLYWIT We met a company with hampers after 'em.
>
> SIR BOUNTEOUS Oh, those were they, those were they, a pox hamper 'em!
>
> FOLLYWIT [*aside*] Bless us all again!
>
> SIR BOUNTEOUS They have hamper'd me finely, sirrah.
>
> FOLLYWIT How, sir?
>
> SIR BOUNTEOUS How, sir? I lent the rascals properties to furnish out their play, a chain, a jewel, and a watch, and they watch'd their time and rid quite away with 'em.
>
> FOLLYWIT Are they such creatures?
>
> SIR BOUNTEOUS Hark, hark, gentlemen! By this light, the watch rings alarum in his pocket! There's my watch come again, or the very cousin-german to 't. Whose is 't, whose is 't? By th' mass, 'tis he; hast thou one, son? Prithee bestow it upon thy grandsire. I now look for mine again, i' faith. Nay, come with a good will or not at all; I'll give thee a better thing. A prize, a prize, gentlemen!

HAREBRAIN Great or small?

SIR BOUNTEOUS At once I have drawn chain, jewel, watch, and all!

Francis Beaumont in *The Knight of the Burning Pestle* (1607–8) parodies the conventions of old-fashioned chivalry, as a city apprentice
takes parts in a 'play-within-the-play'. Philip Massinger's *A New Way to
Pay Old Debts* (1625–26) remained one of the most popular social
comedies for more than two hundred years. The theme of class
superiority (the upper class, and the rising mercantile middle class)
begins to be popular here, and will assume greater and greater prominence in the literature of the eighteenth century. With characters like
Greedy and Frank Wellborn, Massinger's play brings the city comedy
(here set near Nottingham) to new heights; in Sir Giles Overreach – 'a
cruel extortioner' – it created one of the great comic roles. Here Sir
Giles plans with Wellborn (the name is ironic) to help him make a
useful marriage; but Wellborn also has his own ideas.

OVERREACH   You may wonder, nephew,
　　After so long an enmity between us,
　　I should desire your friendship.
WELLBORN   So I do, sir;
　　'Tis strange to me.
OVERREACH   But I'll make it no wonder;
　　And what is more, unfold my nature to you.
　　We worldly men, when we see friends and kinsmen
　　Past hope sunk in their fortunes, lend no hand
　　To lift them up, but rather set our feet
　　Upon their heads, to press them to the bottom;
　　As, I must yield, with you I practised it:
　　But, now I see you in a way to rise,
　　I can and will assist you; this rich lady
　　(And I am glad of 't) is enamoured of you;
　　'Tis too apparent, nephew.
WELLBORN   No such thing:
　　Compassion rather, sir.
OVERREACH   Well, in a word,
　　Because your stay is short, I'll have you seen
　　No more in this base shape; nor shall she say,
　　She married you like a beggar, or in debt.
WELLBORN [*aside*] He'll run into the noose, and save my labour.

THE END OF THE RENAISSANCE THEATRE

After Shakespeare and the other major dramatists of the time, it is easy for critics to say that drama went into decline. This is, however, to ignore the works of several writers: Jonson continued to write for the theatre well into the 1630s, and some of his later plays, such as *The Staple of News* (printed 1631), deserve to be more widely known and performed.

The same can be said for the plays of Richard Brome and James Shirley. They are quite different in style, but both are highly inventive and versatile within their chosen forms. Shirley's tragedies *The Cardinal* (1641) and *The Traitor* (1631) tackle religious and political themes. Brome's most successful works are comic – *A Jovial Crew* (1641) and *The City Wit* (printed 1653). These works show that, despite Puritan opposition, the theatre continued to be a lively art-form right up until the theatres were closed in 1642.

It should, however, be remembered that Puritanism does not simply represent opposition to theatrical activity and similar pursuits. Several dramatists, most notably Middleton, identified themselves with Puritan beliefs, although not in an extremist way. Puritan thought aimed, in its most literal sense, to purify and simplify the spiritual mindset of the time: only later did the extreme of revolution become an option.

The result of extreme Puritan moralistic pressure was that, in 1642, the Long Parliament put an end to theatrical performances. The closure of the theatres brought to an end the greatest period of English drama. Never again was drama to be the most popular literary genre or such a vital forum for the discussion of the major themes of the age.

Restoration to Romanticism

1660–1789

Thy wars brought nothing about;
Thy lovers were all untrue.
'Tis well an old age is out,
And time to begin a new
              (John Dryden, *The Secular Masque*)

CONTEXTS AND CONDITIONS

The Restoration did not so much restore as replace. In restoring the monarchy with King Charles II, it replaced Cromwell's Common- wealth and its Puritan ethos with an almost powerless monarch whose tastes had been formed in France.

It replaced the power of the monarchy with the power of a parlia- mentary system – which was to develop into the two parties, Whigs and Tories – with most of the executive power in the hands of the Prime Minister. Both parties benefited from a system which encour- aged social stability rather than opposition.

Above all, in systems of thought, the Restoration replaced the prob- ing, exploring, risk-taking intellectual values of the Renaissance. It relied on reason and on facts rather than on speculation. So, in the decades between 1660 and 1700, the basis was set for the growth of a new kind of society. This society was Protestant (apart from the brief reign of the Catholic King James II, 1685–88), middle class, and unthreatened by any repetition of the huge and traumatic upheavals of the first part of the seventeenth century. It is symptomatic that the overthrow of James II in 1688 was called The 'Glorious' or 'Bloodless' Revolution. The 'fever in the blood' which the Renaissance had allowed was now to be contained, subject to reason, and kept under control. With only the brief outburst of Jacobin revolutionary sentiment at the time of the Romantic poets, this was to be the political context in the United Kingdom for two centuries or more.

In this context, the concentration of society was on commerce, on respectability, and on institutions. The 'genius of the nation' led to the founding of the Royal Society in 1662–63 – 'for the improving of Natural Knowledge'. The Royal Society represents the trend towards the institutionalisation of scientific investigation and research in this period. The other highly significant institution, one which was to have considerably more importance in the future, was the Bank of England, founded in 1694.

The beliefs and behaviour of the Restoration reflect the theories of society put forward by Thomas Hobbes in *The Leviathan*, which was written in exile in Paris and published in 1651. Like many texts of the time, *The Leviathan* is an allegory. It recalls mediaeval rather than Renaissance thinking. The leviathan is the commonwealth, society as a total organism, in which the individual is the absolute subject of state control, represented by the monarch. Man – motivated by self-interest – is acquisitive and lacks codes of behaviour. Hence the necessity for a strong controlling state, 'an artificial man', to keep discord at bay. Self-interest and stability become the keynotes of British society after 1660, the voice of the new middle-class bourgeoisie making itself heard more and more in the expression of values, ideals, and ethics. Hobbes describes the effects of war on a society, affirming the need for 'a common Power', a strong state:

> ... it is manifest, that during the time men live without a common Power to keep them all in awe, they are in that condition which is called War; and such a war, as is of every man, against every man.
>
> ...
>
> Whatsoever therefore is consequent to a time of War, where every man is Enemy to every man; the same is consequent to the time, wherein men live without other security, than what their own strength, and their own invention shall furnish them withall. In such condition, there is no place for Industry; because the fruit thereof is uncertain: and consequently no Culture of the Earth, no Navigation, nor use of the commodities that may be imported by

Sea; no commodious Building; no Instruments of moving, and removing such things as require much force; no Knowledge of the face of the Earth; no account of Time; no Arts; no Letters; no Society; and which is worse of all, continual fear, and danger of violent death; And the life of man, solitary, poor, nasty, brutish, and short.

(*The Leviathan*)

Later, Hobbes will stress the notion central to Augustan thinking, the binary of passion and reason:

The Passions that encline men to Peace, are Fear of Death; Desire of such things as are necessary to commodious living; and a Hope by their Industry to obtain them. And Reason suggesteth convenient Articles of Peace, upon which men may be drawn to agreement. These Articles, are they, which otherwise are called the Laws of Nature.

(*The Leviathan*)

After the upheavals of the Commonwealth, there was a strong affirmation of religion and a return to traditional beliefs. In such a context, Milton's *Paradise Lost* (completed in 1667) was read not as a Renaissance text about free will and freedom, but as a commentary on God's supremacy, 'to justify the ways of God to men'. It was read in order to confirm an image of God as the period demanded God should be. Questioning of religious values was not part of the age; once Protestant supremacy had been established after 1688, religious dissent was stifled. *Paradise Lost* took on the authority of a quasi-religious text – an imaginative representation of the beliefs contained in the Authorised Version of the Bible and the Book of Common Prayer, from which these extracts are taken:

We have left undone those things which we ought to have done; And we have done those things which we ought not to have done; And there is no health in us.

Lighten our darkness, we beseech thee, O Lord.

The pomps and vanity of this wicked world.

Those whom God hath joined together let no man put asunder.

Man that is born of woman hath but a short time to live, and is full of misery.

It is a fact of human need to make God in its own image; and it was half-jokingly said, in the nineteenth century, that God must have been an Englishman. If this was so, the image began to be created in the late seventeenth century. *Paradise Lost* and John Bunyan's allegorical *The Pilgrim's Progress* were two fundamental texts for the times.

The growth of a city-based middle-class economic mentality during the early and middle years of the eighteenth century parallels the developments which came to be known as the Industrial Revolution and the Agrarian Revolution. At the same time, several trends can be seen in literary production:

- the rise of the novel as a popular if critically unprestigious genre;
- the growth of journalism and magazines, with a corresponding growth in professional authorship;
- a noticeable increase in literary criticism, leading to the establishment of what was critically acceptable and what was not;
- a decline in the reputation of contemporary drama, while the theatre attracted increasing support;
- a reaction to Augustan neoclassicism in poetry, with moves towards the funereal mode, or the rediscovery of simpler values;
- towards the end of the eighteenth century, an attraction for the fantastic, the exotic and the primitive.

This reflects the turmoil of an age which, in the thirty or so years after the Restoration, was trying to put behind it the shadow of revolution. Cromwell's Commonwealth had destabilised everything and shaken the nation to its roots. The next revolution, when the Catholic King James II was replaced by the Protestant House of Orange, was quickly called the 'Glorious' or 'Bloodless' Revolution. (In Ireland, this Protestant takeover continues to cause bloodshed three centuries later.)

James II's grandson, known as Bonnie Prince Charlie – the Catholic 'Young Pretender' to the British throne – led the second of two unsuccessful rebellions against the new Hanoverian dynasty, in 1715 and 1745. The decisive Battle of Culloden, in 1746, finally ended the Stuart line's claims to the throne.

Revolution was the great nightmare of eighteenth-century British society, and when first the American Revolution of 1776, then the French Revolution of 1789 overturned the accepted order, the United Kingdom exercised all its power so that revolution would not damage its own hard-won security and growing prosperity. Eighteenth-century writing is full of pride in England as the land of liberty (far ahead of France, the great rival, in political maturity), and saw a corresponding growth in national self-confidence accompanying the expansion of empire.

EARLY MILTON

Weep no more, woeful shepherds, weep no more
For Lycidas, your sorrow, is not dead
                                                                    (*Lycidas*)

John Milton has, since his own lifetime, always been one of the major figures in English literature, but his reputation has changed constantly. He has been seen as a political opportunist, an advocate of 'immorality' (he wrote in favour of divorce and married three times), an over-serious classicist, and an arrogant believer in his own greatness as a poet. He was all these things. But, above all, Milton's was the last great liberal intelligence of the English Renaissance. The values expressed in all his works are the values of tolerance, freedom and self-determination, expressed by Shakespeare, Hooker and Donne. The basis of his aesthetic studies was classical, but the modernity of his intellectual interests can be seen in the fact that he went to Italy (in the late 1630s) where he met the astronomer Galileo, who had been condemned as a heretic by the Catholic church for saying the earth moved around the sun.

Milton's early poems, from the 1620s and 1630s, include several which remain as models of their kind. *L'Allegro* and *Il Penseroso* are companion pieces advocating contrasting styles of life, the carefree and the studious. Of his sonnets, *On His Blindness* is perhaps the best known, with its last line:

They also serve who only stand and wait.

Lycidas is one of the most-quoted elegies in English, moving from its commemoration of his Cambridge university friend, Edward King, to reflections on the writer's own mortality and ambitions; finishing in the remarkable optimism of a renewal, with the words:

> Weep no more, woeful shepherds, weep no more,
> For Lycidas, your sorrow, is not dead
> . . .
>
> Thus sang the uncouth swain to the oaks and rills,
> While the still morn went out with sandals grey;
> He touched the tender stops of various quills,
> With eager thought warbling his Doric lay.
> And now the sun had stretched out all the hills,
> And now was dropped into the western bay;
> At last he rose, and twitched his mantle blue:
> Tomorrow to fresh woods, and pastures new.

Like all Milton's works, *Lycidas* has been interpreted as specifically Christian. Such a reading can be supported by the poet's ambitions to join the church and by many explicitly Christian references in his writings. But his beliefs go beyond any single doctrine, as can be seen from the wide range of political and social pamphlets he wrote between 1640 and 1660 – a time when he wrote only a few poems. Milton's prose can be related to the writings of Browne and Burton, with the major difference that Milton engages in polemic as well as touching upon philosophical concerns.

In these twenty years, the United Kingdom (of Great Britain and Ireland) went through the only real revolution in its history. It overthrew the monarchy. And, after only a few years, Parliament decided to recall the executed King's son to the throne. It was a time when a great many of the issues which had arisen since the Reformation came to a head: religion, politics, power and freedom were questioned as never before. It was no accident that Milton's first polemic pamphlet was entitled *Of Reformation in England and the Causes that Hitherto Have Hindered It* (1641). He addressed such varied subjects as divorce (in four pamphlets), education, and, famously, the freedom of the press, in *Areopagitica* (1644). In this extract, he anticipates his great epic *Paradise Lost* by more than twenty years.

It was from out the rind of one apple tasted, that the knowledge of good and evil as two twins cleaving together leapt forth into the World. And perhaps this is that doom which Adam fell into of knowing good and evil, that is to say of knowing good by evil. As therefore the state of man now is; what wisdom can there be to choose, what continence to forbear without the knowledge of evil? . . .

Since therefore the knowledge and survey of vice is in this world so necessary to the constituting of human virtue, and the scanning of error to the confirmation of truth, how can we more safely, and with less danger scout into the regions of sin and falsity that by reading all manner of tractats, and hearing all manner of reason? And this is the benefit which may be had of books promiscuously read.

Milton argued, in 1649, after the execution of Charles I, that a people 'free by nature' had a right to overthrow a tyrant; a subject that recalls vividly the questions examined by Shakespeare in his major tragedies about fifty years before.

Milton continued to defend his ideals of freedom and republicanism. But at the Restoration, by which time he was blind, he was arrested. Various powerful contacts allowed him to be released after paying a fine, and his remaining years were devoted to the composition – orally, in the form of dictation to his third wife – of his epic poem on the fall of humanity, *Paradise Lost*, which was published in 1667.

It is interesting that – like Spenser and Malory before him, and like Tennyson two centuries later – Milton was attracted to the Arthurian legends as the subject for his great epic. But the theme of the Fall goes far beyond a *national* epic, and gave the poet scope to analyse the whole question of freedom, free will, and individual choice. He wished, he said, to 'assert eternal providence,/And justify the ways of God to men'. This has been seen as confirmation of Milton's arrogance, but it also signals the last great attempt to rationalise the spirit of the Renaissance: mankind would not exist outside Paradise if Satan had not engineered the temptation and fall of Adam and Eve. For many critics, including the poets Blake and Shelley, Satan, the figure of the Devil, is the hero of the poem. Satan asserts his own freedom in his reasoning between heaven, from which he is expelled (as Adam and Eve are from the Garden of Eden), and hell, where he will be free and reign supreme:

> The mind is its own place, and in itself
> Can make a heaven of hell, a hell of heaven.
> What matter where, if I be still the same,
> And what I should be, all but less than he
> Whom thunder hath made greater? Here at least
> We shall be free; the Almighty hath not built
> Here for his envy, will not drive us hence:
> Here we may reign secure, and in my choice
> To reign is worth ambition, though in hell:
> Better to reign in hell than serve in heaven.

When Eve yields to Satan's temptations and bites the forbidden fruit, the effect is of loss, but the loss will later turn to gain – the gain of a future for humanity on earth.

> . . . her rash hand in evil hour
> Forth reaching to the fruit, she plucked, she eat.
> Earth felt the wound, and Nature from her seat
> Sighing through all her works gave signs of woe,
> That all was lost.

Like the ending of *Lycidas*, the final image of *Paradise Lost* is profoundly forward-looking, an image of gain through loss. As Adam and Eve go hand in hand towards the future, the loss of Paradise is seen as humanity's gain:

> The world was all before them, where to choose
> Their place of rest, and Providence their guide:
> They, hand in hand, with wandering steps and slow,
> Through Eden took their solitary way.

Just are the ways of God,
And justifiable to men
(*Samson Agonistes*)

Milton's *Samson Agonistes*, a verse drama, and *Paradise Regained*, a sequel in four books to *Paradise Lost*, were both published in 1671, four years after *Paradise Lost*. Both works show a different conception of the hero from the ambiguous interplay between God, Man, and Satan, found in *Paradise Lost*. The fundamental difference between Adam and Eve in *Paradise Lost* and the heroes of the other two poems – the former probably written during the Commonwealth, the latter nearer the end of Milton's life – is humanity: both Samson and Christ are superhuman, indeed beyond the bounds of normal human beings. As such, their triumphs and conquests are less clearly explorations of *human* qualities. As Samson destroys the Philistines and their temple, or as Jesus Christ repels the temptations of Satan (the seductive hero of *Paradise Lost*, now overthrown), they lack the element of human identification. Instead they become ideal *exempla*, as in morality plays or mediaeval poems, of what humanity *should be* rather than what it is. This does not indicate a deliberate return to earlier ways of thinking on Milton's part, but perhaps does reflect a need to accommodate his poetic expression to an age which would develop a taste for what was called 'heroic' tragedy. Milton returns to the theme of blindness in some of the darkest lines of English poetry, as Samson describes his being 'exiled from light':

> Eyeless in Gaza at the mill with slaves.
>
> O dark, dark, dark, amid the blaze of noon,
> Irrecoverably dark, total eclipse
> Without all hope of day!
>
> The sun to me is dark
> And silent as the moon,
> When she deserts the night
> Hid in her vacant, interlunar cave.
>
> To live a life half-dead, a living death.

The poem is a journey *from* darkness, as Samson moves from his prison to his final act of strength, pulling down the temple of his foes. Some critics have seen this as echoing Milton's own situation after the loss of his early political ideals. The final note is, however, one of calm:

> Of true experience from this great event
> . . .
> And calm of mind, all passion spent.

It is remarkable that John Bunyan's *The Pilgrim's Progress*, published in two parts in 1678–79 and 1684, and probably the most widely read text in all English literature over the next two hundred years, uses two forms which are pre-Renaissance: the moral fable or allegory, and the dream-vision. The pilgrim, Christian, is on his journey 'from This World, to that which is to come'. The Renaissance fascination with transience, impermanence – symbolised so often in the theatre – is replaced with the pre-Renaissance structure of earth, heaven (reward) and the implied hell (punishment).

This re-establishes an unquestioned moral order, justifying God's ways to men. The century had seen the effects of the kind of questioning the Renaissance had proposed: the result was the chaos of an executed king, and the dissolution of society as it was known. Bunyan's work helped to replace that uncertainty and instability with a clarity of purpose which was rooted in the realities of everyday life.

The author has a dream, in which the hero, Christian, undergoes his pilgrimage through life – leaving his wife and family in the City of Destruction. He visits the Slough of Despond, the Valley of the Shadow of Death, Vanity Fair, Doubting Castle, and encounters such figures as Mr Worldly Wiseman and Giant Despair. In the meantime, his wife and children, accompanied by Great-heart, follow a similar pilgrimage to the same destination – the Celestial City. The closest text to *The Pilgrim's Progress* is perhaps the mediaeval play *Everyman* (see page 47). The images of Giant Despair and Doubting Castle are among the most resonant in the allegory. Here Great-heart destroys them.

> Now Giant Despair, because he was a Giant, thought no man could overcome him, and again, thought he, since heretofore I have made a conquest of angels, shall Great-heart make me afraid? So he harnessed himself and went out. He had a cap of steel upon his head, a breastplate of fire girded to him, and he came out in iron shoes, with a great club in his hand. Then these six men made up to him, and beset him behind and before; also when Diffidence, the Giantess, came up to help him, old Mr Honest cut her down at one blow. Then they fought for their lives, and Giant Despair was brought down to the ground, but was very loth to die. He struggled hard, and had, as they say, as many lives as a cat, but Great-heart was his death, for he left him not till he had severed his head from his shoulders.

Then they fell to demolishing Doubting Castle, and that you know might with ease be done, since Giant Despair was dead. They were seven days in destroying of that; and in it of pilgrims, they found one Mr Despondency, almost starved to death, and one Much-afraid his daughter; these two they saved alive.

(*The Pilgrim's Progress*)

The immediate appeal of the story led to *The Pilgrim's Progress* becoming the most popular work of the imagination in English for more than two centuries. Its language, setting, and characters entered the national consciousness, almost as much as did stories from the Bible. Bunyan's other works include *Grace Abounding* (1666), a kind of spiritual autobiography, and a later allegory, *The Life and Death of Mister Badman*, published in 1680.

Bunyan's language reached an enormous number of people and, together with the Book of Common Prayer (a final version was published in 1662) and the Authorised Version of the Bible (1611), helped to shape the English language (see pages 85–9 and 131). The prayerbook, first published in 1549, is still in use in the Church of England (but not in the Church of Scotland or the Roman Catholic Church). As Jonathan Swift confirmed: 'For those Books being perpetually read in Churches, have proved a kind of Standard for Language, especially to the common People.' This is popular literature in the clearest sense of the term, far removed from the more refined circles of 'Augustan' literature – the self-consciously artistic writing of the time.

RESTORATION DRAMA

The theatre of the Restoration was quite different from Shakespeare's theatre, with the audience now largely upper class. There were only two licensed, or 'patent', theatres – the Theatre Royal, Drury Lane, and Duke's House at Lincoln's Inn, which moved to the Covent Garden Theatre in 1732. Actresses could now perform on stage, the first being a Mrs Coleman, in a private performance of Sir William D'Avenant's *The Siege of Rhodes* in 1656, when theatre performances were still officially suppressed.

The lifting of the ban led to an explosion of dramatic writing, but of a very different kind from the drama of Shakespeare and his successors. Shakespeare's plays were still presented, but usually in adapted versions (often with music), to make them more acceptable to the new tastes of the times. In *The Tempest*, for instance, Prospero's crisis of knowledge, echoing Marlowe's *Doctor Faustus*, is completely absent. Marlowe's play was, in fact, also rewritten in 1697 to meet Restoration tastes – as a farce!

The more worrying of Shakespeare's excesses had to be trimmed to find acceptance in Restoration society. Nahum Tate (author of the Christmas carol *The First Nowell*) reworked *King Lear* to provide it with a happy ending. He cut the more disturbing elements, such as the putting out of Gloucester's eyes. With harmony restored, and family virtues upheld, Shakespeare's most probing and tragic examination of man's inhumanity to man becomes a moral and reassuring tract. Tate's *King Lear* was to be the standard version of the work for almost two centuries.

Restoration tragedy is 'heroic' tragedy. *All for Love* (1678), by John Dryden, is a good example of the type. This play takes the story of Shakespeare's *Antony and Cleopatra* but makes a distinct and new play, in an elaborately formal, neoclassical style. It respects the formal unities of time, place, and action. It concentrates on the final hours in the lives of the hero and heroine, rather than presenting the huge political, historical, and passionate panorama which Shakespeare's drama had enacted.

Thomas Otway was the major original tragedian of the Restoration period, his *The Orphan* (1680) and *Venice Preserv'd* (1682) remaining popular for over a century. They are tragedies of failure, remorse, and suicide, rather than of ambition, corruption, and destiny. *Venice Preserv'd* is about the inadmissibility of dissent, about how a 'foe to Venice' – the hero Jaffeir – eventually kills his best friend and himself, in order that the social order should not be overturned. Jaffeir is a 'hero' because he affirms the *status quo*, rather than questioning and re-examining it. In this way he contrasts with the heroes of Elizabethan and Jacobean tragedy. At first, revenge and freedom are closely linked:

JAFFEIR   . . . from this hour I chase
    All little thoughts, all tender human follies

Out of my bosom. Vengeance shall have room.
Revenge!
PIERRE   And Liberty!
JAFFEIR   Revenge! Revenge!

Later, Jaffeir becomes an outcast, as his plans and friendships fail:

JAFFEIR How cursed is my position, tossed and jostled
From every corner; fortune's common fool,
The jest of rogues, an instrumental ass
For villains to lay loads of shame upon,
And drive about just for their ease and scorn.

The Elizabethan domestic tragedy form finds a new middle-class setting in the plays of George Lillo, notably *The London Merchant* (1731), and his treatment of the Arden of Faversham story, staged in 1736. In *The Fatal Curiosity* (1736), a domestic tragedy set in Cornwall, Wilmot, spurred on by his wife Agnes in a scene reminiscent of *Macbeth*, murders a visiting stranger, in the hope of monetary gain:

AGNES The stranger sleeps at present, but so restless
His slumbers seem, they can't continue long.
Come, come, dispatch! Here, I've secured his dagger.
OLD WILMOT Oh, Agnes, Agnes! If there be a hell, 'tis just
We should expect it.
                                [*Goes to take the dagger but lets it fall.*]
AGNES Nay, for shame! Shake off this panic, and be more yourself!
OLD WILMOT What's to be done? On what had we determined?
AGNES You're quite dismayed. I'll do
The deed myself.
                                [*Takes up the dagger.*]
OLD WILMOT   Give me the fatal steel.
'Tis but a single murder
Necessity, impatience, and despair,
The three wide mouths of that true Cerberus,
Grim poverty, demands. They shall be stopped.

The tragedy is that the young murdered man is Wilmot and Agnes's son, which explains the original alternative title, *Guilt, Its Own Punishment*. The influence of Lillo's plays on European theatre was extensive (the story of *The Fatal Curiosity* was used by Albert Camus as late as 1945), although they have tended to be ignored on the British stage.

It is, however, for comedy that Restoration drama is better known. It was called 'the comedy of manners' because it mirrored directly the manners, modes, and morals of the upper-class society which was its main audience. The main subject of Restoration comedy was sex: sexual attraction, sexual intrigue, and sexual conquest. Sex, and the search for sex, becomes entertainment.

This is usually represented as reflecting the frivolous concerns of the aristocrats who had recently returned from exile at the French court, which, to English tastes, was dissolute. Yet French drama of this period reaches the highest peaks of achievement in the works of Racine and Molière, and it bears very little relation to most English Restoration drama.

We see a concentration on acquisitiveness and an amorality that contrasts with the concerns of Bunyan's Christian. The plays manifest excesses of freedom, now that the constraints of the Puritan Commonwealth have been thrown off. The new comedy – of values and appetites – lacks any of the philosophical concerns found, for example, in Shakespeare's earlier comedies, such as *Love's Labour's Lost*, or in Ben Jonson's 'humours'.

The characters are obsessed with fashion, gossip and their own circle in society. Strong contrasts are made between innocence and knowingness; often these are represented as contrasts between rustic country manners and the refinements of the city. In Restoration comedy, women are such types as predatory young widows, or older ladies still trying to be attractive to young men. The best comedies reflect an amoral and frivolous society. They could be comedies of action, such as Aphra Behn's *The Rover* (1677–81), or comedies of character and chatter, such as George Etherege's *The Man of Mode*.

The age reflects a wide variety of opinions and critical discussions on the nature of comedy, of tragedy, of character and plot, of representation and verisimilitude, with the result that the extensive and very rich theatrical repertoire of the time cannot be easily classified: it is second only to the Elizabethan and Jacobean period in its diversity and range.

One of the first comedies was *The Comical Revenge* (1664) by George Etherege, which, as its title suggests, takes a theme, revenge, which was previously a subject for tragedy, and balances it with a realistic, up-to-date love plot involving a country knight with more money than sense, a valet with ideas above his station, and a rich widow who is in pursuit of the libertine hero. This was the forerunner of many such plots, and it owes as much to the plots of the city comedies earlier in the century as it does to French or Italian theatrical traditions.

The contrast between town manners and country pretensions, and the concern with fashion, are seen again in Etherege's two later works, *She Wou'd if She Cou'd* (1668) and *The Man of Mode* (1676). The final play brings its interwoven plots together in what is perhaps the subtlest light comedy of the time, counterpointing youth and age, town and country, male and female, in a play which satirises the mindless foppery of Sir Fopling Flutter at the same time as it questions the values of all its characters. Here we see something of Sir Fopling's vanity:

[SIR FOPLING *dancing by himself.*]

YOUNG BELLAIR See Sir Fopling dancing.

DORIMANT You are practising and have a mind to recover, I see.

SIR FOPLING Prithee Dorimant, why hast not thou a glass hung up here? A room is the dullest thing without one?

YOUNG BELLAIR Here is company to entertain you.

SIR FOPLING But I mean in case of being alone. In a glass a man may entertain himself.

DORIMANT The shadow of himself indeed.

SIR FOPLING Correct the errors of his motion and his dress.

MEDLEY I find, Sir Fopling, in your solitude you remember the saying of the wise man, and study yourself.

SIR FOPLING 'Tis the best diversion in our retirements.

The Country Wife (1675) by William Wycherley has frequently been held up as the most obscene and amoral of Restoration plays. It is a comedy of seduction and hypocrisy. Its hero, Horner, pretends to be impotent in order to make his conquests, and Mrs Pinchwife claims in all 'innocence' to be behaving as ladies do in town.

HORNER You would not take my advice to be gone home before your husband came back; he'll now discover all. Yet pray, my dearest, be persuaded to go home and leave the rest to my management. I'll let you down the back way.

MRS PINCHWIFE I don't know the way home, so I don't.

HORNER My man shall wait upon you.

MRS PINCHWIFE No, don't you believe that I'll go at all. What, are you weary of me already?

HORNER No, my life, 'tis that I may love you long. 'Tis to secure my love, and your reputation with your husband. He'll never receive you again else.

MRS PINCHWIFE What care I? D'ye think to frighten me with that? I don't intend to go to him again. You shall be my husband now.

HORNER I cannot be your husband, dearest, since you are married to him.

MRS PINCHWIFE Oh, would you make me believe that? Don't I see, every day at London here, women leave their first husbands and go and live with other men as their wives? Pish, pshaw! You'd make me angry, but that I love you so mainly.

HORNER So, they are coming up. – In again, in, I hear 'em.

[*Exit* MRS PINCHWIFE.]

Such was the reaction to Wycherley's work that a swell of opinion against the theatre began to grow in the later decades of the century. The complaints were largely against the subversive morality of the society depicted in the comedies. There was also an element of censure of the irresponsible but now less powerful upper classes in the affirm-ation of a new middle-class ethic. The emergence of new social classes and divisions, which began at this time, became more and more signifi-cant over the following century. Inevitably, religious attitudes came into play. One outcome was a pamphlet published by a clergyman, Jeremy Collier, in 1698, *Short View of the Immorality and Profaneness of the English Stage*. Collier complained about mockery of the clergy, and about profanity and bad language, topics already aired in Puritan stric-tures against the theatre seventy years before. But the effect of his *Short View* was considerable: writers and actors were prosecuted and fined, and, despite many playwrights' strong defences of the drama, Collier contributed a deadly blow to theatrical writing. The immediate result was a royal order prohibiting 'the acting of anything contrary to religion and good manners'. Less than forty years later, censorship became official.

Just as the first blows were being struck against it, Restoration drama produced its greatest masterpieces, in the plays of William Congreve, Sir John Vanbrugh (also an eminent architect), and George Farquhar, who was to die before he was 30, just as his final play, *The Beaux' Stratagem*, achieved renown.

Congreve also reached success by the age of 30, and then wrote nothing else for the stage. His first three comedies in the 1690s – *The Old Bachelor, The Double Dealer,* and *Love for Love* – lead to the climactic work of all Restoration comedy, *The Way of the World* (1700).

MILLAMANT I'll never marry, unless I am first made sure of my will and pleasure.

MIRABELL Would you have 'em both before marriage? Or will you be contented with the first now, and stay for the other till after grace?

MILLAMANT Ah, don't be impertinent – My dear liberty, shall I leave thee? My faithful solitude, my darling contemplation, must I bid you then adieu? Ah-y adieu – my morning thoughts, agreeable wakings, indolent slumbers, all ye *douceurs,* ye *sommeils du matin,* adieu – I can't do it, 'tis more than impossible. – Positively, Mirabell, I'll lie a-bed in a morning as long as I please.

MIRABELL Then I'll get up in a morning as early as I please.

MILLAMANT Ah! Idle creature, get up when you will – And d'ye hear, I won't be called names after I'm married; positively, I won't be call'd names.

MIRABELL Names!

MILLAMANT Ay, as wife, spouse, my dear, joy, jewel, love, sweetheart, and the rest of that nauseous cant, in which men and their wives are so fulsomely familiar, – I shall never bear that. – Good Mirabell don't let us be familiar or fond, nor kiss before folks, like my Lady Fadler and Sir Francis: not go to Hyde Park together the first Sunday in a new chariot, to provoke eyes and whispers; and then never be seen there together again; as if we were proud of one another the first week, and ashamed of one another ever after. Let us never visit together, nor go to a play together, but let us be very strange and well-bred: let us be as strange as if we had been married a great while; and as well-bred as if we were not married at all.

MIRABELL Have you any more conditions to offer? Hitherto your demands are pretty reasonable.

MILLAMANT Trifles, – as liberty to pay and receive visits to and from whom I please; to write and receive letters, without interrogatories or wry faces on your part; to wear what I please; and choose conversation with regard only to my own taste; to have no obligation upon me to converse with wits that I don't like, because they are your acquaintance; or to be intimate with fools, because they may be your relations. Come to dinner when I please, dine in my dressing-room when I'm out of humour, without giving a reason. To have my closet inviolate; to be sole empress of my tea-table, which you must never presume to approach without first asking leave. And lastly wherever I am, you shall always knock at the door before you come in. These articles subscribed, if I continue to endure you a little longer, I may by degrees dwindle into a wife.

What raises Congreve above many of his contemporaries is the acute observation of the social and emotional pressures on characters who are more richly drawn than traditional stereotypes. Like many later writers of comedy, Congreve was something of an outsider, having been brought up in Ireland, and perhaps the outsider's eye gave him a privileged viewpoint on the society he portrayed with such insight, sympathy, and wit.

Vanbrugh's *The Relapse* and *The Provok'd Wife* (1696 and 1697) particularly outraged Jeremy Collier. They take linked plots to new heights, with richly drawn characters – such as Sir Novelty Fashion, Sir Tunbelly Clumsy, Sir John and Lady Brute, Lord Foppington, Lady Fancyfull – and a series of intrigues and impersonations, which bear out the implications of the characters' names and attributes. Here, Loveless has his way with Berinthia – notice how she objects!

BERINTHIA Heavens, what do you mean?

LOVELESS Pray, what do you think I mean?

BERINTHIA I don't know.

LOVELESS I'll show you.

BERINTHIA You may as well tell me.

LOVELESS No, that would make you blush worse than t'other.

BERINTHIA Why, do you intend to make me blush?

LOVELESS Faith, I can't tell that, but if I do, it shall be in the dark.

[Pulling her.]

BERINTHIA O heavens! I would not be in the dark with you for all the world.

LOVELESS I'll try that.

[*Puts out the candles.*]

BERINTHIA O Lord! are you mad? What shall I do for light?

LOVELESS You'll do as well without it.

BERINTHIA Why, one can't find a chair to sit down.

LOVELESS Come into the closet, madam, there's moonshine upon the couch.

BERINTHIA Nay, never pull, for I will not go.

LOVELESS Then you must be carried.

[*Carrying her.*]

BERINTHIA [*very softly*] Help, help, I'm ravished, ruined, undone. O Lord, I shall never be able to bear it.

(*The Relapse*)

Farquhar's plays are rather different. They are more realistic in setting and tone, and are more morally concerned and humanly sympathetic. *The Recruiting Officer* (1706) reminds us that at this time the country was at war: the War of the Spanish Succession involved considerable English army losses on the Continent. The 'stratagem' of Captain Plume and his sergeant, Kite, to catch a rich wife is echoed in *The Beaux' Stratagem* (1707), where Aimwell and his friend Archer plot to win the hand of Dorinda, the daughter of rich Lady Bountiful. Both plays are set in county towns, away from the high society of London. They use Restoration themes and plot devices, but explore the comedy of human motivation in a new context. Here, Mrs Sullen is enchanted by Archer, who has been hiding in her closet:

MRS SULLEN Ah!

[*Shrieks, and runs to the other side of the stage.*]
Have my thoughts raised a spirit? – What are you, Sir, a man or a devil?

ARCHER A man, a man, Madam.

[*Rising.*]

MRS SULLEN How shall I be sure of it?

ARCHER Madam, I'll give you demonstration this minute.

[*Takes her hand.*]

MRS SULLEN What, Sir! do you intend to be rude?

ARCHER Yes, Madam, if you please?

MRS SULLEN In the name of wonder, whence came ye?

ARCHER From the skies, Madam – I'm a *Jupiter* in love, and you shall be my *Alemena*.

MRS SULLEN How came you in?

ARCHER I flew in at the window, Madam; your cousin *Cupid* lent me his wings, and your sister *Venus* opened the casement.

MRS SULLEN I'm struck dumb with admiration.

ARCHER And I with wonder.

> [*Looks passionately at her.*]

MRS SULLEN What will become of me?

> (*The Beaux' Strategem*)

Farquhar, again, was an Irishman, and his comedies are a significant contribution to the opening up of local settings for social comedy.

The plays of Susannah Centlivre, first presented around the turn of the century, were among those which continued to enjoy great success throughout the 1700s. *A Bold Stroke for a Wife* (1718) is particularly memorable, combining the battle of the sexes with witty satire on religious narrow-mindedness. In Act V, both the women (Mrs Prim and Mrs Lovely) and Colonel Fainwell, who wants Mrs Lovely, are disguised as Quakers, the colonel as 'Simon Pure':

> [*Enter* COLONEL *in a Quaker's habit.*]

PRIM Friend Pure, thou art welcome; how is it with Friend Holdfast and all Friends in Bristol? Timothy Littlewit, John Slenderbrain, and Christopher Keepfaith?

COLONEL [*aside*] A goodly company! – [*Aloud.*] They are all in health, I thank thee for them.

PRIM Friend Holdfast writes me word that thou camest lately from Pennsylvania; how do all Friends there?

COLONEL [*aside*] What the devil shall I say? I know just as much of Pennsylvania as I do of Bristol.

PRIM Do they thrive?

COLONEL Yes, friend, the blessing of their good works fall upon them.

> [*Enter* MRS PRIM *and* MRS LOVELY.]

PRIM Sarah, know our Friend Pure.

MRS PRIM Thou art welcome.

> [*He salutes her.*]

COLONEL [*aside*] Here comes the sum of all my wishes. How charming she appears, even in that disguise.

PRIM Why dost thou consider the maiden so intentively, friend?

COLONEL I will tell thee. About four days ago, I saw a vision – this very maiden, but in vain attire, standing on a precipice; and heard a voice, which called me by my name and bade me put forth my hand and save her from the pit. I did so, and methought the damsel grew to my side.

MRS PRIM What can that portend?

PRIM The damsel's conversion, I am persuaded.

MRS LOVELY [*aside*] That's false, I'm sure.

PRIM Wilt thou use the means, Friend Pure?

COLONEL Means! What means? Is she not thy daughter and already one of the faithful?

MRS PRIM No, alas. She's one of the ungodly.

PRIM [*to* MRS LOVELY] Pray thee, mind what this good man will say unto thee; he will teach thee the way thou shouldest walk, Ann.

The disguise is the 'bold stroke' of the title.

Between 1707 and 1737, drama went into critical decline although the theatre was still very active and popular. The decline was partly due to opposition from Jeremy Collier and others, and partly because the middle classes were turning to journals, newspapers and the developing new genre of fictional prose to find discussion, entertainment and reinforcement of their values and beliefs. Farce and musical plays became the regular entertainment, and only *The Beggar's Opera* (1728) by John Gay achieved lasting popular success. It is described as 'a Newgate pastoral' – an ironic description, since Newgate was London's principal prison, and frequently features in writing about the lower depths of London society of the time. Gay mixes ballads and songs, vivid characters in the city comedy tradition, burlesque parody of Italian opera, some sentimental scenes, and more than a touch of political satire, to create a highly original piece of theatre which has maintained its considerable influence and success. This scene, between Polly Peachum and the villain/hero Macheath, shows how different *The Beggar's Opera* is from earlier comedies.

MACHEATH Pretty Polly, say,
When I was away,

	Did your fancy never stray
	To some newer lover?
POLLY	Without disguise,
	Heaving sighs,
	Doting eyes,
	My constant heart discover.
	Fondly let me loll!
MACHEATH	O pretty, pretty Poll.

POLLY And are *you* as fond as ever, my dear?

MACHEATH Suspect my honour, my courage, suspect any thing but my love. – May my pistols miss fire, and may my mare slip her shoulder while I am pursu'd, if I ever forsake thee!

It was, however, the element of political satire which was to bring trouble to the theatre in the 1730s. Sir Robert Walpole, the Whig prime minister from 1721 to 1742, objected to satirical attacks on him in *The Beggar's Opera*, and, most particularly, in *The Historical Register for 1736*, by a highly successful writer of farces and satires, Henry Fielding.

The Theatres Licensing Act of 1737 finally introduced censorship in the person of the Lord Chamberlain, who could grant or refuse a licence to any play on political, religious, or moral grounds. This effectively silenced not only virulent political satires but any sexual 'immorality' of the kind attacked by Jeremy Collier as early as 1698. How much this censorship influenced the form and content of future writing is an open question and one which has been widely studied. Of course, plays continued to be written and produced successfully, but the genre went into critical decline for a long period. Fielding turned to the novel, with great success, but drama was effectively silenced as a vehicle for debate until the end of the nineteenth century. The Theatres Licensing Act remained in force, with the Lord Chamberlain as official government censor, until 1968.

ROCHESTER

Whoreing and Drinking, but with good Intent
(*What, Timon?*)

The one individual who epitomises the spirit of the early Restoration is

John Wilmot, Earl of Rochester. His life-style was more notorious than his writing: drunk 'for five years together', with sexual liaisons of every possible variety, Rochester represented the kind of scandalous extremes of behaviour which both titillate and shock 'proper' society. In any age, if such a figure did not exist, it would be almost necessary to invent him – and his deathbed repentance, and conversion to religion, makes the story complete. Although it may be part of a myth-making process by a career chaplain, who was later to become an adviser to the Protestant King William of Orange and who is the only authority for the conversion, it also underscores the polarities of the age: excess of amorality as against excess of religiosity.

The range of Rochester's poetry is considerable. He is a clear link between the later Metaphysical poets, the Cavalier writers of love lyrics, and the Augustans, with their taste for satire. Rochester wrote in all these veins.

> All my past life is mine no more,
>   The flying hours are gone;
> Like transitory Dreams given o'er,
> Whose Images are kept in store
>   By Memory alone.
>   (*Love and Life*)

He is a sexually explicit poet, capable of treating a subject with both delicacy and bawdy humour. His satires are self-mocking (as in *The Maimed Debauchee*) as well as scurrilous about others. His observation of human folly is tinged both with a kind of world-weary tolerance and with vivid, if shocking, imagery, notably in *A Satire against Reason and Mankind*:

> Were I, who to my cost already am
> One of those strange, prodigious Creatures *Man*,
> A spirit free to choose for my own share
> What case of Flesh and Blood I'd please to wear,
> I'd be a *Dog,* a *Monkey* or a *Bear,*
> Or any thing but that vain *Animal*
> Who is proud of being Rational.

The mocking comedy of Rochester is not far removed from the

comic mode of the best Restoration drama, and his railing against the 'Rational' is particularly damning as the Augustan age prided itself, above all, on being rational. Rochester and the comic dramatists share a worldview that is, at the same time, able to point up enjoyment and to see its own faults. Comic point-of-view in drama and satiric intent in verse are closely related in their observation of the new society of the late seventeenth century.

Instead of expanding, as it did so rapidly in the previous two centuries, the world was becoming more closed, contained and inward-looking. So the comedy and satire become self-referential, with the subject matter often being highly topical and the characters particular rather than universal.

DRYDEN

Soothed with the sound the king grew vain
Fought all his battles o'er again
(Alexander's Feast)

At a time when people were taking sides (Whig or Tory, Protestant or Catholic, middle class or aristocrat) and establishing social, political, and religious identities for themselves, it is not surprising that there should be criticisms and friction between the parties concerned. A great deal of this is found in the satire of the 1670s to the 1730s.

Satire was at first largely expressed in poetry; the form of poetry perhaps tempered the virulence a little, giving the writing a degree of respectability. It was part of the age's return to the classical precedents of the Roman Augustan age that the poetry of Horace and the Satires of the later poet Juvenal were held up as models of this kind of poem, which mocked the follies, vices, and preoccupations of the day. The 'new' classicism took what it saw as the highest point of classical culture, and applied its techniques, forms, and models to create a new Augustan age, the neoclassical, which lasted some sixty or seventy years from the early 1670s.

Restoration satire could be of two types: the kind of very general, sweeping criticism of mankind found in poetry in *A Satire against Reason and Mankind* by Rochester, and in prose in Jonathan Swift's

Gulliver's Travels or *A Modest Proposal* (see page 174); or it could be highly specific, with allusions to real figures in politics and society.

This specifically targeted satire is found in the poetry of one of the main literary figures of the Augustan age, John Dryden, notably in his *MacFlecknoe* (1682–84), which is an attack on a literary rival, Thomas Shadwell, and *Absalom and Achitophel* (1681), which uses an allegorical form to comment on the fundamental religious and political issues of the time, issues which would only be resolved by the overthrow of the Catholic monarchy in 1688. The ageing poet Flecknoe (a reference to Richard Flecknoe, a very minor poet who died in about 1678) is deciding who will best succeed him: he chooses Shadwell (1640–92), a playwright, who was clearly not one of Dryden's favourites.

> *Shadwell* alone my perfect image bears,
> Mature in dullness from his tender years.
> *Shadwell* alone, of all my Sons, is he
> Who stands confirm'd in full stupidity.
> The rest to some faint meaning make pretence,
> But *Shadwell* never deviates into sense.
> *(MacFlecknoe)*

Achitophel (in *Absalom and Achitophel*) is identified with the Earl of Shaftesbury, and David is King Charles II. The ambitions and plots remain of their own times – but the scheming and crowd-pleasing can be seen in politicians in any age and nation!

> Oh, had he been content to serve the Crown,
> With virtues only proper to the Gown; . . .
> *David*, for him his tuneful Harp had strung,
> And Heaven had wanted one Immortal song.
> But wild Ambition loves to slide, not stand;
> And Fortune's Ice prefers to Virtue's Land:
> *Achitophel*, grown weary to possess
> A lawful Fame, and lazy Happiness;
> Disdain'd the Golden fruit to gather free,
> And lent the Crowd his Arm to shake the Tree.
> *(Absalom and Achitophel)*

The Medal (1682) follows on from *Absalom and Achitophel*, and predicts much of the religious and political upheaval which was to come in the next few years.

This kind of political satire, in the hands of later writers of novels and plays like Delarivier Manley and Henry Fielding, became less and less acceptable to the people who were its victims. The result would be political censorship of the theatre, and a refining of satirical content into highly political satires used as upper-class entertainment in some of the writings of Alexander Pope who, with Dryden, is the main figure in Augustan poetry.

Dryden was a highly prolific literary figure, a professional writer who was at the centre of all the greatest debates of his time: the end of the Commonwealth, the return of the monarch, the political and religious upheavals of the 1680s, and the specifically literary questions of neoclassicism opposed to more modern trends. He was Poet Laureate from 1668, but lost this position in 1688 on the overthrow of James II. Dryden had become Catholic in 1685, and his allegorical poem *The Hind and the Panther* (1687) discusses the complex issues of religion and politics in an attempt to reconcile bitterly opposed factions. This contains a well-known line which anticipates Wordsworth more than a century later: 'By education most have been misled . . . / And thus the child imposes on the man.' The poem shows an awareness of change as one grows older, and the impossibility of holding one view for a lifetime:

> My thoughtless youth was winged with vain desires,
> My manhood, long misled by wandering fires,
> Followed false lights. . . .

After 1688, Dryden returned to the theatre, which had given him many of his early successes in tragedy, tragi-comedy, and comedy, as well as with adaptations of Shakespeare. His final plays are among his best, and his translations and critical writings, with one or two significant works such as *Alexander's Feast* (1697) and *The Secular Masque* (1700), are his main achievements in his later years. Here the past dominates, rather than the present of Dryden's earlier verse.

> CHORUS:
> Bacchus' blessings are a treasure;

> Drinking is the soldier's pleasure;
> > Rich the treasure,
> > Sweet the pleasure;
> Sweet is pleasure after pain.

Soothed with the sound the King grew vain,
> Fought all his battles o'er again;
And thrice he routed all his foes, and thrice he slew the slain.

> > > > > > > (*Alexander's Feast*)

> All, all of a piece throughout:
> Thy chase had a beast in view;
> Thy wars brought nothing about;
> Thy lovers were all untrue.
> 'Tis well an old age is out,
> And time to begin a new.
> > > > > > (*The Secular Masque*)

Dryden was an innovator, leading the move from heroic couplets to blank verse in drama, and at the centre of the intellectual debates of the Augustan age. He experimented with verse forms throughout his writing life until *Fables Ancient and Modern* (1700), which brings together critical, translated, and original works, in a fitting conclusion to a varied career.

The term 'heroic' was, as we have seen, applied to tragedy in the Restoration period. As satire lost its venom, the heroic couplet adopted a gentler, more humorous tone. It is in this context that the term 'mock heroic' can be best understood. The term is normally applied to Pope's poetry, but can be seen to refer, more widely, to a whole restructuring of values at what was felt to be the beginning of a new age. In all the arts of the age, there is a self-conscious scaling down of terms of reference, which leads to parody, to satire, and to a more restricted, self-referential literature than the Renaissance produced.

Matthew Prior and Samuel Butler were very well known and highly successful in their own day, but their writings have not had the lasting regard that Dryden, for instance, has enjoyed. Butler wrote the long satirical poem *Hudibras,* which was published in three parts between 1663 and 1680 and quickly gained great popularity. In a sense it set the tone of much of the satire which followed, but Butler's poem, in deliberately absurd-sounding octosyllabic couplets, is full of entertaining digressions, obscure learning, and contemporary reference. It starts as a mock romance, but by the final part it becomes a commentary on the events leading up to the Restoration. The tone can be judged from the opening lines:

> When civil dudgeon first grew high,
> And men fell out they knew not why.

Matthew Prior is more a poet of light occasional verse, although his first major work was a satire on Dryden's *The Hind and the Panther*. He became famous as a secret agent working behind the scenes on the Treaty of Utrecht of 1713, which ended the War of the Spanish Succession. As a very popular poet, he covers a wide range of themes and forms, but his poetry remains anchored in the passing events of the age rather than handling themes of continuing relevance and concern: a comparison between Prior's Ode celebrating the arrival of William III, *Carmen Seculare* (1700) and Andrew Marvell's *Horatian Ode upon Cromwell's Return from Ireland*, written exactly fifty years earlier, confirms that Marvell could produce splendid political poetry, whereas Prior was engaged in rather more trivial flattery. Something of the decline in the place of poetry over those fifty years, despite the work of Milton and Dryden, can also be observed in this comparison (see page 111 for Marvell):

> Confess the various Attributes of Fame
> Collected and compleat in William's Name:
> To all the list'ning World relate,
>   (As Thou dost His Story read)
> That nothing went before so Great,
>   And nothing Greater can succeed.
>   (*Carmen Seculare*)

POPE

True wit is nature to advantage dressed,
What oft was thought but ne'er so well expressed
(*Essay on Criticism*)

Alexander Pope was, like Dryden after 1685, a Catholic, and therefore an outsider in the Protestant-dominated society of the early eighteenth century. The two men were, however, of totally different generations and background. Pope was 12 when Dryden died, and was suffering from the spinal disease which left him deformed and sickly for the rest of his life.

Pope had, in common with Dryden, considerable success in translating Greek and Latin classics – especially Homer – into English, and also prepared a noted, if flawed, edition of Shakespeare, in 1725. But he never engaged in serious political, philosophical, and religious debate on the scale that Dryden achieved. Perhaps because of his poor health, Pope was something of a recluse, but he was very involved in high society, and took sides on most of the political issues of his day. His satires are full of savage invective against real or imagined enemies.

Pope's sphere was social and intellectual. *The Rape of the Lock* (1712–14), written when he was in his mid-twenties, is the essence of the mock heroic. It makes a family quarrel, over a lock of hair, into the subject of a playful poem full of paradoxes and witty observations on the self-regarding world it depicts, as the stolen lock is transported to the heavens to become a new star. 'Fair tresses man's imperial race insnare' makes Belinda's hair an attractive trap for all mankind – a linking of the trivial with the apparently serious, which is Pope's most frequent device in puncturing his targets' self-importance.

> This Nymph, to the Destruction of Mankind,
> Nourish'd two Locks, which graceful hung behind
> In equal Curls, and well conspir'd to deck
> With shining Ringlets the smooth Iv'ry Neck.
> Love in these Labyrinths his Slaves detains,
> And mighty Hearts are held in slender Chains.
> With hairy Springes we the Birds betray,
> Slight Lines of Hair surprise the Finny Prey,
> Fair Tresses Man's Imperial Race insnare,

And Beauty draws us with a single Hair.
    Th' Adventurous *Baron* the bright Locks admir'd,
He saw, he wish'd, and to the Prize aspir'd.
                                  (*The Rape of the Lock*)

The Dunciad (1726, expanded in 1743) is Pope's best-known satire. It is again mock heroic in style, and, like Dryden's *MacFlecknoe* some fifty years before, it is an attack on the author's literary rivals, critics, and enemies. Pope groups them together as the general enemy 'Dulness', which gradually takes over the world, and reduces it to chaos and darkness:

See now, what Dulness and her sons admire;
See! what the charms, that smite the simple heart
Not touch'd by Nature, and not reach'd by Art.

Limited though these issues may seem, Pope's intentions in his writing were wide-ranging. His *Moral Essays* from the 1730s, his *An Epistle to Doctor Arbuthnot* (1735), his *An Essay on Man* (1733–34), and the early *Essay on Criticism* (1711) explore the whole question of man's place in the universe, and his moral and social responsibilities in the world.

A little learning is a dangerous thing.
                    (*Essay on Criticism*)

True wit is nature to advantage dressed,
What oft was thought but ne'er so well expressed.
                    (*Essay on Criticism*)

True ease in writing comes from art, not chance,
As those move easiest who have learned to dance.
'Tis not enough no harshness gives offence,
The sound must seem an echo to the sense.
                    (*Essay on Criticism*)

All nature is but art, unknown to thee;
All chance, direction which thou canst not see;
All discord, harmony not understood;
All partial evil, universal good;
And, spite of pride, in erring reason's spite,
One truth is clear, Whatever is, is right.
                    (*An Essay on Man*)

Know then thyself, presume not God to scan;
The proper study of mankind is man.
(*An Essay on Man*)

The *Imitations of Horace* (1733–38) raise issues of political neutrality, partisanship and moral satire, and as such are a key text of the Augustan age. The conclusion of *An Essay on Man*, 'Whatever is, is right', may seem sadly banal; but a great many of Pope's lines are among the most memorable and quotable from English poetry. His technical ability and wit, although firmly based in the neoclassical spirit of the time, raised Pope's achievement to considerable heights.

JOURNALISM

As the market for the printed word expanded around the beginning of the eighteenth century, so production rose to meet demand. The rising middle classes were the readership for a wide range of daily and weekly newspapers and journals founded at this time. *The Tatler*, founded by Richard Steele, ran from April 1709 to January 1711, to be followed by *The Spectator*, run by Steele with Joseph Addison from March 1711 until December 1712, and by Addison alone for several months in 1714. These were journals of coffee-house gossip and ideas in London. *The Spectator* became the journal of a gentleman's club, led by the fictional Sir Roger de Coverley. Its attitudes, in relation to the city and the country, and relations between social classes, are significant indications of the time:

> I am always very well pleased with a Country Sunday, and think, if keeping holy the Seventh Day were only a human Institution, it would be the best Method that could have been thought of for the polishing and civilising of Mankind. It is certain the Country-People would soon degenerate into a kind of Savages and Barbarians, were there not such frequent Returns of a stated Time, in which the whole Village meet together with their best Faces, and in their cleanliest Habits, to converse with one another upon indifferent Subjects, hear their Duties explained to them, and join together in Adoration of the supreme Being. . . .
> My Friend Sir Roger, being a good Churchman, has beautified the inside of his Church with several texts of his own choosing. He has

likewise given a handsome Pulpit-Cloth, and railed in the Communion-Table at his own Expense. He has often told me that at his coming to his Estate he found his Parishioners very irregular; and that in order to make them kneel and join in the Responses, he gave every one of them a Hassock and a Common-prayer Book: and at the same time employed an itinerant Singing-Master, who goes about the Country for that Purpose, to instruct them rightly in the Tunes of the Psalms; upon which they now very much value themselves, and indeed outdo most of the Country Churches that I have ever heard.

As Sir Roger is Landlord to the whole Congregation, he keeps them in very good Order, and will suffer no Body to sleep in it besides himself; for if by Chance he has been surprised into a short Nap at sermon, upon recovering out of it he stands up and looks about him, and if he sees any Body else nodding, either wakes them himself, or sends his Servant to them.

(Joseph Addison, 'A Country Sunday', *The Spectator*, 1711)

This sense of class and social identity is significant in the papers' consideration of market appeal. The coffee-houses of London, or a gentleman's club, thus became the respected centres of 'middle-brow' ideas on society, culture, manners and morals, literature and life. *The Spectator*'s declared objective was 'to enliven morality with wit, and to temper wit with morality'. This well-balanced attitude established a tradition of safe, witty, reassuring observation of and comment on the life and times of eighteenth-century London and England. Addison wrote: 'I live in the world rather as a spectator of mankind than as one of the species.' What emerges as important is, therefore, a point of view, an attitude, rather than a committed engagement with issues and debates – a well-informed distance which is both tolerant and self-protective. In effect, it sets down and perpetuates class values which would remain strong for more than two centuries: the published word begins to become a powerful instrument in society.

The Gentleman's Journal, which was published from 1692 to 1694, was the first magazine of this kind; the similarly named *Gentleman's Magazine* was one of the longest lasting, from 1731 until 1914. *The Grub Street Journal* (1730–37) was a satirical literary magazine, its jokey name synonymous with literary hack work. *The Monthly Review* became, in the later part of the century, the most significant and influential of the literary magazines. The Bedford Coffee-House, in Covent Garden, was in the 1730s 'the emporium of wit, the seat of criticism, and the standard of taste', as London became the cultural capital of Britain, and London tastes dominated and influenced the tastes of the nation.

Despite their seeming decorum, many of the magazines and journals of the eighteenth century did engage in highly critical and controversial debates. Indeed, many of the age's writers used journalism as a vehicle for their ideas, and some fell foul of libel laws and factional disputes and were subject to prosecution for their ideas.

Daniel Defoe, for example, ran *The Review* for several years; he then edited a trade journal, *The Mercator*, before becoming a novelist. His strong opinions landed him in prison on more than one occasion. Defoe is one of the first to write polemically about money, and the new mercantile ethos in society.

> O Money, Money! What an Influence hast thou on all the affairs of the quarrelling, huffing Part of this World, as well as upon the most plodding Part of it! . . .
> And how art Thou to be obtain'd? How must we court thy favour? Truly, just as the rest of the World does, where Thou art, we must seek Thee. . . .
> And this brings me down to the Times; Money is now the Business, raising Money is the Affair, Ways and Means is the Word: . . . and this is the Foundation of what we call Law, Liberty, and Property, and the like modern Words very much in Use.
>
> (Daniel Defoe, in *The Review*, 1707)

Other major figures, from Pope to Dr Johnson, used journalism as an integral part of their literary careers. Writing, with the advent of journalism and the growing popularity of the novel, was now a profession.

SCOTTISH ENLIGHTENMENT, DIARISTS AND GIBBON

In the eighteenth century, the Scottish Enlightenment focused attention on Glasgow and Edinburgh as centres of intellectual activity. The

Scottish Enlightenment was an intellectual movement which originated in Glasgow in the early eighteenth century, and flourished in Edinburgh in the second half of the century. Its thinking was based on philosophical enquiry and its practical applications for the benefit of society ('improvement' was a favoured term). The Enlightenment encompassed literature, philosophy, science, education, and even geology. One of its lasting results was the founding of the *Encyclopaedia Britannica* (1768–71). The effects of the Scottish Enlightenment, especially in the second half of the century, were far-reaching in Britain and Europe.

The philosophical trends ranged from the 'common-sense' approach of Thomas Reid to the immensely influential works of David Hume, notably his *Treatise of Human Nature,* published in 1739. Here, his arguments on God, and the cause and effect of man's relationship with God, are far ahead of their time in the philosophical debate in Britain:

> It is still open for me, as well as you, to regulate my behaviour, by my experience of past events. And if you affirm that, while a divine providence is allowed, and a supreme distributive justice in the universe, I ought to expect some more particular reward of the good, and punishment of the bad, beyond the ordinary course of events; I here find the same fallacy, which I have before endeavoured to detect. You persist in imagining, that, if we grant that divine existence, for which you so earnestly contend, you may safely infer consequences from it, and add something to the experienced order of nature, by arguing from the attributes which you ascribe to your gods. You seem not to remember, that all your reasonings on this subject can only be drawn from effects to causes; and that every argument, deduced from causes to effects, must of necessity be a gross sophism; since it is impossible for you to know any thing of the cause, but what you have antecedently, not inferred, but discovered to the full, in the effect.
>
> (David Hume, *An Enquiry Concerning Human Understanding,* 1748)

Adam Smith's book *The Wealth of Nations* (1776) was probably the most important work on economics of the century, revolutionising concepts of trade and prophesying the growing importance of America as 'one of the foremost nations of the world'. By a remarkable coincidence, the book was published in the very same year as the American Declaration of Independence. One of the comments later used by Napoleon Bonaparte against the British is first found in Smith's *The Wealth of Nations*, again underlining the new mercantile ethos of the time.

> To found a great empire for the sole purpose of raising up a people of customers, may at first sight appear a project fit only for a nation of shopkeepers. It is, however, a project altogether unfit for a nation of shopkeepers; but extremely fit for a nation that is governed by shopkeepers.

And so to bed
(Samuel Pepys, *Diary*)

The growth of the writing profession coincided with a rise in writing which was private and not intended for publication. Diaries and letters were, for the new literate middle class, forms of expression which enjoyed increasingly wider currency.

The *Diary* of Samuel Pepys is probably the best-known example of its kind in all literature. Running from 1 January 1660 until 31 May 1669, the diary was written in a form of code, which was not deciphered until 1825. Essentially private and highly personal, it gives a day-by-day insight into the decade of the Restoration – with visits to the theatre, graphically described amorous encounters, details of Pepys's work as a high-ranking civil servant, and such major events as the Great Plague (1664–65) and the Great Fire of London (1666).

To Pepys, and to his contemporary John Evelyn, we owe first-hand accounts of the new society as it was taking shape. Evelyn is less spontaneous, perhaps more reflective than Pepys; in part, because his *Diary* (or *Memoirs*), first published in 1818, was not written day by day, as Pepys's was. But their contribution to our knowledge of the Restoration is outstanding. Here we can contrast the two commentaries on the Great Fire.

> . . . the fire running further, that in a very little time it got as far as the Steele-yard, while I was there. Everybody endeavouring to remove their goods, and flinging into the river or bringing them into lighters that lay off; poor people staying in their houses as long as till the very

fire touched them, and then running into boats, or clambering from one pair of stairs by the water-side to another. And among other things, the poor pigeons, I perceive, were loth to leave their houses, but hovered about the windows and balconys till they were, some of them burned, their wings, and fell down.

(Samuel Pepys, *Diary*)

The conflagration was so universal, and the people so astonish'd, that from the beginning – I know not by what desponding or fate – they hardly stirr'd to quench it, so that there was nothing heard or seene but crying out and lamentation, and running about like distracted creatures without at all attempting to save even their goods.

(John Evelyn, *Diary*)

Letters gave fiction the basis of the epistolary novel, echoing the newly established fashion of letter-writing among the middle and upper classes. The eighteenth century was the great era of letter-writing. The best-known letters of the century are those written by Lord Chesterfield to his son, from 1737 until the son's death in 1768. They were not intended for publication, and only appeared after the writer's death, in 1773. The letters then became a kind of handbook of good behaviour, a vivid manual of how society saw itself, and an indication of how appearance and 'manners maketh the man'. The letters were much ridiculed, notably by the critic Dr Samuel Johnson, who asserted that they 'teach the morals of a whore and the manners of a dancing-master'. But they remain a unique insight into mid-eighteenth-century upper-class attitudes and life-style.

The writing of history as a contribution to literature can be traced back to the twelfth century and Geoffrey of Monmouth's *Historia Regum Britanniae*. This drew on earlier documents and on British and Welsh traditions to affirm a glorious historical past for the emerging nation of Britain. Later history both affirms the nation's heritage and questions its cultural influences.

In the eighteenth century, with the growth of publishing and with the intellectual climate of the Enlightenment, there was a great demand for new historical writing. The greatest product of this was *The Decline and Fall of the Roman Empire*, a massive six-volume work published between 1776 and 1788, precisely between the American Revolution and the French Revolution. The context is important, as the author Edward Gibbon was examining not only the greatness of Rome, but the forces which brought about its decay. The story of the burning of Rome is rather different from Pepys's or Evelyn's Great Fire of London, and ends with something more legendary than historical.

> In the tenth year of the reign of Nero, the capital of the empire was afflicted by a fire which raged beyond the memory or example of former ages. The monuments of Grecian art and of Roman virtue, the trophies of the Punic and Gallic wars, the most holy temples, and the most splendid palaces, were involved in one common destruction. Of the fourteen regions or quarters into which Rome was divided, four only subsisted entire, three were levelled with the ground, and the remaining seven which had experienced the fury of the flames displayed a melancholy prospect of ruin and desolation. . . .
>
> The voice of rumour accused the emperor as the incendiary of his own capital: and, as the most incredible stories are the best adapted to the genius of an enraged people, it was gravely reported and firmly believed, that Nero, enjoying the calamity which he had occasioned, amused himself with singing to his lyre the destruction of ancient Troy.

Gibbon's interpretation of history was controversial, especially in its examination of the growth of Christianity, but his accurate scholarship and engaging prose style have made *The Decline and Fall* the most enduring work of history in English.

In the eighteenth century, history is seen as a branch of *belles-lettres*, and it subsumes within it scriptural authority on the one hand, and fictional narrative on the other. History is, in effect, the new secular authority of the Enlightenment, and comes to be a very wide-ranging category of writing.

THE NOVEL

There was nothing talked of but this young and gallant slave

(Aphra Behn, *Oroonoko*)

The concern of the Augustan age was not so much with *exploration* – both of the bounds of human potential and of the bounds of geography and the sciences, which were the concerns of the Renaissance – as with *experience*. The novel and fiction became the dominant form and genre in terms of readership, although for more than a century they would be considered 'inferior' by critics.

The novel was not a sudden innovation at the end of the seventeenth century. Accounts of travels, which may or may not have been fictionalised to some extent, go back as far as the *Travels of Sir John Mandeville*, probably published in 1375. Other worlds and cultures, ways of living and believing, became a main characteristic of fiction through the Elizabethan age. Thomas Nashe's *The Unfortunate Traveller* (1594) provides us with one of the earliest picaresque tales in English. It recounts 'the life of Jack Wilton' in a mixture of styles, anticipating the picaresque heroes and heroines of Daniel Defoe and Henry Fielding just over a century later. Sir Thomas More's *Utopia* was also influential in 'fictionalising travel' and thus providing impetus to the growth of the novel (see page 82).

In general, however, the exotic influence in seventeenth- and eighteenth-century literature was to be tamed; subsumed into recognisably English middle-class ways of thinking and brought into line with the worldview of the time. Englishness could always dominate over exoticism: English readers could usually feel they were superior to any of the outlandish behaviour or ways of life they read about. So, although the fascination with the exotic, seen in travellers' tales over the centuries from Mandeville to Raleigh, is a common theme, the concern now was not simply to document but to accommodate experience within recognisable bounds.

The expanding readership was largely female and upper or upper-middle class. The new ethos indicated that all kinds of social behaviour be monitored, regulated, controlled. So, in many novels, a new morality is propounded, covering male/female relationships, figures of authority, and the social awareness of needs, desires, and fantasies. In this context, the first female figure in English literature stands out as a vivid exception to the newly formulated rule.

Aphra Behn's exotic *Oroonoko* uses a tale of a noble African, who is carried off to slavery in the English colony of Surinam, to illustrate the violence of the slave trade and the corruption of the primitive peoples by treacherous and hypocritical Christian colonisers. It is a novel of violence and cruelty and is ahead of its time in its defence of the 'noble savage' and its affirmation of an anti-colonial stance.

> . . . the fame of *Oroonoko* was gone before him, and all people were in admiration of his beauty . . . there was nothing talked of but this young and gallant slave, even by those who knew not that he was a prince.
>
> I ought to tell you, that the Christians never buy any slaves but they give 'em some name of their own, their native ones being likely very barbarous, and hard to pronounce; so that Mr *Trefry* gave *Oroonoko* that of *Caesar*, which name will live in that country as long as that (scarce more) glorious one of the great *Roman*: for 'tis most evident he wanted no part of the world replenished with people and historians, that might have given him his due. But his misfortune was, to fall in an obscure world, that afforded only a female pen to celebrate his fame; though I doubt not but it had lived from others endeavours, if the *Dutch*, who immediately after his time took that country, had not killed, banished and dispersed all those that were capable of giving the world this great man's life, much better than I have done. . . .
>
> For the future therefore I must call *Oroonoko Caesar*; since by that name only he was known in our western world, and by that name he was received on shore at *Parham House*, where he was destin'd a slave.

Behn was a controversial figure, despite considerable success as a writer for the theatre. She was accused of lewdness and of plagiarism. She was also politically active, and, in general, was an uncomfortable presence in the prevailing moral climate of the late seventeenth century. Perhaps it was this which led to her being ignored in literary history for many years.

She cannot be ignored, however, as the writer of some seventeen plays, and thirty works of fiction – some three decades before Daniel Defoe is credited with writing the first proper novels. She herself contended that the fact that she *was* a woman, and spoke out for women's rights and sexual freedom, had a negative effect on how she was received. Charges of immorality meant that even in the twentieth century, when Virginia Woolf and then the feminist critics attempted to retrieve her reputation, some shades of critical doubt remained. Whether this is a sign of critical and moral double standards remains open to debate, but if Defoe is to be considered one of the 'fathers' of the novel, Aphra Behn has more than a claim to be considered one of the genre's 'mothers'.

The works of other writers who were accused of immorality or anti-government sentiments also suffered in this climate. Delarivier Manley is a good example of a hugely successful writer whose voice was silenced amidst scandalous accusations. Her *The New Atalantis* (1709) was a sensational political allegory, not far removed from Swift. It was described by later moralists as 'the most objectionable of novels' for its handling of dangerous topics such as rape, incest and homosexuality. Here, an ageing Duchess (identified as Lady Castlemaine, a mistress of the King) is attracted to a young count, identified as John Churchill, first Duke of Marlborough (Sir Winston Churchill was grandson of the seventh Duke).

> . . . he . . . was newly risen from the bath and, in a loose gown of carnation taffeta, stained with Indian figures, his beautiful long, flowing hair (for then 'twas the custom to wear their own tied back with a ribbon of the same colour) he had thrown himself upon the bed, pretending to sleep, with nothing on but his shirt and night-gown, which he had so indecently disposed that, slumbering as he appeared, his whole person stood confessed to the eyes of the amorous Duchess. His limbs were exactly formed, his skin shiningly white, and the pleasure the lady's graceful entrance gave him diffused joy and desire throughout all his form. His lovely eyes seemed to be closed, his face turned on one side (to favour the deceit) was obscured by the lace depending from the pillows on which he rested.
>
> (*The New Atalantis*)

Manley's *The Secret History of Queen Zarah* (1705) took the kind of refined political satire of Dryden into the sphere of contemporary politics. Each serial volume of the novel was accompanied by a key explaining who the characters were. The novel exposed the corruption of the worlds of high society and politics, and continued a trend of scandal-mongering which has been a mainstay of popular publishing ever since.

Clearly, lines of demarcation were being drawn, and scandalous novels were deemed unacceptable, while satiric verse, for a much more limited readership, could be condoned. But satire, explicitness in sexual terms, religious questioning and threats to the government's *status quo* were consistently muzzled, and driven out of what was considered 'proper' in literature. Propriety became a key concept in literature, and was directly related to the critical concerns of the Augustan, or neo-classical age.

It will be hard for a private history to be taken for genuine

(Daniel Defoe, *A Journal of the Plague Year*)

The novels of Daniel Defoe are fundamental to eighteenth-century ways of thinking. They range from the quasi-factual *A Journal of the Plague Year*, an almost journalistic (but fictional) account of London between 1664 and 1665 (when the author was a very young child), to *Robinson Crusoe*, one of the most enduring fables of Western culture. If the philosophy of the time asserted that life was, in Hobbes's words, 'solitary, poor, nasty, brutish, and short', novels showed ways of coping with 'brutish' reality (the plague; solitude on a desert island) and making the best of it. There was no questioning of authority as there had been throughout the Renaissance. Instead, there was an interest in establishing and accepting authority, and of the ways of 'society' as a newly ordered whole.

Thus, Defoe's best-known heroine, Moll Flanders, can titillate her readers with her first-person narration of a dissolute life as thief, prostitute, and incestuous wife, all the time telling her story from the vantage point of one who has been accepted back into society and improved her behaviour.

> ... every branch of my story, if duly considered, may be useful to honest people, and afford a due caution to people of some sort or

other to guard against the like surprises, and to have their eyes about them when they have to do with strangers of any kind, for 'tis very seldom that some snare or other is not in their way. The moral, indeed, of all my history is left to be gathered by the senses and judgment of the reader; I am not qualified to preach to them. Let the experience of one creature completely wicked, and completely miserable, be a storehouse of useful warning to those that read.

(*Moll Flanders*)

The novel contains much social comment: the conditions of the poor, the gaols (especially Newgate), the suffering of emigrants, all became subjects of concern to novelists, journalists, artists and the well-intentioned middle classes. The new bourgeoisie in some ways reinforced a class distinction between 'haves' and 'have-nots' in this emphasis on middle-class values and middle-class superiority. However, artistic representations of low life continued to be popular for other reasons too. John Gay's theatrical work *The Beggar's Opera* is a good example of the entertainment value of cut-purses, thieves, and their womenfolk. Its hero, Macheath, is one of the lasting figures of 'popular' culture to emerge from this period (see page 149). But few will be as lucky as Moll Flanders, who comes to a 'happy ending' and, importantly, financial security after all her difficulties.

Robinson Crusoe makes a kingdom of the island upon which he is shipwrecked. His relationships, first with Xury, then with his 'man, Friday', lack the kind of respect Behn gave the royal slave in *Oroonoko* (see page 167). Here is how he speaks to Xury, his boy.

'Xury, if you will be faithful to me I'll make you a great man, but if you will not swear to be true to me, I must throw you into the sea too.' The boy smiled in my face and spoke so innocently that I could not mistrust him; and swore to be faithful to me, and go all over the world with me.

(*Robinson Crusoe*)

Crusoe is a coloniser, who establishes on the island a model of his own society which will continue after the end of the tale. Robinson's belief in God, or in what he himself is doing, is never questioned. To paraphrase Pope: whatever Crusoe does, is right. After Xury leaves, Crusoe encounters 'Friday' – and has to convert him to Christianity.

After Friday and I became more intimately acquainted, and he could understand almost all I said to him, and speak fluently, though in broken English, to me, I acquainted him first, with true Christian religion, and then with my own story, or at least so much of it as related to my coming to into the place. . . .

I described to him the country of Europe, and particularly England, which I came from; how we lived, how we worshipped God, how we behaved to one another; and how we traded in ships to all parts of the world.

So this novel, which has become a potent myth of survival, confirms for the reader the ultimate rightness of Crusoe's way of thinking and acting. The novel ends positively in order not to subvert any of the middle-class mercantile values Robinson Crusoe upholds.

I remained in Lisbon to settle my affairs. Within seven months, I received what I was owed from the survivors of the trustees; the merchants for whose account I had gone to sea.

I was now master, all on a sudden, of above £5,000 sterling in money, and had an estate, as I might well call it, in the Brasils, of above a thousand pounds a year, as sure as an estate of lands in England: and in a word, I was in a condition which I scarce knew how to understand, or how to compose myself for the enjoyment of it.

Crusoe, having survived twenty-eight years on his desert island, sees his investments make him rich, and sees his island colonised, without any sympathy for Friday whom he views as the simple native, improved by his master and by his conversion to Christianity. Alternatively, Friday can be seen as the victim of colonialisation whose territory and beliefs are usurped by the coloniser.

It is significant that the Bank of England was founded in 1694, and we recall Defoe's railing against money (page 161). Robinson Crusoe has been seen as one of the first capitalist heroes, who overcomes extreme difficulties to reach economic security. This kind of success story is later repeated through Charles Dickens in the nineteenth century to H.G. Wells and others in the twentieth century, and it embodies many of the aspects of the triumph of the middle-class ethos, where money is the driving force.

Love and romance were not excluded, however. Moll's search is a search for love and identity as well as for social stability and accept-ability. (But Robinson Crusoe's marriage, it has to be said, occupies less than a page of his adventures; an indication, perhaps, of how men's and women's concerns differ.) The heroine of Defoe's *Roxana*, sub-titled *The Fortunate Mistress*, is a kind of superior Moll Flanders, going through a series of rich protectors and becoming very rich herself in the process. Yet this cannot go unpunished. When her Dutch merchant husband discovers her deceit, he leaves her almost penniless, and her end is the opposite of Moll's, dying penitent while in prison for debt.

Roxana's sin has been to take her fortune for granted, and not to appreciate the effort and hard work which has gone into amassing it: her death as a penitent affirms the Puritan ethic which she has spent her life transgressing. She is not the role-model for the woman of the time – she is far too independent, pleasure-loving, and adventurous. It is not long before the novel provides a female role-model in the work of Samuel Richardson.

Satire is a sort of glass, wherein beholders do generally discover everybody's face but their own

(Jonathan Swift, *The Battle of the Books*)

One writer who dared to criticise and mock authority figures, with ever-increasing venom, was Jonathan Swift. It is indicative of how 'dissidents' can be absorbed that his most famous novel, *Gulliver's Travels* (1726), has long been considered a comic fable for children. In fact, it is a severe attack on the political parties of the time, and on the pointlessness of religious controversies between different denomin-ations within Christianity. These differences are symbolised in the tiny Lilliputians and the enormous Brobdingnagians, or in the differences between the Big-endians or Little-endians. The controversy between these two is whether boiled eggs should be opened at the big or the little end.

The novel goes on to satirise some of the new scientific institutions of the time, such as The Royal Society. The culmination of Swift's angry polemic comes when he presents the Houyhnhnms, a race of rational, clean, civilised horses who are contrasted with the foul, brutal, uncivilised Yahoos, a race of ape-like beasts in human form. Gulliver, the traveller who has visited so many different worlds, has to recognise that the Yahoos are, sadly, the closest to his own species – some 133 years before Charles Darwin confirmed their ape-like connections in *On the Origin of Species*.

> . . . several horses and mares of quality in the neighbourhood came often to our house upon the report spread of a wonderful Yahoo, that could speak like a Houyhnhnm, and seemed in his words and actions to discover some glimmerings of Reason. These delighted to converse with me; they put many questions, and received such answers as I was able to return. By all which advantages, I made so great a progress, that in five months from my arrival, I understood whatever was spoke, and could express myself tolerably well.
>
> The Houyhnhnms who came to visit my master, out of a design of seeing and talking with me, could hardly believe me to be a right Yahoo, because my body had a different covering from others of my kind. They were astonished to observe me without the usual hair or skin, except on my head, face and hands.
>
> (*Gulliver's Travels*)

This is the satire of poets like Dryden and Pope taken to a polemical extreme, and seasoned with real anger. The third part of the novel satirises the period's new institutions and schools of learning. The fourth part becomes an out-and-out satire on mankind, with all the disgust that Rochester showed now applied to depict men as monkey-like Yahoos, considerably inferior in all their qualities to the Houyhnhnms, which are horses. In a period when horses were one of the main servants of man, this is an examination of roles which was intended to provoke and offend. It was, however, dismissed as fantastic comedy and, as a result, its satiric power was blunted.

Dislike of the world is not usually well received. Shakespeare's *Timon of Athens*, about the misanthrope who rejects the world, is one of his least performed plays. It becomes something of a requirement that literature be in some way life-affirming; doubts are resolved, happy endings reached, the bad punished, the good rewarded. Swift does not provide such comfort.

In tone, Swift is sometimes not far from Mandeville, over 350 years before him. Mandeville spoke of an island he visited where children were eaten, describing their flesh as 'the best and sweetest flesh in the world'. Swift, in a prose pamphlet (1729) about the situation of Ireland (already a political problem for more than a century), offers, as a solution to the problem, the marketing of Irish children for English consumption. *A Modest Proposal* suggests that:

> . . . a young healthy child well nursed is at a year old a most delicious, nourishing, and wholesome food, whether stewed, roasted, baked, or boiled, and I make no doubt that it will equally serve in a fricassee, or a ragout.

Mandeville's exotic joke here becomes a vehicle for serious political satire; but the English reading public was shocked and horrified, unable to see Swift's humour or his serious concern.

Swift is yet another example of an Anglo-Irish writer, criticising English society ever more strongly. He wrote a great many political pamphlets on a wide range of topics, and, with Defoe, is one of the most prolific of all English authors. But it is his satire that is best remembered: from *A Tale of a Tub* (1704), on corruption in religion and learning, to *The Grand Question Debated*, in 1729. Always a controversial and polemical figure, his *Journal to Stella* (1710–13) and his vividly expressive poetry show a rich span of emotion and verbal invention. For a long time, he was considered merely a mad misanthrope, but that critical opinion – convenient for the tastes of his own day – can now be seen to do less than justice to a writer who used satire with great originality and wit to highlight what he saw as the faults and hypocrisies of his age. His own joking epitaph says much about his perception of himself:

> He knew an hundred pleasant stories,
> With all the turns of Whigs and Tories;
> Was cheerful to his dying day,
> And friends would let him have his way.
> He gave the little wealth he had
> To build a house for fools and mad,
> And showed by one satiric touch,
> No nation wanted it so much.
> That kingdom he hath left his debtor;
> I wish it soon may have a better.
> <div align="right">(<i>Verses on the Death of Dr Swift</i>)</div>

. . . written, though perhaps not intended, with such explicitness (don't be alarmed, my dear!)

(Samuel Richardson, *Clarissa*)

It is with the next generation of novelists that love stories come into their own. Samuel Richardson had worked his way up from poverty to become a prosperous printer. Among the works he published in the late 1730s were books of moral advice and a version for the times of Aesop's *Fables*. The success of these led him to develop a series of 'familiar letters' with their original aim being a manual of letter-writing. But they turned into a major epistolary novel, *Pamela*, published in 1740.

Novels in the form of letters had been popular for several decades, Aphra Behn having published *Love Letters between a Nobleman and his Sister* as early as 1683. Richardson wanted to raise the tone of the novel from the level of this kind of subject matter, and in doing so created a heroine for the times. Poor but virtuous, Pamela suffers a series of trials at the hands of Mr B, culminating in attempted rape. She refuses to become his mistress or his wife until she converts Mr B. Then she agrees to marry him and becomes a paragon of virtue admired by all. The contrast between male domination, with its implied sensuality, and female restraint and submission, with its emphasis on virtue symbolised in chastity, was immediately criticised as hypocritical, and parodied by Henry Fielding in *Shamela*.

Pamela was a huge success. It not only created a fashion for the epistolary novel, but underscored role distinctions which were to become predominant in society for some two centuries: the dominant male as provider and master; the female as victim, preserving her virtue until submitting to 'affection' and the inevitability of the man's dominance. An impression of female independence is given by the creation of a woman's role in society as mistress of a social circle. Thus the female role is established in relation to male roles, and any deviation is seen as both socially and morally reprehensible. Modern psychological commentators have found Pamela's behaviour perplexing, and the discussion of male/female roles since Richardson wrote *Pamela* has kept the novel in the forefront of literary and social interest.

Richardson's next epistolary novel, *Clarissa* (1747–48), marks a major step forward. There are four major letter writers, where in *Pamela* almost all the letters come from the heroine alone. The novel ends in tragedy, and it is interesting to compare Clarissa's tragedy with similar Renaissance precedents. Clarissa's suitor Lovelace (hinting in the name at love's ties that bind) plays with her emotions in devious ways, consigning her to a brothel, attempting rape, and leading to the key question:

> Is not *this* the hour of her trial – And in *her*, of the trial of the virtue of her whole Sex, so long premeditated, so long threatened? – Whether her frost be frost indeed? Whether her virtue be principle?

Finally, Lovelace drugs and rapes her and Clarissa not only begins to lose her reason but also her very identity. The dilemma recalls Isabella's insistence on her chastity in *Measure for Measure*, nearly 150 years earlier. But Shakespeare's concern was for justice; extreme Puritanism was mocked and overcome. Richardson's concern is with male and female roles and identities, and the interplay of his characters' psychology is handled with considerable subtlety and complexity.

Critics have reacted with greatly mixed feelings. Coleridge, writing some sixty years after *Clarissa*, confesses that it vexes him to 'admire, aye greatly admire Richardson. His mind is so very vile a mind, so oozy, so hypocritical' – yet his work excites admiration. Samuel Johnson favoured Richardson over Fielding, praising Richardson's depth against Fielding's superficiality in his famous comparison 'between a man who knew how a watch was made, and a man who could tell the hour by looking on the dial-plate'. But this was the judgement of the first of the great critics, who also pronounced, of Sterne's *Tristram Shandy*, 'Nothing odd will do long'. Some modern critics have seen Clarissa's death as 'an absolute refusal of political society: sexual oppression, bourgeois patriarchy, and libertine aristocracy together', with the heroine as 'a champion of the downtrodden woman of her day and all days'.

The epistolary novel, as a form, gives several correspondents the opportunity to set forth a point of view. Although one character dominates, this multiplicity of viewpoints creates the impression of diversity leading to consensus. Like Dickens, Richardson, in particular, was known to accommodate the views and suggestions of his readers in the composition of the serially published instalments of his novels, especially *Clarissa* and *Sir Charles Grandison* (1754). But the forum of debate was limited by the initial moral intentions of the author. There is a basic didacticism in the novel of the 1740s and Fielding himself is perhaps the clearest example of this.

Richardson, however, remains a vital figure in the history of the novel, and of ideology. He initiates a discourse on sexual roles which, in all its ambiguities, is as relevant to today's society as it was in the mid-eighteenth century and which fills the pages of hundreds of novels after *Pamela* and *Clarissa*.

I describe not man, but manners; not an individual, but a species

(Henry Fielding, *Joseph Andrews*)

Henry Fielding, a highly successful satiric dramatist until the introduction of censorship in 1737, began his novel-writing career with *Shamela*, a pastiche of *Pamela*, which humorously attacked the hypocritical morality which that novel displayed. *Joseph Andrews* (1742) was also intended as a kind of parody of Richardson; but Fielding found that his novels were taking on a moral life of their own, and he developed his own highly personal narrative style – humorous and ironic, with an omniscient narrative presence controlling the lives and destinies of his characters.

Fielding focuses more on male characters and manners than Richardson. In doing so, he creates a new kind of hero in his novels. Joseph Andrews is chaste, while Tom Jones in *Tom Jones* (1749) is quite the opposite. Tom is the model of the young foundling enjoying his freedom (to travel, to have relationships with women, to enjoy sensual experience) until his true origins are discovered. When he matures, he assumes his social responsibilities and marries the woman he has 'always' loved, who has, of course, like a mediaeval crusader's beloved, been waiting faithfully for him. Both of these heroes are types, representatives of their sex.

There is a picaresque journey from innocence to experience, from freedom to responsibility. It is a rewriting of male roles to suit the society of the time. The hero no longer makes a crusade to the Holy

Land, but the crusade is a personal one, with chivalry learned on the way, and adventure replacing self-sacrifice and battle.

The reader is invited to sympathise with the hero, despite his faults or his disreputable ways, trusting the omniscient and frequently intrusive narratorial voice to bring the story to a proper conclusion. Richardson's Puritan insistence on chastity as female virtue is refocused here. 'Respectable' these heroes are not, until brought to respectability by the author. This reinforces the ambiguous contrast, already seen in Defoe, between the vicarious pleasure and excitement ('will she/won't she?') and the moral to be drawn from the fable. It would be wrong for the woman to 'fall', but it is fun for Tom Jones, and the reader, to enjoy sexual relations with Molly Seagrim. The authorial 'I' gives a judgement which excuses the hero for his natural fall:

> Though she behaved at last with all decent reluctance, yet I rather choose to attribute the triumph to her, since, in fact, it was her design which succeeded.
>
> (*Tom Jones*)

'Decent reluctance' and 'her design', together with the omniscient narrator's ever-present voice, manipulate the reader's response to such 'immoral' behaviour in an ambiguous way which is both salacious and moralistic. In a sense, the fable is necessarily contradictory to the moral, and today's reader might justifiably wonder how much reading pleasure depended on the thrill of the forbidden and how much on the correctness of the conclusion.

Jonathan Wild the Great (1743) is, like Defoe's *Moll Flanders*, a story of a criminal, and presents one of the first real anti-heroes in English literature. The intention is, however, satirical, as the criminal hero is set up as a figure admired by all, the 'Great' of the title being seen as highly ironic. The target is, as it was in Fielding's plays, the prime minister, Sir Robert Walpole, who is 'Newgate with the mask on'. Jonathan Wild's career of cheating, robbery, and vice leads him to Newgate, and a sentence of death. He faces it most unheroically, but emerges as a champion of hypocrisy and double-dealing – a devil-figure for the times.

Fielding took the novel forward from the epistolary form to what he called 'comic epics in prose', rich in character and action, revelling in the English landscape and in the manners of the people his hero encounters. He thus created, at the same time as Richardson was writing, a new area of novelistic experience, one which would lead on to the major comic novelists of the early Victorian age. The spirit he portrays comes to be seen as the spirit of the times, almost a traditional evocation of the mid-eighteenth century, untouched by the effects of the Industrial or Agrarian Revolutions.

Critics have argued that Richardson is more forward-looking and Fielding more backward-looking, but any such judgement is open to debate. The novel was developing along several different but complementary lines. Richardson, in many ways, provides models for the psychological novelists who follow him, Fielding for the social and comic writers.

Female writers of the time have been largely ignored in the history of the novel – the accepted canon consisting of Defoe, Richardson, and Fielding – but numerically there were possibly more female than male novelists. There were certainly more female than male readers in the new market for fiction.

To find a woman writer creating a heroine who is comparable to a Fielding hero, we have to turn to Eliza Haywood and *Betsy Thoughtless* (1751). Eliza Haywood ran the periodical *The Female Spectator*, one of the first magazines intended specifically for a female readership. She and Henry Fielding's sister Sarah, above all, deserve to reclaim a place in the history of the novel, both for the quality of their works and for the opinions and attitudes they display.

As with Sarah Fielding's eponymous hero David Simple, the name of the heroine Betsy Thoughtless gives the clue to the character, but the thoughtless heroine undergoes a transformation. While dithering, trying to choose between two possible suitors, Sober and Gaylord, she loses her 'true love', Mr Truelove, who gives up waiting. Thus, she ends up in an unhappy marriage, and the author has to resort to killing off both the husband and Mrs Truelove in order to bring about the happy ending. The sufferings of Haywood's heroine are presented in a more realistic, less rhetorically sentimental vein than those of Pamela or Clarissa. There is humour to lighten the underlying moral, and very little of the vicarious titillation and excitement for the reader of the procrastinated rape and potential near-rapes of Richardson. The heroine is more a victim of her own thoughtlessness than of male machinations.

David Simple is a true innocent, and, in his constant disappointments, he gives the author the opportunity to handle with considerable irony the differences between appearance and reality in human behaviour. Where Henry Fielding's omniscient narrator never allows his hero to be truly innocent, Sarah Fielding creates a character who is 'in search of a real friend', rather than engaged on a process of maturing through experience. It is a 'quest' novel, a search for an ideal, and as such has served as a model for many future novelists. And, being fairly realistic in its examination of character and motive, the novel does not supply the traditional happy ending. Some nine years after the 'moral romance' was first published, in 1744, the story is taken beyond the rich and happy reconciliation of the original. It ends in financial loss, death and the continued suffering of hapless innocence.

David Simple is an unusual, complex and penetrating examination of human motivation. It lacks the wit and exuberance of Henry Fielding's novels, but brings a new note into the novel, a note of struggle and despair, which remains striking and unexpected.

Oliver Goldsmith, successful as poet and comic dramatist, published his novel *The Vicar of Wakefield* in 1766. It is a kind of pastoral parable, an improbable fairy-tale of a vicar whose family is beset by misfortunes; not unlike the unfolding of George Eliot's *Silas Marner* almost a century later, redemption and justice triumph in the end.

Don Quixote, the epic novel of Spanish literature by Cervantes, was a major influence on English writing after the Restoration. It was published in Spain in 1605 as *Don Quixote de la Mancha*, and added to in 1615. The earliest English translation was published in 1616, the year of Shakespeare's death. The most influential translation was by Peter Motteux, published in 1700–3, who had also completed Urquhart's great translation of Rabelais. Many seventeenth-century plays and novels borrowed something from Cervantes – the idea of the 'picaro', or the clever rogue, is often associated with *Don Quixote*, but is in fact nothing to do with that work. The picaresque novels of Fielding, Smollett, and others derive from another slightly earlier Spanish tradition.

The direct influence of Cervantes can be found in Charlotte

Lennox's *The Female Quixote* (1752), where the heroine, Arabella, echoes the Spanish hero's naivety in a challenging world. Samuel Butler's satire *Hudibras* (1663) is in the form of a mock romance, derived from Cervantes, with the hero Sir Hudibras and his servant, the squire Ralpho, paralleling Don Quixote and Sancho Panza.

CRITICISM

At ev'ry word a reputation dies
  (Alexander Pope, *The Rape of the Lock*)

Criticism, or writing about books and their authors, is as old as writing itself. It is thus hardly surprising that the century which saw the greatest expansion in writing and reading should also see the arrival of the professional critic. Critical essays on theory and form, such as Dryden's *Of Dramatic Poesy* (1668), or satirical views of the literary world, such as Swift's *The Battle of the Books* (1697; published 1704 – the battle is between ancient and modern, or between classical and contemporary literature), draw lines between older and newer styles and modes of writing. This is criticism as an aid to the definition and aims of literature. Under the influence of the French writer Nicholas Boileau's *Art Poétique* (1674), criticism in the Augustan age established canons of taste and defined principles of composition and criticism.

This mix of scientific rigour and subjective reaction has remained constant through succeeding generations. Criticism changes almost as much as literature varies, if more slowly, but it can exert very strong influences. And no critic is ever right, at least for any longer than the critical fashion lasts. What is of interest is how much critical writing is of continuing value and influence. Pope, the wisest and wittiest of Augustans, in his *Essay on Criticism*, wrote:

> Whoever thinks a faultless piece to see,
> Thinks what ne'er was, nor is, nor e'er shall be.

LANGUAGE NOTE
The expanding lexicon – 'standards of English'

> ... a down-to-the-point, sound, natural speech; positive expressions, clear meanings, spontaneousness, the greatest possible approximation to mathematical plainness.
>
> (*Statutes of The Royal Society*, 1662)

As we have seen, it has been estimated that between 1500 and 1650 around 12,000 new words were introduced into the English language. At the same time, English grammar and vocabulary, heavily influenced by other languages, none the less became sufficiently nativised and 'Englished' for a number of writers to feel that the *English* language should be more definitively described and recorded. The seventeenth and eighteenth centuries were periods in which several grammars of English, dictionaries of English and even pronunciation guides to English were published. This movement was given impetus by the establishment in 1662 of The Royal Society. The Society's main purpose was to guide and promote the development of science and scientific exploration, but it created a climate in which language itself could be subjected to greater investigation.

The Royal Society also attempted to lay down certain rules regarding the use of the language and encouraged the introduction of a more scientific style. The scientific style emphasised clarity, precision and sober elegance, and in this respect it was in marked contrast to the complexities of earlier seventeenth-century prose styles which made few concessions to readers. The plainer, 'neoclassical' style allowed fuller communication with the expanding middle classes who would come to constitute a significant part of an enlarged readership for a wide range of writing. In poetry, linguistic clarity and precision is illustrated by Pope and Dryden who also did much to develop the heroic couplet, which in turn further reinforces simplicity, balance and harmony in language. Such language choices enact a world of order and coherence – a world which could be scientifically measured and rationally explained. It is not surprising that it was felt that language should be similarly ordered scientifically and 'ascertained'.

The word 'ascertain' means to describe and to fix authoritatively as part of a permanent record. It is used by Jonathan Swift in his essay *A Proposal for Correcting, Improving and Ascertaining the English Tongue* (1712). Swift took the debate a stage further by arguing that constant change in the language led to disorder and corruption:

... I do here, in the name of all the learned and Polite Persons of the Nation, complain ... that our language is extremely imperfect; that its daily improvements are by no means in proportion to its daily Corruptions; that the Pretenders to polish and refine it, have chiefly multiplied Abuses and Absurdities.

The idea of placing the English language in the hands of an Academy, as had been the case in Italy and France, did not take hold, but the concern to fix the language and, by fixing, purify it, continued through the eighteenth century and beyond. In this respect the creation of Samuel Johnson's *Dictionary of the English Language* (1755) and grammars such as Bishop Robert Lowth's *Short Introduction to English Grammar* (1762) and Lindley Murray's *English Grammar* (1794) were felt to be attempts to give stability to the language and to create norms and standards for correct usage.

From the beginning of the nineteenth century, however, it becomes impossible to focus on England alone as the only source of standardisation. There was a parallel development of other forms of English, most notably American English but also, within Great Britain, Scottish and Irish English and, within England itself, regional, 'non-standard' varieties were promoted as marks of allegiance to different regions and social groups. Writers came to see that language was simultaneously stable and unstable, unchanging and changing. They began increasingly to exploit such tensions and to take language itself as a subject for exploration. (See Language notes on pages 338 and 390.)

JOHNSON

Lexicographer. A writer of dictionaries, a harmless drudge

(*Dictionary of the English Language*)

Dr Samuel Johnson is remembered for his *Dictionary*, for one novel, *Rasselas* (1759), written quickly to pay off debts, and as the first major critic in English. The theme of *Rasselas*, subtitled *Prince of Abyssinia*, is 'choice of life'. It is a rather didactic romance, which has echoes in Johnson's best-known poem, *The Vanity of Human Wishes* (1749):

Where then shall hope and fear their objects find?
Must dull suspense corrupt the stagnant mind?

> Must helpless man, in ignorance sedate,
> Roll darkling down the torrent of his fate?

Johnson had been working as a journalist, contributing to many of the magazines of the time, since 1737, and writing poems and plays of varying degrees of success. One of his early pieces was a highly ironic 'defence' of the 1737 Theatres Licensing Act. In 1755, his monumental *Dictionary of the English Language* was published; and the nine years of work it cost him bore immediate fruit, establishing Johnson as the leading literary figure of his age. The *Dictionary* is more than just a set of definitions; it is a rich mine of quotations and references, with a literary rather than a linguistic or etymological bias, and remains a valuable reference work to this day.

> *Lexicographer.* A writer of dictionaries, a harmless drudge.
>
> *Oats.* A grain, which in England is generally given to horses, but in Scotland supports the people.
>
> *Patron.* Commonly a wretch who supports with insolence, and is paid with flattery.

Johnson's *Lives of the English Poets* (1779–81) manifests all the advantages and disadvantages of critical writing.

> About the beginning of the seventeenth century appeared a race of writers that may be termed the *metaphysical poets*. . . . Their thoughts are often new, but seldom natural. . . . The most heterogeneous ideas are yoked by violence together.
>
> ('Cowley')
>
> The *Churchyard* abounds with images which find a mirror in every mind, and with sentiments to which every bosom returns an echo.
>
> ('Gray')
>
> New things are made familiar, and familiar things are made new. . . . If Pope be not a poet, where is poetry to be found?
>
> ('Pope')

There are some hostile points of view and some odd judgements. But these are balanced with influential and lasting statements of opinion which have been praised in the twentieth century by another major critical figure, T.S. Eliot, as having 'a coherence, as well as an amplitude, which no other English criticism can claim'. The work blends biography with literary criticism in a way that later criticism does not generally follow, but it remains a landmark in establishing criteria of taste, and in the documentation of literary history, which was to have a lasting influence on future generations of writers and critics.

Critics have always sought to find the 'best' writers and works, and to hold them up as models. Although his Preface (1765) to Shakespeare is one of the first major critical essays on the subject, Johnson slighted Sterne's *Tristram Shandy*, undervalued Milton's pastoral elegy *Lycidas*, and was strongly prejudiced against Swift. Similar examples can be found in any critic's judgements, and it is therefore more vital to consider critical standpoints as representing theoretical and ideological issues, rather than merely questions of taste.

Johnson's later life, from 1763, is among the best documented of all literary lives. James Boswell gave himself the enormous task, after Johnson's death in 1784, of producing what is now held to be a model of biography; rich in detail and anecdote, a complete picture of the man and his times, traced over a period of more than twenty years. Boswell's *Life of Johnson*, published in 1791, carries on Johnson's own contribution to the growing art of biography, and consolidates Johnson's position as a major literary figure, who, although a poet and a novelist, is remembered more for his academic and critical achievement than for his creative writings.

> My lord [Monboddo] was extremely hospitable, and I saw both Dr Johnson and him liking each other better every hour.
> Dr Johnson having retired for a short time, his lordship spoke of his conversation as I could have wished. Dr Johnson had said, 'I have done greater feats with my knife than this'; though he had eaten a very hearty dinner. – My lord, who affects or believes he follows an abstemious system, seemed struck with Dr Johnson's manner of living. I had a particular satisfaction in being under the roof of Monboddo, my lord being my father's old friend, and having been always very good to me. We were cordial together. He asked Dr Johnson and me to stay all night. When I said we *must* be at Aberdeen, he replied, 'Well, I am like the Romans: I shall say to you, "Happy to come; – happy to depart!"'
> (James Boswell, *Journal of a Tour to the Hebrides with Dr Johnson*, 1785)

STERNE, SMOLLETT AND SCOTTISH VOICES

Digressions, incontestably, are the sunshine; – they are the life, the soul of reading!

(Laurence Sterne, *Tristram Shandy*)

The tradition of the novel from Behn to Defoe, Richardson, and Fielding, even after less than a century of existence, already lent itself to subversive experimentation. The rationalism which seemed to dominate the early years of the eighteenth century began, about the middle of the century, to give way to new forms of humour, to the expression of emotion, to extension of the limits of imagination, and to an awareness of language.

This first age of experiment in fiction upsets previous notions of time, place, and action, and extends the boundaries of what was possible in the novel. No longer just the observation of human actions, with moral overtones, the genre takes on a range and diversity that leads to its pre-eminence as the dominant literary form for the next two centuries.

Laurence Sterne published the first volume of *Tristram Shandy* in 1759, completing the eighth volume of the novel in 1767. The work was attacked by critics such as Johnson, Richardson, and Goldsmith, but has arguably 'lasted' longer and been more influential than any other novel of its time.

What distinguishes Sterne's writing is its originality and wit: he has been seen as the originator of what came in the twentieth century to be known as 'stream of consciousness'. The novel seems, first and foremost, to parody the developing conventions of the novel as a genre, pointing up the absurdities, contradictions, and impossibilities of relating time, space, reality, and relationships in a linear form. Sterne addresses the reader at the outset:

> . . . nothing which has touched me will be thought trifling in its nature, or tedious in its telling. Therefore, my dear friend and companion, if you should think me somewhat sparing of my narrative on my first setting out – bear with me, – and let me go on, and tell my own story my own way: – Or, if I should seem now and then to trifle

upon the road, – or should sometimes put on a fool's cap with a bell to it, for a moment or two as we pass along, – don't fly off, – but rather courteously give me credit for a little more wisdom than appears upon my outside; – and as we jog on, either laugh with me, or at me, or in short, do anything, – only keep your temper.

(*Tristram Shandy*)

The plot of the novel in the early eighteenth century followed the natural order of things: beginning, middle, and end. Sterne was the first to employ these 'not necessarily in that order'. He also played with digressions, episodes going off at a tangent from the 'main' line of the plot. Tristram Shandy, in the novel that bears his name, is conceived right at the beginning, born in Volume III (some 130 pages into the book) – but the story ends four years before this birth. In a famous use of graphological effect, Sterne's narrator, Tristram, displays the difficulty of keeping to one single line of his story (see Figure 4).

'What passes in a man's own mind' is Sterne's main concern; in this, his writing owes a great deal to John Locke's *Essay Concerning Human Understanding*. This philosophical work had been published in 1690, and exercised a great influence on all the Augustans, including Addison and Richardson. But it was Sterne who took up Locke's ideas – on the relativity of time, on random association, on the nature of sensation – to break the newly set rules of novel writing, and to escape from the moral and social restrictions of the genre.

The association of language and thought is important here. The epistolary novel posited an imaginary addresser and an addressee, one person writing the letter and another reading it. Fielding's omniscient author/narrator establishes a direct relationship with the 'dear reader'. Sterne's narrator uses no fictional intermediary device, and frequently addresses the reader directly. His thoughts ramble forward, backwards, sideways, where they will. He describes a wide range of characters, with all their obsessions and peculiarities. He covers every subject under the sun, from sex to science, from war to noses, in a conversational manner that rushes on headlong with no regard for consistency or coherence. Perhaps coincidentally, Sterne has no single ideological or moral position to enforce: his declared aim was to be unique, and to write a 'civil, nonsensical good-humoured Shandean book'.

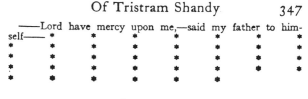

Of Tristram Shandy 347

——Lord have mercy upon me,—said my father to himself——

CHAPTER XL

I AM now beginning to get fairly into my work; and by the
help of a vegetable diet, with a few of the cold seeds, I make no
doubt but I shall be able to go on with my uncle *Toby's* story,
and my own, in a tolerable strait line. Now,

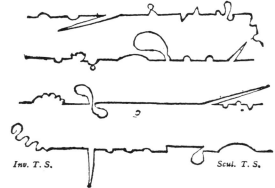

Inv. T. S.   *Scul. T. S.*

These were the four lines I moved in through my first, second,
third, and fourth volumes.[1]—In the fifth volume I have been
very good,——the precise line I have described in it being this:

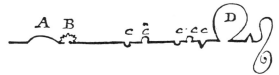

By which it appears, that except at the curve, marked A, where
[1] Alluding to the first edition.

Figure 4 Illustration from *Tristram Shandy* (page 347 from Everyman edition)

L—d! said my mother, what is all this story about? –
A COCK and a BULL, said *Yorick* – And one of the best of its kind, I
ever heard.

Sterne's other contribution to literature is equally unique: *A Sentimental Journey through France and Italy* (1767). It is an account of a
journey in which the narrator, the parson Yorick from *Tristram Shandy*,
only gets as far as Lyons in France. Again, Sterne is parodying a con-

vention – that of the fashionable travel journal – but at the same time his use of 'sentimental' in the title points up, perhaps ironically, a new emphasis on the 'sensibility' of Yorick. The person of sentiment was to bring a whole new range of emotions into literature in the last decades of the eighteenth century.

Our satiety is to suppurate
(Tobias Smollett, *Humphry Clinker*)

The 'outsider', as observer of and commentator on English society (usually London-based society) is an important figure in British writing. Spenser, in the Elizabethan age, wrote from the distant exile of Ireland, as did Swift a century later. Although he was born, educated, and spent most of his life in Ireland, Swift would never have consented to being called Irish. The dramatist William Congreve, also educated in Ireland, was a Yorkshireman; conversely, Laurence Sterne was born in Ireland, but educated in Yorkshire.

The Anglo-Irish contribution to English literature is highly significant, from Spenser to the present day. Scottish writing, little known in England since the Reformation, became a major presence late in the eighteenth century. The important figures were Johnson's biographer Boswell, the novelists Tobias Smollett and Henry Mackenzie, and the poets Robert Fergusson, Ossian and Robert Burns. Smollett was Scottish. This was important in the context of the Union of the Parliaments in 1707, which, 104 years after the Union of the Crowns, theoretically made the United Kingdom a whole. Smollett's finest novel, *Humphry Clinker* (1771) is one of many works, in the novel and in poetry, and by a wide range of authors, which underline difference rather than unity in the newly United Kingdom.

Like many of his contemporaries, including Goldsmith, Smollett used journalism as a vehicle for his ideas. From Defoe to Dickens, magazines gave their readership a weekly or monthly forum for ideas from across the political spectrum. While Addison and Steele, early in the century, had kept their writing comfortably 'middle-brow', Smollett's various ventures into magazine publication are dominated by anger. He was constantly involved in litigation for libel.

His novels put some of this contentiousness to good use. His picaresque heroes (Roderick Random, Ferdinand Count Fathom, Sir Launcelot Graves, and finally, in 1771, Humphry Clinker) reflect the author's interests, experiences (he had been a naval surgeon's mate), and profound concern with the state of the world.

As we have seen, the term 'picaresque' is often used to describe the kind of novel which Smollett wrote, and has also been applied to any novels of trickery and rogues, including *Moll Flanders* and *Tom Jones*. The term was first used in 1829, but can usefully cover the eighteenth-century novel which takes its hero or heroine on a journey, or through a series of events and misadventures, out of which he or she emerges triumphant.

Smollett's characters encompass all levels of society, with servants always having significant identities and key roles. The range of experiences his characters undergo is also vast. Roderick Random, for example, goes from penniless outcast to surgeon's apprentice, to sailor, through graphically described suffering in battle, kidnap, prison, and, not surprisingly, despair. Smollett does not avoid the harsh realities of life in his tales, and is equally straightforward about introducing controversial issues, impassioned debate, and polemical satire. *Ferdinand Count Fathom* creates one of the first truly monstrous anti-heroes in fiction – a more thoroughly evil creature even than Fielding's Jonathan Wild. *Peregrine Pickle* is anti-authoritarian, and highly satirical about the kind of grand tour which Sterne also mocks in *A Sentimental Journey*. *Humphry Clinker* finally takes the chaotic rambling narrative of Smollett's other novels and disciplines it into the old-fashioned form of the epistolary novel, centred on one family and their travels round Britain in search of health and social harmony. The health in question is not just the health of Matthew Bramble, however, but of the nation and of all society, from the semi-literate servant Win to the frustrated spinster aunt Tabitha, from the young Oxford student Jery to the young and impressionable Lydia.

This is the first 'state of the nation' novel, a story in which a family tries to achieve harmony, to reach a kind of utopia. They reach 'this Scottish paradise' at Loch Lomond, near (ironically) Smollett's own birthplace, Dumbarton, the farthest point of their journey. Glasgow, described as a 'dear green place' in Defoe's *A Tour Through the Whole Island of Great Britain* (1724–26) almost fifty years earlier, is here 'one of the prettiest towns in Europe ... one of the most flourishing in Great Britain'. This was the height of both Scotland's mercantile success and the Scottish Enlightenment: Smollett's English characters derive considerable benefit from their contact with this world, and quite the opposite from their contact with the seething metropolis of London.

Class and social judgement are, however, not eliminated; and, in the mauling and mishandling of the English language by some of the letter-writers, Smollett shows a mastery of linguistic disparity, subconscious sexual desires, and divergent moral standpoints, reaching a climax in the multi-level punning of the final letters, when some kind of 'union' is reached. But separating/suppurating seems to be the future prospect: 'our satiety is to suppurate' being the conclusion of an examination of 'satiety' ('society') in all its discordant elements.

Smollett's non-fictional output was also vast. His *Complete History of England* (1757–58) was controversial, but very successful financially; his immense *The Present State of All Nations* (1768–69) is a work of tremendous breadth and complexity. Linguistically and philosophically, Smollett's work recalls the French satirist Rabelais, whose sixteenth-century *Gargantua and Pantagruel* had been translated in the 1650s by another Scots polymath, Sir Thomas Urquhart. The carnivalesque enjoyment of bodily functions, vitriolic argument, splenetic rage, and plentiful scurrility represent a popular tradition which eighteenth-century English society tended to suffocate. In English literature, the free play of bawdiness is found from Chaucer through Skelton to Shakespeare, Jonson, and Donne. But when it resurfaces in the sexual concerns of Restoration drama it becomes the object of criticism and concern. Only Rochester continues the tradition, although the novels of Fielding and Richardson play at titillation. With Smollett, and later the poetry of Burns, the earthy tradition is kept alive; rude word play and comic scurrility are brought into the service of healthy social observation and criticism.

A certain sexual openness begins to emerge in the novel in the mid-eighteenth century. Smollett's *Roderick Random* (1748) contains a not totally serious defence of (and invitation to) homosexuality, citing the Roman satirist Petronius as precedent. (Swift had also touched on this in Book Four of *Gulliver's Travels*.) In the same year, *Memoirs of a Woman of Pleasure* by John Cleland was published. Better known as *Fanny Hill,* the book gave rise to an indecency charge and became a huge seller. History repeated itself in the 1960s, when the book was again the subject of scandal – with resultant success. *Fanny Hill* is a rather breathless examination of both male and female sexuality, in detail and in considerable variety. The occasional moment of quasi-respectability in language and tone serves only to underline the basic titillating ethos of the novel.

Coincidentally, 1771 saw the publication both of Smollett's masterpiece *Humphry Clinker* and the novel which most typifies the opposing tendency towards 'sensibility', *The Man of Feeling* by Henry Mackenzie, another Scot. One of the shorter novels of its time, it creates a new kind of hero: a man who cries. Harley is something of an innocent, not unlike David Simple, but there is the new element of cultivation of sensibility and a kind of self-absorption in Mackenzie's work. This is Harley's reaction to meeting a woman in the madhouse (it was fashionable to visit madhouses such as Bedlam to see the inmates, as in a zoo):

> 'I am a strange girl; – but my heart is harmless: my poor heart! it will burst some day; feel how it beats.' – She press'd his hand to her bosom, then holding her head in the attitude of listening – 'Hark! one, two, three! be quiet, thou little trembler; my Billy's is cold! – but I had forgotten the ring.' – She put it on his finger. – 'Farewel! I must leave you now.' She would have withdrawn her hand; Harley held it to his lips. – 'I dare not stay longer; my head throbs sadly: farewel!' – She walked with a hurried step to a little apartment at some distance. Harley stood fixed in astonishment and pity! his friend gave money to the keeper. – Harley looked on his ring. – He put a couple of guineas into the man's hand: 'Be kind to that unfortunate' – He burst into tears, and left them.

This move towards the acceptance of 'feminine' elements in the masculine hero is, in a sense, a continuation of the exploring and defining of sexual roles in contemporary society, which Richardson and Fielding used in their novels. It was to have an enormous influence outside Britain: Johann Wolfgang von Goethe, who is one of the central figures of European literature of the time, acknowledged the influence of Mackenzie's novel on his *Sorrows of Young Werther* (1774), which gave the figure of the sensitive, suffering and finally suicidal hero both a universal dimension and lasting popularity.

Mackenzie's novel takes the form of a mutilated manuscript – 'scattered chapters, and fragments of chapters' – from which pages and whole sections have been 'lost'. The story is thus disjointed and episodic. In a sense, the failure of the hero, Harley, in any of the traditional ways of worldly success is echoed in this experimental abandoning of the traditional novel form.

The doubtful manuscript also features in the work of another Scottish writer, who was to have a similarly enormous influence on Goethe and on European literature for about a century. James Macpherson is practically forgotten today, but, as the producer of *Fingal* (1762) and *Temora* (1763), which purported to be translations of Gaelic epics by Ossian, he became the favourite writer of characters as diverse as Young Werther and Napoleon Bonaparte. More than a century later, the major Victorian critic and poet Matthew Arnold wrote, of Ossian's impact, 'what an apparition of newness and power [the works] must have been to the eighteenth century'.

Macpherson's project was not, however, just an exercise in sentimental primitivism, but part of a larger attempt – in which Thomas Gray and Thomas Percy, editor of the highly influential *Reliques of Ancient English Poetry* (1765), can also be seen to have taken part – to relocate the origins of British literature in a Northern cultural context, as opposed to a Southern classical context. As such, it was part of a nationalistic enterprise that touched many aspects of literature and culture in the century and more after the Union of the Parliaments in 1707; the making of the United Kingdom. Matthew Arnold's mid-Victorian epic *Balder Dead* (1855) continues this Northern cultural shift of emphasis, almost a century after Ossian.

What created such an impact on the European imagination in the 1760s was the idea of the 'primitive'; a return to simple, natural values, as against the luxurious 'city' values of sophisticated society. To a certain extent, this was also a reaction against neoclassical theory and practice, a return to a time of innocence and goodness. Macpherson's 'newness and power' exactly caught the taste for elemental worlds, and for a primitive local culture. However, the critics were not so easily persuaded.

In Macpherson's own day, the major critic was Dr Samuel Johnson, who was highly sceptical of Ossian's existence. Macpherson, when asked for the Gaelic originals of the works, fabricated them. In 1805, a committee chaired by Henry Mackenzie concluded that Macpherson's work was a mixture of his own invention with only a few Gaelic insertions. But the works of Ossian had an imaginative grip on their readers which lasted far beyond critical debates on their authenticity, and which created an image of Scotland that was to have an influence on writers, composers, and artists throughout Europe in the late eighteenth and early nineteenth centuries.

This ever-expanding influence of literature in English becomes more and more noticeable as publishing turned into an international business. The colonies, and Europe, were eager markets for books of all kinds, and the era of the international bestseller was dawning.

DRAMA AFTER 1737

The Theatres Licensing Act of 1737 did not altogether kill drama, but did successfully stifle it. The history of eighteenth-century theatre becomes the history of actors rather than of plays, although most of the literary figures of the time did try writing for the theatre at one time or another. Dr Johnson's tragedy *Irene* ran for nine performances in 1749, for example, and Richard Steele, of *Spectator* fame, left a heritage of sentimental comedies which held the stage for more than sixty years after his death in 1729. Oliver Goldsmith and Richard Brinsley Sheridan were both Irishmen and the only two writers of theatrical comedy who managed to write lasting masterpieces which go against the prevailing trend of sentimentalism in the late eighteenth century.

Goldsmith's *She Stoops to Conquer* (1773) is seen as the first successful reaction to the sentimental comedy originated by Steele. The comic premise is that the hero, Marlow, is shy with ladies of his own social level, but quite open with servants and barmaids. So the heroine, Miss Hardcastle, 'stoops' to an acceptable level to 'conquer' him.

> MISS HARDCASTLE ... his fears were such, that he never once looked up during the interview. Indeed, if he had, my bonnet would have kept him from seeing me.
> PIMPLE But what do you hope from keeping him in his mistake?

MISS HARDCASTLE In the first place, I shall be *seen*, and that is no small advantage to a girl who brings her face to market. Then I shall perhaps make an acquaintance, and that's no small victory gained over one who never addresses any but the wildest of her sex. But my chief aim is to take my gentleman off his guard, and like an invisible champion of romance examine the giant's force before I offer to combat.

PIMPLE But are you sure you can act your part, and disguise your voice, so that he may mistake that, as he has already mistaken your person?

MISS HARDCASTLE Never fear me. I think I have got the true bar cant. – Did your honour call? – Attend the Lion there. – Pipes and tobacco for the Angel. – The Lamb has been outrageous this half hour.

The comedy of character took over from the comedy of delicacy and sentiment in Goldsmith, and in Sheridan, the most successful playwright of the time. *The School for Scandal* (1777) presents London society as a hotbed of gossip and intrigue:

MRS CANDOUR My dear Lady Sneerwell, how have you been this century? – Mr Surface, what news do you hear? – though indeed it is no matter, for I think one hears nothing else but scandal.

JOSEPH Just so, indeed, ma'am.

MRS CANDOUR Ah! Maria! child, – what, is the whole affair off between you and Charles? His extravagance, I presume – the town talks of nothing else.

MARIA I am very sorry, ma'am, the town is not better employed.

MRS CANDOUR True, true, child: but there's no stopping people's tongues. I own I was hurt to hear it, as I indeed was to learn, from the same quarter, that your guardian, Sir Peter, and Lady Teazle have not agreed lately as well as could be wished.

MARIA 'Tis strangely impertinent for people to busy themselves so.

MRS CANDOUR Very true, child: – but what's to be done? People will talk – there's no preventing it. Why, it was but yesterday I was told that Miss Gadabout had eloped with Sir Filigree Flirt. – But, Lord! there's no minding what one hears; though, to be sure, I had this from very good authority.

MARIA Such reports are highly scandalous.

MRS CANDOUR So they are, child – shameful, shameful! But the world is so censorious, no character escapes.

Sheridan's *The Critic* (1779) is a burlesque comedy, based on a

Restoration farce, which makes the device of a theatrical rehearsal the vehicle for a neat satire on the conventions, and the critics, of the time.

POETRY AFTER POPE

The short and simple annals of the poor
(Thomas Gray, *Elegy*)

It was perhaps inevitable that there would be a reaction to the highly formal, self-consciously heightened, and satirically self-referential poetry of the Augustans. During the remainder of the eighteenth century there was an exploration in poetry of new themes, handled in more low-key language and forms, without the bite of satire, and, in most cases, without the wit and humour of the Augustan age.

The most important single poem of the mid-eighteenth century is arguably Gray's *Elegy*, published in 1751. Its full title is *Elegy Written in a Country Churchyard*, and, as such, its subject matter is much more 'the short and simple annals of the poor' and 'to teach the rustic moralist to die' than the graveyard itself. The *Elegy* has often been associated with the rather earlier 'graveyard school' of poetry, such as Edward Young's *Night Thoughts* (1742–45) – pretentiously subtitled *On Life, Death, and Immortality* – and Robert Blair's *The Grave* (1743). These poets revel at great length in death – 'that dread moment' – and morbidity, creating an atmosphere of 'delightful gloom'. The trend towards this kind of melancholy travelled to Europe and became fashionable during the height of European Romanticism.

> The melancholy ghosts of dead renown,
> Whisp'ring faint echoes of the world's applause,
> With penintential aspect, as they pass,
> All point at earth, and hiss at human pride,
> The wisdom of the wise, and prancings of the great.
>
> (Edward Young, *Night Thoughts*)

Thomas Gray's *Elegy* is considerably different in emphasis, although suffused with a gently humanist melancholy. It is, in some senses, a life-affirming reconsideration of rural values, although the ending is often read as involving the poet's suicide. The elegaic element concerns the passing of the poet's own life, and the consideration of 'loss' in the village's lack of ambition:

> Let not ambition mock their useful toil,
> Their homely joys and destiny obscure;
> Nor Grandeur hear, with a disdainful smile,
> The short and simple annals of the poor.

A realistic pastoral in four-line verses, quatrains, echoing some of Pope's classically inspired eclogues, the *Elegy*'s affirmation of simple lives and their value – in unadorned language – met the mid-century mood and became hugely popular.

> Full many a gem of purest ray serene
> The dark unfathomed caves of ocean bear:
> Full many a flower is born to blush unseen
> And waste its sweetness on the desert air.

The *Elegy* can be read as a poem *against* mourning, anticipating Wordsworth's concern with agricultural life and 'useful' labour; finding meaning in the life lived, rather than in the death feared. In the concluding Epitaph, however, many readers identify the 'youth' with the poet himself:

> Here rests his head upon the lap of earth
> A youth to fortune and to fame unknown.
> Fair Science frowned not on his humble birth,
> And Melancholy marked him for her own.

Gray, an unassuming man, refused public acclaim and the Poet Laureateship. The real continuation of the graveyard school's influence is more to be found in the imaginative terrors of the Gothic novel, rather than in the 'village-life' writings which came to be seen as 'pre-Romantic'.

James Thomson's *The Seasons*, published season by season between 1726 and 1730, can be seen as the first eighteenth-century work to offer a new view of nature. Written largely in blank verse, Thomson's vision of nature as harsh, especially in winter, but bountiful, stresses the 'pure pleasures of the rural life' with no denial of the pain these pleasures can involve. Celebration of nature is closely allied with a sense of desolation, of hard work and harsh landscapes, so the tone of

The Seasons is far removed from the classical idyll. His works were very popular, and are an excellent contrast with Keats's Odes, such as *Ode to Autumn*, almost a century later (see page 237). Thomson sees the negative side of a 'philosophic melancholy' which is very much of its own time, just as the sensuousness of Keats is clearly Romantic.

> Now Nature droops;
> Languish the living herbs with pale decay,
> And all the various family of flowers
> Their sunny robes resign. The falling fruits,
> Through the still night, forsake the parent-bough,
> That, in the first grey glances of the dawn,
> Looks wild, and wonders at the wintry waste.
>   (*The Seasons*, 'Winter')

The true successors to Gray's poetry are Oliver Goldsmith's *The Deserted Village* (1770), William Cowper's *The Task* (1785), and George Crabbe's narrative poems of rural life, such as *The Village* (1783) and *The Borough* (1810). These range from blank verse to heroic couplets and poetic 'letters', in their search for a form that could document the real life of the rural poor. This was the time of the Agrarian Revolution, when many people were forced to move from the country to the newly industrialised cities in search of work. The resulting desolation is the subject of Goldsmith's poem, for example, which contrasts an idyllic past, of the 'loveliest village of the plain', with the harsh reality of the present.

William Cowper's *The Task*, a blank-verse poem in six books, was, with Thomson's *The Seasons*, one of the most lastingly popular of poems on the theme of nature and the simple life. Its famous distinction 'God made the country, and man made the town' underlines the search for tranquillity in a hectic world. It affirms, celebrates and describes a closer relationship between man and nature. These lines from *The Task*, from the section subtitled 'Rural Sights and Sounds', anticipate Wordsworth in their affirmation of the countryside. It is important to note the sense of appreciation, with only a touch of reflection here.

> Nor rural sights alone, but rural sounds,
> Exhilarate the spirit, and restore

The tone of languid nature. Mighty winds,
That sweep the skirt of some far-spreading wood
Of ancient growth, make music not unlike
The dash of ocean on his winding shore,
And lull the spirit while they fill the mind.

Goldsmith has a stronger note, in *The Deserted Village*, of regret, of something lost:

How often have I blessed the coming day,
When toil remitting lent its turn to play,
And all the village train, from labour free,
Led up their sports beneath the spreading tree,
While many a pastime circled in the shade,
The young contending as the old surveyed;
And many a gambol frolicked o'er the ground,
And sleights of art and feats of strength went round.

To a certain extent, Goldsmith can be accused of idealising a lost idyll of country life. Certainly Crabbe, in *The Village*, thirteen years after Goldsmith's poem, reacted against any such view of a lost 'golden age', stressing the trials of real life, and rejecting the kind of Arcadian ideal which had been found in poetry since Sir Philip Sidney two centuries before.

Ye gentle souls, who dream of rural ease,
Whom the smooth stream and smoother sonnet please;
Go! if the peaceful cot your praises share,
Go, look within, and ask if peace be there:
If peace be his – that drooping weary sire,
Or theirs, that offspring round their feeble fire,
Or hers, that matron pale, whose trembling hand
Turns on the wretched hearth th' expiring brand.
Nor yet can time itself obtain for these
Life's latest comforts, due respect and ease;
For yonder see that hoary swain, whose age
Can with no cares except its own engage;
Who, propped on that rude staff, looks up to see
The bare arms broken from the withering tree,
On which, a boy, he climbed the loftiest bough,
Then his first joy, but his sad emblem now.

It was more than a quarter of a century before Crabbe continued his bleak descriptions of country life in *The Borough*, a precise and detailed view of Aldeburgh, in Suffolk – where he spent most of his life. The poem was written as twenty-four letters, and Crabbe wanted to show country life 'as Truth will paint it, and as Bards will not'. This is an important reaction against both the idealisation of rural life and the over-sentimental identification with it, in which city fashion often indulged.

This was a time when women writers, through both the novel and poetry, were making their presence felt, and recent critics and anthologisers have brought a great deal of women's writing to the attention of modern readers. It is perhaps a sign of history's marginalisation of women's writing that, even now, we tend to group the work of several women together. However, many shared themes and concerns confirm the importance of their work. Subjects such as the loss of a child, frustration at an unhappy marriage, difficult servants, the tedium of housework, are treated by these women writers in a variety of manners and forms quite different from but clearly complementary to the concerns of the male Augustans. Mary Leapor's *An Essay on Woman* (published posthumously in 1751) sums up the less than positive aspects of an eighteenth-century woman's lot: she, in fact, was one of the first lower-class female voices in poetry; a kitchen maid from Northamptonshire, who died in her early twenties.

> Woman, a pleasing but a short-lived flow'r,
> Too soft for business and too weak for pow'r:
> A wife in bondage, or neglected maid;
> . . .
> Yet with ten thousand follies to her charge,
> Unhappy woman's but a slave at large.

Anne Finch, Countess of Winchelsea, is highly regarded among women poets of the late seventeenth and early eighteenth centuries, but by no means all of them were from the upper classes. Elizabeth Thomas spoke for generations of women with her line 'Unhappy sex! how hard's our fate', when complaining that she had been instructed (by a man, obviously) not to read, as books would make her mad. Women were, despite the influence of the bluestocking group, 'denied th'improvement of our minds', as she goes on to say in the same poem. Mehetabel (Hetty) Wright's tone is also one of complaint. She was the sister of the founders of Methodism, John and Charles Wesley, but her writings reveal her as a quite different spirit from her brothers, speaking of an unhappy marriage as 'a living death, a long despair', and, in *Address to her Husband,* asserting 'I will not brook contempt from thee!' Wright's short elegy *To an Infant Expiring the Second Day of its Birth* (1733) is a useful female contrast to Blake's later *Songs of Innocence*:

> Tender softness, infant mild,
> Perfect, purest, brightest child;
> Transient lustre, beauteous clay,
> Smiling wonder of a day:
> Ere the last convulsive start
> Rends the unresisting heart;
> Ere the long-enduring swoon
> Weighs thy precious eyelids down;
> Oh! regard a mother's moan,
> Anguish deeper than thy own!
> Fairest eyes, whose dawning light
> Late with rapture blessed my sight,
> Ere your orbs extinguished be,
> Bend their trembling beams on me.
> Drooping sweetness, verdant flow'r,
> Blooming, with'ring in an hour,
> Ere thy gentle breast sustains
> Latest, fiercest, vital pains,
> Hear a suppliant! Let me be
> Partner in thy destiny!

Joanna Baillie, from Bothwell near Glasgow, is a distinctive Scottish lyrical voice; Alison Cockburn and Jane Elliot wrote versions of *The Flowers of the Forest*, one of the best known of all Scottish airs. Women who were distinguished in other genres are also now seen to be interesting poets: Susannah Centlivre, better known as a dramatist, Clara Reeve, Charlotte Lennox and Frances Burney, novelists, and perhaps most interestingly of all, Lady Mary Wortley Montagu, who was one of the great letter-writers of the age, and famously had a long drawn-out and highly public quarrel with Alexander Pope. She castigates him in these words:

> Satire should like a polished razor keen,
> Wound with a touch that's scarcely felt or seen.
> Thine is an oyster's knife, that hacks and hews;
> The rage but not the talent to abuse.

LANGUAGE NOTE
Metrical patterns

Metre is the pattern of stressed and unstressed syllables in lines of poetry. Lines of poetry in English have been traditionally categorised by the length of the line and by the number and type of syllables (also known as 'feet') which they contain. For example, the most common metrical pattern in English poetry – the iambic pentameter – consists of ten syllables and five feet, each metrical foot consisting of a stressed and unstressed syllable. For example:

> If music be the food of love, play on,

The dominant pattern here is one of stressed followed by unstressed syllable (iambic) in five feet (pentameter). Other lengths of line are, of course, also possible so that tetrameter would have four feet and hexameter six feet, and so on. Although the iambic pentameter is the heartbeat of English poetry, it cannot simply be followed mechanically and in the best poetry there are always variations on this basic pattern. For example, in these lines from Thomas Gray's *Elegy Written in a Country Churchyard*, the first line begins with a stressed syllable (ˊ), followed by two unstressed syllables (˘), before the lines settle into the more standard iambic pattern:

> Fár frŏm thĕ máddĭng crówd's ĭgnóblĕ strífe,
> Their sober wishes never learned to stray.

In the following octameter written by Robert Browning the basic iambic rhythm is overridden by the rhythm and tempo of the speaking voice in which the speaker is likely to give particular weight to the word 'soul' and to pause on the words 'I wonder':

> What of soul was left, I wonder, when the kissing had to stop?

In English verse the following metres are the most common:

iambic   dactylic   anapaestic   spondaic   trochaic

Line lengths can extend from one foot monometer to eight feet octameter, including dimeter (2), trimeter (3), tetrameter (4), pentameter (5), hexameter (6), heptameter (7).

Coleridge's poem *Metrical Feet* helps to illustrate these main patterns:

> Trochee trips from long to short
> From long to long in solemn sort
> Slow spondee stalks; strong foot yet ill able
> Ever to come up with the dactyl trisyllable
> Iambics march from short to long.
> With a leap and a bound the swift anapaests throng.

Rhythm and rhyme go together, but blank verse, which is the staple of the poetic line in Shakespearean drama, consists of a basic core of iambic movement but with rhyme occurring very rarely. Milton's *Paradise Lost* and many of the poems by Wordsworth and Coleridge use blank verse.

In the poetry of the twentieth century, traditional systems are not systematically followed. There is more extensive use of free verse, which has no regular line length and depends much more on the rhythms of speech and on tempo and intonation. Here is an example from D.H. Lawrence's *Snake*:

> A snake came to my water trough
> On a hot, hot day, and I in pajamas for the heat
> To drink there.
>
> In the deep, strange-scented shade of the great dark carob tree
> I came down the steps with my pitcher
> And must wait, must stand and wait, for there he was . . .

MELANCHOLY, MADNESS AND NATURE

The *Odes* of William Collins had a considerable influence on the poetry of the second half of the eighteenth century, although they received little recognition during their author's short lifetime. His poetry is visionary and intensely lyrical, and some of his poems, such as *How sleep the brave*, have become very well known.

> How sleep the brave, who sink to rest,
> By all their country's wishes blest!

When Spring, with dewy fingers cold,
Returns to deck their hallowed mould,
She there shall dress a sweeter sod
Than Fancy's feet have ever trod.
(*Ode Written in the Beginning of the Year 1746*)

Collins grew melancholic, and produced very little poetry after the *Odes* of 1746; he died before he reached the age of 40. Another visionary poet lapsed into madness – Christopher Smart, having begun his poetic career in the 1750s with clever satires and elegant light verse, was overcome with religious fervour, and spent several years in an asylum. He produced *A Song to David* in 1763, a highly charged poem in praise of the biblical figure of David. His *Jubilate Agno* was not published until 1939, more than 150 years after his death. It is an extraordinary, quite unique work, again a poem of praise, in some ways not unlike William Blake's work – and Blake was frequently considered mad too. This time Smart's praise is for the whole of creation, from the days of the week to the toad, from the nations of Europe to his famous lines in praise of his cat, 'For I will consider my cat, Jeoffrey'. Smart's use of the language of the Bible and his simple straightforward style in the expression of his belief and his joy in the world give him a place among religious writers who *celebrate* their faith rather than negotiate with their God – a phenomenon rare in English poetry.

In 1771, the same year as two important novels by Scottish writers were published (Smollett's *Humphry Clinker* and Mackenzie's *The Man of Feeling*), the first poems by Robert Fergusson appeared in an Edinburgh magazine. Edinburgh was the centre of the Scottish Enlightenment, and for more than fifty years there had been a growing move towards the rediscovery of Scottish language and culture. The poetry and song collections of Allan Ramsay in the 1720s and 1730s brought the work of such writers as Dunbar and Henryson back into wide circulation. Fergusson was the first contemporary writer to move away from the imitation of English writing to the vigour of Scots. *Auld Reekie*, his celebration of the city of Edinburgh, is still quoted. The Muse, he says, has left the city too long. With its classical references and local description, *Auld Reekie* is still a familiar Scottish name for the city of Edinburgh, deriving from the smoke – 'reek' – as seen from across the River Forth, in Fife.

> Auld Reekie, wale o' ilka town
> That *Scotland* kens beneath the moon;
> Whare couthy chiels at e'ening meet
> Their bizzing *craigs* and *mou's* to weet;
> And blythly gar auld care gae bye
> Wi' blinkit and wi' bleering eye:
> O'er lang frae thee the Muse has been
> Sae frisky . . .

The language is not a nostalgic return to tradition, but an assured affirmation of a living language which the Union of the Kingdom in 1707 had threatened but not submerged. Fergusson, like several other poets of the time, died mad, and tragically young, but not before he had satirised both Dr Johnson and Mackenzie's bestseller, two of the great literary eminences of the day. His influence was great, especially on Robert Burns, but he deserves to be considered as a major Scots poet in his own right. The use of Scots permitted Fergusson – and later Burns – to explore the kind of low life or risqué subject matter which English gentility forbade. With Smollett's sustained satire against the utopia of the Union in *Humphry Clinker,* and Fergusson's attacks on English literary dominance, they are effectively maintaining a tradition of popular expression, lively, humorous and linguistically inventive, which the writings of Ossian and Scott would romanticise, and almost submerge, until MacDiarmid recovered the Scots language for poetry in the twentieth century.

Robert Burns is the most lyrical of the rural poets, and perhaps the most universal. A ploughman himself, he was the closest to nature of his contemporaries. When he turns up a fieldmouse's nest with his plough, he realises that he has destroyed a complete world, wrecked the hopes and plans of a 'sleeket, cowran', tim'rous beastie'.

> But Mousie, thou art no thy-lane,
> In proving foresight may be vain:
> The best laid schemes o' Mice an' Men,
>   Gang aft agley,

> An' lea'e us nought but grief an' pain,
>   For promis'd joy!
>   (*To a Mouse*)

His linking here of 'the best laid schemes o' Mice an' Men' has become almost proverbial both in the kind of humanity it displays and in its identification with the smallest and most helpless of creatures.

These qualities are linked in Burns to a storytelling ability which opens up new areas of experience to literature. *The Cotter's Saturday Night* (1786) is an intimate, affectionate, unsentimental portrait of agricultural family life, written in Scots and English.

> From scenes like these, old Scotia's grandeur springs,
> That makes her lov'd at home, rever'd abroad:
> Princes and lords are but the breath of kings,
> 'An honest man's the noble work of God:'
> And *certes*, in fair Virtue's heavenly road,
> The *Cottage* leaves the *Palace* far behind:
> What is a lordling's pomp? a cumbrous load,
> Disguising oft the *wretch* of human kind,
> Studied in arts of Hell, in wickedness refin'd!

Tam O'Shanter (1791) was a racing tale of a drunk man pursued by witches and spirits while his wife sits at home, 'nursing her wrath to keep it warm'. Much of Burns's work is in the dialect of his Ayrshire home, but there are moments when he shows himself capable of as vivid imagery in English as any of his contemporaries with whose work he was familiar.

> But pleasures are like poppies spread,
> You seize the flow'r, its bloom is shed;
> Or like the snow falls in the river,
> A moment white – then melts for ever.
>   (*Tam O'Shanter*)

The love lyric, largely unexplored in English since the time of Lovelace in the 1640s, reached new heights of both simplicity and precision of imagery in Burns more than a century later. He used a tradition of Scottish songs and ballads as the basis of many of his lyrical poems, some of which – like *Auld Lang Syne* and *My Love Is Like a Red, Red Rose* – have become universally known.

Should auld acquaintance be forgot
And never brought to mind?
Should auld acquaintance be forgot,
And auld lang syne?
(Auld Lang Syne)

As fair art thou, my bonnie dear,
So deep in love am I;
And I will love thee still, my dear,
Till all the seas gang dry.
(My Love Is Like a Red, Red Rose)

Burns lived close to the land, and to poverty, all his life. The image of him perpetrated by Wordsworth, walking 'in glory and joy' behind his plough, is as false as was Goldsmith's Arcadia: the poets who brought their own lived experience of the natural world to bear on their writing use no exaggeration or glorification in the picture they give of rural life. Burns, Crabbe, and, later, John Clare are peasant poets of the land, in a way that the Romantic poets would never be.

There were, of course, many women poets at the time; but Charlotte Smith stands above the rest. Her *Sonnet Written at the Close of Spring* (1782) provides a link between James Thomson, early in the century, and the Romantics – with their concerns of nature and time:

Ah! poor humanity! so frail, so fair,
Are the fond visions of thy early day,
Till tyrant passion, and corrosive care,
Bid all thy fairy colours fade away!
Another May new buds and flowers shall bring;
Ah? why has happiness – no second Spring?

Smith also wrote expressively in *The Emigrants* (1793) of her disillusionment with the French Revolution. Her maturity and wit can be seen in *Thirty-Eight*, a poem to a woman friend on reaching that august age, which is not unlike Lord Byron's thoughts on reaching 30!

With eye more steady, we engage
To contemplate approaching age,
And life more justly estimate;
With firmer souls and stronger powers,
With reason, faith, and friendship ours,

We'll not regret the stealing hours,
That lead from *thirty-* e'en to *forty-eight!*
(Charlotte Smith, *Thirty-Eight: To Mrs H–*, 1791)

You've passed your youth not so unpleasantly,
And if you had it o'er again – 'twould pass –
So thank your stars that matters are no worse . . .
(Lord Byron, *Growing Old*, 1819)

All these poets, except Byron and Clare, are often described as pre-Romantic. It is true that, in their concern for nature, their use of simple spoken language, and their rejection of neoclassicism, they anticipate many of the concerns of the Romantic poets. But, above all, the difference between these poets and Wordsworth, in particular, is one of ideals and intentions. Reflection and recollection take on a greater emphasis in Wordsworth than description, first-hand experience, and direct identification with the subject matter of rural experience.

THE GOTHIC AND THE SUBLIME

You see how enormous his performances are in every way;
what would be the consequence should he get at my wives!
(William Beckford, *Vathek*)

There is a degree of emotional impact in the nature poetry of the eighteenth century which marks a shift in sensibility towards what came to be called 'the sublime'. The concept, from classical Greek, came to England through the French of Boileau, and reached its definitive explication in Edmund Burke's *Philosophical Enquiry into the Origin of Our Ideas of the Sublime and the Beautiful* (1757–59). This is a key text of the times, displaying an emphasis on feelings and on imagination, which is almost the antithesis of the neoclassical insistence on form and reason. Burke's idea of the sublime goes beyond natural beauty (although the beauty of nature is very much a part of it) and goes into the realms of awe, or 'terror'. The sublime is, for Burke, 'productive of the strongest emotion which the mind is capable of feeling'. Terror, emotion, feeling: all these represent a break from the intellectual rigours of the Augustan age, and are in one sense a reaction against the new pressures of society and bourgeois concerns.

A direct line can be traced from Thomson's *The Seasons* to the poetry of nature of the first generation of Romantics, seventy or so years later, with Gray's *Elegy* as the central text which unites nature, emotion, simplicity and eternity.

The link between the sublime and terror is most clearly seen in the imaginative exaggeration of the Gothic novel – a form which concentrated on the fantastic, the macabre and the supernatural, with haunted castles, spectres from the grave and wild landscapes.

It is significant that the term 'Gothic' originally had mediaeval connotations: this is the first of several ways of returning to pre-Renaissance themes and values which is found over the next hundred years or so. The novels of the 1760s to the 1790s, however, gave the term 'Gothic' the generic meaning of horror fantasy.

The Castle of Otranto (1764) by Horace Walpole (son of the prime minister Sir Robert Walpole) was the first of its kind, and the sub-genre has flourished ever since. It is a story of mediaeval times, set in Southern Italy, with castles, vaults, ghosts, statues which come to life, appearances and disappearances, sudden violent death, forest caves, and the whole paraphernalia of horror. Passion, grief and terror are the mainstays of the plot, which moves between the unlikely and the totally incredible. Strange religious characters abound in Gothic novels, from Friar Jerome in Walpole to Ambrosio, the hero of *The Monk* (1796) by Matthew Lewis, one of the most successful novels of its kind.

The Gothic novel's immediate widespread popularity, in the hands of such accomplished writers as Ann Radcliffe, can be seen in the fact that parodies of the form became common. Jane Austen's first mature novel, *Northanger Abbey* (1798–1803; published in 1818) sets out to take a critical but affectionate perspective on *The Mysteries of Udolpho* (1794), Radcliffe's most successful work, transmuting its exaggerations and extravagances into the (sometimes rather sinister) realities of day-to-day life which were to become Jane Austen's primary subject matter.

Clara Reeve, with *The Old English Baron* (1777, published a year earlier as *The Champion of Virtue; a Gothic Story*), enjoyed even greater success than her model, Walpole's *The Castle of Otranto*. Her virtuous hero undergoes all sorts of horrific trials until he reaches his rightful reward: an example of the Gothic novel affirming the good. Among her other works, Clara Reeve's critical study in dialogue form, *The Progress of Romance* (1785), is interesting as one of the comparatively few analyses of the novel by a novelist in this period.

Thomas Love Peacock also mocks the Gothic in *Nightmare Abbey* (1818) and *Gryll Grange* (1860–61), written at a distance of more than forty years; but aspects of the Gothic continue to appear throughout the mainstream Victorian novel, from the Brontës and Dickens to Stevenson and Wilde. In some ways, it is the most resistant continuous strain in the history of the novel, leading to psychological insights as well; at its best in works like *Frankenstein* (by Mary Shelley, 1818) and *Dracula* (by Bram Stoker, 1897) which create images that can thrill the reader even today.

Frankenstein is not properly Gothic in the way *The Castle of Otranto* and most of the novels of Clara Reeve are, where the virginal female victim is subjected to increasingly exaggerated horrors. In *Frankenstein* the 'hero', the young doctor Victor Frankenstein, wants to create a perfect human being. The creature turns out to be an eight-foot tall hideous monster: this is the 'horror' element of the story.

Modern readings of *Frankenstein* have reacted against the cinematic image of the monster and have read the tale as a psychological exploration of creation, childbirth and responsibility, with an emphasis on the creature as an outcast. He is an innocent who has had human life thrust upon him and who is destined to roam the icy wastes (a prevision of twentieth-century wastelands) in solitude. The creature's own point of view is given full voice in the epistolary form of the novel, balancing with pathos the horror which other narrative voices describe. Here the creature utters his first words ('Pardon this intrusion') to another human being:

> My heart beat quick; this was the hour and moment of trial which would decide my hopes or realize my fears. The servants were gone to a neighbouring fair. All was silent in and around the cottage; it was an excellent opportunity; yet, when I proceeded to execute my plan, my limbs failed me, and I sunk to the ground. Again I rose; and, exerting all the firmness of which I was master, removed the planks which I had placed before my hovel to conceal my retreat. The fresh

air revived me, and, with renewed determination I approached the door of their cottage.
I knocked. 'Who is there?' said the old man – 'Come in'.
I entered; 'Pardon this intrusion,' said I, 'I am a traveller in want of a little rest; you would greatly oblige, if you would allow me to remain a few minutes before the fire.'

Frankenstein was inspired, the story goes, by an evening which Mary Shelley spent with the poets Byron and Shelley and their friend John Polidori on the shores of Lake Geneva in 1816. All four of them were to write something 'supernatural'. Byron and Shelley incorporated the ideas into poems. Polidori wrote *The Vampire*, published in 1818, a story which started a long line of vampire tales in English.

A fashion for exotic locales and action, closely related to the Gothic, led to such outrageous works as *Vathek* (1786) by William Beckford. This 'Arabian tale' involves a cruel hero, Caliph Vathek, palaces for the indulgence of the five senses, child sacrifice, and considerable high-pitched excitement. Its exaggerations are tempered with a degree of irony which make the book very funny, although many readers and critics have taken its strangeness at face value. *Vathek* was the precursor of many such oriental tales, and in some ways anticipates the 'aesthetic' temperament which was to develop in Romanticism, such as *Lalla Rookh* (1817), four hugely successful verse tales with a linking narrative, by the Irish writer Thomas Moore.

Like the Gothic terrors, Beckford's exoticism is more the product of imagination and fantasy than of realism, an extension of the imaginative range of the novel which brings together several trends: the fascination of far-off places, the exaggerations of Mandeville and Hakluyt, and an enjoyment of sensuality and sensation.

LANGUAGE NOTE
Point of view

As the form of the novel developed, so the uses of point of view became more sophisticated. We see in Defoe's novels, for example, all the action through the eyes of the main character – Robinson Crusoe, Moll Flanders, Roxana, and others, all of whom use a first-person narration. As narrative developed in, for example, the novels of Richardson and Fielding, other points of view came into play – and readers were invited to evaluate the points of view expressed. In the epistolary novel, different letter-writers' points of view are contrasted, and the reader's sympathy and judgement alter as the reading progresses.

Fielding introduces an omniscient third-person narrator, who frequently nudges the reader – 'dear reader' – pointing out moments when the reader might judge (positively or negatively) a character's behaviour and motivations. This explicit narratorial manipulation generally disappears in the novels of Jane Austen, where irony determines something of the point of view shared between an invisible third-person narrator and the reader: 'It is a truth universally acknowledged, that a single man in possession of a good fortune must be in want of a wife.' This opening sentence of *Pride and Prejudice* effectively gives the reader a *premise* on which the author will work: the reader is invited to share that premise before proceeding with the reading, and thus colludes with the author/narrator in the telling of the tale. So, when the author uses free indirect speech, or uses adjectives which represent the characters' own opinions and attitudes rather than the author/narrator's, the reader is being silently manipulated into a situation of plural points of view: author/narrator's and character's, explicit and implicit, shared and unshared.

Later novelists will refine the expression of point of view, taking it to extremes of interiorisation in the 'stream of consciousness' technique, where the 'author' is imagined to have disappeared completely, and only the character's consciousness is represented.

In the following extract, for example, which is taken from the end of Chapter 16 of Jane Austen's *Mansfield Park*, the central character, Fanny Price, is on her own, and reflecting on a conversation with her cousin Edmund for whom she has considerable feelings but who appears to Fanny to be compromising moral standards in the house (by allowing a play to be performed and agreeing to act in it himself) because he is blinded by the attractions of Mary Crawford:

> He went; but there was no reading, no China, no composure for Fanny. He had told her the most extraordinary, the most inconceivable, the most unwelcome news; and she could think of nothing else. To be acting! After all his objections – objections so just and so public! After all that she had heard him say, and seen him look, and known him to be feeling. Could it be possible? Edmund so inconsistent. Was he not deceiving himself? Was he not wrong? Alas! it was all Miss Crawford's doing.

The point of view here shifts between the author and Fanny. Fanny is not allowed to appear entirely in the light of her own point of view because the report of her thinking is in the third person. However, her own voice emerges consistently in phrases such as 'it was all Miss Crawford's doing' and 'Could it be possible?' and 'To be acting!' In passages like this the narrative is carried not just by the author and not just by the character but by the two together. This narrative strategy was one which Jane Austen, in particular, refined, enabling her to reveal a character's feelings more directly while still providing readers with her own (here quite ironic) view of the character.

The Romantic period

1789–1832

Bliss was it in that dawn to be alive
(William Wordsworth, *The Prelude*)

CONTEXTS AND CONDITIONS

The dates of the Romantic period of literature are not precise and the term 'romantic' is itself not widely used until after the period in question. Conventionally, the period begins in 1798, which saw the publication by Wordsworth and Coleridge of their *Lyrical Ballads*, and ends in 1832, a year which saw the death of Sir Walter Scott and the enactment by Parliament of the First Reform Bill. These years link literary and political events. The Romantic period was an era in which a literary revolution took place alongside social and economic revolutions. In some histories of literature the Romantic period is called the 'Age of Revolutions'.

The period was one of rapid change as the nation was transformed from an agricultural country to an industrial one. The laws of a free market, developed by the economist Adam Smith in his book *Wealth of Nations* (1776), dominated people's lives. At the same time a shift in the balance of power took place. Power and wealth were gradually transferred from the landholding aristocracy to the large-scale employers of modern industrial communities. An old population of rural farm labourers became a new class of urban industrial labourers. This new class came to be called the working class. These workers were concentrated in cities and the new power of an increasingly large and restive mass began to make itself felt.

The Industrial Revolution created social change, unrest, and eventually turbulence. Deep-rooted traditions were rapidly overturned.

Within a short period of time the whole landscape of the country changed. In the countryside, the open fields and communally worked farms were 'enclosed'. The enclosure movement improved efficiency and enabled the increased animal farming necessary to feed a rapidly expanding population; but fewer labourers were required to work the land, and that led to an exodus to the cities of large numbers of people seeking employment. Increasing mechanisation both on the land and in the industrial factories meant continuing high levels of unemployment. Workers in the rural areas could no longer graze the animals on which they partly depended for food and income. Acute poverty followed.

These developments literally altered the landscape of the country. Open fields were enclosed by hedges and walls; in the cities, smoking factory chimneys polluted the atmosphere; poor-quality houses were built in large numbers and quickly became slums. The mental landscape also changed. The country was divided into those who owned property or land – who were rich – and those who did not – who were poor. A new world was born, which Benjamin Disraeli, who was both a novelist and Prime Minister of Britain under Queen Victoria, was later to identify as 'Two Nations'.

The Industrial Revolution paralleled revolutions in the political order. In fact, Britain was at war during most of the Romantic period, with a resultant political instability. Political movements in Britain were gradual, but in countries such as France and the United States political change was both more rapid and more radical. The American Declaration of Independence (from Britain) in 1776 struck an early blow for the principle of democratic freedom and self-government, but it was the early years of the French Revolution, with its slogan of 'Equality, liberty and fraternity', which most influenced the intellectual climate in Britain. In this respect the storming of the Bastille in 1789, to release political prisoners, acted as a symbol which attracted the strong support of liberal opinion.

Debate in Britain was, however, polarised between support for radical documents such as Tom Paine's *Rights of Man* (1791), in which he called for greater democracy in Britain, and Edmund Burke's more conservative *Reflections on the Revolution in France* (1790). Later in the 1790s, more measured ideas are contained in the writings of William

Godwin, an important influence on the poets Wordsworth and Shelley, who advocated a gradual evolution towards the removal of poverty and the equal distribution of all wealth. Such a social philosophy caused much enthusiasm and intellectual excitement among many radical writers and more liberal politicians; but these ideas also represented a threat to the existing order. Positive use of the words 'Jacobin' or 'radical' was dangerous in the 1790s. 'Jacobin', in particular, which derived from French, implied strong sympathy with ideals of absolute social equality.

However, as the French Revolution developed, support for it in Britain declined. There was violence, extremism and much bloodshed as sections of the old aristocracy were massacred, as the members of the new French Republic fought among themselves and with other countries, and as Napoleon Bonaparte became emperor and then dictator of France. In Britain these events were witnessed with some dismay. In *The Prelude*, a long autobiographical poem, Wordsworth wrote that in the early years of the French Revolution 'Bliss was it in that dawn to be alive'. But he later recorded his feeling that the leaders of the French Republic had:

> become Oppressors in their turn.
> Frenchmen had changed a war of self-defence
> For one of Conquest, losing sight of all
> Which they had struggled for.

Support for the spirit of the early years of the French Revolution remained. Among more liberal and radical thinkers there was a feeling of ambivalence when England went to war against France and, after many years, finally defeated Napoleon at the Battle of Waterloo in 1815. The victory was followed by years of social unrest at home. The end of the war led to a decline in manufacturing output and to unemployment, as soldiers returned from war to a world in which the divisions between the 'two nations' were becoming sharper. In the immediate aftermath of the Napoleonic wars the government and ruling classes adopted especially repressive measures. These culminated in the 'Peterloo Massacre' of 1819, in which government troops charged a large group of workers who were meeting in Manchester to demand social and political reforms. Nine were killed and thousands more injured. The word 'Peterloo' ironically recalls the Battle of Waterloo.

The period from 1820 to 1832 was a time of continuing unrest. The unrest took place against a background of the cycles of economic depression which so characterise the modern world. The prevailing economic philosophy was that of *laissez-faire*, meaning 'leave alone'. The consequences were that the government did not intervene directly in economic affairs. It let the free market and private individual decisions control the course of events. During this time, the wealth of the country grew, although it had become increasingly concentrated in the hands of the new manufacturing and merchant classes.

This new middle class wanted to see its increased economic power reflected in greater political power. A general alliance arose between working-class reformers, liberal (called Whig) politicians and this new middle class, resulting in pressure on the Tory government for political reform. After many struggles, and with the threat of national disorder not far away, the first Reform Act was passed by Parliament in 1832. The bill extended voting rights to include a more representative proportion of the country. The immediate benefits were limited, but the bill was of great symbolic importance and a movement was started which would lead, decades later, to universal suffrage and greater democracy in the country.

In terms of literary history, the publication of *Lyrical Ballads* in 1798 is seen as a landmark. The volume contains many of the best-known Romantic poems. The second edition in 1800 contained a Preface in which Wordsworth discusses the theories of poetry which were to be so influential on many of his and Coleridge's contemporaries. The Preface represents a poetic manifesto which is very much in the spirit of the age. The movement towards greater freedom and democracy in political and social affairs is paralleled by poetry which sought to overturn the existing regime and establish a new, more 'democratic' poetic order. To do this, the writers used 'the real language of men' (Preface to *Lyrical Ballads*) and even, in the case of Byron and Shelley, got directly involved in political activities themselves.

The Romantic age in literature is often contrasted with the Classical or Augustan age which preceded it. The comparison is valuable, for it is not simply two different attitudes to literature which are being compared but two different ways of seeing and experiencing life.

The Classical or Augustan age of the early and mid-eighteenth century stressed the importance of reason and order. Strong feelings and flights of the imagination had to be controlled (although they were obviously found widely, especially in poetry). The swift improvements in medicine, economics, science and engineering, together with rapid developments in both agricultural and industrial technology, suggested human progress on a grand scale. At the centre of these advances towards a perfect society was mankind, and it must have seemed that everything was within man's grasp if his baser, bestial instincts could be controlled. The Classical temperament trusts reason, intellect, and the head. The Romantic temperament prefers feelings, intuition, and the heart.

There are further contrasts in the ways in which children are regarded and represented in Classical and Romantic literature. For the Augustan writer the child is only important because he or she will develop into an adult. The child's savage instincts must be trained, making it civilised and sophisticated. For the Romantic writer the child is holy and pure and its proximity to God will only be corrupted by civilisation. The child then is a source of natural and spontaneous feeling. When Wordsworth wrote that 'the Child is father of the Man' (in *My Heart Leaps Up*) he stressed that the adult learns from the experience of childhood.

The two ages may be contrasted in other ways: the Classical writer looks outward to society, Romantic writers look inward to their own soul and to the life of the imagination; the Classical writer concentrates on what can be logically measured and rationally understood, Romantic writers are attracted to the irrational mystical and supernatural world; the Classical writer is attracted to a social order in which everyone knows their place, Romantic writers celebrate the freedom of nature and of individual human experience. In fact, the writings of the Augustan age stress the way societies improve under careful regulation; Romantic literature is generally more critical of society and its injustices, questioning rather than affirming, exploring rather than defining.

The language and form of the literature of the two ages also shows these two different ways of seeing. The Augustans developed a formal and ordered way of writing characterised by the balance and symmetry of the heroic couplet in poetry and by an adherence to the conventions of a special poetic diction. The Romantics developed ways of writing which tried to capture the ebb and flow of individual experience in forms and language which were intended to be closer to everyday speech and more accessible to the general reader. Here is an extract from the Preface to *Lyrical Ballads* (in the revised version of 1802):

> The principal object, then, which I proposed to myself in these poems was to choose incidents and situations from common life, and to relate or describe them, throughout, as far as was possible, in a selection of language really used by men; and, at the same time, to throw over them a certain colouring of imagination, whereby ordinary things should be presented to the mind in an unusual way.

Contrasts between the Augustan and Romantic ages are helpful but there are always exceptions to such general contrasts. For example, eighteenth-century writers such as Gray, Collins and Cowper show a developing Romantic sensibility, and Romantic poets such as Byron were inspired by Augustan poetic models. Romanticism was not a sudden, radical transformation, but grew out of Augustanism. Furthermore, English Romanticism contrasts with mainland European Romanticism which, for example, tends to be more politically motivated and philosophically radical. It is therefore unwise to make too many unqualified generalisations about Romanticism.

One final introductory point can be made about the Romantic period. The English Romantic literature discussed in the following sections grew out of specific historical contexts. The Industrial Revolution led to an increasing regimentation of the individual. Small towns and villages, where everyone knew their neighbours, began to disappear. They were replaced by a more impersonal, mechanised society, fed and clothed by mass production. In this new world individuals lost their identity. The writers of this time wanted to correct this imbalance by giving greater value to the individual sensibility and to the individual consciousness. Their poetic revolution aimed at greater individual freedoms.

'Bliss was it in that dawn to be alive' are words written by

Wordsworth (in *The Prelude*) at what he felt to be the dawn of a new age. It was an age in which the uniqueness of the individual would be celebrated. It was a time of war, a time of ideals, a time of freedom, and of oppression. Its conflicts and contradictions breathed new life into literature and, in particular, into poetry.

The Romantic period is seen today as a crucial time in history. It embodies many of the conflicts and ideological debates which are still at the heart of the modern world; political freedom/repression, individual and collective responsibility, masculine and feminine roles (until recently the traditional canon of Romanticism was almost exclusively male), past, present, and future. These issues recur time and again in Romantic writing. It was a time when ideologies were in the melting-pot, when radicalism and tradition, change and stability, the old and the new, were just as vital as the more traditionally literary themes of innocence/experience, youth/age, country/city, man/nature, language/expression. Many of these issues are as alive today as they were two hundred years ago. The recovery of many female writers' works in recent years is one significant sign that our relationship to the Romantic period is an ongoing and ever-changing one. In many ways, we are all post-Romantics.

LANGUAGE NOTE
William Cobbett, grammar and politics

William Cobbett (1763–1835) was a farmer, journalist and writer who became an MP in 1832. In 1802 Cobbett began a weekly newspaper called *The Political Register*. Cobbett was a Tory, but he increasingly supported radical causes, particularly causes of social and parliamentary reform, using his own newspaper to give greater publicity to the causes, and campaigning more and more vigorously against social injustice and government corruption.

Cobbett was the son of a farmer and self-educated. He took a particular interest in language and in the grammars of Standard English which had been written during the previous century and in his writings makes frequent mention of how he had taught himself the standardised 'correct' grammar of English. Cobbett regularly links grammar and the issue of social class, and stresses the importance of mastering standard grammar:

Without understanding this, you can never hope to become fit for anything beyond mere trade or agriculture. . . . Without a knowledge of grammar, it is impossible for you to write correctly; and, it is by mere accident that you speak correctly; and, pray bear in mind, that all well-informed persons judge of a man's mind (until they have other means of judging) by his writing or speaking.

(*Advice to Young Men*, 1829)

Here, Cobbett recognises the social implications of non-standard language. He often makes reference in his writings to the ways in which petitions to parliament (for voting reform) were dismissed by the government on account of the 'vulgarity' of language used by the petitioners. In the eighteenth century the language of the working classes was deemed not to conform to the standards of the grammar as described in the new standardised grammars of Bishop Lowth and others (see Language note page 182); linguistically 'inferior' language use was seen as a token of inferior thought and also of dubious moral value. Such ideas about language were used to protect the government from criticism and to resist movements for political change.

William Cobbett's solution was to try to ensure that ordinary working people had access to standard grammar. He wrote his grammar book in the form of a series of letters to his son, arguing that to learn standard grammar was both a right of all people and ultimately a way to extend their rights and liberties. Cobbett considered grammar as an integral part of the class structure of Britain and the learning of grammar as an act of class warfare. His views contrast with writers such as Hardy and Lawrence, who believed that dialects were equally valid, equally rule-governed systems, that they gave an identity to people from different social and regional groups, and that losing individual non-standard modes of language would lead to standardised people.

BLAKE, WORDSWORTH AND COLERIDGE

The Child is father of the Man
(William Wordsworth, *My Heart Leaps Up*)

William Blake achieved little fame in his own lifetime but in the twentieth century he has come to be recognised as a poetic genius. Blake was also an engraver, and illustrated many of his poems so that they could be read visually as well as verbally. His life was spent in rebellion against the rationalism of the eighteenth century and he rejected, in particular, the formal restrictions of Augustan poetry, writing in a lyrical visionary style and developing, in the process, an individual view of the world. A characteristic feature was a tendency to see the world in terms of opposites. Blake wrote that 'Without Contraries is no Progression' (*The Marriage of Heaven and Hell*) and much of his poetry illustrates this. The major opposition reflected in his poetry is a contrast between the order of the eighteenth century and the sense of liberation felt in the 1790s as a new century approached.

Blake makes extensive use of symbolism in his poetry. Some of the symbols are straightforward: innocence is symbolised by children, flowers, lambs, or particular seasons. Oppression and rationalism are symbolised by urban, industrial landscapes, by machines, by those in authority (including priests), and by social institutions. The symbolism in some of his later poems, such as the epic *Milton*, is less easy to interpret. Blake sometimes creates a mythological world of his own. For example, the giant Los, who represents the human imagination, is set against his opposite Urizen, who represents the restrictions of law and order. Blake's best-known symbol is that of the tiger in his poem *The Tyger*. The tiger has been interpreted differently by successive generations but its basic meaning is the natural and creative energy of human life, an inspiring shape ('symmetry') which no one should try to control:

> Tyger! Tyger! burning bright
> In the forests of the night,
> What immortal hand or eye
> Could frame thy fearful symmetry?

Images of childhood have a central place in Blake's poetry, as they do in the work of many Romantic poets. Blake's most famous collection of poetry, *Songs of Innocence and Experience*, published separately in 1789 (*Songs of Innocence*) and 1793 (*Songs of Experience*), and together in 1794, abounds in images of children in a world in which people are exploited. (A good example is Blake's poem *The Chimney Sweeper*.) The child in Blake's poetry stands for the poet's dissatisfaction with society and for his belief in the power of uncorrupted feeling and imagination. Through the images of childhood, Blake dramatises the conflict between nature and social order, between natural innocence and the pressures of social experience.

In the volume *Songs of Innocence and Experience*, several poems are written in pairs, contrasting states of human innocence and experience. In them, Blake reveals a profound understanding of psychology and an ability to explore the spiritual side of human existence, both of which are remarkably modern.

Blake was also conscious of the effects on the individual of a rapidly developing industrial and commercial world. He saw the potential dangers of a mass society in which individuals were increasingly controlled by systems of organisation. In his poem *London* he refers to these systems as the result of 'mind-forg'd manacles'. In *London* even the River Thames has been 'charter'd' (given a royal charter to be used for commercial purposes). The repetition of words and structures seems to underline a monotonous regimentation:

> I wander thro' each charter'd street
> Near where the charter'd Thames does flow,
> And mark in every face I meet
> Marks of weakness, marks of woe.
>
> In every cry of every Man,
> In every Infant's cry of fear,
> In every voice, in every ban,
> The mind-forg'd manacles I hear.

This political view of London contrasts with Wordsworth's *Sonnet Composed Upon Westminster Bridge* (1802) in which the poet's personal elation at the 'majesty' of London is recorded: Blake's vision is social where Wordsworth's is personal.

There are some similarities between Blake's poetry and the poetry of William Wordsworth, particularly his emphasis on the value of childhood experience and its celebration of nature. Central to Wordsworth's vision of nature is the importance of the impact and influence of nature on the human mind. Wordsworth's poetry is essentially empirical: that is, he records the evidence of his senses, looking inward rather than outward. Nevertheless, he does describe the world of nature and of the characters who inhabit the natural landscape. In fact, Wordsworth gives detailed accounts of the lives of ordinary people in poems such as *The Old Cumberland Beggar* and *The Leech Gatherer* – characters of a low social position not normally represented in Augustan poetry. Wordsworth celebrates the spirit of man, living in harmony with his natural environment and away from the corrupt city. However, the essence of his poetry lies not in the description of this world of nature but rather in the development of the inner mind which records it.

In Wordsworth's long autobiographical poem *The Prelude* (1805; final version 1850) the main concern is the psychology of the individual. Such an emphasis on the formation of the individual sensibility has since become a major characteristic of Western literature. One of its original titles was *A Poem on the Growth of an Individual Mind*. It is characteristic of the Romantic period that its major epic poem should be about this subject. In many parts of *The Prelude*, and in poems such as *Tintern Abbey* and *Ode: Intimations of Immortality*, Wordsworth records a personal search for the moments of insight and understanding which, he believed, only nature could give. Time, and the passing of time, become recurring themes, as in 'Five years have passed' in *Tintern Abbey*, where memory of the past, together with the effects of nature, allow the poetic 'I' 'to see into the heart of things' in the present. He believed in the truth of his own senses and imagination and he sometimes describes moments in which he perceives mystical and transcendental truths:

> A presence that disturbs me with the joy
> Of elevated thoughts; a sense sublime
> Of something far more deeply interfused,
> Whose dwelling is the light of setting suns,
> And the round ocean and the living air,
> And the blue sky, and in the mind of man.
> (*Tintern Abbey*)

Throughout his poetic career, however, Wordsworth continued to regard the child as the single most important source of wisdom and truth. In his *Ode: Intimations of Immortality* the child, as a symbol of all that is holy and good, is directly addressed:

> Thou best philosopher, who yet dost keep
> Thy heritage, thou eye among the blind,

That, deaf and silent, read'st the eternal deep,
Haunted forever by the eternal mind.

The child is seen here as father of the man. Although lines such as these do not strictly adhere to Wordsworth's poetic principles of simple and unadorned language, many of his poems do create a new poetic language. Wordsworth's language frequently moves towards the language of everyday speech and the lives of ordinary people. It breaks with the artificial diction of the previous century, creating a more open and democratic world of poetry. Wordsworth stated later in his life that he had aimed to show that men and women 'who do not wear fine clothes can feel deeply'.

Wordsworth did not always achieve his aim of writing poetry according to the manifesto in the Preface to *Lyrical Ballads*. Sometimes it is direct, simple and close to ordinary spoken language. For example:

A slumber did my spirit seal;
I had no human fears:
She seemed a thing that could not feel
The touch of earthly years.

Sometimes he uses more complex grammar and vocabulary, as we can see from the above examples. Words like 'heritage' and 'deeply interfused' and the long sentences with several clauses in them seem a long way from his poetic ideals.

Wordsworth's search to record the insights of the imagination and the power of human memory could not always be sustained. Imagination fails. Memories fade, shine brightly and then fade again. Wordsworth revised *The Prelude* throughout his life; in each version he tries to capture more accurately the lasting insights of his past. But later drafts lack the excitement of earlier versions of the poem. It is also possible that the failure of the French Revolution affected the course of Wordsworth's own poetry and life.

In the formative stages of his poetic career Wordsworth collaborated with Samuel Taylor Coleridge. Both contributed to *Lyrical Ballads*, but Wordsworth alone was responsible for the important Preface, which was to influence the whole of the Romantic movement and much subsequent poetry in English. Wordsworth's poetry is concerned with the ordinary, everyday world and with the impact of memory on the present; Coleridge's poetry frequently communicates a sense of the mysterious, supernatural and extraordinary world. Wordsworth stated that he wanted to explore everyday subjects and give them a Romantic or supernatural colouring; by contrast, Coleridge wanted to give the supernatural a feeling of everyday reality.

One of Coleridge's best-known poems is *The Rime of the Ancient Mariner*. In the poem an old sailor or mariner narrates the terrible sequence of events which followed when he shot an albatross and was cursed. His ship is becalmed, he is subjected to nightmare visions and to a long period of suffering and his water supply runs out in punishment for his deed. When the mariner blesses some sea-creatures, his offence against the power of nature is forgiven and he is able to return home, a wiser man through his suffering. The whole poem is written in the form of a mediaeval ballad.

> Day after day, day after day,
> We stuck, nor breath nor motion;
> As idle as a painted ship
> Upon a painted ocean.
>
> Water, water, every where
> And all the boards did shrink;
> Water, water, every where,
> Nor any drop to drink.

Even from these few lines it is possible to see something of the allegorical and symbolic power of the poem. The lack of water represents the dryness of spirit, the becalmed ship symbolises the aimless soul of a man who has sinned and who awaits eventual redemption. The explicit moral is essentially Christian:

> He prayeth well who loveth well
> Both man and bird and beast.
>
> He prayeth best who loveth best,
> All things both great and small.
> For the dear God, who loveth us,
> He made and loveth all.

The conclusion, 'A sadder and a wiser man/He rose the morrow morn', underscores the passage from innocence to experience, from past to present, which is central to a great deal of Romantic writing. (The sadder, wiser man is the wedding guest to whom the mariner's story has been recounted.)

Other poems by Coleridge explore a mystical and supernatural world. Unlike Wordsworth, who concentrates on the everyday world of the present, Coleridge turns to the romance and mystery of the past. *Christabel*, also written in a mediaeval ballad form, is another allegory in which sinister and grotesque images from a distant past have an everyday reality. In *Kubla Khan*, Coleridge presents an exotic landscape which has often been interpreted as symbolising the movement of the creative imagination. The poem opens with a basic contrast between the River Alph, a potentially destructive force, and the pleasure-dome, a source of deep perception and understanding:

> In Xanadu did Kubla Khan
> A stately pleasure-dome decree:
> Where Alph, the sacred river, ran
> Through caverns measureless to man
> Down to a sunless sea.

In *Kubla Khan,* Coleridge embodies the essence of the poetic imagination, the most powerful of the human senses which is alone capable of perceiving the underlying harmony of all things and of understanding the truth about the world. The subtitle to the poem is *A Fragment*. It was reported that Coleridge did not complete the poem because he was interrupted by a visitor during its composition. The poem is indeed a fragment of a powerful vision, but it is a complete statement of a vision which can only be communicated in parts and fragments.

Coleridge's *Christabel* is also an 'unfinished' poem. Several Romantic poems are fragments, almost as if they represent the impossible nature of the Romantic quest for complete meaning and fulfilment. Yet such is the power of the poet's imagination that an unfinished journey can still reveal insights of lasting significance. Even Coleridge's poem *Dejection: An Ode*, which explores an occasion on which the poetic imagination fails, captures a permanent truth. Coleridge's determination to continue his search for transcendental understanding led him to take drugs such as opium. Like a number of Romantic writers, he wished to extend the power of his senses and intuitions as far as possible, even if that were to risk serious damage to his health.

> My genial spirits fail;
> And what can these avail
> To lift the smothering weight from off my breast?
> If it were a vain endeavour,
> Though I should gaze for ever
> On that green light that lingers in the west:
> I may not hope from outward forms to win
> The passion and the life, whose fountains are within.
>
> (*Dejection: An Ode*)

It is important to compare and contrast the poetry of Wordsworth and Coleridge. They created a new kind of poetry, innovating in form, language and subject matter and creating a lasting influence on English poetry. Although their particular styles and methods were generally in contrast, it is necessary to stress that they shared important goals, particularly the goal of making poetry closer to the rhythms and diction of everyday language.

Coleridge's 'conversation poems' are in this respect very close to many of Wordsworth's poems. Poems such as *Christabel* and *Kubla Khan* do indeed represent exotic and intensely mystical flights of the imagination. Yet poems such as *Dejection*, *Frost at Midnight* and *This Lime-Tree Bower My Prison* are based on everyday observation. They reflect on universal issues such as the relationship between parents and children and are intimate and conversational in tone. A good example of Coleridge's dialogic, conversational style is found in *Frost at Midnight* in which the poet addresses his son Hartley:

> My babe so beautiful! it thrills my heart
> With tender gladness, thus to look at thee,
> And think that thou shalt learn far other lore,
> And in far other scenes! For I was reared
> In the great city, pent 'mid cloisters dim,
> And saw nought lovely but the sky and stars.
> But *thou*, my babe! shalt wander like a breeze
> By lakes and sandy shores, beneath the crags
> Of ancient mountain, and beneath the clouds. . . .

We note here a contrast between the natural world and the world of the city, but the choices of language capture the movement of a speaking voice in conversation. The exclamation marks, the use of italics for emphasis, the steady pace of the rhythm, all serve to express a quiet speaking voice revealing intimate thoughts.

While some critics have judged that Wordsworth's later poetry (for example, long poems such as *The Excursion*) lacked the vitality of his earlier work, Coleridge complained that poetic inspiration had deserted him and he wrote no poetry during the last thirty years of his life. Instead he dedicated himself to philosophy and to literary criticism. In 1817 he published *Biographia Literaria*, which contains important discussion of the workings of the poetic imagination and reveals the extent of his thinking about the nature of literature. It has become one of the most influential of works of criticism. Together with Wordsworth's Preface to *Lyrical Ballads*, it also reveals another aspect of the modern writer: almost simultaneously the writer produces both literary work and self-conscious critical reflections on that work and on literature in general. In more ways than one, the Romantics are genuine forerunners of the Modern movement in literature and the arts.

LANGUAGE NOTE
The 'real' language of men

> Remuneration! O that's the Latin word for three farthings.
> (William Shakespeare, *Love's Labour's Lost*)

> I heard among the solitary hills
> Low breathings coming after me, and sounds
> Of undistinguishable motion, steps
> Almost as silent as the turf they trod.
> (William Wordsworth, *The Prelude*)

In the Preface to *Lyrical Ballads* (1800; revised 1802) Wordsworth makes the first theoretical argument in the history of English poetry for a radical review of the language of poetry. His argument is that conventional poetic diction should be replaced by a language closer to the everyday speech of ordinary people. It is an essentially democratic statement, arguing that ordinary words should be admitted into the society of the poem. Wordsworth and Coleridge wanted to purify and renew the language of poetry. From a different starting point Pope and Dryden in the seventeenth century and T.S. Eliot in the twentieth century attempted similar processes of renewal.

At the time of writing, the classical, Latinate style of Milton and his poetic descendants tended to be regarded as the norm. It was an appropriately elevated 'diction' which conferred dignity on lofty thoughts and feelings. Such diction was rejected in the Preface as being too elitist and too remote from the language of 'a man speaking to men'. Here are two examples which illustrate the argument. One is taken from mid-eighteenth-century poetry; the other is taken from a poem by Wordsworth.

> Say, Father Thames, for thou hast seen
> Full many a sprightly race
> Disporting on thy margent green
> The paths of pleasure trace,
> Who foremost now delight to cleave
> With pliant arm thy glassy wave?
> (Thomas Gray, *Ode on a Distant Prospect of Eton College*)

> In the sweet shire of Cardigan,
> Not far from pleasant Ivor-hall,
> An old man dwells, a little man,
> I've heard he once was tall. . . .

> Full five and twenty years he lived
> A running huntsman merry;
> And, though he has but one eye left,
> His cheek is like a cherry.
>   (William Wordsworth, *Simon Lee*)

Although they are less than fifty years apart, the poems show marked contrasts in language. Wordsworth believed that the kind of poetry written by Gray was too affected and ornate with its mainly Latin vocabulary and its deliberate choices of words and phrases which are far removed from everyday language use (for example, 'disporting': playing; 'margent green': river bank; 'cleave with pliant arm': swim) and which conform to Gray's own theory that the language of poetry should have an elevated diction of its own. In *Simon Lee*, Wordsworth writes in unaffectedly simple language, although the demands of such poetic conventions as rhythm and metrics mean that the language can never be entirely similar to ordinary language.

In poetic practice, however, there are limitations to Wordsworth's theory of poetic language. Some would say, for example, that poems like *Simon Lee* are too banal, and that in trying to explore the ordinary feelings of ordinary people in ordinary settings Wordsworth runs the risk that he will fail to find the style which can elevate the poem into a memorable and durable artefact. Indeed, when Wordsworth does achieve poetic heights he does so by using language which is so elevated and Latinate that it falsifies his theory. An example would be the lines cited at the beginning of this language note, which in fact mix 'low' and 'high' styles and in the process chart the ebb and flow of perception and understanding. The lines also, however, illustrate another basic paradox of much Romantic poetry: that the poet is forced to use language to describe experiences which are outside or beyond language.

On the other hand, some critics feel that in groups of poems, such as the 'Lucy' poems published in *Lyrical Ballads*, Wordsworth comes very close to achieving his poetic ideals. A frequently cited example is the poem *She Dwelt Among th' Untrodden Ways*, which combines complexity of insight with simplicity of expression.

KEATS

Beauty is truth, truth beauty, — that is all
Ye know on earth, and all ye need to know
(John Keats, *Ode on a Grecian Urn*)

John Keats is likewise a poet who reflected on the nature of poetry. Keats's letters are important documents and offer many revealing insights into the nature of poetry and many critical precepts which are still cited today as a basis for the evaluation of poetry. Keats wrote that 'we hate poetry that has too palpable a design upon us'. By this he means that we distrust poetry which tries overtly to persuade or convert us to the poet's point of view. According to this statement, poetry should be more indirect, communicating through the power of its images without the poet making his own presence too obvious.

Like other Romantic poets, Keats wrote poems which were incomplete; unfinished fragments of a larger vision. He also, like other Romantic artists, died at a very young age before fulfilling his potential and completing the poetic journey he had begun. However, by the age of 25, he had written a major body of work containing some of the most memorable poems in the English language. Keats's best-known poetry was composed twenty years after the publication of *Lyrical Ballads* and, although his poetry contrasts with that of Wordsworth and Coleridge, they remained an important influence on his work and his theories of poetry.

A main theme of Keats's poetry is the conflict between the everyday world and eternity: the everyday world of suffering, death and decay, and the timeless beauty and lasting truth of poetry and the human imagination. His earliest poetry consists mainly of long poems, some of them epic in style and concept. *Endymion* (1818) is written in four books and is derived in style and structure from Greek legends and myths, the main theme being the search for an ideal love and a happiness beyond earthly possibility. A more ambitious long poem is *The Fall of Hyperion* (1819) which is heavily influenced by John Milton and was not finished by Keats, in part because he wished to develop his own style and identity as a poet. It tells of the downfall of the old gods and the rise of the new gods who are marked by their strength and beauty. Although the poem has been criticised for a lack of control in the writing, there are several places where sensuousness and precision of rhythm and image are combined:

> No stir of air was there,
> Not so much life as on a summer's day
> Robs not one light seed from the feathered grass,
> But where the dead leaf fell, there did it rest.
> 　　　　　　　　　(*Hyperion*)

Keats continued to write long narrative poems which allowed him to develop a characteristic feature of the style of all his poems: lush, sensuous imagery which supports precise descriptive detail. Keats, like Coleridge, was also attracted to exotic settings for his narratives. These include mythic classical backgrounds and mediaeval contexts of high Romance. The poems *Isabella*, *Lamia*, *The Eve of Saint Agnes* and *La Belle Dame Sans Merci* explore familiar Romantic themes: the relationship between emotion and reality; the impermanence of human love; the search for an elusive beauty. Unlike poets and philosophers of the classical, eighteenth-century period, who saw the mediaeval era as one of darkness and superstition, Keats, along with other Romantic poets, was attracted by those times.

> Oh, what can ail thee, knight-at-arms,
> Alone and palely loitering;
> The sedge is withered from the lake,
> And no birds sing.
> (*La Belle Dame Sans Merci*)

Keats was particularly fascinated by Thomas Percy's *Reliques of Ancient English Poetry* (1765) and by the 'pre-Romantic' figure of the poet Thomas Chatterton, who committed suicide in 1770 at the age of 18 and who forged copies of mediaeval ballads.

> Mie love ys dedde,
> Gon to hys death-bedde,
> Al under the wyllowe tree.

> Waterre witches, crownede wythe reytes,
> Bere me to yer leathalle tyde.
> I die; I comme; mie true love waytes.
> Thos the damselle spake, and dyed.
> (Thomas Chatterton, *Song to Aella*, 1769–70)

The ballads written by Chatterton were attributed to the fictional Thomas Rowley but they are 'pre-Romantic' because they point the way, in the late 1760s, to a poetry of direct utterance which escaped the ornamentation of much of the verse of the time. Keats's admiration for the Middle Ages allows him to make particular use of the ballad form to explore aspects of the irrational, unconscious and supernatural world.

Keats's ballads were written within a two-year period (1818–20); in fact, the years saw an intensely creative period of Keats's life and during the same period he wrote the odes in which the rich and sensuous variety of human experience is set against the transience of human life. The odes explore fundamental tensions and contradictions. Keats finds melancholy in delight, pleasure in pain, and excitement in both emotional sensations and intellectual thoughts. He contrasts dreams and reality, the imagination and the actual, the tangible and the intangible. He celebrates beauty but at the same time he knows that all things of beauty must fade and die. He experiences love and death with equal intensity, knowing that they are closely connected. He shared with both Wordsworth and Coleridge the view that suffering is necessary for an understanding of the world and that great poetry grows from deep suffering and tragedy. In one of his letters Keats wrote: 'Do you not see how necessary a world of pains and troubles is to school an intelligence and make it a soul?'

The ode is a complex poetic form, and Keats is generally regarded as one of the masters of the form. At the same time he develops a poetic language appropriate both to the form of the ode and the nature of his themes. Keats's language renders experience precisely; it captures the rhythm and movement of thoughts and feelings; it registers a full range of sense impressions. For example, in the following lines from *Ode to a Nightingale* the poet asks for a drink of cool wine:

> O, for a draught of vintage! that hath been
> Cooled a long age in the deep-delved earth,
> Tasting of Flora and the country green,
> Dance, and Provencal song, and sunburnt mirth!

The description is an example of synaesthesia – a feature which recurs frequently in Keats's poetry and in the poetry of others, such as the twentieth-century poets Wilfred Owen and Dylan Thomas, who have been much influenced by Keats. Synaesthesia is a use of imagery and language choices which describe sensory impressions in terms of other senses. In the lines above, Keats manages to appeal to sight, colour, movement, sound, and heat almost simultaneously. For example, the movement of dancing and the sound of song is described as a taste. 'Sunburnt mirth' describes the sight of sunburnt faces at the same time as we hear the same people laughing. Keats also created a rich poetic music. An example of his control of the rhythmic movement and syntax is the following lines from the *Ode to Autumn*:

> Then in a wailful choir the small gnats mourn
> Among the river sallows, borne aloft
> Or sinking as the light wind lives or dies.

Here the rise and fall in the rhythm of the lines matches the flight of the gnats. Keats's characteristic representation of the physical world, his total immersion in an experience of things outside himself, his delight in sensuous but precise words can be further exemplified from the same poem, where autumn is seen as:

> Close bosom-friend of the maturing sun;
> Conspiring with him how to load and bless
> With fruit the vines that round the thatch-eves run;
> To bend with apples the mossed cottage-trees,
> And fill all fruit with ripeness to the core.

Instead of the expected picture of falling leaves and decay here, the view of autumn is positive and life-affirming (as in James Thomson's *The Seasons*; see page 197). The final lines take the reader through winter, symbolised by the robin redbreast, and on to the future sounds of spring; moving, in effect, through almost the whole calendar in its appreciation of the riches of autumn.

> Then in a wailful choir the small gnats mourn
> Among the river sallows, borne aloft
> Or sinking as the light wind lives or dies;
> And full-grown lambs loud bleat from hilly bourn;
> Hedge-crickets sing; and now with a treble soft
> The redbreast whistles from a garden-croft;
> And gathering swallows twitter in the skies.

Keats's pursuit of the eternal truths of poetic art and the imagination are powerfully expressed in *Ode on a Grecian Urn*. In the poem the urn itself suggests that:

> Beauty is truth, truth beauty, – that is all
> Ye know on earth, and all ye need to know.

The Grecian urn and the artistic carvings on it represent the permanence of art and celebrate the power of the artist to immortalise human activity, to make it permanent, preserving it against mortality and the passing of time. The beauty of art is seeing the real truth of existence.

Keats also gives us occasional glimpses of solitude and desolation. In his famous letters, he calls the world 'The Vale of Soul-Making'; in his sonnet beginning 'When I have fears that I may cease to be', he depicts a desolate shore which anticipates John Clare and Matthew Arnold in its emptiness. The sonnet is all the more poignant when we know that Keats died at the age of 26, a tragically young age, with a poetic career of even greater fulfilment in front of him. He was the Romantic poet *par excellence*: his continuing dedication to poetry in the knowledge that he was dying (from tuberculosis) made him a symbol for the Romantic movement. At the time of his death, the first generation of Romantics, Wordsworth and Coleridge, could no longer write the intense poetry of their early years. He became an emblem of transience, and Shelley's visionary essay *Adonais* on Keats's death depicts the exquisite early flowering and then sudden death of Keats, the man and poet.

SHELLEY

The lone and level sands stretch far away
(Percy Bysshe Shelley, *Ozymandias*)

The poetry of Percy Bysshe Shelley is similar to that of Keats in a number of respects, but, unlike Keats, Shelley explores political and social questions more explicitly. Shelley represents the more revolutionary and non-conformist element in English Romanticism and was constantly critical of conventional authority. He was the individualist and idealist who rebelled against the institutions of family, church, marriage and the Christian faith and against all forms of tyranny. He started writing and publishing poetry while at Oxford University, some three years before Keats's first publication.

One of Shelley's first major poems, published in 1813, was *Queen Mab*. In the poem he attacks institutional religion and codified morality, portraying a utopian vision of man's need for simple virtue and straightforward happiness. Shelley's ideas were anarchic and dangerous in the eyes of the conservative society of his time. He believed that original sin did not exist and that it was possible to attain human perfection on earth if humans could only free themselves from the chains of a repressive society. A year before *Queen Mab*, Shelley had gone to Dublin to distribute a pamphlet – *Address to the Irish People* – and to take part in campaigns for Catholic emancipation and for social justice for oppressed and poverty-stricken people. In a pamphlet entitled *The Necessity of Atheism*, Shelley argued that the existence of

God could not be proved. His refusal to withdraw the pamphlet led to his being expelled from Oxford by the university authorities. At the time of writing *Queen Mab*, Shelley was under the influence of the social philosopher William Godwin who was also influential on the thinking of Wordsworth and other Romantic poets.

Other major poems by Shelley also addressed social and political issues. *The Mask of Anarchy* was a direct response to the Peterloo Massacre of 1819. Like the sonnet *England in 1819*, it closes with a vision of the future revolution of the working classes: 'a glorious phantom may/Burst, to illumine our tempestuous day.'

In *Prometheus Unbound* (1820), generally regarded as one of Shelley's most successful long poems, he employs the Greek myth of Prometheus, who was punished for stealing the gift of fire from the gods and giving it to mankind; but in Shelley's poem he is redeemed by the power of love and acts as a symbol of human fulfilment resulting from a change in his imaginative vision. Prometheus represents archetypal humanity and, as in *The Ancient Mariner*, an apocalyptic change in his life reveals limitless possibilities; above all, a new way of seeing the world.

> To suffer woes which Hope thinks infinite;
> To forgive wrongs darker than death or night;
> To defy Power, which seems omnipotent;
> To love, and bear; to hope till Hope creates
> From its own wreck the thing it contemplates;
> Neither to change, nor falter, nor repent;
> This, like thy glory, Titan, is to be
> Good, great and joyous, beautiful and free;
> This is alone Life, Joy, Empire, and Victory.

Shelley's *Julian and Maddalo* (1824) can in many ways be taken as a central text of English Romanticism. It is described as 'a conversation', and its couplets reflect a chatty and intimate tone. The two characters, Julian and the Count Maddalo, clearly represent Shelley himself and Byron. Their conversation is naturalistic, rather than idealistic, and takes in the life and atmosphere the two characters observe as they ride on the sands, or sail around Venice. The city, and in particular its lunatic asylum ('the madhouse and its belfry tower'), take on a universal significance as the discussion ranges around free will, religion, progress, frustration, and love: like the sonnet *Ozymandias*, it is an evocation of a wasteland, both literally and metaphorically. The lido inspires the phrase 'I love all waste/And solitary places', aspiring to the boundless possibilities of the human soul; but the city and the asylum return the characters to real life, and the prisons of the soul, ending the 'conversation' in a silence which is astonishingly modern in its resonances.

> 'And such,' – he cried, 'is our mortality,
> And this must be the emblem and the sign
> Of what should be eternal and divine! –
> And like that black and dreary bell, the soul,
> Hung in a heaven-illumined tower, must toll
> Our thoughts and our desires to meet below
> Round the rent heart and pray – as madmen do
> For what? they know not. . . .'

Like so many works of Romantic literature, from the novels of Scott to Shelley's own *The Triumph of Anarchy*, this clash between the ideal and the real, between the general and the particular and between past, present and future reflects the principal anxiety of the time: that the necessity of revolutionary change causes individual anguish in the process. This foreshadows a major concern with the suffering of victims at all levels of society, but particularly the lower classes, throughout Victorian literature.

The poem was profoundly influential, especially on the dramatic monologues of Robert Browning later in the century – his *Childe Roland to the Dark Tower Came*, published in 1855 (see page 325), in many ways carries forward the disturbing preoccupations found in *Julian and Maddalo*.

Shelley also wrote many intense short lyrics which draw direct inspiration from nature and are written in controlled, sparse language:

> A widow bird sat mourning for her love
> Upon a wintry bough;
> The frozen wind crept on above,
> The freezing stream below.

There was no leaf upon the forest bare,
No flower upon the ground,
And little motion in the air
Except the mill wheel's sound.
                    (*A widow bird*)

Here the images from nature are employed to express inner feelings and states of mind. A sense of loss and emotional numbness is conveyed through the cold, the emptiness of the scene and the overall lack of movement. Shelley has often been criticised for putting his own feelings too directly at the centre of his poems and for being too self-indulgent and self-pitying. There are certainly lines in some poems where this is the case. For example:

Oh, lift me as a wave, a leaf, a cloud!
I fall upon the thorns of life! I bleed!
                    (*Ode to the West Wind*)

I could lie down like a tired child,
And weep away the life of care
Which I have borne and yet must bear.
            (*Stanzas Written in Dejection, near Naples*)

A widow bird and numerous other lyrics (for example, *To a Skylark, The Cloud, With a Guitar to Jane, The Indian Serenade*) do not, however, fall into that category. In one of his best-known lyrics, *Ode to the West Wind*, Shelley makes the wildness of the wind a controlled symbol of his deepest personal aspirations for human freedom. The wind sweeps away the old life and spreads the seeds which will produce a new ideal life:

O wild West Wind, thou breath of Autumn's being,
Thou, from whose unseen presence the leaves dead
Are driven, like ghosts from an enchanter fleeing,

Yellow, and black, and pale, and hectic red,
Pestilence-stricken multitudes: O thou,
Who chariotest to their dark wintry bed

The wingèd seeds, where they lie cold and low,
Each like a corpse within its grave, until
Thine azure sister of the Spring shall blow . . .

Like several of his contemporaries, Shelley believed that poetry could reform the world. Central to this belief is that the creative power of the imagination and the poet's quest for beauty and the eternal truths of beauty will show the way to a better society. According to Shelley this makes poets 'the unacknowledged legislators of the world'. In his *A Defence of Poetry* (written in 1821 but not published until 1840), Shelley wrote a poetic manifesto for these beliefs, making the poet a missionary, a prophet, a potential leader for a new society. The following extract from *A Defence of Poetry* illustrates these main points:

> It exceeds all imagination to conceive what would have been the moral condition of the world . . . if a revival of the study of Greek literature had never taken place; if no monuments of ancient sculpture had never taken place; if no monuments of ancient sculpture had been handed down to us; and if the poetry of the religion of the ancient world had been extinguished together with its belief. The human mind could never, except by the intervention of these excitements, have been awakened to the invention of the grosser sciences, and that application of analytical reasoning to the aberrations of society, which it is now attempted to exalt over the direct expression of the inventive and creative faculty itself.

The view of the creative artist as hero was later embraced by other writers in the Victorian and modern periods.

BYRON

I need a hero
(George Gordon, Lord Byron, *Don Juan*)

It is appropriate that Byron should be the last major Romantic poet we examine, for many readers, especially in the nineteenth century, regarded Byron as the prototype of the Romantic poet, and many writers across the whole of Europe were influenced by his approach. Like Shelley, Byron was heavily involved with contemporary social issues and became particularly well known for his verse satires. The heroes of his long narrative poems were often imitated; in fact, the Byronic hero almost became a literary fashion. The hero is usually a melancholy and solitary figure who in his actions often defies social conventions; almost, indeed, the poet as reclusive pop star.

The long poem *Childe Harold's Pilgrimage* – the term 'childe' is a mediaeval word for a young nobleman waiting to become a knight – was the work which made Byron's name. The hero, Childe Harold, is often identified with Byron himself. He is a restless wanderer, alternating between despair and great energy and commitment to new, usually forbidden experiences. The poem was published when Byron was only 24 years of age, in 1812. It made him famous overnight and his public career as a popular and scandalous figure was launched.

> I live not in myself, but I become
> Portion of that around me; and to me
> High mountains are a feeling, but the hum
> Of human cities torture: I can see
> Nothing to loathe in nature, save to be
> A link reluctant in a fleshly chain,
> Classed among creatures, when the soul can flee,
> And with the sky, the peak, the heaving plain
> Of ocean, or the stars, mingle, and not in vain.

A more developed example of the Byronic hero comes in his dramatic poem *Manfred* (1817). Manfred is a particularly passionate outcast and rebel whose typically Romantic heroism contrasts with the restraint and humility of the typical Augustan, classical hero. Manfred's disdain for ordinary humanity, his unidentified guilt, his sense of gloom and doom, make him, paradoxically, a deeply attractive, even erotic figure. He seems to be beyond good and evil and to define his own moral codes. His unsatisfied quest makes him not so much a hero as an anti-hero, with literary descendants in characters such as Heathcliff in Emily Brontë's *Wuthering Heights* (1847). Here Manfred rails against a spirit which wants to make him feel guilty:

> Back to thy hell!
> Thou hast no power upon me, *that* I feel;
> Thou shalt never possess me, *that* I know:
> What I have done is done; I bear within
> A torture which could nothing gain from thine:
> The mind which is immortal makes itself
> Requital for its good or evil thoughts,

Its own origin of ill and end,
And its own place and time.
                    (*Manfred*)

Byron's semi-autobiographical *Don Juan* is an example of the more satiric side to his poetry. The tone of the poem is light-hearted and comic throughout, even when the subject matter is at its most serious, moving easily through black comedy and the pathos of tragedy. This is in part due to the *ottava rima* rhyme scheme and partly due to the mixture of different styles, from the most formal poetic diction to the most informal colloquial and everyday English. In particular, the rhyme scheme, which demands regular full rhymes, is difficult to achieve in English without comic effects. The following lines describe Don Juan's first seduction:

And Julia's voice was lost, except in sighs,
Until too late for useful conversation;
The tears were gushing from her gentle eyes,
I wish, indeed, they had not had occasion,
But who, alas! can love, and then be wise?
Not that remorse did not oppose temptation;
A little still she strove, and much repented,
And whispering 'I will ne'er consent' – consented.

Don Juan is an adventure poem as well as an ongoing series of love stories. It begins with a shipwreck and continues by exploring the results that follow. Its essence is the restless, amorous adventures of a young Spaniard, but there are departures from the main plot line so that Byron, as narrator, can advance his own ideas on a range of subjects and can satirise many aspects of contemporary life and of his own contemporaries. Byron himself insisted that *Don Juan* is a satire on abuses of the present state of society but, in several places, judgement is passed upon many of the institutions and values of Western society. However, Byron's poetry cannot be properly compared with the Augustan satires of Dryden or Pope. He saw Pope as his main technical model, but his satires are not based on a vision of positive moral values. The character of Don Juan is a constant seeker of meaning rather than one who already knows the moral basis for his actions. He is not a complete anti-hero; but neither is his quest wholly heroic. Byron's own view of his hero is ironic in places, as in the following instance:

He pored upon the leaves, and on the flowers,
And heard a voice in all the winds; and then
He thought of wood-nymphs and immortal bowers,
And how the goddesses came down to men:
He missed the pathway, he forgot the hours,
And when he looked upon his watch again,
He found how much old Time had been a winner –
He also found that he had lost his dinner.

Here Juan is first described as a kind of mock Romantic poet (with perhaps a slight hint of Wordsworth and *Tintern Abbey*); the final two lines show his love of nature to be over-indulgent. He is brought comically down to earth in a sharp colloquial reminder which contrasts ironically with the more elevated language and topic at the beginning of the stanza.

Such sudden changes in style are common in Byron's poetry. Byron learned from the mock-heroic style of Pope and Dryden, and uses colloquial language widely (which the Augustans did not). In fact, although Wordsworth had advocated the use of the language of ordinary men, *Don Juan* contains more everyday language than *The Prelude* and *The Excursion* put together. The famous short lyric *So we'll go no more a-roving* (1817) shows how simple and heartfelt Byron can be:

So we'll go no more a-roving
So late into the night,
Though the heart be still as loving,
And the moon be still as bright.

For the sword outwears its sheath,
And the soul wears out the breast,
And the heart must pause to breathe,
And love itself have rest.

Though the night was made for loving,
And the day returns too soon,
Yet we'll go no more a-roving
By the light of the moon.

Byron also likes to play with his readers by following amusing and sometimes trivial digressions. In this respect, he is similar to the eighteenth-century novelist, Laurence Sterne. He invites his readers to participate in his poetry, to laugh with him at his heroes and to question their own values. In these lines from *Don Juan*, he warns his readers that the love affair between Juan and Haidée is unlawful and dangerous because they are not married.

> Then if you'd have them wedded, please to shut
> The book which treats of this erroneous pair,
> Before the consequences grow too awful;
> 'Tis dangerous to read of loves unlawful.

Don Juan was judged an immoral poem by many of Byron's contemporaries but it is never clear how far this is a judgement on Byron himself, who scandalised society with a series of well-publicised affairs and who seemed compelled to try forbidden experiences: society's contempt for his incestuous relationship with his half-sister Augusta Leigh led Byron to leave England forever in 1816. As a Lord, he held an unconventional liberal (Whig) view of society, supporting Catholic emancipation and the Nottingham weavers, who were made unemployed as a result of new technology in the industry.

Don Juan begins with the narrator saying 'I need a hero'. The need to identify with heroic struggle, to map out a heroic quest and to push one's self to the limits of heroism is an aspect of Romanticism which remained with Byron throughout his life. Byron died at the age of 36, fighting on the side of the Greeks in their war for independence from Turkey.

Robert Southey was one of the most prolific of all writers of the Romantic period. A great friend of Coleridge, they collaborated while at Oxford University, and shared many idealistic enthusiasms, which disappeared in Southey's later works. His poems from the late 1790s contain some famous ballads, such as *The Inchcape Rock*, and echo the aim of *Lyrical Ballads* to break away from eighteenth-century poetic constraints. Although he became Poet Laureate and remained one of the Lake Poets, living in the Lake District near Wordsworth, Southey devoted his later career more to history and biography than to poetry.

He attacked Byron in the Preface to *A Vision of Judgement*, and as a result Byron wrote a parody called *The Vision of Judgement* a year later, in 1822. It is ironically for this, and for the many mocking mentions of Southey in Byron's *Don Juan*, that the Poet Laureate of the Romantic period from 1813 is largely remembered rather than for the early poems which brought him fame.

CLARE

I am – yet what I am none cares or knows
(John Clare, *I Am*)

The poetry of John Clare is sometimes studied alongside the Romantic poets. It is also sometimes studied as Victorian poetry, since Clare wrote major poetry until his death in 1864. Clare's poetry is, however, difficult to categorise, in more ways than one. Like Blake, he was largely neglected during his lifetime. Like Burns, he is a genuine peasant poet in that he was inspired by the ballads and folk-songs of rural labourers. (His father was a thresher and ballad singer who knew over a hundred songs.) He is a nature poet but his poetry is different from other Romantic poets. Clare knew the world of nature from direct experience; his observations are as much those of a naturalist as they are of a poet. He also witnessed at first hand the rapid break-up of the traditional agricultural world in the first decades of the nineteenth century, mainly as a result of the enclosure movement. John Clare could make a living neither as a farm worker nor as a poet.

Clare's poetry stresses the spoken voice, with intimate rhythms and, often, local dialect words. It registers unique feelings in distinctive tones. The feelings are usually of sadness, regret, and of love lost. Nature is accurately recorded but the poet is always self-conscious and aware of his own position:

> Brown are the flags and fading sedge
> And tanned the meadow plains
> Bright yellow is the osier hedge
> Beside the brimming drains
> The crows sit on the willow tree
> The lake is full below
> But still the dullest thing I see
> Is self that wanders slow
> (*Child Harold*)

Clare's awareness of his self and identity, most apparent in poems such as *Remembrances* and *I Am*, was acute, but always conscious that the 'I' is fragile and easily broken. In this respect Clare's *I Am* compares well with Keats's poem *When I have fears that I may cease to be* in its emphasis on solitude and desolation (see page 238). It may have contributed to the madness of his later years, as he took longer and more detailed journeys between external nature and internal landscapes of the mind.

The metaphor of the journey or quest is central to Romantic poetry. Literally, the journey for some Romantic poets meant leaving England in search of new experiences and radical social or political causes. In their poetry, the journey is an interior one. Poems of epic length explore the growth and development of the self. Lyrics show a search for identity and a genuine spiritual home. There is a close relationship between the poem and the poet's own personal circumstances, but there is almost always something heroic about the journey, and in the longer poems the reader is invited to identify with the hero as he moves through various crises and stages of growth. The poem then becomes a form of spiritual autobiography.

ROMANTIC PROSE

In prose, too, these years saw parallel growth, particularly in the form of personal essays and autobiographies. Charles Lamb and William Hazlitt wrote a large number of letters and essays on a range of topics, literary and otherwise, and in the process established the importance of the literary form of critical essay which came to particular prominence in Coleridge's *Biographia Literaria*. Some prose works were personal confessions, the most famous of which was Thomas De Quincey's *Confessions of an English Opium Eater*. This is an autobiographical account of his opium addition. In *Confessions* he penetrates the depths of his own subconscious world, describing the simultaneously nightmarish and ecstatic experience with great precision and lyrical intensity. Opium provided the Romantic writer with a starting point for a further journey of the imagination into extreme feelings and experiences.

> Oh! just, subtle, and mighty opium! that to the hearts of poor and rich alike, for the wounds that will never heal, and for 'the pangs that

tempt the spirit to rebel,' bringest an assuaging balm; eloquent opium! that with thy potent rhetoric stealest away the purposes of wrath ... and 'from the anarchy of dreaming sleep,' callest into sunny light the faces of long-buried beauties, and the blessed household countenances, cleansed from the 'dishonours of the grave.' Thou only givest these gifts to man; and thou hast the keys of Paradise, oh, just, subtle, and mighty opium!

De Quincey, Lamb, Leigh Hunt, Hazlitt and other writers revolutionised the form of the essay and gave it a new literary impetus. Like the Romantic poets, the essayists rebelled against eighteenth-century conventions. They developed new styles and wrote on a wider range of topics. Instead of describing the leisure pursuits of the upper and middle classes, these essayists wrote about the lives of clerks, chimneysweeps and prize-fighters. Instead of an elaborate formal style, they developed looser, more subjective and impressionistic uses of language, giving each essay their own personal stamp. Like the Romantic poets, the essayists of the Romantic period put their own responses to experience at the very centre of their work.

> The poet is far from dealing only with these subtle and analogical truths. Truth of every kind belongs to him, provided it can bud into any kind of beauty, or is capable of being illustrated and impressed by the poetic faculty. Nay, the simplest truth is often so beautiful and impressive of itself, that one of the greatest proofs of his genius consists in his leaving it to stand alone, illustrated by nothing but the light of its own tears or smiles, its own wonder, might, or playfulness.
>
> (Leigh Hunt, *What Is Poetry?*, 1844)

> No young man believes he shall ever die. It was a saying of my brother's, and a fine one. There is a feeling of Eternity in youth, which makes us amends for every thing. To be young is to be as one of the Immortal Gods. One half of time indeed is flown – the other half remains in store for us with all its countless treasures; for there is no line drawn, and we see no limit to our hopes and wishes. We make the coming age our own.
>
> (William Hazlitt, *On the Feeling of Immortality in Youth*, 1850)

Thomas Love Peacock was a friend of Shelley's as early as 1812, although his final work was published almost fifty years after that. He spans the Romantic and Victorian ages and was deeply involved in the issues of both periods. His poetry is now neglected, although *Rhododaphne* (1818) is one of the most significant longer poems of the lesser-known Romantic poets, and worthy of rediscovery. Peacock's reputation rests on his novels of ideas expressed in conversation – and he deserves recognition as an original contributor for the way he introduces the characters and issues of the time into his works: for example, in *Nightmare Abbey* (1818) Coleridge, Byron and Shelley are satirised, their works, attitudes and life-styles criticised, and the 'morbidities' of modern literature comically questioned. Perhaps surprisingly, Shelley was full of praise for the book.

Peacock worked for many years in the East India Company and at the end of his career returned to his preferred genre of the satirical novel of ideas and conversation – the novel as commentary on the times – in *Gryll Grange* (1860–61), where a collection of characters debate such themes as schools for all, the boring nature of lectures, and the faithfulness of wives.

> I'm afraid we live in a world of misnomers and of a worse kind than this. In my little experience I have found that a gang of swindling bankers is a respectable old firm; that men who sell their votes to the highest bidder, and want only 'the protection of the ballot' to see the promise of them to both parties, are a free and independent constituency; that a man who successfully betrays everybody that trusts him, and abandons every principle he ever professed, is a great statesman, and a Conservative, forsooth, a *nil conservando*; that schemes for breeding pestilence are sanitary improvements; that the test of intellectual capacity is in swallow, and not in digestion; that the art of teaching everything, except what will be of use to the recipient, is national education; and that a change for the worse is reform.

By this time, Peacock's thinking was almost self-consciously old-fashioned: he enjoyed being a Tory reactionary, and something of a parody of himself. But Peacock's questioning throughout his career touches on vital issues; his essay *The Four Ages of Poetry* (1820) can be seen in many ways to have been the spark which inspired Shelley to write his *A Defence of Poetry*.

Peacock's novels are unusual in making the form a mixture of genres, from sub-Gothic to semi-pastoral, with the essential element of conversation, which occasionally develops into an early kind of stream of consciousness. As such, they have an urbanity of ideas and stylish refinement of debate that remain almost unique in the English novel. Recent critical revaluation has given Peacock a major role as an influence on the ideas of the Romantic poets.

The Romantic journey was usually a solitary one. Although the Romantic poets were closely connected with one another, and some collaborated in their work, they each had a strong individual vision. Romantic poets could not continue their quests for long or sustain their vision into later life. The power of the imagination and of inspiration did not last. Whereas earlier poets had patrons who financed their writing, the tradition of patronage was not extensive in the Romantic period and poets often lacked financial and other support. Keats, Shelley and Byron all died in solitary exile from England at a young age, their work left incomplete, non-conformists to the end. This coincides with the characteristic Romantic images of the solitary heroic individual, the spiritual outcast 'alone, alone, all, all alone' like Coleridge's Ancient Mariner and John Clare's 'I'; like Shelley's Alastor, Keats's Endymion, or Byron's Manfred, who reached beyond the normal social codes and normal human limits so that 'his aspirations/ Have been beyond the dwellers of the earth'. Wordsworth, who lived to be an old man, wrote poems throughout his life in which his poetic vision is stimulated by a single figure or object set against a natural background. Even his projected final masterpiece was entitled *The Recluse*. The solitary journey of the Romantic poet was taken up by many Victorian and twentieth-century poets, becoming almost an emblem of the individual's search for identity in an ever more confused and confusing world.

By the mid-1820s the high point of Romanticism in England had passed. The hopes and ideals expressed by Wordsworth in the first decade of the nineteenth century grew weaker. Wordsworth himself constantly revised his poems, in an effort to capture the poetic and idealistic intensity of his youth. He wrote more and more in regretful memory of lost opportunities.

The roots of European Romanticism lie much more in political and philosophical ideas and there the Romantic movement was influential in all spheres of society, not only in artistic circles. By contrast, the political involvements of Wordsworth and, more directly, Shelley and Byron, appear amateurish and more concerned with heroic gestures than with long-term political commitment. European Romanticism continued through the 1830s and 1840s, reaching into another age of revolutions which began in 1848. The political instabilities in Europe contrasted with the more stable climate in England where the movements for political reform were much more gradual.

THE NOVEL IN THE ROMANTIC PERIOD

Oh! it is only a novel!
(Jane Austen, *Northanger Abbey*)

Romantic poetry can be easily labelled, while it could be argued that there is no such thing as 'the Romantic novel'. During the eighteenth century, the novel had evolved into a wide-ranging genre. In the forty or so years after the French Revolution in 1789, novelists brought new themes, new approaches to the novel; and, in doing so, they raised it from the inferior level of critical esteem – 'only a novel', as one of Jane Austen's characters puts it – to the most significant, most popular, and most highly regarded genre of literary expression.

The intellectual climate of the time is reflected in the wide range of issues, themes, and settings which the novel was now beginning to encompass: high-class society contrasts with the primitive; national concerns with regional; male points of view with female; present with past, as more and more new subjects become the raw material for fiction.

William Godwin's *Caleb Williams* (1794), subtitled *Things As They Are*, is a novel of propaganda, but it contains elements of crime, detection, pursuit, and punishment which are remarkably innovative. It is one of the first novels to give a psychological portrait of character at the same time as illustrating conflicts of political ideals and beliefs.

The subtitle of *Hermsprong* (1796) by Robert Bage, *Man As He Is Not*, and the title of his *Man As He Is* (1792), echo Godwin's subtitle and show a similar concern to examine views and values in what can be seen as a more 'truthful', realistic way. The 'truth' in this case is found, as with much of Romantic poetry, in a return to nature. *Hermsprong* is the novel which, more than any other, makes its hero a 'natural' man – a primitive, brought up by American Indians without the constrictions of civilised religion, morality, and ethics. It thus becomes a satire on the values which Hermsprong finds in the civilised society to which he returns. Many views – for example on social class and privilege, and on equality for women – are aired in ways which are critical of conventional English society.

> 'It should seem,' Mr Hermsprong said, 'that Nature, in her more simple modes, is unable to furnish a rich European with a due portion of pleasurable sensations. He is obliged to have recourse to masses of inert matter, which he causes to be converted into a million of forms, far the greatest part solely to feed that incurable craving known by the name of vanity. All the arts are employed to amuse him, and expel the *taedium vitae*, acquired by the stimulus of pleasure being used till it will stimulate no more; and all the arts are insufficient. Of this disease, with which you are here so terribly afflicted, the native Americans know nothing. When war and hunting no more require their exertions, they can rest in peace. After satisfying the more immediate wants of nature, they dance, they play; – weary of this, they bask in the sun and sing. If enjoyment of existence be happiness, they seem to possess it; not indeed so high raised as yours sometimes, but more continued and more uninterrupted.'

Equality, and rights for women, had been the subject of discussion among educated women for several decades. In 1792, these views reached their most noted expression in Mary Wollstonecraft's *A Vindication of the Rights of Woman*, a work which was to have a lasting impact on future women thinkers and writers.

> Probably the prevailing opinion that woman was created for man, may have taken its rise from Moses' poetical story; yet as very few, it is presumed, who have bestowed any serious thought on the subject ever supposed that Eve was, literally speaking, one of Adam's ribs, the deduction must be allowed to fall to the ground, or only to be so far admitted as it proves that man, from the remotest antiquity, found it convenient to exert his strength to subjugate his companion, and his invention to show that she ought to have her neck bent

under the yoke, because the whole creation was only created for his convenience or pleasure.

The novels read by most women of the 1790s were more likely to be by Frances (Fanny) Burney or Clara Reeve than to be Mary Wollstonecraft's *Mary* (1788), or *St Leon* (1799) by her husband, William Godwin, in which she was portrayed after her death in childbirth. The daughter, also called Mary, was to become a novelist herself, and the wife of another Radical figure and Romantic poet, Percy Bysshe Shelley.

Frances Burney's novels, from *Evelina* (1778) through *Cecilia* (1782) to *Camilla* (1796), are novels of how a young woman grows up and develops as she enters and experiences the society of her day. The tone is gently satirical, with vivid observation, continuing in the vein which Eliza Haywood had exemplified in the mid-eighteenth century. Society, and aspirations to be part of it, are the main concerns in Burney's novels. The only female novelist who shared Robert Bage's concern with 'primitive' values was, not surprisingly, a friend of William Godwin's, Elizabeth Inchbald. Her *A Simple Story* (1791) and *Nature and Art* (1796) stress 'a proper education', and the bad effects of civilisation, but in a tone that is more romantic than polemical.

JANE AUSTEN

Three or four families in a Country Village is the very thing to work on

(Jane Austen, Letters)

Jane Austen is quite different from any novelist before her, and an important part of the difference is that for many years she was not consciously writing for publication. Female writers were not unusual: indeed, many of the most notable writers of the thirty or so years before Austen were women – Clare Reeve, Elizabeth Inchbald, and Frances Burney in particular.

In Austen's own time, Maria Edgeworth established herself very significantly as a writer of small-scale, so-called 'provincial' novels, set in Ireland, at the time when the Act of Union (1801) brought Ireland fully into the United Kingdom, in both a political and legal sense. Her *Castle Rackrent* (1800) is particularly significant, both as a regional novel and as an evocation of history, being set 'before the year 1782'.

> Then we were all bustle in the house, which made me keep out of the way, for I walk slow and hate a bustle, but the house was all hurry-skurry, preparing for my new master. – Sir Murtagh, I forgot to notice, had no childer, so the Rackrent estate went to his younger brother – a young dashing officer – who came amongst us before I knew for the life of me whereabouts I was, in a gig or some of them things, with another spark along with him, and led horses, and servants, and dogs, and scarce a place to put any Christian of them into; for my late lady had sent all the feather-beds off before her, and blankets, and household linen, down to the very knife cloths, on the cars to Dublin, which were all her own, lawfully paid for out of her own money. – So the house was quite bare, and my young master, the moment ever he set foot in it out of his gig, thought all those things must come of themselves, I believe, for he never looked after any thing at all, but harum-scarum called for every thing as if we were conjurers, or he in a public-house. For my part, I could not bestir myself any how; I had been so used to my late master and mistress, all was upside down with me, and the new servants in the servants' hall were quite out of my way; I had nobody to talk to, and if it had not been for my pipe and tobacco should, I verily believe, have broke my heart for poor Sir Murtagh.

'The great Maria', as she came to be called, was one of the best-known literary figures of her time, writing several more novels about Irish society, such as *The Absentee* (1812), and many books for children. But her reputation did not last long; and Jane Austen soon came to be regarded as the greatest woman writer of her time.

What Jane Austen did – and no author before her had attempted it so successfully – was to apply the techniques of the novel to the acute observation of society in microcosm: 'three of four families in a Country Village' was 'the little bit (two Inches wide) of Ivory on which I work,' she wrote in her letters. That her intentions were not small-scale, however, is clear from her next words – 'so fine a brush, as produces little effect after much labour'.

Jane Austen deliberately avoids effect, exaggeration and excess. Going against the trend of the novels of her time, she applies the microscope to human character and motivation, with no great didactic, moral, or satiric purpose, but with a gentle irony and perspicacity which make her novels unique, as representations of universal patterns of behaviour, and as documentation of an aspect of the provincial society of her time.

It was a time of war: and, in the history of the novel, it was the time when the Gothic novel was at its most popular. War is only touched upon slightly (for instance, the Battle of Trafalgar in 1805 is mentioned in *Persuasion*) but novels and reading are quite significant in Austen's writing, especially *Northanger Abbey*.

Jane Austen was already writing in the early 1790s, as the debates raged on Radicalism, women's rights, and primitivism. The first versions of the novels now known as *Sense and Sensibility* and *Pride and Prejudice* probably date from 1795–97; after several failed attempts, it was *Sense and Sensibility* which was her first novel to be published, in 1811, and this gave her the impetus, in the last few years of her life, to revise her earlier work and start writing again after a gap of some three or four years.

Northanger Abbey was probably the first of Jane Austen's novels to be completed, around 1798. It was actually sold to a publisher in 1803, but was only published, with the late novel *Persuasion*, in 1818, the year after the writer's death. *Northanger Abbey* gently satirises the 1790s enthusiasm for the Gothic novel, by contrasting day-to-day life with the imagined horrors of Ann Radcliffe's work, which have had a considerable effect on the impressionable heroine, Catherine Morland. The author's distanced, slightly ironic observation of the heroine, and of the love intrigues in fashionable Bath, already displays the tone and the point of view which Austen was to refine in her later works, which are less obviously intended to ridicule and more concerned with acute depiction of character and interaction.

She continues to focus on young heroines: the contrasting Elinor (sense and self-control) and Marianne (sensibility and impulsiveness) in *Sense and Sensibility*; Elizabeth Bennet in *Pride and Prejudice*; Fanny Price in *Mansfield Park*; Emma in the novel that bears her name; and Anne Elliot in *Persuasion*. Sisters are often contrasted, and the closely worked out plots usually involve the twists and turns of emotion in the search for love, marriage, happiness and social status.

Where other writers had used the novel to create fictional models, to give moral examples, to ridicule manners and morals, to describe real or imagined worlds and ways of life, Jane Austen's achievement was to create in each novel a fully realised and populated world, strictly limited in scope, such that the reader can observe – without being made to judge – a group of characters whose emotions are recognisable, whose faults are human, whose traits are familiar. The 'issues' may seem small-scale, when compared to the wars being waged outside the limits of the village; but it is precisely the universality of the characters' preoccupations that makes these issues, and their expression, attractive in a lasting way to a great many readers.

When discussing Jane Austen's work, critics tend to speak of her delicacy and irony, her femininity and her lack of ambition and scope. This is to undervalue her and to prettify a group of novels which are considerably more than 'novels . . . about the gentry and addressed to the gentry'. Neither should she be seen as 'typical' of her age: the major artist is probably the least typical representative of any age. But Austen shows 'the form and pressure of the time' on a society which was undergoing many radical changes; the questions her characters face, 'anti-Jacobin' though their conclusions may be, are just as significant as the questions of social class and Irish identity examined by Maria Edgeworth, the pursuit of truth in Godwin, and the anti-aristocratic satire of Bage. Jane Austen too criticises the 'gentry': her characters stage an 'anarchic' play in *Mansfield Park* (a play, incidentally, by Elizabeth Inchbald); she portrays an older order of values that is changing, at a time when the gap between the gentry and the poor is widening. Her young female characters, in search of the best prospect for marriage, end up marrying a country clergyman or a landed gentleman. Only Anne Elliot breaks with this 'Cinderella' tradition (which, for example, is the mainstay of Frances Burney's novels) by marrying a sailor. But the choices, the options, are indicative: what Jane Austen emphasises is community in microcosm, the search for order in a world beset by chaos, threatened on all sides, not only by war, or class division, but by such human fears as loneliness, uncertainty and failure.

LANGUAGE NOTE
Jane Austen's English

Jane Austen and the Romantic writers of the early nineteenth century write in an English which is recognisably a modern variety. Shakespeare and Chaucer can be read but most will need to have recourse to an etymological dictionary or to an editor's footnotes to help in understanding the words and idioms which are no longer part of the contemporary language or which have meanings which are far removed from those established for the words today. The novels of Jane Austen, the writings of Peacock or Hazlitt, or the poetry of Wordsworth can normally be read without any such reference to dictionaries or special editions.

Such a position is broadly true, but it should not deceive us into thinking that the language has not changed at all during the course of the past two hundred years. There are some subtle differences in the English used by Jane Austen when it is compared, for example, with the present-day language. When, on the second page of Jane Austen's *Mansfield Park*, we read the following sentence, we might note that 'injury' (upset/hurt), 'comprehended' (included) and 'intercourse' (communication) are words with changed meanings in contemporary English:

> Mrs Price in her turn was injured and angry; and an answer which comprehended each sister in its bitterness, and bestowed such very disrespectful reflections on the pride of Sir Thomas, as Mrs Norris could not possibly keep to herself, put an end to all intercourse between them for a considerable period.

As further illustration, the following words, phrases and structures are all extracted from Jane Austen's novels with 'translations' provided in brackets.

> Three or four officers were **lounging** together. [walking/strolling]
> She made her first **essay**. [attempt]
> Suppose you **speak for** tea. [order]
> She must know herself too secure of the **regard** of all the rest of you. [affection]
> For a day or two after the affront was given, Henry Crawford has endeavoured to **do it away** by the usual attack of gallantry and **compliment**. [remove/pass it off] [flattery]
> So you **are come** at last. [have come]

Most writers of the Romantic period engage deeply in an ideological conflict between the past and the future. In many cases, the past wins – in Wordsworth and Scott, most notably. In her settling of plot in the future of marriage, Jane Austen is not succumbing to an ethos of the past, but is endeavouring to confront the realities of a difficult future, without taking recourse to the falsity of a comfortable happy ending.

SCOTT

Where Jane Austen deliberately limited her area of concern, Walter Scott opened up the novel to the full panorama of revolution, dissent, rebellion and social change. Having written verse romances with great success for several years, he published his first novel only in 1814, at the very end of the Napoleonic wars when Britain was triumphant. And, equally significantly, the settings of his novels are in the past, rather than the immediate and highly troubled present.

After the Napoleonic wars, Britain entered a time of severe social unrest, of high unemployment, of widening gaps between rich and poor, employers and workers, upper, middle and lower classes. These contemporary concerns, vividly espoused by writers from the poet Shelley to the social campaigner William Cobbett, are absent from Scott's work.

Scott does, however, use the historical framework of his novels to give a detailed portrait of turmoil. Most of the early Waverley novels, from *Waverley* (1814) to *The Bride of Lammermoor* (1819), are set in times of revolution and rebellion. There is an old-fashioned code of chivalry, which is fundamentally undermined, as the individual comes to terms with the changes in his world. By the end, most of Scott's heroes or heroines have lived through traumatic times, close to what Britain had recently emerged from; and they have resolved *not* to be heroes. The system, the whole mechanism of society, the forces of history, are all greater than any individual, no matter how idealistic or heroic his aspirations. This leads to a kind of accommodation with history, which has given rise to the definition of the historical novel as 'the epic of a world forsaken by God'. Scott alludes to Byron's 'sublime and beautiful' in his description of landscape in *The Monastery* (1820):

The scene could neither be strictly termed sublime nor beautiful and scarcely even picturesque or striking. But its extreme solitude pressed on the heart; the traveller felt that uncertainty whither he was going, or in what so wild a path he was to terminate which, at times, strikes more on the imagination than the grand features of a show scene, when you know the exact distance of the inn where your dinner is bespoke and at the moment preparing. These are ideas, however, of a far later age, for at the time we treat of, the picturesque, the beautiful, the sublime, and all their intermediate shades, were ideas absolutely unknown to the inhabitants and occasional visitors to Glendearg.

Scott's return to history takes in many periods, from the Jacobite rebellion of 1745 in *Waverley* (1814) to the twelfth-century Crusades in *The Talisman* (1825), from the clash between Saxon and Norman in *Ivanhoe* (1819) to the time of Mary, Queen of Scots in *The Abbott* (1820), and on to the Porteous riots in Edinburgh in 1736 in *The Heart of Midlothian* (1818), which has been seen as the most successful of the novels. *Ivanhoe* is, with *Rob Roy* (1817), probably the best known of Scott's novels, with Robin Hood and King Richard the Lionheart among its characters. The appearance of Ivanhoe himself at Ashby-de-la-Zouch is memorable:

As the Saracenic music of the challengers concluded one of those long and high flourishes with which they had broken the silence of the lists, it was answered by a solitary trumpet, which breathed a note of defiance from the northern extremity. All eyes were turned to see the new champion which these sounds announced, and no sooner were the barriers opened than he paced into the lists. As far as could be judged of a man sheathed in armour, the new adventurer did not greatly exceed the middle size, and seemed to be rather slender than strongly made. His suit of armour was formed of steel, richly inlaid with gold, and the device on his shield was a young oak-tree pulled up by the roots, with the Spanish word *Desdichado*, signifying Disinherited. He was mounted on a gallant black horse, and as he passed through the lists he gracefully saluted the Prince and ladies by lowering his lance. The dexterity with which he managed his steed, and something of the youthful grace which he displayed in his manner, won him the favour of the multitude, which some of the lower classes expressed by calling out, 'Touch Ralph de Vipont's shield –

touch the Hospitaller's shield; he has the least sure seat, he is your cheapest bargain.'

The champion, moving onward amid these well-meant hints, ascended the platform by the sloping alley, which led to it from the lists, and, to the astonishment of all present, riding straight up to the central pavilion, struck with the sharp end of his spear the shield of Brian de Bois-Guilbert until it rung again. All stood astonished at his presumption, but none more than the redoubted Knight whom he had thus defied to mortal combat, and who, little expecting so rude a challenge, was standing carelessly at the door of the pavilion.

In *The Heart of Midlothian*, the heroine Jeanie Deans has gone to London to ask for mercy for her sister Effie who has been condemned to death. Here she talks to the Queen, in the presence of the Duke of Argyle:

the Duke made a signal for Jeanie to advance from the spot where she had hitherto remained watching countenances, which were too long accustomed to suppress all apparent signs of emotion, to convey to her any interesting intelligence. Her Majesty could not help smiling at the awe-struck manner in which the quiet demure figure of the little Scotchwoman advanced towards her, and yet more at the first sound of her broad northern accent. But Jeanie had a voice low and sweetly toned, an admirable thing in woman, and eke besought 'her Leddyship to have pity on a poor misguided young creature,' in tones so affecting, that, like the notes of some of her native songs, provincial vulgarity was lost in pathos.

'Stand up, young woman,' said the Queen, but in a kind tone, 'and tell me what sort of a barbarous people your countryfolk are, where child-murder is become so commonplace as to require the restraint of laws like yours?'

'If your Leddyship pleases,' answered Jeanie, 'there are mony places beside Scotland where mothers are unkind to their ain flesh and blood.'

It must be observed, that the disputes between George the Second, and Frederick, Prince of Wales, were then at the highest, and that the good-natured part of the public laid the blame on the Queen. She coloured highly, and darted a glance of a most penetrating character first at Jeanie, and then at the Duke. Both sustained it unmoved; Jeanie from total unconsciousness of the offence she had given, and the Duke from his habitual composure. But in his heart he thought, My unlucky protegee has, with this luckless answer, shot dead, by a kind of chance-medley, her only hope of success.

Scott acknowledged his debt to Maria Edgeworth, but what he himself did with the historical novel as a form was to have an influence on European and world literature which went far beyond the use of regional setting and historical reconstruction. In effect, Scott rewrote history, re-creating for the nineteenth century the real historical figures and bringing them to life in the turmoil of their times, fictionalising history and historicising fiction until the two became almost inextricably linked in the minds of his readers. He moves from the mediaeval ethos of chivalry into an accommodation with the historically determined mercantile ethos of modern times. In an *Essay on Chivalry* (1818), he writes:

> As the progress of knowledge advanced, men learned to despise its fantastic refinements; the really enlightened undervaluing them, as belonging to a system inapplicable to the modern state of the world. . . . The system of chivalry, as we have seen, had its peculiar advantages during the Middle Ages. . . . We can now only look back on it as a beautiful and fantastic piece of frostwork, which has dissolved in the beams of the sun!

Before he turned to the novel, Walter Scott was a hugely successful poet, writing highly original narrative poems such as *The Lay of the Last Minstrel* (1805) and *Marmion* (1808). There is something of the sense of loss and desolation of *Deor's Lament* (see page 7) in the minstrel's (Harper's) plight:

> Old times were changed, old manners gone;
> A stranger fill'd the Stuarts' throne;
> The bigots of the iron time
> Had call'd his harmless art a crime.
> A wandering Harper, scorn'd and poor,
> He begg'd his bread from door to door,
> And tuned, to please a peasant's ear,
> The harp a king had loved to hear.
> (Introduction to *The Lay of the Last Minstrel*)

Scott was also important as a collector of songs and ballads of the Borders, notably in *The Minstrelsy of the Scottish Border*, published in three volumes in 1802–3. He had translated Goethe, and was instrumental in setting up the *Quarterly Review*, the Tory response to the *Edinburgh Review*. Scott was therefore a major figure in the literary establishment when Byron began to attack his poetry – and then Byron began to be more popular than Scott in the genre of narrative poetry. After *Waverley*, Scott only wrote two more long poems, abandoning that form for the novel, which he brought to great popularity and to new levels of achievement.

Sir Walter Scott (he was knighted in 1820) published all his novels anonymously until 1827 – perhaps an indication of the low consideration the novel still had until his own worldwide success. He was the first hugely popular, international bestselling author, reaching vast numbers of readers in many languages, paying off huge debts in his final years through the success of his writing.

As a novelist, Scott's influence was immense: his creation of a wide range of characters from all levels of society was immediately likened to Shakespeare's; the use of historical settings became a mainstay of Victorian and later fiction; his short stories helped initiate that form; his antiquarian researches and collections were a major contribution to the culture of Scotland.

Yet in the twentieth century Scott's reputation drastically declined. This was perhaps due to the fact that the late Victorian writers who used his works as a model and inspiration frequently surpassed his achievement. But he can now be seen to be a great original, almost inventing Scotland as a fictional setting, and illustrating, as only Shakespeare's history plays had before him, the place of the individual in the context of historic events. Historical necessity, the complex interaction of circumstance, character, and change in creating history, is made tangible in his writings. The novels of Scott gave the nineteenth-century world, and especially nineteenth-century Britain, its sense of historical identity. The novels seemed to affirm a chivalric ethos, the constant value of humanity, despite the turmoil of the world. Yet Scott did not affirm static values: his novels are all about movement, the fluctuations of fortune, the rise and fall of families and nations, the ambivalence of good and evil.

The Victorian age perhaps read into Scott an affirmation of the clear-cut values they wanted to affirm in their own society. In many ways the Victorians wished to put times of crisis and upheaval behind them; but almost all Scott's novels are set in times of crisis, and his characters inevitably have to take sides, and make moral decisions. The French novelist George Sand described Scott as 'the poet of the peasant, soldier, outlaw, and artisan'. In introducing the transforming power of history, and its effects on every character's life, Scott transformed the very nature, the scope, and the future of the novel.

FROM GOTHIC TO *FRANKENSTEIN*

Mary Shelley, wife of Percy Bysshe Shelley, is best known as the author of *Frankenstein* (1818). Mary Shelley's father, William Godwin, was a radical political philosopher and her mother, Mary Wollstonecraft, was also a radical writer, responsible for the famous work *A Vindication of the Rights of Woman*, published in 1792. *Frankenstein* is a Gothic horror story in the tradition established in the late eighteenth century by Ann Radcliffe, William Beckford and Horace Walpole (see page 209). The story concerns the creation by Frankenstein, an idealistic scientist, of a living creature from the bones of the dead. Frankenstein believes he has found the secret of creating life, but his creation turns out to be a destructive monster which no one, not even Frankenstein, can control. *Frankenstein*, together with other novels by Mary Shelley such as the futuristic *The Last Man* (1826), *Caleb Williams* by her father William Godwin (1794), C.R. Maturin's *Melmoth the Wanderer* (1820) and James Hogg's *The Private Memoirs and Confessions of a Justified Sinner* (1824), continued the Gothic traditions established at the end of the eighteenth century. The importance of this tradition is underscored by the way in which it is satirised in novels in the Romantic period, such as Austen's *Northanger Abbey* and Peacock's *Nightmare Abbey* and later *Gryll Grange*.

In the context of the Romantic period of literature, 'Gothic' writers are central insofar as they continue a tradition which challenges the emphasis on reason, control and order which characterises early eighteenth-century literature. Gothic novels such as *Frankenstein* explore the deepest recesses of human psychology, always stressing the macabre, the unusual and the fantastic and preferring the realities of the subjective imagination. *Frankenstein* underlines a shift in sensibility and a movement towards the uncanny, the marvellous, the rationally uncontrollable and the psychologically disjunctive. Such a shift also has political repercussions in that the worlds depicted represent a clear challenge to the existing order and to rational modes of thought and of social organisation. The Gothic novels of the Romantic period were to exert a considerable influence on the novels of the nineteenth century. Novels by Dickens and the Brontës, the romances of R.L. Stevenson, Bram Stoker's *Dracula,* the 'fantastic' science fiction of H.G. Wells, the melodramas of Victorian fiction and drama were all to be a part of a continuing exploration of increasingly mainstream 'Gothic' themes and preoccupations.

The Gothic is a subversive tradition in writing (as well as in modern film), though it should never be forgotten that it attracts and continues to attract a wide and popular audience. In the Victorian period, Sheridan Le Fanu and Wilkie Collins, in particular, emerged as bestsellers of novels of the sinister and supernatural. In America in the nineteenth century the works of Edgar Allan Poe derive substantially from these roots. In the Modern period this tradition of the Romantic Gothic novel has continued with British English writers such as Emma Tennant and Angela Carter.

THE SCOTTISH REGIONAL NOVEL

After the Scottish Enlightenment of the early to mid-eighteenth century, Edinburgh became a major publishing centre, and several of the most influential magazines of the nineteenth century were based there. Byron's famous attack on Walter Scott, *English Bards and Scottish Reviewers* (1809), is in part a satire on the *Edinburgh Review*, which was founded in 1802 (an earlier review with the same name had lasted two years in the mid-1750s) and became one of the most significant magazines of the century. Like its main rival *Blackwood's Magazine* (known as 'the Maga'), it published essays, articles, stories, and fiction by a great many of the leading figures of English literature of the time. *Blackwood's* was founded in 1817 as a Tory rival to the *Review*, which was Whig-oriented. The *Review* lasted until 1929, 'the Maga' until 1980.

After Maria Edgeworth, the regional novel began to flourish. Susan Ferrier's three novels of Scottish life – *Marriage* (1818), *The Inheritance* (1824) and *Destiny* (1831) – contain the acute social observation of Austen, but with rather more didactic intent.

John Galt's *The Ayrshire Legatees* and *Annals of the Parish* (both 1821) use the small-town setting to underscore the humour of social pretentions. *The Provost* and *The Entail* (both 1822) expand Galt's range, bringing themes of power, the abuse of power, and greed to significantly new expression. *The Provost* uses a self-revealing first-person narration to create a complete picture of the manipulations of Mr Pawkie, the small-town politician.

> I have had occasion to observe in the course of my experience, that there is not a greater mollifier of the temper and nature of man than a constant flowing in of success and prosperity. From the time that I had been Dean of Guild, I was sensible of a considerable increase of my worldly means and substance; and although Bailie M'Lucre played me a soople trick at the election, by the inordinate sale and roup of his potatoe-rig, the which tried me, as I do confess, and nettled me with disappointment; yet things, in other respects, went so well with me, that about the eighty-eight, I began to put forth my hand again into public affairs, endowed both with more vigour and activity than it was in the period of my magisterial functions.

The Entail is a portrait of a selfish obsession with inheritance and property, and the tragic consequences for an entire family. These two novels are forerunners of many works on similar themes in later English and European literature: Galt's influence is less obvious than Scott's, but it can be seen in the themes of many French and Russian novelists later in the century.

Galt's parochial, small-town novels show a quite different Scotland from that of the Edinburgh of the eighteenth century. That was the time of the Scottish Enlightenment, when Edinburgh was one of the intellectual capitals of Europe, with the philosopher David Hume as one of its leading lights. The economic theorist Adam Smith, a close friend of Hume's, was professor of logic and moral philosophy in Glasgow, the country's trade and business capital.

After Scott, in particular, and after the Romantic writings of Ossian and the homely tones of Galt, the image of Scotland changed profoundly and, out of considerable diversity, a kind of national cultural identity was created. Perhaps the most significant single Scottish novel of the time was James Hogg's psychological study of what is now called a 'split personality' – *The Private Memoirs and Confessions of a Justified Sinner*, published in 1824. The fanatical narrator sees it as his mission to commit a series of murders, 'justified' because of his own faith and religious superiority. It is one of the earliest novels of 'a second self', anticipating Stevenson's *The Strange Case of Doctor Jekyll and Mister Hyde* by some sixty years, and is one of the strangest and most disturbing novels of the entire nineteenth century. Here, Hogg's narrator uses a kind of *alter ego* to kill his own brother:

> There was scarcely an hour in the day on which my resolves were not animated by my great friend, till at length I began to have a longing desire to kill my brother, in particular. Should any man ever read this scroll, he will wonder at this confession, and deem it savage and unnatural. So it appeared to me at first, but a constant thinking of an event changes every one of its features. I have done all for the best, and as I was prompted, by one who knew right and wrong much better than I did.

The nineteenth century

God's in his heaven —
All's right with the world!
(Robert Browning, *Pippa Passes*)

CONTEXTS AND CONDITIONS

The term 'Victorian age' is often used to cover the whole of the nineteenth century. Queen Victoria came to the throne in 1837, at a time when the monarchy as an institution was not particularly popular. But as the success of the nation reached its peak and then began to decline, the monarch assumed a greater and greater symbolic import-ance. Victoria, widowed in 1861, became Empress of India, and by her death in 1901 had come to represent the nation in a way which only Queen Elizabeth I had done in the past.

A history of the Victorian age records a period of economic expan-sion and rapid change. If change can be measured by change to the capital city of a country, then the history of the growth of London during this century is revealing. When Queen Victoria came to the throne, the population of London was about two million inhabitants; at her death in 1901, the population had increased to 6.5 million. The growth of London and of other major cities in Great Britain marked a final stage in the change from a way of life based on the land to a modern urban economy based on manufacturing, international trade and financial institutions.

Great Britain was one of the first countries of the world to indus-trialise, to establish markets and to reinvest the profits in further manufacturing developments. Britain became the centre of the new philosophy of Free Trade, of new technology and of continuing industrial inventions. The country became the workshop of the world, and from the 1870s onwards had become the world's banker. In a period of little more than sixty years of Queen Victoria's reign, the major invention of steam power was exploited for fast railways and ships, for printing presses, for industrial looms and for agricultural machinery. An efficient postal service was developed, the telephone invented and communications improved. The country of the United Kingdom, indeed the world as a whole, became a smaller place. One commentator remarked that 'we have been living, as it were, the life of three hundred years in thirty'. The age was characterised by optimism and a sense that everything would continue to expand and improve. Beneath the public optimism and positivism, however, the nineteenth century was also a century of paradoxes and uncertainties.

The contrast between social unrest, with related moves towards change, and the affirmation of values and standards which are still referred to as 'Victorian values', is an essential part of the paradox of the age. 'The Victorian compromise' is one way of seeing this dilemma. It implies a kind of double standard between national success and the exploitation of lower-class workers at home and of colonies overseas; a compromise between philanthropy and tolerance (the abolition of slavery, 1833; tolerance for Catholics, 1829) and repression (the punishment of the Tolpuddle Martyrs, 1834; the conditions of the poor).

The literature of the time reflects these concerns from the very beginning. The Jacobin novels of the 1790s had already outlined some areas of discontent. These novels had been suppressed, as also were the Romantic poets' political statements – such as Shelley's pamphlets on the Irish problem and the necessity of atheism. With the younger Romantic poets in exile after 1815, the government was still severely criticised: when riots by unemployed ex-soldiers and others were violently suppressed in 1819, the so-called 'Peterloo Massacre' became the subject of one of Shelley's most virulent satires.

The 1820s saw the deaths of Byron, Keats and Shelley, but they also saw the greatest success of Sir Walter Scott, whose influence on nineteenth-century literature worldwide was immense. Indeed, the

1820s and 1830s can be described as the era of the historical novel, with such followers of Scott as Edward Bulwer-Lytton (who wrote *The Last Days of Pompeii*, 1834) and Harrison Ainsworth commencing their careers at the same time as Benjamin Disraeli, who was later to become prime minister of Great Britain. The novel as a form became hugely popular and it was the novelists rather than the poets who became the literary representatives of the age.

It was Disraeli whose political novels give us one of the main 'labels' of the Victorian age. *The Two Nations* – i.e. the Rich and the Poor – was the subtitle of his novel *Sybil*, published in 1845. It underlines the fact that social concern and reform were sympathetic subjects for a novel many years before Disraeli himself actually implemented some of the reforms described. Thirty years after the Battle of Waterloo, the working-class Chartist movement was still considered too radical and dangerous to be tolerated. This movement arose directly as a result of the First Reform Bill of 1832, which, although it extended the franchise and gave more people the right to vote, excluded the working classes by its insistence on property ownership. It was not until 1918 that universal suffrage, the first claim of the Chartists, was reached in Britain. Even then, it was not until 1928 that the vote was given to all adult women.

There is thus a movement throughout the Victorian period towards democracy, as there was in the rest of Europe. But where mainland Europe suffered revolutions and political upheavals (1848 came to be called The Year of Revolutions), the British government kept a strong hold on power. Working-class movements, republican groups, trade unions and similar dissident expressions were contained as far as possible. In literature, however, such expression flourished.

DICKENS

The History of England is emphatically the history of progress

(Thomas Babington Macaulay, *Historical Essays*)

The life of Charles Dickens can be seen to mirror the intellectual patterns of the Victorian age, in which he became the dominant literary figure. He started his career as a journalist, and his first success came with *Sketches by Boz* (1836), the kind of light humorous writing which had been popular for more than a century. The extension of this form into the novel *The Pickwick Papers* (1836–37) established Dickens as a comic novelist in the eighteenth-century tradition represented by Smollett, whom he acknowledged as one of his masters. The vein of good-natured comedy, well-observed character, humorous use of class and dialect difference, and 'traditional' values will be found repeatedly in Dickens's work after *The Pickwick Papers*. *A Christmas Carol* (1843) is the high point of one of these trends, bringing together a touch of the Gothic, the clash between wealth and poverty, and the sentimental assertion of fireside and family values. This is the happy ending:

> 'God bless us every one!' said Tiny Tim, the last of all.

However, a more serious tone soon enters Dickens's works, as he begins to play on his readers' awareness of social problems and the growing conscience of the age. *Oliver Twist* (1837–38) highlighted the problems of poor city children who after the Poor Law Act of 1833 ended up in the workhouse, or at the mercy of crooks like Fagin and Bill Sykes. One of the most memorable images in the novel is when Oliver asks the workhouse master for more to eat:

> He rose from the table; and advancing to the master, basin and spoon in hand, said: somewhat alarmed at his own temerity: 'Please, Sir, I want some more.'

This is the city as portrayed in Blake's *London*, rather than Wordsworth's *Sonnet Composed Upon Westminster Bridge*. In many of Dickens's novels he portrays the diversity and disorder of the rapidly growing capital. The suffering of children continues in the Yorkshire schools described in *Nicholas Nickleby* (1838–39); money emerges as the main influence behind the action here, a role it continues to play in late novels of the century. Sentiment takes over in *The Old Curiosity Shop* (1840–41) with its heroine, Little Nell, the epitome of the helpless Victorian female victim. The death of Little Nell is the climax of the sentimental trend started by Henry Mackenzie in his novel *The Man of Feeling*. However, the change in taste between 1841 and the end of the century is wittily underlined in Oscar Wilde's comment on the lachrymose death scene: 'One must have a heart of stone to read the death of Little Nell without laughing.'

In the 1840s, Dickens described increasingly realistically the society of his time, but with a faith and optimism which reaches a climax in the semi-autobiographical *David Copperfield* (1849–50). Like all his works, it was published in serial form, building up a huge worldwide readership for each monthly issue. 'I like this the best,' said Dickens later of this novel, and indeed it marks the high point of the first phase of his writing – where the hero could achieve success, marry his (rather vapid) sweetheart Dora, and, after her death, the faithful Agnes, and where even the debt-ridden Mr Micawber achieves respectability. Dickens's plots and portrayals of character are regarded by some critics as melodramatic and sentimental, but his insights into human situations are frequently profound and always accessible. He remained a bestseller all his life, giving numerous public readings of his work, travelling widely, but at the same time putting great strain on his health.

Dickens's next novel (1852–53) begins to mark a change in sensibility and attitude. Even the title *Bleak House* reveals a negative feeling. Rain and fog come to represent the gloom that has settled over the characters. 'Lady Dedlock sat again looking at the rain': it is always raining in the heart of Lady Dedlock. The city of London, which had given hope and a future to Dickens's heroes Oliver Twist, Nicholas Nickleby, Paul Dombey (*Dombey and Son*, 1846–47), and David Copperfield, is shrouded in fog in the opening chapter of *Bleak House*. This might be read as a symbol of what was happening to Victorian optimism and self-confidence:

> Fog everywhere. Fog up the river, where it flows among green aits and meadows; fog down the river, where it rolls defiled among the tiers of shipping, and the waterside pollutions of a great (and dirty) city.

Dickens's scope expands greatly during the 1850s, from the concentration on the individual hero to examinations of society, the law, industrialism, trade unions, historical ideals (*A Tale of Two Cities*, 1859), and on to the re-examination of the semi-autobiographical concerns of *David Copperfield* in the ironically titled *Great Expectations* (1860–61).

Hard Times (1854), subtitled *For These Times*, is the most familiar of Dickens's 'state of the nation' novels, perhaps because it is one of his shortest. It contains a picture of the industrialised English Midlands which emphasises the dehumanising aspects of the Industrial Revolution: Jeremy Bentham's philosophy of utilitarianism – 'the greatest happiness of the greatest number' – is called into question. And education, one of Dickens's concerns throughout his life, finds a memorable embodiment in Mr Gradgrind, the educator who insists on 'Facts' at the expense of imagination:

> 'Now, what I want is, Facts. Teach these boys and girls nothing but Facts. Facts alone are wanted in life. Plant nothing else, and root out everything else. You can only form the minds of reasoning animals upon Facts: nothing else will ever be of any service to them. This is the principle on which I bring up my own children, and this is the principle on which I bring up these children. Stick to Facts, sir!'

Hard Times is actually one of the less rich and rewarding of Dickens's novels, but is in many ways his most accessible critique of the society he lived in.

Great Expectations marks a change from *David Copperfield*. Here the hero – bearing a close resemblance to Dickens himself – does not achieve the success and happiness which crowned the earlier novel. Disappointment and disillusionment dominate, with such memorable images as Miss Havisham, eternally ready for the marriage which will never happen:

> I saw that everything within my view which ought to be white had been white long ago, and had lost its lustre, and was faded and yellow. I saw that the bride within the bridal dress had withered like the dress, and like the flowers, and had no brightness left but the brightness of her sunken eyes. I saw that the dress had been put upon the rounded figure of a young woman, and that figure upon which it now hung loose, had shrunk to skin and bone.

Philip Pirrip is one of the first modern anti-heroes, a character whom life treats in a way readers would recognise as 'real', rather than romanticised. This echoes the American writer H.D. Thoreau's statement (in *Walden*, 1854) that 'the mass of men lead lives of quiet desperation'.

This despairing tone becomes the keynote of much literature in the later decades of the century.

The last decade of Dickens's own life produced only one major novel, *Our Mutual Friend* (1864–65) as well as the unfinished Gothic novel *The Mystery of Edwin Drood* (1870). In *Little Dorrit* (1855–57) and *Our Mutual Friend*, Dickens's disgust with the hypocrisies of Victorian society reached new heights of savage comic expression. Characters have comic names, but the evil characters of the early novels (Fagin in *Oliver Twist*, Quilp in *The Old Curiosity Shop*) have become more realistic, credible characters. Mr and Mrs Merdle, in *Little Dorrit*, anticipate a fixation with the worst elements of society:

> For by that time it was known that the late Mr Merdle's complaint had been simply Forgery and Robbery. He, the uncouth object of such wide-spread adulation, the sitter at great men's feasts, the roc's egg of great ladies' assemblies, the subduer of exclusiveness, the leveller of pride, the patron of patrons . . . he, the shining wonder, the new constellation to be followed by the wise men bringing gifts, until it stopped over a certain carrion at the bottom of a bath and disappeared – was simply the greatest Forger and the greatest Thief that ever cheated the gallows.

The fixation with filth and corruption fills the time of Mr Boffin, the Golden Dustman in *Our Mutual Friend*. In *Little Dorrit*, the Circumlocution Office satirises bureaucracy mercilessly; Mr and Mrs Veneering (in *Our Mutual Friend*) are the epitome of social falsity, and Mr Podsnap could represent all the worst of Victorian mentality and attitudes:

> Mr Podsnap was well to do, and stood very high in Mr Podsnap's opinion. Beginning with a good inheritance, he had married a good inheritance, and had thriven exceedingly in the Marine Insurance way, and was quite satisfied. He never could make out why everybody was not quite satisfied, and he felt conscious that he set a brilliant example in being particularly well satisfied with most things, and, above all other things, with himself.
> Thus happily acquainted with his own merit and importance, Mr Podsnap settled that whatever he put behind him he put out of existence. There was a dignified conclusiveness – not to add a great

convenience – in this way of getting rid of disagreeables, which had done much towards establishing Mr Podsnap in his lofty place in Mr Podsnap's satisfaction. 'I don't want to know about it; I don't choose to discuss it; I don't admit it!'

The high point of Victorian success and self-esteem was probably the Great Exhibition of 1851. The exhibition was held in the Crystal Palace in London which was specially built to display Britain's achievements at home and abroad, and to show Britain at the height of its wealth, power and influence. The guiding spirit behind this display of industrial and commercial domination was the Queen's husband, Prince Albert. He insisted that 'it should not merely be useful and ornamental; it should preach a high moral lesson'. This didacticism underlines the feeling of superiority in mid-century, the role the Victorians gave themselves as moral leaders and exemplars – though it was soon to be undermined. Albert's death, ten years later, left Victoria a widow, and this is how she is generally remembered. It also marks the beginnings of a growth in public sympathy for the Queen as a symbol of the nation. This was to be brilliantly manipulated by the prime minister, Disraeli, in his imperialist policies of the 1870s, reinforcing the image of the monarch by her nomination as Empress of India.

However, public faith had been shaken in the 1850s by two unrelated events. The Crimean War (1853–56) was the first war Britain had been involved in (from 1854) since the victory at Waterloo in 1815; it was a war in a distant place, and for no clear purposes – as Vietnam was for America in the 1960s and 1970s. Like that war, it was covered by the 'mass media': William Russell of *The Times*, the first war reporter, kept his readers informed of what was happening. The lack of a clear-cut victory, the losses recalled in Alfred Tennyson's *The Charge of the Light Brigade* (1854), and the sheer waste of the war brought a whole new sense of doubt to the nation's recent high self-esteem.

The publication of Charles Darwin's *On the Origin of Species* in 1859 was another severe blow to mid-Victorian self-esteem. Indeed, Darwin, foreseeing the kind of effect his doctrine of 'natural selection' would have on the religious beliefs and moral attitudes of Victorians, postponed publication of his scientific work for almost thirty years. Its effect was profound, greater perhaps than any other single publication of the nineteenth century. Darwin showed the determining factors of chance and necessity in the 'survival of the fittest', and totally undermined the higher values of religion and morality which, for centuries, society had done so much to create and affirm.

> Man . . . still bears in his bodily frame the indelible stamp of his lowly origin.

Statements of this kind from Darwin were the source of continuing moral and existential uncertainties. The period was a time of intellectual and moral ferment. In a volume entitled *Essays and Reviews*, published in 1860, many of the religious thinkers of the established church caused profound shock in their attempts to come to terms with scientific theories and discoveries.

The influence of Darwin was immediate, partly because his ideas had been circulating for so many years. Walter Bagehot's *The English Constitution* (1867) and *Physics and Politics* (1872) are determinedly post-Darwinian in their thinking: the latter volume was described as 'an attempt to apply the principles of natural selection and inheritance to political society'. Bagehot's works have remained the classics in their field.

The disillusion and doubt which exist in the later novels of Dickens became ever more dominant in late Victorian and early twentieth-century literature, especially in the novel. The novel, published in weekly or monthly parts, became both increasingly popular and the forum for the expression, discussion and shaping of ideals and ideas. The history of the period, then, was *not* always as 'emphatically the history of progress' as Macaulay asserted.

VICTORIAN THOUGHT AND VICTORIAN NOVELS

Harrison Ainsworth was the biggest-selling historical novelist after Sir Walter Scott. By 1841, he was second only to Dickens in fame and income as a writer; and Dickens could not quite match him in producing novels for the market. Ainsworth's history brought together elements of the Gothic, the adventure story, and the detailed 'archaeological' sense which the mid-nineteenth century took as authenticity. In fact, his history is fanciful rather than factual; early pulp-fiction rather than well-researched history, transformed into fiction. His subjects are often figures who are partly historical and partly mythical: Dick Turpin (in *Rookwood*, 1834), Guy Fawkes (1841) and Jack Sheppard (1839) in the novels which bear their names are good examples. Later, Ainsworth used places with historical associations as his background: the Tower of London, Old St Paul's and Windsor Castle give their names to three of Ainsworth's novels of the 1840s. Later still, *The Lancashire Witches* (1848) took a well-known and much mythologised series of events as the basis for a popular novel, which led to many more with similar settings.

Harrison Ainsworth was an entertainer first, a historian much later. He cashes in on the early/mid-Victorian taste for historical fantasy, making little use of the kind of serious social observation of the past, in relation to the present, which characterises the best of Scott's works. The nearest twentieth-century equivalent is the Hollywood historical epic: research is taken over by the glamour of the hero and the pace of the action. This can be seen as escapist use of history, rather than well-researched authenticity. Ainsworth writes swashbuckling page-turners with few pretensions to offering more than that. For today's readers there is the added attraction of the 'Victorian hero' bestseller ethos, anticipating H. Rider Haggard and Anthony Hope (see page 318). Instead of far-off colonies, or Ruritania, Ainsworth's romanticisation of history is always set solidly in English history and myth, and with a lovable rogue at its heart rather than a stiff-upper-lipped gentleman hero.

As in the eighteenth century, creative writers came under the influence of philosophers of a wide spectrum of different opinions. Dickens, for example, was greatly affected by the writings of Thomas Carlyle. Translator of the German national poet Goethe, and historian of the French Revolution, in the 1840s Carlyle became occupied with 'the Condition-of-England question', anticipating in many of his ideas the social novels of Gaskell, Dickens, and others. His views on strong leadership (in *On Heroes, Hero-Worship and the Heroic in History*, 1841) have been criticised for their apparent support of dictatorship, but they are more relevant to the coming manifestation of the anti-hero in late Victorian and twentieth-century writing. The concept of the hero, the great man as model of behaviour, was beginning to lose its appeal; Carlyle, in affirming the importance of 'Great Men' at a moment of historical and ideological crisis, highlights a crucial shift in awareness. He stressed the need for heroic behaviour in an increasingly unheroic age. *Past and Present*, written in two months in 1843, expresses Carlyle's anger (and compassion) at the statistics which announced that there were 1,429,089 'paupers' in England and Wales. Carlyle's essay praises work, and berates the system which deprives so many of work. He questions liberty, and gives us a continuing sense of the social anger found in Shelley:

> The liberty especially which has to purchase itself by social isolation, and each man standing separate from the other, having 'no business with him' but a cash-account: this is such a liberty as the Earth seldom saw; — as the Earth will not long put up with, recommend it how you may. This liberty turns out, before it have long continued in action, with all to die by want of food; for the Idle Thousands and Units, alas, a still more fatal liberty to live in want of work; to have no earnest duty to do in this God's-World any more. What becomes of a man in such predicament?

The novelist George Eliot described Carlyle's influence in glowing terms: 'there is hardly a superior or active mind of this generation that has not been modified by Carlyle's writings.' Hers was one of the most 'superior or active' minds of the age and, like Carlyle, was considerably influenced by German thought – especially by David Friedrich Strauss's *Life of Jesus*, which she translated in 1846, and Ludwig Feuerbach's *Essence of Christianity*, which she translated in 1854. These works fuelled George Eliot's conviction that religious belief is an imaginative necessity and a projection of concern for mankind; this is a humanist tendency which goes beyond any single doctrine, and allows Eliot to welcome Darwin's scientific theses without the great crisis of belief which affected many of her contemporaries. Apart from Carlyle, John Stuart Mill was probably the most influential of Victorian philosophers; his writings cover such topics as utilitarianism, liberty, logic, and political economy. They reflect the intellectual concerns of the day, rather than make a wholly original contribution to the history of thought.

In the nineteenth century, the novels of Sir Walter Scott gave a totally fresh view of the mixed history which united the once-divided Scotland, and later the once-divided United Kingdom. The leading non-fictional historian of the age was Thomas Babington Macaulay, whose *Essays Critical and Historical* (1834) reached a wide audience. Compared to Edward Gibbon (see page 164), however, Macaulay is less balanced, more prejudiced and dogmatic. His *History of England*, published in four volumes between 1849 and 1855, can now be seen to reflect Victorian attitudes and complacency, although his reconstructions of historical events, under Scott's influence, are still effective.

Probably the most famous and influential work of its kind, written in England, was *Das Kapital* by Karl Marx, published in 1867. *Das Kapital*, in effect a theory of political economy, is a negative critique of the capitalist system which concentrates wealth in the hands of fewer and fewer people, at the expense of the labouring class. Marx, with Friedrich Engels, had made a close study of Britain's industrial system and its effects. Engels's study *The Condition of the Working Class in England* (1845) praises Carlyle's awareness of workers' conditions, and anticipates the kind of situation which Elizabeth Gaskell was to describe, three years later, in *Mary Barton*.

Marx has been blamed for many things which *Das Kapital* does not suggest. But the abolition of private property, the advocacy of class war, and the slogan 'From each according to his abilities, to each according to his needs' are vital to his doctrines, and brought to the age a new awareness of social class, means of production, and working-class exploitation. His ideas were to become more important as the century progressed.

Marxism is a social and materialist philosophy contrasting with more religious and spiritual views of the world. After the Catholic Emancipation Act of 1829, there was a movement towards the Catholic church on the part of some members of the Anglican faith. The Oxford Movement, as it was known, was a small but significant eddy in the tide of Victorian faith. The theme, however, remains of interest right up to the present, in the novels of Barbara Pym and some of the early novels of A.N. Wilson; but now the subject is treated as delicate social comedy, rather than as the serious issue it was in the 1840s. John Henry Newman – Cardinal Newman, as he became in 1879 – was the leading figure of the Oxford Movement, the author of an important autobiography, *Apologia pro Vita Sua* (1864), of novels including *Loss and Gain* (1848) which portray the intellectual and religious life of Oxford at the time, and of the visionary poem *The Dream of Gerontius* (1865). The fact of religious debate is significant, echoing some of the controversies of the Elizabethan age, between high church and low church. In the nineteenth century, the move towards faith, especially towards the Catholic church, is a vital contrast with the move away from faith of many of the writers and thinkers of the time.

In the mid-nineteenth century there was a vogue for handbooks on self-improvement, and these became among the bestselling books of their time. They were the first 'how to' books. The best known of these was *Self-Help* by Samuel Smiles, first published in 1859, and translated into many languages. For many, this book and other Smiles' titles such as *Character* (1871), *Thrift* (1875), and *Duty* (1880) represent the negative aspects of the Victorian bourgeois ethos. Smiles was also the biographer of such nineteenth-century worthies as George Stephenson and Josiah Wedgwood.

Charles Kingsley was highly regarded as a novelist and critic in his own day, but is now remembered more for his controversial attacks on Newman and some interesting reforming novels of social concern such as *Alton Locke* (1850). His *Westward Ho!* (1855) is memorable as a patriotic statement re-evoking the Elizabethan age, just at the time when the Crimean War was denting national pride.

The novels of Benjamin Disraeli tend to be overshadowed by his political career: he became Tory prime minister for a few months in 1868, and then held the office from 1874 to 1880. But, he declared, 'my works are my life', and his many portrayals of high society and politicians are ironic and well-observed, if often rather rhetorical in manner. Disraeli is best known for the trilogy *Coningsby* (1844), *Sybil* (1845), and *Tancred* (1847). These are perhaps the first truly political novels in English; Disraeli wanted to influence public opinion through them. *Sybil* echoes Carlyle's *Past and Present* in its concern with the plight of the poor, one of the two nations which Disraeli's novel identified. His later novel *Lothair* (1870) is quite different. A huge success when first published, it in some ways foreshadows Wilde for its irony and wit. Lothair searches for Christian truth, while all sorts of struggling patriots (mainly Italian) try to control and influence him, in order to have access to his wealth. In its treatment of such themes as money, religion, aristocracy, and patriotism, *Lothair* brings together the verve and wit of Byron and the end-of-the-century cynical realism of Oscar Wilde.

William Makepeace Thackeray can be seen to follow Dickens's example in beginning his career in light, sketch-type journalism, and, like Dickens's pen-name Boz, Thackeray's 'Michael Angelo Titmarsh' became a well-known voice. But the lightness of the humour of his early works begins to darken in the late 1840s and early 1850s. *Vanity Fair* (1847–48) gives an unusual perspective on the Napoleonic wars, focusing a satirical eye on high society. The heroine, Becky Sharp, is a penniless orphan, and is contrasted throughout the novel with rich, spoiled Amelia Sedley. The background of the war, with Waterloo a climax of death in the private world of the heroines at the moment of greatest national triumph, underscores the hollowness behind the achievement. Thackeray anticipates Dickens's later concern with money and society: Becky can impress society on 'nothing a year' with the facade of respectability which is soon revealed to have no substance.

Pendennis (1848–50) and *The History of Henry Esmond* (1852) – the first, like *David Copperfield*, a story of the growth of the hero from childhood to adulthood, the second a historical novel – confirm the darker side of Thackeray's outlook in the creation of characters whose lives are 'a series of defeats' to be overcome rather than a simple progress to prosperity. Thackeray, who was born in Calcutta (the first major novelist to be born in the colonies), continued the Henry Esmond story in *The Virginians* (1857–59), one of many English novels of the age to be set in America, which is viewed with a critical eye. Dickens's own reactions to America in *American Notes* (1842), and then in the novel *Martin Chuzzlewit* (1843–44), had offended his American readership considerably. Thackeray's melancholy tone, and the characters' fixations with money, inheritance and social status, confirm that, since Scott, the historical novel had made considerable progress as a vehicle for social observation and comment. Dickens's portraits of Victorian society are broader than Thackeray's, and George Eliot explores psychological and moral issues in greater depth; but Thackeray contributed substantially to the growth of the nineteenth-century novel.

The Newcomes (1853–55) even experiments with a kind of 'alternative ending', anticipating John Fowles's *The French Lieutenant's Woman* (1969) by over a century. Thackeray is the omniscient author *par excellence*: he sees himself as a kind of puppet master, in control of his characters and their destinies, as we see at the end of *Vanity Fair*:

> Ah! *Vanitas Vanitatum!* which of us is happy in this world? Which of us has his desire? or, having it, is satisfied? – Come, children, let us shut up the box and the puppets, for our play is played out.

This self-conscious authorial role recalls Henry Fielding, but later Victorian novelists tend to point their moral in a more compassionate rather than manipulative way; the author's point of view becomes more sympathetic, often almost participatory.

The growth of the provincial novel in both Ireland and Scotland is an important development in the early nineteenth century. Two novels by Lady Morgan, *The Wild Irish Girl* (1806) and *The O'Briens and the O'Flahertys* (1827), are significant 'national tales' which brought their author such renown that she was the first woman to be granted an annual pension for her services to the world of letters. The works of Maria Edgeworth and Lady Morgan open up areas of non-cosmopolitan experience, but, equally significantly, begin to give a clear identity to the province of Ireland. This would grow and develop throughout the century, eventually leading to political separation in the twentieth century. Many writers are now described as Anglo-Irish, and the distinction between Irish and Anglo-Irish will assume greater importance in all later discussions of writing in and about Ireland.

The English novelist Anthony Trollope, for example, set his first two novels in Ireland: *The Macdermots of Ballycloran* (1847) and *The Kellys and the O'Kellys* (1848) remain important portrayals of Ireland, published at a time when it was much talked about because of the Great Famine. Trollope was to return twice more to the subject of Ireland, in *Castle Richmond* (1860) and the unfinished *The Landleaguers* (1882). Two out of four of his titles echo Edgeworth and Morgan's earlier Irish novels. Trollope knew their work well, and was also considerably indebted to the Irish writer William Carleton's novel of the Famine, *The Black Prophet* (1846–47). Carleton's *Traits and Stories of the Irish Peasantry* (1830–35) and *Tales of Ireland* (1834) are seminal in their impact on all subsequent writing about the province, initiating both a concern with local character and life, as well as effectively establishing the new tradition of tales and short stories, which were to become a major feature of Irish writing.

In the mid-nineteenth century, the novels of Charles Lever enjoyed great popularity for their racy, anecdotal style. *The Martins of Cro'Martin* (1847) was published in the same year as Trollope's first novel, also set in Ireland, and was a considerably more successful portrayal of family life in the West of Ireland. *Lord Kilgobbin* (1872) is Lever's most significant novel, one of the major contributions to Irish literature between Edgeworth and Joyce. It handles the theme of the misrule of Ireland by the English, and instead of the rollicking homely warmth of much Irish writing, including much of Lever's own, it presents a wide-ranging canvas illustrating chaos and despair, decay and discontent. It is close to late Dickens or George Eliot in its serious analysis of the Irish problems of the period.

The novels of Anthony Trollope offer considerable insight into the 'progress' of society in Victorian England. He was the most industrious of writers, the most prolific since Scott, writing every day while at the same time maintaining a career and travelling all over the country and abroad as a Post Office civil servant. His *Autobiography* (1875–76, published posthumously in 1883) shows a man of immense self-discipline and energy; he is even credited with the invention of the pillar-box. His novels have been seen as the epitome of conservatism, but the undercurrents flowing through them reflect the changing times in which he lived. His insistence that 'on the last day of each month recorded, every person in [the] novel should be a month older than on the first' shows a concern with time and its effects that is vital in the development of the novel.

Trollope wrote two great series of interconnected novels: the Barsetshire novels (1855–67), set in a fully realised West Country area, and the Palliser novels (1864–80), which are the most politically contextualised novels of the nineteenth century.

The fictional county of Barsetshire gives Trollope the opportunity to expand upon Jane Austen's desire for the novel to explore 'three or four families in a Country Village'. The series examines the religious tendencies of the time in a local situation, and the social behaviour of a wide cast of characters is observed: ambition, career, belief and personality are portrayed through the clashes and conflicts that occupy them.

The Palliser novels move on to the national political stage, with a similarly careful observation of social influences on public life. Women's roles are particularly important in this series – 'love and intrigue' being a main feature of the plots. Trollope's novels trace the rise and fall of Victorian characters, shading in their ideals and aspirations with a gentle irony, rather than with the social concern of Dickens or Gaskell, the moral weight of George Eliot, or the sharpness and later melancholy of Thackeray.

Trollope's plots contain all the manifold contrivances and complications which have come to be seen as typical of the Victorian novel: inheritances, intrigues, scheming and cheating, property and propriety. They are novels of behaviour rather than of manners; novels which, quietly and undramatically, reveal as much about the second half of the nineteenth century as any of the more acclaimed works of 'greater' writers. By the time of *Orley Farm* (1862) – his most complex inheritance plot – Trollope was already a master of how situations evolve and develop, and the processes behind action. It is this which gives him his status as a major writer. By the time of *The Way We Live Now* (1875), his writing could be seen not just as a highly readable social observation of character and intrigue, but also as a fully worked out criticism of capitalist ethics and 'the commercial profligacy of the age'. The financier Augustus Melmotte, the leading character in this novel, is one of the best examples of Victorian hypocrisy; behind the hugely wealthy facade is a sordid and corrupt reality that recalls Mr Merdle in Dickens's *Little Dorrit* and Bulstrode in Eliot's *Middlemarch*.

> He had not far to go, round through Berkeley Square into Bruton Street, but he stood for a few moments looking up at the bright stars. If he could be there, in one of those unknown distant worlds, with all his present intellect and none of his present burdens, he would,

he thought, do better than he had done here on earth. If he could even now put himself down nameless, fameless, and without possessions in some distant corner of the world, he could, he thought, do better. But he was Augustus Melmotte, and he must bear his burdens, whatever they were, to the end. He could reach no place so distant but that he would be known and traced.

Trollope is in a long line of Victorian writers who continually explore and question what is meant by historical 'progress' in the context of the nineteenth century.

Towards the end of the nineteenth century, George Meredith was considered the 'grand old man' of English literature. He was the model, early in his career, for the famous painting of the death of the young poet Chatterton, by Henry Wallis, in 1851. From poor beginnings, he gradually established an immense reputation, although few of his novels enjoyed great popularity in his lifetime. Only *Diana of the Crossways* was a considerable bestseller when it was published in 1885. This novel shows many of Meredith's qualities – an unusual capacity for portraying female characters and a good ear for the presentation of dialogue. His major novels, from *The Ordeal of Richard Feverel* (1859), which caused a scandal when first published, to *The Egoist*, twenty years later, and the political novel *Beauchamp's Career* (1876), are all concerned with the psychology of misunderstanding. Characters in Meredith's novels are not understood, or do not understand themselves, with personal, social, and even political consequences. They are therefore novels of discovery and self-discovery, and as such are often considered to be very Modern in outlook, especially as regards the role of women. But Meredith's style tended to become precious and overwritten in his later works, and his high reputation declined after his death.

Meredith's *Modern Love*, published in 1862, is a remarkable series of fifty sixteen-line 'sonnets' about the decline of a marriage, reflecting his own disillusionment after his wife, the daughter of Thomas Love Peacock, left him for the painter Wallis. Often considered to be one of the first psychological love poems, *Modern Love* has kept Meredith's fame as a poet alive: like his younger contemporary, Thomas Hardy, Meredith always considered himself a poet rather than a novelist. But it is his novels, his influential essay *The Idea of Comedy* (1897; originally a lecture in 1877), and his role as a 'grand old man' of letters which give him his place in literary history.

THE BRONTËS AND ELIOT
A Woman is a foreign land
(Coventry Patmore, *The Angel in the House*)

Women writers and female characters had been part of novel-writing since the time of Aphra Behn and Delarivier Manley, and it is a commonplace that women were the main readers of the genre in the eighteenth century. After Sir Walter Scott made the novel popular worldwide, it was, for two decades, seen largely as a man's genre. Women writers were expected to write the kinds of novel which George Eliot was to condemn in an essay as *Silly Novels by Lady Novelists* – the sub-genres of romance, fantasy and sensation. But several of the major figures of the Victorian novel are women; and the heroines they created began to throw off the victim's role that male authors had created, from Moll Flanders, Pamela, and Clarissa onwards. Jane Eyre's 'Reader, I married him' close to the end of Charlotte Brontë's novel (1847) that bears the character's name, shows the reversal of roles and the decision-making capacities that the new generation of socially aware women could demonstrate.

On the whole, Dickens's women are not well portrayed; but from Trollope to Thomas Hardy and Henry James, a desire to present fully rounded and complex female characters can be traced. George Eliot (née Mary Ann Evans) took a male name partly in order to rise above the 'silly novels' syndrome, but such writers as Elizabeth Gaskell and the Brontë sisters had already made a notable contribution to the flourishing of female writing in mid-century.

The Brontë sisters, Charlotte, Emily and Anne Brontë, not only contributed much to the growth of the novel, but also to the position of women at this time. They did much to alter the way in which women were viewed, demonstrating new social, psychological and emotional possibilities for women. Like George Eliot, however, they adopted pseudonyms (Currer, Ellis and Acton Bell) in order not to draw attention to the fact that they were women. Charlotte and Emily

Brontë are in many ways both opposites to Jane Austen. They are distinctly romantic in temperament, exploring in their novels extremes of passion and violence. Although there are some features of romanticism in Jane Austen's novels, her work is essentially Augustan in spirit. She prefers exploration of the individual within clear boundaries of decorum and restraint.

Charlotte Brontë's first novel *Jane Eyre* was published in 1847 to considerable critical acclaim. Like Dickens's *David Copperfield* it is a *Bildungsroman* (a novel of growing up). Jane Eyre, the character whose name forms the title of the novel, begins life as an orphan, undergoes many difficulties working as a governess, and finally marries the man she loves, Rochester, who is her social superior and a man of wealth. On one level, the novel is a rags-to-riches story. On another level, it is a novel of love, mystery and passion which poses profound moral and social questions. The good characters win, but only after they have suffered and been forced to examine their own conscience and to explore their moral selves. The plot is characterised by melodramatic incidents, but in each phase Jane grows in maturity and understanding. She becomes increasingly independent and self-reliant in her judgements. Like the heroine in *Villette* (1853), she is not strikingly beautiful but plain, and, on the surface at least, reticent. However, she is passionate and unafraid of her strong feelings. In *Jane Eyre*, Charlotte Brontë sends out a signal that ordinary women can experience deep love and begin to take responsibility for their own lives.

Emily Brontë's only novel *Wuthering Heights* was also published in 1847. It is a novel which contains a degree of emotional force and sophisticated narrative structure not seen previously in the history of the English novel. Many of the early reviewers of the novel thought that it must have been written by a man of a particularly uncontrolled temper. *Wuthering Heights* is a cyclical novel in structure. It moves in a tragic circle from relative peace and harmony to violence, destruction and intense suffering, and finally back into peace and harmony again. It is a work of extreme contrasts set in the wild moorland of Yorkshire, which is appropriate to the wild passions it describes between the two main characters, Cathy and Heathcliff. Here is an episode from the novel in which one of the narrators, Lockwood, 'dreams' of Cathy. She is beating at his window in Wuthering Heights, a house situated at the top of a desolate and isolated hill, literally at the edge of the normal world:

> Terror made me cruel, and finding it useless to attempt shaking the creature off, I pulled its wrist on to the broken pane, and rubbed it to and fro till the blood ran down and soaked the bed clothes: still it wailed, 'Let me in!' and maintained its tenacious grip, almost maddening me with fear.

In the novel the incident is described as if it were a dream, but there is a strong emotional and psychological reality to it. It is poised between dream and reality, lucidly capturing the extreme feelings of Cathy. Another incident, narrated in a matter-of-fact way by a boy who was himself only told about it by someone else, describes how the ghosts of Heathcliff and Cathy walk across the moors after their deaths. Heathcliff himself is a man of dark and brooding passions, whose love for Cathy has no boundaries. At times, their love for each other is violent and destructive; at others, it appears to be a completely natural phenomenon. Cathy says: 'My love for Heathcliff resembles the eternal rocks beneath: a source of little visible delight, but necessary.' The tragic outcome to the novel is inevitable, but the depths of their mutual feeling endure. *Wuthering Heights,* a novel of unique imaginative power, was Emily Brontë's only novel, for she died the year after it was published at the age of 30.

The third sister, Anne, wrote *The Tenant of Wildfell Hall* (1848), which has been overshadowed by Charlotte and Emily's more spectacular successes. It is, however, an important novel in its own right. In the novel Anne Brontë depicts a bitterly unhappy marriage followed by the departure of the wife, Helen Huntingdon, and her search for new freedom. One critic wrote that the 'slamming of Helen's bedroom door against her husband reverberated throughout Victorian England'.

The Brontë sisters opened up new possibilities for the form of the English novel; at the same time they provided a basis for which psychological exploration became a key component in the development of the genre of the novel. They also offered new possibilities for the portrayal of women in fiction. Women became even more of a 'foreign land', but increasingly familiar and central as subjects for fiction.

In the works of George Eliot, the English novel reached new

depths of social and philosophical concern, and moral commitment. For some twentieth-century critics, Virginia Woolf and F.R. Leavis among them, her writings are seen to have brought the novel to new heights of maturity. She shares with the greatest European writers of her century – Balzac, Flaubert, Dostoevsky, and Tolstoy – a concern for her characters' vulnerability and weakness in the face of 'progress' and the moral imperatives of duty and humanity.

The scope of Eliot's writing is considerable. From the early stories in *Scenes of Clerical Life* (1857–58), published anonymously but recognised by Dickens as certainly by a female hand, to the massive *Middlemarch* (1871–72), and *Daniel Deronda* (1876), she touches on many of the major issues of her day. Such issues have not lost their pertinence over a century later: how a wife copes with a drunken husband (*Janet's Repentance* in *Scenes of Clerical Life*); what happens when an unmarried girl is accused of murdering her infant child (*Adam Bede*, 1859); how an orphan child brings humanity to a miserly social outcast (*Silas Marner*, 1861); and how a sister and brother achieve reconciliation in the moment of tragedy after bankruptcy, moral compromise, and ostracism have separated them (*The Mill on the Floss*, 1860). *Janet's Repentance* is particularly vivid in its evocation of the woman's plight:

> Poor Janet! how heavily the months rolled on for her, laden with fresh sorrows as the summer passed into autumn, the autumn into winter, and the winter into spring again. Every feverish morning, with its blank listlessness and despair, seemed more hateful than the last; every coming night more impossible to brave without arming herself in leaden stupor. The morning light brought no gladness to her: it seemed only to throw its glare on what had happened in the dim candle-light – on the cruel man seated immovable in drunken obstinacy by the dead fire and dying lights in the dining-room, rating her in harsh tones, reiterating old reproaches – or on a hideous blank of something unremembered, something that must have made that dark bruise on her shoulder, which ached as she dressed herself. Do you wonder how it was that things had come to this pass – what offence Janet had committed in the early years of marriage to rouse the brutal hatred of this man?

These are the themes of Eliot's early novels, and show her concern for the outsider in society. Her search for illustration illuminated the moral areas of experience which more traditional Victorian thought would have tried to handle in absolute terms – black and white, wrong and right. The moral simplicity of early Victorian thinking and writing, influenced (as indeed Eliot was) by Scott's return to a mediaeval ethos, had to change with the times, and encompass a much wider range of problems and experience.

George Eliot's novels are largely set in the realistically presented location of the Midlands area of her childhood – Warwickshire – and her characters tend to be ordinary, unheroic people caught up in circumstances which are greater than any individual. The necessity of heroic behaviour in an unheroic age (advocated by Carlyle) reaches its highest expression in *Middlemarch*, which Virginia Woolf described as 'one of the few English novels written for adult people'. Here the 'heroine', Dorothea Brooke, is seen very much not to be a heroine.

> She was open, ardent and not in the least self-admiring: indeed it was pretty to see how her imagination adorned her sister Celia with attractions altogether superior to her own. . . . Dorothea, with all the eagerness to know the truths of life, retained very childlike ideas about marriage. . . . The really delightful marriage must be that where your husband was a sort of father, and could even teach you Hebrew, if you wished it.

In the final sentence, Dorothea's own voice emerges through the standard third-person narrative perspective. It enables Dorothea's own thoughts and feelings to be heard more clearly, but it also allows George Eliot to distance herself from them. Dorothea appears in the light of her own point of view. George Eliot can present her ironically and critically. It is an approach which many novelists were subsequently to adopt.

Dorothea Brooke is both complementary to and a contrast with Romola in the novel of the same name (1863), set in the 1490s in Florence, at the peak of the Renaissance; *Romola* is George Eliot's most historically researched novel. Both Dorothea and Romola have to seek and find their calling by experiencing and rejecting various ways of life: religion, good works, love and marriage, betrayal and disappointment. As always, Eliot makes use of the standard Victorian plot devices – inheritances, secrets hidden and revealed, and natural disasters. But it is in *Middlemarch* that she finds the imagery perfectly to match her theme: the 'Dead Hand' of the past on the living pulse of the city. Middlemarch is a town in the Midlands in 1832, at the time of the First Reform Act. Readers in the 1870s could see how much or how little progress had been made since then: in politics, in medicine, in transport (the clash between horse-drawn transport and the railways is particularly remarkable), in social concern for the poor, in dedication to humanity. Corruption and stasis are tempered by duty and hope. The downfall of the 'villain' of the piece, the banker Mr Bulstrode, is a vividly dramatic moment of public denunciation and personal self-recognition.

George Eliot's last novel, *Daniel Deronda*, moves on to grander themes of dedication in the professional, artistic and nationalistic senses, following Gwendolen Harleth's career through disillusionment to self-sacrifice. The fight for a Jewish nation, and a wider worldview than English provincial life, are keynotes of this work; a novel which, like much of George Eliot's work, was to have a considerable influence on future generations of writers, most notable among them Henry James.

OTHER LADY NOVELISTS

After the flourishing of women's writing towards the end of the eighteenth century, the nineteenth century brought great popularity to many female authors. Equality was still some way off, as is shown by Mary Ann Evans's choice of pen-name, George Eliot, when she began to write fiction. As already mentioned, it was George Eliot, in an essay called *Silly Novels by Lady Novelists*, who attacked the lightweight nature of the writing by many of her contemporaries.

However, there were many whose work was very distinguished. F. (Frances) Trollope is remembered as the mother of Anthony Trollope, but in her own day she was the author of one of the first 'visit America' books, *Domestic Manners of the Americans* (1832). She followed this with books on Austria and Italy and a long series of 'silver fork' novels of high society, which became enormously popular in the 1840s.

Mrs Craik (Dinah Maria Mulock) is remembered best for *John Halifax, Gentleman* (1856). Set near Tewkesbury, in the west of

England, it is the classic tale of the poor orphan boy who reaches the level of 'gentleman' by his own efforts, and marries the heroine, Ursula March, for love. It is the last flush of mid-Victorian realism, exactly between Dickens's *David Copperfield* and the more disillusioned *Great Expectations*. Mrs Craik's huge output was frequently in the area of children's literature.

Many of the women writers of the Victorian age were enormously prolific. Mrs Margaret Oliphant, for example, wrote too many novels for her reputation's good: over one hundred. Her series *Chronicles of Carlingford* (1863–76) is witty and observant, similar in some ways to Anthony Trollope's Barsetshire novels. Carlingford is a small town near London, and Mrs Oliphant handles many of the topical themes of class, religion, and progress with immense verve. If the series were to be dramatised on television, as many Victorian novels have been, Mrs Oliphant might reach an enormous new audience. Her series *Stories of the Seen and Unseen* (from 1880) exploits the late Victorian fascination with death and the soul.

Mrs Oliphant proclaimed that she was shocked by the works of Mary Elizabeth Braddon, whose sensational *Lady Audley's Secret* (1862) was one of the lasting successes of the time. It introduced 'the fair-haired demon of modern fiction', the scandalous woman, whose role would become more and more serious and socially significant towards the end of the century – in works by Thomas Hardy, George Moore, and Oscar Wilde. *Lady Audley's Secret* and *Aurora Floyd* (1863) are the two best-known novels of over seventy works by Miss Braddon.

East Lynne (1861), the first novel by Mrs Henry Wood (born Ellen Price), was similarly sensational and similarly successful. It was the first of her many mysteries in middle-class settings, which are forerunners of the crime genre so successful in the twentieth century. Mrs Henry Wood's novels are distinguished not only for their careful plotting and detailed settings, but there is usually also a degree of social awareness: strikes and unemployment feature often. This is not escapist fiction, but entertainment with something of a conscience.

Mrs Eliza Lynn Linton was something of a reactionary, attacking feminism and concepts of 'the New Woman'. Her collected journalism, *The Girl of the Period* (1883), gives a memorable counterblast to the burgeoning ideas of female liberation. Of her many novels, historical and contemporary, *Rebel of the Family* (1880) is probably the best remembered, although the earlier *Joshua Davidson* (1872) is a remarkably socialist novel in its sympathies.

Mrs Humphry (Mary Augusta) Ward was from the same family as Matthew Arnold, and her novels reflect the intellectual and religious ambience of Oxford and the Oxford Movement (see page 282). *Robert Elsmere* (1888) was her most famous work; *Helbeck of Bannisdale* (1898) one of the most distinctive. Her works are quite different from those of Mrs Oliphant and Miss Braddon: they are full of high moral purpose, an earnestness which had gone out of fashion more rapidly than wit and sensation. Mrs Humphry Ward was an early feminist, and follows George Eliot as one of the most distinguished of serious women writers of the late Victorian period.

LATE VICTORIAN NOVELS

The nineteenth century dislike of Realism is the rage of Caliban seeing his own face in a glass

(Oscar Wilde, Preface to *The Picture of Dorian Gray*)

As the novel expanded in range and scope in the nineteenth century, so the range of characters and localities grew. Novelists in the eighteenth century like Smollett and Sterne had brought in a wide range of dialects and discourses; for example, naval language in Smollett. With Maria Edgeworth and Scott, Irish and Scottish voices began to be heard. In poetry, Burns and Fergusson had revitalised Scots, and in the nineteenth century the Dorsetshire dialect writings of William Barnes were to be a considerable inspiration to Thomas Hardy in the characterisation and settings of his Wessex novels.

Dickens's cockney characters, such as Sam Weller in *The Pickwick Papers* and Sarah Gamp in *Martin Chuzzlewit*, are classics of their kind, but Dickens's choice of dialect is more normally used for comic effect than for social criticism. In the novels of Elizabeth Gaskell, as later with Hardy, dialect often reflects conflicts between social classes; linguistic collisions come to symbolise social issues. George Eliot tries to bring different speech communities into greater social harmony in her works, making linguistic integration an emblem of a new social order.

Dialects have always been part of English literature. They are a central feature of English as a polyglot language. In literature, they have also been used to underline the values of community and of individual identity, especially as set against the standardising centrist tendencies of London and the South East. From Chaucer's *Canterbury Tales* through Henryson's fifteenth-century Scottish fables, of which *The Town Mouse and the Uplandis Mouse* is a good example, through Shakespeare to the Victorians and beyond, dialect shows the difference between the city and the country, between aristocrat and peasant, and often between rich and poor. The Victorian novel is rich in linguistic variation as the genre explores differences in social class and expands the boundaries of nationhood and social identity. Colonial expansion will bring a very much wider range of voices, dialects, and Englishes into modern writing.

The industrial novel, of which Dickens's *Hard Times* is the best-known example, originated as early as 1832 with *A Manchester Strike* by Harriet Martineau – one of the most successful female polemicists of all time, a fiercely independent reformer and social observer. She wrote few novels, but maintained an output of fiery and significant journalism for another forty years. Benjamin Disraeli's *Coningsby* (1844) and *Sybil* (1845) also explore industrial worlds and contexts.

The sub-genre can be seen to acquire force and commitment in the works of (Mrs) Elizabeth Gaskell, starting with *Mary Barton* (1848). Dickens recognised her worth, and published much of her writing in his magazines *Household Words* and *All the Year Round*. It is significant, however, that Gaskell's *Cranford* (1853), a village story not far removed from Jane Austen, was for many years her best-remembered work. But her social concern, her realistic use of character, setting, and speech, and her pleas for humanity and reconciliation have been restored in recent years to a prominent place. Her contribution to the Victorian novel is now recognised as one of considerable social commitment and artistic achievement. *North and South* (1855), with its contrast between the rural South and the industrial North, is a valuable companion piece to the bleaker *Hard Times*, published in the previous year. George Eliot's *Felix Holt, the Radical* (1866) is perhaps the most complex of all the 'industrial' novels, bringing together the inheritance plot, social change, and political ideals in an optimistic but deeply serious tragicomic creation.

Later in the century, social awareness and realism in the novel go hand in hand. As Oscar Wilde was to put it in his Preface to *The Picture of Dorian Gray* (1891), 'The nineteenth century dislike of Realism is the rage of Caliban seeing his own face in a glass'. Like Shakespeare's half-man half-beast Caliban in *The Tempest*, the Victorians did not necessarily want to see reality in the novels they read. Like Dickens's character, Mr Podsnap, they wanted to put it behind them, for it offended them.

The ever-stronger insistence on the more distasteful side of society in the later novels of Dickens was, in part, an attempt to bring his readers to a recognition that unpleasantness cannot be avoided. Moral questions – such as illegitimacy and cohabitation – are clearly raised in both the life and works of George Eliot. But the wider public was still easily shocked, and the realistic novels of the 1880s and 1890s aroused storms of protest and reaction.

Another novelist critical of the basis of Victorian society was Samuel Butler. His *The Way of All Flesh* (1903) marks a shift in attitude. Butler openly satirises major Victorian idols such as family life and Victorian fathers as the moral centre of society. His novel *Erewhon* (1872) (erewhon is almost 'nowhere' backwards) presents a utopian society which is used to satirise Victorian concepts of duty and religion. Like William Morris's *News from Nowhere* (1890–91) and later Aldous Huxley's *Brave New World* (1932), the form of a utopian novel, dating back to Sir Thomas More's *Utopia* (1515), is used with a satirical aim.

George Gissing's novels, from *Workers in the Dawn* (1880) and *The Unclassed* (1884) to *The Nether World* (1889) and *New Grub Street* (1891), show a concern and sympathy for the deprived which is not far removed from Dickens. Gissing was a 'naturalist' writer in that he described everyday life in great detail.

> With the first breath of winter there passes a voice half-menacing, through all the barren ways and phantom-haunted refuges of the nether world. Too quickly has vanished the brief season when the sky is clement, when a little food suffices, and the chances of earning that little are more numerous than at other times; this wind that vies

utterance to its familiar warning is the vaunt-courier of cold and hunger and solicitude that knows not sleep. Will the winter be a hard one? It is the question that concerns the world before all others, that occupies alike the patient workfolk who have yet their home unbroken, the strugglers foredoomed to loss of such scant needments as the summer gifted them withal, the hopeless and the self-abandoned and the lurking creatures of prey. To all of them the first chill breath from a lowering sky has its voice of admonition; they set their faces; they sigh, or whisper a prayer, or fling out a curse, each according to his nature.

(The Nether World)

Gissing's naturalism was partly based on the writings of the French novelist Emile Zola (1840–1902). In places, however, he shows a greater degree of sentiment and social concern.

George Moore was associated with various kinds of writing during his long career. After a period as an art student in Paris in the 1870s and early 1880s, he wrote *A Modern Love* (1883), a novel set in Bohemian artistic society. This was banned by the circulating libraries, and inspired Moore to fight censorship for the rest of his career. He wrote several plays, including *Martin Luther* (1879), one of the few literary works in English to feature Luther as a tragic hero. The realistic novel *Esther Waters* made his name in 1894 as a scandalous novelist in the new realistic mode of Gissing and the French novelist Emile Zola. It is similar in some ways to Thomas Hardy's treatment of the woman as victim in *Tess of the D'Urbervilles*, published three years earlier. Esther is a servant girl from a religious background, who is seduced and deserted by another servant. (In the three other major novels on this theme, the seducer is of a higher class than the girl: Arthur Donnithorne is the squire who seduces Hetty Sorrel in George Eliot's *Adam Bede* (1859), and Alec D'Urberville is Tess's social superior in Hardy's novel of 1891. Ruth Hilton, in Elizabeth Gaskell's *Ruth* (1853), is seduced and abandoned by Henry Bellingham, who is a wealthy young man of a higher class.) The realism of *Esther Waters* lies in its depiction of poverty, and in its settings, which include the world of the racing establishment, a lying-in hospital and the workhouse. It takes the line of 'seduction novels' on to a new level of social realism, and although its ending is less tragic than some, it caused considerable scandal at a time when many novels were banned if they offended the tastes of the great circulating libraries, from which a large number of readers borrowed novels.

Moore's earlier novel *Mike Fletcher* (1889) is of particular interest as the only real decadent novel of the time, featuring a sensitive artistic hero whose sufferings and sensibility dominate the whole tale: the modern novel as a chronicle of artistic sensibility is importantly anticipated in this neglected work, which can find a comparison only in Wilde's *The Picture of Dorian Gray* (1890–91) as a novel of an aesthetic life lived for its own sake. The discussion here anticipates Wilde's novel quite strikingly.

> 'You must consider the influence of impure literature upon young people,' said John.
> 'No, no; the influence of a book is nothing; it is life that influences and corrupts. I sent my story of a drunken woman to Randall, and the next time I heard from him he wrote to say he had married his mistress, and he knew she was a drunkard.'
> 'It is easy to prove that bad books don't do any harm; if they did, by the same rule good books would do good, and the world would have been converted long ago,' said Frank.

In his later work, Moore's Irish background comes more to the fore, and he is a major figure in the development of the short story in Ireland – *The Untilled Field* (1903) being a significant collection. His later novels, such as *The Brook Kerith* (1916), explore religious themes. Moore lived to become one of the grand old men of English letters, and at the same time worked with Yeats on plans for the Irish National Theatre. His reputation has declined since his death, but several of his works are being rediscovered and re-evaluated.

The 'proletarian' novel, describing, in realistic detail, working lives and conditions, had, in fact, been in existence since the 1830s and 1840s, in the form of broadsheets and cheap (penny) periodicals which carried all kinds of fiction, and began to include somewhat melodramatic tales in recognisably working-class settings. These works are more a sign that there was a commercial market for fiction among the poorly educated, rather than showing any upsurge of popular discontent in the novel. That discontent could be found in the ballads of

Ebenezer Elliott (for example, *Corn Law Rhymes*, 1830), but not yet in an authentic 'working-class art', which would come many years later.

The works of Arthur Morrison – *Tales of Mean Streets* (1894) and *A Child of the Jago* (1896) – are perhaps the most successful fictionalised accounts of working-class life. But no novels compare with the documentary work of Henry Mayhew, whose *London Labour and the London Poor* (1851) and *London Children* (1874) gave detailed records of real suffering, and had a considerable effect on the public awareness of the need for reform.

Taken with the writings of Friedrich Engels, these documents give the clearest insight into the harsh reality behind the Victorian facade, and perhaps confirm that the aims of novelists will always go beyond mere documentary realism towards some wider purpose. Victorian novelists do not express direct anger, perhaps because the victims of society were not educated to read and write until after the Education Act of 1870 (incidentally, the year of Charles Dickens's death). The generations which benefited from the Act would largely make their voices heard in the twentieth century, in the works of writers such as Robert Tressell and Walter Greenwood (see pages 417 and 442).

Thomas Wright, who, as the 'Journeyman Engineer', left us a fascinating series of documentary writings, turned to the novel with *The Bane of a Life* (1870); but, despite its first-hand account of working-class life, the polemical issues are toned down for a middle-class readership. John W. Overton, in *Harry Hartley* (1859) and *Saul of Mitre Court* (1879), makes his working-class concerns the basis of a philosophical approach to a new society along positivist lines. Overton was one of the earliest self-educated working-class intellectuals, and his contribution to the growth of socialist thinking was considerable.

W.E. Tirebuck's *Miss Grace of All Souls* (1895) has been described as 'the most important industrial novel' to be published in England since *Hard Times* forty years earlier, and it was the most successful portrayal of independent working-class life since *Mary Barton*. This 'industrial' trend in the novel made the 'two nations' theme especially vivid, with the workers' cause strongly maintained, with no possibility of compromise. *Miss Grace* is the continuation of a line in fiction which Disraeli began in *Sybil*, and of which *Mary Barton* and Kingsley's *Alton Locke* are perhaps the most significant examples.

Two women writers of the end of the century attempted to bring this industrial or working-class novel to a new readership, but their work is now little read. Constance Howell shows the conversion of an upper-class woman to socialism, in a novel of 'class repentance' called *The Excellent Way* (1888). Margaret Harkness (using a male pen-name, John Law) took realism to new levels of directness with *A City Girl* (1887) and her major novel *Out of Work* (1888).

> Competition has had its day; it *must* give place to co-operation, because co-operation is the next step in the evolution of society; it has a scientific basis. Individualists may try to stop it, but it cannot be stopped. The organisation of labour and the brotherhood of men are scientific truths which *must* be demonstrated. Join them in the struggle. Be Socialists.
>
> *(Out of Work)*

In 1890, John Law published both *In Darkest London* and *A Manchester Shirtmaker*. The brutality of her descriptions comes across with immense force:

> An old woman came to us last night and asked if we would take her to the doctor. Her little grandchild led her in. Her husband had knocked her eye out. She is stone blind now; for he knocked out her right eye when she was fifty, and last night he knocked her left eye out of its socket. I know six women close by this house whose husbands have knocked their eyes out.
>
> *(In Darkest London)*

A revolutionary tone pervades the work of all these 'socialist' writers, and, perhaps because the English establishment has always kept down revolutionary elements, these writers' works have remained obscure. But today's readers would still find them striking and vivid, a useful further viewpoint on the social conditions described by better-known writers. George Eliot had handled similar themes in *Janet's Repentance* (in *Scenes of Clerical Life*, 1857–58), but with fictional intent balancing the anger which Harkness's writing reveals. Like so much of Victorian writing, these later flourishings of working-class concern lead directly to the writings of Oscar Wilde: in this case, to his essay *The Soul of Man Under Socialism* (1891).

All art is quite useless
(Oscar Wilde, Preface to *The Picture of Dorian Gray*)

The development of fantasy writing, set in other worlds or expressing other realities, became a popular phenomenon of the second half of the nineteenth century. Of course, the exotic had been a theme in literature from Mandeville to Beckford, and the Romantics had brought many oriental themes into their writings. The bestselling book of its day, *Lalla Rookh* (1817) by Thomas Moore (1779–1852), was a series of oriental tales in verse, anticipating Edward Fitzgerald's *The Rubaiyat of Omar Khayyam* (1859) in its appeal.

Such fantasy expanded its range as the real Victorian world became less and less positive and acceptable. The new genre of science fiction was one result; the detective story, ghost stories (extending the Gothic novel's range), utopian writing, and fantasy writing for children, all represent the escapist search for other worlds in ways which were to become increasingly popular in the twentieth century.

Lewis Carroll's *Alice's Adventures in Wonderland* (1865) and *Through the Looking Glass* (1872) are the most lasting mid-Victorian fantasies, requiring modern adjectives like 'surreal' and 'absurd' to describe their dream-like transformations and humour. Unlike a great deal of writing for children at the time, there is no overt moral or didactic intent, but the play of an absurd logic, perhaps influenced by the author's career as a mathematics lecturer. Both the linguistic experiments and the dream-type fluidity of character and plot anticipate trends in the innovative writing of the twentieth century. Much of Carroll's writing depends on ambiguities, such as the following extract from *Through the Looking Glass*:

> Here the Red Queen began again.
> 'Can you answer useful questions?' she said. 'How is bread made?'
> 'I know that!', Alice cried eagerly. 'You take some flour –'
> 'Where do you pick the flower?' the White Queen asked: 'In a garden or in the hedges?'

The detective story, originating in America with Edgar Allan Poe in the 1840s, finds its first full expression in novels such as *The Moonstone* (1868) by Wilkie Collins. The genre is a variant on the theme of the 'hidden secret' or the 'dead hand', which was a common theme in

Victorian fiction – reaching great heights of complexity in Charles Dickens's *Bleak House*, George Eliot's *Middlemarch*, and Wilkie Collins's other highly successful novel, *The Woman in White* (1860). What the detective novel offers is a solution to the mystery, rather than the resolution of a tangled past in the present, as in the 'dead hand' stories. The detective, starting with Inspector Bucket in *Bleak House*, becomes with Sergeant Cuff (in *The Moonstone*) a fully fledged character who solves the mystery. From this official level, he moves on, in Arthur Conan Doyle's Sherlock Holmes stories (published from 1887 to 1927), to the omniscient amateur who stuns the world with brilliant solutions to impenetrable mysteries.

Sheridan Le Fanu was Irish, and a dominant figure in Dublin's literary life from the 1840s to the 1860s. His political interests are reflected in some patriotic popular ballads, but he is remembered for his continuation of the later Gothic strain found in C.R. Maturin's *Melmoth the Wanderer* (1820). Le Fanu's murder story *The House by the Churchyard* (1863) is one of the earliest novels of its kind, written at exactly the same time as Wilkie Collins was producing his novels of sensation. *Uncle Silas* (1864) is a classic of grotesque mystery and complicated plotting, a direct link between the fantasy of *Frankenstein* earlier in the century and *Dracula*, by another Irishman, Bram Stoker, published in 1897.

It is tempting to see the popularity of detective and mystery stories since the mid-nineteenth century as reflecting both the reader's interest in deviant psychology, and the satisfaction of a solution actually being offered – something which, in real life and in more 'serious' fiction, is less and less possible.   Science fiction, in the sense of time travel and space fantasy, became popular in the works of the French writer Jules Verne (1828–1905), although Swift's *Gulliver's Travels* (1726) contains elements of fantasy, travel, and social observation used by most modern writers in the genre.

William Morris's *News from Nowhere* (1890–91) is a socialist utopian fantasy set far in the future, when all the contemporary ills of society (industrialism, government, squalor, even money) have been superseded after a bloody revolution which takes place in 1952. Morris is, in effect, proposing an alternative society whose values (the beauty of handicrafts, the practical application of the Pre-Raphaelite ideals which Morris had shared early in his career) are clearly the opposite of the actual values of the age. His earlier *A Dream of John Ball* (1888) takes the genre back to 1381 – John Ball being one of the leaders of the Peasants' Revolt – and the historical fantasy is a clear protest against exploitation. The book wants to encourage a modern workers' revolt against the society and values of the 1880s.

With the growth of middle-class literacy in the nineteenth century, there was a corresponding growth in writing for children. This was usually heavily moral, full of 'good' children and didacticism. Charles Kingsley's *The Water Babies* (1865), for example, with characters such as Mrs Doasyouwouldbedoneby and Mrs Bedonebyasyoudid, recounts the transformation of a dirty chimney-sweep, Tom, into a clean little boy, worthy of middle-class Ellie. School stories, such as *Tom Brown's Schooldays* (1857) by Thomas Hughes (1822–96), family sagas like *The Daisy Chain* (1858) by Charlotte Yonge (1823–1901), and animal stories – for example, *Black Beauty* (1877) by Anna Sewell (1820–78) – set a trend which has continued to the present day.

Tom Brown's Schooldays portrays Rugby School and its headmaster Dr Thomas Arnold, father of the poet and critic Matthew Arnold. The character of Flashman is the archetypal bully, and the mid-century ethos which the novel affirms is very much the 'muscular Christianity', stiff-upper-lip way: strength of character and physical strength being seen as on a par; emotions and sensitivity being signs of weakness. For many readers this was the best of the British Empire; for others it was the worst!

Some so-called 'children's' writing, like Carroll's *Alice* books, or the adventure stories of Ballantyne and Stevenson, achieved success with adult readers too. Conversely, such adult novels as *The Pilgrim's Progress*, *Robinson Crusoe*, and *Gulliver's Travels* were widely read as suitable for children. Books written specially for children are one result of the Romantic age's view of childhood. Meeting the needs of children, who are a special group of people with unique perceptions, was thought to be vital, though several Victorian books for children were, as we have seen, didactic and heavily moralistic.

Robert Louis Stevenson rises above any attribution of his work to the field of 'children's literature', although *Treasure Island* (1883), with its infamous pirate Long John Silver, has been consistently popular with young readers. Stevenson, like Wilde, was a writer in many genres, from drama to travel writing, from fiction to verse. He was one of the first writers to become a world traveller; writing anywhere, but referring constantly to his Calvinist background and upbringing in Scotland. Most of his best novels have a Scottish setting, but Stevenson's Scotland is markedly different from the historical romanticism of Walter Scott.

Stevenson probes the identity of his characters, finding constant contrasts: between the violent, unscrupulous devil-figure of the Master of Ballantrae (in the novel of the same name, 1889), and his more decorous, righteous younger brother; between the tyrannical 'hanging judge', Lord Hermiston, and his son Archie in the unfinished *Weir of Hermiston* (published posthumously in 1896). This is one of the few unfinished novels in English literature which is generally considered to be a masterpiece, taking Robert Louis Stevenson's reputation on from his most famous tale, *The Strange Case of Doctor Jekyll and Mr Hyde* (1886).

> He put the glass to his lips and drank at one gulp. A cry followed; he reeled, staggered, clutched at the table and held on, staring with injected eyes, gasping with open mouth; and as I looked there came, I thought, a change – he seemed to swell – his face became suddenly black and the features seemed to melt and alter – and the next moment, I had sprung to my feet and leaped back against the wall, my arm raised to shield me from that prodigy, my mind submerged in terror.
> 'O God!' I screamed, and 'O God!' again and again; for there before my eyes – pale and shaken, and half fainting, and groping before him with his hands, like a man restored from death – there stood Henry Jekyll!

This is the classic story of the *alter ego*, personifying good and evil in one character. This dichotomy, essential to Calvinist thinking, runs through all Stevenson's works, and can be seen to embody a part of the general Victorian crisis of identity – where good and bad cannot be easily delineated, where moral ambiguity, masks of social behaviour covering up shocking secrets, and the disturbing psychological depths of the human character are revealed. Stevenson is a writer who reveals realism behind the social mirror. Such writing caused even further discomfort for Victorian readers.

The 'double' in Scottish fiction can be traced back to James Hogg's *The Private Memoirs and Confessions of a Justified Sinner* (1824). This was one of the first novels which could be called 'psychological' in its examination of an evil *alter ego* – the devil in the seemingly normal person. Hogg plays with point of view and psychology in a surprisingly modern way. He anticipates the concern with masks and faces which was to be exploited so successfully by Stevenson and Oscar Wilde more than sixty years later.

In *The Amateur Emigrant* (1892–95), a travel book which examines the phenomenon of emigration to and across the United States – at a time when people were flooding into that land of freedom and hope – Stevenson summed up in one simple phrase much of the philosophising of the age: 'We all live by selling something.' He thus undercuts with directness and simplicity the moral and philosophical ideas of mid-Victorian society. The end-of-the-century capacity for such brevity, without moralising, reaches its highest point in the epigrammatic and paradoxical witticisms of Oscar Wilde.

WILDE AND AESTHETICISM

The Aesthetic movement's insistence on 'Art for Art's sake' was just as much a search for new values as any philosophical or political movement, but its values and motivations have been called into question through the fate of Oscar Wilde (the movement's most prominent figure from about 1878) and the lack of other writers of stature to affirm the doctrine of aesthetic beauty.

Aestheticism may be traced back to Keats's affirmation, 'Beauty is truth, truth Beauty' (in *Ode on a Grecian Urn*, 1819). The giving of absolute values to such abstracts as art, beauty, and culture, is part of the late Victorian search for constants in a fast-changing universe. Matthew Arnold's *Culture and Anarchy* (1869) is an important book in this context (see page 330), with its concept of philistinism. The re-evaluation of art, and the philosophical consequences of this, are found more significantly in the works of two of the most influential critics of the age – John Ruskin and Walter Pater.

Ruskin has been described as the first real art critic. His early concerns were to recognise and preserve architecture in the face of industrialism, and to attack the 'pseudo-science' of John Stuart Mill and the economist David Ricardo (1773–1823). Later he founded the Guild of St George, a utopian society which anticipates much of William Morris's utopian writing. Ruskin's importance lies in his considerable influence on late Victorian ways of thinking about art, architecture and the reclaiming of earlier ideals. His criticism ranged from genuine re-evaluations of painters such as Giotto to all-encompassing critiques of social concerns, which became angrier and more political as he grew older – as, for instance, in *Fors Clavigera* (1871–78).

Walter Pater was less of a polemicist than Ruskin. He was an academic, and much of his writing is in the form of lectures; it was at Oxford University that he began to influence the generation which included Oscar Wilde. In *Studies in the History of the Renaissance* (1873), Pater continued Ruskin's work in the re-evaluation of Italian Renaissance painting (notably Botticelli and Leonardo da Vinci); *Marius the Epicurean* (1885) used the form of fictional biography to explore his concerns with Christianity, paganism and the classical world; *Appreciations: with an Essay on Style* (1889) confirmed his status both as a writer and an 'aesthete'. It was Pater who introduced the phrase 'the desire for beauty, the love of art for art's sake' into English, deriving it from Theophile Gautier (1811–72) who had used the phrase *l'art pour l'art* as early as 1835.

In the 1880s and 1890s, the Aesthetic movement became associated with the kind of pale young man parodied in Gilbert and Sullivan's operetta *Patience* (1881) as:

> A pallid and thin young man
> A haggard and lank young man

who would

> walk down Piccadilly
> With a poppy or a lily
> In his mediaeval hand.

The image of Pre-Raphaelite mediaevalism and delicate sensibility, combined with affectation and sentimentalism, did little to attract public sympathy.

Many tendencies in late Victorian writing come together in the works of Oscar Wilde. His image as a dandy made his name known long before his professional career as a journalist did, and the contrast between image and reality can be seen to run through all his later creative writing.

Wilde is remembered best as the author of theatrical comedies, and for the humiliating end to his career when he was sentenced to two years' hard labour for homosexual offences (made illegal in 1885). The dichotomy between the elegant social witticisms and the seeming frivolity of the comic plots, and the shame and scandal of Wilde's private life, are almost emblematic of the whole crisis of Victorian morals. Wilde's 'transgressive ethic' was a fully conscious playing with Victorian assumptions: 'How I used to toy with that Tiger, Life', as he expressed it after his release from prison. One of Oscar Wilde's stories, which effectively explores Victorian assumptions and values about a variety of issues including art, is *The Picture of Dorian Gray*. It is the story of a beautiful young man and his portrait. As he ages, he keeps his good looks and indulges himself in all kinds of sensual pleasure (the details of which are carefully left to the reader's own imagination) without regard to moral consequences. But, as the action proceeds, his portrait changes, reflecting the corruption of his soul. Wilde, the author, remains detached and refuses to pass judgement. Wilde's view of art is that the artist can have no ethical sympathies. It was, and continues to be, a controversial story, and has been read as a criticism of the 'art for art's sake' movement, as a criticism of superficial self-love, and as a criticism of a society, Victorian society, which does not recognise its moral responsibilities.

> All art is at once surface and symbol. Those who go beneath the surface do so at their peril. Those who read the symbol do so at their peril.
>
> (Preface to *The Picture of Dorian Gray*)

Wilde's essays reveal a serious, concerned thinker behind the aesthetic masks. *The Truth of Masks* (1885) and *The Soul of Man Under Socialism* (1891) probe behind the Victorian facade into the details and implications of some of the standard hypocrisies of the age. He continues a realism of portrayal which the nineteenth century did not want to applaud or even acknowledge.

> A man is called selfish if he lives in the manner that seems to him most suitable for the full realisation of his own personality. . . . It is not selfish to think for oneself. A man who does not think for himself does not think at all.
>
> (*The Soul of Man Under Socialism*)

Wilde's name and reputation have also been associated with *Teleny*, a homosexual novel, explicitly the 'reverse of the medal' of *The Picture of Dorian Gray*. This was published, with no author's name, in 1893 by Leonard Smithers, who was to publish most of Wilde's later writing, after his conviction in 1895. Always limited in its circulation because of its highly explicit sexual content, *Teleny* was only made available to a wide readership in its original form in 1986. Many of Wilde's biographers ignore it completely: others suggest that he may only have been marginally involved in the book's writing. Nothing can be proved, as no original manuscript exists, but *Teleny* remains highly significant as a gay text, and as the expression of a minority voice, which would only be properly heard a century later.

HARDY AND JAMES

In more far-reaching ways, the novel form also documented the social changes of the time. The move from the high moral didacticism of mid-century to the exploration of moral issues and responsibilities can be seen particularly clearly in the novels of Thomas Hardy. Like so many of the major writers of the time, Hardy was something of an outsider. He came from the rural county of Dorset, which in his novels becomes Wessex, the fictional countryside with a long historical past which is markedly distant from the capital city, London, or the industrial North. In this scene from Hardy's *Tess of the D'Urbervilles* (1891), Tess delivers milk on a cart to the local station as the milk train arrives:

> Then there was the hissing of a train, which drew up almost silently on the wet rails, and the milk was rapidly swung can by can into the truck. The light of the engine flashed for a second on Tess Durbeyfield's figure, motionless under the great holly tree. No object could

have looked more foreign to the gleaming cranks and wheels than this unsophisticated girl, with round bare arms, the rainy hair and face, the suspended attitude of a friendly leopard at pause, the print gown of no date or fashion, the cotton bonnet drooping on her brow.

Tess is presented here as 'foreign', as an outsider in a rural world which has seen rapid change, including the mechanisation of transport. But Hardy presents this new world largely through the eyes and inner thoughts of Tess. She is an uneducated farm labourer who speaks in the local dialect of her region and who possesses sharp insight, natural intelligence and deep feelings. Tess is one in a line of such heroines in Hardy's novels, including Bathsheba Everdene in *Far From the Madding Crowd* (1874) and Grace Melbury in *The Woodlanders* (1887), whose natures make them outsiders in their own society as they fall victim to forces and changes, economic, social and sexual, which are outside their control.

Here Grace finds herself alone: the world of nature awakens before her eyes, but with an air of mystery and uncertainty, related to her own emotional turmoil:

> It was even now day out of doors, though the tones of morning were feeble and wan, and it was long before the sun would be perceptible in this overshadowed vale. Not a sound came from any of the out-houses as yet. The tree-trunks, the road, the out-buildings, the garden, every object, wore that aspect of mesmeric passivity which the quietude of daybreak lends to such scenes. Helpless immobility seemed to be combined with intense consciousness; a meditative inertness possessed all things, oppressively contrasting with her own active emotions. Beyond the road were some cottage roofs and orchards; over these roofs and over the apple-trees behind, high up the slope, and backed by the plantation on the crest, was the house yet occupied by her future husband, the rough-cast front showing whitely through its creepers. The window-shutters were closed, the bedroom curtains closely drawn, and not the thinnest coil of smoke rose from the rugged chimneys.
> Something broke the stillness. The front-door of the house she was gazing at opened softly, and there came out into the porch a female figure, wrapped in a large cloak, beneath which was visible the white skirt of a long loose garment like a night-dress. A grey arm, stretching from within the porch, adjusted the cloak over the woman's

shoulders; it was withdrawn and disappeared, the door closing behind her.

(*The Woodlanders*)

Most of Hardy's novels are tragedies, or they reveal the cosmic indifference or malevolent ironies which life has in store for everyone, particularly for those unable to curb the demands of their own natures. His last two major novels were *Tess of the D'Urbervilles* (1891) and *Jude the Obscure* (1895). *Tess* is a deeply pessimistic novel, revealing how an intelligent and sensitive girl can be driven to her death by a society which is narrow in morality and in spirit. *Jude the Obscure* has another central character, Jude Fawley, whose sensual nature cannot be accommodated by a rigid and inflexible social system. The novel has been seen by many as Hardy's most direct attack on Victorian chains of class-consciousness and social convention. Both Tess and Jude are ambitious and articulate working-class people whose lives cannot be properly fulfilled. Tess is a modern version of 'the ruined maid' (a ballad of the same title is used in the novel). Hardy brings together such traditional forms and concepts, sets them in a literary context which goes back to Greek tragedy, and brings out issues which are highly relevant to his own day.

Hardy's vision has been called tragic, and the fate of many of his characters is indeed bleak. Henchard in *The Mayor of Casterbridge* (1886) rises to power, then brings about his own fall in a manner that recalls the classical forms of tragic drama. But his intention is also social. Tess, 'a pure woman', as the subtitle of the novel calls her, is the victim of a hypocritical sexual morality. She finally kills Alec, the man who caused her disgrace. But then society punishes her for that crime too.

Jude Fawley's 'crime' is to want an education. The university town of Christminster is always just beyond his reach. Poverty, marriage and family combine to keep him from his ambition. In one of the most tragic scenes, his children are all found dead one morning, with a note left by his son: 'Done because we are too menny.' Jude tries to comfort their mother Sue, saying:

It was in his nature to do it. The doctor says there are such boys springing up amongst us – boys of a sort unknown in the last generation – the outcome of new views of life. They seem to see all its terrors before they are old enough to have staying power to resist them. He says it is the beginning of the coming universal wish not to live.

This is a savage attack on the restrictions of late Victorian society. The book caused a terrible scandal, as had *Tess of the D'Urbervilles* four years earlier. It was burned, banned and denounced. Hardy became so discouraged by this reaction that he stopped writing novels, publishing only *The Well-Beloved* (1897; it had been serialised in 1892) before dedicating himself entirely to poetry.

The 1890s, and the end of Hardy's career as a novelist, also mark the end of the dominance of the 'triple-decker' long Victorian novel, usually published in instalments. From this time, novels in general become shorter, and are usually published in volume form. The power of circulating libraries began to decline too. They were the places where people paid to borrow books, and the libraries could damage a book's success by refusing to have it. Some of Hardy's novels suffered in this way. But shorter novels were also cheaper, and a new era of book-buying was about to begin.

Hardy's Wessex is not a romanticised landscape; contrary to the view taken by some of his critics, Hardy's world is one of considerable social upheaval as settled communities face the disruption caused by the mechanisation of agriculture in the late nineteenth century. His last novels embody these changes technically. Hardy focuses less on plot, more on the lyrical revelation of character, using techniques of episodic structure; in this respect, though written at the end of the nineteenth century, his novels are frequently regarded as 'Modern' texts. He is one of the writers who best represent the transition from nineteenth to twentieth century.

LANGUAGE NOTE
Dialect and character in Hardy

Mrs Durbeyfield habitually spoke the dialect; her daughter, who had passed the Sixth Standard in the National School under a London-trained mistress, spoke two languages; the dialect at home, more or less; ordinary English abroad and to persons of quality.

(*Tess of the D'Urbervilles*)

Hardy did not consider the dialect of his native Wessex to be inferior to Standard English and he did not consider that representing the speech of his characters in dialect form was simply an entertaining embellishment for his readers. Unlike several nineteenth-century writers, he did not employ dialect-speaking characters who were idiosyncratic, lacked education, or who were exaggeratedly 'low' in society (see Language note, page 338); Hardy took local dialects seriously. In his obituary for the poet William Barnes he wrote:

> In the systematic study of his native dialect . . . he has shown the world that far from being . . . a corruption of correct English, it is a distinct branch of Teutonic speech, regular in declension and conjugation, and richer in many classes of words than any other tongue known to him.

Of course, Hardy knew that to transcribe local speech too accurately would cause problems for his readers, but he believed it was important to retain the spirit of the talk of certain of his characters. He was, however, primarily interested in using speech differences to distinguish between his characters, particularly with reference to their social position and to the social and psychological contexts in which they find themselves. In *Tess of the D'Urbervilles* Tess's ability to move between different speech forms – for example, the dialect of her home and the more standard dialect of Alec D'Urberville – illustrates the linguistic and social dualities and clashes in values produced by new cultural processes. Hardy was also aware that speaking the dialect of the speech community of which you are a part is a natural act embodying who you really are.

For example, Henchard in *The Mayor of Casterbridge* moves towards more standard speech when he begins to achieve material success and a successful position within the community, but when his status changes he begins increasingly to use dialect forms. Here he comments on a man who aspires to his former position as mayor:

> A fellow of his age going to be Mayor, indeed! . . . But 'tis her money that floats en upward. Ha-ha – how cust odd it is. Here be I, his former master, working for him as man, and he the man standing as master.

More commonly, however, characters speak in the local Wessex dialect when under the pressure of emotion. For example, Gabriel Oak in *Far from the Madding Crowd* is moved to speak to Bathsheba:

> If wild heat had to do wi' it, making ye long to overcome the awkwardness about your husband's vanishing, it mid be wrong. The real sin, ma'am, in my mind, lies in thinking of ever wedding wi' a man you don't love honest and true.

Although Hardy was among the first English novelists who understood the social and personal significance of dialects in relation to Standard English, he remained for the most part constrained by the Victorian convention that main characters in a novel, especially those characters who are meant to engage the sympathy of the reader, should consistently speak Standard English. Paradoxically, therefore, major characters such as Tess and Jude (the Obscure) only rarely speak in local dialects, in spite of their social positions. What is important, however, is that Hardy represents his characters as speaking in a way which would be normal both for other characters and readers. He wanted to capture the spirit of independence in his characters but could not risk underlining this by an over-reliance on dialect speech.

In many respects, however, Hardy paved the way for twentieth-century novelists such as D.H. Lawrence, who made working-class characters central to his fiction and who in turn made more extensive use of dialect in their language and as a central element in the representation of values in ways suggested by the nineteenth-century poet and writer William Barnes:

> [Dialect] will not, however, be every-where immediately given up as the language of the land-folk's fire-side, though to outsiders they may speak pretty good English, since 'fine-talking' (as it is called) on the lips of a home-born villager, is generally laughed at by his neighbours as a piece of affectation.

Many of the novelists of the end of the Victorian age can be considered outsiders for one reason or another. Hardy was from the West Country, Gissing from the industrial North. Wilde was an outsider twice over, as an Irishman and a homosexual. This preponderance of outsiders becomes even more noticeable between the 1890s and 1914: Henry James was born in America, Joseph Conrad in the Ukraine (to a Polish family), Rudyard Kipling in India where much of his work is set, and George Bernard Shaw was another Irishman. As we move into the twentieth century, literature's horizons and influences expand in a broader vision. E.M. Forster, although of the southern English middle class, was homosexual, and his work reflects an outsider's concern with Englishness. D.H. Lawrence was from the working class, and spent much of his life in exile from England. T.S. Eliot was born in America; James Joyce was Irish; Ford Madox Ford was of German extraction, changing his original surname, Hueffer, to the more English-sounding Ford in 1919.

An American by birth, Henry James also stands 'outside' Britain, although his education was divided between America and Europe. He was deeply attracted to European culture but explored it from the perspective of a sophistcated New York background. When the First World War broke out in 1914, James became a British citizen.

His early novels, such as *The Americans* (1877), *Daisy Miller* (1879) and *The Portrait of a Lady* (1881), explore differences between European and American high society. The main point of view is that of an 'innocent' character who undergoes conflicts between innocence and experience. The novels are written in the manner of a *Bildungsroman* (a growing-up novel) and in them he reveals considerable depths in understanding female psychology. In *What Maisie Knew* (1897), the narrative is recounted almost completely from the point of view of a child's consciousness and understanding. Maisie is 6 years old when her parents divorce and she is forced to live alternately with both of them. The novel is a considerable technical and formal achievement, as James manages to re-create a child's world and to use language to represent her thought-processes and perceptions. In later novels such as *The Wings of the Dove* and *The Ambassadors*, James's style is even more subtle, in order to render complexities of thought and feeling in the 'stream of consciousness' of the main characters who are each in different ways 'outsiders' in their society.

James was always deeply concerned with art, and how art both shapes and reflects life. From the short story *The Figure in the Carpet*, which shows a concern with the mysteries and intricacies of a design, to his fine novel *The Golden Bowl*, art, artifice and their role in human life are probed and evaluated.

> The Prince continued very nobly to bethink himself. 'Didn't we get you anything?'
>
> Maggie waited a little; she had for some time, now, kept her eyes on him steadily; but they wandered, at this, to the fragments on her chimney. 'Yes; it comes round, after all, to your having got me the bowl. I myself was to come upon it, the other day, by so wonderful a chance; was to find it in the same place and to have it pressed upon me by the same little man, who does, as you say, understand Italian. I

did "believe in it", you see – must have believed in it somehow instinctively; for I took it as soon as I saw it. Though I didn't know at all then,' she added, 'what I was taking *with* it.'

The Prince paid her for an instant, visibly, the deference of trying to imagine what this might have been. 'I agree with you that the coincidence is extraordinary – the sort of thing that happens mainly in novels and plays. But I don't see, you must let me say, the importance or the connexion –'

'Of my having made the purchase where you failed of it?' She had quickly taken him up; but she had, with her eyes on him once more, another drop into the order of her thoughts, to which, through whatever he might say, she was still adhering. 'It's not my having gone into the place, at the end of four years, that makes the strangeness of the coincidence; for don't such chances as that, in London, easily occur? The strangeness,' she lucidly said, 'is in what my purchase was to represent to me after I had got it home; which value came,' she explained, 'from the wonder of my having found such a friend.'

(*The Golden Bowl*)

James's language and syntax are carefully modulated – at the same time delicate and convoluted. His sentences and paragraphs can reach considerable length and complexity, but, in so doing, his admirers affirm that they reflect the deep care and precision with which he worked to achieve the full expression of a highly refined consciousness. The opening sentence of *The Wings of the Dove* is a good example:

She waited, Kate Croy, for her father to come in, but he kept her unconscionably, and there were moments at which she showed herself, in the glass over the mantel, a face positively pale with the irritation that had brought her to the point of going away without sight of him.

Here the constant increase in the clauses, the additional interrupting phrases ('in the glass over the mantel'), even the slight delay in the mention of Kate Croy's name, are characteristic. They show a concern to make language fit the delicate feelings of Kate as she hesitates, reflects, justifies and pauses in her actions and her thoughts about the relationship with her father. The 'outsiders' sense is vital to the ability of James and other writers to look at society objectively, to criticise it from a secure viewpoint and to create a fully realised world in their works.

These writers could bring a multiplicity of viewpoints and subject areas into the novel, which contrast with the London-centred viewpoints of many Victorian writers. The novel begins to represent a worldview rather than a national or regional concern, and its horizons begin to expand outwards geographically at the same time as the earliest studies in psychology begin to expand characters' inner horizons as well. It is perhaps no accident that the term 'stream of consciousness' was a concept first described in 1890 by the American psychologist, William James, who was brother of the novelist Henry James. In the twentieth century, as concepts of society changed and things (as the poet W.B. Yeats said) began to 'fall apart', the fragmentation of all that held society together was expressed in the novel partly by the use of 'stream of consciousness', allowing the psychological revelation of what a character feels deep inside through constantly fluctuating points of view and by a fluid expansion and contraction of time. Although these emphases were new, and do depart from conventional representation in the nineteenth-century novel, the seeds of such developments lie in the techniques used in the eighteenth century by Laurence Sterne, especially in *Tristram Shandy*, in the 'monologues' of some of Charles Dickens's characters, such as Mrs Lirriper in the Christmas story *Mrs Lirriper's Lodgings* (1863), and in the experiments with viewpoint in Jane Austen and George Eliot's depiction of characters.

Something of an outsider in literary life, John Meade Falkner was an industrialist; but he wrote three remarkable novels, each of which is unique in its way. *Moonfleet* (1898) is a classic adventure yarn of smugglers, set on the south coast of England. *The Nebuly Coat* (1903) has echoes of Hardy in its setting and its vivid picture of the ending of a society. *The Lost Stradivarius* (1895) is a mysterious tale of drugs and decadence, set in Naples. Falkner has a fascination with word games, heraldry, and tradition, which lends his stories a mixture of puzzle, history and the unusual.

Adventure novels came to enjoy enormous popularity. They reached a high point towards the end of the nineteenth century in the jingoistic colonial tales of H. Rider Haggard (such as *King Solomon's Mines*, 1886, and *She*, 1887) and the Ruritanian fantasies of Anthony Hope (*The*

Prisoner of Zenda, 1894). In their works, the stiff-upper-lip ethic triumphs over all sorts of devilish plots in the exotic locales of another 'outside'.

VICTORIAN POETRY

Its melancholy, long, withdrawing roar
(Matthew Arnold, *Dover Beach*)

Victorian poetry is generally considered to be in the shadow of the popular genre of the novel: a reversal of the situation in the Romantic age, and largely due to the success of the novels of Walter Scott, who transferred his energies from poetry to the novel in 1814. Victorian poetry is, however, of major importance, and the most popular poet of the age, Alfred (later Lord) Tennyson, is as much a representative figure as Dickens.

In Memoriam A.H.H. is the key work of Tennyson; a series of closely linked but separate poems, it is, in effect, an elegy on the death of a close friend, Arthur Henry Hallam, who died in 1833 at the age of 22. Tennyson worked on the poem between 1833 and 1850, and it was published anonymously in 1850. Its publication appropriately marks a central point in nineteenth-century sensibilities, and the note of doubt and despair of *In Memoriam* matched the tone of the times perfectly, in the very year in which the first of the great Romantics, William Wordsworth, died.

In Memoriam became hugely popular, especially with Queen Victoria after the death of her husband, Prince Albert, in 1861. Its melancholy tone, not without a degree of self-pity, became a keynote of late Victorian taste and sentiment:

> I hold it true, whate'er befall;
> I feel it when I sorrow most
> 'Tis better to have loved and lost
> Than never to have loved at all.

Such melancholy is sometimes reinforced in poems such as *The Lady of Shallot* by a background of mediaeval legend, in which a dream-like atmosphere of brooding tragedy is created.

However, there is more than emotion and simple feelings in

Tennyson's work. *The Brook* gives a first-person voice to a stream, in a vision of eternity:

> For men may come and men may go,
> But I go on for ever.

Tennyson's observation is personal, deeply felt, and in many ways simplifies the worldview of the Romantic poets. But his view of nature could hardly be more different from the Romantics:

> Nature red in tooth and claw
> (*In Memoriam*)

is nature at its most violent, dangerous, threatening, rather than being the solace and inspiration it was to Wordsworth. Although Tennyson is not normally regarded as an observer of social realities, in *Locksley Hall* he presents a vision of social unrest and disturbance which was later to influence W.H. Auden in the 1930s:

> Slowly comes a hungry people, as a lion, creeping nigher,
> Glares at one that nods and winks behind a slow-dying fire.

In such poems he continues a Romantic tradition of social prophecy.

Tennyson's emotion is recollected in regret, rather than in Wordsworth's 'tranquillity'. His sense of loss, doubt and anxiety gives his work a tone of melancholy which contrasts with much Romantic optimism, commitment and wit. Before the publication of *In Memoriam*, Tennyson had published a wide range of poems, of which *Poems*, published late in 1832, is taken as the starting point of his career. (*Poems, Chiefly Lyrical* – published in 1830 – does, however, contain some significant work.)

The best of Tennyson's early poems are dramatic monologues, a form which became highly developed in the hands of his contemporary, Robert Browning. *Mariana*, published by Tennyson in 1830, already contains a note of despair, as the abandoned heroine (inspired by Shakespeare's *Measure for Measure*) waits for her lost lover. Other dramatic monologues, such as *Ulysses* and *Tithonus*, also convey a characteristic melancholy, with a foretaste of Arnold's 'long, withdrawing roar':

> The woods decay, the woods decay and fall,
> The vapours weep their burden to the ground,

Man comes and tills the field and lies beneath,
And after many a summer dies the swan.
(*Tithonus*, 1833; published 1860)

These lines also illustrate Tennyson's musicality, his belief that language should recreate the sights, sounds, and rhythms of vision of life, as witnessed here by the falling movement of each melancholic line. However, such poems also show a stronger, fighting spirit, in the face of challenges:

To strive, to seek, to find, and not to yield.
(*Ulysses*, 1833; published 1842)

After the death of the nation's hero, the Duke of Wellington (commemorated by Tennyson as 'the last great Englishman' in an *Ode*, 1852), the Crimean War introduced a note of futility, and *The Charge of the Light Brigade* commemorates one of the most futile moments of heroism in that war:

All in the valley of Death
Rode the six hundred . . .
Someone had blundered:
Theirs not to make reply,
Theirs not to reason why,
Theirs but to do and die . . .

This note of courage against all odds is the beginning of the characteristic 'stiff-upper-lip' behaviour which came to be seen as typifying British emotions. The contrast between early Victorian sentiment and this denial of emotion is remarkable. On the one hand, it can be seen as a denial of human feelings, of a blindness to reality; on the other hand, of courage in difficult situations, even of heroism. Commentators have frequently accused Tennyson of sentimentality and self-pity. He has also been criticised for being more concerned with sensations than with ideas, and with simply conveying experience, rather than reflecting on it. But such accusations may be overstated. The sentimentality of, for example, Little Nell's death in Dickens's *The Old Curiosity Shop*, represents the final scene in a tearful mode of writing initiated in Mackenzie's *The Man of Feeling* in 1771. Tennyson's emotion is contained, although strongly felt. More than any other writer, he embodies – especially in his more heroic verse – a certain nobility, the peculiarly British colonial unemotional stiffness found in *The Charge of the Light Brigade* and throughout Kipling's more patriotic pieces. It reaches its height in Tennyson's *Idylls of the King* (1859–91), with its note of nostalgic heroism, and in *If* (1892) by Rudyard Kipling:

> If you can keep your head when all about you
> Are losing theirs and blaming it on you. . . .

Recently, Kipling's *If* was voted the most popular and best-loved poem by general readers in Britain. The poem very much reflects a stiff-upper-lip late Victorian ethos, and in fact does not give any idea of the range of Kipling's verse, which uses dialect to express the feelings of the ordinary soldier in India with unusual sympathy and innovative rhythms: this example comes from *Gunga Din* in *Barrack-Room Ballads* (1892):

> The uniform 'e wore
> Was nothin' much before . . .
> You're a better man than I am, Gunga Din!

Kipling, although awarded the Nobel Prize for Literature in 1907, is seen more as a Victorian figure than a modern writer. His novels, such as *Plain Tales from the Hills* (1888) and *Kim* (1901), are usually read as children's stories. They reflect a significant understanding of the culture of the Indian subcontinent, but are often seen as representing the colonial sentimentality alone. Kipling's short stories often rise above this rather negative judgement. *The Jungle Book* (1894) is a vital text in establishing a colonial ethos. This relates to the efforts of General Sir Robert Baden-Powell, a British hero of the Boer War (1899–1902), who founded the Boy Scout movement and used Kipling's text to establish a basis of discipline for the Wolf-Cubs, an organisation which brought together boys between the ages of 7 and 11, now known as Cub-Scouts. Akela, leader of the pack of wolves in Kipling's *The Jungle Book*, became a well-known name for many young boys in England, as leader of their quasi-military group of young associates. More recently, *The Jungle Book* has become well known as an animated feature film from Disney Studios.

Vitae Lampada by Sir Henry Newbolt (1862–1938) – 'Play up! play up! and play the game!' – has been severely mocked for the 'public-school' ethos it embodies, but this way of thinking is central to the concepts of duty and conduct of the Victorian empire-builders. No less a figure than the Duke of Wellington is credited with the affirmation that 'the Battle of Waterloo was won on the playing fields of Eton'. This shows how central the public-school ethos was to the whole age.

It is remarkable that Tennyson turned, both at the beginning and at the height of his career, to the myth of King Arthur and the Knights of the Round Table as a source of inspiration. Malory had used the myth in *Le Morte D'Arthur* as England endured the Wars of the Roses, and Milton had thought of writing an English epic after the Civil War and the Commonwealth, before turning to the more universal myth of the Garden of Eden in *Paradise Lost*.

This recourse to the most potent English national myth at times of crisis is interesting in its wish to affirm English nationalism, history, and a sense of national identity. *Idylls of the King* incorporates Tennyson's *Morte d'Arthur* from 1833 in a series of poems covering the whole tale of Arthur and Guinevere, through romance and chivalry, to adultery, denunciation, and the end of the kingdom, with the great sword Excalibur cast into the lake. The 'moral' is one of change; not just change and decay, however:

> The old order changeth, yielding place to new.
> (Tennyson, *Idylls of the King*)

What sets Tennyson apart as a major poet is his capacity to bring together sound and sense, mood and atmosphere, to make an appeal to the emotions of the reader.

> Tears, idle tears, I know not what they mean,
> Tears from the depths of some divine despair.
> (*Tears, idle tears*)

His is emotive rather than intellectual poetry, only *naming* the 'divine despair' rather than investigating or challenging it, as Gerard Manley Hopkins was to do. It was perhaps inevitable that his poetry should fall from its high regard in the general reaction against Victorianism during the first half of the twentieth century. His reputation has recovered, however, and Tennyson now stands high among the lyrical poets.

Tennyson's melancholy is the first sign of a darkening vision in poetry after the Romantics. Victorian poetry moves progressively closer to despair during the century, coming, by the time of Hopkins and Hardy, to a sense of gloom which anticipates much of the desperation of the early twentieth century.

Tennyson's career, and the parable of the *Idylls*, mirror the mood of late Victorianism, without the early optimism found in the novel form. The poetry of Robert Browning – who was seen as Tennyson's rival throughout their careers, but generally considered superior since – develops the dramatic monologue to its greatest heights. In the early *Porphyria's Lover* (1836), he already shows how the first-person speaker can tell a surprisingly vivid story of love and violence:

> That moment she was mine, mine, fair,
> > Perfectly pure and good: I found
> A thing to do, and all her hair
> > In one long yellow string I wound
> > Three times her little throat around,
> And strangled her . . .
> And thus we sit together now,
> > And all night long we have not stirred,
> > And yet God has not said a word!

My Last Duchess (1842), probably the most widely known of Browning's poems, is also a tale of love and violence, as the speaker reveals to a diplomatic emissary the true situation behind the facade of polite words: he had his previous wife murdered:

> I gave commands;
> Then all smiles stopped altogether.

These two poems were contained in *Dramatic Lyrics*, published in 1842. His later volumes often have similar titles: from *Dramatic Romances and Lyrics* (1845) to *Dramatis Personae* (1864), and two series of *Dramatic Idylls* (1879 and 1880). Some of Browning's best characters are contained in *Men and Women* (1855), where the monologues are spoken by such characters as the painters Fra Lippo Lippi and Andrea del Sarto:

Ah, but a man's reach should exceed his grasp,
Or what's a heaven for?

(Andrea del Sarto)

and by Bishop Blougram, who 'apologises' for his life.

Browning's dramatic monologues enable him to explore extreme and usually extremely morbid states of mind. But his use of different characters and a range of different voices does not allow the reader to identify the speaker with Browning the author. The dramatic monologues, which Browning developed after his experience of writing for the London theatre, act as a kind of mask. They anticipate the monologues of Modernist poets such as Ezra Pound and T.S. Eliot (for example, *The Love Song of J. Alfred Prufrock*). The 'mask' allows the writer to explore the human soul without the soul-searching being too directly personal. It distances Browning from the more subjective style of a poet such as Shelley, who was a considerable formative influence on his writing.

We also find in Browning's monologues many contrasts in language and style with the poetry of Tennyson. Tennyson's poetry is in a tradition which includes Spenser, Milton, and Keats. Stylistically, they favour a polished poetic texture and smooth, harmonious patterns of sound. Browning draws on a different tradition which includes the soliloquies of Shakespeare, the poetry of John Donne, and, later in the Victorian period, the sonnets of Gerard Manley Hopkins. Such poets use more colloquial language, draw on the more discordant sounds of spoken language, and employ contrasting stylistic tones which are often shocking and unpredictable, but serve to startle us into awareness of a world of everyday realities. An example is provided by the following lines from Browning's *The Bishop Orders His Tomb*:

Shrewd was that snatch from out the corner south
He graced his carrion with, God curse the same

in which the dying bishop curses his rival in worldly and unspiritual tones.

Childe Roland to the Dark Tower Came (in *Men and Women*, 1855) is the most intense and mysterious of Browning's mid-century poems. Its title (and last line) uses a line from one of the darkest moments in

Shakespeare's *King Lear* (in Act III, scene iv). Childe Roland is a figure associated with Arthurian legend, a 'childe' being a kind of apprentice knight. He narrates his own journey across a frightening wasted landscape to the mysterious 'Dark Tower'; the poem ends with his arrival – and no sign of what happens next.

> There they stood, ranged along the hill-sides, met
> To view the last of me, a living frame
> For one more picture! in a sheet of flame
> I saw them and I knew them all. And yet
> Dauntless the slug-horn to my lips I set,
> And blew, '*Childe Roland to the Dark Tower Came.*'

In many ways, this poem is an anticipation of twentieth-century themes: the proto-'wasteland', the lack of identity or purpose in the hero, the non-resolution of the story, the mysterious symbol of the tower itself. These are the kind of negative, empty, ambiguous images which became more and more common in poetry, as poetic certainties diminished and romantic ideals disappeared into history.

Browning's was a very productive career, from *Pauline* (published anonymously in 1833) and *Paracelsus* (1835) to *Asolando*, published, coincidentally, on the day of his death in 1889. *The Ring and the Book* (1869–70) was his greatest single success. It employs the dramatic monologue in a multi-viewpoint historical reconstruction in blank verse, telling the story of a seventeenth-century Italian murder, examining relative 'truth', 'imagination', character and setting, in a 'novel in verse' quite unlike any other.

More than any other writer, Browning used his verse to go beneath the surface appearance given by his speakers. He examines 'between the lines' a wide range of moral scruples and problems, characters and attitudes. He is the widest-ranging of Victorian poets in his intellectual and cultural concerns, and spent much of his life in Italy. Many of his poems have Renaissance settings which enabled Robert Browning to explore differences and continuities between Renaissance and Modern worlds.

He met Elizabeth Barrett (Browning) in 1845, and eloped with her the following year to Italy, where they lived until her death in 1861. She was highly regarded as a poet on the strength of *Poems* (1844), and in her lifetime was more famous than her husband. An adventurous experimenter in form and style, she is now best remembered for her 'novel in verse', *Aurora Leigh* (1857), the life story of a woman writer, which anticipates Virginia Woolf's *A Room of One's Own* in its strongly feminine affirmation of an independent viewpoint. The poem is a female *Prelude* (following Wordsworth), a portrait of the artist as a young woman committed to an art which embraces social and political realities.

> The works of women are symbolical.
> We sew, sew, prick our fingers, dull our sight,
> Producing what? A pair of slippers, sir,
> To put on when you're weary – or a stool
> To stumble over and vex you . . . 'curse that stool!'
> Or else at best, a cushion, where you lean
> And sleep, and dream of something we are not
> But would be for your sake. Alas, alas!
> This hurts most, this – that, after all, we are paid
> The worth of our work, perhaps.
>
> (*Aurora Leigh*)

Elizabeth Barrett Browning is one of the earliest female writers on the social responsibilities of the woman writer, like Charlotte Brontë and Elizabeth Gaskell, and later, George Eliot. Her poetry records a constant search for poetic identity. As with Robert Browning, this search sometimes involved masks and disguises. For example, the cause of Italian nationalism enabled her to explore many contemporary social and moral issues; her *Sonnets from the Portuguese* are presented as a translation from Portuguese, but in fact record the stages of her love for Robert Browning. The following lines from one of the forty-four 'Portuguese' sonnets show Elizabeth Barrett Browning to be, as Virginia Woolf described her, 'the true daughter of her age':

> I love thee freely, as men strive for Rights;
> I love thee purely, as they turn from Praise,
> I love thee with the passion put to use
> In my old griefs, and with my childhood's faith.

The year Darwin's *On the Origin of Species* was published (1859) also saw the publication of a poem which was to become one of the most popular and widely read of any age – Edward Fitzgerald's translation of *The Rubaiyat of Omar Khayyam*. A very free version of a twelfth-century Persian poet, it catches an escapist, irresponsible mood which might seem at odds with the seriousness of the time. But, in echoing the Renaissance preoccupation with the fleeting nature of time and the transience of human glory, Fitzgerald's injunction to seize the moment gives almost the only purely sensual enjoyment in mid-Victorian verse, and a suitable antidote to Tennyson's dominant tone of resignation.

> Ah, my Beloved, fill the Cup that clears
> Today of past Regrets and future Fears:
>   Tomorrow? – Why, Tomorrow I may be
> Myself with Yesterday's Sev'n thousand years.
>   . . .
> Ah, make the most of what we yet may spend,
> Before we too into the Dust descend;
>   Dust into Dust, and under Dust, to lie,
> Sans Wine, sans Song, sans Singer, and – sans End!

The wit of Browning is matched in some of the irreverent writings of Arthur Hugh Clough, who has been described as having 'the sympathetic modern accent'. The tone which might find most modern approval is in his *The Latest Decalogue* (published posthumously in 1862), a satirical rewriting of the biblical Ten Commandments:

> Thou shalt have one God only; who
> Would be at the expense of two?

Similarly,

> There is no God, the wicked saith,
> And truly it's a blessing . . .
>
> And almost everyone when age,
> Disease, or sorrows strike him,
> Inclines to think there is a God,
> Or something very like him.

This is one of the few highly ironic commentaries on the crisis of faith of the age. Clough is usually represented in anthologies by his shorter poems, but he is also an innovator in longer poems. His *The Bothie of Tober-na-Vuolich* (1848) is a novel in verse, recording an autobiographical undergraduate love story. In collections of poems such as *Dipsychus* (1850) he explores in depth and detail the extent of his religious uncertainties.

If one single poem brings together the major concerns of mid-Victorian writing, it is *Dover Beach* (1867) by Matthew Arnold. Set in a room overlooking the Straits of Dover, it describes love, faith, and desolation, bringing together classical and modern allusions, to conclude with a vision of the world more completely negative than any in the previous two centuries. Arnold begins with a version of a world of endless sadness:

> Listen! you hear the grating roar
> Of pebbles which the waves draw back, and fling
> At their return, up the high strand,
> Begin, and cease, and then begin again,
> With tremulous cadence slow, and bring
> The eternal note of sadness in

and ends with a vision of bleak nothingness in which meaningless wars are fought for meaningless causes. Against such a background, human love has no purpose:

> And we are here as on a darkling plain
> Swept with confused alarms of struggle and flight,
> Where ignorant armies clash by night.

It is a world which has neither 'certitude, nor peace, nor help for pain'.

This is the twentieth-century 'wasteland', half a century before the First World War brought 'no man's land' into the language. The vision of despair is the antithesis of the 'high moral lesson' of mainstream Victorianism, but it is a vision for which Tennyson, Dickens and others had amply prepared the ground. The reaction to despair might be the jingoism of Kipling, or the pessimism of Hardy and Conrad, or the positivist sense of duty of George Eliot, but the 'eternal note of sadness' was now part of Victorian literature.

Arnold was no pessimist, however: 'love, let us be true to one another' is the saving emotion in *Dover Beach*. But he was an acutely aware social observer. Like Trollope, he followed a professional career; he was a schools inspector for some thirty-five years, and became, like Dickens, an ardent campaigner for educational reform. His poems, from 1849, show a concern with solitude and doubt, notably in *Empedocles on Etna* (1852) with its 'dwindling faculty of joy'.

Arnold's poetry, although imbued with the disillusionment of the mid-nineteenth century, has a wide range of theme, form and tone. *The Scholar-Gypsy* (1853) is a pastoral of the Oxford countryside which reached a wide readership with its observation of 'the strange disease of modern life'. The author himself was displeased with the melancholic tone of the poem. *Sohrab and Rustum*, published in the same year, moves towards epic in its tale of a son's search for his father. But it is in *Balder Dead* (1858) that Arnold reaches the greatest heights in a long poem. It is the major poetic epic of the Victorian age, and is based on a Norse myth of the death of a god. It is an epic of things ending, of doubt, and celebrates the ritual of passing on. With none of the heroic elements of Tennyson, Arnold's hero Balder becomes a more human god, his death a reflection of the condition of mankind. With *Balder Dead,* the English epic is brought back to the human level of the end of *Paradise Lost.*

> And the Gods stood upon the beach, and gazed.
> And while they gazed, the sun went lurid down
> Into the smoke-wrapt sea, and night came on.
> Then the wind fell, with night, and there was calm;
> But through the dark they watch'd the burning ship
> Still carried o'er the distant waters on,
> Farther and farther, like an eye of fire.
> And long, in the far dark, blazed Balder's pile;
> But fainter, as the stars rose high, it flared,
> The bodies were consumed, ash choked the pile.
> And as, in a decaying winter-fire,
> A charr'd log, falling, makes a shower of sparks –
> So with a shower of sparks the pile fell in,
> Reddening the sea around; and all was dark.
>
> (*Balder Dead*)

Dover Beach is the culmination of Arnold's poetic work, published at a time when he was becoming recognised as the leading critic of the day. *Culture and Anarchy* (1869) is the collection of essays which contains his central arguments, and its importance lies in its difference from Carlyle, Mill, and the Victorian philosophers. Arnold starts from social observation rather than philosophical reflection, and stresses the importance of seeing 'things as they really are'. Culture, seen as a striving towards an ideal of human perfection, is regarded as the opposing spirit to barbarism, philistinism, and the consequent anarchy – which would mean, in Shakespeare's words, that 'chaos is come again'. In *Culture and Anarchy*, Arnold asserted that

> Our society distributes itself into Barbarians, Philistines, and Populace. . . . The pursuit of perfection, then, is the pursuit of sweetness and light. . . . *Philistine* gives the notion of something particularly stiff-necked and perverse in the resistance to light and its children; and therein it specially suits our middle-class.

So, ten years after Darwin's affirmation of man's animal origins, Arnold's affirmation of culture as raising humanity above the level of Barbarians takes on a particular resonance. A new vision of what culture, art, and society mean will emerge as the century moves to its close.

> . . . the world which seems
> To lie before us like a land of dreams
> So various, so beautiful, so new,
> Hath really neither joy, nor love, nor light,
> Nor certitude, nor peace, nor help for pain.
> (Dover Beach)

There is an undercurrent of social comment all through Victorian poetry, although the novel was the main vehicle of social criticism. Thomas Hood, best remembered for humorous punning verses for children, wrote as early as 1843 a searing piece against the condition of a poor woman at work:

> With fingers weary and worn,
> With eyelids heavy and red,
> A Woman sat, in unwomanly rags,
> Plying her needle and thread –

> Stitch! stitch! stitch!
> In poverty, hunger, and dirt,
> And still with a voice of dolorous pitch
> She sang the 'Song of the Shirt'!
>
> 'Work! work! work!
> While the cock is crowing aloof!
> And work – work – work,
> Till the stars shine through the roof!
> (*The Song of the Shirt*)

The late Victorian sense of gloom and despondency is well exemplified in the long poem *The City of Dreadful Night* (1874) by James Thomson, also known by the initials B.V. His poem echoes Milton and Blake in its savage depiction of human misery, and it remains a vital text of the times. In his denial of God, there is none of the lightness of Clough; more, an almost existentialist despair:

> There is no God; no Fiend with names divine
> Made us and tortures us; if we must pine,
> It is to satiate no Being's gall.
>
> It was the dark delusion of a dream,
> That living Person conscious and supreme,
> Whom we must curse for cursing us with life;
> Whom we must curse because the life He gave
> Could not be buried in the quiet grave,
> Could not be killed by poison or by knife.

Towards the end of the century, the Scottish ballad poet John Davidson handled the theme of poverty in a first-person narration called *Thirty Bob a Week* (1894). The narrator is a clerk, and one of the earliest positive voices of the 'respectable' working class who would feature in the novels of H.G. Wells and others. For T.S. Eliot, this poem was 'to me a great poem for ever', and some critics have considered Davidson, and his 'dingy urban images', a precursor of twentieth-century Modernism. The tone of the opening verse is lively, but subversive. By the end of the poem, it is bleak and angry:

> I couldn't touch a stop and turn a screw;
> And set the blooming world a-work for me,

Like such as cut their teeth – I hope, like you –
On the handle of a skeleton gold key;
I cut mine on a leek, which I eat it every week;
I'm a clerk at thirty bob as you can see.

. . .

It's a naked child against a hungry wolf;
It's playing bowls upon a splitting wreck;
It's walking on a string across a gulf
With millstones fore-and-aft about your neck;
But the thing is daily done by many and many a one;
And we fall, face forward, fighting, on the deck.

At about the same time that Tennyson was returning to Arthurian myth for his subject matter, a new movement in art and literature was setting about a revolution against the ugliness of contemporary life. The Pre-Raphaelite Brotherhood – as they called themselves when their work first appeared at the Royal Academy – stressed their admiration for the Italian art of the period before the High Renaissance (which Raphael, who died in 1520, was taken as symbolising). A mediaeval simplicity, a closeness to nature in representational clarity, and a deep moral seriousness of intent distinguish the Brotherhood, of whom the main figures were the painters John Millais and William Holman Hunt, and the brothers Dante Gabriel and William Michael Rossetti. Dante Gabriel was a painter first, but became well known as a poet; William Michael edited the group's periodical, *The Germ*, which published four issues in 1850, originally with the significant subtitle *Thoughts towards Nature in Poetry, Literature, and Art*.

Nature for the Pre-Raphaelites is different from the nature of the Romantics or of Tennyson: there is a mysticism in, for example, Dante Gabriel Rossetti's *The Blessed Damozel* (1850) which uses lilies and a white rose for essentially symbolic purposes. This symbolism, and a concern with generalities of life, love, and death, permeates Rossetti's verse for some thirty years, but his writing also carries an erotic charge which is new in Victorian verse, and led to accusations of obscenity when it was identified as 'the Fleshly School of Poetry'. Here is an example from *The Blessed Damozel*:

> Her robe, ungirt from clasp to hem
> No wrought flowers did adorn,
> But a white rose of Mary's gift,
> For service meetly worn;
> Her hair that lay along her back
> Was yellow like ripe corn.

The Pre-Raphaelite influence, however, was stronger on the visual arts than on writing. It was an attitude to visual art and representation which had a profound and lasting effect, but the Brotherhood's writings had a much less enduring impact on literature.

The poetry of Algernon Swinburne brings together many of the ideas of the Pre-Raphaelites, with what Tennyson called a 'wonderful rhythmic invention'. But, more than any of the works of the Pre-Raphaelites, his writings shocked the Victorians, with their emphasis on sadism, sexual enchantment, and anti-Christian outlook. A prolific poet, using a wide range of forms from drama to ballad, Swinburne had a considerable influence on the generation of the 1890s, by which time his own inspiration was failing. But, from the drama *Atalanta in Calydon* (1865) and *Poems and Ballads* (1866) to his second series of *Poems and Ballads* (1878), Swinburne was the new original spirit in English poetry, a spirit of luscious sensuality which was both a moral and spiritual challenge to the ethos of the day. His love poems, in particular, do not so much celebrate the nature of love as explore the pain which often comes with human love. Here is an example from Swinburne's *A Forsaken Garden* (1878):

> And men that love lightly may die – but we?
> And the same wind sang and the same waves whitened,
> And for ever the garden's last petals were shed,
> In the lips that had whispered, the eyes that had
> lightened,
> Love was dead.

In his own life, Swinburne rebelled against established codes, rather in the manner of Shelley. In religion he was a pagan, and in politics he wanted to see the overthrow of established governments. In poetry, his work confirms a collapse of conventional Victorian poetic standards. The poem *Ave Atque Vale*, an elegy to the nineteenth-century

French poet Charles Baudelaire, continues a traditional line from Milton's *Lycidas* and Shelley's *Adonais*, but is almost wholly preoccupied with death and with the extremes of pleasure, pain, and suffering which characterise Baudelaire's own poetry. The following morbid and languid lines are from the final stanza of the poem:

> Thin is the leaf, and chill and wintry smell,
> And chill the solemn earth, a fatal mother,
> With sadder than the Niobean womb,
> And in the hollow of her breasts a tomb.
> (*Ave Atque Vale*)

William Morris was the most significant figure to take up and develop Pre-Raphaelite ideas in his writings and other artistic works. The Aesthetic movement was to have a more sustained and significant literary impact, and acknowledged its debt to Pre-Raphaelites and to Swinburne in its formulation of a more lasting artistic doctrine.

Like Tennyson, Ernest Dowson had a gift for the melancholy line, as in 'I have been faithful to thee, Cynara! in my fashion', but his was the aesthetic sensibility of the 1890s rather than the stoical self-doubt of the mid-Victorians. His poems emphasise the transience of a period in which *The Yellow Book* flourished. This was a short-lived publication (1894–97), famous for its illustrations by Aubrey Beardsley, which came almost to symbolise the Aesthetic movement.

> They are not long, the weeping and the laughter,
>   Love and desire and hate:
> I think they have no portion in us after
>   We pass the gate.
>
> They are not long, the days of wine and roses:
>   Out of a misty dream
> Our path emerges for a while, then closes
>   Within a dream.
> (Ernest Dowson, *Vitae Summa Brevis Spem Nos Vetat Incohare Longam*)

There is in these lines a sense of ending, not only of the century but of much of what it represented. Dowson died in 1900, the same year as Oscar Wilde, the man who, more than any other, embodied the Aesthetic motto 'Art For Art's Sake'. In the poem he wrote on his release from prison, *The Ballad of Reading Gaol* (1898), Wilde gave us a line which sums up much of the late Victorian dilemma of attachment to the past and inevitable movement towards a new century:

> Each man kills the thing he loves . . .
>
> . . .
>
> Some kill their loves when they are young,
>> And some when they are old;
> Some strangle with the hands of Lust,
>> Some with the hands of Gold:
> The kindest use a knife, because
>> The dead so soon grow cold.

No worst, there is none
(Gerard Manley Hopkins)

Victorian despair in verse reaches its climax in the poetry of Gerard Manley Hopkins, which was largely written in the 1870s and 1880s but not published until 1918. Before 1918 his poetry was known only to a small circle of friends, including the poet Robert Bridges who eventually published it. Hopkins is therefore the poet who bridges the centuries, and carries Victorian doubt to the other side of the First World War and into 'Modernism'. He has caused critics some difficulty in categorising him, because of his formal experimentation and his highly personal theories of 'inscape' and 'sprung rhythms'. In some anthologies, Hopkins is classified as a 'Modern' twentieth-century poet; in others he is classified as a late Victorian poet.

Hopkins was a highly original poet, bringing a new energy into his wrestling with doubt, sensuality, and the glories of nature. Although his anguish is very similar to George Herbert's, Hopkins is negotiating with a God who must exist, but can only truly be seen in nature:

> Glory be to God for dappled things.
>> (*Pied Beauty*)

His major single poem is *The Wreck of the Deutschland* (1876), inspired by the deaths, amongst many, of five nuns.

> Five! the finding and sake
> And cipher of suffering Christ.

> Mark, the mark is of man's make
>> And the word of it Sacrificed.
> But he scores it in scarlet himself on his own bespoken,
> Before-time-taken, dearest prized and priced –
> Stigma, signal, cinquefoil token
> For lettering of the lamb's fleece, ruddying of the rose-flake.

Many of Hopkins's sonnets take the bounds of human suffering to levels not attempted since *King Lear*. Shakespeare's words 'Nothing will come of nothing' find an echo in Hopkins's *No worst, there is none*. But Hopkins rejects, rather than indulges in, the negative emotion of despair:

> Not, I'll not, carrion comfort, Despair, not feast on thee.
> Not untwist – slack they may be – these last strands of man
> In me or, most weary, cry *I can no more*.
>> (*Carrion Comfort*)

Hopkins rejects an ultimate despair, because he continues to believe in the existence of God. But his doubts are radical doubts. He questions a world in which right and wrong appear to him to be reversed. In the poem *Thou art indeed just, Lord*, he takes these questions directly to God:

> Thou art indeed just, Lord, if I contend
> With thee; but, sir, so what I plead is just.
> Why do sinners' ways prosper? and why must
> Disappointment all I endeavour end?

This is poetry in the tradition of the metaphysical poetry of John Donne and George Herbert. It is sensuous and intensely spiritual, and, in some poems, involves the description of violent emotions. In a sequence of sonnets, written between 1885 and 1886 and referred to as the 'terrible' or 'dark' sonnets, Hopkins writes from the deepest agonies of despair at a world which is, for him, a spiritual wilderness. Indeed, his explorations at times reveal a wilderness and emptiness within his own soul.

The honest statements of doubt and despair prefigured those of twentieth-century poets such as T.S. Eliot, and explain why his work became so influential on the literature of the modern period when it was published. But Hopkins also experimented and innovated in his poetry and influenced many other poets' forms and techniques. He believed that every object, experience, or happening had its own unique pattern, and much of his poetic technique aims to reveal that uniqueness or 'inscape'. His sprung rhythm means that he exploits every aspect of language – sound, syntax, choices of words (often dialect words) – to render the precise nature of what he describes. For example, in *The Windhover* the language captures both the excited feelings of the poet and the movement of the bird in the air:

> I caught this morning morning's minion, king-
> dom of daylight's dauphin, dapple-dawn-drawn Falcon, in
> his riding . . .

Hopkins breaks with conventional poetic rhythm to produce this unique 'inscaped' description. Many modern poets were influenced by the ways in which he broke linguistic rules in order to express a deeper view into the nature of things. His inventive collocations of words, his grammatical inventiveness, and his individual use of rhythm were to be very influential on the generations of poets who discovered Hopkins's work in the 1920s and beyond.

LANGUAGE NOTE
The developing uses of dialects in literature

Before Modern English developed in the sixteenth century, most writing had been in local varieties of English. As standard English developed, some writers took pains to maintain the importance of local or regional varieties and dialects in their writings.

In the seventeenth century, Robert Fergusson's poetry brought the spoken language of Edinburgh to a wide readership. Robert Burns, clearly influenced by Fergusson's work, was equally at home in using his local southern Scottish dialect as in using English in his writing.

In the nineteenth century, Tennyson used his local Lincolnshire dialect in many of his poems – although these have tended to be forgotten. And, as we have seen in the Language note (page 314), Thomas Hardy acknowledged the considerable influence of William Barnes, the Dorset poet, in many of his uses of language in the Wessex novels and in his own poetry.

Dickens's use of cockney dialect in creating lower-class London characters is perhaps the best-known example of dialect used to delineate social class. It is widely found in the Victorian novel, both for comic effect and as part of the social milieu. Sir Walter Scott used Scots for similar reasons in several of his Waverley novels.

The sense of pride in local dialect can be traced through the works of many Irish and Scottish writers such as Maria Edgeworth and John Galt, reaching major levels of affirmation in the early twentieth century in such works as the mining plays of D.H. Lawrence (using Nottinghamshire dialect), and the plays of the Irish writers J.M. Synge (using the dialect speech of the Aran Islands off the West Coast of Ireland), and Sean O'Casey (Dublin).

The increasing use of dialects in the novel allowed the voices of Northeast Scotland to be heard in the works of Lewis Grassic Gibbon in the 1930s; more recently the voices of the larger cities in the novels of James Kelman and Jeff Torrington (Glasgow) and Irvine Welsh (Edinburgh) have reached a wide readership. The spread of Irish dialect has been more rapid, especially since the writing of James Joyce. Flann O'Brien, Samuel Beckett, and generations of younger novelists and poets have made Irish a distinct voice – and they have not always agreed that it should be considered part of *English* literature. Although there are social and political messages conveyed by the uses of dialects, there is also a strong sense that dialects are natural expressions of individual identity.

Here is an illustration from a poem by Tennyson, *Northern Farmer, New Style* (1829), in which a farmer talks about his attachment to property and gives his son down-to-earth advice on love and marriage.

> Thim's my noätions, Sammy, wheerby I means to stick;
> But if thou marries a bad un, I'll leäve the land to Dick
> Coom, oop, proputty, proputty – that's what I 'ears im saäy –
> Proputty, proputty, proputty – canter an' canter awaäy.

Standard English version:

> That's how I think, Sammy, and I'll stick to my views
> But if you marry a bad one, I'll leave the land to Dick.
> Come on, property, property – that's what I hear him say –
> Property, property, property – canter and canter away.

One interesting question raised by the representation of non-standard English in pre-twentieth-century literature is that writers generally employ it to represent the lower classes, those on the fringes of mainstream society, the uneducated, or the simply idiosyncratic. Non-standard English parallels what are represented as being non-standard people.

VICTORIAN DRAMA

Never speak disrespectfully of Society, Algernon. Only people who can't get into it do that.

(Oscar Wilde, *The Importance of Being Earnest*)

The censorship of plays by the Lord Chamberlain, between the Theatres Licensing Act of 1737 and its abolition in the Theatres Act of 1968, meant that for some 230 years a wide range of subjects could not be handled in dramatic form. Initially a political move, the censorship of plays expanded to cover religious and moral themes, 'bad' language and 'indecency', and anything which was 'likely to deprave and corrupt' the potential audience.

This became a central problem for dramatists in the second half of the nineteenth century, when, as with the novel, social and moral issues became the subject matter of plays. The trend towards a kind of realistic drama began in the 1860s, with the plays of Tom (T.W.) Robertson. Their titles give an indication of their themes – *Society* (1865), *Caste* (1867), *Play* (1868) and *School* (1869) – far removed from the usual theatrical fare of melodrama, farce and burlesque. Robertson was the first playwright to insist on the stage-setting of a room having a real ceiling, and on real properties; this gave rise to his plays being called 'cup and saucer' dramas, almost a hundred years before 'kitchen sink' plays brought such attention to realistic detail back to the stage.

> POLLY You must call me 'my lady', though, or you shan't have any ham.
> HAWTREE Certainly, 'my lady'; but I cannot accept your hospitality, for I'm engaged to dine.
> POLLY At what time?
> HAWTREE Seven.
> POLLY Seven! Why, that's half-past tea-time. Now corporal, you must wait on me.
> HAWTREE As the pages did of old.
> POLLY My lady.
> HAWTREE My lady.
> POLLY Here's the kettle, corporal.
> [*Holding out kettle at arm's length.* HAWTREE *looks at it through eye-glass.*]

HAWTREE Very nice kettle!
POLLY Take it into the back kitchen.
HAWTREE Eh!
POLLY Oh! I'm coming too.
HAWTREE. Ah! that alters the case.

(*Caste*)

The social issues, presented fairly uncontroversially by Robertson, became highly controversial in the 1880s and 1890s. This was the time when the realistic novels of the French writer Emile Zola and the major novels of Thomas Hardy were publicly burned because of the moral outrage they caused. In drama, equivalent outrage was caused by the English translations of the plays of the Norwegian, Henrik Ibsen.

Ibsen's early plays were written in the late 1860s, but it was not until 1880 that *The Pillars of Society* was staged in England, and almost ten years later *A Doll's House* received a successful production. George Bernard Shaw's essay *The Quintessence of Ibsenism,* published in 1891 (the same year as Oscar Wilde's important *The Soul of Man Under Socialism*), gave the first great impetus to Ibsen's work, and to the concept of the 'play of ideas' (see page 382). The new flood of ideas – socialist, Fabian (Shaw's brand of socialism), and aesthetic – was leading to a re-evaluation of the role of artistic expression in helping to formulate public opinion.

> For in art there is no such thing as a universal truth. A Truth in art is that whose contradictory is also true. And just as it is only in art-criticism, and through it, that we can apprehend the Platonic theory of ideas, so it is only in art-criticism, and through it, that we can realise Hegel's system of contraries. The truths of metaphysics are the truths of masks.
>
> (Oscar Wilde, *The Truth of Masks*, 1885)

Wilde's successful plays were all written and performed in a period of three years, between 1892 and 1895. They are brilliantly witty and epigrammatic comedies, whose surface polish conceals considerable social concern: the title of Wilde's essay *The Truth of Masks* is the clue to his comedies, which always handle dangerous and compromising secrets. Illegitimate birth in *A Woman of No Importance* (1893), culpable indiscretions in *Lady Windermere's Fan* (1892) and *An Ideal Husband*

(1895), obscure social origins in *The Importance of Being Earnest* (1895) – these are the dark background to the light comedy of Oscar Wilde. The revelation of a hypocritical society, behind 'the shallow mask of manners', gives a resonance to the plays which Wilde's own destiny was to underscore. (His biblical tragedy *Salome*, written in 1891–92, was another play to be banned by the censor, even though it was written in French!)

MRS ARBUTHNOT All love is terrible. All love is a tragedy. I loved you once, Lord Illingworth. Oh, what a tragedy for a woman to have loved you!

LORD ILLINGWORTH So you really refuse to marry me?

MRS ARBUTHNOT Yes.

LORD ILLINGWORTH Because you hate me?

MRS ARBUTHNOT Yes.

LORD ILLINGWORTH And does my son hate me as you do?

MRS ARBUTHNOT No.

LORD ILLINGWORTH I am glad of that, Rachel.

MRS ARBUTHNOT He merely despises you.

LORD ILLINGWORTH What a pity! What a pity for him, I mean.

MRS ARBUTHNOT Don't be deceived, George. Children begin by loving their parents. After a time they judge them. Rarely if ever do they forgive them.

(A Woman of No Importance)

LADY BRACKNELL I have always been of opinion that a man who desires to get married should know either everything or nothing. Which do you know?

JACK [*after some hesitation*] I know nothing, Lady Bracknell.

LADY BRACKNELL I am pleased to hear it. I do not approve of anything that tampers with natural ignorance. Ignorance is like a delicate exotic fruit; touch it and the bloom is gone. The whole theory of modern education is radically unsound. Fortunately in England, at any rate, education produces no effect whatsoever. If it did, it would prove a serious danger to the upper classes, and probably lead to acts of violence in Grosvenor Square.

(The Importance of Being Earnest)

While Wilde's career flourished, the other main figure in the theatre was Arthur Wing Pinero. His comedies, such as *Dandy Dick* and *The*

Magistrate, are well-made farces. With *The Second Mrs Tanqueray* (1893) Pinero touched successfully on the theme of social scandal, also handled by Wilde the year before in *Lady Windermere's Fan*. But his comedy lacks the bite and wit of Wilde, or the forceful debating ideas of George Bernard Shaw, whose early plays were first produced in the 1890s. Pinero's contemporary, Henry Arthur Jones, was a more socially committed dramatist, his end-of-the-century plays handling fashionable themes such as the double standards of behaviour concerning men and women but without the controversy of Shaw. *The Liars* (1897) and *Mrs Dane's Defence* (1900) are among his more significant plays.

The twentieth century

1900–45

CONTEXTS AND CONDITIONS

The twentieth century really begins before the end of the nineteenth century. Queen Victoria's Jubilee in 1887 was felt by many to represent the end of an era. An end-of-century stoicism, and a growing pessimism among writers and intellectuals, may be traced to several sources, not least the publication in 1859 of Charles Darwin's *On the Origin of Species* which put the existence of God into radical question. Across the whole population, and in the face of rapid economic and social changes, radical doubts about the stability of the existing order were expressed.

By the end of the nineteenth century the pre-industrial economy and way of life had almost disappeared. In 1911 nearly 70 per cent of the country's 45 million inhabitants lived in urban areas. The sense of 'local' community was being lost: a greater anonymity of the individual in the urban context was a result. Society became more fragmented and individual identities more fluid.

The British Empire, which had expanded under Queen Victoria and in 1900 had reached 13 million square miles, also began to disintegrate. The Boer War (1899–1902), which was fought by the British to establish control over the Boer republics in South Africa, marked the beginning of rebellion against British imperialism. The British won but it was a hollow victory, and the war inspired other colonies to rebel. Liberal beliefs in the gradual transition to a better world began to be questioned. The mass destruction of the First World War led many towards more extreme affiliations, and both Fascism and Marxism held attractions for many intellectuals and workers, particularly during the 1930s.

A strong social ethic, continued from the Victorian times of Dickens and Disraeli, began increasingly to influence the political character of the country and its institutions. The Gladstone Parliament of 1880–85 was the 'no-man's land' between the old Radicalism and the new Socialism, but thereafter the aristocracy and upper classes exerted less influence and the state began to organise itself more in the interests of majority community needs. Institutions became more democratic. The Socialist Party grew as Liberalism declined. In 1928 universal suffrage for women was obtained, paradoxically during a time when growing economic depression and slump appeared to lend increasing weight to Marxist analyses of the inevitable failure of capitalist economic systems.

Culturally too, increasing access to literacy, and to education in general, led to profound changes in the reading public. The Education Act of 1870 made elementary education compulsory for everyone between the ages of 5 and 13. This led to the rapid expansion of a largely unsophisticated literary public, the rise of the popular press, and the mass production of 'popular' literature for a semi-literate 'low-brow' readership. By the time of the First World War there was a whole new generation of young soldiers who not only could read but, very important, were able for the first time in the history of war to write letters home describing war in all its unheroic horror. The twentieth century has seen more and more of this broadening of artistic trends, extending into the other cultural forms of radio, television, cinema and popular music. Some writers reacted to this situation by concentrating on a narrow, highly educated audience who would understand their alienation from this changing world; thus, the avant-garde era in writing began. This 'intellectualisation' has been criticised as restricting literature to a cultural and academic elite. However, this tendency has been balanced by other writers who have made use of popular forms in order to communicate with a wider audience.

A tension in writing between the popular and the esoteric, and the popular and specialised, the commercial and the avant-garde, became a feature of twentieth-century literature. Isolation and alienation, together with experimental forms of expression, came to characterise serious literature, while cinematic techniques and the elaboration of popular genres came to dominate other forms of cultural expression.

To some writers, the alienation they felt and depicted was an exploration of the individual sensibility in a world which it was felt was becoming ever more standardised and uniform, an age of the masses.

Looking back on the nineteenth century, it is easy to see it as falling into distinct moments: before and after the defeat of Napoleon in 1815; before and after the accession of Queen Victoria in 1837 (in effect, she gives her name to almost the whole century); and, in intellectual terms, before and after Darwin. Although *On the Origin of Species* was published in 1859, its ideas had been circulating for some thirty years before then, and their currency and effects define the later years of the century.

It is less easy to define the twentieth century. The First and Second World Wars (1914–18 and 1939–45 respectively) mark, in time and in their effects, momentous changes on a global scale: this kind of worldwide effect is a phenomenon of the century. Before 1914, English literature and ideas were in many ways still harking back to the nineteenth century: after 1918, *Modern* begins to define the twentieth century. But as literacy increased after the 1870 Education Act and, as a result, many more people could read and write, the effect on literature was to expand its range, to fragment its solidity, to enlarge and profoundly change its audience, its forms and its subject matter.

From the perspective of the end of the century, a few major names stand out as those who will probably define the 1900s – and it is easier to pick out such names from the first part of the century (say, to 1945) than it is from the second half. Novelists such as Virginia Woolf, James Joyce and D.H. Lawrence will probably remain among the most significant of the century; poets from Thomas Hardy and W.B. Yeats to T.S. Eliot and W.H. Auden will probably still be read in a hundred years' time. It is more difficult to point to major dramatists after the Irish theatre's flowering with J.M. Synge and Sean O'Casey: the plays of W. Somerset Maugham have lost much of their appeal, and the early comedies of Noël Coward are now often seen as light and insignificant.

This serves to underline the difficulty of reaching lasting critical judgements on a period which is close to the present. There is also the fact that there is much more literature, more cultural production in general, in the twentieth century than in any previous period.

Modernism is one of the key words of the first part of the century. Among its influences were the psychological works of Sigmund Freud and the anthropological writings of Sir James Frazer, author of *The Golden Bough* (1890–1915), a huge work which brought together cultural and social manifestations from the universe of cultures. Modernism is essentially post-Darwinian: it is a search to explain mankind's place in the modern world, where religion, social stability and ethics are all called into question. This resulted in a fashion for experimentation, for 'the tradition of the new' as one critic, Harold Rosenberg, memorably put it. The workings of the unconscious mind become an important subject, and all traditional forms begin to lose their place: 'a beginning, a middle and an end, but not necessarily in that order' might, half-jokingly, sum this up. What went out was narrative, description, rational exposition; what emerged focused on stream of consciousness, images in poetry (rather than description or narration), a new use of universal myth, and a sense of fragmentation both of individuality and of such concepts as space and time. As such, it relates closely to Impressionism in the visual arts, and shares many structural features with the new medium of the cinema, which reached great heights of achievement and influence in the first decades of the twentieth century.

Against Modernism it was said that it produced chaotic and difficult writing, that it moved beyond the capacity of many readers and became elitist. Indeed, it is true that readers need a background awareness of psychology, anthropology, history and aesthetics to master some of the literature of the early years of Modernism: T.S. Eliot even furnished footnotes to help the reader with his *The Waste Land*. But all through what might be termed the period of Modernism there were writers who kept working away in more traditional modes. Often they enjoyed greater popular success than the experimenters, but it is largely the innovators who are seen to have defined the new tastes of the times. Figures like John Galsworthy and Arnold Bennett in the novel tend now to be consigned to history as relics of Victorianism, rather than being read as contemporaries of Woolf, Joyce and Eliot. What is significant is that both kinds of writing could flourish at the same time.

MODERN POETRY TO 1945

Things fall apart; the centre cannot hold
(W.B. Yeats, *The Second Coming*)

Queen Victoria died in 1901, but most of the certainties of the Victorian age had disappeared long before. So had the certainties of Victorian poetry in its sounding public voice and its conviction in the existence of a distinct poetic language everyone could accept and enjoy. The year 1900 marked only a chronological entry into the twentieth century; many of the new tones of voice, the new anxieties and difficulties that we associate with modern writing had already begun. This was apparent in the poetry of the 1890s – the decade of Aestheticism and Decadence. It was largely a poetry of urban themes; the Romantic dependence on nature had already declined. The poet was less likely to appear as the Victorian sage than the outrageous bohemian, conscious of the artifice of both life and art. Narratives gave way to lyrics, above all to 'impressions', capturing the sensation of an immediate scene or moment; a development paralleled in the 'Impressionist' painting of artists like Sickert and Whistler.

Above all, poetry was not statement or felt sensation, but 'art'. In 1899, Arthur Symons, one of the poetic 'aesthetes' of the 1890s, published his study *The Symbolist Movement in Poetry*, which would have great influence on modern poets like W.B. Yeats and T.S. Eliot. He brought home to British poets the significance of French experimental symbolists like Rimbaud, Verlaine, Laforgue, and Mallarme, and observed that with them literature 'becomes itself a kind of religion, with all the duties and responsibilities of the sacred ritual'. Yeats himself quickly drew the lesson that 'We must purify poetry', which was to continue, through movements like Imagism and Vorticism, up to the outbreak of the Great War in 1914, the period when the Modern movement in poetry was formed.

There were many changes in this period to the language of poetry. Throughout the Victorian and Georgian periods the language of poetry was felt to have a special decorum and to be different from everyday language. It was seen to consist of a special diction which gave a unity to the poem and which was appropriate for the expression of elevated feelings and ideas. In the Modern period, there is a movement from poetic diction to a new poetic language. Modern poetry contains language that is closer to the idioms of everyday speech and to a more diverse range of subject matter. Instead of a single unified poetic diction, different styles coexist more frequently. This is first noticeable in Hopkins and Hardy, and continues through Eliot and Auden to Larkin and more recently to Tony Harrison, Simon Armitage, and Benjamin Zephaniah. Dialect words, colloquial expressions, specialist terminology, poeticism, and foreign words may be found in the same poem. Such a rich use of language expresses a view of reality which is more fluid, uneven, intertextual than before and which is less patterned and unified. Poetry has become more polyglot. The language mix reflects a sense that there is no longer a fixed language of poetry just as there is no longer one English (if there ever was). Socio-cultural dislocation is reflected in stylistic mixing, which occurs in the work both of modernist experimental poets and in many of the more traditional and conservative poets.

LATER HARDY

Few poets better convey the uneasy transition from Victorianism to Modernism than Thomas Hardy. His novels, written between 1870 and 1895, made him not only the recorder of his distinctive region of 'Wessex', but the explorer of the transition of lives and minds from the age of traditional values and religious certainties to the age of godlessness and modern tragedy, a transition sometimes described as 'the clash of the modern'. After the hostile reception of his tragic and bitter novel *Jude the Obscure* in 1895, he devoted himself largely to poetry and poetic drama until his death in 1928. In 1898 he published his *Wessex Poems*, verse that he had written over the previous thirty years. His poems are largely traditional in theme, form, and structure, and show a continuity with the Wordsworthian art of recording the impact of ordinary daily events on an individual and sensitive mind; they in turn became a major influence on the work of writers like Robert Graves, W.H. Auden, John Betjeman, and Philip Larkin. Yet behind Hardy's verse the unease is plain. The familiar world is progressively growing darker, more unfamiliar and the drama of existence is lived in an uncertain, fated, and godless age.

Hardy was a prolific poet, author of some 900 poems with an extensive range of feelings and attitudes. Some of the poems are gently ironic; some are strongly felt love poems, especially those he wrote following the death of his wife in 1912; some are written in a mordantly comic light verse. Others lament the brevity and fragility of human life; some are bleak and darkly pessimistic. The perspective constantly shifts from ordinary simple events and feelings to a more cosmic awareness, contrasts between 'life's little ironies' and the global randomness of things. In *During Wind and Rain* (1917) a sudden sense of death and impermanence pervades pastoral moments of domestic happiness:

> They are blithely breakfasting all –
> Men and maidens – yea,
> Under the summer tree,
> With a glimpse of the bay,
> While pet fowl come to the knee . . .
> Ah, no; the years O!
> And the rotten rose is ript from the wall.

The preoccupation with death indicates neither total pessimism nor a negative view of humanity. It is because he appreciates the moments of individual human life so fully that Hardy faces the reality of existence so directly. Frequently the result is a macabre humour, as in *Ah! Are You Digging My Grave?* (1914), but it would also extend to the tragic sensibility of his verse drama *The Dynasts* (1904–8), which is preoccupied with the power of fate.

On the last day of the old century, 31 December 1900, Hardy wrote what is perhaps his most famous poem *The Darkling Thrush*. Writing on the bridge between two centuries, Hardy is uncertain what the future holds. A typically Romantic situation is described. The landscape of the work is bleak and funereal:

> The land's sharp features seemed to be
> The Century's corpse outleant.

The voice of a thrush is heard 'upon the growing gloom'. The beauty of the bird's song does not dispel the dark vista. Unlike Keats's *Ode to a Nightingale* or Shelley's *To a Skylark*, the poet in this poem sees no cause for song and cannot accept the hope or sense of unchangingness over time that the birdsong might express. The poem uses a Romantic mechanism, but does not reach a Romantic resolution. It is stern and unpitying and the final stanza reads as follows:

> So little cause for carolings
>   Of such ecstatic sound
> Was written on terrestrial things
>   Afar or nigh around,
> That I could think there trembled through
>   His happy good-night air
> Some blessed Hope, whereof he knew
>   And I was unaware.

So the poem ends in suspension, caught between hope and pessimism. Hardy does not accept one single mood; neither the Romantic hope the bird might express, nor his own sense of historical doubt. He simply acknowledges that, as the corpse of the previous century is prepared for burial, both hope and hopelessness coexist.

Other poems, like *The Oxen*, carry the same mood, a sense of being suspended between a secure community and a world of isolation and uncertainty. Hardy looks back to the nineteenth century for security and forward to a twentieth century 'in the gloom'. He considers the possibility of belief in a beneficent God, but suggests no confidence in his existence. The same attempt at balance is evident in his choice of poetic language. He does not reject completely the poetic voice of the High Victorians, but lets dialect words, colloquialisms, specialised terms, and the vernacular note into his verse (like the unusual word 'outleant' in the opening quotation, referring to the macabre subject of a corpse leaning out of its coffin). In the poem *After a Journey*, seals 'flop' lazily by the sea – a colloquial word which would not have been considered poetic by an earlier generation. When he titled one of his eight volumes of poems *Satires of Circumstance* (1912), contemporary readers knew just what he meant.

In their experiments with language, many poets explored their local dialects. Tennyson wrote many highly significant poems in the dialect of Lincolnshire, for example. Hardy was a major experimenter with the dialects of the West Country, and the Dorsetshire poet William

Barnes is considered to have been a major influence on this side of his work, introducing him to the expressive possibilities of linguistic inventiveness that dialect grammar and vocabulary presented.

It is in his influence on Tennyson and Hardy, and on the poetry of Gerard Manley Hopkins, that Barnes has affected English poetry, but he may still reclaim a place of his own as an individual and original voice, an outsider in Victorian poetry, anticipating many of the linguistic developments in poetry in the modern age.

LANGUAGE NOTE
The fragmenting lexicon

> LOGOPOEIA, 'the dance of the intellect among words', that is to say, it employs words not only for their direct meaning, but it takes count in a special way of habits of usage, of the context we expect to find with the word, its usual concomitants, of its known acceptances, and of ironical play. It holds the aesthetic content which is peculiarly the domain of verbal manifestation, and cannot possibly be contained in plastic or in music. It is the latest come, and perhaps most tricky and undependable mode.
>
> (Ezra Pound, *How to Read, or Why* (1929–31))

The Modernist poet and critic Ezra Pound noted the existence of logopoeia in modern poetry, believing it to be characteristic of much poetry in the early twentieth century. Logopoeia occurs, in particular, when different layers and levels of vocabulary are mixed in a text. Here is an example from the first stanza of a poem by Thomas Hardy, *After a Journey*:

> Hereto I come to view a voiceless ghost;
> > Whither, O whither will its whim now draw me?
> Up the cliff, down, till I'm lonely, lost,
> > And the unseen waters' ejaculations awe me.
> Where you will next be there's no knowing,
> > Facing round about me everywhere,
> > > With your nut-coloured hair,
> And gray eyes, and rose-flush coming and going.

The poem as a whole displays a number of different styles: archaisms and poeticisms ('hereto'; 'whither'; 'twain'; 'wrought division' (stanza 2)); formal, Latinate, almost technical vocabulary ('ejaculations'); colloquial spoken grammar and lexis ('Where you will next be there's no knowing'); romantic, popular song style ('rose-flush coming and going'; 'when you were all aglow' (stanza 3)). It is almost as if there are several different voices playing off against one another in the poem and as if the poet seems unable to stay with any one uniform language or a single or fixed point from which to register the reality of the speaker's perceptions. The lexical fragmentation encodes a kind of fragmentation of the self, a profound psychological disturbance and dislocation which a conventionally unitary and harmonious 'poetic' diction consisting of uniformly elevated words and phrases could not possibly capture.

Such play with vocabulary and point of view is, as Pound observes, common in the poetry of this period as poets sought to enact in their poetry a wider sense of the uncertainties of belief and the ambiguities of action. In the case of the poetry of T.S. Eliot and in Ezra Pound's own poetry, the lexical mixing goes beyond all previously accepted norms of poetic language, extending even to the mixing of words and phrases from different world languages as they sought to give expression to an almost inexpressible sense of social and cultural breakdown in Western civilisation. In Modernist poets such as Eliot and Pound the fragmentation is reflected in a collapse in syntax (see page 371) as well as in vocabulary:

> What is the city over the mountains
> Cracks and reforms and bursts in the violet air
> Falling towers
> Jerusalem Athens Alexandria
> Vienna London
> Unreal
> (T.S. Eliot, *What the Thunder Said*, from *The Waste Land*)

A.E. Housman's volume *A Shropshire Lad*, first published privately in 1896, became one of the bestselling and best-loved books of poetry of the twentieth century. It is said that it was the one volume most of the soldiers in the trenches in the First World War carried with them. The poems speak of love and loss, of the English countryside and seasons, the passing of time, and death, reflecting a lost love and the ending of a passionate attachment in the writer's own life:

> Because I liked you better
> Than suits a man to say,
> It irked you, and I promised
> To throw the thought away.

The sense of loss recalls Tennyson's loss of his friend A.H. Hallam, who inspired *In Memoriam*. Housman's poems are spare and simple, keeping emotion under control and evoking the world of nature in his native county of Shropshire. As with Tennyson's poem, it was an outside event which brought the work to a wider public – in Tennyson's case, the death of the Prince Consort, in Housman's, the First World War, which brought the loss of a whole generation of young men of exactly the age of Housman's 'lad'. In 1922, the year of publication of several of the most influential modern texts, Housman's *Last Poems* were also published, and again were very popular. *More Poems* followed in 1936, and Housman's reputation has continued to flourish.

GEORGIAN AND IMAGIST POETRY

The poetry which is termed 'Georgian' takes its name from the King (George V) who reigned from 1910 to 1936, but in effect it covers a much shorter period. A great many of the most significant poets of the time – including Rupert Brooke, D.H. Lawrence, Siegfried Sassoon and Isaac Rosenberg – were published in the series *Georgian Poetry* (five volumes, between 1912 and 1922), but they cannot be properly classified together. Ezra Pound and T.S. Eliot later severely criticised these volumes, but the reputations of many of the individual poets have remained high.

Robert Graves was one of the central figures in English poetry for more than fifty years. His first published work appeared during the First World War and he was associated with the publication of *Georgian Poetry*. He wrote a considerable amount of poetry between then and his *Collected Poems* in 1975, and was an influence on several generations of younger poets. He is not experimental, preferring classical forms and technical mastery to any of the prevailing fashions in writing. He uses a wide range of poetic forms and subjects, but it is for his love poetry that he is best known, encompassing a wide range of feelings and attitudes at a time when intellect rather than emotion tended to dominate literary taste. Graves was never popular as a poet, but towards the end of the century (after the *Collected Poems* of 1975) his reputation has enjoyed something of a revival, and he is now seen as a major lyric poet, in a century when lyricism was rarely fashionable.

More significant than Georgian poetry, although short-lived as a movement, were the Imagist poets, whose first anthology – *Des Imagistes* (1914) – was edited by the American exile Ezra Pound. Imagist poems tend to be short, sharp glimpses, which contrast with the lushness of Romantic and Victorian verse. Imagism was a movement designed to replace the 'soft', discursive narrative voice of Victorian verse with a harder, more condensed, Imagistic language – 'nearer the bone'. James Joyce was among contributors to *Des Imagistes*, and D.H. Lawrence's poetry can frequently be considered Imagist, although he was not directly associated with the group.

D.H. Lawrence was a prolific poet, especially of nature. His close-up descriptions of flowers (*Bavarian Gentians*) or animals (*Snake, Kangaroo, Mountain Lion, Bat*) penetrate deep into the essence of living things, and are among the most carefully observed depictions of nature in English poetry. He ranged from descriptive to love poetry, from light satirical verse to philosophical meditation (*The Ship of Death*). Had his reputation not been made by his novels, Lawrence would be remembered as an important poet of the 1920s, outside the main poetic current of his times, but reflecting the re-emerging concern with the natural world which would appear in the post-Second World War work of Dylan Thomas and Ted Hughes. *Love Poems* (1913), *Look! We Have Come Through!* (1917), and *Birds, Beasts and Flowers* (1923) are significant volumes. *Collected Poems* (1928) brings together his prodigious poetic output.

Of later poets working in the 1930s, perhaps only Norman Cameron came close to Imagism in his use of a single image to make a poem. The poet Dylan Thomas said, 'a poem by Cameron needs no more than one image'. Writing against the current of the times, Cameron's poetry (*Collected Poems*, 1957, with an Introduction by his friend and mentor Robert Graves) has been critically neglected, as has Graves's, but both are likely to undergo critical re-evaluation.

Charlotte Mew became well known for her first volume of poetry *The Farmer's Bride* (1915). Although she was a contemporary of the Georgians, her poems have a combination of restraint and passion which set her apart. Her second volume *The Rambling Sailor* appeared after her death by suicide in 1928.

FIRST WORLD WAR POETRY

The Poetry is in the pity
(Wilfred Owen, Preface to *Poems*)

At the beginning of the First World War the characteristic response to it was that to serve in the war was a matter of duty. Poetry was written in order to express a sense of honour and to celebrate the glories of war. A typical example is the first part of Rupert Brooke's *The Soldier*:

> If I should die, think only this of me:
> That there's some corner of a foreign field
> That is for ever England.

The poem is a romantic sonnet and is deeply patriotic. It almost celebrates the values of the liberal culture of Brooke and his contemporaries which sees death as a sacrifice which all young men should freely make for the sake of their country.

The image of Rupert Brooke as a golden boy from a golden age persisted after his death (from blood-poisoning) on the way to the Dardanelles campaign. *The Old Vicarage, Grantchester* (1911), with its famous lines:

> Stands the Church clock at ten to three?
> And is there honey still for tea?

is an image of time that has stopped, a world that is frozen forever. *The Soldier* ('If I should die . . .') (1915) is one of the last poems which unashamedly evoked patriotism: it contrasts significantly with the irony of Wilfred Owen's *Dulce et decorum est*, published just five years later. The same Latin line is also used in Ezra Pound's *Provincia Deserta*, written in 1916, and, like much of Owen's poetry, it prefigures the image of the wasteland which was to dominate post-First World War writing.

The horrors of the First World War marked the end of a phase of Western European liberal culture. In four years from 1914 to 1918, over nine million lives were lost from Europe, the British Commonwealth, and the USA. Deep psychological wounds were caused in the minds of the survivors and a physical and metaphysical wasteland was created across Europe. This desolation was increasingly reflected in the poetry of these years. It became difficult to continue to believe in the heroic liberal values expressed in Brooke's *The Soldier*. There is a clear sense that the previous century and its values are, in fact, a 'corpse outleant', to use Hardy's phrase.

The reaction of poets such as Siegfried Sassoon, Isaac Rosenberg, and Ivor Gurney was to write vivid and realistic poetry satirising the vainglory and incompetence of many in the officer class whose actions caused the unnecessary deaths of some of the finest young men. In poems such as *They* and *The General*, Sassoon was one of the first poets to point to the consequences of war for the maimed and disfigured soldiers who had to live with the horrors long after the war had finished. The language of Sassoon's poetry is deliberately anti-Romantic in its rejection of conventional poetic diction in favour of sharp and biting colloquialisms.

> 'Good morning; good morning!' the General said
> When we met him last week on our way to the line.
> Now the soldiers he smiled at are most of 'em dead,
> And we're cursing his staff for incompetent swine.
> 'He's a cheery old card,' grunted Harry to Jack
> As they slogged up to Arras with rifle and pack.
>
> But he did for them both by his plan of attack.
>
> (*The General*)

The major poet of the First World War, Wilfred Owen, began writing poetry in the manner of Keats, but his poetry underwent stylistic changes as he toughened and tightened his language under the pressure of traumatic, front-line experience of war. One of his most bitterly ironic poems, *Dulce et decorum est*, describes the horrors of a gas attack while commenting ironically on the limits of patriotism. (The complete title to the poem – from a Latin epigraph – translates into the phrase 'It is sweet and honourable to die for one's country'.) Owen came to see it instead as a duty to warn of the horrors of war and to ask why political rulers allowed such mass destruction to continue for so long. He also questioned the necessity of war, stressed the common humanity of both sides in war, and linked the futility of the deaths of individual soldiers to the cosmic indifference of a world from which God was conspicuously absent. The following lines from the poem entitled *Futility* underline this stance:

Was it for this the clay grew tall?
O what made fatuous sunbeams toil
To break earth's sleep at all.

This plays ironically on the link between the clays of the earth and the biblical meaning of clay (the human body). The introduction of religious connotations here reinforces the poem's sense of spiritual emptiness.

One of Wilfred Owen's technical qualities is also illustrated in these lines. Owen's innovative use of half-rhyme (e.g. tall/toil) is a pervasive feature of his poetry. Whereas full rhyme would inappropriately underscore a sense of pattern and completeness, the use of half-rhyme reinforces a sense of things not fitting and being incomplete. It is an aspect of poetic form which is highly appropriate for the tone and subject matter of much of Owen's poetry; the bleak landscape which is the background to this poetry. Owen also concentrated on the immediate sound effects of his poems. The result is lines which reproduce the sounds of war:

What passing-bells for those who die as Cattle?
– Only the monstrous anger of the guns . . .
Can patter out their hasty orisons.
                                        (*Anthem for Doomed Youth*)

After Wilfred Owen died, among his papers a draft Preface was found for a future volume of poems. The most famous part of it is the following:

This book is not about heroes. English poetry is not yet fit to speak of them. Nor is it about deeds, or lands, nor anything about glory, honour, might, majesty, dominion, or power, except War. Above all I am not concerned with Poetry. My Subject is War and the pity of War. The Poetry is in the pity . . . all a poet can do today is warn. That is why the true Poets must be truthful.

The contrast with the sentiments expressed in Rupert Brooke's *The Soldier* is very marked. When Owen says he is 'not concerned with Poetry', he means the kind of poetry associated with Brooke. The First World War saw the death of millions of men; it saw the death of Victorian forms of poetic expression and the radical questioning of liberal values. But it also saw the birth of a new realism and a determination to face the facts of the modern world and to write about them as honestly as possible.

Charles Hamilton Sorley, who only left some thirty-seven completed poems when he was killed in the trenches in 1915, was considered by Robert Graves as one of the three major poets of the war. The opening line of his best-known poem sums up the loss and destruction:

> When you see millions of the mouthless dead . . .

The poetry of nature was not ignored during the war – the work of Edward Thomas is based in the English countryside, like Housman's, as in *As the Team's Head Brass*, which is at the same time a celebration of the land and of working on the land, and a reminder that the country's young men are dying not far away in the fields of France. Thomas's best-known poem is *Adlestrop*, which is an evocative nostalgic remembering of a train stopping at a deserted country station.

> Yes. I remember Adlestrop –
> The name, because one afternoon
> Of heat the express-train drew up there
> Unwontedly. It was late June.
>
> The steam hissed. Someone cleared his throat.
> No one left and no one came
> On the bare platform. What I saw
> Was Adlestrop – only the name
>
> And willows, willow-herb, – and grass,
> And meadowsweet, and haycocks dry,
> No whit less still and lonely fair
> Than the high cloudlets in the sky.
>
> And for that minute a blackbird sang
> Close by, and round him, mistier,
> Farther and farther, all the birds
> Of Oxfordshire and Gloucestershire.

This poem can be read as a text 'out of time': a poem of memory, its positive recollections are tinged with a sense of loss, of an era that is lost, rather than just a fleeting memory. The geographical opening up in the final lines might be seen as moving the poem from the personal remembering of 'I' to a wider and wider sense of loss.

IRISH WRITING

As Irish literature moved into the twentieth century, there was an upsurge in interest in Celtic myth and legend. Often called the Celtic Twilight, this is more of a renaissance than a decline, but it tended to be looked on rather in the same way as the sentimental Scottish Kailyard School at around the same time. It is true that it shares some of the Kailyard's homely sentimentalism, but its inspiration is more concerned with national identity and cultural individuality. Writers began to find a confidence in their own ground, place, and speech, expressing themselves in English and Irish. The poet W.B. Yeats, whose career spans the end of the nineteenth century, the struggle for Irish nationhood and the period between the two world wars, used Sligo for much of his inspiration, just as J.M. Synge used the setting, the language, the *otherness* of the Aran Islands in his plays.

The Celtic Twilight was in fact the title of a collection of stories published by W.B. Yeats in 1893. The slightly negative connotations which the term came to have are due to the emphasis on the belief in fairies expressed in some of the tales. But much more positive is the rediscovery of myth and legend which allowed Yeats and other writers to bring such figures as Cuchulain and Finn McCoull into their works as symbols and expressions of Irishness past and present.

The prose fantasy *The Crock of Gold* (1912) by James Stephens is the high point of Irish whimsy, but the book is closer to the world of Pan found in Forrest Reid, and to the magical realism of the 1980s, than it is to late Victorian sentimentality. Stephens edited volumes of fairytales, but he also wrote more realistic works such as *The Charwoman's Daughter* (1912) which confirm that the best writers could work with myth and legend and with more modern subjects side by side.

Many poets contributed to the Irish Renaissance, although Yeats rapidly left them behind: Seamus O'Sullivan's *The Twilight People* (1905) is illustrative of precisely the self-indulgent tone which gave the movement a rather negative reputation.

W.B. YEATS

Like Thomas Hardy, W.B. Yeats is a poet whose poetry stretches across the whole period of the late Victorian and Early Modern ages. However, Yeats's poetry undergoes more marked changes during these years than that of Hardy. Yeats is not as restlessly experimental as T.S. Eliot, but he is not as content as Hardy to work with traditional forms and poetic subject matter. Yeats's first poetry was published in 1885 and he continued writing until his death in 1939.

There are three main stages to Yeats's development as a poet. The first phase, when he was associated both with the Aesthetic movement of the 1890s and the Celtic Twilight, is characterised by a self-conscious Romanticism. The poetry is sometimes based on Irish myth and folklore and has a mystical, dream-like quality to it. Yeats at that time wanted his poetry to be seen as a contribution to a rejuvenated Irish culture but he also wanted it to have a distinctive stamp, and the structure and imagery of many of these poems have considerable clarity and control. Yeats was also regularly in the habit of revising his poems, and when he revised many of these early poems he sharpened the language in an attempt to clarify the imagery. A key early poem is *The Lake Isle of Innisfree*, a poem of idealistic escape, which dates from Yeats's stay in London in 1890.

> I will arise and go now, and go to Innisfree,
> And a small cabin build there, of clay and wattles made . . .

The second main phase of Yeats's poetic career was dominated by his commitment to Irish nationalism, and it was Irish nationalism which first sent Yeats in search of a consistently simpler, popular, and more accessible style. As Yeats became more and more involved in public nationalist issues, so his poetry became more public and concerned with the politics of the modern Irish state.

In one of his most famous poems, *Easter 1916*, Yeats describes the Easter Rising of 1916 in which (as part of their continuing struggle for independence) Irish nationalists launched a heroic but unsuccessful revolt against the British government. A number of the rebels, who were known to Yeats personally, were executed. The callous and unfeeling treatment of the uprising moved Yeats to deep anger and bitterness. Yeats recognised, however, that the causes of violence, disorder, and repression are complex and have to be confronted and understood. For example, his poem *The Second Coming* (1921) is a chilling vision of impending death and dissolution. It contains the famous lines:

> Things fall apart; the centre cannot hold;
> Mere anarchy is loosed upon the world . . .

but the dissolution is part of a cycle of history which also guarantees order, joy and beauty. There is gaiety and celebration in Yeats's poetry in these years as well as terror and fear of anarchy. The refrain of *Easter 1916* is that 'A terrible beauty is born'. Terror and beauty are contraries, yet a recognition of the essentially cyclical nature of life and of history helped Yeats to resolve many of the contraries and paradoxes he experienced. It is not surprising, therefore, that Yeats's poetry at this time contains many images of winding staircases, gyres, spinning-tops, and spirals. Yeats developed an elaborate symbolic system which was private to him, in certain particulars drawn from traditions of esoteric thought which almost compensated for a lost religion. But his greatness as a poet lies in communicating both precisely and evocatively to readers who may know nothing of his sources.

Between the First World War and 1930, the most significant volumes Yeats published include *The Wild Swans at Coole* (1917), *Michael Robartes and the Dancer* (1921), *The Tower* (1928), and *The Winding Stair* (1929). Yeats handles themes of age and myth in poems such as *Sailing to Byzantium* (from *The Tower*), which opens with the line:

> That is no country for old men.

The concern is with the new Ireland, and its future; the poet 'returns' to the holy city of Byzantium as a symbol of artistic/creative perfection. The concern with the passing of time, a major concern in many Modernist writers, becomes clear in the poem's last line, which speaks 'Of what is past, or passing, or to come'.

In the final phase of his career, Yeats reconciles elements from both his earlier periods, fusing them into a mature lyricism. The poetry is less public and more personal. He develops his theories of contraries and of the progression which can result from reconciling them, but he also writes about the eternity of art, producing in the process many memorable poems which have come to be seen as having enduring value. The later poems explore contrasts between physical and spiritual dimensions to life, between sensuality and rationality, between turbulence and calm. Yeats's *Among School Children* (also from *The Tower*) places the 'sixty-year-old smiling public man', now a senator in the newly independent Ireland, among the new generation. His own uncertainties dominate the later poems, until his final words, in *Under Ben Bulben* (1938), when he instructs the younger generation of Irish writers:

> Irish poets, learn your trade,
> Sing whatever is well made.

Like T.S. Eliot, Yeats creates a modern idiom for poetry, particularly in merging formal and colloquial styles. He adheres, however, more strictly to traditional forms than Eliot and is more comfortable than his contemporary with the direct expression of a personal self. He is less ironic and less distrustful of Romanticism than Eliot. He is also less willing than Eliot to embrace a single religious vision.

T.S. ELIOT

These fragments I have shored against my ruins
(*What the Thunder Said*, from *The Waste Land*)

The ruins created across Europe as a result of the First World War enter the world of T.S. Eliot's poetry indirectly. There is little direct reference to the war. Eliot's major poem, *The Waste Land*, published in 1922, is not a land literally laid waste by war, a real wasteland which poets such as Owen and Rosenberg had graphically described. It does not mention the economic dislocation which would eventually lead to the unemployment and economic crises of the late 1920s. Instead the poem depicts a cultural and spiritual waste land, a land populated by people who are, physically and emotionally, living a kind of death in the midst of their everyday lives:

> A crowd flowed over London Bridge, so many
> I had not thought death had undone so many.
> (*The Burial of the Dead*, from *The Waste Land*)

The people move across a desolate landscape of fragmented images; they do not relate to one another. The many different voices we hear in the poem speak not to each other but past each other. There is no uniting belief in one transcendent God. In this sense, Eliot echoes the post-Darwinian concerns of an unstable world, and many of the ideas owe a lot to Frazer's *The Golden Bough* (see page 350).

To many of T.S. Eliot's contemporaries, the whole poem was written in the accent of its times – an unmistakably twentieth-century, indeed post-war poem which records the collapse in the values of Western civilisation. The main examples of this collapse are sterile, unloving sexual relationships, cultural confusion, and spiritual desolation. Eliot sees the root of the modern world's unhappiness and alienation in the fact that people are unable to bring together the different areas of their experience to make a complete whole. Their social, sexual, and religious experiences are fragmentary and not unified.

Eliot's poetry breaks radically with much of the other poetry written during these years. Like the War Poets, he felt that the poetic idiom available to him was exhausted and had to be changed. Different experiences needed different styles and uses of language. Eliot's poetry went much further than that of the War Poets, however. His poetry was formally more experimental and innovative, and intellectually more complex and philosophical.

In an essay on *The Metaphysical Poets* (1921) – which reveals the influence on him of seventeenth-century poetry – Eliot wrote about complex modern poetry for complex modern times:

> Our civilization comprehends great variety and complexity, and this variety and complexity, playing upon a refined sensibility, must produce various and complex results. The poet must become more and more comprehensive, more allusive, more indirect, in order to force, to dislocate if necessary, language into his meaning.

Instead of the traditional lyric rhythms and conventionally beautiful and 'poetic' images of the pre-war poets, Eliot uses images that shock and bewilder. They are images which are original and novel, striking and obscure, drawn from a discordant urban rather than a harmonious rural life:

What is the city over the mountains
Cracks and reforms and bursts in the violet air
Falling towers
Jerusalem Athens Alexandria
Vienna London
Unreal
        (*What the Thunder Said,* from *The Waste Land*)

There is no doubt that this kind of poetry is difficult to read. A main cause of difficulty for the reader is that Eliot suppresses all direct connections between these images. The reader has to work hard to build up meanings without overt explanation from the poet. The reader has to rebuild the fragments by an indirect process of association.

The three principal qualities which characterise Eliot's work have been neatly summarised as: first, his particular sense of the age in which he lived; second, his conviction that poetry, although using the poet's emotions as its starting point, becomes 'impersonalised' by the tradition in which the poet works; and third, his use of quotations from and allusions to other poets' work for reference, parody, irony, and a sense of continuing intertextual communication and community. 'Immature poets borrow; mature poets steal,' he wrote; 'bad poets deface what they take, and good poets make it into something better, or at least something different'.

It is important to note Eliot's use of rhythm and metre: he strongly maintained he had no time for 'free verse', which he said 'does not exist'. He continues the tradition of the dramatic mono-logue, especially that used by Browning, and while alluding to the whole tradition of English poetry he exploits the past for use in the present. He requires of the reader an 'auditory imagination' rather than just a capacity to understand his poetry. In his essay *The Use of Poetry and the Use of Criticism* (1933), he sees this as 'the feeling for syllable and rhythm, penetrating far below the conscious levels of thought and feeling ... returning to the origin and bringing some-thing back, seeking the beginning and the end'. Bringing together 'the old and obliterated and the trite' with 'the current and the new and surprising' was Eliot's poetic intention, and in many ways his achievement.

Eliot saw himself as English and the traditions he was working in as European rather than American, although he was born in Missouri. He was considerably influenced by French contemporaries such as Henri Alain-Fournier (author of the novel *Le Grand Meaulnes*) and by the critic and philosopher Henri Bergson; earlier figures such as Jules Laforgue and Charles Baudelaire helped to shape his Modernism, with its particular intensity and urban imagery. Historically, Dante was a lifelong inspiration and influence.

Difficulties are created by Eliot's frequent allusions to other literatures, languages, and cultures. Many of these references are difficult to follow, require a specialised knowledge, or are simply highly personal to Eliot's own individual reading. *The Waste Land* contains end notes which Eliot, perhaps not without some irony, supplies himself and which explain some of the more cryptic references. For example, in the lines:

> Son of Man
> You cannot say, or guess, for you know only
> A heap of broken images . . .
> (*The Burial of the Dead,* from *The Waste Land*)

the allusion to 'Son of Man' is taken from the Bible (the Book of Ezekiel) and refers to God who addresses Ezekiel direct. In Eliot's poem, communication between God and man is at best indirect, if it takes place at all. The 'broken images' are also the false idols of Israel, which God has destroyed. In the modern world the false and broken images are all that remain. Eliot achieves an ironic contrast by highlighting differences between ancient and modern worlds. One possible result of this poetic method is obscurity but it is an important part of Eliot's overall purpose, as he explains himself:

> Any obscurity in the poem, on first readings, is due to the suppression of 'links in the chain', of explanatory and connecting matter, and not to incoherence, or love of cryptogram. The justification of such abbreviation of method is that the sequence of images coincides and concentrates into one intense impression of barbaric civilization.

Fragments broken from a whole are all that twentieth-century civilisation has to interpret the world. At the end of *The Waste Land*, however, T.S. Eliot succeeds in suggesting that a spiritual whole can be created from the parts. Timeless values still exist and can be recovered. The wasteland can be regenerated and fragments from the past can be used to survive the ruins of a collapsed civilisation.

In an earlier poem, *The Love Song of J. Alfred Prufrock* (published in Ezra Pound's *Poetry* magazine in 1915), Eliot first demonstrates an almost total break with the conventions of Romantic poetry. He applies to poetry a technique similar to that of the stream of consciousness (see pages 418 ff.), giving fragments of the thoughts passing through the mind of the lonely Mr Prufrock, who seems to be a failed lover. It is a poem more in the tradition of the dramatic monologue developed by Robert Browning. It is not an ordinary love poem and Prufrock continually gives voice to feelings of disorientation. The poem is ironic – as suggested by the rather ridiculous name of the main character – and the character cannot be directly equated with the poet himself. Indeed there are, as it were, different Prufrocks. There is no consistent point of view or single self explored in the poem.

> Let us go then, you and I,
> When the evening is spread out against the sky
> . . .
> In the room the women come and go
> Talking of Michelangelo.

An interesting question is whether Eliot effectively embodies the spirit of his times: that is, whether Eliot uses a technique of fragmentation in order to depict a fragmented society or whether he simply indulges his own personal view of the broken images of a modern world. Critics disagree whether poems like *Prufrock* or *The Waste Land* are socially responsible pictures of the modern world or essentially private and personal pieces of self-expression.

Eliot was an American, deeply drawn towards the British Anglican tradition, and his later poetry is characterised by a quiet searching for spiritual peace. Poems like *Marina* explore aspects of religious revelation; and his major poetic sequence *Four Quartets*, with its many allusions to the Bible, to mystical religious literature, and to Dante, presents a sustained exploration of the relations between moments in human time and moments of spiritual eternity. (Eliot's plays deal, directly or indirectly, with religious themes.) The later style and uses of language still retain features from his earlier poems. *Marina*, for example, presents a sequence of images which are difficult to connect and require some knowledge on the part of the reader of Shakespeare's late play *Pericles*, in which Pericles's daughter, Marina, is lost as a young child and then found by her father again as a young woman. The images in the poem of the father rediscovering his daughter can be equated with images of religious awakening:

> What seas what shores what granite islands towards my timbers
> And woodthrush calling through the fog
> My daughter.

The images here are fragments; there is no punctuation but there is a sequence of interconnected feeling and awareness, based on a developing spiritual knowledge, which has no parallel in Eliot's earlier poetry.

LANGUAGE NOTE
Modernist poetic syntax

One of the aims of Modernist poets was to articulate a representation of the world and of a way of seeing which expressed a profound sense of a spritual and psychological condition which was not readily definable and certainly not easily definable within conventional poetic resources. For these purposes the limits of expression in rhythm, the use of images and symbols, allusion and reference and word choice were extended: at the same time the limits of syntax as a resource for the expression of meaning were explored. Here is an example from the opening of T.S. Eliot's *The Love Song of J. Alfred Prufrock*, first published in 1915:

> Let us go then, you and I,
> When the evening is spread out against the sky
> Like a patient etherised upon a table;
> Let us go, through certain half-deserted streets,
> The muttering retreats
> Of restless nights in one-night cheap hotels
> And sawdust restaurants with oyster shells:

Streets that follow like a tedious argument
Of insidious intent
To lead you to an overwhelming question . . .
Oh, do not ask, 'What is it?'
Let us go and make our visit.

The 'I' here is a persona created in the poem but the character of the 'you' is not at all clear. It could refer to us, the readers, or it might be someone who is invited within the speech situation to accompany the 'I', or it may possibly be another part of the personality of the 'I' with the result that the speaker in the poem is addressing another self, an *alter ego*. Neither the identity of the 'I' nor the 'you' is entirely clear and as a result of such indefinite pronoun use a sense of psychological unease and division is suggested. The syntactic structure of the poem also does not wholly cohere. Is it the streets or the argument that leads to the 'overwhelming question'; and how can streets follow and lead at the same time? And why is the question not asked? Attempts to try to answer these questions by examining the details of the text only lead to further questions and further problems as the reader begins to perceive that the journey is more metaphorical than literal. It is a progress through fragments of thoughts, memories, and dialogues out of which no arrival seems feasible.

The syntactic dislocation and disorientation are compounded by an Imagistic confusion: does the 'etherised' state refer to the sky or to the condition of the visitors? Similarly, the irregular verse movement is brought back to a pattern of rhyme at the end of the paragraph but the rhyme frames a trite and deliberately dismissive rhythm, appropriate perhaps to the dismissal of unanswerable questions.

Both Eliot and Yeats used fragments from earlier cultural expression to resist the ruins of the contemporary civilisation which they saw around them. Both poets sought order and significance in a variety of different traditions, myths, and beliefs. Eliot expresses this diversity in the different styles, languages, and voices of his early poetry. In his later poetry he writes in a more consistent style, as he attempts to bring together diverse ideas and different areas of experience into a more unified whole. He seeks a single poetic voice and single religious viewpoint.

Throughout the different stages of his career, Yeats made more direct and personal poetic statements. His poetic styles never became as fragmented as those of Eliot. Unlike Eliot, however, Yeats did not occupy a single viewpoint and was always ready to explore a contrary position. Yeats continued to see things cyclically, making the fragments of his ideas into a whole, then breaking them into fragments again. For Yeats, a deeper understanding and a creative joy in life resulted from this process.

The following much-quoted lines from Yeats's poem *The Second Coming* illustrate these points:

> And what rough beast, its hour come round at last,
> Slouches towards Bethlehem to be born?

In the modern world a new Christ is unlikely to be born. It is more likely to be an unidentifiable but violent beast. We should note, too, the use of the colloquial word 'slouches'. It is more precise, say, than a word such as 'moves'; it is rougher, less conventionally 'poetic', more shocking. It is part of a modern idiom of mixed styles of language which the poem creates.

Eliot consulted Ezra Pound over the writing of *The Waste Land* and dedicated it to him as *il miglior fabbro*, or the greater poet. Pound advised Eliot on the arrangement and editing of the fragments which make up the text.

Pound's own career after the publication of *Hugh Selwyn Mauberley* in 1920 was spent largely in Italy, and was devoted to the writing of the *Cantos*, the first three of which had been published in 1917 in the magazine *Poetry*. The *Cantos* are an immensely ambitious, allusive, multi-cultural poetic voyage through numerous aspects of twentieth-century thought and experience. Although daunting to the reader, they are a major contribution to modern writing – and possibly the poetic text that was longest in its writing, the last *Cantos* being published in 1970.

POPULAR POETS

While Eliot and Pound were bringing Modernism into poetry, and Yeats was at his most productive, the two bestselling poets of the 1920s were the Poets Laureate Robert Bridges and John Masefield.

Bridges is best remembered for bringing the poetry of Gerard Manley Hopkins to a wide public in 1918, but his own poetry reached a considerably greater readership, notably with *The Testament of Beauty* in 1929.

Masefield's subject was the sea, and in his prolific career he wrote poems, novels such as *Sard Harker* (1924), stories and adventure yarns. The well-known short poem *Cargoes* was published in *Ballads and Poems* (1910), and his *Collected Poems* (1923, the year after the publication of *The Waste Land*) was a bestseller. He continued to write prolifically as Poet Laureate from 1930 until his death in 1967, the second longest term in office as Laureate, exceeded only by Tennyson.

If Masefield was the poet of the open sea, W.H. Davies was the poet of the open road. His *The Autobiography of a Super-Tramp* (1908) continues a tradition established with George Borrow's *Lavengro* in 1851: picaresque pictures of life on the road – a style which Jack Kerouac would later Americanise successfully. Davies's poetry reached a wide readership, affirming countryside and rural values with great success.

> What is this life if, full of care,
> We have no time to stand and stare.
>
> No time to stand beneath the boughs
> And stare as long as sheep and cows.
> 			(*Leisure*)

THIRTIES POETS

Consider this and in our time
As the hawk sees it or the helmetted airman
			(W.H. Auden, *Consider*)

Most writers between the wars displayed an engagement with the issues of the time. In essays, criticism, and journalism a wide range of views are aired which might not find their way into novels or poetry. In the 1930s, political commitment became a more noticeable part of creative writing, especially in the poetry of Auden.

These lines, from the poem *Consider* by W.H. Auden, published in 1930, characterise much writing in the 1930s. The word 'consider' – in the imperative form – addresses the reader directly, proposing action or at least inviting some thought before any action is taken. The poet stresses the present, asking us to consider 'this', which suggests something close to us. We also consider something which is contemporary and 'in our time', with Auden inviting us to see more clearly what is taking place before our own eyes.

In order to see more clearly, we have to develop a proper perspective on our world. We should regard things as if from a great height, like a hawk or an airman who can consider events clinically and objectively. The use of the present tense 'sees' is a universal present, expressing a general truth and underlining how important it is to view things in this way. Auden stresses that such a viewpoint is particularly relevant at the time of writing the poem.

In the decade of the 1930s the skies contained both natural and man-made objects – the hawk and the helmetted airman. The airman may be in a battle helmet, his plane is likely to be a war-plane, his actions are threatening the coming decade. One of the tasks of the poet is to warn us to consider our times and be prepared for appropriate action.

One of the main European political events of the 1930s, which drew a response from writers was the Spanish Civil War (1936–39). They felt that its outcome would shape the future, particularly since a second world war seemed close. In 1937, Auden wrote a poem entitled *Spain*. In the poem, he sees the war as a battle between good and evil forces. The forces of evil are associated with Fascism and the regime of the dictator General Franco; the forces of good are associated with the Republican army which had the support of the majority of the ordinary people of Spain. Auden stresses the importance of the struggle 'today' because it affects the future 'tomorrow':

> Tomorrow the rediscovery of romantic love,
> The photographing of ravens; all the fun under
> > Liberty's masterful shadow.
> Tomorrow . . . the eager election of chairmen
> By a sudden forest of hands. But today the struggle.

Auden saw the struggle for Spain as a political struggle. Victory would ensure that democracy ('election' by voting with a show of hands) prevailed. But he also saw a struggle between opposing moral and psychological forces, with one side representing negative feelings and the other side a positive democracy of feeling which is at the heart of all humane action:

> Madrid is the heart. Our moments of tenderness blossom
> > As the ambulance and the sandbag;
> Our hours of friendship into a people's army.

This poetry is noticeably different from the poetry of the 1920s. Eliot's poetry explores a private condition; Auden's poetry explores a more public situation. Eliot is searching primarily for spiritual solutions; Auden is stressing that our private worlds cannot be separated from social and political contexts. T.S. Eliot uses form and language to embody the confusions and complexities of individual identity in the modern world. As a result, his poetry is often obscure and difficult. W.H. Auden during this period uses form and language to communicate a more social perspective on the modern world. As a result, his poetry is more accessible and more popular. However, both Auden and Eliot share the same poetic quest for a meaning to life amidst images of a contemporary world which fail to form a coherent whole.

Although W.H. Auden's poetic voice was powerful and influential throughout the 1930s, many other writers responded to the events of that decade with equal energy and commitment. They also considered 'this' and 'in our time', and their writing fused the private and public worlds, attempting to win a wider readership.

A number of these poets were called the Auden Group because they developed a style and viewpoint similar to W.H. Auden. The most important members of this group were Louis MacNeice, C. Day Lewis and Stephen Spender. Their poetry is diverse but there is again a focus on social themes and on a use of clear, ordinary language and popular forms. In this extract by Day Lewis, from a *Song* for the child of poor parents, one aim is to awaken greater social awareness:

> The stars in the bright sky
> Look down and are dumb
> At the heir of the ages
> Asleep in a slum
>
> Thy mother is crying,
> Thy dad's on the dole,

Two shillings a week is
The price of a soul.

The setting of such poems is often urban while the environment is often seen as twisted out of its natural shape.

In *The Pylons* by Stephen Spender, as in the opening lines to W.H. Auden's *Consider*, the natural and the man-made coexist:

Now over these small hills they have built the concrete
That trails black wire:
Pylons, these pillars
Bare like nude, giant girls that have no secret.

The mood here is not one of overt protest. Spender does not appear to know how best to react, but he does feel a duty to record what he sees and to catalogue the details – here twentieth-century images of huge electricity pylons crossing the country. Part of his message seems to be that we do not sufficiently consider the implications for the future of what we see and what we know.

Louis MacNeice catalogues his environment in great detail and in forms, like a letter, diary, or journal, which appear ordinary and every-day. MacNeice's poetry contains many observations on life in the 1930s and seems to suggest that poetry itself is not special but is democratically open to all readers and their experiences:

Now the till and the typewriter call the fingers
    The workman gathers his tools
For the eight hour day, but after that the solace
    Of films and football pools . . .
                                        (*Autumn Journal*)

Yet while he is sympathetic to the daily routine of most lives, MacNeice also expresses his concern about the mechanised, modern world which is dependent on material values rather than on the values which *Eclogue for Christmas* represents.

The jaded calendar revolves,
Its nuts need oil, carbon chokes the valves,
The excess sugar of a diabetic culture
Rotting the nerve of life.

These lines illustrate a further characteristic use of language in thirties poetry: the use of the definite article 'the'. It is, for instance, present in the already quoted opening lines of *Consider*. The word 'the' suggests something familiar and recognisable. The thirties poets regularly present a clinical catalogue of familiar objects, places, and ideas. Readers feel comfortable with familiar objects but their perception is challenged by placing the objects in unfamiliar contexts, giving a new perspective. The listing style does not always clarify how one object or place or idea relates to another. The poem retains an ambiguity which the readers have to elaborate for themselves.

At the end of the 1930s, poets looked back on the decade and tried to evaluate the rapid and radical changes that had taken place. In the poem *1st September 1939*, W.H. Auden wrote:

> I sit in one of the dives
> On Fifty Second Street,
> Uncertain and afraid
> As the clever hopes expire
> Of a low dishonest decade.

Auden, somewhat disillusioned, emigrated to America and during the following thirty years his poetry became more personal and more spiritual. It also came to reflect a belief that poetry cannot by itself create a better world even when it attempts to communicate with a wider reading public. One wry conclusion which Auden reached at the end of the 1930s was that, as he put it in the poem *In Memory of W.B. Yeats*, 'poetry makes nothing happen'.

Later in his career, Auden wrote: 'Poets are, by the nature of their interests and the nature of artistic fabrication, singularly ill-equipped to understand politics or economics.' This affirmation, in an essay (*The Poet and the City*, in *The Dyer's Hand*, 1962), effectively undermines and questions the commitment of a generation. The question remains as to how much its political idealism was subjective or objective, fashionable or self-conscious, genuine or fleeting; and such a question can probably never be fully answered.

The decade that began with *Consider* and the need to alert readers of poetry to immediate contemporary events ended with a message that poetry cannot really influence things. Auden's own departure from

England to America to some extent symbolised this change of attitude from commitment to withdrawal.

SCOTTISH AND WELSH POETRY

Scottish literature has always been polyglot: the linguistic influences of the Highlands, the Lowlands, Norway, England, France, and Rome have all shaped the language, thought, and style of Scottish writing. Gaelic, the Celtic language of the far North, was suppressed for many years, but in the twentieth century there has been a considerable revival of Gaelic speaking and writing, led by such poets as Sorley Maclean.

Although it does not contain the kind of mythical tales found in Welsh literature, in *The Mabinogion*, Scotland has provided a great deal of Romantic literature through the eighteenth- and nineteenth-century rewriting of its myth and history by Ossian and, most significantly, Sir Walter Scott.

The major Scottish poet of the twentieth century, Hugh MacDiarmid, attempted in the 1920s to create a Scottish poetic language based on Lowlands (Lallans). This has sometimes been called synthetic Scots, but it is in fact a return to the language used in a long tradition, from Henryson and Dunbar around 1500 to Burns in the eighteenth century. MacDiarmid was a strong Scottish nationalist, and his attempts to throw off English linguistic domination helped to create a nationalistic cultural identity at a time when political identities and ideals were being questioned all over the world.

A Drunk Man Looks at the Thistle (1926) is MacDiarmid's best-known work, and is held by many to be one of the major long poems of the century. His *First Hymn to Lenin* (1931) and *Second Hymn to Lenin* (1932) are highly significant as examples of the earliest left-wing poems, establishing what was to become a major trend in the 1930s. His later work, in English as well as in Scots, kept him in the forefront of cultural debate for a further four decades, with no loss of power and invention. He remains a major poet, both lyrical and polemical, and a very influential cultural presence.

> Hauf his soul a Scot maun use
> Indulgin' in illusions,

And hauf in getting rid o' them
And comin' to conclusions
Wi' the demoralisin' dearth
O' onything worthwhile on Earth.
    (*A Drunk Man Looks at the Thistle*)

The Perth poet, William Soutar, who spent much of his life bed-
ridden as an invalid, offers a bleak vision of what a poet, or makar,
leaves unsaid in 'the lawland tongue':

Nae man wha loves the lawland tongue
but warsles wi' the thocht –
there are mair sangs that bide unsung
nor a' that hae been wrocht.
                    (*The Makar*)

Edwin Muir, while less politically committed, is a more international
poet than MacDiarmid. Born in the Orkney Islands, he returns frequently to their wild landscapes in his poetry (*Chorus of the Newly Dead*,
1926, and several other volumes, until *Collected Poems 1921–1951*). He is
also remembered, with his wife Willa, as the first translator of Kafka
into English, the fruit of a long stay in Prague in the 1920s. Deeply
influenced by Freud and Germanic culture, Muir's use of dreams, and
his examinations of insecurity and hidden menace, caught the mood
of their times as effectively as did the contemporaneous novels of
Christopher Isherwood. One of his best-known poems is *The Horses*,
describing a world after some kind of holocaust:

Barely a twelvemonth after
The seven days war that put the world to sleep,
Late in the evening the strange horses came.
By then we had made our covenant with silence,
But in the first few days it was so still
We listened to our breathing and were afraid.
On the second day
The radios failed; we turned the knobs; no answer.
On the third day a warship passed us, heading north,
Dead bodies piled on the deck.

Norman MacCaig, a Scot, wrote in English. Although he uses both the Highlands and Edinburgh for his inspiration, he has a wider sphere of reference than many of his contemporaries. A prolific poet, from *Far Cry* (1943), the 1960s was his most productive decade, including the highly popular *Measures* (1965) and *Surroundings* (1966). MacCaig's *Collected Poems* were published in 1990.

Like Scotland and Ireland, Wales is a multilingual country: Welsh is the most widely spoken of the Celtic languages, and Welsh culture has flourished since the time of the ballads. The name of Taliesin, a bard supposed to have lived in the sixth century, is associated with the fourteenth-century *Book of Taliesin*, a collection of poems of various kinds, sources, and dates. The *Book of Aneurin* is a thirteenth-century collection of poems ascribed to one bard, the seventh-century Aneurin. It is remembered for the elegiac battle poem *Gododin*, which gives one of the earliest mentions of that seminal figure, King Arthur. Aneurin, Caedmon, and Taliesin probably wrote at around the same time, but Welsh culture remained more localised, as English became the dominant language and culture of the British Isles.

Welsh writing in English (known until recently as Anglo-Welsh writing) received an enormous boost with the Education Act of 1870 and the establishment of the University of Wales in 1893. Many important names in literature are from Wales, even though they might not be seen as Welsh, from the metaphysical poet Henry Vaughan to the Second World War poet Alun Lewis and the critic and novelist Raymond Williams. In the twentieth century, Dylan Thomas and R.S. Thomas have become internationally known poets, and Richard Llewellyn's novel *How Green Was My Valley* (1939) was a worldwide bestseller.

Every year at the Eisteddfod – the 'session' or congress of Welsh bards – the tradition of poetry in Welsh, and the declamation which maintains the oral convention, is celebrated. The bard of the Eisteddfod is crowned in triumph for the best poem of the festival. Unfortunately, there is little acknowledgement of this tradition in mainstream English literature. Dylan Thomas, one of the major poets of the twentieth century, has been appropriated for English literature rather than remaining distinctly Welsh, despite the Welsh setting of some of his best works such as the radio drama *Under Milk Wood* (1953).

MODERN DRAMA TO 1945

Th' whole worl's in a terrible state o'chassis
(Sean O'Casey, *Juno and the Paycock*)

Henrik Ibsen's play *Ghosts*, given a single performance in 1891, was famously described as 'an open sewer', because of its theme of hereditary syphilis. George Bernard Shaw, a champion of the Norwegian Ibsen, himself began to write plays on similarly controversial themes: *Mrs Warren's Profession* (written in 1894; published in 1898) is about prostitution. It was not allowed a full public performance until the 1920s, although it was privately performed in London in 1902. Shaw always wrote a Preface to the published texts of his plays, justifying his 'determination to accept problems as the normal material of the drama'.

> The notion that prostitution is created by the wickedness of Mrs Warren is as silly as the notion – prevalent, nevertheless, to some extent in Temperance circles – that drunkenness is created by the wickedness of the publican. Mrs Warren is not a whit a worse woman than the reputable daughter who cannot endure her. Her indifference to the ultimate social consequence of her means of making money, and her discovery of that means by the ordinary method of taking the line of least resistance to getting it, are too common in English society to call for any special remark. Her vitality, her thrift, her energy, her outspokenness, her wise care of her daughter, and the managing capacity which has enabled her and her sister to climb from the fried fish shop down by the Mint to the establishments of which she boasts, are all high English social virtues.
>
> (Preface to *Mrs Warren's Profession*)

In a career which lasted over sixty years, Shaw continued to treat contemporary problems and issues in a total of over fifty plays. The first, *Widowers' Houses*, written in 1892, dealt with a slum landlord's exploitation of the poor; *Candida* (1895) with female equality; *John Bull's Other Island* (1904), his first real success, with the Irish question. Shaw's are plays of ideas, debate, and discussion, rather than dramas of character, action, and passion. This has led to his characters being criticised as 'mere mouthpieces' for the views they express; but the best of the plays remain theatrically viable, and many have entered the twentieth-century consciousness: *Man and Superman* (1903), with its idea of a 'Life Force'; *Heartbreak House* (published 1919) which, more than any other, charts the decline of Britain as a power; *Pygmalion* (1912) which reveals Shaw's constant fascination with language, famously presented in Eliza Doolittle's cockney English; and *Saint Joan* (1924), based on the French martyr Joan of Arc, who was canonised in 1920. In the 'pre-feminist' play *Candida*, the heroine asserts her rights:

MORELL We have agreed – he and I – that you shall choose between us now. I await your decision.

CANDIDA [*slowly recoiling a step, her heart hardened by his rhetoric in spite of the sincere feeling behind it*] Oh! I am to choose, am I? I suppose it is quite settled that I must belong to one or the other.

MORELL [*firmly*] Quite. You must choose definitely.

MARCHBANKS [*anxiously*] Morell: you dont understand. She means that she belongs to herself.

CANDIDA [*turning on him*] I mean that, and a good deal more, Master Eugene, as you will both find out presently. And pray, my lords and masters, what have you to offer for my choice? I am up for auction, it seems. What do you bid, James?

At the end of *Heartbreak House* the discussion is about the survival of England:

HECTOR And this ship that we are all in? This soul's prison we call England?

CAPTAIN SHOTOVER The captain is in his bunk, drinking bottled ditch-water; and the crew is gambling in the forecastle. She will strike and sink and split. Do you think the laws of God will be suspended in favour of England because you were born in it?

HECTOR Well, I dont mean to be drowned like a rat in a trap. I still have the will to live. What am I to do?

CAPTAIN SHOTOVER Do? Nothing simpler. Learn your business as an Englishman.

HECTOR And what may my business as an Englishman be, pray?

CAPTAIN SHOTOVER Navigation. Learn it and live; or leave it and be damned.

ELLIE Quiet, quiet: youll tire yourself.

MAZZINI I thought all that once, Captain; but I assure you nothing will happen.

[*A dull distant explosion is heard.*]

HECTOR [*starting up*] What was that?

CAPTAIN SHOTOVER Something happening.

Pygmalion famously gave rise to one of the more farcical episodes in the history of stage censorship: Shaw was allowed to keep the word 'bloody' in Eliza's famous line 'Walk! Not bloody likely. I am going in a taxi', only if he cut several other expletives. The word 'bloody' was not to be allowed on the English stage again for another twenty-five years. Shaw was able to make considerable use of this linguistic idiocy in the play, which remains his funniest work. Shaw was an Irishman, as was Oscar Wilde. Their outsiders' view of British society allowed them a freedom to observe it critically, which is not found so clearly in any English dramatist of the turn of the century.

The plays of Harley Granville-Barker in the early years of the century also had considerable political content. Granville-Barker was well known as a theatre director, and his highly practical Prefaces to twelve of Shakespeare's plays (1927–47) remain an important contribution to the study of Shakespeare in the theatre. Granville-Barker's plays, such as *The Madras House* (1910), *The Voysey Inheritance* (1905), and *Waste* (1907), caused controversy (*Waste* was banned) and, with the plays of Shaw, gave the theatre a brief moment of glory as the forum for debate on social issues, such as class and hypocrisy and double standards in public life. Granville-Barker also directed several of the social debate plays of John Galsworthy (see page 396).

IRISH DRAMA

Shaw and Wilde were Irishmen who, for the most part, used English subjects for their plays, staged in London, but there was also a very strong movement for native Irish drama. For instance, 1899 saw the foundation of the Irish Literary Theatre by the poet and playwright W.B. Yeats, with Lady Augusta Gregory and Edward Martyn, whose play *The Heather Field* (1899) was one of the first the group staged. From 1904, the Abbey Theatre in Dublin was the home of the Irish

National Theatre Society, as the Irish Literary Theatre was renamed. It became the centre for a flourishing in dramatic expression which lasted until well after the state of Eire was finally created in 1922.

John Millington Synge's plays *Riders to the Sea* (1904), *The Playboy of the Western World* (1907), and *Deirdre of the Sorrows* (1910) use the language of Ireland – and in particular of the Aran Islands, off the West Coast – to create potent images of the culture and the people, in both tragedy and comedy.

NORA [*in a whisper*] Did you hear that, Cathleen? Did you hear a noise in the north-east?

CATHLEEN [*in a whisper*] There's someone after crying out by the seashore.

MAURYA [*continues without hearing anything*] There was Sheamus and his father, and his own father again, were lost in a dark night, and not a stick or sign was seen of them when the sun went up. There was Patch after was drowned out of a curagh that turned over. I was sitting here with Bartley, and he a baby lying on my two knees, and I seen two women, and three women, and four women coming in, and they crossing themselves and not saying a word. I looked out then, and there were men coming after them, and they holding a thing in the half of a red sail, and water dripping out of it – it was a dry day, Nora – and leaving a track to the door.

(*Riders to the Sea*)

Sean O'Casey's plays are set in the city rather than the country, but have a similar intention: to portray, in realistic language and action, the Irish character, and the issues of patriotism, self-deceit, resignation, and tragedy. As with Synge's work, O'Casey's plays aroused controversy. They did not conform to the myth-making ideals of some supporters of Irish Revival, but they came to be seen as crucial statements of identity and consciousness – despite, and perhaps even because of, the stir they caused.

Juno and the Paycock (1924) is O'Casey's best-known play (Juno being the wife of the 'peacock', Jack Boyle), with its Dublin tenement setting, and the tragedy of its inhabitants' self-deceptions. The famous statement of chaos – 'Th' whole worl's in a terrible state o' chassis' – is one of the most poignant final lines in modern drama.

JUNO Give your hat an' stick to Jack, there . . . sit down, Mr Bentham . . . no, not there . . . in th' easy chair be the fire . . . there, that's betther. Mary'll be out to you in a minute.

BOYLE [*solemnly*] I seen be the paper this mornin' that Consols was down half per cent. That's serious, min' you, an' shows the whole counthry's in a state o' chassis.

MRS BOYLE What's Consols, Jack?

BOYLE Consols? Oh, Consols is – oh, there's no use tellin' women what Consols is – th' wouldn't undherstand.

BENTHAM It's just as you were saying, Mr Boyle . . .

[MARY *enters, charmingly dressed.*]

BENTHAM Oh, good evening, Mary; how pretty you're looking!

MARY [*archly*] Am I?

BOYLE We were just talkin' when you kem in, Mary; I was tellin' Mr Bentham that the whole counthry's in a state o' chassis.

MARY [*to* BENTHAM] Would you prefer the green or the blue ribbon round me hair, Charlie?

MRS BOYLE Mary, your father's speakin'.

BOYLE [*rapidly*] I was jus' tellin' Mr Bentham that the whole counthry's in a state o' chassis.

MARY I'm sure you're frettin', da, whether it is or no.

The Shadow of a Gunman (1923) and *The Plough and the Stars* (1926) were the last plays O'Casey wrote in Ireland. The latter caused riots when it was staged at the Abbey Theatre. O'Casey moved to England, where he continued to write plays but without reaching the success of his earlier works. His six-volume autobiography, published between 1939 and 1954, remains one of the most valuable insights into the period of Irish liberation that inspired his best work.

D.H. LAWRENCE

The plays of D.H. Lawrence are much less well known than his novels, short stories, and poems. But his use of naturalistic settings and local accents makes him much closer to O'Casey than is often realised.

A great many of the successful novelists of the early part of the twentieth century tried their hand at writing for the theatre. The realistic mining plays of D.H. Lawrence are the first lasting examples of 'kitchen-sink' drama of the twentieth century. They are written mainly in dialect, and with a carefully naturalistic description of the life of the Nottinghamshire mining community where Lawrence had grown up. These plays – *A Collier's Friday Night* (1909), *The Daughter-in-Law* (1912), and *The Widowing of Mrs Holroyd* (1914) – relate very closely to Lawrence's short stories and novels. In fact, as his career in fiction developed, Lawrence wrote less for the theatre, although his biblical play on the David and Jonathan theme of male solidarity, *David* (1926), is a powerful drama.

Lawrence's plays did not achieve wide recognition until the 1960s, when 'kitchen-sink' realism had found new favour. The well-known novelist was suddenly 'discovered' as a dramatist, and as a significant forerunner of a modern theatrical trend. As with the Irish dramatists, the use of local dialects in Lawrence's plays contrasts with the more common standard English in the drama of the time. They underline the criticisms of society made by these dramatists, and reinforce the realistic settings and local identities of the plays. In this scene, the miner father is washing in front of the fire, as the son Ernest (seen as the Lawrence character) discusses books and college with his mother:

FATHER If you 'anna the money you canna 'a'e 'em, whether or not.

MOTHER Don't talk nonsense. If he has to have them, he has. But the money you have to pay for books, and they're no good when you've done with them! – I'm sure it's really sickening, it is!

ERNEST Oh, never mind, Little; I s'll get 'em for six shillings. Is it a worry, *Mutterchen?*

MOTHER It is, but I suppose if it has to be, it has.

ERNEST Old Beasley is an old chough. While he was lecturing this afternoon Arnold and Hinrich were playing nap; and the girls always write letters, and I went fast asleep.

FATHER So that's what you go'n to Collige for, is it?

ERNEST [*nettled*] No, it isn't. Only old Beasley's such a dry old ass, with his lectures on Burke. He's a mumbling parson, so what do you expect?

[*The* FATHER *grunts, rises, and fetches a clean new bucket from the scullery. He hangs this on top of the boiler, and turns on the water. Then he pulls off his flannel singlet and stands stripped to the waist, watching the hot water dribble into the bucket. The pail half-filled, he goes out to the scullery on left.*]

Do you know what Professor Staynes said this morning, Mother? He

said I'd got an instinct for Latin – and you know he's one of the best
fellows in England on the classics: edits Ovid and what-not. An
instinct for Latin, he said.

MOTHER [*smiling, gratified*] Well, it's a funny thing to have an instinct
for.

(A Collier's Friday Night)

POPULAR AND POETIC DRAMA

Each decade of the twentieth century saw one or two dramatists
achieve considerable success, but the tastes and fashions of one decade
have seldom retained their popularity much beyond their own time.
W. Somerset Maugham, also remembered for his novels and short
stories, had four plays running simultaneously in London in 1908: a
feat repeated only by Noël Coward in 1925, Alan Ayckbourn in 1975,
and by the musicals of Andrew Lloyd Webber in the 1980s.

Maugham's plays are largely treatments of middle-class attitudes to
love and money. *The Circle* (1921) and *The Constant Wife* (1926), in which
the main female character asserts her independence in a choice of
partner, are still revived; but they have dated badly, and lack the argumentative power of Shaw's plays of the same period.

The use of poetry in drama has a long history. In the first half of
the twentieth century, several poets contributed to a short-lived revival
of poetic drama. T.S. Eliot's *Murder in the Cathedral* (1935), on the
subject of the martyrdom of Saint Thomas à Becket in Canterbury
Cathedral in 1170, had a considerable impact; but the plays which
followed, most notably *The Cocktail Party* (1950), blend the London
West End theatrical conventions with poetic diction rather less
comfortably.

The last temptation is the greatest treason:
To do the right deed for the wrong reason.
(Murder in the Cathedral)

In the 1930s, the poet W.H. Auden also contributed to several plays,
usually on political themes and in collaboration with the novelist Christopher Isherwood. *The Dog Beneath the Skin* (1935) and *The Ascent of F6*
(1936) show traces of the influence of German expressionism (both

writers had lived in Germany), but Auden and Isherwood's concern with drama was not continued after *On the Frontier* (1938).

Noël Coward's comedies have stood the test of time more successfully than Maugham's. In particular *Private Lives* (1930), about a divorced couple who meet again on their honeymoons with new partners, *Hay Fever* (1925), about a self-obsessed theatrical family, *Design for Living* (1933), about a successful love triangle, and *Blithe Spirit* (1941), in which an eccentric medium helps a first wife to return to torment her husband and his new wife, have a sense of wit, style, and underlying pain, which guarantee them a place in the tradition of English comedy.

AMANDA What's happened to yours?

ELYOT Didn't you hear her screaming? She's downstairs in the dining-room I think.

AMANDA Mine is being grand, in the bar.

ELYOT It really is awfully difficult.

AMANDA Have you known her long?

ELYOT About four months, we met in a house party in Norfolk.

AMANDA Very flat, Norfolk.

ELYOT How old is dear Victor?

AMANDA Thirty-four, or five; and Sibyl?

ELYOT I blush to tell you, only twenty-three.

AMANDA You've gone a mucker alright.

ELYOT I shall reserve my opinion of your choice until I've met dear Victor.

AMANDA I wish you wouldn't go on calling him 'Dear Victor'. It's extremely irritating.

ELYOT That's how I see him. Dumpy, and fair, and very considerate, with glasses. Dear Victor.

AMANDA As I said before I would rather not discuss him. At least I have good taste enough to refrain from making cheap gibes at Sibyl.

ELYOT You said Norfolk was flat.

AMANDA That was no reflection on her, unless she made it flatter.

ELYOT Your voice takes on an acid quality whenever you mention her name.

AMANDA I'll never mention it again.

ELYOT Good, and I'll keep off Victor.

AMANDA [*with dignity*] Thank you.

(*Private Lives*)

In the 1930s, J.B. Priestley achieved considerable success with several plays on the theme of time – *Dangerous Corner* (1932), *Time and the Conways*, and *I Have Been Here Before* (both 1937) being the best known. But fashionable ideas can date as well, and, despite the technical accomplishment of some further fifty plays, Priestley's most lasting success is the rather facile psychological drama *An Inspector Calls* (1946), about guilt and self-torment within a family.

In the late 1940s, the plays of Christopher Fry were hailed as a major contribution to the poetic revival. *A Phoenix Too Frequent* (1946), *The Lady's Not for Burning* (1949), *Venus Observed* (1950), and *A Sleep of Prisoners* (1951) were the highpoint of this vogue; but it faded as the 1950s progressed, and a greater degree of realism entered British drama in the work of playwrights like Osborne and Wesker.

LANGUAGE NOTE
Literature about language

POLONIUS What do you read, my Lord?
HAMLET Words, words, words.
(William Shakespeare, *Hamlet*)

Words are not the sunlight
After the dark night or terrible tempest of grief.
(Elizabeth Jennings, *Justice*)

Language has always been a constant subject in literary discourses and many writers have reflected on both the power and limitations of language. The phenomenon of literature about language is, however, especially marked in the twentieth century. It takes a variety of different forms, a number of which are described briefly in other parts of these final sections.

Literature about language is often made up of texts which explore the nature of communication and, in particular, the difficulties of communication. In such texts language comes increasingly to be understood as a problem. It is a problem for a poet such as T.S. Eliot, for whom words fail adequately to capture elusive meanings:

Trying to learn to use words . . .
Because one has only learnt to get the better of words
For the thing one no longer has to say, or the way in which
One is no longer disposed to say it.
> (T.S. Eliot, *East Coker*, from *Four Quartets*)

Words are especially inadequate for capturing the nature of spiritual experience which extends beyond language. Paradoxically, the poet is forced to use language to express the 'unsaid', what cannot be put into arbitrary and imprecise words.

Living to live in a world of time beyond me; let me
Resign my life for this life, my speech for that unspoken.
> (T.S. Eliot, *Marina*)

The impossibility of communicating the incommunicable is also a topic to which playwrights such as Beckett and Pinter return. Indeed, their plays (and in the case of Beckett his prose fiction too) contain many instances where silence is preferred to language and the limitation of words; at the same time, however, they also exploit dramatic language to illustrate a human condition in which we can be trapped by and within language and explore the powerful discourses that can be created by those who wish to control and coerce others.

In William Golding's *The Inheritors* (1957), language itself is a major theme in the novel and is shown to be enslaving. One group of people, who belong to one phase of the human evolutionary process, is defeated and superseded by another group whose greater command of language allows them more powerful categories of thought and enables them to classify their experience in a more 'advanced' way.

Above all, it is the inadequacy and arbitrariness of language which is most often addressed in twentieth-century literature. At best, language allows us to make only indeterminate, surrealistic sense of our world, and animals may be blessed in having left language to their 'betters' who are lost and isolated within it. Brief extracts from poems by Sylvia Plath and W.H. Auden underline such insights:

I'm a riddle in nine syllables,
An elephant, a ponderous house,
A melon strolling on two tendrils.
> (Sylvia Plath, *Metaphor*)

Let them leave language to their lonely betters
Who count some days and long for certain letters;

We, too, make noises when we laugh or weep:
Words are for those with promises to keep.
(W.H. Auden, *Their Lonely Betters*)

THE NOVEL TO 1945

I have, I am aware, told this story in a very rambling way

(Ford Madox Ford, *The Good Soldier*)

For many critics the years 1900–1945 are the high point in the development of the English novel, a time when not only the greatest twentieth-
century novels but the greatest novels in the English language were
written. Many commentators stress, in particular, the technical and aesthetic advances which occurred during this period and it was indeed a
time of extensive formal innovation and experimentation. In this
respect, developments in the novel parallel developments in poetry.

The novels of this era contrast markedly with most nineteenth-
century novels. The English fiction of the early nineteenth century was
written at a time of great confidence in the basic structure of society
and the place of individuals within it. Towards the end of the century,
however, novelists realised that there was no longer a shared and
agreed community of values; a general background of belief which
united them with their readers no longer existed after Darwin; and the
certainties that lay behind the progress and prosperity of the Victorian
age were collapsing. Hence the challenging, questioning nature of
many late Victorian novelists, who brought in the outsiders' more
critical viewpoint.

SUBJECTIVITY: THE POPULAR
TRADITION

Together with the increase in objectivity given by outsiders, which
permitted a different view of English society – or, in Conrad,
Kipling, and Forster, a clearer depiction of colonialism and its effects
– there can also be found a greater degree of subjectivity in the

novels of writers whose concern was more with the inner life of characters.

Of course, objectivity and subjectivity are to be found everywhere: no novelist is only one or the other. It is indicative of the widening range of the novel that the years between 1880 and 1930 should produce the novels of Hardy and Gissing, Wilde and George Moore, as well as the realism of Arnold Bennett and John Galsworthy, and the new 'great tradition' of writers such as James, Conrad, Lawrence, Joyce, and Woolf.

Instead of drawing on an existing world of public values, writers felt they had to build up a world of private values. The definite shape of a novel's *plot*, which organises characters and events, gave way to less logical and sequential modes of organisation. There was a stress on the individual's sense of what is valid in experience, and techniques of subjectivity were evolved to represent this.

The whole nature of what made a fictional hero or heroine was also questioned. The individual could no longer be a *model* for behaviour, which had been the case since Richardson and Fielding, but was to be seen as an example. Since every example was different, novelists had to find different ways of exploring and describing these differences. What is called the 'stream of consciousness' technique was developed in various ways by writers in order to render directly and in depth the experience of individual characters.

There was at this time, too, a related change in attitudes to *time*. Writers no longer simply wrote 'he said' or 'she recalled', or 'this reminded him of', or 'she decided in future to . . .'. Time was not a series of separate chronological moments and consciousness was seen as a continuous flow, with past and present merging. Under the general influence of work by psychologists such as Sigmund Freud and Carl Jung, writers came to believe that we *are* our memories, that the present is the sum of our past and that the form and style of the novel have to capture this understanding. One result was that the novel concentrated less on a social, public world and more on the inner world of unique and isolated individuals or the shapeless, unstructured sensations of life. In all, the novel became a less rigid, plotted, and naturalistic form.

The themes which preoccupied many of the major novelists in the period 1900–1930 were accordingly themes of loneliness and isolation and the difficulties of relationships both with other individuals and with a wider social and cultural community. Humans are unique individuals and need privacy; they are also social beings and need communion. This is a dilemma which was explored extensively in the works of the greatest novelists and short-story writers of the period against a background of cultural crisis and social dislocation.

Yet it would be inaccurate to suggest that the period of the modern novel was one of total change. Many writers continued the traditions of the nineteenth century without making a radical departure from the main themes or from the main forms which sustained that tradition. The novels and short stories of Rudyard Kipling, for example, were written with a confidence that readers would accept much the same values and points of view as the writer. Many of Kipling's prose works are set not in England but in the countries of the British Empire. Born in India and intimately acquainted with the workings of Empire and colonialism, Kipling wrote about areas of experience new to literature – the psychological and moral problems of living among people who are subject to British rule but of a different culture. Kipling confirmed the importance and value of an Empire and the white man's responsibility to create a single rich civilisation among diverse races, cultures, and creeds. In *Kim* (1901), the Indians are treated with an equal sympathy to the Victorian ruling classes.

THE KAILYARD SCHOOL

In the 1890s there was a flowering of the Scottish provincial novel in a highly sentimental and romanticised form which came to be known as the Kailyard School. The kailyard was the cabbage patch at the back of a village house, and it designates the small-town preoccupations with which the novelists dealt. Much more limited in scope than the novels of John Galt earlier in the century, and without his hard-hitting social observation, these novels – by James Barrie (later to write many successful plays, including the perennial *Peter Pan*), Ian Maclaren, and S.R. Crockett – enjoyed considerable popularity in their day. Barrie's *A Window in Thrums* (1889), based on his home town of Kirriemuir in Angus (the Thrums of the title), remains the best known of this short-lived burst of parochial, vernacular romanticism.

PROVINCIAL NOVELS

A novel by George Douglas Brown called *The House with the Green Shutters* (1901) returned to the harsher view of small-town life. Set in Barbie, closely resembling Douglas Brown's own village of Ochiltree, it portrays the rise and fall of John Gourlay, a small-town tyrant who recalls both Stevenson's Weir of Hermiston, in the novel of the same name, and Thomas Hardy's Michael Henchard in *The Mayor of Caster-bridge*. The house of the title becomes Gourlay's obsession in life, and the relationship with his own son and with the village lead to tragedy. Douglas Brown died young, a year after the novel's publication, and it was John Macdougall Hay who was to carry on the small-town realist novel in Scotland with his *Gillespie* (1914), set in Brieston, Hay's home village of Tarbert. Like so much Scottish writing, these novels have a preoccupation with the presence of evil. It has moved on from the metaphysical evil found in James Hogg a century before to a more modern concern with the contrast between rural stability and the commercial and industrial pressures of the city – and the exploitation, treachery, and potential disaster this contrast brings. This concern aligns these two highly individual Scottish novels with the novels of Hardy, but in a quite different moral atmosphere: Hardy's Wessex, with the brooding historical presence of the heath as a symbol of a kind of 'wasteland', is in the Scottish context replaced by a religious and moral background derived from Calvinism. It is possibly harsher, certainly less mythical, but equally powerful as an indictment of the clash of the modern with the traditional world.

Traditional forms were also adopted and extended by Arnold Bennett. Bennett's novels are set in 'the Five Towns', the area in the English Midlands known as the Potteries and which has been the centre for the manufacture of chinaware. Bennett's novels – he was influenced by the French naturalists – give a detailed picture of people confined in difficult and drab conditions. His best-known novels are *The Old Wives' Tale* (1908) and *Clayhanger* (1910), holding out little hope that the conditions in which people live can be changed. What remains is a well-documented portrayal of ordinary people caught in the grip of oppressive social conditions, but displaying great dignity and humanity in their struggles to survive. *Riceyman Steps* (1923), set in

London, is seen by many critics as the best of Bennett's later work. He was a figure of immense influence, one of the last of the truly popular literary figures, a widely read critic and a prosperous professional writer, continuing the tradition of Scott, Dickens, and Trollope.

SOCIAL CONCERNS

John Galsworthy is also deeply concerned with issues of class and social awareness. He is best known for his *Forsyte Saga* (1906–34), a series of nine novels which covers late Victorian days to the early 1920s and traces the fortunes of an upper-class English family who gradually witness the death of the ruling elite they represent. Galsworthy is ambiguous in his attitudes towards the family; his initial aim was satire, but his characters became typical figures from the British bourgeoisie. The novels are traditional insofar as major crises of plot are shown through changes in the social, marital, or financial status of the main characters.

It is fascinating that the first three novels of *The Forsyte Saga* (the sequence is continued later with another two trilogies) should have been published together in 1922, the same year as James Joyce's *Ulysses*. The 'saga' title is ironic, but its overtones of epic do show how some driving forces – the acquisition of property, wealth, and power – remain fundamental in human terms, from the time of Beowulf to the twentieth century.

By contrast, H.G. Wells took many of his characters from a lower social level, for example *Kipps* (1905) and *The History of Mr Polly* (1910). His characters – modern figures, seizing new social opportunities – are generally energetic and positive and, though not always successful, in the end more fully understand what they need to be happy. Wells is nowadays better known for his earlier scientific novels, and is important as a reforming writer who expresses a socialist-liberal vision of the future. Wells wanted to destroy all the inequalities and inconsistencies associated with the Victorian era, particularly the economic and social privileges granted to only a few. He believed that the advances of science could create a rational, and more enlightened, society, indeed a new world order, though some of his suggested methods for doing so have recently been labelled as fascist and racist. In works of great imagination, he creates worlds in which the old certainties and fixed order of the world disappear. Man can travel to the moon; we can move backwards and forwards in time; we can be attacked by people from Mars; human size can be increased indefinitely; we can sleep for two hundred years and wake up in a strange scientific future. The seventeenth-century scientific world of Newton, which provided the agreed basis of understanding in the nineteenth century, is radically displaced in novels like *The Time Machine* (1895), *The Invisible Man* (1897), and *The War of the Worlds* (1898). Yet, though radical in his social vision – *Ann Veronica* (1909) is a novel about the equal status of women with men – the form and shape of Wells's novels are conservative.

The short stories of Saki, the pen-name of H.H. Munro, present a satiric, rather cynical view of pre-First World War society, of children and of animals, which often manage to wreak revenge on humankind. *The Chronicles of Clovis* (1911) and *Beasts and Super-Beasts* (1914) are the best-known collections. Saki's novel *The Unbearable Bassington* (1912) is a remarkable mix of social satire and serious intent. It clearly echoes Conrad's *Heart of Darkness,* with its hero taken into the depths of the jungle to undergo a kind of moral transfiguration. That this image of colonialism should be used again for a moral purpose is an indication of Saki's moral intention, and reinforces an association between comic writing and satiric anger, which will be found in another major comic novel, Evelyn Waugh's *A Handful of Dust* (1934). In this novel too, the 'hero' ends up in the jungle, up the River Amazon this time, as a kind of punishment or cure for his moral shallowness.

LIGHT NOVELS

From the time of the rise of journalism in the early eighteenth century, through the novels of R.S. Surtees and the early Dickens and Thackeray, there had been a tradition of light, humorous writing, largely in journalism, which in the late nineteenth and early twentieth centuries flourished in the comic novel. Jerome K. Jerome's *Three Men in a Boat* (1889) is an outstanding example of this. It is the story of three young men and their dog on a boating holiday on the Thames, and contains a great many comic set pieces which have hardly dated.

P.G. Wodehouse mined a comic vein which used the English

perception of class as its source. In a long series of novels, from *My Man Jeeves* (1919) and *The Inimitable Jeeves* (1923) through to the 1970s, he uses the contrast between the dim upper-class Bertie Wooster and the resourceful butler Jeeves to create a world of manners and attitudes that remains fixed in a timeless age. It is a world of country-house weekends, frightful aunts, and a vision of the rightness of things which probably never existed. In creating this escapist world, Wodehouse is a master of character, plot, and language and the world of Wooster is for many readers worldwide the classic image of an England which was out of date long before Wodehouse started writing about it.

Ronald Firbank is an unusual figure in early twentieth-century literature. His stories and novels are very much an acquired taste, combining high camp, outrageous comedy, and a sense of aestheticism and fantasy which remains inimitable, and distinctively of its 'modern' time. *Valmouth* (1919) and *Concerning the Eccentricities of Cardinal Pirelli* (1926) are perhaps the best examples of Firbank's innovative use of language, imagery, and style. His influence on writers such as Evelyn Waugh and Ivy Compton-Burnett is considerable, and his reputation is enjoying something of a recovery.

GENRE FICTION

Escapist literature goes hand in hand with serious concerns all through the twentieth century: the comedy of Wodehouse lasts through the Jazz age of the 1920s; the threat of Fascism, the fascination with Communism, and the Depression of the 1930s; the War and later austerity in the 1940s and 1950s. The trend has continued through to the present day.

Novels of adventure maintained their popularity. In the twentieth century, fantastic schemes for world domination become fact rather than fiction, although losing none of their pace and excitement in the medium of the novel. John Buchan, historian and statesman, wrote some of the most famous of the genre, including *The Thirty-nine Steps* (1915), which has been filmed several times. These novels reflect the preoccupation with the genuine threat of chaos in a disintegrating world. As Buchan put it in the first of his 'shockers', *The Power House* (serialised in 1913), 'you think a wall as solid as the earth separates civilisation from barbarianism. I tell you the division is a thread, a sheet of glass.' It is interesting to note that this was written before 'the war to end all wars', before the sense of things falling apart became a common concern. With the ending of all certainties, the fragmentation of the world was of interest to writers in every genre, serious and popular.

Novels of spying and adventure have become a mainstay of twentieth-century fiction. *The Scarlet Pimpernel* (1905) by the Hungarian-born Baroness Orczy was one of the earliest successes of the genre; a more overtly political kind of thriller is found in *The Riddle of the Sands* (1903) by Erskine Childers, who was shot by a firing squad in 1922 as a result of his work for Irish republicans. This novel involves German plans to invade England. This kind of threat to stability (and English authority) is vital to the genre. Later masters of the thriller included 'Sapper' (Herman Cyril McNeile), with his hero 'Bulldog' Drummond; Ian Fleming, who created James Bond; and John Le Carré, whose 'cold war' novels such as *The Spy Who Came In From the Cold* (1963) have taken the genre forward to the status of major novels, according to many critics.

Since the development of the detective story from Wilkie Collins to Arthur Conan Doyle, it has become one of the most popular of all genres. Agatha Christie, 'the Queen of Crime', has been the most successful of all crime writers. From *The Mysterious Affair at Styles* (1920) to *Poirot's Last Case* (1976) she wrote over sixty detective novels featuring Hercule Poirot and Miss Marple as her sleuths. Some of her works are considered classics: *The Murder of Roger Ackroyd* (1926) and *Murder on the Orient Express* (1934) in particular. Her play *The Mousetrap* has been running constantly in London since 1952.

Dorothy L. Sayers with her detective Lord Peter Wimsey introduces the popular upper-class sleuth in novels such as *Murder Must Advertise* (1933) and *The Nine Tailors* (1934). J.I.M. Stewart, an academic and critic, brought the highbrow, academic detective story to high peaks of achievement, writing as Michael Innes: from *Death at the President's Lodging* (1936) to *Hamlet, Revenge* (1937), *A Night of Errors* (1948) and *Lament for a Maker* (1938) (based on Dunbar's late mediaeval poem).

The novels of Buchan, Bennett, Christie, Galsworthy and Wells were more likely to be bestsellers than, for example, the novels of Joseph Conrad or Henry James. Innovative forms and concerns often have a less immediate appeal for readers. Wells, in particular, was a master of controversial, futuristic ideas, but he expressed them in forms which were less challenging to his readers than the forms and techniques of writers who are now hailed as significant innovators. This is one sign of a growing divergence between popular writing and intellectual literature.

MODERNISM AND THE NOVEL

Modernism has been described as one of the most profound changes and upheavals ever to have occurred in the history of literature. It is not limited to English literature, of course, nor to the twentieth century, but reflects a shift in knowledge and understanding, in sensibility and expression, as the world approaches the twenty-first century. What D.H. Lawrence called in a poem 'the struggle of becoming' is explained in any age and in any culture: however, Modernism is now seen to have encompassed the changes which overtook society's expression of its concerns in the first half of the twentieth century, a time when values and systems which had been more or less stable for a century and longer were questioned and, in many cases, overthrown.

What drives the Modern is the need to redefine: the redefinition covers practically every aspect of society, past, present, and future. To attempt to classify Modernism in a few words would be impossible. Every individual voice made its own contribution to the Modern; in literature, as in all the other forms of artistic expression.

Modern writing has given rise to unprecedented amounts of commentary, exegesis, and criticism, precisely because each individual creative voice can be seen to be distinctive: it is not as easy to classify writers into groups, trends, and movements. Even groups like the Bloomsbury Group and the Auden Group are full of diverse personalities and divergent creative achievement. A significant by-product of Modernism in literature is a new age of critical writing – much of the best of it by the creative writers themselves.

Modernism adopted new techniques, especially in narration. In this, the cinema, the popular new art-form of the century, was hugely influential, especially in cross-cutting, in close-up and in bringing a

visual awareness of image, character, and story-telling to a mass audience. Cinema also influenced worldwide ideas of humour (from
Charlie Chaplin and Mack Sennett onwards), of glamour and escapism,
especially in the Depression years of the 1930s, and of propaganda.

FORSTER, CONRAD AND FORD

Only connect . . .
(E.M. Forster, *Howards End*)

E.M. Forster offers a more detailed critique than many of his contemporaries of the social and cultural world of the early part of twentieth century and of the values which held the British Empire together.
Like Kipling, Forster spent time in India; but his view of the country is
different from Kipling and in his last novel, *A Passage to India* (1924), he
questions whether the dualities of East and West, the Indian people
and the ruling British, can be truly brought together. 'East is East and
West is West,' Kipling had written, 'and never the twain shall meet.'
Forster tries to bring them together, but in doing so he illustrates the
complexities of the colonial situation. Life is rarely simple in Forster's
novels. In *A Passage to India*, Forster can admire the detachment of the
Hindu mind, at the same time criticising the inflexibility of the British
approach to life. His heroine's response to the openness and freedom
of India is praised but it brings into the open the impossibility of
making a whole out of two different peoples, societies, attitudes, and
religions.

> 'You went alone into one of those caves?'
> 'That is quite correct.'
> 'And the prisoner followed you.'
> 'Now we've got 'im,' from the Major.
> She was silent. The court, the place of question, awaited her reply.
> But she could not give it until Aziz entered the place of answer.
> 'The prisoner followed you, didn't he?' he repeated in the mono-
> tonous tones that they both used; they were employing agreed
> words throughout, so that this part of the proceedings held no
> surprises.
> 'May I have half a minute before I reply to that, Mr McBryde?'
> 'Certainly.'

Her vision was of several caves. She saw herself in one, and she was also outside it, watching its entrance, for Aziz to pass in. She failed to locate him. It was the doubt that had often visited her, but solid and attractive, like the hills. 'I am not –' Speech was more difficult than vision. 'I am not quite sure.'

'I beg your pardon?' said the Superintendent of Police.

'I cannot be sure . . .'

'I didn't catch that answer.' He looked scared, his mouth shut with a snap. 'You are on that landing, or whatever we term it, and you have entered a cave. I suggest to you that the prisoner followed you.'

She shook her head.

'What do you mean, please?'

'No,' she said in a flat, unattractive voice.

Contrasts are central to Forster's novels. In *Where Angels Fear to Tread* (1905) and *A Room with a View* (1908) he contrasts refined English gentility and sensuous Italian vitality. In this scene from *A Room with a View*, Lucy is in the square in Florence, hoping for something to happen:

Then something did happen.

Two Italians by the Loggia had been bickering about a debt. 'Cinque lire,' they had cried, 'cinque lire!' They sparred at each other, and one of them was hit lightly upon the chest. He frowned; he bent towards Lucy with a look of interest, as if he had an important message for her. He opened his lips to deliver it, and a stream of red came out between them and trickled down his unshaven chin.

That was all.

Howards End (1910) also explores contrasts in relationships. The overt contrasts are drawn between two families, the Schlegels and the Wilcoxes. The Wilcoxes represent material values and the effective management of the outer life; the Schlegels represent the inner life and the importance of spiritual values. The heart of the novel is Forster's attempt to explore the relationship between these two kinds of reality. On a symbolic level, the two families struggle for the house named in the title, which in a sense stands for England itself. Symbolically, too, the house is within sight of and increasingly surrounded by the suburban, anonymous housing of a new middle-class Britain – which the Schlegels regard as 'civilised' in only the most superficial and mechanised way.

As the epigraph to the novel puts it, 'only connect'. If there were some connection between these different worlds, these contrasting attitudes of mind, and these opposing values, then individuals and societies might form complete and healthy wholes and human love might flourish. The lower-middle-class character Leonard Bast becomes something of a symbol of how these ideals of connection are threatened by class differences, poverty, and a lack of 'culture'. The connection must involve the whole of the personality and must not be dictated merely by social codes or conventions or by external necessity. As a homosexual, Forster had great difficulty in reconciling his private world with the codes of behaviour expected during the times in which he lived. This conflict emerges in his novel *Maurice* (written 1913, published in 1971) – a novel about homosexual love which was only published following the author's death.

> He moaned, half asleep. There was something better in life than this rubbish, if only he could get to it – love – nobility – big spaces where passion clasped peace, spaces no science could reach, but they existed for ever, full of woods some of them, and arched with majestic sky and a friend. . . .
> He really was asleep when he sprang up and flung wide the curtains with a cry of 'Come!' The action awoke him; what had he done that for? . . .
> But as he returned to his bed a little noise sounded, a noise so intimate that it might have arisen inside his own body. He seemed to crackle and burn and saw the ladder's top quivering against the moonlit air. The head and the shoulders of a man rose up, paused, a gun was leant against the window sill very carefully, and someone he scarcely knew moved towards him and knelt beside him and whispered, 'Sir, was you calling out for me? . . . Sir, I know . . . I know,' and touched him.

LANGUAGE NOTE
Metaphor and metonymy

Here are two openings to two classic novels, Dickens's *Bleak House* and
E.M. Forster's *A Passage to India*:

> LONDON. Michaelmas Term lately over, and the Lord Chancellor sitting in
> Lincoln's Inn Hall. Implacable November weather. As much mud in the
> streets, as if the waters had but newly retired from the face of the earth, and
> it would not be wonderful to meet a Megalosaurus, forty feet long or so,
> waddling like an elephantine lizard up Holborn Hill. Smoke lowering down
> from chimney-pots, making a soft black drizzle, with flakes of soot in it as
> big as full-grown snowflakes – gone into mourning, one might imagine, for
> the death of the sun. Dogs, undistinguishable in the mire. Horses, scarcely
> better; splashed to their very blinkers. Foot passengers, jostling one anoth-
> er's umbrellas, in a general infection of ill-temper, and losing their foot-hold
> at street-corners, where tens of thousands of other foot passengers have
> been slipping and sliding since the day broke (if this day ever broke), adding
> new deposits to the crust upon crust of mud, sticking at those points
> tenaciously to the pavement, and accumulating at compound interest.
>
> (*Bleak House*)

> Except for the Marabar Caves – and they are twenty miles off – the city of
> Chandrapore presents nothing extraordinary. Edged rather than washed by
> the river Ganges, it trails for a couple of miles along the bank, scarcely
> distinguishable from the rubbish it deposits so freely. There are no bathing
> steps on the river front, as the Ganges happens not to be holy here; indeed
> there is no river front, and bazaars shut out the wide and shifting panorama
> of the stream. . . . There is no painting and scarcely any carving in the
> bazaars. The very wood seems made of mud, the inhabitants of mud mov-
> ing. So abased, so monotonous is everything that meets the eye, that when
> the Ganges comes down it might be expected to wash the excrescence back
> into the soil. Houses do fall, people are drowned and left rotting, but the
> general outline of the town persists, swelling here, shrinking there, like some
> low but indestructible form of life.
>
> (*A Passage to India*)

The critic David Lodge, basing his analysis on the work of the Russian
linguist Roman Jakobson, has argued that two major literary tropes, *metaphor*
and *metonymy*, constitute the basis of two major literary styles of modern
writing. According to Lodge, metaphor corresponds to Modernism and Symbolism, while metonymy corresponds to anti-Modernism and Realism. In

terms of the historical development of literature from Romanticism through Realism to Symbolism and Modernism, there has been an alternation of style from the metaphoric to the metonymic back and forth through the twentieth century, in prose and poetry and drama.

In the first passage above, from *Bleak House*, the key description occurs at the end of the passage. What is striking is Dickens's use of metaphor, particularly in the final sentence of this first paragraph, where references to money amplify the description by adding this new element. London is the capital city and at that time the world city of capital. By equating references to money ('accumulating', 'deposits', 'compound interest') with mud and dirt, Dickens employs a poetic metaphor indirectly and critically to suggest the ways in which capital may have contributed to London's growth. The pervasive trope is metaphor and the passage accordingly takes on symbolic, poetic, and non-realistic modes of representation. Using a metaphor involves substituting one thing for another in a context and requires the reader to interpret what the substitution stands for or implies in that context.

In the second passage above, from *A Passage to India*, the basic descriptive style is metonymic. Metonymy involves a shift from one element in a sequence to another or from one element in a context to another. Parts, aspects, and contextual details of things are used by the writer to evoke a whole context. Thus, reference to the sight of 'sails' on the horizon is taken metonymically to refer to ships; we refer to a 'cup' of something when we refer to its contents or to 'turf' when we refer to horse-racing. Like metaphor, metonymy requires a context and we work out meanings by referring one element in the context to another element in the context. Lodge argues that this is one of the principal ways in which realism operates.

In the opening to *A Passage to India*, one key sentence is:

> The very wood seems made of mud, the inhabitants of mud moving.

The description works here not so much symbolically as by reference to real mud of which the inhabitants of Chandrapore are literally a part. Chandrapore itself is presented through one selected aspect; it is not, as in the case of London in *Bleak House*, obliquely and indirectly presented in terms of poetic images of capital and prehistoric monsters.

Paradoxically, in the case of these passages, the nineteenth-century novel is in metaphoric and the twentieth-century novel in metonymic mode. More often the reverse would be the case. The distinction between metaphoric and metonymic cannot, of course, be mechanically applied. There are other novels by Dickens which are more realistic and metonymic in style but the modes of metaphor and metonymy do allow a useful categorisation of dominant styles in relation to historical period, author, and genre.

Joseph Conrad was another novelist who used the wider world beyond England as the setting for his explorations in character and motive. Conrad's novels have a variety of locations which reflect his own extensive travels, mainly as a merchant seaman. Like several of the important writers of the time, he came to Britain as an exile from elsewhere. He was born Jozef Teodor Konrad Korzeniowski of Polish parents and did not learn English until his early twenties. He joined the British merchant navy, and became a naturalised British subject in 1896. He brought to his novels experiences and attitudes which were unusual for a writer of his time. He shared with both Kipling and Maugham a fascination with different cultures, especially the Far East and Africa, but he has more wide-ranging and explicit political insights than these writers normally express.

In his early novels, Conrad uses his sea experiences in remote places as a means of exploring human character and English codes of honour and loyalty in particular. His situations are often extreme and test human beings to their limits. *Lord Jim* (1900) is the story of a young Englishman who panics and deserts his ship. Lord Jim later dies an honourable death but not before his moral conflicts are explored in detail. Innocence and experience, and the resulting moral growth which the character undergoes, turn Jim into a Conradian hero.

Nostromo is often considered to be Conrad's masterpiece. It was published in 1904, the same year as Henry James's *The Golden Bowl* (see page 316). The two novels are in many ways opposites: where Conrad is concerned with the effects on his characters of extreme stress and danger, James looks at the complexities and the refinements of art. Both writers are, however, engaged with the unfolding of deep mysteries, with the establishing of true identities and valid relationships in a flawed world.

The bowl in James's novel is as much a symbol of human frailty as is the treasure of silver which corrupts Nostromo in Conrad's novel. The 'incorruptible' Emilia in *Nostromo*, in her relationship with the Italian sailor who is the book's hero, has a similar innocence to Maggie Verver's in her relationship with the Italian prince, Amerigo, in *The*

Golden Bowl. Where James's characters find their truth in Europe rather than America, Conrad places his characters in the imaginary South American country of Costaguana.

Nostromo, like many of Conrad's novels, involves a journey towards discovery in a vividly described and richly peopled country of the mind. *Nostromo* has a more clearly defined social and political setting than most of his works, but it is the moral struggle which is paramount.

> He mistrusted his superior's proneness to fussy action. That old Englishman had no judgement, he said to himself. It was useless to suppose that, acquainted with the true state of the case, he would keep it to himself. He would talk of doing impracticable things. Nostromo feared him as one would fear saddling one's self with some persistent worry. He had no discretion. He would betray the treasure. And Nostromo had made up his mind that the treasure should not be betrayed.
>
> The word had fixed itself tenaciously in his intelligence. His imagination had seized upon the clear and simple notion of betrayal to account for the dazed feeling of enlightenment as to being done for, of having inadvertently gone out of his existence on an issue in which his personality had not been taken into account. A man betrayed is a man destroyed.

Themes of trust and betrayal, ignorance and self-knowledge dominate Conrad's works, and will be taken up again in many forms by later twentieth-century writers from Graham Greene to John Le Carré and beyond.

The critic F.R. Leavis places Conrad firmly in what he called 'the great tradition' of novelists whose moral affirmations make them stand out as major contributors to literature. Many other critics have questioned this 'tradition'. Jane Austen, George Eliot, and Henry James also gain Leavis's approval, and few would deny that these are all highly significant writers. The importance of their writings goes beyond moral and aesthetic values, and they can be critically considered from several other viewpoints (for example, social, political, popular, cultural) without in any way diminishing their significance.

Conrad was indeed a profoundly moral novelist but he recognised the moral complexities of his age which stemmed in part from the absence of any clearly shared set of values between people. In order to present this world fictionally, Conrad develops techniques of multiple points of view. A hero like Lord Jim is not judged directly by Conrad but his behaviour is seen from different narrative viewpoints, including the viewpoint of a narrator distinct from Conrad himself. He is a master of complex narrative techniques such as time-shifting and flashbacks, which prevent a reader from adopting too simplistic an interpretation of events.

Conrad wrote long novels, short stories, and novellas, with his most famous novella being *Heart of Darkness* (1899). In it Conrad describes a long journey to a place deep inside the Belgian Congo, the heart of darkness of the title. The story is again told by the intermediate narrator Marlow, who retraces his first visit to colonial Africa and his growing awareness of the evils he encounters. The story contrasts Western civilisation in Europe with what that civilisation has done to Africa. Early in the novel, while on the River Thames near London, Marlow speaks:

> 'And this also,' said Marlow suddenly, 'has been one of the dark places of the earth.' . . .
> 'I was thinking of very old times, when the Romans first came here, nineteen hundred years ago – the other day. . . . Light came out of this river since – you say Knights? Yes; but it is like a running blaze on a plain, like a flash of lightning in the clouds. We live in the flicker – may it last as long as the old earth keeps rolling! But darkness was here yesterday.'

The theme of darkness leads to the figure of Kurtz, the central character, a portrait of how the commercial and material exploitation of colonial lands can make men morally hollow, and create a permanent nightmare in the soul. The fears Conrad expresses find an echo in T.S. Eliot's poetry, especially in his poem *The Hollow Men* with the epigraph 'Mistah Kurtz – he dead' – a direct quotation from Conrad's novella.

> His was an impenetrable darkness. I looked at him as you peer down at a man who is lying at the bottom of a precipice where the sun never shines. . . .
> Anything approaching the change that came over his features I have never seen before, and hope never to see again. Oh, I wasn't

touched. I was fascinated. It was as though a veil had been rent. I saw on that ivory face the expression of sombre pride, of ruthless power, of craven terror – of an intense and hopeless despair. Did he live his life again in every detail of desire, temptation, and surrender during that supreme moment of complete knowledge? He cried in a whisper at some image, at some vision – he cried out twice, a cry that was no more than a breath –

'The horror! The horror!'

I blew the candle out and left the cabin. The pilgrims were dining in the mess-room, and I took my place opposite the manager, who lifted his eyes to give me a questioning glance, which I successfully ignored. He leaned back, serene, with that peculiar smile of his sealing the unexpressed depths of his meanness. A continuous shower of small flies streamed upon the lamp, upon the cloth, upon our hands and faces. Suddenly the manager's boy put his insolent black head in the doorway, and said in a tone of scathing contempt –

'Mistah Kurtz – he dead.'

Conrad also shares with other writers of this time a sense of impending anarchy and the collapse of moral and political order. His most explicitly political novels are *Nostromo* (1904), *The Secret Agent* (1907), and *Under Western Eyes* (1911). Throughout his fiction he depicts human isolation, the conflict between different parts of one's personality and external fate as well as the difficulties of human communication. He writes with a deep pessimism reminiscent of Thomas Hardy and he appreciates E.M. Forster's need to 'only connect'. Formally and technically, however, Conrad is a more innovative and influential writer and closer to Modernists than Hardy or Forster. The word 'Modern' is again important here. It came into use in the nineteenth century in the context of art and architecture. Only later did writers begin to use it – George Meredith's sonnet sequence *Modern Love* (1862) and George Moore's novel *A Modern Lover* (1883) being significant examples.

Ford Madox Ford was a contributor to *Des Imagistes*, a collaborator with Joseph Conrad on the novels *The Inheritors* (1901) and *Romance* (1903), and a critic, being the founder of *The English Review*, from 1908 to 1910. He became one of the most influential figures in literature during and after the First World War, encouraging new writing, founding the *Transatlantic Review* and assisting in the spread of new trends, in an untiring and hugely productive career. Noted in his own day as poet, editor, and autobiographer, Ford is now best remembered in his own right for *The Good Soldier* (1915), subtitled *The Saddest Story Ever Told*, which has been described as 'the greatest tragedy of sexuality in English prose'. It is recounted by a first-person narrator, John Dowell, whose unreliability undermines every scene in the novel, rendering the whole story ambiguous. Full of time-shifts, and with a mysterious death which is only resolved on the last page, it has remained both fascinating and influential. Something of the ambiguity and necessary uncertainty of the narration can be gauged in this paragraph:

> I have, I am aware, told this story in a very rambling way so that it may be difficult for anyone to find their path through what may be a sort of maze. I cannot help it. I have stuck to my idea of being in a country cottage with a silent listener, hearing between the gusts of the wind and amidst the noises of the distant sea, the story as it comes. And, when one discusses an affair – a long, sad affair – one goes back, one goes forward. One remembers points that one has forgotten and one explains them all the more minutely since one recognizes that one has forgotten to mention them in their proper places and that one may have given, by omitting them, a false impression. I console myself with thinking that this is a real story and that, after all, real stories are probably told best in the way a person telling a story would tell them. They will then seem most real.

Ford's 'Impressionist' trilogy, *Fifth Queen* (1907–8), and the tetralogy *Parade's End* (1924–28), with its hero Tietjens, were notable contributions to the experimentation with narrative techniques and styles which Ford spent his life promoting. The trilogy is about one of the wives of Henry VIII, Catherine Howard; the tetralogy follows its hero through intrigues of passion and the experience of the war, bringing together personal and universal themes, tracing the breakdown of the old order and the emergence of the new, in a way that few other novels have done.

Like many other creative writers, Ford published a great deal of criticism. Henry James had constantly commented on his own and others' writing in *The Art of Fiction* (1885) and *The Art of the Novel*

(1893). Shaw had used the prefaces to his plays to raise social issues. Artists frequently used their position to discuss, evaluate, and pronounce on the rapidly changing world in which they lived. D.H. Lawrence's essays cover a vast range of topics, from psychology to American literature; T.S. Eliot is, by many, as highly regarded as a critic as he is for his poetry and drama; Virginia Woolf's two volumes of *The Common Reader* (1925; 1932), discuss a wide range of writing, with a concern for the values it expresses; E.M. Forster's *Aspects of the Novel* (1927) was immensely influential; and Ford's own overview, *The English Novel* (1930), is a complementary survey, concluding with Conrad. Ford's *The March of Literature* (1935) is the last of this kind of personal, polemical critical writing, which flourished between the wars. The quality and quantity of critical writing at this time is a sign of how much all these writers were crucially absorbed by the role of literature and by the changes in writing and reading which were happening in their own lifetimes. It is a testimony to the urgency of the debate that most of what they wrote is still vivid, relevant, and illuminating, whether of the earlier writers they examined or of later writing.

D.H. LAWRENCE

Another distinctively modern writer for whom the phrase 'only connect' had considerable significance was D.H. Lawrence. Lawrence was born in the mining village of Eastwood, Nottinghamshire, in the English Midlands. His father was a coal-miner and his mother an ex-teacher. Lawrence's mother fought to lift her children out of the working class. She was determined her son would not become a miner and encouraged him to take up teaching. His first major novel *Sons and Lovers* (1913) is largely autobiographical, and chronicles the domestic conflicts in his own home between a coarse, inarticulate father and a self-consciously genteel mother. The novel also explores the theme of the demanding mother who exercises a strong emotional influence over her son and frustrates his relationships with other women; it is also, like several other novels of the time, a portrait of the birth of an artist. Later in his life, Lawrence felt that his mother had prejudiced him against his father and against the working class. He grew to believe that people like his father had a vital, whole personality that was lacking in middle-class culture, with its material and social ambitions. Early in the novel, something of the distance between the miner and his wife is clearly seen:

> Morel sitting there, quite alone, and having nothing to think about, would be feeling vaguely uncomfortable. His soul would reach out in its blind way to her and find her gone. He felt a sort of emptiness, almost like a vacuum in his soul. He was unsettled and restless. Soon he could not live in that atmosphere, and he affected his wife. Both felt an oppression on their breathing when they were left together for some time. Then he went to bed and she settled down to enjoy herself alone, working, thinking, living.

Lawrence's next major novel was *The Rainbow*, which was published in 1915 but suppressed a month later as indecent. The novel deals with three generations of the Brangwen family, from the middle of the nineteenth century to the early years of the twentieth century. Like many of Lawrence's novels, *The Rainbow* explores human individuality and all that might hinder or fulfil that essential individuality. At the heart of individual fulfilment is a proper basis for marital relationships, and the elemental symbols which Lawrence employs represent the deepest rhythms and impulses in the relationships between men and women. At the end of *The Rainbow*, Ursula Brangwen, the main character, rejects a future life with her fiancé because he is insufficiently aware of her as a unique individual. For Lawrence, awareness of the essential 'otherness' of one's partner is fundamental to a truly harmonious relationship. If either partner is too weak or seeks to dominate the other, then mutual destruction will follow.

In *The Rainbow* and its sequel *Women in Love* (1921), Lawrence explores human relationships with psychological precision and with intense poetic feeling. He combines a detailed realism with poetic symbolism in ways which make us believe in his characters at the same time as we understand the most deeply buried aspects of their selves. Although technically more innovative and experimental, Lawrence's novels owe much to the nineteenth-century tradition of realism developed by George Eliot, in which a central task of the novelist was to depict the formation and development of an individual character. Much of *Women in Love* – including an opening chapter which was suppressed for many years – discusses the close male–male relationship between Gerald Crich and Rupert Birkin. Here, they have just had a wrestling match:

> 'It was real set-to, wasn't it?' said Birkin, looking at Gerald with darkened eyes.
> 'God, yes,' said Gerald. He looked at the delicate body of the other man, and added: 'It wasn't too much for you, was it?'
> 'No. One ought to wrestle and strive and be physically close. It makes one sane.'
> 'You do think so?'
> 'I do. Don't you?'
> 'Yes,' said Gerald.
> There were long spaces of silence between their words. The wrestling had some deep meaning to them – an unfinished meaning.
> 'We are mentally, spiritually intimate, therefore we should be more or less physically intimate too – it is more whole.'
> 'Certainly it is,' said Gerald. Then he laughed pleasantly, adding: 'It's rather wonderful to me.' He stretched out his arms handsomely.
> 'Yes,' said Birkin. 'I don't know why one should have to justify oneself.'
> 'No.'
> The two men began to dress.

A similar closeness between women is found in a noted scene from *The Rainbow*. Given the context of society in 1915, and Lawrence's scandalous attachment to a German woman, it is hardly surprising that the novel was banned:

> Now, ah now, she was swimming in the same water with her dear mistress. The girl moved her limbs voluptuously, and swam by herself, deliciously, yet with a craving of unsatisfaction. She wanted to touch the other, to touch her, to feel her.
> 'I will race you, Ursula,' came the well-modulated voice.
> Ursula started violently. She turned to see the warm, unfolded face of her mistress looking at her, to her. She was acknowledged. Laughing her own beautiful, startled laugh, she began to swim. The mistress was just ahead, swimming with easy strokes. Ursula could see the head put back, the water flicker upon the white shoulders, the strong legs kicking shadowily. And she swam blinded with passion.

> Ah, the beauty of the firm, white, cool flesh! Ah, the wonderful firm
> limbs. If she could but hold them, hug them, press them between
> her own small breasts! Ah, if she did not so despise her own thin,
> dusky fragment of a body, if only she too were fearless and capable.

It was not simply in relationships between men and women that
Lawrence sought to 'only connect'. There are creative tensions both in
his novels and extensively in his short stories between different generations, between man and his environment and between human reason
and human instinct. Above all he wanted the tensions to be creative
and not sterile. The area in Nottinghamshire in which he was brought
up highlighted the contrasts between industrial and natural worlds. The
coal-miner walking home from the waste of an industrial site often
passed through relatively unspoilt countryside. Lawrence saw indus-
trialisation as a threat to a natural, fulfilled life. The industrial world is
associated with mechanised feelings and with the death of spontaneous, instinctive responses to life.

There is a sense in much of Lawrence's writing of overcoming the
huge moral, spiritual, and indeed physical crises which afflict the world.
The title of the collection of poems *Look! We Have Come Through!*
(1917) is an indication of this consciously optimistic viewpoint, shared
perhaps in Molly Bloom's defiant 'Yes' at the end of James Joyce's
Ulysses (1922) and reached with difficulty at the end of the novels of
Virginia Woolf, Dorothy Richardson and others. There is, despite the
horrors to be lived through, a sense of optimism deep in the heart of
the nature which Lawrence so clearly describes.

The theme of freedom from inhibition is also vital to this positive
outlook: complete honesty between lovers will lead to greater self-
knowledge, deeper fulfilment, and a stronger will to live. This is found
between men in the highly charged chapters of *Women in Love* (1921)
(including the opening chapter which was originally suppressed), and
in *The White Peacock* (1911), between women in *The Rainbow* (1915), and
between man and woman most clearly in *Lady Chatterley's Lover* (1928).
It is a theme shared, perhaps surprisingly, by E.M. Forster: the bathing
scene in *A Room with a View* (1908) has the same liberating intention
between men as a similar scene in *The White Peacock* (1911), where the
narrator says:

Our love was perfect for a moment, more perfect than any love I have known since, either for man or woman.

Lawrence travelled constantly, and his travel writing underlines both his dissent from English life and his joy in the freshness of new experiences, in places as far apart as Australia, Mexico, and Cornwall. His is always a search for the primitive, for the gods of a place, as in *Etruscan Places*, posthumously published in 1932, or, in fiction, in *The Plumed Serpent* (1926) set in Mexico. *Lady Chatterley's Lover*, written in Italy, and published in 1928, is Lawrence's most notorious novel, banned in England for its sexual content until a trial in 1960 allowed it to be widely read.

Lady Chatterley's Lover brings together Lawrence's industrial and social concerns with the account of Lady Constance Chatterley's sexual liaison with the lower-class Mellors, a gamekeeper. Her husband, Sir Clifford, had been wounded in the First World War, and the relationship with Mellors has been seen by many critics as a vivid symbol of social and class shifts as a result of the war. Increasingly, in Lawrence's work, death comes to be associated with genteel culture, the middle-class world of his mother, and the forces of social convention. In many of his short stories and novellas, he sets the restricting life of middle-class convention in contrast with liberating forces from outside – the world of a gypsy, a peasant, a primitive of some kind, or someone coming from the warm instinctive south in opposition to the more rational and cold north. Men and women often form the basis for contrasts and attempt to achieve a loving relationship against prejudice, class-consciousness, or social convention. Something of the social 'ugliness' that Lawrence railed against all his life is clear in this scene from *Lady Chatterley's Lover*. The love between Connie and Mellors is a challenge to this kind of 'dirt':

> The car ploughed uphill through the long squalid straggle of Tevershall, the blackened brick dwellings, the black slate roofs glistening their sharp edges, the mud black with coal-dust, the pavements wet and black. It was as if dismalness had soaked through and through everything. The utter negation of natural beauty, the utter negation of the gladness of life, the utter absence of the instinct for shapely beauty which every bird and beast has, the utter death of the human

intuitive faculty was appalling. The stacks of soap in the grocers' shops, the rhubarb and lemons in the greengrocers! the awful hats in the milliners! all went by ugly, ugly, ugly, followed by the plaster-and-gilt horror of the cinema with its wet picture announcements, 'A Woman's Love!', and the new big Primitive chapel, primitive enough in its stark brick and big panes of greenish and raspberry glass in the windows.

Tension in sexual feeling is a recurring theme in Lawrence's fiction. Lawrence saw sexuality as a driving force in human relationships which could be both creative and destructive. Sexual love could be destructive if it were too mechanical or based on rationality or reason; if it were created on an instinctive level it would be positive and could help individuals achieve a wholeness of personality through their love for each other. He described relationships with uncompromising original-ity and genuinely sought ways of reconciling tensions and contrasts, of 'only connecting' seemingly irreconcilable opposites. Above all, Lawrence was concerned to find ways of describing the deepest experi-ences of his characters. He once wrote that the human personality was like an iceberg, with the major part of it under the surface. His art attempts to capture the submerged parts of the self and to develop forms and techniques in the novel which render those intense experi-ences. To this end, readers have to abandon conventional understand-ings of 'plot' and 'character', and immerse themselves in the total pattern of rhythm, episodic structure, and poetic symbolism which is the experience of reading his fictional work. A relevant comment on his own practice as a novelist is contained in a letter by Lawrence to a friend, Edward Garnett. He wrote (about the writing of *The Rainbow*):

> You mustn't look in my novel for the old stable ego of character. There is another ego, according to whose actions the individual is unrecognisable and passes through, as it were, allotropic states which it needs a deeper sense than we've been used to exercise to discover.

Not all his fiction is so successful, however. Some of the later novels such as *Aaron's Rod* (1922) or *The Plumed Serpent* (1926) are uneven, somewhat formless, and given to preaching rather than exploring ideas: some of D.H. Lawrence's writing in the 1920s has been accused of displaying Fascist ideas (of racial superiority). But a full belief in such ideas would go against his consistent display of sympathy with a wide range of cultures and classes. Lawrence's prolific output covers novels, short stories, travel writing, criticism, drama, and poetry.

D.H. Lawrence wrote about the pressures of working-class life from close quarters, but then moved on. One major novel of the early years of the twentieth century is a document of working-class life, written by one who never actually lived in the situation described in his novel. *The Ragged-Trousered Philanthropists* was published in 1914, three years after the death of its author, Robert Tressell. It is set in Mugsborough, and the 'mugs' are a group of poor house-painters who accept their lot without rebelling against it. The novel is one of the most vivid and realistic portraits of an unvarnished Hell, following on from the late Victorian novels of John Law and Arthur Morrison, with no sweetening of its powerful impact. This scene echoes Thomas Hardy's *Jude the Obscure*:

TERRIBLE DOMESTIC TRAGEDY

WIFE AND TWO CHILDREN KILLED
SUICIDE OF THE MURDERER

It was one of the ordinary poverty crimes. The man had been without employment for many weeks and they had been living by pawning or selling their furniture and other possessions. But even this resource must have failed at last, and when one day the neighbours noticed that the blinds remained down and that there was a strange silence about the house, no one coming out or going in, suspicions that something was wrong were quickly aroused. When the police entered the house, they found, in one of the upper rooms, the dead bodies of the woman and the two children, with their throats severed, laid out side by side upon the bed, which was saturated with their blood.

Examine for a moment an ordinary mind on an ordinary day.

(Virginia Woolf, *The Modern Novel*)

D.H. Lawrence is a novelist who was concerned to represent the innermost thoughts and feelings of his characters. In his development as a novelist, the story or plot line of his novels became less important than the shifts in feeling and the stream of consciousness of his characters. While probing this deeply into the recesses of his characters' psychology, Lawrence externalises their relationships with the outside world, particularly the world of nature. Other writers focus more on the inner workings of their characters' minds in a way that is much more appropriately defined as 'stream of consciousness'.

Stream of consciousness is a term widely used in discussions of the twentieth-century novel. It is usually used to refer to particular techniques of presentation which a number of Modernist novelists developed. The term refers to the flow of impressions, perceptions, and thoughts which stream unbidden through our minds. These impressions can be stimulated by something that happens to us or by subconscious impulses; the stream of consciousness can be illogical and random. We can be aware of various impressions in no particular order; past memories may intermingle with present actions or thoughts of the future; saying something to a friend may be quite different from the thoughts or impressions passing through the mind at the same time; sounds, smells, and sights are all registered and may stimulate unpredictable feelings. For many modern novelists it became a central task to find a way of recording this kind of subjective 'flow' in the language and form of the novel.

Time had always been important in the fiction: from Defoe's Robinson Crusoe measuring the length of his stay on the island, to Sterne's playing with time, to Trollope's careful handling of characters in time, the novelist is always aware of 'Time's wingèd chariot hurrying near', as Marvell put it. In the twentieth century, the treatment of time becomes, however, a major concern for writers. The last novel to be published by Thomas Hardy – *The Well-Beloved* (see page 313) – opened up this area of exploration. This novel had a particularly strong influence on Marcel Proust (1871–1922), whose *A la recherche du temps perdu* (1913–27) is the major 'time-novel' of the century.

The Well-Beloved is quite different from any other of Hardy's more socially concerned works, telling the story of Jocelyn Pierston's search for the love of Avice Caro in the same place in Wessex, at three different periods. Character and time become fluid; motivation and landscape eternal. What became important as a result of such experiments was a sense of the fluidity and flexibility both of time and memory. Virginia Woolf, in particular, experiments very successfully with the concept of 'Time on the clock and time in the mind'.

> 'Time passed' (here the exact amount could be indicated in brackets) and nothing whatever happened. . . .
> An hour, once it lodges in the queer element of the human spirit, may be stretched to fifty or a hundred times its clock length; on the other hand, an hour may be accurately represented on the timepiece of the mind by one second. This extraordinary discrepancy between time on the clock and time in the mind is less known than it should be and deserves fuller investigation. . . .
> It would be no exaggeration to say that he would go out after breakfast a man of thirty and come home to dinner a man of fifty-five at least. Some weeks added a century to his age, others no more than three seconds at most.
>
> (Virginia Woolf, *Orlando*, 1928)

WOOLF AND JOYCE

Novelists such as D.H. Lawrence and, more particularly, Virginia Woolf and James Joyce felt that the demands of the traditional novel with its emphasis on external realism were restricting. Such a form of the novel emphasised a plot development and a logical order which was not consistent with experience. New stylistic techniques were needed to reflect that experience.

Virginia Woolf was born into a large, talented, upper-class, intellectual family in London. She was the daughter of Leslie Stephen, a famous Victorian biographer, critic, and philosopher. Her mother died when she was 13, after which she suffered the first of many nervous breakdowns. Her father exerted a powerful inhibiting influence over her, and she later confessed that she could never have written her stories and novels while he was alive. After his death, she was at the centre of the 'Bloomsbury Group' – an artistic and literary group renowned for their rebellion against Victorian puritanism and which had great influence on British culture from 1920 to the 1940s. Mental illness affected Virginia Woolf throughout her life. In 1941, at a time of deep personal depression with the Second World War, and deeply dissatisfied with her own writing, she committed suicide.

Virginia Woolf's first novels were relatively traditional in form, but she later rebelled against what she called the 'materialism' of novelists such as H.G. Wells, Arnold Bennett and John Galsworthy. Her characteristic method appears in her third novel, *Jacob's Room*, published in 1922. She renders the flow of experience through a stream of consciousness technique, but her work is also particularly characterised by an intensely poetic style. She utilises poetic rhythms and imagery to create a lyrical impressionism in order to capture her characters' moods with great delicacy and detail. The novel shows her breaking free from traditional forms and the traditional concerns with external reality – the 'materialism' which she felt to be untrue to life.

As diversity in individual character portrayal increased, so also did novelists' concept of setting and space. Shakespeare had Hamlet say:

> I could be bounded in a nutshell and count myself a king of infinite space.

In the modern novel, space can equally be enclosed or infinite, often at the same time, in one character's mind.

Virginia Woolf's main novels are *Mrs Dalloway* (1925), *To The Lighthouse* (1927) and *The Waves* (1931). *Mrs Dalloway* describes the events of one single day in central London through the mind of one character, Clarissa Dalloway, who is to be the hostess of a party for high-society friends later the same evening. It is a finely shaded portrait of an individual personality:

> Mrs Dalloway said she would buy the flowers herself.
> For Lucy had her work cut out for her. The doors would be taken off their hinges; Rumpelmayer's men were coming. And then, thought Clarissa Dalloway, what a morning – fresh as if issued to children on a beach.
> What a lark! What a plunge! For so it had always seemed to her when, with a little squeak of the hinges, which she could hear now, she had burst open the French windows and plunged at Bourton into the open air. How fresh, how calm, stiller than this of course, the air was in the early morning; like the flap of a wave; the kiss of a

wave; chill and sharp and yet (for a girl of eighteen as she then was) solemn, feeling as she did, standing there at the open window, that something awful was about to happen; looking at the flowers, at the trees with the smoke winding off them and the rooks rising, falling; standing and looking until Peter Walsh said, 'Musing among the vegetables?' – was that it? – 'I prefer men to cauliflowers' – was that it? He must have said it at breakfast one morning when she had gone out on to the terrace – Peter Walsh. He would be back from India one of these days, June or July, she forgot which, for his letters were awfully dull; it was his sayings one remembered; his eyes, his pocket-knife, his smile, his grumpiness and, when millions of things had utterly vanished – how strange it was! – a few sayings like this about cabbages.

The novel contains many flashbacks to Clarissa Dalloway's past experience as she seeks to bring together past memory and present action and as she endeavours to balance a need for privacy with a need for communication with other people.

In *The Waves*, Virginia Woolf takes six characters who are all at different stages in their lives. She explores how each one of these characters is affected by the death of a person they all knew well. In *To The Lighthouse*, two days in the life of a family on holiday are recorded: one before the Great War, one after it, when some of the characters have died. Again, Virginia Woolf is more interested in her characters' mental processes than in their visible actions. Mrs Ramsay is a powerful figure in the family who is searching for a truth which lies beneath surface facts. Her husband, Mr Ramsay, is more literal-minded and contrasts with Mrs Ramsay. In the second part of the novel we learn that Mrs Ramsay has died, but she continues to exert a spiritual influence over all those who return to the holiday home years later. The narrative and emotional focus of the novel is on Mrs Ramsay, but the inner worlds of many of the characters are communicated. Some readers have felt that in places the novel breaks away from prose and becomes something closer to poetry. The novel is also marked by a use of poetic symbolism, most strikingly in the 'lighthouse' of the title. The lighthouse is a suggestive and ambiguous symbol which takes on uniquely different meanings for each character in the novel and for each reader who attempts to interpret it.

Several Modernist novels during this period are centred on key poetic (rather than realistic) symbols. Other examples are *The Rainbow*, *The Waves*, *Kangaroo* and *Heart of Darkness*. This contrasts with the normal practice of nineteenth-century novelists. The nineteenth-century novelists do not avoid symbolism but it is associated with clearly identifiable places, people or human qualities. Examples are *Mansfield Park*, *Jane Eyre*, *Pride and Prejudice* and *Middlemarch*. The use of poetic symbols suggests a more indirect, oblique, and tenuous approach to reality. For a writer such as Virginia Woolf, who has no definite or fixed vision of reality, the suggestiveness of these symbols is an essential part of her art.

Virginia Woolf was also a highly influential journalist and critic. In *A Room of One's Own* (1928) she gives a unique account of why a woman must have money and a room of her own in order to write fiction. It has become a classic statement of feminism. Some of her many reviews and critical essays are collected in *The Common Reader* (1925; second edition, 1932). With her husband, Leonard Woolf, Virginia founded the Hogarth Press in 1917. The press published Virginia Woolf's own work and the work of other Modernists such as T.S. Eliot.

Here is an example of Virginia Woolf's prose style: a brief extract from *To The Lighthouse*. Lily Briscoe is one of the characters who return to the Ramsays' holiday home. Mrs Ramsay's efforts to persuade Lily to marry have come to nothing but her influence is still pervasive. The extract reveals some of the thoughts and feelings passing through Lily's mind:

> But the dead, thought Lily, encountering some obstacle in her design which made her pause and ponder, stepping back a foot or so, oh, the dead! She murmured, one pitied them, one brushed them aside, one had even a little contempt for them. They are at our mercy. Mrs Ramsay had faded and gone, she thought. We can override her wishes, improve away her limited, old-fashioned ideas. She recedes further and further from us. Mockingly she seemed to see her there at the end of the corridor of years saying, of all the incongruous things, 'Marry, marry!' (sitting very upright early in the morning with the birds beginning to cheep in the garden outside). And one would have to say to her, it has all gone against your wishes.

We can note here how Virginia Woolf represents Lily's 'stream of consciousness'; particularly how her memories of the past mingle with perceptions of the present and how the constant switches in tense capture the simultaneous nature of her experiences. There is no simple chronology to 'what happens'; that would be false to the immediacy of Lily's experience. In fact, there is only minimal reference to an outside world (for example, 'stepping back a foot or so') – actions and external movement which would receive more emphasis in traditional novels and which contrast here with a varied and complex inner movement. The point of view here is also complex and varied. It seems to belong both to Virginia Woolf, the author, and to Lily, the character, but not clearly to either. In a traditional novel, the thoughts and speech of the characters would be clearly marked by *she said* or *she thought* with appropriate quotation marks and with the point of view of the author definitely present. The effect is less certain for the reader who has to work harder to make meanings, and there is very little direction given by the author who does not directly interpret for her readers what is happening.

The term 'stream of consciousness' is widely used, indeed perhaps over-used. The concern of writers is to 'examine for a moment an ordinary mind on an ordinary day', as Virginia Woolf put it herself in an essay entitled *Modern Fiction*. But the techniques are employed differently by different writers. A major, some think *the* major, Modernist writer who shares Virginia Woolf's concern to render the inner life of characters is James Joyce. Joyce's techniques of stream of consciousness are different from Virginia Woolf's. The following extract from his novel *Ulysses* (1922) provides an interesting comparison. The main character in the novel is Leopold Bloom:

> He entered Davy Byrne's. Moral pub. He doesn't chat. Stands a drink now and then. But in leapyear once in four. Cashed a cheque for me once. What will I take now? He drew his watch. Let me see now. Shandygaff? ---- Hellow, Bloom! Nosey Flynn said from his nook. ---- Hello, Flynn. ---- How's things? ---- Tiptop ---- Let me see ---- Sardines on the shelves. Almost taste them by looking. Sandwich? ---- What is home without Plumbtree's potted meat? Incomplete. What a stupid ad! ---- Eat, drink and be merry. Then casual words full after. Heads bandaged. Cheese digests

all but itself. Mighty cheese. ---- Have you a cheese sandwich? ----
Yes, sir.

There is some overlap between the narrator's voice and the character's voice and the same concentration on Bloom's interior monologue. The movement of the prose is, however, more staccato and
less poetic in rhythm and imagery. In linguistic terms, the fragmentation of narration is often represented by unusual cohesion, or
changes in the normal ways of linking sentences, paragraphs, and
narration. This leads to unusual jumps, juxtapositions, and connections, often also marked by unusual or missing punctuation, which
can create unexpected visual or graphological effects on the page.
Stream of consciousness takes these effects to extremes, often abandoning cohesion, syntax, and punctuation and lexical correctness
which previously brought order and clarity to narration. Much modern writing has continued these linguistic experiments introduced in
the 1920s.

The world recorded here reflects the presence of the everyday in
Bloom's consciousness. It is in keeping with the character of Bloom
himself who is portrayed as an ordinary, average man, most of whose
thoughts tend to be about the immediate world around him. Bloom's
stream of consciousness is made up of strange, inconsequential
associations. Memories are prompted, unusual ideas connected, playful
links created between words of similar sound or meaning. The style is
kaleidoscopic and the language often ungrammatical, but rules are
broken in order to represent the workings of Bloom's mind.

In other parts of *Ulysses*, Joyce's experiments with language are even
more innovative and experimental. Here is an extract from the famous
interior monologue of Molly Bloom, Leopold Bloom's wife, which
occurs at the end of the novel. It is at the end of the day (the novel
describes one day in the life of the characters in June 1904), and Molly
Bloom is lying in bed, half-awake and half-asleep. Molly's monologue
lasts for almost fifty pages and is totally without punctuation:

what shall I wear shall I wear a white rose those cakes in Liptons I
love the smell of a rich big shop at 7½d a pound or the other ones
with cherries in them of course a nice plant for the middle of the
table I love flowers Id love to have the whole place swimming in

roses God of heaven theres nothing like nature the wild mountains
then the sea and the waves rushing –

The stream of consciousness here is in a freer, looser style and captures
something of Molly's excited reverie. The lack of punctuation reflects
the way in which thoughts and ideas merge into one another. This is in
many ways the epitome of the stream of consciousness technique.

Not all the linguistic experiments in the form and structure of the
novel are easy to comprehend and there are places where it is difficult
to follow the stream of consciousness. Neither is there one single
appropriate style. Different characters have different inner lives and
different writers perceive and represent the inner mind in contrasting
ways. In the hands of Modernist writers like Joyce and Woolf, brilliant
insights into the workings of the human mind are revealed which were
not possible within the limits of the nineteenth-century novel and
which have not been consistently surpassed since.

However, James Joyce's contribution to the development of the
novel in English in the twentieth century goes beyond particular techniques of formal experimentation. His contribution was a major one
on several levels. Joyce was born in Dublin, educated in Ireland and
spent most of his adult life in Europe, mainly in France, Italy, and
Switzerland. In Europe he was at the centre of literary circles but he
remained, throughout his life of voluntary exile from Ireland, a deeply
Irish writer and he wrote only and always about Dublin. To write about
Dublin and its people was for Joyce to write about all human experience. Joyce wrote something in each of the principal genres before
concentrating on fiction: *Chamber Music* and *Pomes Penyeach* (poetry);
Exiles (play), and *Dubliners* (short stories).

His first short stories, published in the collection *Dubliners* (1914),
depict the lives of the ordinary people of the city with clarity and
realism. The stories are carefully organised so that meanings arise not
only from the individual sketches but also from the relations between
them. The best known of these stories – *The Dead* – is the final one in
the sequence, to which many of the previous stories point. It is a story
in which a husband is shocked out of his self-satisfaction and egotism
by learning of his wife's love for a young man she had known many
years before:

The air of the room chilled his shoulders. He stretched himself cautiously along under the sheets and lay down beside his wife. One by one, they were all becoming shades. Better pass boldly into that other world, in the full glory of some passion, than fade and wither dismally with age. He thought of how she who lay beside him had locked in her heart for so many years that image of her lover's eyes when he had told her that he did not wish to live.

Generous tears filled Gabriel's eyes. He had never felt like that himself towards any woman, but he knew that such a feeling must be love. The tears gathered more thickly in his eyes and in the partial darkness he imagined he saw the form of a young man standing under a dripping tree. Other forms were near. His soul had approached that region where dwell the vast hosts of the dead. He was conscious of, but could not apprehend, their wayward and flickering existence. His own identity was fading out into a grey impalpable world: the solid world itself, which these dead had one time reared and lived in, was dissolving and dwindling.

A few light taps upon the pane made him turn to the window. It had begun to snow again. He watched sleepily the flakes, silver and dark, falling obliquely against the lamplight. The time had come for him to set out on his journey westward. Yes, the newspapers were right: snow was general all over Ireland. It was falling on every part of the dark central plain, on the treeless hills, falling softly upon the Bog of Allen and, farther westward, softly falling into the dark mutinous Shannon waves. It was falling, too, upon every part of the lonely churchyard on the hill where Michael Furey lay buried. It lay thickly drifted on the crooked crosses and headstones, on the spears of the little gate, on the barren thorns. His soul swooned slowly as he heard the snow falling faintly through the universe and faintly falling, like the descent of their last end, upon all the living and the dead.

The theme of many of the stories in *Dubliners* is the attempts of many of the citizens to free themselves from lives in which they feel paralysed by relationships, by social, cultural, and religious traditions, or by their own natures. Joyce's treatment shows a mastery of the short-story form and becomes increasingly detached and neutral.

Joyce's first major novel, *A Portrait of the Artist as a Young Man* (1916), is semi-autobiographical and tells the story of Stephen

Dedalus from the very earliest days of his life, showing him growing into adulthood and independence under the powerful influences of Irish national, political, and religious feelings. The novel shows how he gradually frees himself from these influences and decides to become an exile from Ireland and to dedicate his life to writing. He also develops a view of the writer as necessarily alienated from the values of society and committed only to artistic values. Like T.S. Eliot in poetry, Stephen (who may or may not represent Joyce's ideas) believed that the true artist had to be objective and not simply give direct expression to his feelings. He compared the artist to the God of creation who 'remains within or behind or beyond or above his handiwork, invisible, refined out of existence, indifferent, paring his fingernails'.

> *April 26.* Mother is putting my new secondhand clothes in order. She prays now, she says, that I may learn in my own life and away from home and friends what the heart is and what it feels. Amen. So be it. Welcome, O life! I go to encounter for the millionth time the reality of experience and to forge in the smithy of my soul the uncreated conscience of my race.
>
> *April 27.* Old father, old artificer, stand me now and ever in good stead.
>
> (*A Portrait of the Artist as a Young Man*)

Ulysses is the high point of Modernism, bearing the same relationship to the development of the novel as *The Waste Land* does to poetry. Both were published in 1922. In addition to its innovative techniques of 'stream of consciousness', the novel exhibits a wealth of forms and styles and explores a rich variety of ideas. Most striking is the use of Homer as a model. The characters and episodes of the novel have parallels in ancient Greek stories although the comparisons are often deliberately comic or ironic. For example, like Ulysses, Leopold Bloom wanders from one place to another but his adventures are distinctly unheroic. Each chapter corresponds to an episode from Homer's *Odyssey* but, instead of being written in a uniform, elevated language, each has a distinct style of its own. For example, in a scene set in a maternity hospital, which Bloom visits, the prose imitates English literary styles from *Beowulf* to the Victorian age which also reflect the growth of a baby in the womb from conception to the moment just before its birth in the present.

However, the connection with episodes from Homer's *Odyssey* gives the novel a wider, more universal significance. *Ulysses* tells the story of one day in the lives of Dublin citizens and vividly evokes the life of the city. Joyce's Leopold Bloom becomes a modern Ulysses, an Everyman in a Dublin which becomes a microcosm of the world.

Joyce's last work, *Finnegans Wake* (1939), took fourteen years to write. In the novel, Joyce attempted to present the whole of human history as a dream in the mind of a Dublin innkeeper, H.C. Earwicker. Any attempt to depict life realistically is abandoned. Devices of literary realism are replaced by a kind of dream language in which as many associations as possible are forced into words and combinations of words. In many ways, the novel is about language itself: Joyce uses puns and plays on words within and across both English and other languages. He pushes language to the absolute limits of experiment and for most readers the result is a very demanding, sometimes incomprehensible experience.

> Sobs they sighdid at Fillagain's chrissormiss wake, all the hoolivans of the nation, prostrated in their consternation and their duodisimally profusive plethora of ululation. There was plumbs and grumes and cheriffs and citherers and raiders and cinemen too. And the all gianed in with the shoutmost shoviality. Agog and magog and the round of them agrog. To the continuation of that celebration until Hanandhunigan's extermination!

The use of language suggests the merging of images in a dream. It enables Joyce to present history and myth as a single image with all the characters of history becoming a few eternal types, finally identified as Earwicker, his wife, and three children. This corresponds with a cyclical view of history which Joyce developed and in which the events of human life are like a river that flows into the sea from which rain clouds form to feed once again the source of the river. Thus, life is always renewed.

In his cyclical view of history, Joyce, like the poet W.B. Yeats, was influenced by the eighteenth-century Italian philosopher Giambattista Vico, who proposed a four-stage circular process of human time. As did Yeats, Joyce saw his own generation as in the final stage awaiting the anarchy and collapse that would eventually return them to the first stage. Joyce even builds this cyclical view into the structure of his novels. The final word of *Ulysses* is 'yes', which reverses the letters 's' and 'y' of the first word 'stately' and signifies a triumphant new beginning; the end of *Finnegans Wake* is a half-complete sentence and, to complete it, the reader has to return to the very first sentence of the novel, which begins 'riverrun, past Eve and Adam's, from swerve of shore to bend of bay . . .'.

LANGUAGE NOTE
Irish English, nationality and literature

> A rich language. A rich literature . . . full of mythologies of fantasy and hope and self-deception – a syntax opulent with tomorrows. It is our response to mud cabins and a diet of potatoes; our only method of replying to . . . inevitabilities.
>
> (Brian Friel, *Translations*, 1981)

Ireland was England's first colony, its local culture and languages absorbed by a Protestant English-speaking culture. Anglo-Norman knights invaded parts of Gaelic-speaking Ireland in the twelfth century and English law was introduced. During the Tudor period, settlers from England and Scotland took over large plantations of land and attempts at rebellion by the Irish were quashed in a number of military campaigns, one of which was led by Oliver Cromwell. In 1801 the Act of Union made Ireland part of the United Kingdom, a situation which remained until the 1920s when there was a partition between the mainly Catholic South (Eire) and the mainly Protestant North (Ulster). Paradoxically, however, after eight centuries of contact with English and considerable linguistic domination, Irish Gaelic (Erse) became the official national language of the newly independent Irish state of Eire.

In spite of the official status of Gaelic and numerous attempts to revive and extend the language, the linguistic reality is none the less that English is used throughout Ireland, with Gaelic only extensively used in the West of Ireland. Above all, Gaelic retains an emblematic importance and since the nineteenth century numerous writers have attempted to recognise the position of Gaelic as an example of the need to impart a specifically Irish identity to Irish literature written in English. One central question posed was whether English could be sufficiently re-created so that a distinctive Irish English voice emerged. In this re-creation the Irish writers have to avoid the cultural and linguistic imposition of English at the same time as they have to avoid an unduly romantic and nostalgic regard for the position of Gaelic. Seamus Heaney has described well the sense of dislocation induced in the Irish by the English language:

> History, which has woven the fabric of English life and landscape and language into a seamless garment, has rent the fabric of Irish life, has effected a breach between its past and present, and an alienation between the speaker and his speech.

Irish (or Hiberno-English) has distinctive varietal features of pronunciation, vocabulary, and grammar, although patterns vary considerably between North and South and East and West. In grammar, for example, tense and aspect are structured differently from standard southern English. *I do be* is a habitual present tense and the form 'after' is used in Irish English to record a completed act or to express recency: thus, *they're after leaving* has the meaning of 'they have just left', and *he was after saying* means he had just said. The variety also has distinctive discourse and conversational patterns: for example, it is common for a question to answered with a question: A: *Can you tell me where the post office is?* B: *Would it be stamps you're looking for?*; Gaelic-influenced word order in questions is also common: *Is it ready you are?*; and standard English 'but' is used with the meaning of 'though': He still went there *but*. (See also the quotation from J.M. Synge, page 385.)

Writers regularly attempted to exploit the distinctive patterns of Irish English but, as is the case with writers such as Hugh MacDiarmid and Scots, invented or 'forged' artificial versions, which retain as much intelligibility as the writer judges proper for a wide English-speaking reading public, are actually used. In the many sections of Joyce's fiction which involve narrative recounts, Irish colloquial speech patterns are prevalent:

> What was he after doing it only into the bucket of porter.
> (*Ulysses*)

> I know you are a friend of his and not like some of those others he does be with.
>
> (*Grace*)

> But still and all he kept on saying that before the summer was over he'd go out for a drive one fine day just to see the old house again where we were all born down in Irishtown, and take me and Nannie with him. If we could only get one of them new-fangled carriages that makes no noise that Father

O'Rourke told him about, them with the rheumatic wheels, for the day cheap.

(The Sisters)

The other distinctive expressive feature in Irish English writing is a constant verbal 'play' with the resources of the language as a whole, in which the whole fabric of idiom, allusion, derivations, etymologies, parody, pastiche and figurative expression is exploited to create a world in which there is no single vantage point. It is a linguistic artifice appropriate to Modernism which also reinforces mutiple ways of seeing, but it in part underlies the strong connection between much modern Irish writing and the formal inventiveness of modernism.

Its apotheosis is Joyce's *Finnegans Wake* which is simultaneously no language and every language, a heteroglot of words and structures, a kind of world English but one which Joyce himself called 'the last word in stolentelling', recognising that this inventively fabricated English has its roots in the everyday English of the Ireland of his birth.

> Sobs they sighdid at Fillagain's chrissormiss wake, all the hoolivans of the nation, prostrated in their consternation and their duodisimally profusive plethora of ululation. There was plumbs and grumes and cheriffs and citherers and raiders and cinemen too. And the all gianed in with the shoutmost shoviality.

NOVELS OF THE FIRST WORLD WAR

Wyndham Lewis – like Henry James, Ezra Pound, and T.S. Eliot – was born in the United States of America. With Pound he edited *Blast* (1914–15), which expressed the views of the Vorticists. This was primarily an artistic movement, influenced by Futurism and Cubism, determined to replace Victorian sentimentality with abstract art and writing. Perhaps the First World War achieved the Vorticists' aim for them: the old ways changed rapidly, and the movement petered out after 1915. But Lewis went on to write several novels and a great many critical essays, which have been neglected despite their explorations of the hollowness of modern values and beliefs. *Tarr* (1918) and *The Apes of God* (1930) are energetic depictions of artistic life in Paris and London, attacking several of the literary figures of the time. His essay

Time and Western Man (1927) is a challenging view of the intellectual collapse of the modern world; like his novels, it was not designed to win the author many friends, but it is an important counterbalance to the intellectual currents of the time.

Several novels were written about the First World War. Unlike the great poetry, which was written in the trenches during the fighting, the novels were mostly composed long after the events they describe. The title of Robert Graves's autobiography, *Goodbye to All That*, published in 1928, indicates the extent to which the author felt that the war marked the end of an era. Graves later became one of the more important lyric poets of the century, and he also wrote the historical tales of Ancient Rome, *I, Claudius* and *Claudius the God* (both 1934), which confirmed his status as a popular historical novelist.

Her Privates We (1929) by Frederic Manning is a good example of how the colloquial language of the common soldier can be used to write a documentary novel exploring the futility of war that Owen described in his poetry.

> 'Them poor, bloody Jocks,' he said in a slow, pitiful whisper.
> What the casualties were they did not know, though various rumours gave precise, and different, details; one shell did all the damage, the others exploding in an empty field. The sympathy they felt with the Scotsmen was very real; the same thing might so easily have happened to themselves; and as they talked about it, the feeling turned gradually into resentment against an authority, which regulated, so strictly, every detail of their daily lives. The shell falling where it did, at that particular time, would probably have caused a certain number of casualties; even if the men had been moving about freely; but this kind of discipline, excusable enough when men have to be kept under control, as with a carrying party lined up at a dump, was unnecessary on this moment; and, for that reason alone, it was wiser to avoid assembling a large number of men at any one point. They remembered their own experience at Philosophe.

C.E. Montague's *Disenchantment*, published in that seminal literary year 1922, gives in its title a key to the attitudes which characterised the whole generation of writers who experienced the war at first hand.

T.E. Lawrence, Lawrence of Arabia, is one of the legendary figures of the century. His exploits in the Middle East during the First World

War made him a hero, and *The Seven Pillars of Wisdom* (1926–35) is one of the few essentially romantic books to come out of that war. It is heroic, just at the time when the heroism of war was questioned as it never had been before in history. Lawrence's own self-doubt and anxiety led him to change his identity, and he wrote a document-ary account of army life which is anything but heroic, *The Mint*, first published in America in 1936 'by 352087 A/C Ross'.

Lewis Grassic Gibbon's Scottish trilogy *A Scots Quair*, comprising *Sunset Song* (1932), *Cloud Howe* (1933), and *Grey Granite* (1934), shows how the war affected the provincial life of a young woman, Chris Guthrie, in the north-east of Scotland. Her young husband is killed in the war, and the trilogy tells of how she survives the rapidly changing post-war world far from the city and the main trends of society.

ALDOUS HUXLEY

Aldous Huxley was the grandson of T.H. Huxley, an eminent Victorian philosopher and writer who championed the ideas of Charles Darwin. In the 1920s Aldous Huxley published a number of novels which satirised contemporary society. The novels do not always have Evelyn Waugh's penetrating wit, comic anarchy, and invention, but among the best known of them are *Crome Yellow* (1921), *Antic Hay* (1923), which has many similarities with T.S. Eliot's *The Waste Land*, and *Point Counter Point* (1928).

Huxley's best-known novel, published in 1932, is *Brave New World*. The title is an ironic quotation from Shakespeare's *The Tempest*: 'O brave new world, that hath such people in it' – innocent and sincere words given to Miranda and used without irony. *Brave New World* is often compared with George Orwell's dystopia in *Nineteen Eighty-four*.

Brave New World depicts a scientifically perfect society based on a caste system in which human beings are 'conditioned' to occupy a place on a social scale. Manual workers (Epsilons) are brought up in nurseries and are segregated from intellectuals (Alphas) who are brought up in a different environment. Both groups are conditioned to accept their social position. The novel provides a prophecy of a world of test-tube babies, genetic engineering, and social control. It is a book which captures the particularly negative and destructive elements of the times.

> A squat grey building of only thirty-four stories. Over the main entrance the words CENTRAL LONDON HATCHERY AND CONDITIONING CENTRE, and, in a shield, the World State's motto, COMMUNITY, IDENTITY, STABILITY.
> The enormous room on the ground floor faced towards the north. Cold for all the summer beyond the panes, for all the tropical heat of the room itself, a harsh thin light glared through the windows, hungrily seeking some draped lay figure, some pallid shape of academic goose-flesh, but finding only the glass and nickel and bleakly shining porcelain of a laboratory. Wintriness responded to wintriness. The overalls of the workers were white, their hands gloved with a pale corpse-coloured rubber. The light was frozen, dead, a ghost. Only from the yellow barrels of the microscopes did it borrow a certain rich and living substance, lying along the polished tubes like butter, streak after luscious streak in long recession down the work tables.
> 'And this,' said the Director opening the door, 'is the Fertilizing Room.'

Aldous Huxley became disillusioned with war in Europe and moved to California, where he became preoccupied with the kinds of visionary experience which hallucinogenic drugs can produce. *The Doors of Perception* (1954) and *Heaven and Hell* (1956) – both titles which suggest links with the visionary Romantic poet, William Blake – record these experiences. In 1962, Huxley wrote the novel *Island*, which appears to describe a society which is a genuine utopia – the opposite of *Brave New World* – where a good and optimistic life exists. This world is, however, eventually destroyed by a brutal and materialistic dictator, not only echoing the political threats of the 1920s and 1930s but also reflecting the terror of a post-war world which now possessed nuclear weapons.

WOMEN WRITERS

Virginia Woolf is the most influential and probably the most widely studied woman writer and one of the most influential of all writers in the twentieth century. Nevertheless, her presence should not over-shadow a great many other women writers, several of whom were more daring or more explicit than Woolf in introducing a metaphorical 'room of one's own', where women could express themselves in novels and other forms.

While Virginia Woolf is the best known in this area, it was Dorothy Richardson who used the stream of consciousness technique most fully. She wrote a sequence of novels, under the overall title *Pilgrimage* (1915–38), exploring her characters' psychology and motivations in a way that echoes Woolf, but with a more rigorous attention to detail. Virginia Woolf described Dorothy Richardson as inventing 'the psychological sentence of the female gender' – Woolf was no great admirer of Joyce, so would not countenance Molly Bloom's soliloquy.

May Sinclair's use of stream of consciousness is perhaps more accessible than Dorothy Richardson's. She uses it to particularly good effect in her novels *Mary Olivier: A Life* (1919) and *The Life and Death of Harriet Frean* (1922), which chart the growth of a heroine from girl-hood to unmarried middle age. May Sinclair herself was a keen supporter of women's suffrage, and was deeply interested in the psychoanalytical works of Freud and Jung; both the political and the psychological concerns are clear in her twenty-four novels. *The Three Sisters* (1914) echoes the lives of the Brontë sisters in its recounting of frustration and creativity. May Sinclair's work anticipates many of the trends of women's writing in the second half of the twentieth century, especially Doris Lessing's novels of psychological growth and Anita Brookner's novels exploring the lives of unmarried women.

The Well of Loneliness (1928), by Radclyffe Hall, holds a significant position as the major lesbian novel of its time. It caused considerable controversy, and was prosecuted and banned, like many works of the time, for its explicitness and 'obscenity'. Where D.H. Lawrence's *Lady Chatterley's Lover* stayed banned until after a famous trial in 1960, *The Well of Loneliness* was republished in 1949. The novel, though dated, remains a landmark in gay writing.

Among the later generation of novelists to have been influenced by May Sinclair are Rebecca West and Rosamund Lehmann. Rebecca West, like May Sinclair, was closely involved in the struggle for women's suffrage, and there is a political note in much of her writing.

Her first novel *The Return of a Soldier* (1918) is the first major description in literature of what it meant to come home from the war, shell-shocked and effectively destroyed as a man. Although it is an early work, it is remarkably powerful in evoking what was to become, both realistically and symbolically, an image of how the First World War affected the generation which survived it. After the Second World War, Rebecca West's book on the Nuremberg Trials – *The Meaning of Treason* (1949) – is equally significant as an examination of the motivations for betrayal of not only national values, but of humanity. Her later novels include *The Fountain Overflows* (1956) and *The Birds Fall Down* (1966). Noted for her journalism, Rebecca West's name has been associated with intellectual and combative polemic; and her novels are fine examples of committed and serious writing which remain unrestricted by the label 'feminist' and should take their place in the mainstream of the century's literature.

Rosamund Lehmann's novels are less polemical in content, but created considerable scandal for their frankness. *Dusty Answer* (1927) handles a young woman's emotional and sexual awakening in a way that is not far from the style of D.H. Lawrence, but with quite a different sensibility. *A Note in Music* (1930) is similarly frank on the theme of homosexuality; *The Weather in the Streets* (1936) takes its heroine through a failed marriage, adultery and abortion. Lehmann's novels have been criticised for being romantic and soft-centred, but she is ahead of her time in being able to handle controversial themes within the framework of the traditional novel. Her heroines carry on where George Moore's Esther Waters left off in the 1890s, and brings women's experience into the male-dominated novel at a time when it was still difficult for a woman writer who handled controversial subjects frankly to be published.

IRELAND

Southern Ireland became the separate state of Eire in 1922, but many writers have continued to be described as Anglo-Irish even after that date. Since earliest times, writers in Ireland have used English (as well as the local Erse language) as a medium for fables, tales, poetry, songs, and other forms of imaginative writing. In the tradition of English literature, a great many major writers were born or lived in Ireland: Spenser, Swift, Goldsmith, Farquhar, Edgeworth, as well as Wilde, Shaw, Synge, Yeats, Joyce, and Beckett. These are all in some ways Irish, and many of them are described as Anglo-Irish. Later writers, such as Iris Murdoch, Brian Moore, or William Trevor, are described as Anglo-Irish, even though they may have settled elsewhere.

Some writers have traced changing relations between England and Ireland – Elizabeth Bowen is a significant example. *The Last September* (1929) is set in an upper-class country house during the Troubles – the fight for an independent Ireland from 1916 to 1922. It is a novel which charts the decline of a social system and of the relationships it entailed, and was one of the few novels to document the period from an upper-class point of view while retaining sympathy with the struggle.

Ireland, after William Carleton in the 1830s, produced a great number of short-story writers: major writers such as James Joyce and Samuel Beckett also made significant contributions to the genre, Joyce in *Dubliners* (1914), Beckett in *More Pricks than Kicks* (1934).

Samuel Beckett was, like James Joyce in the 1920s, an Irish writer who based himself in Paris and whose writing is as much European as 'English'. With Beckett, this is almost literally the case since he wrote in French, then translated his novels and several of his short stories into English. Beckett lived in France from the late 1920s, and collaborated with James Joyce. The critical essay entitled *Our Exagmination and Factification Around His Work In Progress* was one of the first of Beckett's published writings, as well as the the first study of *Finnegans Wake* while it was still 'in progress'.

Beckett's own novels tend to be monologues, with a whole universe encompassed in a rambling flow of discourse. Only *Murphy* (1938) and the stories contained in *More Pricks than Kicks* (1934) were published before the Second World War. After the war, and his experiences with the French resistance, Beckett's work reaches its full flowering in the novels and plays which won him the Nobel Prize for Literature in 1969.

For many, the major figure in modern Irish short-story writing is Sean O'Faolain. Since his first volume, *Midsummer Night Madness and Other Stories* (1932), he has explored Irish frustrations and the aspirations of Irish nationalism, missed opportunities, and the limitations of provincial life. His *Collected Stories* were published in 1981, and his novels and biographies have consolidated his reputation as a major voice.

Flann O'Brien is, for many, one of the great comic writers in the Irish tradition. His real name was Brian O'Nolan, and he wrote with equal facility in English and Gaelic. *At Swim Two-Birds* (1939) and *The Third Policeman* (written in 1940, but not published until 1967) are extravagant multi-layered explorations of Irishness, considered by many critics to have been influenced by Joyce, but having their own eccentricities, their own mix of realism and fantasy, their own capacity to reveal a grim reality in the midst of hilarious satire. *An Beal Bocht*, written in Gaelic in 1941, was published in English in 1973 as *The Poor Mouth*.

EARLY GREENE AND WAUGH

Decline and Fall
(Evelyn Waugh)

Graham Greene was a convert to Catholicism and in much of his work he explores problems of good and evil and the moral dilemmas this entails. In several of his novels, characters who are failures in life are shown to be closer to God as a result; indeed, salvation in Greene's world can sometimes only be achieved through sin.

Greene's career before the Second World War culminates in *Brighton Rock* (1938). For some critics, this remains his best novel, and it continues to be one of the most popular. It brings together the detective thriller genre (the plot derives from an incident in his earlier novel *A Gun For Sale*), religious concerns, and allusions to the post-*Waste Land* world. Greene's Catholicism is important in his portrayal of Pinkie, the young amoral 'hero', who is one of the major anti-heroes of modern literature. He can be read as a personification of evil, a modern devil: Catholic belief in God implies belief in the Devil, and in many of his works Greene will examine the continuing presence of evil and corruption. In *Brighton Rock*, Pinkie's pleasure in killing and tormenting his victims, especially his girlfriend Rose, takes the reader into a new perception of unredeemed evil: it has rarely been pointed out that this novel's publication coincided with the rise of Nazism, and that the 'hero-ism' of evil in modern times is one of the major moral ambiguities that artists have difficulty in facing. Greene is one of the few writers to examine evil closely, which he did throughout his writing career, but his Catholicism has been seen as in some way justifying his fascination with the negative aspects of humanity, as if redemption will solve all problems. More and more, however, Greene makes it clear that there are no easy solutions: Pinkie's death at the end of *Brighton Rock* does not bring his evil influence to an end; the Devil is always with us.

Evelyn Waugh's career as a novelist, like Graham Greene's, spanned the central years of the twentieth century – from the Jazz age to the 1960s. Waugh's work may be divided into two periods: in the first period he wrote brilliant satires on the lives of the wealthy upper classes; in the second period he explores the place of Catholicism in the modern world with deep seriousness while always retaining a satir-ical eye for human absurdity. His best-known earlier novels are *Decline and Fall* (1928), *Vile Bodies* (1930), and *A Handful of Dust* (1934). *Decline and Fall* depicts the innocent adventures of a young man, Paul Pennyfeather, who becomes a schoolteacher in a seedy school in North Wales. The novel satirises public school life (Paul's fellow teachers are either petty criminals or mad) by showing how the characters of the ruling classes are formed.

> 'Silence!' said Paul again.
> The ten boys stopped talking and sat perfectly still staring at him. He felt himself getting hot and red under their scrutiny.
> 'I suppose the first thing I ought to do is to get your names clear. What is your name?' he asked, turning to the first boy.
> 'Tangent, sir.'
> 'And yours?'
> 'Tangent, sir,' said the next boy. Paul's heart sank.
> 'But you can't both be called Tangent.'
> 'No, sir, *I'm* Tangent. He's just trying to be funny.'
> 'I like that. *Me* trying to be funny! Please, sir, I'm Tangent, sir; really I am.'

'If it comes to that,' said Clutterbuck from the back of the room, 'there is only one Tangent here, and that is me. Anyone else can jolly well go to blazes.'

Paul felt desperate.

'Well, is there anyone who isn't Tangent?'

Four or five voices instantly arose.

'I'm not, sir; I'm not Tangent. I wouldn't be called Tangent, not on the end of a barge pole.'

In *Vile Bodies* the emptiness and lack of values in the lives of the 'bright young things' – the younger generation in the inter-war years – are cruelly exposed. *A Handful of Dust* (the title is a quotation from T.S. Eliot) is the story of the break-up of a marriage against the background of the dissolution of an ancient country estate. A contrast is established between a cynical and frivolous modern world and the gradual disappearance of a world of order and stability associated with an aristocratic past. Unlike Jane Austen or Henry Fielding, however, Waugh does not normally use irony and satire to judge or offer solutions, but presents the world as black comedy.

THIRTIES NOVELISTS

The three Powys brothers wrote several massive, complex and ambitious novels which achieved great critical regard, but never reached a wide readership. They used the West Country as a background and examined themes of vast scope in complex and controversial ways. John Cowper Powys's *Wolf Solent* (1929), *A Glastonbury Romance* (1933), and *Weymouth Sands* (1934) include the eternal struggle between good and evil and the legends associated with the West of England. T.F. Powys's *Mr Weston's Good Wine* (1927) is an allegory of God's coming to earth in an English village. This kind of personification is found throughout T.F. Powys's work and is his way of handling the huge themes found in the works of all three brothers. Llewelyn Powys was perhaps the most prolific of the three. *Impassioned City* (1931) is his most all-encompassing account of humanity's predicament and, like *Love and Death* (1939), confronts the extremes of experience in a way that brings together the concerns of Thomas Hardy with a vision close to that of Samuel Beckett: the whole imbued with the vast compass of reference to myth, religion, and cosmology, which identifies all the Powys brothers' writing.

Several writers looked forward rather than back in their novels, tackling new themes or experimenting with form in an innovative way. Christopher Isherwood, a friend of and collaborator with W.H. Auden, uses cinematic techniques in his Berlin novels *Mr Norris Changes Trains* (1935) and *Goodbye to Berlin* (1939). The narrator says 'I am a camera' and proceeds to tell his stories with the kind of distanced objectivity a camera can lend. These novels remain valuable impressions of Germany at a crucial time in its history, and the lack of emotional involvement in the author's style takes on a highly ambiguous and chilling note as the 1930s moved rapidly towards the Second World War.

A trilogy published by Edward Upward in 1977, *The Spiral Ascent*, is one of the clearest illustrations of the ideological, political and cultural conflicts in English intellectual life of the 1930s. A close friend of Isherwood's, Upward and he concocted a fantasy world, Mortmere, which appears in Upward's *The Railway Accident and Other Stories* (1969) and is described in Isherwood's *Lions and Shadows* (1938), in which Upward is the character Allen Chalmers. Upward's need for escape into a surreal fantasy world is at the opposite extreme from his strong commitment – stronger than Auden's or Isherwood's – to the Communist Party. Mortmere is a kind of antidote to the profoundly negative forces which were working against the idealism of the early 1930s.

Rex Warner's *Poems* (1937) established him as close to Auden and Day Lewis in his sympathies. His novel *The Aerodrome* (1941) is a Kafkaesque parable, reflecting the increasingly pessimistic outlook of 1930s Europe as the decade shifted from idealism to civil and then total war.

William Gerhardie is also interesting in the context of the early twentieth-century novel. He was born in St Petersburg of English parents, and many of his works have Russian connections, including his studies of Chekhov and the Romanovs. His first novel *Futility*, a novel on Russian themes, was published in 1922, the same year as *Ulysses*, *The Waste Land*, and *Jacob's Room*, but has tended to be ignored by recent critics despite being widely admired at the time. Gerhardie catches the mood of futility combined with wild hope that is characteristic of the post-First World War era. *The Polyglots*, a semi-autobiographical novel published in 1925, is his best-known work, combining comedy and tragedy in an international setting filled with trivia; it is a representative mixture of the confusion and alienation in early twentieth-century Europe.

Walter Greenwood's *Love on the Dole* (1933) is a novel of the 1930s Depression, which still carries resonances over half a century later. It represents contemporary working-class concerns in a language that blends with romantic fictional conventions. Greenwood in some senses prepares the way for the working-class provincial novelists of the 1950s, and is an important link between Arnold Bennett early in the century and those writers of the post-Second World War era.

Forrest Reid has been called the greatest Ulster novelist, but he does not allow the troubles in his province to colour his writings. Rather, Reid uses his novels to explore an ideal world of innocence. His Tom Barber trilogy, comprising *Uncle Stephen* (1931), *The Retreat* (1934), and *Young Tom,* (1944) traces the passage from innocence to awareness in the hero, Tom, as he grows from the age of 10 to 15. These are not novels of childhood, however. They are full of classical references, explorations of consciousness, and realism which make a potent mixture, producing a 'paradise lost' of modern times.

> He was not offended; he had been talking really, towards the end, as much to himself as to his companion; and now he felt too drowsy to wonder at what point Pascoe had ceased to hear him. That, he would learn tomorrow, and in the meantime he was content to lie in dreamy contemplatation of a world shifting uncertainly between recollection and imagination. Nor was he surprised to see, amid drifting scenes and faces, Ralph himself standing between the window and the bed. By that time, too, he must have forgotten Pascoe, or surely he would have awakened him, whereas all he did was to murmur sleepily; 'Why have you come?'
> The voice that answered him was faint and thin as the whisper of dry corn. 'I don't know. I don't think I have come. I don't think this is real. . . . Or perhaps I can only come when you are dreaming, for I think you are dreaming now. . . .'
> There was a silence – deep, wonderful, unbroken – as if all the

restless murmuring whispers of earth and night were suddenly stilled. . . .

'Listen!'

Tom listened, but somehow Ralph was no longer there; and far, far away he could hear the sound of waves breaking, and surely he had heard that low distant plash before – many times perhaps, though when and where he had forgotten.

(*Young Tom*)

At the time of the war, Henry Green, Ivy Compton-Burnett, and George Orwell had written several major novels. Indeed, in many ways their early work qualifies them as 'thirties novelists'. They span the war, like Greene and Waugh, and the continuity they represent in English writing carries itself forward into the post-war years, into a new and deeply changed world.

The twentieth century

1945 to the present

What do we do now, now that we are happy?
(Samuel Beckett, *Waiting for Godot*)

CONTEXTS AND CONDITIONS

The ending of the Second World War did not bring with it stability. The world had moved into the Atomic age with the dropping of bombs on Hiroshima and Nagasaki in 1945. With the atomic bomb, the world was on a knife-edge: the world might end at any moment. This threat hung over the world until the end of the so-called cold war between the Communist bloc and 'the West' in the late 1980s. The 'Iron Curtain' divided the world politically into Communist and non-Communist. The United States of America, which had entered the First World War in 1916, entered the Second World War in late 1941 – and being on the winning side each time helped it become the dominant economic and cultural force in the world, a position which was strengthened by the fall of Communist regimes in the late 1980s and early 1990s.

The war accelerated the break-up of the British Empire and forced upon Great Britain a reassessment of its place in the world. The wartime prime minister, Winston Churchill, after the Labour government was elected in 1945, devoted much of his time to writing a six-volume history of *The Second World War* (1945–54) and *A History of the English-Speaking Peoples* (four volumes; 1956–58). He won the Nobel Prize for Literature in 1953.

The years since the end of the Second World War have seen a decline in British influence and continuing failure to compete successfully with the newly developing economies of the world. In national terms, the country has also seen decentralisation. The regions have competed with London for economic, social, and cultural influence. Nowadays, regional accents are heard as regularly on BBC television and radio programmes as standard English accents. These changes have corresponded to changing inflections in writing in the English language worldwide, with the result that the term 'literatures in English' is now often preferred to English literature.

In social terms, a long period of austerity led to the boom years of the 1960s, when the post-war youth culture began to find expression, and a new affluence and optimism filled Britain. The pendulum swung back in the 1970s, with a great deal of social unrest; and it swung back again to affluence and the 'me' generation of yuppies in the 1980s.

Underlying these swings have been continuing polarities – South/North; London/provinces; Conservative/Labour; management/trades unions; rich/poor – and continuing conflicts in Ulster, in international wars, and, to a lesser extent, in claims for autonomy for Wales and Scotland.

What stability there is tends to be seen as economic, and therefore political. Culture questions, but frequently ends up by affirming a *status quo*; humour is a useful safety valve; the most widely followed narratives are television soap operas. But there has probably never been greater variety, richness, and sheer productiveness in literary expression. It is fashionable to say there are no great novelists/poets/playwrights, and to look back to the past of an imaginary golden age – when very probably the same complaint could have been heard! The literary imagination has charted the last fifty years with no lack of inventiveness and imagination.

In spite of the growth of other media, in the final years of the twentieth century more books are being published than ever before, and more books are being read than ever before. It is impossible to say which of today's writers will be considered 'important' in a hundred years' time. However, trends can be identified – preoccupations, kinds of writing, and directions in which literature is moving.

After the Second World War, the changes in society – in ways of thought and in literature – were every bit as deep and far-reaching as they were after the First World War. The sense of fragmentation developed into a sense of absurdity, of existential futility, which echoes and goes beyond the kind of futility expressed in the poems of Wilfred Owen. There is a veritable explosion of expression around the question of the atomic bomb, around the possibility that all life could end at a moment's notice. Each decade, as the century moves towards its close, has had a distinct and different feeling: the 1950s were the age of austerity; the 1960s, the age of youth; the 1970s, an age of anxiety; the 1980s, an age of new materialism; the 1990s, an age of recession and preoccupation.

For the novelist A.S. Byatt, there is, throughout this time, a new richness and diversity in English writing, a continuing of the search for a post-Darwinian security in creativity: 'A wonderful mix of realism, romance, fable, satire, parody, play with form and philosophical intelligence.' Byatt notes an 'almost obsessive recurrence of Darwin in modern fiction'. Where nineteenth-century writers – novelists in particular – wrote about the ending of certainty, especially religious certainty, late twentieth-century writers have largely concerned themselves with (again according to Byatt) 'what it means to be a naked animal, evolved over unimaginable centuries, with a history constructed by beliefs which have lost their power'. This is a useful perception of the common themes underlying much of modern writing, and indeed much of the Modern or post-Modern perception of the world we live in.

Where *Modern* was a keyword for the first part of the twentieth century, the term *post-Modern* has been widely used to describe the attitudes and creative production which followed the Second World War. Post-Modernism almost defies definition. Rather, it celebrates diversity, eclecticism, and parody in all forms of art, from architecture to cinema, from music to literature. All the forms which represent experience are mediated, transformed, and the 'truth' of experience thus becomes even more varied than it has ever been before.

The mix of 'post-Darwin' and post-Modern is indicative of the binary linking of traditional and new elements in literature: the subject matter is still, essentially, the human condition, but the means and methods of exploring it are infinitely richer and more varied than ever before. There are no more heroes, as there might have been in the time of Beowulf. There is the individual; solitary, responsible for his or her own destiny, yet powerless when set against the ineluctable forces of the universe. This is one of the basic conflicts of the post-Modern condition, and one which gives rise to the immense variety of explorations of recent writings in English. Identity is a common theme: sexual identity, local identity, national identity, racial identity, spiritual identity, intellectual identity. All of these, and more, recur.

It is almost impossible to classify modern authors in terms of their lasting contribution to the literature of their time. A few figures have attained critical impregnability: Samuel Beckett would seem to have a secure place among the major dramatists of the century; Seamus Heaney's winning the Nobel Prize for Literature in 1995 assures his place in Irish poetry after Yeats. In the novel, it is much more problematic. For every exploration of history or myth, there will be a forward-looking exploration of future worlds in science fiction or a near-documentary examination of life on the streets today. Past, present, and future coexist in literature today as never before.

Just as the earlier part of the twentieth century opened up literature to many hitherto unheard or ignored voices, so more recent years have opened up the literary world to voices from a wide range of countries, and from differing social and sexual orientations. Added to this, modern critical studies have recovered a great many voices from the past, and, with the critical approach designated New Historicism, have revisited many periods, gaining new perceptions of them.

All this adds to the post-Modern celebration of diversity in writing, making the end of the twentieth century the most diverse and rich mixture of old and new, English and non-English, standard and non-standard, male and female, public and private, universal and individual, certain and uncertain, in the ongoing search to express the contemporary world we live in.

It is an ongoing concern with humanity that keeps literature alive. The twenty-first century will no doubt see new trends, new forms of expression, a new literature to set beside the continuing story that began more than thirteen centuries ago.

DRAMA SINCE 1945

Nothing happens, nobody comes, nobody goes, it's awful!
(Samuel Beckett, *Waiting for Godot*)

The theatre was dominated until the 1950s by well-made plays in standard English for middle-class audiences: few problem areas were touched on, although both Noël Coward and George Bernard Shaw had found ways of making serious moral points, despite the censor's presence. However, the language of drama in the twentieth century has undergone significant changes. From Oscar Wilde in the 1890s to Noël Coward from the 1920s to 1940s, it was consistently elevated and stylish, the formal elaborate speech modes matching the high social status of many of the characters. Shaw, Lawrence, Synge, and O'Casey brought in dialect and lower-class accents and helped the transition to a more working-class voice in the theatre which emerged in post-Second World War drama. The plays of Beckett, Osborne, Pinter, or Orton in the 1950s and 1960s are more colloquial and slangy, in keeping with the setting and the characters: tramps, gangsters, newspaper vendors, unemployed youths. Their language is more naturalistic and shows gaps, repetitions, silences, and incoherences, modelled on normal conversation.

LANGUAGE NOTE
Drama and everyday language

In the 1950s the language used in the theatre was deliberately elevated in keeping with the elevated social position of the majority of characters. In plays such as the poetic dramas of T.S. Eliot and Christopher Fry, which though written in previous decades were regularly performed at this time, the expectation of audiences was that they would encounter characters on stage who expressed lofty sentiments, often on issues of great moral or religious significance and who expressed such sentiments in conventional poetic diction and sometimes in verse drama which rhymed.

In T.S. Eliot's *The Cocktail Party* the characters, who are all members of the upper class, speak lines which are dominated by an iambic rhythmic movement and by a constant engagement with ideas:

EDWARD
Your responsibility is nothing to mine, Lavinia.
LAVINIA
I'm not sure about that. If I had understood you
Then I might not have misunderstood Celia.
REILLY
You will have to live with these memories and make them
Into something new. Only by acceptance
Of the past will you alter its meaning.
JULIA
Henry, I think it is time that I said something:
Everyone makes a choice, of one kind or another,
And then must take the consequences.

In the following couplet from *Murder in the Cathedral*, rhyme is employed to underscore the memorability of the lines:

The last temptation is the greatest treason:
To do the right deed for the wrong reason.

By contrast, here are extracts from two plays first performed in the 1950s in which the definition of what is or is not appropriate dramatic language is brought sharply into question. The first is from Samuel Beckett's *Waiting for Godot* (written in French, 1953). The two characters, who are often depicted as tramps in stage productions, engage in talk about how to fill the time they have while they wait for Godot (who does not in any case materialise):

VLADIMIR That passed the time.
ESTRAGON It would have passed in any case.
VLADIMIR Yes, but not so rapidly.

[*Pause.*]

ESTRAGON What do we do now?
VLADIMIR I don't know.
ESTRAGON Let's go.
VLADIMIR We can't.
ESTRAGON Why not?
VLADIMIR We're waiting for Godot.

The next extract is from Harold Pinter's *The Birthday Party* (1957), in which Goldberg and McCann are two characters who turn up claiming to have known about Stanley, the third character, as Webber in the past. Here, Stanley is being questioned by Goldberg and McCann. The purpose of the interview is not altogether clear and this adds to the note of menace, but one aim of the 'interviewers' appears to be to humiliate Stanley and thereby exercise dominance and control over him:

GOLDBERG Why did you never get married?
MCCANN She was waiting at the porch.
GOLDBERG You skedaddled from the wedding.
MCCANN He left her in the lurch.
GOLDBERG You left her in the pudding club.
MCCANN She was waiting at the church.
GOLDBERG Webber! Why did you change your name?
STANLEY I forgot the other one.
. . .
GOLDBERG Do you recognise an external force?
STANLEY What?
GOLDBERG Do you recognise an external force?
MCCANN That's the question!
GOLDBERG Do you recognise an external force, responsible for you, suffering for you?
STANLEY It's late.
GOLDBERG Late! Late enough! When did you last pray?
MCCANN He's sweating!

The dialogue in these plays does not conform to the expected norms of poetic dialogue. There are no extended poetic tropes, no soliloquies, no linguistic embellishment or elaboration and no obvious effort to create language which is memorable for its expression of ideas. Instead, the language is deliberately ordinary and everyday, in keeping with characters who are distinctly 'lower' in the social order and whose use of language pretends to no obvious distinction between the language of the theatre and the language of everyday discourse.

Dramatic language remains, of course, different from everyday conversation in which there are frequent interruptions and overlaps, but the plays of Pinter and Beckett and others in the 1950s set out to establish new themes and characters, new types of interaction, and new dramatic language. Rather than poetry in the theatre, they created poetry of the theatre in which messages communicated indirectly and between the lines were as significant as those conveyed overtly within crafted 'poetic' speeches.

The plays of Terence Rattigan – from the comedy *French Without Tears* (1936), to the highly moral dramas of *The Browning Version* and *The Winslow Boy* in the 1940s, and on to *In Praise of Love* (1973) – have been heavily criticised for playing to the mindless average audience, symbolised in the figure of 'Aunt Edna'. But ironically, it was Rattigan himself who invented this mythical middle-brow figure. The 'Aunt Edna' mentality probably never saw the deeper sense of solitude, injustice, and quiet desperation, which are at the heart of Rattigan's carefully crafted plays.

In the 1950s, a reaction set in. Working-class accents and dialects, younger voices, ardent social concern, suddenly returned to the theatre. The 'angry young man' appeared, most significantly in the figure of Jimmy Porter in *Look Back in Anger* by John Osborne, staged at the Royal Court Theatre in 1956. This play was seen as the testament of a new generation, heralding a new spirit in drama, and in culture in general. Osborne followed it with several major plays, making the historical figure of *Luther* an angry young man (1961), using the Austrian Empire as the setting for what is arguably his richest and most controversial play *A Patriot for Me* (1965), and giving the actor Sir Laurence Olivier one of his most unusual roles, as a fading music-hall performer, in *The Entertainer* (1957).

> JIMMY [*quickly*] Did you read about the woman who went to the mass meeting of a certain American evangelist at Earl's Court? She went forward, to declare herself for love or whatever it is, and, in the rush of converts to get to the front, she broke four ribs and got kicked in the head. She was yelling her head off in agony, but with 50,000 people putting all they'd got into 'Onward Christian Soldiers', nobody even knew she was there.
>
> > [*He looks up sharply for a response, but there isn't any.*]
>
> Sometimes, I wonder if there isn't something wrong with me. What about that tea?
>
> CLIFF [*still behind paper*] What tea?
>
> JIMMY Put the kettle on.
>
> > [ALISON *looks up at him.*]
>
> ALISON Do you want some more tea?
>
> JIMMY I don't know. No, I don't think so.
>
> ALISON Do you want some, Cliff?
>
> JIMMY No, he doesn't. How much longer will you be doing that?
>
> ALISON Won't be long.
>
> JIMMY God, how I hate Sundays! It's always so depressing, always the same. We never seem to get any further, do we? Always the same ritual. Reading the papers, drinking tea, ironing. A few more hours,

and another week gone. Our youth is slipping away. Do you know
that?

CLIFF [*(throws down paper]* What's that?

JIMMY [*casually*] Oh, nothing, nothing. Damn you, damn both of you,
damn them all.

CLIFF Let's go to the pictures.

(Look Back in Anger)

But the anger of one generation may be of less interest to the next
generation. Much of Osborne's work is now seen as documenting a
moment in the post-war move towards new values and more open
expression; a step on the way, rather than a major theatrical
innovation.

The realistic room setting, found in Tom Robertson's plays almost a
century before, returns to the stage in a group of plays of the late
1950s, generally called 'kitchen sink dramas'. Osborne himself, and
Arnold Wesker (one of whose works was, in fact, called *The Kitchen*)
were the most significant figures in this reaction, of lower-class
domestic realism, against the 'drawing-room comedies' which had
dominated the stage since the time of Maugham.

ADA . . . I must go.

SARAH [*wearily*] Go then! Will we see you tomorrow?

ADA Yes, I'll come for supper tomorrow night. Good night. [*Calling.*]
Good night, Ronnie.

RONNIE [*appearing from kitchen*] 'Night, Addy.

SARAH You washing up, Ronnie?

RONNIE I'm washing up.

SARAH You don't have to worry about – but your sister runs away. At
the first sight of a little bother she runs away. Why does she run
away, Ronnie? Before she used to sit and discuss things, now she
runs to her home – such a home to run to – two rooms and a
shadow!

RONNIE But, Ma, she's a married woman herself. You think she hasn't
her own worries wondering what it'll be like to see Dave after all
these years?

SARAH But you never run away from a discussion. At least I've got you
around to help me solve problems.

RONNIE Mother, my one virtue – if I got any at all – is that I always imagine you can solve things by talking about them – ask my form master! [*Returns to kitchen.*]

SARAH [*wearily to* HARRY] You see what you do? That's your daughter. Not a word from her father to ask her to stay. The family doesn't matter to you. All your life you've let the family fall around you, but it doesn't matter to you.

HARRY I didn't drive her away.

SARAH [*bitterly*] No – you didn't drive her away. How could you? You were the good, considerate father.

[HARRY *turns away and hunches himself up miserably.*] Look at you! Did you shave this morning? Look at the cigarette ash on the floor. Your shirt! When did you last change your shirt? He sits. Nothing moves him, nothing worries him. He sits! A father! A husband!

HARRY [*taking out a cigarette to light*] Leave me alone, please leave me alone, Sarah. You started the row, not me, you!

SARAH [*taking cigarette from his hand*] Why must you always smoke? – talk with me. Talk, talk, Harry.

HARRY Sarah! [*He stops, chokes, and then stares wildly around him.*] Mamma. Mamma. [*He is having his first stroke.*]

(Arnold Wesker, *Chicken Soup with Barley*)

A different kind of realism is found in the plays of Samuel Beckett and Harold Pinter. Their works were for several years rather misleadingly labelled 'theatre of the absurd'. The critic who first applied the term 'absurd', Martin Esslin, has since revised his terms of reference for the word 'absurd', but it can still be applied, if in a slightly different sense. The existential philosophy of writers such as Jean-Paul Sartre – which posited the individual as 'the source of all value' – met the mood of a time which was to become more and more concerned with material comforts, acquisitiveness, and wealth. A vision of the world as essentially meaningless, peopled with helpless but selfish characters with no particular sense of identity, was not new. It can be traced back in poetry, through T.S. Eliot and Wilfred Owen, as far as Matthew Arnold's *Dover Beach*, and in the use of 'wasteland' or 'no man's land' as an image.

Beckett's characters inhabit these empty wastelands, and one of Pinter's plays has the title *No Man's Land*. Although accepting the 'absurdity' of existence and human behaviour, neither playwright can be described as entirely pessimistic. Where, in *Dover Beach*, the line 'Ah, love, let us be true to one another' offered some reassurance against the bleakness of the world, Beckett's characters 'always find something, eh Didi, to give us the impression we exist'. *Waiting for Godot* (in English, 1955), probably Beckett's best-known play, is based on waiting, in the eternal hope that 'tomorrow everything will be better'.

The two tramps Vladimir and Estragon spend their time in the same place, day after day, filling in time, waiting for things to happen. The audience might feel, with Estragon, that 'Nothing happens, nobody comes, nobody goes, it's awful!' But the spirit of Beckett is highly comic even in the face of bleakness and sameness. It is the same spirit informing the absurd situations presented in the silent films of the early twentieth century. Beckett's characters have much in common with those played by the stars of silent films like Charlie Chaplin and Buster Keaton, in that their 'routines' (both verbal and physical), their very appearance, all deliberately recall these 'Everyman' figures of the century.

VLADIMIR You must be happy, too, deep down, if you only knew it.
ESTRAGON Happy about what?
VLADIMIR To be back with me again.
ESTRAGON Would you say so?
VLADIMIR Say you are, even if it's not true.
ESTRAGON What am I to say?
VLADIMIR Say, I am happy.
ESTRAGON I am happy.
VLADIMIR So am I.
ESTRAGON So am I.
VLADIMIR We are happy.
ESTRAGON We are happy. [*Silence.*] What do we do now, now that we are happy?
VLADIMIR Wait for Godot.

[ESTRAGON *groans. Silence.*]

      Things have changed since yesterday.
ESTRAGON And if he doesn't come?
VLADIMIR [*after a moment of bewilderment*] We'll see when the time comes.

In his later plays, Beckett reduces his theatre to its essentials: from two acts in *Waiting for Godot* and *Happy Days* (1961), to one, starting with *Endgame* (1957); from five characters to four, then two, then one, and finally – in *Breath* (1970), which lasts only about thirty seconds – there are no characters at all. This move towards minimalism is a *reductio ad absurdum*, which can perhaps allow the term 'absurd' to be reclaimed in a theatrical context. The setting is a 'stage littered with miscellaneous rubbish', and the sounds of birth, breath and death are heard. This is the ultimate image of the wastelands of twentieth-century literature, where 'we are born astride of a grave', and 'the light gleams an instant, then it's night once more', as Vladimir says in *Waiting for Godot*.

Beckett takes drama to new extremes, and pushes his characters to the limits of solitude, non-communication and hopelessness. Yet they all survive, and any thoughts of suicide are dispelled. Hamlet's age-old question, 'To be or not to be', is answered in the affirmative, even though Beckett takes his characters closer to the extremes of despair and hopelessness of *King Lear* than any other writer since Shakespeare. Critics have tended to see close parallels between *King Lear*, in particular, and the plays of Beckett – citing this as proof of Shakespeare's modernity. Equally, it might be evidence for Beckett's universality in the face of seemingly tragic situations. Yet in Beckett there is no tragic climax; continuing the struggle to remain alive is offered as the unavoidable and necessary conclusion. His novel *The Unnamable* (1958) sums up the paradox of the 'absurd' life human-kind leads in the words, 'Where I am, I don't know, I'll never know, in the silence you don't know, you must go on. I can't go on, I'll go on.'

Harold Pinter's plays have many superficial resemblances to Beckett's drama. The two men were friends, and Beckett is certainly a major influence on Pinter, as he is on many writers of the late twentieth century. All the same, Pinter is more concerned with the dangers inherent in the silences between characters, the menace in the meaning of what is said and not said. His characters do not have the capacity, that Beckett's characters have, to fill their time with memories, chat, tortured reflections. They are much less self-sufficient and more dependent on the unstable ties that bind them to each other.

The Caretaker (1960) and *The Homecoming* (1965) are full-length plays of menace, ambiguity and unfulfilled ambitions. Like Beckett, Pinter has developed the one-act play into a major theatrical form. *The Dumb Waiter* (1957), about two characters, Gus and Ben, whose situation is more and more threatened by the machinery of the title, was one of the plays which established Pinter's name. The year 1969 saw the first production of *Silence*, arguably his most fully realised and innovative work, in which three characters rehearse their interlinked memories without ever relating directly to each other. Their words resemble a kind of musical fugue, in which silence becomes – ever more clearly – the dominant presence.

[ELLEN *moves to* RUMSEY.]

ELLEN It's changed. You've painted it. You've made shelves. Everything. It's beautiful.

RUMSEY Can you remember . . . when you were here last?

ELLEN Oh yes.

RUMSEY You were a little girl.

ELLEN I was.

[*Pause.*]

RUMSEY Can you cook now?

ELLEN Shall I cook for you?

RUMSEY Yes.

ELLEN Next time I come. I will.

[*Pause.*]

RUMSEY Do you like music?

ELLEN Yes.

RUMSEY I'll play you music.

[*Pause.*]

RUMSEY Look at your reflection.

ELLEN Where?

RUMSEY In the window.

ELLEN It's very dark outside.

RUMSEY It's high up.

ELLEN Does it get darker the higher you get?

RUMSEY No.

[*Silence.*]

In a speech in 1962, Pinter underlined the importance of silence:

When true silence falls we are still left with echo but are nearer nakedness. One way of looking at speech is to say that it is a constant strategem to cover nakedness.

Since *Old Times* (1971), *No Man's Land* (1975), and *Betrayal* (1978), Pinter has himself moved closer to silence. His more recent work, such as *Mountain Language* (1988), is a powerful examination of language, power, and freedom, which brings a directly political dimension to his writing – introducing a new focus of concern, not obviously present in early Pinter. *Ashes to Ashes* explores similar territory to *Old Times*.

The comic tradition exemplified in Wilde and Coward reaches a high point in the subversive farces of Joe Orton. Homosexual, like his two predecessors (as well as, incidentally, the more reticent Maugham and Rattigan), Orton allows his sexual viewpoint to determine much of the satiric attack on society's hypocrisies. *Loot* (1966) is a black comedy, involving the taboo subject of death, hilariously mixed up with sex and money. *Entertaining Mr Sloane* (1964) is a comedy of forbidden sexual attraction, a theme developed in Orton's last play *What the Butler Saw* (1969), which takes sexual and psychological subversion to new heights of farcical exploration. The climax of this play takes comedy back to its original Greek roots, of the God Pan, and the *panic* which comic chaos can create. In this scene from *Loot*, Truscott, the authority figure, is trying to obtain information:

TRUSCOTT Understand this, lad. You can't get away with cheek. Kids nowadays treat any kind of authority as a challenge. We'll challenge you. If you oppose me in my duty, I'll kick those teeth through the back of your head. Is that clear?

HAL Yes.

[*Door chimes.*]

FAY Would you excuse me, Inspector?

TRUSCOTT [*wiping his brow*] You're at liberty to answer your own doorbell, miss. That is how we tell whether or not we live in a free country.

[FAY *goes off left.*]

[*Standing over* HAL] Where's the money?

HAL In church.

TRUSCOTT Don't lie to me!

HAL I'm not lying! It's in church!

TRUSCOTT [*shouting, knocking* HAL *to the floor*] Under any other political system I'd have you on the floor in tears.

HAL You've got me on the floor in tears.

TRUSCOTT Where's the money?

(*Loot*)

No other comic dramatist reaches Orton's level of anarchic invention, but the plays of Tom Stoppard bring a new level of intellectual
comic gymnastics to the theatre. *Rosencrantz and Guildenstern Are Dead*
(1966) makes two minor characters in Shakespeare's *Hamlet* the leading
players in a comedy of identity, and lack of it, with Hamlet as a very
minor character. Like Beckett's Vladimir and Estragon, Rosencrantz
and Guildenstern are waiting for something to happen, to give them a
reason for existing. They exist, however, in 'the irrational belief that
somebody interesting will come on in a minute', finding their justifica-
tion in what happens around them, over which they clearly have no
control. Here they comment on what has happened to Hamlet:

ROS [*lugubriously*] His body was still warm.

GUIL So was hers.

ROS Extraordinary.

GUIL Indecent.

ROS Hasty.

GUIL Suspicious.

ROS It makes you think.

GUIL Don't think I haven't thought of it.

ROS And with her husband's brother.

GUIL They were close.

ROS She went to him –

GUIL – Too close –

ROS – for comfort.

GUIL It looks bad.

ROS It adds up.

GUIL Incest to adultery.

ROS Would you go so far?

GUIL Never.

ROS To sum up: your father, whom you love, dies, you are his heir, you
come back to find that hardly was the corpse cold before his young
brother popped onto his throne and into his sheets, thereby

offending both legal and natural practice. Now why exactly are you
behaving in this extraordinary manner?

GUIL I can't imagine!

[*Pause.*]

But all that is well known, common property. Yet he sent for us. And
we did come.

The Real Inspector Hound (1968) is a one-act farce, parodying the genre
of detective fiction. *Jumpers* (1972) moves into the world of philosophical speculation, with real gymnasts as a visual counterpoint to
mental acrobatics. Stoppard, like many writers of the period, is also a
significant writer for radio and television. His most recent plays for the
theatre have extended his idiom into the love comedy (*The Real Thing*,
1982), and spy intrigue (*Hapgood*, 1988). *Arcadia* (1993) moves back and
forth between the Romantic era and the present day, bringing together
a literary mystery story, reflections on landscape, and the emotional
involvements of the characters. *Indian Ink* (1995) examines conflicts of
cultural identity in post-colonial India.

The comedies of Alan Ayckbourn are the most consistently successful depictions of middle-class family life in modern theatre.
Viewed by some as 'traditional' comedies, they are seen by others as
deeply serious observations on certain social malaises in late twentieth-
century Britain. *The Norman Conquests* (1975), an interlinked trio of
simultaneous-action comedies, is one of the high points of Ayckbourn's career. *Season's Greetings, Absurd Person Singular,* and *Henceforward*
are among his major plays in a prolific output during the 1970s and
1980s. Ayckbourn is probably the one dramatist who, like Greene as a
novelist, has enjoyed great commercial success while retaining a following among the more intellectual or academic communities.

In the 1960s, following on from the social content of the 'angry' plays
of Osborne and the 'kitchen-sink' dramas of Wesker and others, a
new, directly political theatre began to emerge – often from small,
untraditional theatres, and from travelling groups with no affiliation to
the normal channels of production, which continued to focus on the
West End theatres of London.

Edward Bond's *Saved* (1965) caused considerable controversy, when censorship was still in force, because of the staged stoning to death of a baby, but *Saved* emerges as a key play in the recent political development of the theatre. Bond's *Lear* (1971) takes Shakespeare's tragedy as a starting point for an examination of human cruelty: it is interesting that Edward Bond and Samuel Beckett should examine the geography of the human soul in divergent ways, concentrating on cruelty and on despair respectively – but with reference, direct or indirect, to the Shakespearean tragedy which critics have always seen as the most pessimistic. This is a reflection of the rediscovery of the power of the theatre as a vehicle for the deeper examination and discussion of issues, which Ibsen and Shaw had initiated, and which continues to be a focus for the drama.

Bond's *Bingo* (1973) actually puts the character of Shakespeare on stage, in an examination of the clash between artistic and capitalist values. The play shows Shakespeare in his retirement in Stratford, as a property owner rather than the cultural colossus history has made him. Bond's Marxist viewpoint makes Shakespeare a class enemy, an enemy of the people, in his support for the enclosures of common land. On the cultural level, an encounter with Ben Jonson also undermines the traditional ideas of Shakespeare, the man, and the playwright:

JONSON What are you writing?
SHAKESPEARE Nothing.

> [*They drink.*]

JONSON Not writing?
SHAKESPEARE No.
JONSON Why not?
SHAKESPEARE Nothing to say.
JONSON Doesn't stop others. Written out?
SHAKESPEARE Yes.

> [*They drink.*]

JONSON Now, what are you writing?
SHAKESPEARE Nothing.
JONSON Down here for the peace and quiet? Find inspiration – look for it, anyway. Work up something spiritual. Refined. Can't get by with scrabbling it off in noisy corners any more. New young men.

Competition. Your recent stuff's been pretty peculiar. What was *The Winter's Tale* about? I ask to be polite.

Similar clashes of values are the basis of several of the plays of David Hare, from *Knuckle* (1974) through *Plenty* (1975) to *Racing Demon* (1989), which is a highly satirical portrayal of the relationship between the church and the state, part of a trilogy of 'state of the nation' plays; the second – *Murmuring Judges* (1992) – examines the judicial system. Hare's *The Secret Rapture* (1988) is a family tragedy, where politics and pragmatic financial policies – echoing the concerns of the Thatcher years – are seen as no solution to the eternal human questions of emotional truth and lasting values. This is the kind of conflict which David Hare dramatises best; where contemporary political ideas and ideals are set against more basic human characteristics.

Skylight (1995) is his most popular play. It brings together a highly successful businessman, a 1980s figure, and a socially conscious schoolteacher who has rejected his life-style to live and work in an economically deprived area of London. *Skylight* is a social debate play, in the tradition of Shaw, but with constant reversals of sympathy, shifting of standpoints, and theatrical surprises. In the final scene, the younger generation (the businessman's rejected son) provides a Ritz-style breakfast in Kyra Hollis's cold flat: this is one of Hare's recurring scenes of celebration (a huge wedding scene in his earlier co-written play *Brassneck* is equally memorable). *Skylight* is very much a play of 1990s issues.

One of the most controversial plays of the 1980s was Howard Brenton's *The Romans in Britain* (1980), which, in a scene of homosexual rape, effectively paralleled the Roman occupation of Britain with the contemporary situation in Northern Ireland. Contrasting scenes of the two 'occupations', Brenton draws on epic theatre conventions: this is theatre of war, but with a deeply human concern for history's victims. At the end of the play, we return to the aftermath of the Romans' departure from Britain, as the native characters try to identify something, maybe mythical maybe real, that they can hold on to from the nightmare of their recent past. As so often in British history, the past they evoke reverberates with the name of King Arthur:

CORDA What poem you got then? In your new trade?
FIRST COOK 'Bout a King!

[*A silence*]

CORDA Yes?
FIRST COOK King. Not any King.
CORDA No?
FIRST COOK No.
CORDA Did he have a Queen, this King?
SECOND COOK Yes. [*He hesitates*] Yes, oh very sexy –
FIRST COOK Look let me do the meat, right?
SECOND COOK Oh yeah, I do the vegetables even when it comes to fucking poetry.
FIRST COOK Actually, he was a King who never was. His Government was the people of Britain. His peace was as common as rain or sun. His law was as natural as grass, growing in a meadow. And there never was a Government, or a peace, or a law like that. His sister murdered his father. His wife was unfaithful. He died by the treachery of his best friend. And when he was dead, the King who never was and the Government that never was – were mourned. And remembered. Bitterly. And thought of as a golden age, lost and yet to come.
CORDA Very pretty.
MORGANA What was his name?
FIRST COOK Any old name dear. [*To the* SECOND COOK] What was his name?
SECOND COOK Right. Er – any old name. Arthur? Arthur?

Brenton's plays have often confronted political themes: from *Brass-neck* (co-written with David Hare, 1973) – a panorama of industrial capitalism – and *The Churchill Play* (1974), a dystopian view of the future. Hare and Brenton also collaborated on *Pravda* (1985), one of the most significant plays of the 1980s; it is set in the context of the press, examining the roles of individuals and institutions in a way which anticipates Hare's later trilogy.

Peter Shaffer's concern is less with the political situation of the present than with universal mysteries. He has written several epic dramas with a historical or psychological basis. *The Royal Hunt of the Sun* (1964) is set at the time of the Spanish conquest of the Inca Empire; *Equus* (1973) is a probing psychological drama of sexual deficiency;

and *Amadeus* (1980) examines the life and the myth of Mozart. Shaffer's subject is the mystery, the magic, of motivation; and, in their spectacle and their humanity, his plays (as one critic put it) 'take us nearer to God'. Here the disturbed boy, Alan, is watched by his father and a psychoanalyst, Dysart, as he praises his own god-figure, Equus, the horse:

FRANK As I came along the passage I saw the door of his bedroom was ajar. I'm sure he didn't know it was. From inside I heard the sound of this chanting. . . .

ALAN And Legwus begat Neckwus. And Neckwus begat Fleckwus, the King of Spit. And Fleckwus spoke out of his chinkle-chankle!

[*He bows himself to the ground.*]

DYSART What?

FRANK I'm sure that was the word. I've never forgotten it. Chinkle-chankle.

[ALAN *raises his head and extends his hands up in glory.*]

ALAN And he said, 'Behold – I give you Equus, my only begotten son!'

DYSART Equus?

FRANK Yes. No doubt of that. He repeated that word several times. 'Equus, my only begotten son.'

ALAN [*reverently*] Ek . . . wus!

DYSART [*suddenly understanding; almost 'aside'*] Ek . . . Ek . . .

FRANK [*embarrassed*] And then . . .

DYSART Yes: what?

FRANK He took a piece of string out of his pocket. Made up into a noose. And put it in his mouth.

[ALAN *bridles himself with invisible string, and pulls it back.*]

And then with his other hand he picked up a coat hanger. A wooden coat hanger, and – and –

DYSART Began to beat himself?

[ALAN, *in mime, begins to thrash himself,*
increasing the strokes in speed and viciousness. Pause.]

FRANK You see why I couldn't tell his mother. – Religion. Religion's at the bottom of this.

DYSART What did you do?

FRANK Nothing. I coughed – and went back downstairs.

(*Equus*)

Caryl Churchill's *Cloud Nine* (1979), *Top Girls* (1982), and *Serious*

Money (1987) were seen as innovative and highly topical plays of the 1970s and 1980s. *Cloud Nine* shows up the sexual ambivalences behind the facade of the British Empire, with a fascinating time-shift when a century passes but the characters only age by twenty-five years. Churchill mixes her times again in *Top Girls*, with contrasting types of feminism from Chaucer to a female Pope. In *Serious Money* she was among the first to use currency speculators as a paradigm for 1980s Thatcherism.

Timberlake Wertenbaker is altogether a different kind of playwright. She uses history and myth, art and intertextual references, in a range of plays which are lyrical and poetic while maintaining a strong level of social observation and comment. She uses Greek theatre, Greek myth (*The Love of the Nightingale*, 1988), and, in *Our Country's Good* (1987), the Farquhar play *The Recruiting Officer* (see page 147) is woven into the modern plot. *Three Birds Alighting on a Field* (1991) is a critical look at the Britain of the 1980s and 1990s, using the market for works of art as its basis. *Break of Day* (1995) looks at relationships in time, and contains echoes of the Russian dramatist Chekhov's *Three Sisters* in its rich tapestry of themes and allusions.

The Abbey Theatre continues to provide Irish dramatists with a stage for their ideas. In recent years, the works of Frank McGuinness – such as *Observe the Sons of Ulster Marching Towards the Somme* (1985) and *Someone Who'll Watch Over Me* (1992) – and particularly of Brian Friel, have shown that Irish drama continues to flourish. Friel has reached audiences worldwide with *Philadelphia! Here I Come!* (1968), *Translations* (1986), and *Dancing at Lughnasa* (1990) – plays which combine the Irish sense of dislocation and chaos with an evocation of the past in lyrical, yet realistic, terms.

Theatre has expanded enormously since the 1950s. There are 'alternative' theatres and groups of every kind; and the monolithic presence of the major dramatist has given way to creative enterprise on many levels. Local theatre, community theatre, childrens' theatre all flourish with little regard for the more traditional West End London theatre scene.

A great deal of drama is produced on television and radio, and most dramatists have at some time worked in these media, and in the cinema. For example, David Hare has written and directed several films;

Harold Pinter has written many screenplays; and Samuel Beckett wrote several of his one-act dramas for radio, as well as the unique *Film* for (and with) Buster Keaton.

Alan Bennett, whose stage plays include *Forty Years On* (1968) and *The Madness of George III* (1991), has written some of his best work for television, including the series of six monodramas, *Talking Heads* (1987).

> [*Come up on* GRAHAM *sitting on an upright chair. Evening.*]
>
> GRAHAM This morning I went to Community Caring down at the Health Centre. It caters for all sorts. Steve, who runs it, is dead against what he calls 'the ghetto approach'. What he's after is a nice mix of personality difficulties as being the most fruitful exercise in problem-solving and a more realistic model of society generally. There's a constant flow of coffee, 'oiling the wheels' Steve calls it, and we're all encouraged to ventilate our problems and generally let our hair down. I sometimes feel a bit out of it as I've never had any particular problems, so this time when Steve says 'Now chaps and chappesses who's going to set the ball rolling?' I get in quick and tell them about Mother and Mr Turnbull. When I'd finished Steve said, 'Thank you, Graham, for sharing your problem with us. Does anybody want to kick it around?'
>
> First off the mark is Leonard, who wonders whether Graham has sufficiently appreciated that old people can fall in love and have meaningful relationships generally, the same as young people. I suppose this is understandable coming from Leonard because he's sixty-five, only he doesn't have meaningful relationships. He's been had up for exposing himself in Sainsbury's doorway. As Mother said, 'Tesco, you could understand it.'
>
> (*A Chip in the Sugar*, from *Talking Heads*)

Alan Bleasdale and Dennis Potter wrote more for the television than the stage. Potter is widely regarded as the first major television dramatist, such series as *The Singing Detective* (1986) and *Pennies from Heaven* (1978) reaching very much larger audiences than most stage plays. Although Potter achieved fame for his television plays including the series *Karaoke* and *Cold Lazarus*, broadcast in 1996 after his death, a stage revival of *Blue Remembered Hills* (1979, staged in 1996) proved that his work could be very powerful in the traditional medium. In this play adults take the roles of children growing up in the West Country during the Second World War. Time and memory, adult and child, become telescoped in a daring exploration of the theme of 'the child is father of the man', with the present healing the past and the man forgiving the child who was his father.

Bleasdale is a political dramatist: *Boys from the Blackstuff* (1982) focused on unemployment and social deprivation; *GBH* (1991) on political and social violence; *The Monocled Mutineer* (1986) on class division and hypocrisy, in a First World War setting.

The history of British theatre since the 1860s may appear to be cyclical, moving from social dramas about a 'state o' chassis' to plays where 'nothing happens', to an intensely political theatre. Yet each cycle also takes things forward, pushing back new frontiers of subject matter and expression and continuing to explore how drama can best represent the human condition.

POETRY OF THE SECOND WORLD WAR

History is now and England
(T.S. Eliot, *Little Gidding* from *Four Quartets*)

By the end of the Second World War, W.B. Yeats, James Joyce, and Virginia Woolf were dead; T.S. Eliot had completed his *Four Quartets* (1936–42); W.H. Auden and Christopher Isherwood had become American citizens; and H.G. Wells, the last (and most modern) of the Victorians, was in the final year of his long life. In 1945, he had written his ultimate forward-looking work, *Mind at the End of its Tether*. The most profound changes were universal rather than local: there was a new consciousness of world politics, and of the dawn of the atomic age.

The writing of the immediate post-war era reverberates with a sense of nostalgia, of ending, and later with a sense of emptiness. The opening lines of *Burnt Norton*, the first of T.S. Eliot's *Four Quartets*, might stand as an epigraph to the period's growing concern with time:

> Time present and time past
> Are both perhaps present in time future,
> And time future contained in time past.

If all time is eternally present
All time is unredeemable.
What might have been is an abstraction
Remaining a perpetual possibility
Only in a world of speculation.
What might have been and what has been
Point to one end, which is always present.
Footfalls echo in the memory
Down the passage which we did not take
Towards the door we never opened
Into the rose-garden.

This idea had featured strongly in the plays of J.B. Priestley just before the war, but now took on a sense of lost time – time never to be regained. W.H. Auden's long poem of 1948, *The Age of Anxiety*, is often seen as giving a 'label' to the second half of the twentieth century.

Eliot's *Four Quartets* was the major poetic achievement of the war years. It was written at a distance from the action of war, unlike the poetry of Owen, Rosenberg, and others in the First World War. With the anxieties of the pre-war years already well documented, the role of poets on active service in the Second World War was different. Like the poets of the First World War, they were participants and observers, rather than critics or commentators.

The three most important Second World War poets were Alun Lewis, Keith Douglas, and Sidney Keyes. All were killed in the war, all in their twenties. Alun Lewis was Welsh: there is a sense of pessimism in his work which can be felt in his best-known poem, *All Day It Has Rained*. *Raiders' Dawn* (1942) and a volume of stories, *The Last Inspection*, were published in his lifetime. Keith Douglas's only volume before his death was *Selected Poems* (1943), but for many critics he was the most promising of the Second World War poets. Like Lewis, he frequently wrote about death, as in his noted *Simplify Me When I'm Dead*. The posthumously published *Alamein to Zem Zem* (1946) was a highly innovative narrative of war. Douglas's *Collected Poems* appeared in 1951. There were two collections of the poems of Sidney Keyes: *The Iron Laurel* (1942) and the posthumous *The Cruel Solstice* (1943). His elegiac tone expresses regret rather than anger. Keyes's *Collected Poems* appeared in 1945.

Henry Reed survived the war. His *Naming of Parts* has become one of the best-known single poems of the Second World War:

> Today we have naming of parts. Yesterday,
> We had daily cleaning. And tomorrow morning,
> We shall have what to do after firing. But today,
> Today we have naming of parts. Japonica
> Glistens like coral in all of the neighbouring gardens,
>   And today we have naming of parts.

This poem appeared in 1946, in the volume *A Map of Verona*. Reed went on to become a noted radio dramatist.

POETRY SINCE 1945

Sexual intercourse began
In nineteen sixty-three
(Which was rather late for me) –
Between the end of the Chatterley ban
And the Beatles' first LP
                    (Philip Larkin, *Annus Mirabilis*)

The years after 1945 saw both continuities and changes in English poetry. Some poets, despite Modernism, continued Romantic traditions, writing deeply personal responses to the world and engaging with 'eternal', 'elemental' themes. The central viewpoint in their poems is an 'I', a single voice, recording experiences directly and shaping them in generally traditional poetic forms. Other poets are not as clearly in the Romantic tradition. The 'I' in their poems is more indirect, and experience is presented more ironically. The focus is restricted, concentrating more on the particulars of everyday life. However, no poet fits neatly into the categories of 'Romantic' or 'anti-Romantic' and some resist this useful but simplified categorisation.

In 1934, Dylan Thomas's first volume, entitled *Eighteen Poems*, won widespread acclaim. Thomas (who was Welsh) was felt to be a poet who could restore to poetry in English a Romantic vigour and flamboyance after the anxious, uncertain tones of T.S. Eliot, the more cautious Romanticism of W.B. Yeats, and the social preoccupations of

W.H. Auden. Throughout Dylan Thomas's greatest poems there is an intensity born out of the struggle to give expression to very powerful feelings. Many of his poems are dense in meaning and the images are frequently wild and surreal but his tone is bold and affirmative. Thomas's poetry is sometimes obscure; it is sometimes moving in its simplicity; it is frequently very original in its selection and combinations of words. A good example is the poem *Fern Hill*. The poem describes Thomas's childhood holidays on his aunt's farm in Wales:

> All the sun long it was running, it was lovely, the hay
> Fields high as a house, the tunes from the chimneys, it was air
> And playing, lovely and watery
> And fire green as grass.

Thomas's choice of phrases is original. He sees smoke coming from chimneys as if it made tuneful sounds; the grass is so hot it is as if it were on fire; the sun shines all the day long – 'all the sun long'. Words like green are used both literally and non-literally, exploiting connotations of youth, happiness, and innocence. The ending to *Fern Hill* is especially poignant, linking the innocence of youth with an inevitable death while asserting the importance of the self through the poetry ('singing'):

> Time held me green and dying
> Though I sang in my chains like the sea.

At times, Dylan Thomas's reputation for hard drinking and riotous behaviour attracted more attention than his poetry, especially in America, where he went on several poetry-reading tours in the early 1950s. During the fourth of these American tours, in 1953, he suddenly collapsed and died.

Thomas was born and brought up in Wales, and the Welsh traditions of the power of the spoken word, especially in matters of religion, are present in his poetry. He writes with an elegiac appreciation of natural forces, the forces of birth, sex, and death, and with a rhapsodic regret for all that is lost in death. His best poems affirm with great passion and vigour the joys and beauties of life, even in the midst of death. In a famous poem to his dying father, written in the form of a villanelle, Thomas urges him to resist:

Do not go gentle into that good night,
Old age should burn and rave at close of day;
Rage, rage against the dying of the light.

Much of modern poetry continues Dylan Thomas's affirmation of life over death, particularly poignant in the nuclear age of post-war writing.

John Betjeman was immensely popular as a poet. His *Selected Poems* (1948) brought him considerable attention, although he had been publishing poetry since 1930 and was close to the Auden Group. A passionate defender of Victorian architecture and heritage, he wrote witty poetry which had public appeal and dealt with everyday subjects, for example *Sudden Illness at the Bus-Stop*, with sympathy and concern. He came to be identified as a representative middle-brow voice of the present, adjusting to the past. His verse autobiography *Summoned by Bells* (1960) became a bestseller and was followed by an expanded *Collected Poems* (1962). There is an underlying melancholy in Betjeman's best work which relates him closely to Philip Larkin, who was one of his greatest admirers, and in many ways his successor in the depiction of modern urban life.

At the same time as the angry young man was appearing in novels and plays, poetry took on a new tone with The Movement. Although it was short-lived, and was never very homogeneous as a group, its aim to rid poetry of high-flown Romanticism and bring it down to earth can be seen to have been realised in the work (most notably) of Philip Larkin, and of Donald Davie, D.J. Enright, and Elizabeth Jennings. Their work deliberately contrasted both with the high emotion and verbal effusion of Dylan Thomas and with the Modernist tradition of T.S. Eliot and Ezra Pound. The novelists Kingsley Amis and John Wain were also associated with The Movement in the mid-1950s, notably in the 1956 anthology, *New Lines. A Way of Looking* (1955) by Elizabeth Jennings contains in its title something of what the group represented – a different way of perceiving the world – but she cannot really be grouped with the others. Most of her poetry is of personal suffering and struggle, rather than the detached, slightly ironic writing of the more socially acute poets such as Larkin.

D.J. Enright, whose *Collected Poems* were published in 1981, taught

English literature, largely in the Far East, and his view of cultural difference and misunderstanding is a distinctive and ironic one. Donald Davie's work is more obscurely erudite and philosophical, moving, as he put it, 'among abstractions'. Like Enright, he was a critic and academic, using his poetry to express a worldview rather than a provincial English one, which a great deal of writing in the 1950s and 1960s emphasised.

The poetry of Philip Larkin plays with and against the Romantic tradition in poetry. Larkin does not assert the importance of his own personal experience. His vision is realistic and unsentimental, preferring to be indirect and ironic. He continues, however, the tradition of Romantic poets such as Wordsworth and later poets, particularly Thomas Hardy, by exploring eternal themes of death and change within established rhythms and syntax, and he generally uses conservative poetic forms. Like Hardy, he writes about what appears to be normal and everyday, while exploring the paradox that the mundane is both familiar and limited. He is also a Hardyesque poet in the way he presents experiences which many readers recognise and feel they can share. He is, however, more of a social poet than Hardy, frequently commenting on the tawdry superficial aspects of modern urban living. Although his poetry can seem patronising in tone, the intention is always to see things as honestly as possible.

In *Poetry of Departures*, Larkin contrasts the decisive Romantic gesture of action with the more cautious decision to leave things as they are. He knows that this is less likely to be approved:

> Sometimes you hear, fifth-hand
> As epitaph:
> He chucked up everything
> And just cleared off,
> And always the voice will sound
> Certain you approve . . .

but it is more realistic. He has his own world with its detested limits:

> We all hate home
> And having to be there:
> I detest my room
> Its specially-chosen junk . . .

but he prefers it to action which is likely to lead nowhere. The different languages in the poem – the colloquial slang and the plain – embody the differences in life-style. In *The Whitsun Weddings* he describes couples attempting to give their lives some happiness and order, but concludes that happiness is something which only happens elsewhere, outside our lives, in the past rather than in the present.

In the Introduction to his controversial anthology *The Oxford Book of Twentieth-Century English Verse* (1973), Larkin underlines the importance of a native English tradition, as opposed to the Modernist influence, and gives considerable space to Chaucer, Wordsworth, Hardy, and Auden, with Hardy seen as the major poet of the Modern period. Larkin's 'I' is quiet and unsentimental. He appears to be simultaneously a Romantic poet who is distrustful of certain aspects of Romanticism. He is certainly not a poet who can 'sing in his chains like the sea' or use such language as 'Time held me green and dying'. Nevertheless, he represents and records his experience with fidelity and with great sensitivity.

Thom Gunn's work also appeared in the 1950s in *New Lines*, and already he had a distinctive voice in his depiction of the new young culture of leather-clad motorbikers, their attitudes and passions. His later poems, in such volumes as *My Sad Captains* (1961), *The Passages of Joy* (1982), and *The Man with Night Sweats* (1992) show a growing technical mastery and an ever more uninhibited expression of gay themes. Gunn has lived in San Francisco since 1960, and is one of the few English poets to have moved West; while retaining the detached ironic viewpoint of The Movement, he has a touch of American verve, to which his poetry on AIDS brings a note of sadness.

> My thoughts are crowded with death
> and it draws so oddly on the sexual
> that I am confused
> confused to be attracted
> by, in effect, my own annihilation.
> Who are these two, these fiercely attractive men
> who want me to stick their needle in my arm?
> They tell me they are called Brad and John,
> one from here, one from Denver, sitting the same
> on the bench as they talk to me,
> their legs spread apart, their eyes attentive.

> I love their daring, their looks, their jargon,
> and what they have in mind.
> (*In Time of Plague*, from *The Man with Night Sweats*)

In the 1960s, a wave of pop poetry reached a wide audience, and writers such as Roger McGough, Brian Patten, and Adrian Henri, all from Liverpool, have continued to produce a great deal of lighter verse, considered unworthy of serious comment by some critics, but using language, imagery, and contemporary reference in ways which many British readers find accessible, enjoyable and significant.

> He wakes when the sun rises
> Gets up   Exercises
> Breakfasts with one whom he despises
> Chooses one of his disguises
> and his gun   Fires his
> first bullet   It paralyses
> Drives into town   Terrorizes
> Armed police in vizors
> materialize   His demise is
> swift   No surprises.
> (Roger McGough, *No Surprises*, from *Defying Gravity*)

Both Dylan Thomas and D.H. Lawrence influenced the work of Ted Hughes, who in 1985 succeeded John Betjeman as Poet Laureate. Hughes's poetry emphasises the pitiless and violent forces of nature. Many of his poems focus on animals who pursue their lives with a single-minded strength and power. Some of the animals he depicts are not so much violent as vigorous, with a sharp sense of survival. Hughes makes his readers aware of the prehistory of the natural world, stressing its indifference to man. Poems such as *Pike*, *Jaguar*, *Thrushes*, or *Wind* are totally without sentimentality, the natural forces viewed with a harsher eye than Lawrence's.

In one of his best-known poems, *Hawk Roosting*, which is cast as a monologue, Hughes presents the hawk as a powerful bird which catches and eats smaller birds and animals. The hawk states that everything in nature has been arranged for its own convenience. It assumes that the existence of other birds and animals as his prey is part of the purpose of creation. His eye and a strong personality ('I' in a pun on 'eye') will ensure that this situation does not change.

I kill where I please because it is all mine
My manners are tearing off heads, the allotment of death.

The sun is behind me.
Nothing has changed since I began;
My eye has permitted no change.
I am going to keep things like this.

Many critics have equated this state of mind with the psychology of a totalitarian dictator. The hawk's words and actions relate to forces underlying both human and animal experience. The word 'hawk' is applied to politicians who believe in the use of force to resolve political problems.

In his later work, Hughes has become more preoccupied with myths and legends. In *Crow* (1971) he retells the creation story from the point of view of a violent, anarchic consciousness – the crow himself – who emerges as a kind of anti-Christ. The poems in this volume, and in *Gaudete* (1977), are sparse dramas in which traditional metrical patterning and realistic presentation are abandoned. Ted Hughes's poetry is often contrasted with Larkin's gentle, urbane and introspective manner.

Seamus Heaney is a poet who writes directly and obliquely about politics, speaking in a clearly personal voice. As an Irishman, many of his poems deal with the horrors which continue to afflict Northern Ireland. In his early poems, Heaney writes of the countryside and the natural world in ways which suggest the influence of D.H. Lawrence and Ted Hughes. In one of his earliest poems, *Digging*, he establishes a metaphor which recurs in different ways in several subsequent poems.

Between my finger and my thumb
The squat pen rests.
I'll dig with it.

He digs into his own memory, into the lives of his family, into the past of Irish history and into the deeper levels of legend and myth which shape the character of the people of his country. Heaney attempts to go beyond the terrible daily events of life in Northern Ireland to discover the forces beneath the history of that country which might restore hope and comfort. But he does not hide the deep-rooted tribal passions of revenge and honour which endure in contemporary society.

The award of the Nobel Prize for Literature to Seamus Heaney in 1995 set the seal on his worldwide reputation as the major Irish poet of the second half of the twentieth century, and, indeed, as one of the finest poets writing in the English language. It was the volume of poems *North* (1975) which established Heaney's fame and popularity, after *Door Into the Dark* (1969). More recent collections of verse have examined the 'bog people', the poet's own relationships, and the complex relationships between individual and society, cult and history. In these lines from the poem *North* the poet looks back to the hidden imperial roots of the English language in Viking Ireland and Norse culture:

> 'Lie down
> in the word-hoard, burrow
> in the coil and gleam
> of your furrowed brain.
>
> Compose in darkness.
> Expect aurora borealis
> In the long foray
> But no cascade of light.
>
> Keep your eye clear
> As the bleb of the icicle,
> Trust the feel of what nubbed treasure
> Your hands have known.'

In his essays and academic writings, Seamus Heaney is perceptive, and sometimes polemical. He is particularly acute in his writings on poets and poetry. His early lecture *Yeats as an Example?* ends with words of praise for one of Yeats's last poems, *Cuchulain Comforted*: words which might, in some way, also stand for Heaney's own creative work.

> It is a poem deeply at one with the weak and the strong of this earth, full of a motherly kindness towards life, but also unflinching in its belief in the propriety and beauty of life transcended into art, song, words.

Charles Tomlinson and Geoffrey Hill share a concern with time, history, tradition, and place. Tomlinson's *The Way of the World* (1969) and *The Shaft* (1978) are direct examinations of continuity and change: this goes against the notion that most contemporary poetry is about chaos and disorder. Some poets do indeed concentrate on breakdown, Sylvia Plath in particular. But Tomlinson, Hill, and others take the constants of their landscape as the basis of their work. For Hill, this means the landscape of Mercia, as in *Mercian Hymns* (1971) which celebrate, in a kind of prose poetry, Offa, 'the presiding genius of the West Midlands' in early English history. Where Plath's violence is emotional, personal, suicidal – *Collected Poems* (1981) – Hill's is latent, hidden in the past and brooding to produce perhaps the most complex and allusive of recent poetry.

In an essay entitled *Englands of the Mind*, Seamus Heaney discusses the poetry of Ted Hughes, Philip Larkin, and Geoffrey Hill. He contrasts Hill's primitive landscapes and Larkin's city-scapes. Hill is a poet of another England; he searches for the roots of English identity, in historical, linguistic, and cultural terms, in the region of Mercia – the West Midlands. Hill's search is not far removed from Heaney's own digging into the depths of his own Irishness. In this extract from *Mercian Hymns*, Geoffrey Hill celebrates the work of English needle-workers, in echoes of the Victorian celebration of mediaeval work found in the works of Thomas Carlyle and William Morris:

> In tapestries, in dreams, they gathered, as
> it was enacted, the re-entry of
> transcendence into this sublunary world.
> *Opus Anglicanum*, their stringent mystery
> riddled by needles: the silver veining, the
> gold leaf, voluted grape-vine, masterworks
> of treacherous thread.
>
> They trudged out of the dark, scraping their
> boots free from lime-splodges and phlegm.
> They munched cold bacon. The lamps grew
> plump with oily reliable light.

C.H. Sisson shares Hill's fascination with the genius of the past, especially distant English and classical history. His *Collected Poems* (1984) shows a wide span of reference, a concern with the fallen nature of man, and a rich range of cultural images.

Edwin Morgan is one of the foremost Scottish poets of the century. Noted for experimental 'concrete' poetry, which makes visual images of words and letters, he is also a lyric poet, and acute observer of the city of Glasgow, where he has lived and worked most of his life. Like many poets, he is also an academic, and his volume of essays, interviews, and observations, *Nothing Not Sending Messages* (1992), gives useful insights into his *Collected Poems* published in 1990.

> When love comes late, but fated,
> the very ground seems on fire with tongues of running time,
> and conscious hearts are speaking
> of the long vistas closed in clouds
> by lonely waters, all goodbyes
> where the swallow is a shadow
> swooping back, like youth, to silence,
>
> If all goodbyes could be drowned in one welcome,
> and the pains of waiting be washed from a hundred street-corners,
> and dry rebuffs and grey regrets, backs marching into rain
> slip like a film from the soiled spirit made new –
> I'd take that late gift, and those tongues
> of fire would burn out in our
> thankful fountains, to the sea.
>
> (*The Welcome*)

Douglas Dunn, with *Terry Street* (1969), *Elegies* (1985), *Northlight* (1988), and *Dante's Drum Kit* (1993), has been called the major Scottish poet of his generation. Strongly political in much of his work, he challenges Sir Walter Scott's turning 'our country round upon its name/ And time'. Dunn's nationalist sentiment is concerned with common, popular experience, underlying recorded history. The elegies written on the death of his wife – *Elegies* (1985) – display an emotional range allied with a technical mastery which has taken Dunn's work on to new levels of achievement.

Some of the major poetry of recent years focuses on place, and the language used to evoke its setting. Seamus Heaney has described Ted Hughes's sensibility as 'pagan in the original sense; a heath-dweller', in direct contrast with the urban concerns of Larkin. Heaney, himself attracted to the peatbog, its wildness, and its capacity to preserve, celebrates his contemporaries, saying, 'all that I really knew about the art [of poetry] was derived from whatever poetry I had written'. His observations on Hughes, Larkin, and Geoffrey Hill focus on their sense of place: Hughes's heath is as much 'England as King Lear's heath', Larkin's 'landscape . . . is dominated by the civic prospects' and the poet a 'humane and civilised member of the . . . civil service'; Hill's Mercia is seen with 'a historian and school's eye', with the poet seeming, to the Irishman's objective eye, to be 'celebrating his own indomitable Englishry'.

When Seamus Heaney's poems were included in the 1982 *Penguin Book of Contemporary British Poetry*, Heaney riposted, in *An Open Letter* (1983) that 'My anxious muse . . . Has to refuse/ The adjective,' – concluding 'British, no, the name's not right'. This is a crucial assertion of the Irishness of modern writing in Ireland, whether in the North (Ulster) or Eire.

Heaney's first volume after winning the Nobel Prize for Literature in 1995 was *The Spirit Level* (1996). The title brings together his spiritual side and his practical nature, and the volume consolidates his position as a poet of nature, politics and humanity who can make major poetry out of the essential mundane. It is interesting that, although Heaney rejected the label 'British', he has always written in English rather than using any regional Irish dialect. In *The Spirit Level* he illustrates how, growing up a Catholic in a divided province, then becoming an emblematic exile in England and America, has given him the capacity to voice images of universal healing rather than division, to find 'personal solutions to a shared crisis, momentary stays against confusion'. Like Samuel Beckett, his vision is to 'gain an inch against the darkness'.

Heaney travels widely and his poetry and myth-making are international: Tollund in Denmark features frequently in his poems (it is where the 'Bog People' were found); America, Africa, and ancient Greece are visited and imaginatively revisited. To this international experience Heaney brings a deep awareness of English linguistic and poetic traditions. From Anglo-Saxon poetry through the Metaphysicals, Wordsworth, Gerard Manley Hopkins, and W.H. Auden, to Yeats and Ted Hughes, Heaney revels in the historical voices to which he is now compared. His range and depth, from local to international, from deeply personal to easily universal, has given new strength to poetry in English:

> You are like a rich man entering heaven
> Through the ear of a raindrop.
> Listen now again.
> (*The Rain Stick*, from *The Spirit Level*)

Poets such as Tom Paulin, Mebdh McGuckian, Paul Muldoon, Paul Durcan, Eavan Boland, Michael Longley and Derek Mahon – together with Heaney, and the older generation of Pearse Hutchinson, Brendan Kennelly and Thomas Kinsella – have given Irish poetry a new vitality, which brings North and South together in common concern.

Eavan Boland has emerged as Ireland's foremost female poet: volumes like *Outside History* (1990) and *In a Time of Violence* (1994) show, like Seamus Heaney, an awareness of history, a sense of national pride, and, in Boland's case, a feminist sense of the potential for the growth of her country.

> we will live, we have lived
> where language is concealed. Is perilous.
> We will be – we have been – citizens
> of its hiding place. But it is too late
>
> to shut the book of satin phrases,
> to refuse to enter
> an evening bitter with peat smoke,
> where newspaper sellers shout headlines
> and friends call out their farewells in
> a city of whispers
> and interiors where
>
> the dear vowels
> *Irish Ireland ours* are
> absorbed into Autumn air,
> are out of earshot in the distances
> we are stepping into where we never
> imagine words such as *hate*
> and *territory* and the like – unbanished still
> as they always would be – wait

and are waiting under
beautiful speech. To strike.
(Beautiful Speech)

Contemporary Irish poetry can be urban working class, polemical, feminist, occupied with history and tradition, and at the same time open to international influences and concerns. Poets like Pearse Hutchinson and Michael Davitt, to name only two, are reinvestigating the tradition of poetry in the Irish language, bringing together the strands of history, legend, literature and language, which give Ireland its modern identity and heritage.

MARTIANS AND GORGONS

In the late 1970s Craig Raine came to be known as leader of the 'Martian' school of poetry. It was not so much a 'school' as a defamiliarising mode of perception which derived from the poem *A Martian Sends a Postcard Home* (1979). This plays with ways of seeing; books are 'Caxtons', the toilet is 'a punishment room' where 'everyone's pain has a different smell'. From *The Onion Memory* (1978) through to *Clay: Whereabouts Unknown* (1996), Raine has continued in this vein, bringing unexpected perspectives to everyday things: 'a pug like a car crash' and the moon fading in the morning 'like fat in a frying pan'. He is, more than any other, the poet who sees likes in unlikes. More ambitious projects like the long poem *History* (1995) have less of this distinctive characteristic and have enjoyed less success.

Tony Harrison regards poetry as 'the supreme form of articulation' and sees the poet's role as to 'reclaim poetry's public function'. His writing, often set in his home county of Yorkshire, as in *V* (1985–88), uses colloquial forms, natural speech, and local dialect in perfectly scanning rhymes to explore matters like education and class, violence and language, questions of social conflict. The letter *V* stands for 'versus', punning on 'verses', and the traditional V for Victory; the poem was written during the miners' strike of the mid-1980s, causing scandal when it was broadcast on television. Harrison's work, often for theatrical performance, is a vital assertion of poetry and language, with none of the safe, ironic detachment of some of his contemporaries:

Harrison's is committed, dramatic poetry which is never comfortable and always challenging.

The Gaze of the Gorgon (1992), a long poem for television written in the wake of the Gulf War, has shown that his energy and creativity are constantly developing, making Harrison one of the most accessible and exciting poets now writing. He is also an accomplished translator, especially from classical Latin and Greek. The range of poetic and dramatic reference in his works is immense. *A Kumquat for John Keats* finds the fruit to celebrate the famous poet; *U.S. Martial* (1981) punningly transposes the Latin epigrammatist Martial into 1980s New York. *The Pomegranates of Patmos Martial* (from the 1992 volume *The Gaze of the Gorgon*) is an apocalytic vision:

> I'm so weary of all metaphorers.
> From now on my most pressing ambition's
> to debrainwash all like Prochorus
> made Moonies by metaphysicians.
>
> But my poor brother could never respond.
> I couldn't undermine his defences.
> His brain went before him to the Beyond.
> He took all leave of his senses.
>
> My brother's heart was turned to stone.
> So my revenge on St John's to instil
> in lovers like these, who think they're alone,
> the joy John and his ilk want to kill,
>
> and try any charm or trick
> to help frightened humans affirm
> small moments against the rhetoric
> of St Cosmocankerworm.

Few modern poets are as observant as Harrison about class, or about how speech reflects class. *Them and Us* (phonetic rendering (u:z)) recalls his schooldays, when his accent 'murdered' the words of Keats: at least, according to his English master. Later, the poem *Y* (the initial stands for the cheapest form of airline travel) shows the same perception on a flight across the Atlantic:

the First Class can pay
while the Y class gapes

pour encourager . . .
any man can fly
Premium if he can pay
(or his company).

We curtain the classes
while they eat,
the plastics from glasses,
we are so discreet!

Women poets, after the emotionally charged verses of Sylvia Plath, have tended to mix emotion with humour, passion with acute observation, penetration with pleasure rather than pain. Jenny Joseph, Anne Stevenson, U.A. Fanthorpe, and Scottish-born Carol Ann Duffy are particularly noteworthy. Here is Duffy's subversive version of a Valentine:

Not a red rose or a satin heart.

I give you an onion.
It is a moon wrapped in brown paper.
It promises light
like the careful undressing of love,

Here.
It will blind you with tears
like a lover.

Wendy Cope has reached a wide audience with a form of witty and pungent light verse, such as *Making Cocoa for Kingsley Amis* (1986).

Stevie Smith is something of an outsider; she wrote spare, inventive, often humorous verse with 'a particular emotional weather between the words', as Seamus Heaney put it. She is a compassionate observer of the modern tragedy of isolation, memorably in the much anthologised poem *Not Waving but Drowning* (1957). Her *Collected Poems* was published in 1975.

Nobody heard him, the dead man,
But still he lay moaning:

I was much further out than you thought
And not waving but drowning.

Poor chap, he always loved larking
And now he's dead
It must have been too cold for him his heart gave way,
They said.

Oh no no no, it was too cold always
(Still the dead one lay moaning)
I was much too far out all my life
And not waving but drowning.

Andrew Motion, author of important biographies of Philip Larkin and John Keats, quotes Stevie Smith in one of his own poems: *Close*, in *Love in a Life* (1991). The title covers both the close escape and the feelings for his family.

The afternoon I was killed
I strolled up the beach from the sea
where the big wave had hit me, . . .
Nobody spoke about me
or how I was no longer there.
It was odd, but I understood why:
when I had drowned I was only
a matter of yards out to sea
(not *too far out* – too close),
still able to hear the talk
and have everything safe in view.

Motion is a poet of contrasts, working with that kind of intimacy: he also writes larger-scale, longer poems, such as *Bathing at Glymenopoulo*, in *Dangerous Play: Poems 1974–1984* (1985), and *Scripture*, in *Natural Causes* (1987).

Basil Bunting, whose *Collected Poems* appeared in 1978, was for many years the forgotten man of modern English poetry. He had been a disciple of Pound's in the 1920s, but his achievement was not widely recognised until the publication of his lengthy autobiographical poem *Briggflatts* in 1966. Set in his home county of Northumberland, it is an account of the county and the century, bringing Pound's influence up to our own day.

Furthest, fairest things, stars, free of our humbug,
each his own, the longer known the more alone,
wrapt in emphatic fire roaring out to a black flue.
Each spark trills on a tone beyond chronological compass,
yet in a sextant's bubble present and firm
places a surveyor's stone or steadies a tiller.
Then is Now. The star you steer by is gone,
its tremulous thread spun in the hurricane
spider floss on my cheek; light from the zenith
spun when the slowworm lay in her lap
fifty years ago.

R.S. Thomas is the most significant Welsh poet since Dylan Thomas. He has been described as 'our best living religious poet', and there is some truth in this, although many poets discuss religion in their works. Thomas is, in fact, a clergyman and his work in a rural parish imbues his poetry with a harsh, bleak, pastoral quality, reflecting the landscape and the history of Wales. 'There is no present in Wales/ And no future;/ There is only the past', he affirms, contradicting T.S. Eliot. His poetry has a roughness to it, a challenge to 'the English/ Scavenging among the remains/ of our culture'. *Pietà* (1966) and *Selected Poems 1946–68* (published in 1973) are representative of his best work.

What's living but courage?
Paunch full of hot porridge,
Nerves strengthened with tea,
Peat-black, dawn found me

Mowing where the grass grew,
Bearded with golden dew.
Rhythm of the long scythe
Kept this tall frame lithe.

(*Lore*)

TOWARDS THE TWENTY-FIRST CENTURY

If Irish poetry is undergoing something of a renaissance, there is no lack of variety in English writing. Craig Raine's 'Martian' school, after

A Martian Sends a Postcard Home (1979), enjoyed a vogue, but more recently the vivid urban expression of Simon Armitage, in *Zoom!* (1989), *Kid* (1992), and *The Dead Sea Poems* (1995), and Glyn Maxwell, in *Tale of the Mayor's Son* (1990) and *Out of the Rain* (1992), have attracted considerable acclaim. Their technical accomplishment, in the tradition of Larkin and Harrison, has become a vital part of poetic achievement. Simon Armitage's *Xanadu* (1992) is a film poem, set in Lancashire, using twenty-six alphabetically named blocks of flats – being demolished – as the background for his reflections on social deprivation.

> I have to say I'd never thought
> of this place as a ski resort.
>
> Ashfield Valley
> and its thousand chalets,
>
> a case of the half-light
> making me snow-blind.
>
> In any case,
> this house of cards, these Meccano apartments
> thirty years ago were the cat's pyjamas.
>
> So instead
> of putting the cart before the horse
> I should trace this rumour back to its source;
>
> the place: perhaps a council chamber,
> the date: nineteen-sixty something or other . . .

Writers like Ben Okri, born in Nigeria – where his Booker Prize-winning novel *The Famished Road* is set – Grace Nicholas, and John Agard, born in Guyana, and Benjamin Zephaniah, born in Birmingham but brought up in Jamaica and the UK, are bringing new rhythms, performance styles, social and racial concerns into current British poetry. Zephaniah's *The Dread Affair* (1985) and his nomination for the post of Professor of Poetry at Oxford University, confirm his status as a new voice in the multi-faceted revitalisation of poetry in English. 'I think poetry should be alive,' he has said. 'You should be able to dance to it.' *As a African* shows something of the range of minorities Benjamin Zephaniah is speaking for in his poetry.

> As a African a plastic bullet hit me in Northern Ireland,
> But my children overstood and dey grew strong.
> As a African I was a woman in a man's world,
> A man in a computer world,
> A fly on the wall of China,
> A Rastafarian diplomat
> And a miner in Wales.
>
> I was a red hot Eskimo
> A peace loving hippie
> A honest newscaster
> A city dwelling peasant,
> I was a Arawak
> A unwanted baby
> A circumcised lady,
> I was all of dis
>
> And still a African.

THE NOVEL SINCE 1945

The decades following the Second World War have seen a considerable increase in the numbers of novels published and in the variety of themes and subjects they cover. Yet at the same time there has been no shortage of critics who have been quick to pronounce 'the death of the novel'. This is related to the phenomenon of the intellectualisation of literature which began in the 1920s, when some writers – for example, T.S. Eliot, James Joyce, and Virginia Woolf – consciously distanced themselves from 'popular' taste; and it was helped by the industry which has continued to grow around the academic study of literature in universities and schools. It is noticeable that several writers, such as Graham Greene, made a distinction in their writing between their popular novels – 'shockers' or thrillers – and their more 'serious' books. This distinction would have been far less likely to occur to a writer in any previous century.

Among the voices which can be more clearly heard in the novel in recent years are those of the young and the lower classes, the voice of the new educated middle classes, the voices of women, racial minorities, gays, and outsiders of many other types. Various sub-genres of novel have become bestsellers while retaining intellectual acceptability – for example, the working-class novel, the Hampstead novel, the academic novel, the Scottish novel, the women's novel, the magic realist novel.

At the same time there have been numerous bestsellers which have never reached intellectual acceptability – for example, romances, thrillers, and historical novels. Some genres, like the detective story and the spy story, have, however, begun to receive critical acclaim, and to be recognised as major contributions to literature. The growth in cultural studies has meant that many previously unconsidered areas of written expression have come under scrutiny in the late twentieth century.

LANGUAGE NOTE
Discourse, titles and dialogism

The titles of the earliest novels written in English are designed to suggest a certain solidity. The names of people predominate; for example, *Tom Jones, Joseph Andrews, Roderick Random, Moll Flanders* all indicate the writer's attempt to blur a distinction between fiction and real-life biography at a time when there were suspicions that a novel was merely something invented, a fiction or romance which need not be taken seriously. Similarly, the names of 'real' places serve as titles, reflecting a not dissimilar realist pretension to truth; for example, *Mansfield Park, Wuthering Heights, Cranford, Waverley, Middlemarch.* As moral concerns come increasingly to the fore, so the titles signal the serious-ness of the issues which the novelist sets out to explore; for example, *Sense and Sensibility, Pride and Prejudice.*

Modernist writers generally prefer titles which are more oblique and symbolic and which require an act of interpretation from the reader. They do not always provide the reader with any definite anchor in recognisably realistic people and places; for example, *Ulysses, The Rainbow, Heart of Darkness.*

In the titles of a number of post-war British novels another trend is discernible. Some titles carry a clearly marked imprint of the speaking voice. The voice may or may not be that of the author, suggesting in turn that the author's voice may only be one among several voices in the novel and may not necessarily be the most authoritative or the one which offers a secure and stable vantage point. It may not be the singular voice of the moral centre from which the world of the novel can be interpreted. Here are some representative titles from this period:

An Awfully Big Adventure (1990) Beryl Bainbridge
How Late It Was, How Late (1994) James Kelman
Now That You're Back (1994) A.L. Kennedy
Take A Girl Like You (1960) Kingsley Amis
You Can't Do Both (1994) Kingsley Amis
Ginger, You're Barmy (1962) David Lodge
How Far Can You Go? (1980) David Lodge
Burning Your Boats (1995) Angela Carter
A Far Cry From Kensington (1988) Muriel Spark

The titles are stylistically marked by features which recur more frequently in spoken than in written discourse. Personal pronouns, in particular, set up a tone of involvement and the use of imperatives and interrogatives establish dialogic interaction. Titles such as these also draw, however, on formulaic, idiomatic phrases ('a far cry from..'; 'burn your boats') and everyday spoken lexis ('barmy', 'awfully big') in ways which suggest a direct and evaluative tone of voice. It is not immediately clear where the voice is coming from and a point of view cannot be easily established. Such a voice is, however, not expected and is perceived by most readers to be deliberately intrusive and unsettling.

The terms 'discourse' and 'dialogue' are regularly used in the literary theoretical writings of the Russian literary critic and theorist Mikhail Bakhtin (1895–1975). For Bakhtin, the novel in its most basic form is characterised by a collage of different styles, voices, and points of view. There is thus no such thing as *the* language or *a* unitary style of the novel. In contrast with conventional lyric or epic poetry, the novel is a 'dialogic' form and in this respect no one voice can ever be seen to prevail, even that of the author. In certain periods in the development of the novel, the author may be seen to have tried to impose a single vision or a particular preoccupation (and the title may reflect this) but the novel as an art-form none the less embraces the different voices and speech styles of many characters and resists singular perspectives.

The discourse of the novel, according to Bakhtin, is always contradictory and challenging, and in this respect it is an essentially democratic form, not imposing any single voice or vision. The British post-war, post-Modernist novel has a variety of different titles, including the names of people and places as well as more allusive and symbolic titles; but there is no single discourse of titles and thus the novelistic worlds which are represented are more relativistic, multi-voiced and consistently dialogic.

The novels of J.R.R. Tolkien created a fictional world that encompasses mythology, fable, and fantasy – and reached a huge worldwide readership. Tolkien himself was a philologist and professor of mediaeval language and literature, and his fiction contains many influences from that period. His hero Bilbo Baggins is a hobbit whose adventures take him through a range of landscapes and encounters with heroes and villains in a modern epic in the form of a series of novels: *The Hobbit* (1937), the three volumes of *The Lord of the Rings* (1954–55), and *The Silmarillion* (1977).

LATER GREENE

Graham Greene's most serious novels are: *The Power and the Glory* (1940); *The Heart of the Matter* (1948); *The Quiet American* (1955) and *A Burnt Out Case* (1961). Greene initially appeared to regard several of his other novels as less serious since he referred to them as 'entertainments'. In these novels he uses the popular conventions of the thriller or the spy story. These books include: *The Confidential Agent* (1939); *The Third Man* (1950) and *Our Man in Havana* (1958). Greene later dropped this distinction, realising that the 'thriller' could be a 'serious' novel. Throughout all his fiction he remained fascinated by people who are capable or incapable of judging between good and evil. His novels are carefully constructed, with powerful plots and a strong sense of place.

During the Second World War, Graham Greene had largely remained in London, working for a time in the Ministry of Information. This gave rise to his novel *The Ministry of Fear* (1943). But it is his 1940 novel *The Power and the Glory* which remains – with *Brighton Rock* (see page 438) – his classic of this period. Again, the fascination with guilt and salvation is reflected in his thrillers just as much as in his more serious novels. In the world of spies violence, betrayal, treachery and human weakness are brought into play in terms of plot before they become moral or spiritual issues. So, although his 'shockers' are superficially novels of escape, like Maugham's influential *Ashenden* stories (1928) or Buchan's Richard Hannay novels, they reveal a more serious purpose. His work creates an identifiable 'Greeneland' – a world of constant anxiety rather than easy excitements. Greene's technique – his strengths in plotting and cutting from one scene to the next – and the sinister atmosphere of the thriller were influenced by his time spent as a cinema critic in the late 1930s.

Greene's late fables, such as *Doctor Fischer of Geneva* or *The Bomb Party* (1980), take the anxiety level of Greeneland to a new pitch: greed and total amorality threaten the superficial veneer of civilised behaviour, as they have done in all the threatened landscapes Greene has visited, as traveller, critic or novelist. From West Africa to Indo-China, Brighton to Cuba, wartime London to the Stamboul Train, the threats of betrayal are the same. In *A World of My Own: A Dream Diary* (1992), published after his death, Greene makes a close analysis of how dreams and anxieties are related throughout his long writing career, leaving us with the thought, 'God is suffering the same evolution as we are, perhaps with more pain'.

POST-WAR WAUGH

In the Second World War, Evelyn Waugh served in the Royal Marines and this provided him with material for a satirical trilogy about the English at war: *Men at Arms* (1952); *Officers and Gentlemen* (1955), and *Unconditional Surrender* (1961), published together as *Sword of Honour* in 1965. In this trilogy, considered by some critics to be the best English fiction about the Second World War, the hero, Guy Crouchback, always tries to do his moral best but ends up doing something foolish or inconsequential. The publication of *Brideshead Revisted* (1945) had introduced a more sustained note of seriousness into Waugh's work. It is a novel about a fascinating but decadent aristocratic family and the powerful influence on them of the Roman Catholic faith. The house of Brideshead, similarly to Howards End in the novel of the same name by E.M. Forster, represents a part of English society – the aristocracy – which was disappearing from the post-war world.

Waugh is widely recognised as the pre-eminent novelist who charted that decline and fall. Something of the emptiness of English bravado can be seen in this scene, together with the note of time passing, and regret.

> 'We'll give Europe a good strong line. Europe is waiting for a speech from Rex.'
> 'And a speech from me.'
> 'And a speech from me. Rally the freedom-loving peoples of the world. Germany will rise; Austria will rise. The Czechs and the Slovaks are bound to rise.'
> 'To a speech from Rex and a speech from me.'
> 'What about a rubber? How about a whisky? Which of you chaps will have a big cigar? Hullo, you two going out?'
> 'Yes, Rex,' said Julia. 'Charles and I are going into the moonlight.'
> We shut the windows behind us and the voices ceased; the moonlight lay like hoar-frost on the terrace and the music of the fountain crept in our ears; the stone balustrade of the terrace might have been the Trojan walls, and in the silent park might have stood the Grecian tents where Cressid lay that night.
> 'A few days, a few months.'
> 'No time to be lost.'
> 'A lifetime between the rising of the moon and its setting. Then the dark.'
>
> (*Brideshead Revisited*)

The Second World War did not stimulate the enormous explosion of major writing produced during and after the First World War. Among the reasons for this is the fact that, for the first time, many more of the soldiers who fought in the First World War were able to record and write home about their experiences. The Second World War was much more dominated by the broadcast media: the cinema, both for information and for escapist entertainment, and the radio, which allowed direct contact with what was happening on the war front around the world. The major novels about the war, such as Waugh's *Sword of Honour* trilogy, or Charles Morgan's Resistance novel *The River Line* (1949), often take a slightly distanced, ironic standpoint, rather than the deeply involved and involving narrations found in the prose centred on the First World War.

The River Line is a novel of intrigue and betrayal, both personal and public, set among workers in the French Resistance. It brings together a thrilling plot, a love triangle, and major moral issues to make a disturbing and compelling story. Rarely does an apparent thriller touch on such profound questions as *The River Line*. In this conversation, destiny and responsibility are under discussion, in relation to the war in Europe.

'Responsibility within our destiny?' he repeated. 'Will you translate? Destiny's a difficult word for me.'

'You went westward across the Atlantic,' she answered, 'then westward across your own continent; others followed, not of English blood, from every nation of the world, to become American, away from their first homes; always westward, away from Europe and her struggles and confusions. It was like the consistent movement of a great salmon up-river. Now geographically there is no further to go; now spiritually there is no further to go – *that* way. The time has come to return, as it comes to the salmon. Destiny, which sent you out, is drawing you back again.'

'And responsibility?'

'For democracies – desperately hard. First: to know what it is and where it lies – from day to day, from hour to hour.'

'Next?'

'To accept it – rather than bread and circuses. Hardest of all: to require others to accept it. There are no exemptions. Democracy is not an almshouse, even for the common man.'

'And then?'

'To act – in time. Having acted, rightly or wrongly, not to regret but to pay. Having paid, not to ask the price back. In action – above all, in thought – not to wish to have it both ways.'

ORWELL

It was a bright cold day in April and the clocks were striking thirteen.

(George Orwell, *Nineteen Eighty-four*)

In any age there is a tension between the desire for a stable order and the challenges to that stability. Hamlet talked of these forces as 'the form and pressure of the time', insisting that 'the purpose of playing' theatre, and by extension all art, was to illustrate this. The opening sentence of George Orwell's *Nineteen Eighty-four* (1949) shows how time and security in the immediate post-war world could have a semblance of normality, but with something distinctly odd: clocks do not strike thirteen. The time, echoing Hamlet again, was 'out of joint', or not functioning as it normally did.

George Orwell (real name Eric Blair) had come to prominence in the 1930s, commenting incisively on the social and political world of his day in such non-fiction works as *Burmese Days* and *Down and Out in Paris and London*, as well as the novels *A Clergyman's Daughter* and *Keep the Aspidistra Flying* (all published between 1933 and 1936). *Burmese Days* (1934), *Down and Out in Paris and London* (1933), and the novels *The Road to Wigan Pier* (1937) and *Coming Up for Air* (1939) are studies in social realism, using traditional forms of the novel and blending documentary fact with artistic invention in original ways. *Keep the Aspidistra Flying* (1936) is a study in how the dominance of a powerful cultural elite inhibits the central character, Gordon Comstock, and prevents him from becoming a successful artist. Needless to say, Comstock triumphs in the end, but the relationship between class, money, and culture remains a significant concern, despite the positive ending. The novel is semi-autobiographical in its examination of a working-class author's struggle to get his work published.

> Gordon gazed at the thing with wordless hatred. Perhaps no snub in the world is so deadly as this, because none is so unanswerable. Suddenly he loathed his own poem and was acutely ashamed of it. He felt it the weakest, silliest poem ever written. Without looking at it again he tore it into small bits and flung them into the wastepaper basket. He would put that poem out of his mind for ever. The rejection slip, however, he did not tear up yet. He fingered it, feeling its loathly sleekness. Such an elegant little thing, printed in admirable type. You could tell at a glance that it came from a 'good' magazine – a snooty highbrow magazine with the money of a publishing house behind it. Money, money! Money and culture! It was a stupid thing that he had done. Fancy sending a poem to a paper like the *Primrose*! As though they'd accept poems from people like *him*. The mere fact that the poem wasn't typed would tell them what kind of person he

was. He might as well have dropped a card on Buckingham Palace. He thought of the people who wrote for the *Primrose*; a coterie of moneyed highbrows – those sleek, refined young animals who suck in money and culture with their mother's milk. The idea of trying to horn in among that pansy crowd! But he cursed them all the same. The sods! The bloody sods! 'The Editor regrets!' Why be so bloody mealy-mouthed about it? Why not say outright, 'We don't want your bloody poems. We only take poems from chaps we were at Cambridge with. You proletarians keep your distance?' The bloody, hypocritical sods!

During the Second World War, Orwell worked a great deal for BBC radio, as did his fellow novelist, J.B. Priestley. Orwell's broadcasts are among the most characteristic of his works, their analysis of English-ness and British cultural identity continuing to be keynote texts on the subject.

Orwell is probably best known throughout the world as a political satirist, his allegory *Animal Farm* having been translated into over forty languages. He once admitted: 'where I lacked a political purpose I wrote lifeless books.' Although Orwell was a committed socialist, much of the power of his work derives from his horror of the night-mare of Stalin's Russia and from his longing for a pre-First World War England free from totalitarianism, mass unemployment, and the threat of mass destruction as a result of world war. In 1936, Orwell joined the Republicans in the Spanish Civil War in their fight against the dictatorship of General Franco. Orwell was wounded in 1937 and returned to England, convinced of the decency of the ordinary Span-ish people, a hater of all forms of totalitarianism, and disillusioned with Communism.

Animal Farm (1945) is a parable of the corruption of Communism. It narrates the revolution of farm animals against the exploitation of their masters and how the pigs take over as the new masters. Gradually, however, the pigs create a dictatorship over the other animals which is worse than anything they experienced in the days when the farm was run by human beings. The animals in this political fable correspond to real historical characters – for example, Napoleon the pig is based on Josef Stalin – and the whole book becomes a satire on Communist Russia. The final commandment, which is changed from the original

'All animals are equal' to 'All animals are equal but some animals are more equal than others', has become a famous catchphrase and expresses Orwell's own cynicism.

Orwell's novel *Nineteen Eighty-four* is based on the tendencies in the Europe of the 1930s and 1940s which most disturbed him. It is a vision of the ways in which totalitarian governments, whether right-wing or left-wing, can destroy individual thought and feeling. In the novel, the totalitarian state is supported by a secret police force and every citizen can be observed and heard at all times through a tele-screen. The head of state, Big Brother, the dictator who watches everybody, has to be obeyed. A special official language, 'Newspeak', is created by the state. It is deliberately limited in its expression so that people are limited in their thoughts and ideas. History is rewritten and can be changed to suit the needs of the present rulers. The hero of the novel, Winston Smith, rebels, but he is captured and tortured into submission. This bleak vision of dictatorial power allied to modern technology has made *Nineteen Eighty-four* one of the most famous twentieth-century novels.

> It was a bright cold day in April, and the clocks were striking thir-teen. Winston Smith, his chin nuzzled into his breast in an effort to escape the vile wind, slipped quickly through the glass doors of Victory Mansions, though not quickly enough to prevent a swirl of gritty dust from entering along with him.
> The hallway smelt of boiled cabbage and old rag mats. At one end of it a coloured poster, too large for indoor display, had been tacked to the wall. It depicted simply an enormous face, more than a metre wide: the face of a man of about forty-five, with a heavy black moustache and ruggedly handsome features. Winston made for the stairs. It was no use trying the lift. Even at the best of times it was seldom working, and at present the electric current was cut off during daylight hours. It was part of the economy drive in prepar-ation for Hate Week. The flat was seven flights up, and Winston, who was thirty-nine and had a varicose ulcer above his right ankle, went slowly, resting several times on the way. On each landing, opposite the lift-shaft, the poster with the enormous face gazed from the wall. It was one of those pictures which are so contrived that the eyes follow you about when you move. BIG BROTHER IS WATCHING YOU, the caption beneath it ran.

Inside the flat a fruity voice was reading out a list of figures which had something to do with the production of pig-iron. The voice came from an oblong metal plaque like a dulled mirror which formed part of the surface of the right-hand wall. Winston turned a switch and the voice sank somewhat, though the words were still distinguishable. The instrument (the telescreen, it was called) could be dimmed, but there was no way of shutting it off completely.

Orwell also achieved a lasting reputation as an essayist and as a master of English prose style. He wrote on a wide range of subjects, and his commentaries on English society, culture and politics still have topical relevance more than fifty years after they were written, with themes such as colonialism, popular culture, and tradition recurring. Many of these essays were broadcast on radio. With J.B. Priestley, Orwell was one of the first important writers to achieve a reputation through the broadcasting media.

DIALOGUE NOVELS

One feature of the modern novel which takes on great importance is the use of dialogue and conversation, especially when presented with very little narratorial intervention. This gives the reader the challenge of filling out the 'script' – it is minimalism of quite a different kind from the interior monologue mode. Novelists as different as Evelyn Waugh in the 1920s and 1930s and Iris Murdoch in the 1960s and 1970s (see pages 439 and 523) have experimented with this kind of speech presentation. Arguably the most innovative and successful exponents of the 'conversational novel' are Henry Green and Ivy Compton-Burnett.

Green and Compton-Burnett both had privileged backgrounds, and their novels share a highly distinctive approach to prose, especially to dialogue. Compton-Burnett's novels and their chilling and disturbing picture of family and society are largely written in dialogue, and depict an enclosed world somewhere before the First World War. The author's own life had been severely marked by the war and her novels examine how 'nothing is so corrupting as power' in the deceptively calm and well-ordered society that E.M. Forster also portrays. But Ivy

Compton-Burnett's novels are more frequently compared with post-Impressionism in painting than with the literary fashions of the time. They exude an air of gloom and crime, from the first *Pastors and Masters* (1925) to later work such as *Manservant and Maidservant* (1947), which recalls the corruption expressed in Dickens's *Our Mutual Friend*, and *The Present and the Past* (1953). She reveals, as T.S. Eliot put it in another context, 'the skull beneath the skin' of late Victorian and Edwardian society.

> 'Poor Father!' said Toby suddenly.
> 'Yes, poor Father!' said Cassius. 'Toby's poor old father! But Toby loves him, doesn't he?'
> 'No. Oh, yes, poor Father!'
> 'And Father loves his Toby.'
> 'Yes, dear little boy.'
> 'And dear Father.'
> 'No, dear Toby.'
> 'Will you two elder boys come for a walk with me?'
> 'Yes,' said Guy, approaching him.
> 'We were going for a walk with Mother,' said Fabian.
> 'Well, which do you want to do?'
> 'Well, we had arranged to go with Mother.'
> 'Did you know that, Guy?' said Cassius.
> 'No. Yes. Yes, I did.'
> 'You are as bad as Toby.'
> 'Or as good,' said Flavia. 'They both tried to give you what you wanted.'
> 'Oh, I don't want scraps of attention thrown to me, as if I were a beggar in their path. What a way to regard their father! I am content to go my own way, communing with myself. It may be the best companionship.'
> 'It is the only kind we have,' said Henry.
> 'Oh, you have found that, have you? You are in the same plight as I am. Alone amongst many, as is said.'
>
> (*The Present and the Past*)

Henry Green is also renowned for his dialogue, but in a less restricted and more wide-ranging context. He was from a family of rich industrialists and his novel of the factory floor, *Living* (1929), is a vivid example of his style: colloquial, ungrammatical, and highly revealing about both the workers and the managerial class. This extract brings together Green's working environment and his gift for representing speech.

> Four o'clock. And now men in iron foundry in Mr Dupret's factory straightened their backs for the fan had been started which gave draught in cupola in which the iron was melted. They stood by, two by two, holding ladles, or waiting. Craigan and Joe Gates and Dale stood by their box ready weighted for pouring and in which was mould of one of those cylinders. They said nothing. They had worked all day. The foreman stood near by. They waited. Gates was tired. Foreman stood near by. Mr Craigan threw spade to ground then which had been in his hand. He went up to foreman.
> 'I know there's been three wasters off this job better'n nobody. But man I'll tell you this'ns a good un.'
> 'Right you are Phil' foreman said and moved away. 'I can't sleep at night. I took tablets last night' he told himself 'but did I sleep, no I did not. No I didn't sleep,' he said to himself, moving away.
> 'Dirty bleeder, what call 'as 'e to stand waiting for?' said Mr Gates muttering.
> 'You talk more'n is natural in a man' Mr Craigan said and then no word was said between them not while their eight ton of metal was carried them in a ladle by the crane or after when they fed their casting, lifting their rods up in the risers and letting them down, and again and again.

Many of his novels have one-word titles such as *Caught* (1943), *Loving* (1945), and *Nothing* (1950), which takes the form to new heights, being written almost entirely in dialogue form. *Party Going* (1939), in which a group of rich young people are delayed at a railway station by fog, has been read as a highly symbolic examination of the decline of the class system. His style has been described as combining the upper class with the demotic, which is an accurate reflection of his concerns. In many ways Green's novels mark the transition between the novel of upper- and middle-class concerns and the working-class novels of the 1950s.

THE MID-CENTURY NOVEL

Samuel Beckett is better known for his contribution to modern drama, but novels such as *Murphy* (1938), *Watt* (1953), and his trilogy – *Molloy* (1955), *Malone Dies* (1956), and *The Unnamable* (1958) – are examples of fiction reduced to a minimum of action, in limited settings, and often focused on a single consciousness. In terms of technical invention and experimentation Beckett is very much an heir to the Modernists, and to James Joyce in particular.

Beckett wrote most of his works first in French, then rendered them into English, aiming thereby to reach a purer simplicity of style, a distance from Irish or English traditions. *Malone Dies*, the second volume of Beckett's trilogy, famously opens with an interior monologue:

> I shall soon be quite dead at last in spite of all . . .

and the trilogy ends, 240 pages later,

> . . . it will be the silence, where I am, I don't know, I'll never know, in the silence you don't know, you must go on, I can't go on, I'll go on.
>
> *(The Unnamable)*

L.P. Hartley's trilogy of Eustace and Hilda – *The Shrimp and the Anemone, The Sixth Heaven*, and *Eustace and Hilda* (1944–47) – is similar in aim to Forrest Reid's writing (see page 442) but less rich in its range. *The Go-Between* (1953) is the work of Hartley's which most clearly catches the sense of loss and regret which the novelists of the 1920s to 1940s share. Its opening line has become almost proverbial: 'The past is another country. They do things differently there.'

Part of the nostalgic recall of 'golden' or mythical days after the Second World War led to the success of Laurie Lee's autobiographical account of his country childhood in *Cider With Rosie* (1959). This was one of the consistently biggest-selling books of the last decades of the century, largely because of its arcadian ideal of golden summers and happy innocence, long since lost. A further volume of memories – *As I Walked Out One Midsummer Morning* (1969) – takes the author off to the Spanish Civil War of the late 1930s; and the golden days are gone for ever, except in written memoirs.

After 1945, Christopher Isherwood (like W.H. Auden) remained an American citizen. His writing, like Aldous Huxley's, came to be influenced by Eastern thinking, as exemplified in *Vedanta for the Western World* (1945). Isherwood persisted with a semi-autobiographical strain in his writings, which might usefully be termed 'auto-fiction': from the pre-war *Lions and Shadows* (1938), to *Down There on a Visit* (1962), *A Single Man* (1964), and the directly autobiographical, openly gay, *Christopher and His Kind* (1977).

With Angus Wilson, several strands of the late twentieth-century novel meet. An academic, he wrote about personal relationships in the upper middle classes with a range of characters, often in middle age, who try to balance the conflicting demands of the world they live in: the wild and the tame, the past and the present, conformity and difference – he takes particular care to integrate homosexual characters into his fictional landscapes. Wilson is a writer of satiric wit and sharp social observation. He looks back to Dickens, and gives the novel in the second half of the twentieth century some of its most carefully constructed and richly layered investigations of the human comedy. *Hemlock and After* (1952) was his first novel, followed by *Anglo-Saxon Attitudes* (1956), *The Middle Age of Mrs Eliot* (1958) and *No Laughing Matter* (1967), all contributing to his growing reputation over the following three decades. *No Laughing Matter* is perhaps his most ambitious novel, moving between parody and realistic family saga, exploring narrative techniques and psychological nuances in an intricate tapestry. *Setting the World on Fire* dates from 1980. As a critic, Wilson wrote studies of Dickens and Kipling, and a significant examination of English writing and his own creative processes, in *The Wild Garden* (1963).

V.S. Pritchett's achievement in the short-story form is close to Sean O'Faolain's. Two collected volumes were published in 1982 and 1983. Written during a career which covered more than fifty years, they display a wide range of social observation and irony. Pritchett is generally acknowledged to be the most accomplished English short-story writer this century, and also has a notable reputation as a travel writer and essayist. He is that almost extinct phenomenon in late twentieth-century Britain: a 'man of letters', who has made a career from writing in a number of forms, including criticism, without ever working in an academic institution.

The 1950s tried to classify a generation of writers as 'angry young men', citing Osborne's character Jimmy Porter as the voice of his generation. Perhaps Colin Wilson's *The Outsider* (1956), however, is more clearly representative of the disaffection of a young generation seeking to establish its identity by breaking away from class constraints and social norms. In its portrayal of alienation, this novel stands slightly apart from the trends it was identified as representing and is more of an existential than a social novel.

Provincial novels such as John Wain's *Hurry on Down* (1953), with its university-educated lower-middle-class hero, are, in effect, a continuation of the preoccupations of H.G. Wells, in early twentieth-century novels like *Kipps* (1905), although the characters have moved slightly up the social scale. The novels and stories of Alan Sillitoe explore provincial life and the problems of working-class characters. *Saturday Night and Sunday Morning* (1958), although firmly anchored in its time, remains a highly effective novel of working-class frustration, and the story *The Loneliness of the Long-Distance Runner* (1959) offers a lasting image of rebellion, all the more effective for its first-person narration.

> Walking the streets on winter nights kept him warm, despite the cold nocturnal passions of uprising winds. His footsteps led between trade-marked houses, two up and two down, with digital chimneys like pigs' tits on the rooftops sending up heat and smoke into the cold trough of a windy sky. Stars hid like snipers, taking aim now and again when clouds gave them a loophole. Winter was an easy time for him to hide his secrets, for each dark street patted his shoulder and became a friend, and the gaseous eye of each lamp glowed unwinking as he passed. Houses lay in rows and ranks, a measure of safety in such numbers, and those within were snug and grateful fugitives from the broad track of bleak winds that brought rain from the Derbyshire mountains and snow from the Lincolnshire Wolds. Grey rain splashed down drainpipes and ran across pavements into gutters, a sweet song whether you heard it sitting by a coal fire, or whether you trod through it while on your way to pub, cinema, or the clandestine bed of an uncontrite and married woman. Arthur held his cigarette down in the darkness, caught in a game of fang-and-claw with a dangerous hand of aces, feeling, after each successful foray between Brenda's or Winnie's sheets, that one pitch night the royal flush would stay at the bottom of the pack.
>
> *(Saturday Night and Sunday Morning)*

Sillitoe has not been tempted away from the subject matter he knows best, and has thus remained the most consistent of the new writers of the 1950s – his semi-autobiographical *Raw Material* (1972) is particularly vivid.

The hero of John Braine's *Room at the Top* (1957) is a small-town provincial opportunist, Joe Lampton, prepared to compromise love for money and social progress. Identified as another 'angry young man', he is more of the traditional ambitious hero, who will achieve success at all costs. This he did in *Life at the Top* (1962), in which Braine in some ways echoes the model of Dickens's *Great Expectations*, taking his hero through material success to spiritual and emotional disillusionment.

AMIS, FATHER AND SON

Kingsley Amis's *Lucky Jim* (1954) was one of the most successful novels of its time, anticipating the later campus novel in having as its central character a university lecturer of lower-middle-class origins. The comedy of the novel has been surpassed, but its effect remains considerable; subsequently Amis tried to create similar shock effects, with greater or lesser success. His best novels tackle difficult themes, usually with comedy. *Ending Up* (1974) and *The Old Devils* (1986) are studies of old age, close in theme, but not in style or sympathy, to Muriel Spark's *Memento Mori* (1959). *Stanley and the Woman* (1984) concerns mental disturbance; in *The Riverside Villas Murder* (1973) Kingsley Amis successfully imitates the classic early twentieth-century detective story; in *The Folks That Live on the Hill* (1990) his characters live in Hampstead, that area of London where many writers and media people settled. In many ways this novel shows the progress of the angry young man of the 1950s to the reactionary of the 1980s, with little left to fight for, but with much to complain about! Some critics have accused Amis of misogyny and right-wing attitudes. However, there is little doubt that he was a major figure in continuing the tradition of social and comic realism which is one of the English novel's enduring strengths. *You Can't Do Both* (1994) and *The Biographer's Moustache* (1995) were Amis's final works.

Kingsley Amis's son Martin is a quite different writer from his father, and the differences are more than simply generational: Martin Amis's language and subject matter are violent, reflecting the collapse of the established class system which the 'angry young men' of the 1950s could rail against. A parallel moral and spiritual violence in his novels has caused some shock – when his second novel *Dead Babies* (1975) was published in paperback, the publishers preferred to retitle it *Dark Secrets* in order not to cause offence. *London Fields* (1989) – its very title is paradoxically ironic – is an exploration of morality and murder in the television age: its central character Keith Talent can be seen as a symbol of the 1980s in the way that Jim Dixon in *Lucky Jim* was of the 1950s: he is amoral, fascinated by television ('TV!' is his favourite adjective of praise), and prepared to do anything to achieve fame and fortune by appearing on television as a darts player.

> I sidled up, placed my coin on the glass (this is the pinball etiquette), and said, 'Let's play pairs.' In his face: a routine thrill of dread, then openness; then pleasure. I impressed him with my pinball lore: silent five, two-flip, shoulder-check, and so on. We were practically pals anyway, having both basked in the sun of Keith's patronage. And, besides, he was completely desperate, as many of us are these days. In a modern city, if you have nothing to do (and if you're not broke, and on the street), it's tough to find people to do nothing with.
>
> (*London Fields*)

Perhaps more than any other English-born novelist, Martin Amis has forged a 'new' language: going beyond 'old' language, using new rhythms, incorporating American English, street English, and minority dialect Englishes, to give a representation of some of the range of Englishes spoken in England at the end of the twentieth century.

Time's Arrow (1991) is an experiment in the backward narration of time, returning from the present to the Holocaust of the Second World War. Martin Amis is a daring experimenter in form, style, and content, capable of shock, and capable of clear-sighted social observation. *Money* (1984) and *Success* (1978) may come to be seen as among the most revealing novels about the preoccupations of the 'yuppie' 1980s. Amis has said that one of his favourite themes is 'men doing each other down', and this reaches its high point in *The Information* (1995), where two novelists – one a popular success, the other an ambitious failure – are pitted against each other in their careers, relationships and destinies.

LANGUAGE NOTE
City slang

Different styles of language can reveal different facets of personality and the various speaking styles of narrators, in particular, can reveal much about their attitudes and their ways of seeing. A distinctive speech style can also mark off a narrator or character from the position of the author, allowing a viewpoint to emerge which can be critical of the character, satirising the life-style which the character represents or allowing more ironic perceptions to emerge.

In the following extract from Martin Amis's novel *Money* (1984) the main character, John Self, is revealed through a distinctive use of contemporary slang, in this case a specifically urban speech style cultivated by the character who inhabits a world of decaying social and cultural fabrics:

> In LA, you can't do anything unless you drive. Now I can't do anything unless I drink. And the drink-drive combination, it really isn't possible out there. If you as much as loosen your seatbelt or drop your ash or pick your nose, then it's an Alcatraz autopsy with the questions asked later. Any indiscipline, you feel, any variation, and there's a bullhorn, a set of scope sights, and a coptered pig drawing a bead on your rug.

Slang words and phrases abound. 'Pig' is a term used for a policeman; 'rug' is American slang for a toupee; 'coptered' is a word derived from helicopter; 'drawing a bead' means to take aim and, additionally, we need to know that Alcatraz is a famous prison in San Francisco Bay in California.

The city slang in *Money* is used to create a sense of place which is both every metropolitan city and nowhere. John Self's speech is fast-paced, slick, witty, often obscene, and at the same time constitutes a kind of linguistic litter of easy joking phrases which matches the empty character of Self and the urban wasteland he inhabits. The urban decay is matched by a verbal decay in which communication beyond a small, knowing in-group is not seen to matter.

Slang is generally regarded as below the level of educated speech and is sometimes a way in which less educated characters can be presented to a reader. An important function is, however, to mark membership of a group and to underline in-group identity. Slang is often looked down on as vulgar;

yet it cuts across all social classes and everyone has access to slang in one form or another.

In Thomas Dekker's *The Gulls Hornbook* (1609) the main character uses a well-developed and personalised urban slang and there is a gap between author and character; but the gap here allows much more markedly ironic effects to be created. The title of the book derives from Elizabethan school books (bound between plates of horn) which aim to teach appropriately polite behaviour for the guidance of those seeking to enter polite society, usually in London. Dekker's book offers advice which is sometimes ironically the opposite of what polite society would wish; the word 'gull' itself carries two main meanings: 'fop' and 'dupe or fool'. The book is linguistically rich in the city street slang of cosmopolitan Elizabethan London. Here there is a description of how a 'Gallant' should conduct himself in a playhouse:

> If you can (either for love or money) provide yourself a lodging by the water side: for above the conveniencie it brings, to shun Shoulder-clapping, and to ship away your Cockatrice betimes in the morning it adds a kind of state unto you, to be carried from thence to the staires of your Play-house: . . .

> Now sir if the writer be a fellow that hath epigrammd you, or hath had a flirt at your mistris, or hath brought either your feather or your red beard, or your little legs etc on the stage, you shall disgrace him worse than by tossing him in a blancket, or giving him a bastinado in a Taverne.

Here slang words and phrases include: 'Cockatrice' meaning whore; 'Shoulder-clapping' meaning arrest; 'bastinado' (from Spanish) meaning a beating. The city slang also helps to create a racy spoken idiom which contrasts with the kinds of formal language associated with pretentiousness.

Representations of the city in literature have taken many different forms but there is a tradition of depicting urban speech styles in literature in English over several centuries. Other rich examples include Dekker's *The Shoemaker's Holiday*, Jonson's *Bartholomew Fair*, Middleton's *A Mad World, My Masters*, several novels by Dickens (*Oliver Twist*, in particular), and, in the twentieth century, most notably Anthony Burgess's novel *A Clockwork Orange* where a mechanical teenage slang reflects a world without human feeling.

GOLDING

William Golding's first published novel *Lord of the Flies* (1954) is his best-known work, though some of his later writing has a complexity and resonance deserving greater attention. *Lord of the Flies* became an immediate worldwide success, reflecting post-war disillusionment with human nature; indeed, Golding has explained that the novel originates from his experience of human evil during the atrocities of the Second World War.

Lord of the Flies describes how a group of English schoolboys, who are shipwrecked on a desert island, degenerate into savages. With a combination of fantasy and psychological realism, Golding shows how, when the constraints of civilisation are removed, the essential nature and original sin of man is revealed. Although based on the dynamics of a group of schoolboys, the novel confronts profound questions of innocence, evil and the fall of man, casting doubt on the possibility of any lasting social progress.

> The slanting sticks of sunlight were lost among the branches. At length he came to a clearing in the forest where rock prevented vegetation from growing. Now it was a pool of shadows and Ralph nearly flung himself behind a tree when he saw something standing in the centre; but then he saw that the white face was bone and that the pig's skull grinned at him from the top of a stick. He walked slowly into the middle of the clearing and looked steadily at the skull that gleamed as white as ever the conch had done and seemed to jeer at him cynically. An inquistive ant was busy in one of the eye sockets but otherwise the thing was lifeless.
> Or was it?

Like George Orwell's *Nineteen Eighty-four* and Aldous Huxley's *Brave New World*, Golding's *Lord of the Flies* has been described as a dystopia. Instead of showing an optimistic picture of a perfect world, Golding depicts a pessimistic picture of an imperfect world. The novel is also a revision of the desert-island myth originating in *Robinson Crusoe* and continued in *The Coral Island* (1857), a novel for boys written by R.M. Ballantyne. Ballantyne shows individuals who maintain their humanity in uncivilised places because of their innate goodness and virtue. Golding's novel shows the reverse.

Golding explores related themes of 'decline and fall' in several other major novels. In *The Inheritors* (1955) he examines the evolution of man in primeval times and shows how one tribe supersedes another because it can perform more evil deeds. This is also one of the major explorations of the relationship between language, thought and action in the modern novel. *Free Fall* (1959) explores man's capacity to choose between good and evil, demonstrating how the fall from grace is not predetermined but a matter of human choice. Other novels include *The Spire* (1964), and *Rites of Passage* (1980), the first of a trilogy which takes the narrative of an early sea journey to the Antipodes as a metaphor for the progress of the soul. The trilogy was completed with *Close Quarters* (1987) and *Fire Down Below* (1989).

In 1983 William Golding was awarded the Nobel Prize for Literature. He is in the great tradition of the storyteller, and is not afraid to point up a moral truth while keeping the reader entertained. His final work, the posthumously published, nearly complete *The Double Tongue* (1995) opens up new territory (a female narrator as central character, an ancient Greek setting) and confirms Golding as one of the great explorers of myth, and of how truth and myth interrelate. All his works contrast human potential and the reality of human achievement. As the 'goddess' of his final novel wonders, watching herself being presented to the world *as* a goddess, by Ionides, a cynic and atheist:

> I suppose we all change. I had believed in the Olympians, all twelve of them. How much did I believe now, after years of hearing Ionides inventing speeches for me? How much after years of inventing them myself? How much after years of remembering that the god had raped me, years of part-belief, of searching for a proof that all I had believed in was a living fact and if twelve gods did not live on that mountain, they did in fact, in real fact, live somewhere, in some other mode, on a far greater mountain? It was too much for me. I did not speak out but kept silent, veiling my head completely.

Golding's fictional search for a truth of humanity ties in with A.S. Byatt's idea of a post-Darwinian attempt in fiction to replace or substitute the faith that has been put in question.

FOWLES AND FRAYN

The novels of John Fowles use magic, artifice, the very self-conscious fictionality of writing to carry on that search. They have enjoyed great academic and commercial success in Europe and the USA: they are intellectual, self-conscious experiments with theme and form, and carry warnings for the reader about the nature of the reading experience. In *The French Lieutenant's Woman* (1969), for example, the Victorian novel form is used and then questioned while the reader is left with a choice between two possible endings. For many readers and critics, this is the post-Modern novel *par excellence*; innovative while using traditional form, subversive while telling a good tale, authoritative but questioning. It is, indeed, a major achievement, although its playing with time is not wholly original, and the 'alternative ending' idea had been tried out as early as Thackeray's *The Newcomes* in the 1850s.

Fowles's *The Magus* (1966, revised 1977) plays with reality and myth on a Greek island. Fowles is not associated with any one trend in the novel, moving with ease from the psychological thriller of imprisonment and obsession, in *The Collector* (1963), through short stories, to the Laurie Lee-like evocation of growing up in *Daniel Martin* (1977). Always a writer to keep the reader from falling into preconceptions, his narrator in *A Maggot* (1985) asserts:

> . . . the retrospective we have of remembering and asserting a past age by its Popes, its Addisons and Steeles, its Johnsons, conveniently forgets how completely untypical artistic genius is of most human beings in any age, however much we force it to be the reverse.

Like Golding, Fowles uses time to great effect, clashing past with present across centuries or across a character's memories. His novels play with the imagination of the *reader*, just as much as they revel in the creative imagination of the writer. What remains, therefore, can divide critical opinion more than almost any other writer. Fowles can be fascinating and irritating at the same time – a treasure trove for academics, an enjoyable storyteller for those who simply want to read for pleasure. Several of his works have been filmed, notably *The French Lieutenant's Woman*, for which the dramatist Harold Pinter wrote the screenplay.

Michael Frayn – novelist, playwright, translator and philosopher – brings a note of comedy and philosophy together in such novels as *The Trick of It* (1989), *A Landing on the Sun* (1991), and *Now You Know* (1992). He is one of the most wide-ranging intellectual writers of his time, tempering the intellectual challenge of his ideas (on the nature of artistic creation and love, for instance, in *The Trick of It*) with some of the brightest comedy in the modern novel. His farce *Noises Off* (1982) enjoyed huge worldwide success in the theatre, and was later filmed.

NOVEL SEQUENCES

Several writers in English have followed the French writer Marcel Proust in writing multi-novel sequences, of which Proust's *A la recherche du temps perdu* (1912–27) – in English, *Remembrance of Things Past* – is the prime example (1922–31, revised 1981 and again in 1992 by the poet D.J. Enright with the title *In Search of Lost Time*). Anthony Powell set his twelve-novel sequence *A Dance to the Music of Time* (1951–75) among the upper and middle classes, following a wide range of characters, including the hero Nicholas Jenkins and the ambitious Kenneth Widmerpool, through the period leading up to the Second World War and its aftermath. It presents a panorama of the period, echoing Evelyn Waugh at some stages, but preserving its clear-sighted view of the unfolding tragedy despite frequent passages of high comedy.

The same vein of tragedy and comedy distinguishes Simon Raven's sequence of ten novels *Alms for Oblivion* and seven novels in *The First Born of Egypt* (both series begun in the 1960s), whose strong narratives frequently touch on homosexual themes and give a more rumbustious view of the times they describe than Powell's sequence. C.P. Snow's sequence *Strangers and Brothers* (1940–70) consists of eleven novels following the career of Lewis Eliot in his progress from a humble provincial upbringing, like the author's own, through Cambridge University to a law career and politics. Snow was a scientist, and his famous lecture *Two Cultures and the Scientific Revolution* (1959) was an important attempt to break down barriers between 'the two cultures', the scientific and the humanist. Less rich in characterisation and humour than Powell or Raven, Snow gives a documentary rather than a panoramic view of life in the cloisters of academe and the corridors of power.

Olivia Manning's *The Balkan Trilogy* and *The Levant Trilogy*, which were published between 1960 and 1980, observe the Second World War in Romania, in Greece, and the Middle East, through the eyes of newly married Harriet Pringle. They are novels of character, with a wide range of British expatriate characters. *The Battle Lost and Won* (1978), the second volume of *The Levant Trilogy*, also gives one of the most vivid and harrowing accounts of a battle (Alamein) to be found in any modern novel.

THE CAMPUS NOVEL

In Britain, the academic as novelist tends towards comedy. After Angus Wilson, Malcolm Bradbury (in the same university) and David Lodge continued to explore society in novels which introduce a new element of reader awareness and intellectual subject matter to literature. The setting is often a university or college, the characters often academics or writers. The problems, however, remain the standard concerns of love and money, religion (especially in Lodge, who is arguably the most significant Catholic novelist of his generation), and success or failure. Where, in earlier writing, success was seen in social terms, here the scope is often reduced to academic success, with the result that there is a profoundly comic questioning of the whole ethos of success, failure, career, and private life, extending well beyond the English university system. Both writers use their experience of travel and other cultures to examine the ambivalence of the attitudes of the newly educated mass readership which has benefited from the worldwide expansion in education and social awareness. Both are also highly aware literary critics, particularly strong on Modernism and modern critical theory.

Bradbury, in *Stepping Westward* (1965), and Lodge in *Changing Places* (1975), its sequel *Small World* (1984), and *Paradise News* (1991), are attracted to the United States as a vehicle to examine contrasts between British and American cultures. Bradbury, notably in *Rates of Exchange* (1983) and *Doctor Criminale* (1992), also examines changing relationships within Europe, an indication, as with many other writers, that the English novel's horizons are as England-centred as they were a century before. A new internationalism is very much a keynote of modern fiction.

One of the most vital of all examinations of British/American academic and social contrasts is found in *The Battle of Pollock's Crossing* (1985) by J.L. Carr. He is a writer who cannot be easily classified – he has written about the end of the First World War *(A Month in the Country*, 1980), about frustration and helplessness *(A Day in Summer*, 1963), and about the Second World War *(A Season in Sinji*, 1967), moving from highly localised concerns and settings, to personal drama against a wider background. *The Battle of Pollock's Crossing* is very close to the concerns of Bradbury and Lodge in its portrayal of the clash of cultures, and reveals Carr as one of the less widely recognised but consistently rewarding writers of his time.

> George's foreignness rated close attention for, in those far-off days, Europe was many days distant and only veterans of the 1917 Expeditionary Force had set eyes upon an Englishman. So he was examined with unusual interest, his weight and height calculated, the unsuitability of his clothing marvelled at, his love-quotient assessed, the unjustly high salary with which the School Board had lured him from his green and pleasant island bitterly censured.
>
> 'I shall depart from custom and call upon George G. Gidner to say something,' the Superintendent announced – doubtless to reassure his subordinates that they were not to be burdened with a language problem. No public institution ever before had invited George to address it, but he managed to mutter his delight at finding himself in Palisades and that he was enjoying the unusually settled weather. This drew mild applause and a man in the next seat shook his hand warmly, saying, 'Hadlestadt (Speech and Debate) – say, that was some declam. My old Grandpa was an Englishman from the city of Norfolk and, because of this, I could follow every word you uttered. Am not so aged as you may be supposing. Thirty-two in fact, no more than. My hair I lost being required unjustly to sponsor the Junior Prom four years in a row. Have much hope it will come again: my wife don't like me this way.'

Carr is a male writer who usually works on the kind of small scale that Jane Austen cultivated to perfection.

EXCELLENT WOMEN

Anita Brookner and Barbara Pym have both been compared to Jane Austen, but could hardly be more different from each other. Barbara Pym's novels explore the note of sadness in spinster life in small parishes, often in cities, and touch upon emotional depths in what always seems to be a rather comic setting. From *Excellent Women* in 1952 to the tragic *Quartet in Autumn* in 1977, Pym explores a world that is small in scale, but profound in its emotional impact.

> On my way home, I was just passing the vicarage when Julian Malory came out.
> 'Congratulations,' I said. 'I've just heard your news.'
> 'Thank you, Mildred, I wanted you to be among the first to know.'
> . . .
> 'And I had better hurry into Evensong,' said Julian, for the bell had now stopped. 'Are you coming or do you feel it would upset you?'
> 'Upset me?' I saw that it was no use trying to convince Julian that I was not heartbroken at the news of his engagement.
> 'No, I don't think it will upset me.' Perhaps the consciousness that I was already an orphan and not likely to be a widow was enough cause for melancholy, I thought, as I put my basket down on the pew beside me.
>
> *(Excellent Women)*

Anita Brookner's characters are also frequently spinsters, and her novels of loneliness and pain are among the most classically refined treatments of the theme of solitude in the twentieth century. They continue in some ways from the novels of May Sinclair, but with more of a sense of submission than challenge. Hers is not a world of comedy, or of the consolation of religion, but of solitary struggle and renunciation. Her characters are usually single women of intelligence but restricted means, and her examination of dependency and the rejection of dependency is a marked contrast to traditional feminine 'love-story' fiction. *Hotel du Lac* (1984) is her best-known novel, but *A Friend from England* (1987), *Lewis Percy* (1989) with its male protagonist, *Fraud* (1992), and *Incidents in the Rue Langier* (1995) show her constantly refining and deepening her art as an observer of the darker sides of human isolation.

There was within Sally a kind of readiness for friendship, but for a friendship based essentially on amusement. She was not inclined to, or stimulated by, acts of altruism. Blanche could see that her feeling for Elinor was based on a certain spasmodic camaraderie; and that was why the child, to a limited extent, trusted her. What the child resisted was precisely her pleasure-loving insubstantiality, her desire to be diverted, her readiness to accept the next invitation, her availability. Blanche saw that as a mother, or as a putative mother, Sally was indeed nymph-like; she would provide a temporary shelter for the little girl and educate her to a sort of viability, but it would be senseless to demand of her further guidance. At the age of seven Elinor would be expected to be self-reliant; at the age of ten she would be given her sexual education; at the age of fifteen or sixteen she would be expected to have left home for good. Her refusal to speak was based on her foreknowledge of this fate.

(A Misalliance, 1986)

The strange and haunting novels of Barbara Comyns, such as *Who Was Changed and Who was Dead* (1954), which is about the effects of the plague on a village, deserve mention here too. They combine the everyday with the macabre in a very individual way, and *Our Spoons Came from Woolworth's* (1950) and *Mr Fox* (1987) foreshadow the treatment of poverty found later in the novels of Beryl Bainbridge (see page 520).

Jean Rhys is one of the same generation as May Sinclair (see page 435), but only began writing in Paris in the 1920s. She was born in Dominica in the Caribbean, and it is there that her best-known novel, *Wide Sargasso Sea*, is set. It was published in 1966, after a gap of almost thirty years from her early works, such as a study of Bohemianism in Paris, and the novels *After Leaving Mr Mackenzie* (1930), *Voyage in the Dark* (1934), and *Good Morning, Midnight* (1939). *Wide Sargasso Sea* is set in the 1830s and takes the character of 'the madwoman in the attic': Mrs Rochester in Charlotte Brontë's *Jane Eyre*. The character has come to be seen by feminist critics as something of a symbol of misunderstood female suffering in marriage, and it is this aspect of the character which Jean Rhys explores, with great psychological penetration and sympathy. She depicts the loneliness and bitterness of unhappy marriage in many of her works, and her uncompleted autobiography, *Smile*

Please (1979), reveals how much personal suffering was transmuted into the art of her novels and stories.

Elizabeth Bowen's pre-war novels were often set in Ireland. Later she became known for her short stories. Her best stories are set during the Second World War, and give what Angus Wilson described as 'acute perceptions of the first impact of ever present danger and death upon a great city'. Bowen's *Collected Stories* were published in 1980.

This was three years before the collected stories of William Trevor appeared in a single volume. He is a writer from Ireland who has much in common with Elizabeth Bowen. These stories, and his later volume *The News from Ireland* (1986), return frequently to Ireland, but their subject matter is loneliness, love and loss, rather than a concentration of specifically Irish problems. Trevor's novel *Fools of Fortune* (1983) achieves a similar balance of sympathy to Bowen's classic pre-war Irish novel, *The Last September* (1929), moving the story backwards and forwards in time to show the period of the Troubles, and its consequences more than half a century later. *Felicia's Journey* (1994) is the most successful of Trevor's later novels on these themes.

A.S. Byatt is a former academic whose novels are rich in historical, literary, and mythical allusion. *The Virgin in the Garden* (1978) portrays Yorkshire at the beginning of the new Elizabethan age in 1952, and is an ambitious contrast of the sixteenth-century Elizabethan age with the present. Its sequel *Still Life* (1985) continues the rich observation of England in the 1950s. *Possession* (1990) brought Antonia Byatt wide acclaim, winning several major prizes. Once more it contrasts past and present, with the search for a Victorian poet's past illuminating a contemporary university researcher's life and times.

> Somewhere in the locked-away letters, Ash had referred to the plot or fate which seemed to hold or drive the dead lovers. Roland thought, partly with precise post-modernist pleasure, and partly with a real element of superstitious dread, that he and Maud were being driven by a plot or fate that seemed, at least possibly, to be not their plot or fate but that of those others. And it is probable that there is an element of superstitious dread in any self-referring, self-reflexive, inturned post-modernist mirror-game or plot-coil that recognises that it has got out of hand, that connections proliferate apparently at random, that is to say, with equal verisimilitude, apparently in

response to some ferocious ordering principle, not controlled by conscious intention, which would of course, being a good post-modernist intention, *require* the aleatory or the multivalent or the 'free', but structuring, but controlling, but driving, to some – to what? – end. Coherence and closure are deep human desires that are presently unfashionable. But they are always both frightening and enchantingly desirable. 'Falling in love', characteristically, combs the appearances of the world, and of the particular lover's history, out of a random tangle and into a coherent plot.

Byatt's *Angel and Insects* (1992) explores the background to Tennyson's *In Memoriam* in the context of travel, scientific discovery and inherited wealth. It became a successful film. Byatt's *Babel Tower* (1996) follows on from *The Virgin in the Garden* and *Still Life*. It is an ambitious, long, rather sprawling novel about the 1960s. The period is seen as a time of social and intellectual revolution, but in particularly English terms. It is a novel about words and ideas and contains within it a novel called 'Babbletower' which is prosecuted for obscenity in an echo of the *Lady Chatterley's Lover* trial. Byatt takes post-Modern pastiche, intertextuality and contemporary history to new heights in this extended romp through recent fashions, preoccupations and intellectual concerns.

Similarly, *Restoration* (1989) by Rose Tremain examines a crucial period in English social and intellectual history to reinterpret it in the light of contemporary concerns and attitudes. The novel's central character, Robert Merivel, is a Falstaffian figure whose progress towards a deeper understanding of himself and others is charted with wit and profundity. *Restoration* has established Rose Tremain as an important writer who will almost certainly continue to make a significant contribution to the English novel.

The flowering of writing by women authors since the 1950s has produced a very wide range of achievement. P.D. James, Ruth Rendell, Margaret Yorke, and Joan Smith have taken the crime novel to new heights of psychological and social observation. Since Agatha Christie and Dorothy L. Sayers (see page 399), it is remarkable that the most significant crime writers have been women. What was considered by some to be an inferior genre now stands with equal importance beside mainstream writing – such novels as *Innocent Blood* (1980) and *Devices and Desires* (1989) by P.D. James, *A Small Deceit* (1991) and *Evidence to*

Destroy (1987) by Margaret Yorke, *A Dark-Adapted Eye* (1986, under the pseudonym Barbara Vine), *Live Flesh* (1986), and *Talking to Strange Men* (1987) by Ruth Rendell clearly rise above the constraints of the genre. Their male counterparts, such as Julian Symons, Colin Dexter and Reginald Hill, are similarly adept in their use of crime plots to explore questions of human good and evil.

MURIEL SPARK AND OTHERS

The role of women as inferiors or outsiders in society has concerned many writers. Muriel Spark's female characters cover a wide range, from the Edinburgh schoolmistress in *The Prime of Miss Jean Brodie* (1961) to *The Abbess of Crewe* (1974), a highly satirical fantasy on religious and political themes, and *The Girls of Slender Means* (1963), a tragi-comedy set in 1945, echoed in the more recent *A Far Cry from Kensington* (1988). Many of Spark's works observe similar landscapes to Barbara Pym's: the lonely inhabitants of London's bed-sitters, solitude and attempts at self-sufficiency are recurring themes. Like Pym, she handles religion with comic acerbity.

> 'Good morning, Mrs Hawkins.' This was the Cypriot next door cleaning his bicycle as I left for the office. 'Good morning, Marky.' That was the name he demanded to go by; he was decidedly embarrassed when any of us made to call him Mr something. It was to be a while before I found myself being addressed by my first name. This certainly coincided with the time when I was moved to lose my great weight. Then, I invited people to call me Nancy, instead of Mrs Hawkins as I was to everyone in that summer of 1954, when I went to my office in the morning partly by bus and partly across Green Park, whether it rained or whether it didn't.
> Suicide is something we know too little about, simply because the chief witness is dead, frequently with his secret that no suicide-note seems adequate to square with the proportions of the event. But what we call suicidal action, an impetuous career towards disaster that does not necessarily end in the death of the wild runner, was going on at the Ullswater Press. That spring I had reason to reflect on Martin York's precipitous course towards a heavy reckoning when I heard on the wireless – it was May 6th – that the runner, Roger Bannister, had beaten the world record: a mile in under four

minutes. Martin York, I reflected, was going faster than that, he was going at something like a mile a minute, even when he sat hemmed-in, drinking whisky.

(*A Far Cry from Kensington*)

Spark observes her characters with wit and empathy, taking in all ages and classes – *Memento Mori* (1959) is unusual in being a comedy about old age. Her pastiche thriller *The Driver's Seat* (1970) is a particularly adventurous experiment in form: her middle-aged, unmarried heroine leaves her job, her flat, her normal life, and goes on a journey. On this simple framework, Muriel Spark hangs a comic, threatening, intriguing tale, which asks as many questions as it answers, and takes the reader as close to the edge as any of the fictions of Beckett.

Spark is Scottish, Edna O'Brien Irish. Both use the idea of young girls seeking their independence in the big city as an image of the search for identity and a role in life. O'Brien's *Country Girls* trilogy (1960–63) combines modern female sensuality with the difficulty of escaping from an Irish Catholic tradition. This background is well evoked in the later novel *A Pagan Place* (1971).

A similar exploration of a young female character has continued with Jeanette Winterson's novels in the 1980s and 1990s. She is one of the most outspoken of lesbian writers. In *Oranges Are Not the Only Fruit* (1987) she treats female homosexuality and religious oppression; in *Written on the Body* (1992) the gender of the narrator is not clear, opening up the question of sexual identity. *Art and Lies* (1994) and the essays in *Art Objects* (1995) take such questions on to a wider level of discussion, centring on the role and position of the artist as the new century beckons.

An interest in sexuality and gender, poor backgrounds, and black humour, distinguish the novels of Beryl Bainbridge, whose style is spare, allusive, and wry. *The Bottle Factory Outing* (1974) shows her empathy with the deprived, and such novels as *Injury Time* (1977) and *An Awfully Big Adventure* (1990) confirm her insight into characters who react against the frustrations of their backgrounds, but who never in fact progress very far. *Every Man for Himself* (1996) is a novel concerning the sinking of the *Titanic* in 1912, which was the subject also of a famous poem by Thomas Hardy, *The Convergence of the Twain* (in *Satires of Circumstance*, 1914).

MARGARET DRABBLE

In the novels of Margaret Drabble, however, the characters do make progress, as indeed their author did. From a provincial background, the characters of her 1980s trilogy – *The Radiant Way* (1987), *A Natural Curiosity* (1989), and *The Gates of Ivory* (1991) – achieve success in the new liberated society of London. The achievements and failures of the characters mirror the progress of England in a series of novels which reflects the 'state of the nation' more deliberately than almost any other recent fiction. Drabble's earlier novels, from *A Summer Bird-Cage* (1963) to *The Ice Age* (1977), go further than Edna O'Brien in examining how character and society are interdependent, with female concerns emerging as central. Drabble's writing has been unfairly classed as 'the Hampstead novel', but her novels have ranged from Yorkshire to Cambodia, from Southern Italy to Stratford, and her social and political terms of reference are among the widest of her generation. Drabble's work displays a sense of the social concerns which has been a strong characteristic of the English novel since the eighteenth century, but which is found in only a few writers today. Angus Wilson shares it too, and it is no coincidence that Margaret Drabble is his biographer.

> When Liz Headleand woke on the first day of 1980 and found herself in bed with her husband, she remembered instantly the scene of the night before, and wondered how she could ever have been so upset by it. Lying there at seven o'clock in the morning, suddenly wide awake, as was her manner, it seemed to her quite obvious that she and Charles should get divorced: it had surely long been inevitable, and if Charles really wanted to marry that woman (or had he perhaps been *joking?* – no, perhaps not), well then, let him. She had plenty to get on with meanwhile. Why ever had she taken it so badly? She had an embarrassed recollection of having burst into tears, of demanding to know how long the affair with Henrietta had been going on. I must have been tired, she said to herself reasonably. Tired and a little drunk. All those people in the house. That's what it was.
>
> (*The Radiant Way*)

LESSING, HILL AND WELDON

Doris Lessing's stature as one of the major writers of her time has been assured for many years. Her early stories and novels move between Africa and England, and her five-volume *Children of Violence* series, beginning with *Martha Quest* (1952), is perhaps the richest of the novels of self-discovery of a young woman in post-war years. *The Golden Notebook* (1962), a long novel which combines the political, the social, and the psychological, to narrate the disintegration of a personality, is one of the most highly regarded novels of the 1960s. Since then Lessing has moved on to examine middle age, in *The Summer Before the Dark* (1973), other worlds in the *Canopus in Argos: Archives* series (five novels, 1979–83), and 'inner space', continuing the exploration of the disintegration of a character, in *Briefing for a Descent into Hell* (1971) and *The Memoirs of a Survivor* (1974). Political and committed, Lessing is sometimes not as accessible as some of her contemporaries, but she has expanded the boundaries of fiction, especially of fictional and psychological realism, in ways which will continue to be important.

Susan Hill is not easily classified as a novelist. In the 1970s her novels and short stories of isolation and torment brought her considerable critical acclaim, as she tackled unusually risky themes for a young woman novelist: the relationship between two soldiers in the First World War in *Strange Meeting* (1971), which presages J.L. Carr's *A Month in the Country*; a young widow's desolation in *In the Springtime of the Year* (1974); schoolboy violence in *I'm the King of the Castle* (1970); and a wide range of themes in short stories, such as *A Bit of Singing and Dancing*, a vivid picture of the loneliness of old age. When she married, Susan Hill stopped writing fiction for some time, but *Air and Angels* (1991) marks a return to the novel. Using fragmented time and multiple points of view, it is a moving and original love story.

Fay Weldon is probably the closest of present-day writers to the tradition of May Sinclair, Rebecca West, and Rosamund Lehmann. Her novels, which she refuses to describe as feminist, are concerned with every aspect of female experience, including the (apparently) humdrum experience of being a wife and mother. In making this kind of 'normal' life the material for her numerous novels, Weldon has widened the focus of the modern novel with considerable humour and insight. But her concerns are not limited to explorations of downtrod-den women; she is particularly acute on the difficulty of women's relationships with other women, and on the insecurities of the settled life. From *The Fat Woman's Joke* (1967), through *Down Among the Women* (1971) and *Female Friends* (1975), she expands her range, achieving con-siderable acclaim with *Praxis* (1978), *Puffball* (1980), and *The Life and Loves of a She-Devil* (1983), this last being perhaps her best-known work, having been both televised and filmed. *Letters to Alice on First Reading Jane Austen* (1984) is an enthusiastic defence of the novel and its tradi-tions in the television age, in the form of letters to a student who is beginning to study English literature.

> I speak as one studied by Literature Departments (a few) and in Women's Studies courses (more). . . .

Weldon goes on to affirm the vitality of reading and writing through-out history, whether it is studied or not. 'Fiction,' she asserts, 'on the whole, if it is good, tends to be a subversive element in society', and this is just as true of the fiction of Jane Austen as it is of Fay Weldon herself, or of the addressee of the letters, Alice, who by the end of the book is not only a reader, but a writer too.

IRIS MURDOCH

Iris Murdoch is one of the most significant figures in the modern English novel. A philosopher by training, her later novels have been accused of being rambling philosophical treatises rather than fiction, but they are a clear extension of her prolific output, which has always shown a more philosophical tendency than is usually found in English literature. From the comedy of *Under the Net* (1954), through the novels of relationships from *The Bell* (1958) to *A Fairly Honourable Defeat* (1970), she was extending her range, in terms of character, dialogue, and setting. *The Nice and the Good* (1967) is one of her earliest novels to deal with questions of philosophy and intertextuality. Her novels have always involved a search, complications within a set of relationships, and, very often, a powerful mysterious influence, usually a dominant character, who influences all the others.

> Axel came out, removing his jacket and rolling up his white shirt

sleeves. The sun made gold in his dark hair. 'I've asked the *patron* to bring us a carafe of wine out here straight away. I'm just going up to look at the room. You stay here.'

Simon sat down at the table. The *patron* bustled over wearing purple braces, with a carafe and two glasses. '*Merci.*' Simon poured out some wine and tasted it. It was excellent. The serrated green leaves extended above him, before him, their motionless pattern of angelic hands. The air quivered with warmth and a diffusion of light.

Simon thought, it is an instinct, and not a disreputable one, to be consoled by love. Warily he probed the grief which had travelled with him so far, and he felt it as a little vaguer, a little less dense. His thoughts of Rupert now reached back further into the past, to good times which had their own untouchable reality. He drank some more wine and raised his face to the dazzle of the sun among the leaves and felt his youth lift him and make him buoyant. He was young and healthy and he loved and was loved. It was impossible for him, as he sat there in the green southern light and waited for Axel, not to feel in his veins the warm anticipation of a new happiness.

(A Fairly Honourable Defeat)

Born in Ireland, Iris Murdoch took up the theme of the 1916 Easter uprising in *The Red and the Green* (1965) but it stands outside the usual run of her work, although the central character does have to search for his own identity between Irish and English loyalties. From *The Black Prince* (1973) and *A Word Child* (1975), through *Henry and Cato* (1976), this search takes on a more self-consciously literary tone, with, for example, *Hamlet* and *The Tempest* lying behind the novels as a reference point. *The Sea, The Sea* (1978) is the best known of Murdoch's novels of this period, and won the major literary award, the Booker Prize, which brought it to a wider public. In her novels of the 1980s, such as *Nuns and Soldiers, The Philosopher's Pupil, The Good Apprentice, The Book and the Brotherhood*, and *The Message to the Planet*, the search is more obviously a philosophical one: questions of good and evil, art and life, power and impotence dominate the discussion in *The Green Knight* (1993). More than many novelists, Iris Murdoch revels in intertextuality – using or alluding to a wide range of other writings in her own works. Her terms of reference are vast, covering literature, philosophy, and history, and this gives her works an unusual depth and richness of resonance which few others (A.S. Byatt is one) can match.

All Murdoch's writing – she has also written philosophical works – tends towards the affirmation of good, despite the endemic weakness of humanity, and its temptations to move towards evil. They are novels of the human condition seen in terms of weakness and strength, portrayed in thought rather than action, with a high regard for spiritual values.

INTERNATIONALISM

Anthony Burgess's Malayan trilogy – *Time for a Tiger, The Enemy in the Blanket, Beds in the East* (1956–59) – was written when he had been given only a few months to live – but he survived and went on to produce an enormous range of novels, textbooks, musical works, and journalism. *A Clockwork Orange* (1962) is probably his best-known work, portraying a violent dystopia, with its own slang and high-tech authoritarianism. It was memorably filmed in the 1970s. His Enderby trilogy (1963–74) follows its hero around the world in search of success in literature and love; *Earthly Powers* (1980) combines real characters and history with the fictional memoirs of a first-person narrator with a massive ego, and rewrites the twentieth century in his image. *A Dead Man in Deptford* (1993) is a historical recreation of the life and death of Christopher Marlowe. Burgess's final novel, *Byrne* (1995), is a comic epic written in verse, exploring the nature of creativity through the frustrations and successes of a first-person narrator who is not too far removed from Burgess himself.

In the late 1970s and 1980s a distinctive group of younger writers emerged who had been associated with Malcolm Bradbury at the University of East Anglia. Many share a concern with non-English experience. Kazuo Ishiguro was born in Japan, and Ian McEwan spent part of his childhood outside Britain. Other writers who do not belong to this group, such as William Boyd and Salman Rushdie, were also raised outside the United Kingdom, and Julian Barnes has set his novels in countries as diverse as France and Bulgaria. This echoes the sense of an enlarging world, an ever-growing internationalism, which emerged in writing at the end of the nineteenth century, when 'outsiders' like Shaw and Conrad began to make their mark on English literature.

The decline of the British Empire had been a subject for fiction since Kipling: E.M. Forster's *A Passage to India* is arguably the major novel on the theme in the first half of the century. The novels of Paul Scott, from *Johnnie Sahib* (1952) to *The Raj Quartet* (*The Jewel in the Crown*, 1966; *The Day of the Scorpion*, 1968; *The Towers of Silence*, 1971, and *A Division of the Spoils*, 1975), take the concern with India up to and beyond independence: *Staying On* (1977) is almost a requiem for the colonial era, seen through the eyes of survivors of its modern decline.

The Siege of Krishnapur (1973) by J.G. Farrell was, like *Staying On*, a major prizewinner. It is a detailed historical reconstruction of the events of the Indian Mutiny and it was followed by *The Singapore Grip* (1978) which analysed another of the fatal blows to the British Empire, the fall of Singapore to the Japanese in the Second World War.

J.G. Ballard, one of the widest ranging of modern novelists, exploring science fiction, urban nightmare, and memories of childhood in his many novels, similarly handles the fall of Shanghai to the Japanese, as witnessed by a young boy in *The Empire of the Sun* (1984). This takes Farrell's historical documentation further, making the boy's experience almost a rite of passage of the century: history becomes personal, as it has continued to do in the writing of the new generation.

'INSIDERS' FROM 'OUTSIDE'

The present wave of 'outsiders', or non-Anglo-Saxon writers, covers a wide range of themes, but many share a concern with how the past has influenced and continues to influence the present.

Kazuo Ishiguro's *The Remains of the Day* (1989) examines loyalties, mistaken or otherwise, between the upper classes and a servant in the 1930s, and his *A Pale View of Hills* (1982) brings Japan into English literature in an examination of the post-war consciousness of guilt.

From an Anglo-Chinese background, Timothy Mo examines cross-cultural and post-colonial stresses, both in England – with the black comedy *Sour Sweet* (1982) – and in the Far East, with the huge, historical *An Insular Possession* (1986) and with contemporary politics and war in *The Redundancy of Courage* (1991). Mo had to publish *Brownout on Breadfruit Boulevard* (1995) himself: it was seen by publishers and most critics as badly written, scatological, and ill-conceived. It could alternatively be seen as a graphic, highly satirical critique of third-world corruption.

Its inventive representation of local Englishes, especially in the Philippines, is an exciting contribution to the awareness of new Englishes in modern writing.

> There seemed even more giggling among the girl students than usual, if this was possible. (Carla hadn't thought it was.) She still found it very charming. They were so much more accessible than American teenagers. 'Hey, what's with you guys?'
> More giggling. 'You're not jealous, Mrs Giolitti?'
> 'Jealous? I don't understand. You mean of youth and beauty?'
> Further tittering. 'Maybe you're a fan of Roel Escarcinas? You know him?'
> 'Never heard of him, honey. He's a Philippine heart throb?'
> 'Maribeth going to bed with him every night, mum. She hugs his photo when she goes to sleep.' Screams of protest.
> Carla entered into the spirit of things, light-hearted banter though her guts felt like lead. 'So what's the problem. Is Maribeth accusing me of seducing her picture?'
> 'No, mum. Maribeth can kiss Roel when he's coming here, day before yesterday.'

Salman Rushdie's novels move from realism to what has become known as magic realism. Rushdie was born in India, and the subcontinent is the setting of what many regard as his best works – *Midnight's Children* (1981), about the children born as India passed to self-rule in 1947, and *Shame* (1983) – which are deeply concerned with the culture, politics, and religion of that vast land and its neighbours. Rushdie recalls an oral tradition of storytelling applied in a modern context, evoking sights, sounds, and smells of the world in realistic terms, side by side with the spinning of wild fantasies and improbable tales.

Rushdie is at the same time the most controversial novelist of his time and the most critically acclaimed. *The Satanic Verses* (1988) gave rise to charges of blasphemy, and the Iranian government issued a *fatwa* (death sentence for religious reasons) against the author. The controversy over this – possibly his least exciting novel – has often overshadowed the very real achievements of his major novels. In *Midnight's Children* Rushdie uses the image of chutney, one jar per year, to indicate the glorious rich mixture that is India. Towards the end of the novel, the narrator reflects:

The process of revision should be constant and endless; don't think I'm satisfied with what I've done! Among my unhappinesses: an overly-harsh taste from those jars containing memories of my father; a certain ambiguity in the love-flavour of 'Jamila Singer' (Special Formula No. 22), which might lead the unperceptive to conclude that I've invented the whole story of the baby-swap to justify an incestuous love; vague implausibilities in the jar labelled 'Accident in a Washing-chest' – the pickle raises questions which are not fully answered, such as: Why did Saleem need an accident to acquire his powers? Most of the other children didn't . . . Or again, in 'All-India Radio' and others, a discordant note in the orchestrated flavours: would Mary's confession have come as a shock to a true telepath? Sometimes, in the pickles' version of history, Saleem appears to have known too little; at other times, too much . . . yes, I should revise and revise, improve and improve; but there is neither the time nor the energy. I am obliged to offer no more than this stubborn sentence: It happened that way because that's how it happened.

There is also the matter of the spice bases. The intricacies of turmeric and cumin, the subtlety of fenugreek, when to use large (and when small) cardamoms; the myriad possible effects of garlic, garam masala, stick cinnamon, coriander, ginger . . . not to mention the flavourful contributions of the occasional speck of dirt. (Saleem is no longer obsessed with purity.) In the spice bases, I reconcile myself to the inevitable distortions of the pickling process. To pickle is to give immortality, after all: fish, vegetables, fruit hang embalmed in spice-and-vinegar; a certain alteration, a slight intensification of taste, is a small matter, surely? The art is to change the flavour in degree, but not in kind; and above all (in my thirty jars and a jar) to give it shape and form – that is to say, meaning. (I have mentioned my fear of absurdity.)

One day, perhaps, the world may taste the pickles of history. They may be too strong for some palates, their smell may be overpowering, tears may rise to eyes; I hope nevertheless that it will be possible to say of them that they possess the authentic taste of truth . . . that they are, despite everything, acts of love.

Rushdie's reputation was fully restored with the publication of *East West* (1994) and *The Moor's Last Sigh* (1995). Where *Midnight's Children* took the historical moment of Indian independence, *The Moor's Last Sigh* takes the departure of the Moors from Spain in the fifteenth century as its starting point: what is lost and what is gained are explored in a panoply of fantasies, tales, realism, and magic, which reaffirm Rushdie's place in modern fiction, and show him returning to the height of his creative powers.

V.S. Naipaul is the grand old man of British literature – yet he was not even born in Britain; born in Trinidad, he settled in England in 1955, but is a constant traveller. Naipaul is perhaps the clearest example of the changing cultural identity of Britain, of English, and of literature in English. From *The Mystic Masseur* (1957) to *A Way in the World* (1994) he has written about the processes of history, power, and culture. He moves with ease from high social comedy, such as the glorious Caribbean novel, *A House for Mr Biswas* (1961), to deeply serious examinations of colonialism and third-world problems, such as *A Bend in the River* (1979), set in Africa and redolent with echoes of Joseph Conrad. Naipaul won the Booker Prize for *In a Free State* (1971) and was awarded the first David Cohen British Literature Prize, in 1983. This moment from *A Bend in the River* shows something of his perception and the clashes *within* a post-colonial society:

> Everyone had been waiting to see what the President would do. But for more than a fortnight the President had said and done nothing.
> And what the President said now was staggering. The Youth Guard in our region was to be disbanded. They had forgotten their duty to the people; they had broken faith with him, the President; they had talked too much. The officers would lose their stipend; there would be no government jobs for any of them; they would be banished from the town and sent back to the bush, to do constructive work there. In the bush they would learn the wisdom of the monkey.
> '*Citoyens-citoyennes*, monkey smart. Monkey smart like shit. Monkey can talk. You didn't know that? Well, I tell you now. Monkey can talk, but he keep it quiet. Monkey know that if he talk in front of man, man going to catch him and beat him and make him work. Make him carry load in hot sun. Make him paddle boat. *Citoyens! Citoyennes!* We will teach these people to be like monkey. We will send them to the bush and let them work their arse off.'

Caryl Phillips is seen by some critics as a young Naipaul. His subject matter is often identity and settlement, questioning state, culture, and even the flow of time, in historical and geographical terms. Phillips is West Indian by birth, British by upbringing, but universal in his concerns. Among his novels are *Crossing the River* (1993) and *A State of Independence* (1986).

Ian McEwan came to prominence with two volumes of vivid stories – *First Love, Last Rites* (1975) and *In Between the Sheets* (1978) – involving the kind of graphic revulsion that Martin Amis was also using in the mid-1970s though McEwan's prose is more detached than Amis's. When he moved on to the full-length novel he mined a vein which explores Europe's post-war heritage, and in *The Innocent* (1990) and *Black Dogs* (1992) he has related the nightmare of the cold war to present-day realities, bringing past and present together in an attempt to examine and assuage guilt while exploring a new post-cold war identity. His *The Child in Time* (1987) is also a novel of discovery after loss – about the kidnapping of a child, and the ensuing re-establishment of a life and marriage.

William Boyd made his name as a comic novelist with *A Good Man in Africa* (1981) and followed this by examining a marginal wartime episode in *An Ice-Cream War* (1982), American and British cultural differences in *Stars and Bars* (1984), the history of the twentieth century seen through the eyes of a self-absorbed maniacal film director – *The New Confessions* (1987) which is reminiscent of Burgess's *Earthly Powers* – and anthropology and truth, in *Brazzaville Beach* (1990). Boyd's concerns are huge, and his novels consequently run the risk of failure, but their narrative drive and humour carry them forward with great readability.

Rewriting and reinterpreting the past have been a major concern of recent novelists. Julian Barnes mockingly rewrites the history of the world in *The History of the World in 10½ Chapters* (1989) and reinterprets the life of the French novelist Flaubert in *Flaubert's Parrot* (1984). *Porcupine* (1992), published in Bulgaria a few weeks before it was published in Britain, traces the fall of Communism in a fictional country not too far from Bulgaria. Barnes has also written effective love stories – *Before She Met Me* (1982) and *Talking It Over* (1991) – which play with time and point of view in the search for elusive truths of the heart. *Cross Channel* (1996) returns to France; it is a collection of stories which show Barnes extending his range with humour, simplicity, and gentle cross-cultural perception.

Graham Swift and Nigel Williams are more concerned with English settings, but their subjects are no less wide-ranging. Swift's *Waterland* (1983) is set in the Fens of East Anglia and is a saga of family and growing up which involves history, and even the life cycle of the eel, in a rich and complex novel that is at the same time regional and universal. *Last Orders* (1996), which won the 1996 Booker Prize, is similarly complex and rewarding. It is again a study of a family, this time in London and Kent, preparing for a funeral. Swift plays with time, class, success and failure, in an ambitious novel which, like much of Peter Ackroyd's writing, uses careful local description to give a solid basis to his examination of changing values. Williams is a comic novelist, and his visions of suburban life are highly satirical manipulations of genre with social comedy and high farce, combining to give a highly pointed view of twentieth-century life, only equalled by the similarly irreverent Fay Weldon. *East of Wimbledon* (1993) is a neatly comic mystery and *Star Turn* (1985) a comic view of Britain before and during the Second World War, seen through the eyes of two boys from the East End of London.

Sebastian Faulks's fourth novel, *Birdsong* (1993), achieved great acclaim, being called 'quite simply one of the best novels written about war, and about the First World War in particular'. He recalls the poetry of Edward Thomas in his evocation of the local suffering caused by widescale events.

Some eighty years after the First World War, and more than fifty years after the Second World War, both wars remain favoured subjects and settings for contemporary writers. Pat Barker's trilogy – *Regeneration* (1991), *The Eye in the Door* (1993), and *The Ghost Road* (1995) – uses the First World War to explore the disrupting effects of the conflict on the individual soldier: class, identity and personal responsibility are key questions. The third novel in the trilogy won the Booker Prize in 1995.

Captain Corelli's Mandolin (1994) by Louis de Bernières is a novel about the German occupation of a Greek island. As with de Bernières's other novels, *Captain Corelli's Mandolin* combines 'magic realism' – both fantastic and eerily comic – with a deep concern for the pain inflicted by politics and politicians on innocent victims. Louis de Bernières is one of the few British writers to take South America on, in its own magic realist setting, in such novels as *The War of Don Emmanuel's Nether Parts* (1990), *Senor Vivo and the Coca Lord* (1991), and *The Troublesome Offspring of Cardinal Guzman* (1992). He writes long, well-told novels, to match his long titles, and is one of the best story-tellers among contemporary novelists.

The novels of Peter Ackroyd explore the worlds of literature, art, and culture: *The Last Testament of Oscar Wilde* (1983) purported to be by the great aesthete himself; *The Great Fire of London* (1982) was a cross-referential story based on a fictional film of Dickens's *Little Dorrit*. Ackroyd is also the biographer of William Blake, Charles Dickens, and T.S. Eliot, occasionally incorporating fictional moments into his biographies. His *Chatterton* (1987) is based on the 'marvellous boy' poet, and *Hawksmoor* (1985) moves between present and past as it explores the London of the great church architect. Ackroyd is the most London-centred of modern novelists, using history, culture, and intertextuality in a constant redefining and rediscovery of Englishness and identity. *The House of Doctor Dee* (1993) goes back to Elizabethan times; *Dan Leno and the Limehouse Golem* (1994) to late Victorian popular culture.

LANGUAGE NOTE
English, Scots and Scotland

The earliest systematic records of the Scots literary language date from the second half of the fourteenth century. By the late Middle Ages, Middle Scots had evolved as a separate variety and was as far removed from Old English as Middle English. During the Old English period, most of the people of Scotland spoke Celtic languages (mainly Gaelic) but the numbers speaking varieties of English increased considerably as many English noblemen, some of whom spoke Norman French, settled in Scotland, mainly in the southern areas bordering on Northumbria. Scotland was generally successful in resisting the territorial ambitions of English kings and, after the battle of Bannockburn in 1314, greater Scottish independence was reflected in the increasing use of Scots in the Scottish court, in Parliament, in the law and in educational institutions.

From the end of the fourteenth century to the beginning of the seventeenth century there was a flowering of literature in Scots, reaching its peak in the poetry of William Dunbar and Robert Henryson. The following lines from Dunbar's *Lament for the Makers* (Elegy for the Poets) illustrate that Scots is best seen as a variety of English, not as a dialect, nor as a separate language (the last line is in Latin):

> The stait of man dois change and vary,
> Now sound, now seik, now blith, now sary,
> Now dansand, mery, now like to dee;
> *Timor mortis conturbat me.*

> [The state of man does change and vary,
> Now sound, now sick, now blithe, now sorry,
> Now dancing merry, now seeming to die;
> The fear of death does trouble me.]

However, during the seventeenth and eighteenth centuries the power and prestige of Scots began to decline. In 1603 the Union of Crowns meant that a Scottish king was on the throne but his court was in London, and the Act of Union in 1707 meant that Scotland was administered from England and in English. Lowlands Scots (or 'Lallans') was kept alive in literature, in particular by Robert Fergusson, Robert Burns, and later by Sir Walter Scott. Scott, in particular, remained sensitive to the social and cultural differences between Scots and English and often in his fiction represents the use of Scots as marking warmth, intimacy, and a sense of identity, while by contrast English is represented as impersonal and cold. This literary movement has continued into the twentieth century and Scots English certainly exists as a separate variety of international English with its own distinctive pronunciation and vocabulary, though in grammar differences are not especially marked. For example:

Scottish English	*Standard Southern English*
I doubt she's not in	I expect she's not in
outwith	outside
wee	small
I'll not be going home	I won't be going home

Within Scots there are of course further variations, with many working-class speakers uttering the final sentence as 'I'll no be gaun hame'. And it is important not to forget that the separate and independent language of Gaelic is still maintained within many communities in the West of Scotland.

In modern literature Hugh MacDiarmid has promoted an internationally intelligible version of Scots, though it is in many respects invented rather than authentic; and Lewis Grassic Gibbon achieved similar effects in prose. Recently, varieties of Scots have given great vitality and inventiveness to contemporary Scottish fiction and writers have been generally successful in creating believable characters with their own clear identity who speak a created version of Scots which can be relatively readily understood by all readers of English, as the following extract from Irvine Welsh's novel *Trainspotting* illustrates:

> Whin the auld man shot the craw, ah managed tae cajole ma Ma intae giein us a couple ay her valium. She wis oan them fir six months after Davie died. The thing is, because she kicked them, she now regards hersel as an expert oan drug rehabilitation.

THE CONTEMPORARY SCOTTISH NOVEL

Alasdair Gray and James Kelman have in recent years contributed greatly to the revival of Scottish literature in the vernacular accents of Glasgow. Gray's *Lanark* (1981) is partly magic realism, partly social fantasy, perhaps best described as a phantasmagoria of writing and illustration, as outrageous as Blake, as inventive as Rushdie. Gray's later work can be equally zany, or, as in *Janine 1982* (1984), fairly straightforward storytelling. The prizewinning *Poor Things* (1992) looks at the medical profession in Victorian Scotland, and provides a comic critique of the age. The author himself describes it as 'the funniest book I have ever written'. He then goes on to say: 'it's also the most socialist, really . . . but people don't need to notice that.'

Gray's *Mavis Belfrage* (1996) continues his idiosyncratic progress with a series of stories linked by themes of alienation and loss of identity. Gray, as ever, provides his own cover design and page embellishments, making the presence of the creative writer felt at all stages of the book's production. He has given considerable impetus to a new wave of Scottish writing which has put Glasgow, and to a lesser extent Edinburgh, very much on the literary map of writing in the 1990s. His language is Scottish English, and his concerns are both realisitic (social problems, unemployment) and artistic (the nature of creative endeavour, critical attitude, the role of the artist).

The vitality and humour of Gray are found in many of the new generation of Scottish writers. Janice Galloway and Alison (A.L.) Kennedy have brought women's voices fully into the forefront of the recent flourishing of Scottish writing. Galloway, in *The Trick Is to Keep Breathing* (1989), uses her own training to describe vividly the mind of a woman living alone in a state of psychological collapse. In *Female Friends* (1994) her two heroines travel abroad (to France) in a search for adventure, reality and friendship. Galloway's short stories, in *Blood* (1991) and *Where You Find It* (1996), range through a spectrum of experience, often with undertones of psychological violence. A.L. Kennedy's stories, in *Night Geometry and the Garscadden Trains* (1990) and *Now That You're Back* (1994), share this undercurrent of violence and social concern. Her first novel *Looking for the Possible Dance* (1993) is a narrative of a train journey from Glasgow to London (literal and metaphorical references to trains recur in modern Scottish writing – perhaps because there seem to be fewer and fewer of them but also perhaps as a reversal of the positive images of trains as emblems of progress in the mid-Victorian novel). The journey is also one of memory, of the heroine's relationships and hopes for the future. The climax is among the most strikingly violent in modern women's writing. *So I Am Glad* (1995) continues to keep Alison Kennedy at the forefront of recent Scottish writing.

James Kelman's novels are unrelentingly naturalistic pictures of inner-city desolation, portrayed with a vivid humour and empathy. *The Bus Conductor Hines* (1984) was his first success, and *A Disaffection* (1989), about the frustration of a man on the edge of middle age, enjoyed wide acclaim. *Not Not While the Giro* (1983) is a collection of stories, which was followed by a second collection, *The Burn* (1991). Both Gray and Kelman are highly specific – many readers find the emphasis on local accents and setting daunting – but they represent a strong and imaginative voice handling themes of considerable importance. Jeff Torrington's *Swing Hammer Swing!* (1992), set in the poorest area of Glasgow, the Gorbals, attracted a lot of attention, and has been talked of as the ultimate Glasgow novel 'doing for Glasgow what Joyce did for Dublin'. While this sounds like an over-reaction, it does mean that the author, Jeff Torrington, will be closely watched as he follows this, his first novel, one that was some thirty years in the writing. James Kelman's *How Late It Was, How Late* (1994) won the Booker Prize, and perhaps marks the arrival of the Glasgow novel. It is a long monologue, famously full of violent language which depicts the isolation and blindness of one of society's victims, Sammy. Close to Beckett's novels in style, it has also evoked comparison with Kafka in its picture of frustration; but the music and humour of the language raise it from despair into an affirmation of survival, despite all the odds.

> Now he was chuckling away to himself. How the hell was it happening to him! It's no as if he was earmarked for glory!
> Even in practical terms, once the nonsense passed, he started thinking about it; this was a new stage in life, a development. A new epoch! He needed to see Helen. He really needed to see her man if he could just see her, talk to her; just tell her the score.
> A fucking new beginning, that was what it was! He got out of bed and onto his feet and there was hardly a stumble. The auld life was definitely ower now man it was finished, fucking finished.

Irvine Welsh's novel *Trainspotting* (1993) achieved huge popularity and cult status (also as a play and film) in the mid-1990s, despite being written in broad Edinburgh dialect (noticeably different from Kelman's Glaswegian). It is about a group of drug addicts, their pain and pleasure, and owes a great deal of its success to its accurate and sympathetic depiction of the concerns of a disaffected generation.

> Whin the auld man shot the craw, ah managed tae cajole ma Ma intae giein us a couple ay her valium. She wis oan them fir six months after Davie died. The thing is, because she kicked them, she now regards hersel as an expert oan drug rehabilitation. This is smack, fir fuck's sake, mother dear.
> I am tae be under house arrest.
> The morning wisnae pleasant, but it wis a picnic compared tae the efternin. The auld man came back fae his fact-finding mission. Libraries, health-board establishments and social-work offices had been visited. Research hud been undertaken, advice hud been sought, leaflets procured.
> He wanted tae take us tae git tested fir HIV. Ah don't want tae go through aw that shite again.
> Ah git up fir ma tea, frail, bent and brittle as ah struggle doon the stairs. Every move makes ma blood soar tae ma throbbing heid. At one stage ah thought that it wid just burst open, like a balloon, sending blood, skull fragments and grey matter splattering oantae Ma's cream woodchip.

The auld girl sticks us in the comfy chair by the fire in front ay the telly, and puts a tray oan ma lap. Ah'm convulsing inside anyway, but the mince looks revolting.
– Ah've telt ye ah dinnae eat meat Ma, ah sais.
– Ye eywis liked yir mince n tatties. That's whair ye've gone wrong son, no eating the right things. Ye need meat.
Now there is apparently a causal link between heroin addiction and vegetarianism.
– It's good steak mince. Ye'll eat it, ma faither says. This is fuckin ridiculous. Ah thought there and then about making for the door, even though ah'm wearing a tracksuit and slippers. As if reading ma mind, the auld man produces a set ay keys.
– The door stays locked. Ah'm fittin a lock oan yir room as well.
– This is fuckin fascism, ah sais, wi feelin.

Welsh's later works, *The Acid House* (1994), *Marabou Stork Nightmares* (1995), and *Ecstasy* (1996), continue in a similar vein but with a broader range of locales and experiences. *Marabou Stork Nightmares* takes the reader inside the mind of a man in a coma. It relates his experiences and recollections from childhood in Scotland and South Africa through sexual and drug-related traumas to a conclusion of consider-able ambiguity between life and death, past, present, and future. In many ways Welsh tries to encapsulate in his novels the experience of alienation of the younger generation of the 1980s and 1990s, which is perhaps why his novels have achieved some kind of cult status. Cults often go out of fashion quicker than they came in, but Irvine Welsh's graphic use of language marks a significant broadening of the scope of local English in the context of a new generation of writers and new subject matter. Like many writers before him, he forges a new English for the stories he has to tell.

George Mackay Brown's novels are largely set in his native Orkney Islands, the birthplace also of Edwin Muir, and are concerned with the lives of the fishing people in Hamnavoe, which is Stromness. *Greenvoe* (1972) re-creates a week in the life of the village, intertwining past and present in a way that recalls the poetry of George Crabbe. Mackay Brown is also a poet and short-story writer, and was influenced and encouraged by Muir but, unlike him, decided to return to his native islands for his inspiration. *Magnus* (1973) goes into the history of the islands, showing the influences of folklore, the Norse sagas, history, and legend in the culture of one of the northernmost areas of British culture. *Beside the Ocean of Time* (1994) is a story of a Viking boy who is reborn in several centuries.

Allan Massie is one of the liveliest Scottish novelists writing today. His range has covered Ancient Rome in *Augustus* (1986) and *Tiberius* (1987), Scottish history in the John Buchan mode in *The Hanging Tree* (1990), and novels which explore the related themes of guilt and responsibility in the context of the Second World War, *The Sins of the Father* (1991) and *A Question of Loyalties* (1989). *Change and Decay In All Around I See* (1978) is one of the most indicative titles in modern fiction!

Iain Banks is also a prolific Scottish novelist with a wide range of styles and subjects, from science fiction to pop. *Espedair Street* (1987) is one of the very few novels to use the world of pop music successfully to examine modern solitude, success, and values. *The Wasp Factory* (1984) is an obsessive fantasy which aroused both critical revulsion and acclaim. *Feersum Endjun* (1994) continues Banks's fantastic vein, using a wonderful kind of Scots Internet language which works phonetically:

> Thas thi trubl wif sparos; they got a veri limitid tenshun span & r inclind 2 go witterin on 4 ages b4 they get 2 thi poynt, always flutterin off @ tanjints . . .

THE CONTEMPORARY IRISH NOVEL

Of modern Irish novelists, Brian Moore is probably the most significant of the older generation. His early novels such as *The Lonely Passion of Judith Hearne* (1955), are set in Belfast and *The Emperor of Ice-Cream* (1965) uses the bombing of that city as its background. Moore moved to Canada, then California, and his later works exploit similar tensions on a more international scale. *I Am Mary Dunne* (1968) uses Molly Bloom's monologue in *Ulysses* as a starting point for a woman's search for her true identity, and *Catholics* (1972) shows the author's constant concern with problems of Catholicism. Moore's more recent novel *The Colour of Blood* (1987) is set in an imaginary 'Eastern bloc' country with a cardinal as the central character. With David Lodge, Moore is one of the few writers to explore this subject throughout his work. He returned to an Irish setting with *Lies of Silence* (1993).

The voice of Ireland and, in particular, working-class Dublin has reached a worldwide audience through the works of Roddy Doyle. His novels are bleakly comic descriptions of working-class life in Dublin and are frequently told through conversations. *The Commitments* (1988) is about a white band trying to make its name singing black American music; *The Snapper* (1990) is about the Rabbitte family's reactions to a daughter's pregnancy; and *The Van* (1991) is about a 'mobile' chip shop van as a solution to the problem of unemployment. These novels, known as the Barrytown Trilogy – from the area of Dublin in which they are set – were all made into successful films.

The comic tone takes on a more serious note in *Paddy Clarke Ha Ha Ha* (1993) which won the Booker Prize, and *The Woman Who Walked Into Doors* (1996). Paddy Clarke is a 10-year-old schoolboy and the story follows his own views of his parents' marital break-up. In *The Woman Who Walked Into Doors*, the story is told by a semi-literate alcoholic woman, Paula Spencer, and traces her own marital difficulties. At the end her husband turns out to be a murderer as well as a wife-beater.

Doyle's huge popular success has also brought controversy: he is accused of being uncompromisingly negative about lower-class life in Ireland, but his social observation, authentic dialogue and portrayal of modern Irish humour in increasingly desperate circumstances mark him out as the true successor of Sean O'Casey and Flann O'Brien.

ENDINGS AND BEGINNINGS

Bruce Chatwin was very much an outsider. A traveller in both the physical and spiritual sense, he explores regions of the world and of human sensibility which other writers never even approached. His best works are evocations of travel with the heightened response of the imaginative writer, as in *The Viceroy of Ouidah* (1980), based on the slave-trade in Dahomey (Benin), and *In Patagonia* (1977) which continues the long tradition of the voyage of wonder started by Mandeville in the fourteenth century. Chatwin's novels *On the Black Hill* (1982), set in the Wales more closely associated with the poetry of R.S. Thomas, and *Utz* (1988), set in Eastern Europe, are studies of resilience and survival, a theme which resonates through *The Songlines* (1987), which traces the invisible pathways of aboriginal culture in Australia.

Trade means friendship and co-operation; and for the Aboriginal the principal object of trade was song. Song, therefore, brought peace. Yet I felt the Songlines were not necessarily an Australian phenomenon, but universal: that they were the means by which man marked out his territory, and so organized his social life. All other successive systems were variants – or perversions – of this original model.

The main Songlines in Australia appear to enter the country from the north or the north-west – from across the Timor Sea or the Torres Strait – and from there weave their way southwards across the continent. One has the impression that they represent the routes of the first Australians – and that they have come from *somewhere else*.

How long ago? Fifty thousand years? Eighty or a hundred thousand years? The dates are insignificant compared to those from African prehistory.

And here I must take a leap into faith: into regions I would not expect anyone to follow. I have a vision of the Songlines stretching across the continents and ages; that wherever men have trodden they have left a trail of song (of which we may, now and then, catch an echo); and that these trails must reach back, in time and space, to an isolated pocket in the African savannah, where the First Man opening his mouth in defiance of the terrors that surrounded him, shouted the opening stanza of the World Song, 'I AM!'

Chatwin was a nomad himself, and fascinated by nomads; a wanderer who questioned modern society in a way that is quite different from other writers. His early death, in 1989, meant that his selection of essays and reflections in *What Am I Doing Here?* (1989) became the last testament of this adventurer and romantic's lifelong 'search for the miraculous'. More than any other writer, Chatwin used his travels to the remotest parts of the globe as a means to search for the truths of humanity, *pre-* as well as post-Darwin. A writer such as Bruce Chatwin actually blurs the distinction between fiction and non-fiction, between oral storytelling traditions and modern scientific discourse.

Like Chatwin, Angela Carter was a genre-bender: her essays, stories, and novels are all-encompassing in their verve, imagination, and polemic. Like many modern (or, indeed, post-Modern) writers, she had a great fondness for the intertextuality that pastiche and a wide range of allusions permit. She brings together magic realism, post-modernism, feminism, the Gothic, the real and the surreal. If that all seems a heady mixture, let the final paragraphs of her last novel – *Wise Children* (1991) – speak for her: the twins Dora and Nora Chance (the Chances, illegitimate daughters of Melchior Hazard) celebrate with their own double offspring.

> We put our handbags in the pram, for safety's sake. Then and there, we couldn't wait, we broke into harmony, we serenaded the new arrivals:
>
> > 'We can't give you anything but love, babies,
> > That's the only thing we've plenty of, babies –'
>
> The window on the second-floor front window of 41 Bard Road went up, a head came out. Dreadlocks. That Rastafarian.
> 'You two, again,' he said.
> 'Have a heart!' we said. 'We've got something to celebrate, tonight!'
> 'Well, you just watch it, in case a squad car comes by,' he said. 'Drunk in charge of a baby carriage, at your age.'
> We'd got so many songs to sing to our babies, all our old songs, that we didn't pay him any attention. 'Gee, we'd like to see you looking swell, babies!' and the Hazard theme song, 'Is You Is or Is You Ain't'. Then there were songs from the show that nobody else remembers. '2b or not 2b', 'Hey nonny bloody no', 'Mistress Mine', and Broadway tunes, and paper moons, and lilacs in the spring, again. We went on dancing and singing. 'Diamond bracelets Woolworths doesn't sell.' Besides, it was our birthday, wasn't it, we'd got to sing them the silly old song about Charlie Chaplin and his comedy boots all the little kids were singing and dancing in the street the day we were born. There was dancing and singing all along Bard Road that day and we'll go on singing and dancing until we drop in our tracks, won't we, kids.
> What a joy it is to dance and sing!

The death of Angela Carter in 1992 robbed modern writing of one of its major and most distinctive figures. Feminist and iconoclastic, humorous and passionate, her writing ranges from the retelling of fables – *The Bloody Chamber* (1979) – to extravagant magic realism, in *Nights at the Circus* (1984); from a disturbing examination of love, in *Love* (1971), to the battle between reason and emotion in *The Infernal Desire Machine of Doctor Hoffman* (1972). Her novels illustrate her range and daring, as characters change sex, grow wings, move between reality and fantasy, and explore beyond the range of normal human experience. Her short stories were collected posthumously in *Burning Your Boats* (1995). Like many of her contemporaries, Angela Carter looked back to the traditions which inform all storytelling, and rewrote the history of our own times in her own style.

The note of continuity is the triumph of the writer in the face of eternity. Literature is the triumph of the imagination. As such, it will only die if or when imagination dies. In a novel of only seven-and-a-half short pages, Samuel Beckett takes us to that furthest extreme: the title of the novel, published in 1965, is expressed in the last three words of the opening sentence:

> No trace anywhere of life, you say, pah, no difficulty there, imagination not dead yet, yes, dead, good, imagination dead imagine.

Jeremy Hunter

OLD AND MIDDLE ENGLISH

*c.*410	Roman legions withdrew from Britain (*in Latin:* Britannia)
449	Jutes (from Denmark) occupied Kent (south-east England) under Hengest
477	First invasion of England by Saxons (from northern Germany) under Aelle: south Saxon colony of Sussex established
495	Second Saxon invasion, under Cerdic; west Saxon colony of Wessex established
537	Death of King Arthur, leader of the early sixth-century revolt by the native Britons against continental colonisers: retreat of many Britons in this period to Scotland, Wales, Cornwall, and Brittany. The geographical term 'Great Britain' originates in the sixth century, as later rulers from France were obliged to distinguish between Brittany ('Bretagne') and the island of 'Britannia', which they called 'Grande Bretagne'
547	Norwegians (Vikings), under Ida, established the colony of Northumbria, in northern England
565	Introduction of Christianity to Britain by Saint Columba
597	Saint Augustine established the first Catholic mission in England, at Canterbury
664	Synod of Whitby confirmed Catholicism as the state religion
Eighth century	Rise in political influence of Mercia, in the mid-west of England (particularly under King Offa, reigned 757–795). Colonisers established a 'heptarchy' of seven kingdoms – Northumbria, Mercia, East Anglia, Essex, Kent, Sussex, Wessex – to encourage harmony and co-operation. 'Offa's

Dyke' built to restrict native Britons to land within Wales

802   Egbert of Wessex became leader of the 'heptarchy': in the next few years, Wessex subjected Essex, Kent, and Sussex, thereby controlling the whole of southern England. Egbert is sometimes called the first King of England; certainly, the establishment of an Anglo-Saxon national identity can be dated to the early ninth century, as the old colonisers became fully integrated with the native English

866   The Danish 'Great Army' (also called Vikings) landed in East Anglia, taking control of East Anglia, Northumbria, and much of Mercia

871   Alfred (the Great) became King of Wessex: he led Anglo-Saxon revolt against Scandinavian invaders

878   Battle of Edington: boundary of Danish-held territory in England ('the Danelaw') fixed to the north-east of a line from London to Chester. Political disputes between the English and the Danes were resolved by 885

Tenth century   English forces slowly resumed control of most territories occupied by Danish colonisers

973   Edgar of Wessex proclaimed first King of all England, including the Danelaw. He was succeeded by Ethelred in 978

c.990   Danish armies, under Sven (or Sweyn), invaded southern England; another long territorial dispute followed. King Ethelred (nicknamed 'the Unready') left for France in 1013

1016   Canute, son of Sweyn, became King of England after the death of Ethelred, and married Ethelred's widow, Emma of Normandy

1035   Death of Canute; Danish succession guaranteed with the execution of the English 'pretender', Alfred

1040   Macbeth became King of Scotland on the death of Duncan

1042   Death of Hardicanute, the last Danish king of England. Peaceful restoration of the English monarchy, with Edward ('the Confessor'), son of Ethelred and Emma, who had been brought up in northern France (Normandy)

1045   King Edward married the daughter of the English baron, Godwin, but did not produce an heir. Godwin (who died in 1053) feared the influence of the Norman court. The succession was much disputed in the 1050s and 1060s: the king's nephew Edward ('the Outlaw') died before his uncle, leaving a son, Edgar, as 'pretender'. But 'the Confessor' chose William of Normandy, the son of his cousin, as his successor

1066   Death of Edward the Confessor. Harold, the Queen's brother, proclaimed King. Edgar (aged 14) was proposed instead, but withdrew to Scotland (where his sister Margaret was Queen to Malcolm III, Macbeth's successor). The same year, Norwegian invaders defeated at Stamford Bridge (near York).

The Norman Conquest: William, Duke of Normandy, Edward's nominated successor, invaded England, and Harold was killed at the Battle of Hastings. William was recognised as King. (The arrival of William of Normandy's armies, to claim the throne of England from Harold Godwinson, is claimed to be the last time that foreign powers have successfully invaded British shores)

1086   Publication of *The Domesday Book*, a record of land holdings throughout England and commissioned by William the Conqueror

1087   William I died; succeeded as King of England by his second son, William II (the first son, Robert, became Duke of Normandy)

1095   Beginning of the 'Crusades': so-called 'Holy Wars' in the eastern Mediterranean region to establish the dominance of Christianity over other faiths (principally Islam)

1100   Accession of King Henry I. He married Princess Edith of Scotland, daughter of King Malcolm III and Queen Margaret, but did not have a son. His daughter, Matilda, was proposed as a future queen in the 1120s, but Henry's nephew, Stephen (the only living grandson of William I), became king when Henry died in 1135

1152   Matilda's son Henry (by Geoffrey Plantagenet of Anjou) married Eleanor of Aquitaine, divorced wife of the French king, Louis VII. Henry was King Stephen's nominated successor, and became King Henry II in 1154. In Henry's thirty-seven years as king, England owned most of western France

1153   Nicholas Brakespeare became the first (and only) Englishman to be elected Pope of the Roman Catholic church; he took the title Hadrian VI

1170	Thomas à Becket, the reforming Archbishop of Canterbury, was murdered in the cathedral by Henry II's soldiers
1189	Accession of King Richard I ('the Lionheart'); he was closely involved in foreign wars, including the Middle Eastern 'Crusades' (which continued into the late thirteenth century). Richard died in France in 1199, and his brother John became king
1204	England lost political control of Normandy. There was a strong feeling in the early thirteenth century towards democratic politics and the establishment of a new 'English' national identity after centuries as 'Anglo-Saxons'. This nationalist feeling was encouraged by the heroic status of King Richard I, who died young. His successor, King John, was never popular. One of John's adversaries was Robin Hood, Earl of Huntingdon, who was probably the first democratically inclined nobleman in English history
1210	English colonisation of Ireland began
1215	Pope Innocent III convoked the fourth Lateran Council of the Roman Catholic church, to give new moral guidelines to thirteenth-century Europe
1215	King John signed the Magna Carta at Runnymede; this document transferred many of the King's political powers to landowning noblemen. A new distinction between 'government' (which remained at the royal court) and 'parliament' (which was the prerogative of the aristocracy) emerged at this time. This new division of power was not changed until the First Reform Bill of 1832
1265	Simon De Montfort convoked the first true English Parliament of landowning barons, to advise the court-based government
1282	Wales was subjected to the English forces of King Edward I. In 1284, Edward's heir (later to become King Edward II) was created Prince of Wales – the title for the monarch's first-born son continues to the present day
1286	Death of the Scottish King Alexander III: English forces tried to subject Scotland to English rule. For twenty years there was no Scottish king
1305	The Scottish nationalist William Wallace ('Braveheart') killed by English forces
1306	Robert I ('the Bruce') declared King of Scotland

1314	Battle of Bannockburn: English forces destroyed, and Scottish independence reasserted. In the fourteenth and fifteenth centuries, Scotland frequently sided with France ('the Auld Alliance') against England in territorial wars on the continent of Europe
1339	England invaded France, wishing to reassert the English king's authority and power in the continental lands which he owned; the dispute with French royalist forces continued until 1453 (the so-called 'Hundred Years' War')
1346–7	English military victories over France at Crecy (1346) and Calais (1347; Calais remained an English enclave in France until 1558)
*c.*1348	Bubonic plague – 'the Black Death' – strikes England
1362	The English language becomes the official language of the Law Courts
1371	Death of Scottish King David II: replaced by Robert II, grandson of Robert the Bruce, and son of Walter Stewart. (The spelling of the family name was changed to Stuart, because this was easier to understand at the English court – which still spoke French.) The Stuart dynasty continued in Scotland without a break until 1603
1377	Death of English King Edward III. His first son (Edward, 'the Black Prince') had already died in battle. So the Black Prince's son (aged 9) became King Richard II. Edward III's surviving sons were overlooked: they were John of Lancaster (also known as 'John of Gaunt') and Edmund of York. Both advised the young king, their nephew
1380	First translation of the Christian Bible into English, by John Wycliff
1381	The Peasants' Revolt, led by Wat Tyler. This protest against the conditions for farm workers in Western England is often seen as the beginning of trade unionism
1399	King Richard II deposed and replaced by John of Gaunt's son, a Lancastrian, Henry ('Bolingbroke'), who was declared King Henry IV
1415	Battle of Agincourt: the peak of English supremacy in the Hundred Years' War. English forces were led by King Henry V ('Prince Hal') who succeeded his father as monarch in 1413. Also in this year, Henry established English as the language of the court

1420	Henry V married Princess Catherine, daughter of the French King Charles VI ('Charles the Mad'). King Henry V of England was recognised as 'Regent' of France
1422	Deaths of Henry V and Charles VI. Henry's infant son became King Henry VI of England; the new King of France was Charles VII ('the Dauphin')
1423–24	Scottish King James I imprisoned by the English; he writes his *Kingis Quair*
1431	The French heroine Jeanne d'Arc ('Joan of Arc') was burned to death, not for her political activities but because of alleged offences against the doctrinal law laid down by the Roman Catholic church. (Catholic orthodoxy was strongly promoted by successive Popes, beginning with Gregory II in 1231 and continuing for over three hundred years; this so-called 'Inquisition' reached its height in Spain, under Torquemada, in the 1480s and 1490s)
*c.*1440	Invention of printing in Europe
1453	End of the Hundred Years' War between England and France; England lost political authority over most of its former French colonies
1455	Beginning of 'The War of the Roses' – so called after the emblems of the royal houses of Lancaster (the red rose) and York (the white rose). This civil dispute returns to the succession of 1377; King Henry VI (a Lancastrian) was challenged for the Crown by Richard, Duke of York
1456	Gutenberg's Bible published in Germany; possibly the first printed book
1456	Richard of York killed at the Battle of Wakefield; his son Edward becomes Duke of York, and later (1460) King Edward IV, when Henry VI is defeated at the Battle of Towton
late fifteenth century	Rise of the Medici dynasty in Florence (Italy). The Renaissance (or 'Rinascimento') began with the Medici, whose wealth came from banking and foreign trade. Profits were used to sponsor artists such as Sandro Botticelli, Leonardo da Vinci and Michelangelo Buonarotti
1471	The Earl of Warwick (nicknamed 'the King-maker') – who helped Edward IV to become king – restores Henry VI to the throne; but Edward's Yorkist forces kill the Earl of

Warwick at the Battle of Barnet, and King Henry is executed

1476   William Caxton, who served an apprenticeship in Holland, established the first printing press in England, at Westminster. His first 'bestseller', in 1485, was Sir Thomas Malory's *Le Morte D'Arthur*

1483   Death of King Edward IV; succession passes to his 12-year-old son, Edward V. But the new king and his younger brother Richard ('the Princes in the Tower') are imprisoned in London, and later executed. This may have been ordered by their uncle, who became King Richard III, the last Yorkist king

THE RENAISSANCE

1485   The Battle of Bosworth Field, the end of the Wars of the Roses: death of King Richard. Lancastrian forces were led by Henry Tudor, Earl of Richmond. Henry was grandson of Queen Catherine, widow of Henry V. He became King Henry VII, and initiated the Tudor dynasty. Soon after becoming king, Henry married Princess Elizabeth of York, daughter of Edward IV

1488   Accession of King James IV of Scotland; he later married Henry VII's daughter, Margaret

1490s   The great decade of discovery: Christopher Columbus (Italian, but paid by Spain) – who was the first European to discover the American continent, in 1492; Vasco Da Gama (who sailed around Africa to India, on behalf of Portugal); John Cabot (also Italian) was sponsored by the English – he sailed from Bristol to the north-eastern shores of America (unlike Columbus, whose discoveries were all in the Caribbean region)

c.1500   The Dutch philosopher and religious reformer Erasmus published his views on humanism – stressing the importance and supreme value of mankind in daily life and in relationships with God. For the first time in Europe, the power and even the existence of God could be questioned

1509   Accession of King Henry VIII, second son of Henry VII. Henry VIII's elder brother, Prince Arthur, died before his

	father. Arthur was married to Catherine of Aragon, a Spanish princess. The new king, Henry VIII, married his brother's widow. A daughter, Mary, was born (in 1516), but Henry became frustrated at failing to father a male heir
1513	Niccolo Machiavelli, a Florentine political philosopher, published his major work, *The Prince*. His philosophy acknowledged the use of questionable political expediency – a 'reign of terror' even – to achieve just results, and he was considered 'evil' in England
1521	The German religious reformer, Martin Luther, was excommunicated by the Pope; in the same year, King Henry VIII was granted the title 'Defender of the Faith'
1526	A printed version of the New Testament of the Christian Bible, translated by William Tyndale, was published with great success
1533	Henry defied the Roman Catholic church by divorcing Catherine of Aragon. He married his second wife, Anne Boleyn; his second daughter, Elizabeth, was born the same year
1534	Ignatius Loyola, a Spanish monk, founded the Catholic Society of Jesus ('the Jesuits'). With the 'Act of Supremacy', Henry VIII declared himself the supreme head of a non-conformist (Protestant) Christian church in England. Anglicanism became the state religion; this religious change, after many centuries of Catholicism, was called 'the Reformation'. The king pronounced the 'Dissolution of the Monasteries' – all the Catholic monasteries, with their vast libraries, were destroyed by 1539, with a great deal of violence
1536	Henry VIII married his third wife, Jane Seymour, who was a servant in the royal household. Anne Boleyn was executed. Henry's third child, his only son, Edward, was born in 1537, but Queen Jane died in childbirth. Edward was a very weak child, and Henry married three other wives in the 1530s and 1540s: Anne of Cleves, whom he divorced; Catherine Parr, who was executed; and Catherine Howard (who outlived King Henry)
1538	Pope Paul III excommunicated King Henry VIII from the Roman Catholic church: this merely reinforced Henry's

position as 'Defender of the Faith' for the newly founded Anglican Protestant church

1538   The licensing of books was first introduced, as the monasteries and their libraries continued to be destroyed

1539   The Great Bible, based on the works of two expatriates (Tyndale and Coverdale), published in English

1541   Jean Calvin, a Frenchman, founded a new Protestant church in Geneva (Switzerland); its severe doctrines gained great influence throughout Europe in the 1550s

1543   The Polish astronomer Copernicus's explanation of the solar system was published; it stated that the Earth revolves around the Sun. The Italian, Galileo, continued Copernicus's studies in the 1590s, and was excommunicated by the Catholic church

1547   Death of King Henry VIII; he was succeeded by his only son (from his third marriage), King Edward VI, who was still a child, and in poor health

1549   The first Book of Common Prayer published; this was edited by King Henry VIII's first Archbishop of Canterbury, Thomas Cranmer

1553   King Edward died, aged 16, and his eldest half-sister, Mary (daughter of Catherine of Aragon and wife of Prince Philip of Spain – later King Philip, who sent the Spanish Armada against England thirty-five years later) became Queen. Mary's accession followed a brief protest by Protestant parliamentarians who made Lady Jane Grey the Queen of England for ten days

1556–58   The Catholic Queen Mary I ('Bloody Mary') supported Spain in its war with France, which aimed to spread Catholicism

1558   Elizabeth I (daughter of Henry VIII and Anne Boleyn, after the King's first divorce) became Queen. England now opposed Spain, which continued to fight in Europe for Catholic supremacy

1559   The English were expelled from Calais, their last possession in France

1563   Beginning of the Catholic 'Counter-Reformation' in Germany

1568   Mary, Queen of Scots, who was forced to abdicate the throne of Scotland, fled to England and claimed the

	English throne. (Her infant son became James VI of Scotland. As a Catholic, who did not recognise divorce, she believed Elizabeth I to be illegitimate, especially because Elizabeth's mother, Anne Boleyn, had been executed after accusations of adultery)
1571	Opening of the London Stock Exchange. England's capitalist economy grew very quickly around this time, with large overseas trading interests
1578	Opening of The Theatre, London's first
1577–80	Sir Francis Drake's first voyage around the world
1584	Sir Walter Raleigh established Virginia, the first English colony in America
1587	Mary, Queen of Scots, executed
1588	The Spanish naval fleet ('the invincible Armada'), sailing against England, was repulsed
1592–94	London theatres closed by an outbreak of plague
1594	Foundation of the Bank of England
1600	England's foreign trade continued to spread, with the foundation of the East India Company. (This lasted to 1858, when England established dominion over India)
1603	Elizabeth ('the Virgin Queen') died. James VI of Scotland became James I 'of Great Britain'
1604	At the Hampton Court Conference, bishops of the Church of England denounced both Catholicism and Puritanism (or Protestant extremism)
1605	The Gunpowder Plot. Catholics, led by Guy Fawkes, attempted to blow up the Parliament buildings, in anger at the intolerance of the official Church of England
1609	Galileo published (in Italy) several of his highly influential scientific theories
1611	Publication of the King James or Authorised Version of the Bible. This immediately superseded all former editions of the Bible, and remains the bestselling book in Britain today
1618	Beginning of the Thirty Years' War, initially a religious conflict, in Northern Europe. Britain supported the Protestant powers (France, The Netherlands, Denmark), but did not join the fighting
1620	The Pilgrim Fathers, a group of discontented Puritans, left England to establish new colonies in north-eastern America ('New England')

1625	Charles I became King on the death of his father, James I. The government, which Charles directly controlled, quickly came into conflict with the landowners' Parliament
1628	The Petition of Rights. Parliament demanded assurances from the government against excessive taxes and arbitrary arrest
1629	The Royalist government abolished Parliament
1638	'The War of the Bishops': Scotland resisted the northward spread of the Church of England
1640	Parliament recalled ('the short Parliament'). Most members of Parliament were Puritans, and strongly opposed the government's taxation policies. The popular name changed to 'the long Parliament', as the power of the King was resisted
1642	Parliament closed down all theatres
1642–48	English Civil War. Government forces ('Cavaliers' loyal to King Charles I) opposed parliamentary forces ('Round-heads') led by Oliver Cromwell. Scotland joined on the side of Parliament, and the King was finally arrested
1648	Peace of Westphalia ended the Thirty Years' War in Europe
1649	King Charles I tried and executed. Cromwell became the leader of a republican Britain known as 'the Commonwealth'
1658	Death of Oliver Cromwell
1660	The Commonwealth collapsed because of weak leadership; the son of Charles I was recalled from France (the Restoration) and became King Charles II. The terms 'Whig' and 'Tory' were first applied to landowners who, respectively, welcomed the division of power between the monarchy and the landowners, and those who favoured the retention of all power with the landowners (while not opposing the Restoration)

RESTORATION TO ROMANTICISM

1665	The Great Plague: London's population decimated
1666	The Great Fire of London: Christopher Wren was appointed principal architect for the rebuilding of the city
1667	Britain's colonial expansion continued, with the exchange of Surinam (which became Dutch Guiana) for many states

in north-eastern America (including New York, formerly New Amsterdam)

1672 Third Anglo-Dutch War, involving many European states. Dutch forces were led by the young Prince William of Orange, who was married to King Charles II's niece Mary

1685 Death of Charles II: succession of his brother James II, a devout Catholic. Protestant landowners were disturbed when James became king

1688 The birth of a male heir to King James II (already father to two much older daughters – Mary and Anne) provoked the 'Glorious' or 'Bloodless' Revolution. James was exiled, and his daughter Mary became Queen Mary II with her Protestant husband William of Orange (King William III)

1689 The Declaration of Rights. In the same year, the philosopher John Locke published his *Two Treatises*, justifying the division of government into legislative and executive branches; this is often seen as the birth of party politics

1701 England established the Grand Alliance with the German House of Hanover. William and Mary were childless; if Mary's sister, who became Queen Anne, also died without an heir, the Hanoverians would become constitutional monarchs of Britain (the Act of Settlement)

1707 Union of the Scottish and English parliaments

1709 The first Copyright Act protects the earnings of professional writers

1713 End of the major European war (of Spanish Succession) with the Treaty of Utrecht

1714 The Elector of Hanover succeeded Queen Anne, as King George I (he was great-grandson of King James I, through two female lines. The Hanoverian dynasty continues to the present day)

1721 Robert Walpole (a Whig) became the first prime minister of Great Britain (to 1742). Britain expanded greatly in mercantile trade and colonial development, often coming into conflict with the parallel ambitions of France

1743 Peace of Aix-la-Chapelle: France (allied with Prussia) conceded its claims to territories in Europe to Austro-Hungary (allied with Britain) at the end of the War of Austrian Succession

1754–63	Britain fought with France over territorial claims in the American colonies and in India. Britain gained decisive victories at Plassey (India, 1757) and in eastern Canada (1759–60). The British prime minister at this time, William Pitt (the Elder), Earl of Chatham, is often considered to be a 'Father of the British Empire'. France conceded a vast amount of territory to Britain with the Peace of Paris (1763)
1768	Captain James Cook's first journey to the South Pacific, in the name of colonial expansion as well as scientific discovery (Cook was killed in Hawaii in 1779)
c.1770	The so-called 'Age of Reason' – a term often applied to the whole of the eighteenth century – reached its height. The German word *Aufklärung*, applied to the works of the philosopher Immanuel Kant, was translated into English as 'Enlightenment'. Optimism in Europe was high, as intellectual superiority seemed to be assured. One English offshoot of the Enlightment was the establishment, by John Wesley, of the Methodist church. This Protestant sect rejected any personal extravagance (like the Puritans) but, unlike its predecessor, was born in a spirit of tolerance towards other Protestant sects
1775	The invention of the steam-engine, by the Scotsman James Watt, led to a rapid rise in industralisation and urban growth (the Industrial Revolution)
1776	The American Declaration of Independence (4 July). Britain was at war with America from 1775 to 1783, when independence was recognised

THE ROMANTIC PERIOD

1789	The French Revolution: the monarchy of Louis XVI and Marie Antoinette was overthrown
1793–94	'The Reign of Terror' in France, led by left-wing radicals known as Jacobins (Robespierre, Danton, Marat) who ruthlessly suppressed their political opponents
1793	Britain joined the 'Wars of the Coalition' against France, which was aiming for supremacy throughout Europe. Major British victories were achieved at sea, at Trafalgar (under Lord Nelson, 1805), and on land, at Waterloo (under the Duke of Wellington, 1815)

1801	The Act of Union: Ireland was politically joined to Britain
1804	Napoleon Bonaparte, an army general, became Emperor of France
1811–12	The campaign of the Luddites, who broke factory machinery in a protest about workers' conditions
1812–14	Second War of American Independence: Britain was unable to regain this part of the former Empire
1814	Invention of the railway locomotive by George Stephenson
1815	Congress of Vienna, at the end of the wars against France (the Napoleonic wars). Britain emerged as the most power-ful nation in Europe, and consolidated this position throughout the nineteenth century
1819	The Peterloo Massacre: a workers' uprising in Manchester was brutally suppressed, with many casualties
1824	Trades unions were recognised by the British government
1829	The Catholic Emancipation Act made discrimination against Catholics illegal in Britain
1830	A new liberal (Whig) government was elected in Britain – emulating the upheavals of the so-called 'July revolution' in France, which led to the abdication of King Charles X

THE NINETEENTH CENTURY

1832	The First Reform Bill: voting rights were extended for the first time to men who were not landowners, and most of the privileged seats in Parliament (the rotten boroughs) were abolished
1833	Slavery abolished in British colonies
1833	First Factory Act improved workers' conditions and made factory inspections compulsory
1833	Poor Laws provided accommodation in workhouses for the destitute, but with forced labour
1834	A group of labourers from Dorset (later called 'the Tolpuddle Martyrs') were sentenced to exile for protesting against worker exploitation (remission was granted in 1836)
1837	Victoria became Queen
1839	Industrial uprising of the Chartists, who rebelled against Parliament's rejection of the popular People's Charter of 1836, calling for greater democracy. A general workers' strike was called in 1842, but failed

1845–47	Famine in Ireland, largely due to failure of the potato crop. Irish population declined from 8.5 million to 6.5 million, with one million deaths and one million emigrations, principally to the United States of America
1846	Life for British farmers eased, with the repeal of the Corn Laws
1847	Publication of *The Communist Manifesto* by Karl Marx and Friedrich Engels. Both Christianity and the landowners' control of political power were questioned
1848	The Year of Revolution. Many new regimes were established on the continent of Europe, but Queen Victoria increased her popularity in Britain
1851	The First World Fair (the Great Exhibition) was held in the Crystal Palace, especially erected in Hyde Park, London. The Queen's husband, Prince Albert of Saxe-Coburg-Gotha, is largely credited with this demonstration of British supremacy in science and the arts. The Great Exhibition is widely regarded as the high point of British imperialism
1853–56	The Crimean War: Britain's first war for two hundred years. With other European nations, the Russian claims in the Ukraine were rejected
1857	The Indian Mutiny: Britain's colonial presence was challenged for the first time. In 1858, the East India Company was wound up, and the Indian company became a Vice-Royalty – politically, therefore, a public rather than a private concern
1859	Publication of *On the Origin of Species* by Charles Darwin. This scientific treatise, conducted in the 1830s, challenged orthodox religious beliefs. For the first time, agnosticism and atheism became widespread
1861	Death of Prince Albert. Queen Victoria remained a widow for forty years, until her death in 1901
1861–65	The American Civil War. 'Confederate' states in the southeast wanted to preserve slavery for black immigrants. President Abraham Lincoln supported integration. The southern 'Confederacy' was finally defeated. In 1865, the Confederacy was joined to the already 'United' states (in the north-east). After 1865, the USA expanded towards the Pacific Coast, with territorial concessions from Spain and France

1860s	'Modernism' was recognised as a force in English literature. George Meredith was an early practitioner of Modernism
1860s–1880s	The Conservative party leader Benjamin Disraeli and the Liberal leader William Gladstone alternated as prime minister
1867	Karl Marx published, in England, *Das Kapital*, which was a principal text of Socialist ideology for over a century. (Matthew Arnold's epoch-breaking poem *Dover Beach* dates from the same year)
1867	The Second Reform Bill: the right to vote in parliamentary elections was gradually being expanded in Britain (a third bill was passed in 1884)
1868	Foundation of the British Trades Union Congress, to politicise workers' rights
1870	Education Act makes schooling compulsory for children aged 5 to 13
1870	Political union in Italy
1871	Political union in Germany
1870s	Britain leads international communications with the development of postal services and pioneering work in telecommunications (the Italian inventor of the telephone, Giuseppe Marconi, worked in England)
1877	In order to boost the flagging popularity of the monarchy, Queen Victoria is declared Empress of India by Conservative prime minister Disraeli, reinforcing Britain's colonial ambitions
1879	John Henry Newman, a convert to Catholicism, is created Cardinal of England by the Pope
1880s	Radical Liberalism began to give way to Marxist-influenced Socialism: 1881, the Socialist Democratic Federation: 1884, the Fabian Society, which politicised Marxist ideas in parliamentary terms; 1893, the Independent Labour Party (founded by Keir Hardie) which first contested and won seats in Parliament. The Labour Party (1906) grew decisively in the early 1900s as political Liberalism lost favour (especially after the First World War, 1914–18)
1886	The Liberal prime minister, William Gladstone, introduced the first Irish Home Rule Bill. Many members of his own party opposed him

1887	Queen Victoria celebrated fifty years as monarch (the Golden Jubilee)
1893	Irish issues continued to dominate British politics. Gladstone's revised Home Rule Bill introduced. Keir Hardie's Independent Labour Party, originally supporters of Gladstone in the divided Liberal Party, became a full parliamentary force in 1906 (the Labour Party, under Ramsay Macdonald)
1898	Marxist politics introduced in Russia, with the establishment by Lenin and others of the Russian Socialist Democratic Workers' Party
1899	Establishment in Dublin of the Irish National Theatre
1899–1902	The Boer War: the Boers, from The Netherlands, occupied Transvaal and the Orange Free State in South Africa, and had territorial ambitions in Natal and the Cape Province (British colonies). Britain won the war, and established the Union of South Africa (to 1970)

THE TWENTIETH CENTURY: 1900–45

1901	Death of Queen Victoria, after sixty-four years as monarch
1904	France established many political alliances between states on the continent of Europe; this was called the 'Entente Cordiale'. But the agreements lasted for only ten years, breaking down in 1914
1911	Height of the campaign by suffragettes in Britain; they were women who had not achieved suffrage (the right to vote) in three reform bills. Many people trace the beginning of feminism to the suffragette campaign (women over the age of 30 received the vote in 1918; from 1928, all adult women – aged over 21 – were given the vote)
1912	Defeat of the ruling Liberal Party's Bill for Irish Home Rule. The Conservative opposition were often called Unionists, a name which still exists today (the Ulster vote was decisive)
1914	Opening of the Panama Canal, built by the United States of America. Originally a French project, then widely supported in Europe, the work was conceded to the USA, which demanded the creation of the country of Panama, out of former Colombian territory

1914	Beginning of the First World War in Europe. This was started by the assassination of the Bosnian king in Sarajevo, which led to the collapse of the Entente Cordiale. Britain opposed Germany's territorial ambitions. The bloodiest battles were in Northern France, after Germany's takeover of the Benelux countries (BElgium, NEtherlands, LUxembourg)
1916	US President Wilson sent American forces to Europe, to help British and French forces to fight German aggression. American intervention was vital to the eventual defeat of Germany. While war continued on the Western European continent, the political climate changed elsewhere in Europe
1916	Easter Rising in Ireland, in protest at continued British presence. Several Irish rebels were executed by the English
1917	The Russian Revolution, led by so-called 'Bolsheviks', the majority of Communist sympathisers, led by Lenin. Execution of Tsar Nicholas II and his family. Lenin became head of the Union of Soviet Socialist Republics (to his death in 1924, when he was replaced by Stalin)
1918	End of the First World War (11 November)
1919	The Peace of Versailles. In the redrawing of boundaries in Europe, the Ottoman and Austro-Hungarian empires were dismantled. New states in Eastern Europe included Czechoslovakia and Yugoslavia. Many monarchies, including that of Germany, were replaced by republics. The League of Nations was created, in an attempt to secure future world peace
1922	Ireland finally achieved self-government, with the establishment of the Irish Free State ('Eire'). Six of the nine counties in the North ('Ulster') chose to remain within the United Kingdom
1929	The collapse of the New York Stock Exchange led to economic depression in the Western democracies. Party politics were abandoned in Britain in 1931, until 1945. Ramsay Macdonald, the Labour leader, led the first National government
1933	Adolf Hitler, the leader of the largest single political party in Germany, the National Socialists (Nazis) took power. Right-wing extremism (known as Fascism) had begun in

Italy as a reaction against Bolshevism, and spread to Germany and Spain. Hitler, however, had territorial ambitions for Germany's 'Third Reich' and was viciously racist

1936–39   The Spanish Civil War. Britain did not officially support either side, but many individuals opposed the victorious General Franco's right-wing political challenge to the monarchist *status quo* (which was restored on Franco's death in 1975)

1938   Hitler's German forces occupied Austria, following the failure of diplomatic moves towards unification

1939   Hitler occupied Czechoslovakia, despite warnings from Western neighbours, including Britain, which strengthened alliances with other countries. When Hitler invaded Poland, the Second World War was declared

1940   Winston Churchill (aged 66) became leader of the British National government

1941   Japan, with its own territorial ambitions in Asia, attacked the American naval base at Pearl Harbor in Hawaii. The United States of America joined the war in the Pacific and in Europe

1945   Hitler's forces were defeated in Europe, in the spring. The war against Japan continued until August, when the USA dropped the first two atomic bombs on Hiroshima and Nagasaki

THE TWENTIETH CENTURY: 1945 TO THE PRESENT

1945   Britain's first party political elections for many years rejected Churchill, and a Labour-led government, under Clement Attlee, was elected (to 1951). Major industries (for example, railways, coal-mines) were nationalised

1946   The free National Health Service was established.
The League of Nations was dissolved, having never received a political consensus. In its place, the United Nations Organisation was established. The Western democracies severely distrusted the politics of Stalin's USSR, to whom, as allies who had helped to win the war, a major influence over the whole of Eastern Europe was conceded. The phrase 'Third World', relating to underdeveloped

countries (usually ex-Western colonies), dates from this period; the First and Second Worlds were the Western democracies and the Communist bloc. Their antagonism, notably between the leading nations of the USA and the USSR, was called 'the cold war'. It was Churchill who coined the phrase 'Iron Curtain' to describe the democratic/Communist border between the Baltic and the Adriatic

1947   Britain granted independence to its largest colonial territory, India

1948   British diplomats drew new territorial boundaries in the Middle East (Western Asia), establishing the Jewish state of Israel

1950   Beginning of the Korean War. The USA moved against Communist forces in this former Japanese colony, bordering Communist China. The war ended (1953) with the partition of the country

1954   French colonialists were removed by violence from Indo-China (Vietnam, Cambodia, and Laos). American forces entered Vietnam in 1965, to try and prevent Communist control of the country from China to the north. The Vietnam War lasted until 1972, when President Nixon withdrew all US forces; the war achieved nothing, and the Communist north of Vietnam reunified the divided country

1956   The Suez Crisis: Britain and France encouraged Israel to go to war against Egypt for control of the Suez Canal

1960   With the independence of Ghana, Britain's rapid withdrawal as a colonial power from Africa began. The democratisation of Britain's former colonies in Africa was not always easy: the process in the white-dominated states of Rhodesia (now Zimbabwe) and South Africa was especially difficult. In other states, the handover to a popular black-led Communist regime caused tensions between the UK and the anti-Communist USA

1961   Building of the Berlin Wall. The wall was the ultimate symbol of the cold war, separating the Communist and non-Communist worlds; it was built to prevent East Germans (under Soviet influence) from escaping to a better life in the democratic West. (The wall was demolished in 1989.)

1962   President Kennedy of the USA came into conflict with

Soviet leader Kruschev over the installation of nuclear warheads in the Communist Caribbean state of Cuba. This was the height of the cold war

1963   The assassination of President Kennedy shocked the Western world

1964–70   The Labour Party, under Harold Wilson, achieved the majority in Britain, after thirteen years of Conservative government. The 1960s in Britain were typified by liberal politics, and the growth of a youth-led culture of young people born after the Second World War. British popular culture – fashion, music, etc. – led the world in the late 1960s. The growth of feminist consciousness also led to a reappraisal of gay rights

1968   Soviet forces brutally suppressed democratic movements in Czechoslovakia. (Hungary had earlier rebelled against Soviet domination in 1956)

1969   US astronauts Armstrong and Aldrin landed on the moon. This was the end of a 'space race' with the USSR, begun with the Soviet cosmonaut Yuri Gagarin being the first man to travel in space (in 1961)

1970   The age of becoming an 'adult' in Britain was reduced from 21 to 18. Voting rights were thus extended

1971   Britain, under Conservative prime minister Edward Heath, joins the European Economic Community

1973   First World demand for oil precipitated a crisis, leading to great wealth for oil-rich states in the Middle East when oil prices were greatly inflated. Outrageous wealth was channelled to the Gulf states, while Western Europe and the USA started thinking about 'austerity' again

1979   A new Conservative government elected in Britain, under Margaret Thatcher. (Her Labour opponent, James Callaghan, had lost the trust of the labour movement.) Mrs Thatcher survived as prime minister until 1990; she was a champion of free enterprise. Ideologically, she was ideally in tune with US President Ronald Reagan (1981–89).

Thatcher's regime led to a very stable economy throughout the 1980s. 'Yuppies' were a product of the 1980s (Young Upwardly mobile Professionals). Mrs Thatcher was widely criticised for making new divisions in British society

1985   Mikhail Gorbachev became First Secretary of the USSR

Communist Party. Gorbachev concentrated on foreign policy, with enormous success; he was a conciliator. Gorbachev conceded all Soviet influence over Eastern European countries, and dissolved the 'Warsaw Pact' which determined a common defence policy for Russian satellite states. Gorbachev's concentration on foreign policy led to difficulties at home in Russia, where he was replaced by Boris Yeltsin, an even more liberal reformer, in 1991

1989   Blind devotion to Communism in Eastern Europe broke down, with Gorbachev's policies of 'perestroika' and 'glasnost'. Communist regimes in the region all broke down with the new openness. This led to the independence of Latvia, Lithuania, and Estonia, the reunification of Germany, but the ethnic division of Yugoslavia and Czechoslovakia. Ethnic wars in the former Yugoslavia – particularly in Bosnia – were the major problem in Europe in the early 1990s

1993   With the end of the cold war, with its threat of nuclear warfare between the USA and the USSR, a series of arms limitation talks was concluded. StART 2 (Strategic Arms Reduction Talks 2) marked an agreement to cut dangerous weapons of war, bilaterally, by about 70 per cent

1994   Nearly twenty-five years of terrorist activity by the Irish Republican Army (which wishes to see Ulster reintegrated into a Catholic Ireland) was halted, with the agreement of a ceasefire. The agreement broke down in early 1996

British and Irish winners of the Nobel Prize for Literature

1907 Rudyard Kipling

1923 W.B. Yeats

1925 George Bernard Shaw

1932 John Galsworthy

1948 T.S. Eliot

1953 Winston Churchill

1969 Samuel Beckett

1983 William Golding

1995 Seamus Heaney

Acknowledgements

W.H. AUDEN, *Their Lonely Betters* from *Collected Poems*; *Spain* and *1st September 1939* from *The English Auden*, edited by Edward Mandelson: copyright Faber & Faber Ltd.

Samuel BECKETT, *Malone Dies, The Unnamable, Imagination Dead Imagine, Waiting for Godot*: US Rights 1996 by Grove/Atlantic Inc.

Alan BENNETT, *A Chip in the Sugar* from *Talking Heads*: reproduced with permission of BBC Worldwide Ltd.

Eavan BOLAND, *Beautiful Speech* from *Collected Poems*: copyright Carcanet Press Ltd.

Edward BOND, *Bingo*: copyright Reed Books, US rights copyright 1974 Edward Bond. All rights whatsoever in this play are strictly reserved and application for performance etc. must be made before rehearsal to Casarotto Ramsay Ltd, National House, 60–66 Wardour Street, London W1V 4ND. No performance may be given unless a licence has been obtained.

Howard BRENTON, *The Romans in Britain*: copyright Reed Books, US rights copyright 1980, 1981 Howard Brenton. All rights whatsoever in this play are strictly reserved and application for performance etc. must be made before rehearsal to Casarotto Ramsay Ltd, National House, 60–66 Wardour Street, London W1V 4ND. No performance may be given unless a licence has been obtained.

Anita BROOKNER, *Lewis Percy*, reproduced with permission of A.M. Heath: copyright © Anita Brookner.

Basil BUNTING, *Briggflatts* from *The Complete Poems of Basil Bunting*: copyright 1994 Oxford University Press.

Angela CARTER, *Wise Children*: copyright © Angela Carter 1991. First published by Chatto & Windus in the UK, and Farrar, Straus & Giroux in the

USA. This extract reproduced by permission of the Estate of Angela Carter, c/o Rogers, Colerige & White Ltd, 20 Powis Mews, London W11 1JN.

Bruce CHATWIN, *The Songlines*: copyright Aitken & Stone Ltd.

Noël COWARD, *Private Lives*: copyright © 1930 by Noël Coward, by permission of Michael Imison Playwrights Ltd, 28 Almeida Street, London N1 1TD.

W.H. DAVIES, *Leisure*: copyright Reed Books.

Carol Ann DUFFY, *Valentine* from *Mean Time*: copyright 1993 Anvil Press Poetry.

T.S. ELIOT, *The Metaphysical Poets* from *Selected Essays*: Faber & Faber Ltd; *The Waste Land, The Love Song of J. Alfred Prufrock, Marina, Four Quartets* from *Collected Poems 1909–1962*: Faber & Faber Ltd; *Murder in the Cathedral, The Cocktail Party*: Faber & Faber Ltd. US rights: excerpts from *The Waste Land* in *Collected Poems 1909–1962* by T.S. Eliot, copyright 1936 by Harcourt Brace & Co, copyright 1964, 1963 by T.S. Eliot, reprinted by permission of the publisher.

William GOLDING, *Lord of the Flies, The Double Tongue*: copyright Faber & Faber Ltd.

Thom GUNN, *In Time of Plague* from *The Man with Night Sweats*: copyright Faber & Faber Ltd.

Thomas HARDY, *After a Journey, During Wind and Rain, The Darkling Thrush* from *The Complete Poems*: copyright Papermac.

Seamus HEANEY, *Digging* from *Death of a Naturalist*; *North* from *North*: copyright Faber & Faber Ltd.

Geoffrey HILL, *Mercian Hymns* from *Collected Poems*: UK and Commonwealth rights excluding Canada, Penguin Books, 1985, copyright Geoffrey Hill 1971, 1985.

A.E. HOUSMAN, *A Shropshire Lad*: by courtesy of The Society of Authors as the literary representative of the Estate of A.E. Housman and in the US Henry Holt & Co, Inc.

Ted HUGHES, *Hawk Roosting* from *Lupercal*: copyright Faber & Faber Ltd.

Elizabeth JENNINGS, *Justice* from *Collected Poems*: copyright David Higham Associates.

Philip LARKIN, the quotation from *Poetry of Departures* is reprinted from *The*

Less Deceived by permission of The Marvell Press, England and Australia; *Annus Mirabilis* from *High Windows*, copyright Faber & Faber Ltd.

D.H. LAWRENCE, *A Collier's Friday Night* from *The Complete Plays of D.H. Lawrence*: courtesy of Laurence Pollinger Ltd and the Estate of Frieda Lawrence Ravagli.

Hugh MACDIARMID, *A Drunk Man Looks at the Thistle* from *Complete Poems*: copyright Carcanet Press Ltd.

Louis MACNEICE, *Autumn Journal, Ecologue for Christmas* from *Collected Poems*: copyright Faber & Faber Ltd. World rights courtesy David Higham Associates.

Edwin MORGAN, *The Welcome* from *Collected Poems*: copyright Carcanet Press Ltd.

Andrew MOTION, *Close* from *Love in a Life*: reprinted by permission of the Peters Fraser & Dunlop Group Ltd.

Edwin MUIR, *The Horses* from *Collected Poems*: copyright Faber & Faber Ltd.

Sean O'CASEY, *Juno and the Paycock*: copyright Macmillan General Books.

Joe ORTON, *Loot*: copyright Reed Books. US rights Grove/Atlantic Inc.

George ORWELL, *Keep the Aspidistra Flying*: copyright © The estate of the late Sonia Brownell Orwell and Martin Secker & Warburg Ltd. US rights: copyright 1956 by the Estate of Sonia B. Orwell, reprinted by permission of Harcourt Brace & Co; *Nineteen Eighty-four*: copyright 1949 by Harcourt Brace & Co and renewed 1977 by Sonia Brownell Orwell, reprinted by permission of the publisher.

John OSBORNE, *Look Back in Anger*: copyright Faber & Faber Ltd. US rights Helen Osborne.

Harold PINTER, *The Birthday Party* from *Plays: One*; *Silence* from *Plays: Three*: copyright Faber & Faber Ltd. US rights Grove/Atlantic Inc.

Sylvia PLATH, *Metaphor* from *Collected Poems*: copyright Faber & Faber Ltd.

Henry REED, *Naming of Parts* from *Collected Poems*, edited by Jon Stallworthy: copyright 1991 Oxford University Press.

Salman RUSHDIE, *Midnight's Children*: copyright Aitken & Stone Ltd.

Siegfried SASSOON, *The General*: by permission of George Sassoon.

Peter SHAFFER, *Equus* from *Three Plays*: UK and Commonwealth rights excluding Canada, Penguin Books, 1976. Copyright Peter Shaffer 1973, 1976.

George Bernard SHAW, The Preface to *Mrs Warren's Profession, Candida, Heartbreak House*: by courtesy of The Society of Authors on behalf of the Bernard Shaw Estate.

Stevie SMITH, *Not Waving but Drowning* from *Collected Poems*: copyright Andre Deutsch.

William SOUTAR, *The Makar* from *Poems of William Soutar (A New Selection)*, 1988, Scottish Academic Press: copyright the Trustees of the National Library of Scotland.

Stephen SPENDER, *The Pylons* from *Collected Poems 1928–1985*: copyright Faber & Faber Ltd.

Tom STOPPARD, *Rosencrantz and Guildenstern are Dead*: copyright Faber & Faber Ltd. US rights copyright 1996 Grove/Atlantic Inc.

Dylan THOMAS, *Fern Hill, Do Not Go Gentle Into That Good Night* from *The Poems*: copyright David Higham Associates Ltd. US rights, *Fern Hill* from *The Poems of Dylan Thomas*: copyright 1952 by Dylan Thomas, reprinted by permission of New Directions Publishing Corp; *Do Not Go Gentle Into That Good Night* from *The Poems of Dylan Thomas*: copyright 1945 by The Trustees for the Copyrights of Dylan Thomas, reprinted by permission of New Directions Publishing Corp.

R.S. THOMAS, *Lore* from *Collected Poems 1945–1990*: copyright J.M. Dent.

Evelyn WAUGH, *Brideshead Revisited, Decline and Fall*: copyright the Peters Fraser & Dunlop Group Ltd.

Irvine WELSH, *Trainspotting*: copyright Minerva.

Arnold WESKER, *Chicken Soup with Barley*: copyright Faber & Faber Ltd.

Virginia WOOLF, *Mrs Dalloway, Orlando, To the Lighthouse*: copyright Chatto & Windus. US rights, *Orlando*: copyright 1928 by Virginia Woolf and renewed 1955 by Leonard Woolf, reprinted by permission of Harcourt Brace & Co; *Mrs Dalloway*: copyright 1925 by Harcourt Brace & Co and renewed 1953 by Leonard Woolf, reprinted by permission of the publisher.

Routledge has made every effort to trace copyright holders and to obtain permission to publish extracts. Any omissions brought to our attention will be remedied in future editions.

Index

Page numbers in **bold** indicate the main discussion.

Ackroyd, Peter (1949–) 531, 532
Addison, Joseph (1672–1719)
  159–60, 187, 189
Aelfric (c.955–1010) 86
Aesop (6th century BC) 45, 175
Agard, John (1949–) 488
Ainsworth, Harrison (1805–82) 273,
  279–80
Alain-Fournier (Henri) (1886–1914)
  369
Alcuin (also known as Ealhwine)
  (735–804) 9
Alfred (the Great), King of Wessex
  (848–99) 15, 46, 52
Amis, Kingsley (1922–95) 473, 485,
  491, 505–6
Amis, Martin (1949–) 505–7, 530
Ancrene Rewle (also known as *Ancrene
  Wisse*) 9, 28
Aneurin (7th century?) 381
Anglo-Saxon Chronicle, The 9, 15
Anselm, Saint (1033–1109) 9
Arden of Faversham 122-3, 141
Ariosto, Ludovico (1474–1535) 66
Armitage, Simon (1963–) 352, 488
Arnold, Matthew (1822–88) 193,
  238, 296, 305, 307, 320, **329–31,**
  456-7
Arthur, King (died 537) 6, 323, 381,
  464–5

Arthurian literature 17, 30, 49–50,
  66, 135, 323–4, 326, 333, 381; *see
  also Sir Gawain and the Green Knight*
Auden, W(ystan) H(ugh) (1907–73)
  320, 349, 352, **374–9**, 388-9, 391-2,
  400, 441, 469, 470, 472, 473, 475,
  481, 502
Austen, Jane (1775–1817) 209,
  212–13, 253, **255–60**, 265, 267,
  287, 290, 297, 318, 407, 440, 514,
  515, 523
Authorised Version of the Bible 61,
  85–9, 131–2, 139; *see also* Bible, the
Ayckbourn, Alan (1939–) 388, 462

Bacon, Francis (1561–1626) 53, 61,
  79–80
Bage, Robert (1729–1801) 253–4,
  255, 258
Bagehot, Walter (1826–77) 279
Baillie, Joanna (1762–1851) 201
Bainbridge, Beryl (1934–) 491,
  516, 520
Bakhtin, Mikhail (1895–1975) 491
Ballantyne, R(obert) M(ichael)
  (1825–94) 305, 509
Ballard, J(ames) G(raham)
  (1930–) 526
Balzac, Honoré de (1799–1850) 292
Banks, Iain (1953–) 538

Barbour, John (*c.*1320–95) 44
Barker, Pat (1943–   ) 531
Barnes, Julian (1946–   ) 525, 530–1
Barnes, William (1801–86) 296, 314,
    315, 338, 354–5
Barrett, Elizabeth *see* Browning,
    Elizabeth Barrett
Barrie, James M(atthew)
    (1860–1937) 394
Battle of Maldon, The 14
Baudelaire, Charles (1821–67) 335,
    369
Beaumont, Francis (1584–1616)
    117–18, 125
Beckett, Samuel (1906–89) 339, 391,
    437, 449, 450, 451, 452–3, **456–8**,
    459, 461, 463, 468, 481, 502, 520,
    536, 542
Beckford, William (1759–1844) 211,
    265, 303
Bede, the Venerable (673–735) 9, 46
Behn, Aphra (1640–69) 100, 142,
    167–8, 170, 175, 186, 289
Bennett, Alan (1934–   ) 468
Bennett, Arnold (1867–1931) 350,
    393, 395–6, 399, 420, 442
Bentham, Jeremy (1748–1832) 276
Beowulf 10, 12–15, 27, 35, 42, 57, 68,
    396, 427, 449
Bergson, Henri (1859–1941) 369
Betjeman, John (1906–84) 352, 473,
    476
Bhagavad Gita 3
Bible, the 3, 9, 26, 46–7, 52, 59, 61,
    80, 81, **85–9**, 104, 131–2, 139, 328,
    369, 370
Blair, Robert (1699–1746) 196
Blake, William (1757–1827) 135,
    201, 204, **224–6**, 248, 274, 332,
    434, 532, 534
Bleasdale, Alan (1946–   ) 468, 469
Bloomsbury Group 400, 419
Boccaccio, Giovanni (1313–75) 33

Boethius (Anicius Manlius
    Severinus) (died 525) 33
Boileau, Nicholas (1636–1711) 181,
    208
Boland, Eavan (1944–   ) 482–3
Bond, Edward (1934–   ) 463–4
Book of Common Prayer 131–2, 139
Borrow, George (1803–81) 374
Boswell, James (1740–95) 185, 189
Bowen, Elizabeth (1899–1973) 437,
    517
Boyd, William (1952–   ) 525, 530
Bradbury, Malcolm (1932–   ) 513–14,
    525
Braddon, Mary Elizabeth
    (1837–1915) 295, 296
Braine, John (1922–86) 505
Brenton, Howard (1942–   ) 464–5
Bridges, Robert (1844–1930) 336,
    373–4
Brome, Richard (*c.*1590–1652/3)
    126
Brontë, Anne (1820–49) 210, 266,
    289, 291, 435
Brontë, Charlotte (1816–55) 210,
    266, 289–90, 291, 327, 435, 516
Brontë, Emily (1818–48) 210, 244,
    266, 289, 290–1, 435
Brooke, Rupert (1887–1915) 357,
    359, 360, 361
Brookner, Anita (1928–   ) 435,
    515–16
Brown, George Douglas *see* Douglas
    Brown, George
Brown, George Mackay *see* Mackay
    Brown, George
Browne, Thomas (1605–82) 61, 85,
    134
Browning, Elizabeth Barrett
    (1806–61) 326–7
Browning, Robert (1812–89) 107,
    202, 241, 320, **324–6**, 327, 328,
    368, 370

Buchan, John (1875–1940) 398–9, 493, 538

Bulwer-Lytton, Edward (1803–73) 273

Bunting, Basil (1900–85) 486–7

Bunyan, John (1628–88) 132, 138–9, 142; see also *The Pilgrim's Progress* 305

Burgess, Anthony (John Wilson) (1917–93) 508, 525, 530

Burke, Edmund (1729–97) 208–9, 218

Burney, Frances (also known as Fanny Burney) (1752–1840) 201, 255, 258

Burns, Robert (1759–96) 189, 191, **205–7**, 248, 296, 338, 379, 533

Burton, Robert (1577–1640) 85, 134

Butler, Samuel (1613–80) 155–6, 181

Butler, Samuel (1835–1902) 298

B.V. *see* James Thomson (1834–82)

Byatt, A(ntonia) S(usan) (1936–   ) 449, 510, 517–18, 524

Byron, George Gordon, Lord (1788–1824) 207–8, 211, 220, 222, 240, **243–8,** 251, 252, 253, 260, 264, 266, 272, 284

Caedmon (late 7th century?) 7, 9, 15, 46, 381

Cameron, Norman (1905–53) 358

Camus, Albert (1913–60) 142

Carew, Thomas (*c.*1594–1640) 109, 112

Carleton, William (1794–1869) 286, 437

Carlyle, Thomas (1795–1881) 280–1, 282, 283, 293, 331, 479

Carr, J(ames) L(loyd) (1912–94) 514, 522

Carroll, Lewis (Charles Lutwidge Dodgson) (1832–98) 303, 305

Carter, Angela (1940–92) 266, 491, 540–2

Castiglione, Baldassarre (1478–1529) 81

Castle of Perseverance, The 48

Caxton, William (*c.*1422–91) 28, 42, 49, 57, 483

censorship 150, 177, 184, 192, 194, 299, 340, 435, 518

Centlivre, Susannah (1669–1723) 148–9, 201

Cervantes, Miguel de (1547–1616) 181–2

Chatterton, Thomas (1752–70) 236, 288, 532

Chatwin, Bruce (1940–89) 539–40

Chaucer, Geoffrey (*c.*1343–1400) 20, 23–5, 27, **32–9,** 40, 41, 42, 43, 44, 45, 47, 66, 67, 68, 70, 95, 191, 259, 297, 467, 475

Chekhov, Anton (1860–1904) 441, 467

Chesterfield, Philip Stanhope, 4th Earl of (1694–1773) 164

Childers, Erskine (1870–1922) 399

Christie, Agatha (1890–1976) 399, 518

Christine de Pisan (*c.*1364–1430) 28, 29

Churchill, Caryl (1938–   ) 466–7

Churchill, Winston (1879–1965) 447

Cicero Marcus Tullius (106–43 BC) 52

Clare, John (1793–1864) 207, 208, 248–9, 252

Cleanness 21

Cleland, John (1709–89) 191–2

Clough, Arthur Hugh (1819–61) 328–9, 332

Cobbett, William (1763–1835) 223–4, 260

Cockburn, Alison (*c.*1712–94) 201

Coleridge, Samuel Taylor (1772–1834) 83, 176, 203, 217,

220, 228, **228–32**, 233, 235, 237,
239, 247, 249, 251
Collier, Jeremy (1650–1726) 146,
149, 150
Collins, Wilkie (1824–89) 266,
303–4, 399
Collins, William (1721–59) 203–4,
222
Compton-Burnett, Ivy (1884–1969)
398, 443, 499–500
Comyns, Barbara (1909–94) 516
Condell, Henry (died 1627) 95
Congreve, William (1670–1729)
145–6, 189
Conrad, Joseph (Jozef Teodor
Konrad Korzeniowski)
(1857–1924) 315, 329, 392, 393,
397, 399, **406–9**, 411, 525, 529
Cope, Wendy (1945–   ) 485
Coverdale, Miles (1488–1568) 86–8
Coward, Noël (1899–1973) 349, 388,
389, 451, 460
Cowley, Abraham (1618–67) 184
Cowper, William (1731–1800)
198–9, 222
Crabbe, George (1754–1832)
198–200, 207, 537
Craik, Mrs (Dinah Maria Mulock)
(1826–87) 294–5
Crashaw, Richard (c. 1612–49)
110–11
Crockett, S(idney) R. (1860–1914)
394
Cynewulf (8th or 9th century)
11–12, 15

Dante Alighieri (1265–1321) 33,
369, 370
Darwin, Charles (1809–82) 58, 173,
278–9, 281, 327, 331, 347, 349,
433, 449, 540
D'Avenant, William (1606–68) 139
Davidson, John (1857–1909) 332–3

Davie, Donald (1922–95) 473, 474
Davies, W(illiam) H(enry)
(1871–1940) 374
Davitt, Michael (1950–   ) 483
Day Lewis, C(ecil) (1904–72)
376–7, 441
de Bernières, Louis (1954–   ) 531–2
Defoe, Daniel (1660–1731) 29, 161,
166, 168, **169–72**, 174, 178, 179,
186, 189, 190, 211, 418; *see also*
Robinson Crusoe 305, 509
Dekker, Thomas (c. 1570–1632) 81,
117, 124, 508
Deor's Lament 7–8, 15, 263
De Quincey, Thomas
(1785–1859) 249–50
detective fiction 303–4, 399, 462,
490, 518–19
Dexter, Colin (1930–   ) 519
Dickens, Charles (1812–70) 171,
176, 189, 210, 266, **273–9**, 280,
284–5, 286, 287, 289, 290, 292,
295, 296, 297, 298, 301, 303, 318,
319, 321, 329, 330, 338, 348, 396,
397, 404–6, 500, 503, 505, 506, 532
Disraeli, Benjamin (1804–81) 218,
273, 278, 283–4, 297, 301, 348
Donne, John (1572–1631) 61, 81–2,
83, **105–8**, 109, 112, 133, 191, 325,
337
Dostoevsky, Fyodor (1821–81) 292
Douglas, Keith (1920–44) 470
Douglas Brown, George
(1869–1902) 395
Dowson, Ernest (1867–1900) 335–6
Doyle, Arthur Conan (1859–1930)
304, 399
Doyle, Roddy (1958–   ) 539
Drabble, Margaret (1939–   ) 521
Dream of the Rood, The 9–11
Dryden, John (1631–1700) 113, 140,
152–6, 156, 157, 158, 168, 173,
181, 182, 233, 245, 246

Duffy, Carol Anne (1955–) 485
Dunbar, William (*c.*1456–1513)
  44–5, 204, 379, 399, 532–3
Dunn, Douglas (1942–) 480
Durcan, Paul (1944–) 482

Edgeworth, Maria (1768–1849)
  255–6, 258, 263, 267, 285, 286,
  296, 339, 437
Eliot, George (Mary Ann Evans)
  (1819–90) 180, 281, 285, 286, 287,
  289, **291–4**, 296, 297–8, 299, 302,
  304, 318, 327, 329, 407, 412
Eliot, T(homas) S(tearns)
  (1888–1965) 107, 184, 233, 315,
  325, 332, 337, 349, 350, 351, 352,
  356, 357, 364, **366–73**, 376, 388,
  390–1, 408, 411, 422, 427, 431,
  433, 440, 451–2, 456, 469–70, 471,
  473, 487, 489, 500, 532
Elliot, Jane (1727–1805) 201
Elliott, Ebenezer (1781–1849) 301
Elyot, Thomas (*c.*1490–1546) 81
Encyclopaedia Britannica 162
Engels, Friedrich (1820–95) 282, 301
Enright, D(ennis) J(oseph) (1920–)
  473–4, 512
Erasmus, Desiderius (*c.*1467–1536)
  58–9, 76, 86
Esslin, Martin (1918–) 456
Etherege, George (1634–91) 142–3
Evelyn, John (1620–1706) 163–4,
  165
Everyman 47–8, 138

Falkner, John Meade (1858–1932)
  318
Fanthorpe, U(rsula) A. (1929–) 485
Farquhar, George (*c.*1677–1707)
  145, 147–8, 437, 467
Farrell, J(ames) G(ordon) (1935–79)
  526
Fates of the Apostles, The see Cynewulf

Faulks, Sebastian (1953–) 531
Fergusson, Robert (1750–74) 189,
  204–5, 296, 338, 533
Ferrier, Susan (1782–1854) 267
Feuerbach, Ludwig (1804–72) 281
Fielding, Henry (1707–54) 150, 154,
  166, 175, 176, **177–9**, 180, 186,
  187, 190, 191, 192, 211–12, 285,
  393, 440
Fielding, Sarah (1710–68) 179–80
Finch, Anne, Countess of
  Winchelsea (1661–1720) 200
Firbank, Ronald (1886–1926) 398
Fitzgerald, Edward (1809–83) 303,
  328
Flaubert, Gustave (1821–90) 292,
  530
Flecknoe, Richard (died *c.*1678) 153
Fleming, Ian (1908–64) 399
Fletcher, John (1579–1625) 117
Ford, Ford Madox (originally known
  as Ford Madox Hueffer)
  (1873–1939) 315–16, 409–11
Ford, John (1586–*c.*1640) 117,
  121–2, 123
Forster, E(dward) M(organ)
  (1879–1970) 315, 392, **401–3**,
  404–5, 409, 411, 414, 493, 499,
  526
Fowles, John (1926–) 285, 511
France, Marie de (12th century) 28
Frayn, Michael (1933–) 512
Frazer, James (1854–1941) 350, 367
Freud, Sigmund (1856–1939) 350,
  380, 393, 435
Friel, Brian (1929–) 429, 467
Fry, Christopher (1907–) 390, 451

Galloway, Janice (1956–) 534–5
Galsworthy, John (1867–1933) 350,
  384, 393, 396, 399, 420
Galt, John (1779–1839) 267–8, 339,
  394

Gammer Gurton's Needle 50, 70

Gaskell, (Mrs) Elizabeth (1810–65) 280, 282, 287, 289, 296, 297, 299, 327; *see also Mary Barton* 301

Gautier, Theophile (1811–72) 308

Gawain *see Sir Gawain and the Green Knight*

Gay, John (1685–1732) 149–50, 170

Geoffrey of Monmouth (died 1155) 17, 164

Gerhardie, William (1895–1977) 441

Gibbon, Edward (1737–94) 164–5, 282

Gibbon, Lewis Grassic (James Leslie Mitchell) (1901–35) 339, 433, 533

Gilbert, W(illiam) S(chwenck) (1836–1911) 308

Gilgamesh, The Epic of 3

Gissing, George (1857–1903) 298–9, 315, 393

Gododin 381

Godwin, Mary *see* Shelley, Mary

Godwin, William (1756–1836) 218–19, 240, 253, 255, 258, 265

Goethe, Johann Wolfgang von (1749–1832) 192–3, 264, 280

Golding, William (1911–93) 391, 509–10, 511

Goldsmith, Oliver (*c.*1730–74) 180, 186, 189, 194–5, 198–9, 207, 437

Gothic literature 84, 197, 208–11, 252, 257, 265–6, 279, 303, 304, 540

Gower, John (*c.*1330–1408) 20, 41–2, 45

Granville-Barker, Harley (1877–1946) 384

Graves, Robert (1895–1985) 352, 357, 358, 362, 432

Gray, Alasdair (1934–) 534, 535

Gray, Thomas (1716–71) 184, 193, 196–7, 198, 202, 209, 222, 233–4

Green, Henry (Henry Yorke) (1905–73) 443, 499–501

Greene, Graham (1904–91) 407, **438–9**, 443, 462, 489, **492–3**

Greene, Robert (1558–92) 69, 83–4

Greenwood, Walter (1903–74) 301, 442

Gregory, Lady Augusta (1852–1932) 384

Gunn, Thom (1929–) 475–6

Gurney, Ivor (1890–1937) 360

Haggard, H(enry) Rider (1856–1925) 280, 318

Hakluyt, Richard (1552–1616) 82–3, 90, 211

Hall, Joseph (1574–1656) 39–40

Hall, Radclyffe (1883–1943) 435

Hardy, Thomas (1840–1928) 224, 288, 289, 295, 296, 299, **310–15**, 318, 324, 329, 338, 341, 349, **352–6**, 360, 364, 393, 395, 409, 417, 418, 440, 474, 475, 520

Hare, David (1947–) 464, 465, 467

Harkness, Margaret *see* Law, John

Harrison, Tony (1937–) 352, 483–5, 488

Hartley, L(eslie) P(oles) (1895–1972) 502

Hay, John Macdougall (1881–1919) 395

Haywood, Eliza (*c.*1693–1756) 179–80, 255

Hazlitt, William (1778–1830) 249, 250, 259

Heaney, Seamus (1939–) 430, 450, 477–8, 479, **480–2**, 485

Heminge, John (1556–1630) 95

Henri, Adrian (1932–) 476

Henryson, Robert (*c.*1424–1506) 44–5, 204–5, 297, 379, 532

Herbert, George (1593–1633) 105–6, 107–8, 336–7

Herrick, Robert (1591–1674) 112

Heywood, John (*c.*1497–1580) 69–70
Heywood, Thomas (*c.*1574–1641)
117, 122
Hill, Geoffrey (1932–   ) 478–9, 481
Hill, Reginald (1936–   ) 519
Hill, Susan (1942–   ) 522
Hobbes, Thomas (1588–1679)
130–1, 169
Hoccleve, Thomas (*c.*1369–1426)
42–3
Hogg, James (1770–1835) 265, 268,
307, 395
Homer (8th century BC) 3, 17, 18, 66,
157, 427–8
Hood, Thomas (1835–74) 331–2
Hooker, Richard (*c.*1554–1600) 61,
80–1, 133
Hope, Anthony (Anthony Hope
Hawkins) (1863–1933) 280,
318–19
Hopkins, Gerard Manley (1844–89)
11, 323, 324, 325, **336–8**, 352, 355,
374, 481
Horace (Quintus Horatius Flaccus)
(65–8 BC) 152, 159
Housman, A(lfred) E(dward)
(1859–1936) 356–7, 362
Howard, Henry, Earl of Surrey *see*
Surrey
Howell, Constance (*c.*1860–1910)
302
Hrotsvitha (10th century) 28
Hughes, Ted (1930–   ) 358, 476–7,
479, 480–1
Hughes, Thomas (1822–96) 305
Hume, David (1711–76) 162, 267
Hunt, Leigh (1784–1859) 250
Hutchinson, Pearse (1927–   ) 482,
483
Huxley, Aldous (1894–1963) 298,
433–4, 502, 509
Huxley, T(homas) H(enry)
(1825–95) 433

Ibsen, Henrik (1828–1906) 341, 382,
463
Inchbald, Elizabeth (1753–1821)
255, 258
Innes, Michael *see* Stewart, J.I.M.
Isherwood, Christopher (1904–86)
380, 388–9, 441, 469, 502–3
Ishiguro, Kazuo (1954–   ) 525, 526

Jakobson, Roman (1896–1982) 404
James I, King of Scotland
(1394–1437) 33, 44
James, Henry (1843–1916) 289, 294,
315, **316–18**, 393, 399, 406, 407,
410, 431
James, P(hyllis) D(orothy) (1920–   )
518–19
Jennings, Elizabeth (1926–   ) 390,
473
Jerome, Jerome K(lapka)
(1859–1927) 397
Johnson, Samuel (1709–84) 105, 161,
164, 176, **183–5,** 186, 189, 205
Jones, Henry Arthur (1851–1929)
343
Jones, Inigo (1573–1652) 109,
115–16
Jonson, Ben (*c.*1572–1637) 61, 84,
104, 112, **113–16**, 117, 118, 120,
126, 142, 191, 194, 463, 508
Joseph, Jenny (1932–   ) 458
Joyce, James (1882–1941) 11, 286,
315, 339, 349, 350, 358, 393, 396,
414, 419, **423–9**, 430–1, 435, 437,
438, 469, 489, 502, 535, 538
Julian of Norwich (*c.*1342–1416) 28,
29
Jung, Carl (1875–1961) 393, 435
Juvenal (Decimus Junius Juvenalis)
(60–*c.*136) 39, 152

Kafka, Franz (1883–1924) 380, 441,
536

Keats, John (1795–1821) 198, **234–9**,
    249, 252, 272, 307, 325, 353, 360,
    484, 486
Kelman, James (1946–) 339, 491,
    534, 535–6
Kempe, Margery (*c.*1373–1439)
    29–30
Kennedy, A(lison) L. (1965–) 491,
    534–5
Kennelly, Brendan (1936–) 482
Kerouac, Jack (1922–69) 374
Keyes, Sidney (1922–43) 470
Khayyam, Omar (12th century) *see*
    Fitzgerald, Edward
King Horn 26
King James Bible *see* Authorised
    Version of the Bible
Kingsley, Charles (1819–75) 283,
    301, 305
Kinsella, Thomas (1929–) 482
Kipling, Rudyard (1865–1936) 315,
    322, 329, 392, 394, 401, 406, 503,
    526
Koran, the 3
Kyd, Thomas (1558–94) 70–1, 80, 89

Laforgue, Jules (1860–87) 351, 369
Lamb, Charles (1775–1834) 249, 250
Langland, William (*c.*1330–86) 21,
    27, 39–41, 47
Larkin, Philip (1922–85) 352, 473,
    474–5, 479, 480–1, 486, 488
Law, John (Margaret Harkness)
    (1854–1920) 302, 417
Lawrence, D(avid) H(erbert)
    (1885–1930) 203, 224, 315, 339,
    349, 357, 358, **386–8**, 393, 400,
    411–18, 419, 435, 436, 451, 476,
    479
Lawrence, T(homas) E(dward)
    (1888–1935) 432–3
Layamon (13th century) 16–17, 19,
    20, 21–3, 30, 33

Leapor, Mary (1722–46) 200
Leavis, F(rank) R(aymond)
    (1895–1978) 292, 407
Le Carré, John (David Cornwell)
    (1931–) 399, 407
Lee, Laurie (1914–) 502, 511
Le Fanu, Sheridan (1814–73) 266,
    304
Lehmann, Rosamund (1901–90)
    435, 436, 522
Lennox, Charlotte (1720–1804)
    180–1, 201
Lessing, Doris (1919–) 435, 522
Lever, Charles (1806–72) 286
Lewis, Alun (1915–44) 381, 470
Lewis, Matthew (1775–1818) 209
Lewis, Wyndham (1882–1957)
    431–2
Lillo, George (1693–1739) 141–2
Lindsay, David (*c.*1486–1555) 48–9
Linton, Eliza Lynn (1822–98) 295–6
Llewellyn, Richard (Richard David
    Vivian Llewellyn Lloyd)
    (1907–83) 381
Locke, John (1632–1704) 187
Lodge, David (1935–) 404–5, 491,
    513–14, 538
Lodge, Thomas (1558–1625) 69
Longley, Michael (1939–) 482
Lord Randal 19–20
Lovelace, Richard (1618–57/8) 112,
    206
Lowth, Robert (1710–87) 183, 224
Luther, Martin (1483–1546) 58, 59,
    299, 454
Lydgate, John (*c.*1370–1449) 42–3
Lyly, John (*c.*1554–1606) 78–9

Mabinogion, The (collected 1838–49)
    379
Macaulay, Thomas Babington
    (1800–59) 279, 282
MacCaig, Norman (1910–96) 380–1

MacDiarmid, Hugh (Christopher Murray Grieve) (1892–1978) 205, 379–80, 430, 533

McEwan, Ian (1948–) 525, 530

McGough, Roger (1937–) 476

McGuckian, Mebdh (1950–) 482

McGuinness, Frank (1948–) 467

Machiavelli, Niccolo (1469–1527) 93

Mackay Brown, George (1921–96) 537–8

Mackenzie, Henry (1745–1831) 189, **192–4**, 204, 205, 274, 321

Maclaren, Ian (John Watson) (1850–1907) 394

Maclean, Sorley (1911–96) 379

MacNeice, Louis (1907–63) 376, 377–8

Macpherson, James *see* Ossian

Mahon, Derek (1941–) 482

Mallarmé, Stephane (1842–98) 351

Malory, Thomas (died 1471) 49–50, 52, 57, 66, 135, 323

Mandeville, John (died *c.*1372) 31–2, 166, 173–4, 211, 303, 539

Mankind 48

Manley, Delarivier (1663–1724) 154, 168–9, 289

Manning, Frederic (1882–1935) 432

Manning, Olivia (1908–80) 513

Mannyng, Robert (*c.*1288–1338) 20

Marie *see* France, Marie de

Marlowe, Christopher (1564–93) 27, 61, 69, 70, **72–5,** 83, 84, 89, 93, 140, 525

Martial (Marcus Valerius Martialis) (40–104) 484

Martineau, Harriet (1802–76) 297

Martyn, Edward (1859–1923) 384

Marvell, Andrew (1621–78) 111, 112, 156, 418

Marx, Karl (1818–83) 282

Masefield, John (1878–1967) 373–4

Massie, Allan (1938–) 538

Massinger, Philip (1583–1640) 117, 125

Maturin, C(harles) R(obert) (1782–1824) 265, 304

Maugham, W(illiam) Somerset (1874–1965) 349, 388, 389, 406, 455, 460, 493

Maxwell, Glyn (1962–) 488

Mayhew, Henry (1812–87) 301

Medwall, Henry (late 15th century) 70

Meredith, George (1828–1909) 288–9, 409

Mew, Charlotte (1869–1928) 358

Middleton, Thomas (1580–1627) 117, 118–20, 124–5, 126, 508

Mill, John Stuart (1806–73) 281, 308, 331

Milton, John (1608–74) 27, 53, 61, 85, 112–13, 131, **133–7**, 156, 185, 203, 233, 235, 323, 325, 332, 335; *see also Paradise Lost* 60, 131, 132

Mo, Timothy (1950–) 526–7

'Modern' and Modernist literature 232, 266, 288, 315, 325, 332, 336, 349–50, 351–2, 365, **400–1**, 404–5, 409, 418, 421–2, 425, 427, 431, 449–50, 471, 473, 475, 490–2, 502, 540

Molière (Jean-Baptiste Poquelin) (1622–73) 142

Montagu, Lady Mary Wortley (1689–1762) 201–2

Montague, C(harles) E(dward) (1867–1928) 432

Montaigne, Michel de (1553–92) 79

Moore, Brian (1921–) 437, 538

Moore, George (1852–1933) 295, 299–300, 393, 409, 436

Moore, Thomas (1779–1852) 211, 303

More, Thomas (*c.*1477–1535) 59, 82, 166, 298

Morgan, Charles (1894–1958) 494–5
Morgan, Edwin (1920–　) 480
Morgan, Lady (Sydney Owenson)
　(1776–1859) 285
Morris, William (1834–96) 298,
　304–5, 308, 335, 479
Morrison, Arthur (1863–1945) 301,
　417
Motion, Andrew (1952–　) 486
Motteux, Peter (1660–1718) 180
Muir, Edwin (1887–1959) 380, 537
Muldoon, Paul (1951–　) 482
Murdoch, Iris (1919–　) 437, 499,
　523–5
Murray, Lindley (1745–1826) 183

Naipaul, V(idiadhar) S(urajprasad)
　(1932–　) 529
Nashe, Thomas (1567–1601) 61, 69,
　84, 118, 166
Newbolt, Henry (1862–1938) 323
Newman, John Henry (1801–90)
　283
Nichols, Grace (1950–　) 488
Norton, Thomas (1532–84) 70

O'Brien, Edna (1932–　) 520, 521
O'Brien, Flann (Brian O'Nolan)
　(1911–66) 339, 438, 539
O'Casey, Sean (1880–1964) 339, 349,
　385–6, 451, 539
O'Faolain, Sean (1900–91) 437–8,
　503
Okri, Ben (1959–　) 488
Oliphant, (Mrs) Margaret (1828–97)
　295, 296
Orczy, Baroness (Mrs Montague
　Barstow) (1865–1947) 399
Orton, Joe (1933–67) 451, 460–1
Orwell, George (Eric Blair)
　(1903–50) 433, 443, **495–9**, 509
Osborne, John (1929–94) 390, 451,
　454–5, 462, 504

Ossian (James Macpherson)
　(1736–96) 189, 192–4, 205, 267,
　379
O'Sullivan, Seamus (James Sullivan
　Starkey) (1879–1958) 363
Otway, Thomas (1652–85) 140–1
Outremeuse, Jean d' (14th century)
　31
Overton, John W. (c.1833–90) 301
Ovid (Publius Ovidius Naso)
　(43BC–AD18) 33
Owen, Wilfred (1895–1918) 237,
　359, **360–2**, 366, 432, 449, 456, 470
Owl and the Nightingale, The 25

Paine, Tom (1737–1809) 218
Pater, Walter (1839–94) 307–8
Patience 21, 26, 35
Patten, Brian (1946–　) 476
Paulin, Tom (1949–　) 482
Peacock, Thomas Love (1785–1866)
　210, 250–2, 259, 265, 288
Pearl 21, 27
Peele, George (1556–96) 69
Pepys, Samuel (1633–1703) 163–4,
　165
Percy, Thomas (1729–1811) 193, 236
Petrarch (Francesco Petrarca)
　(1304–74) 33, 34, 60, 65
Petronius (Gaius Petronius Arbiter)
　(died AD65) 191
Phillips, Caryl (1958–　) 529–30
Pinero, Arthur Wing (1855–1934)
　342–3
Pinter, Harold (1930–　) 391, 451,
　452–3, 456, **458–60**, 468, 511
Pisan, Christine de see Christine de
　Pisan
Plath, Sylvia (1932–63) 391–2, 479,
　482
Plautus Titus Maccius (c.254–184BC)
　69, 70, 95
Poe, Edgar Allan (1809–49) 266, 303

Polidori, John (1795–1821) 211
Pope, Alexander (1688–1744) 154,
157–9, 161, 170, 173, 181, 182,
184, 197, 233, 245, 246
Potter, Dennis (1935–93) 468–9
Pound, Ezra (1885–1972) 325,
335–6, 357, 358, 359, 370, 373,
431, 473, 486
Powell, Anthony (1905–   ) 512
Powys, John Cowper (1872–1963)
440
Powys, Llewelyn (1884–1939) 440
Powys, T(heodore) F(rancis)
(1875–1953) 440
Priestley, J(ohn) B(oynton)
(1894–1984) 390, 470, 497, 499
Prior, Matthew (1644–1721) 155–6
Pritchett, V(ictor) S(awdon)
(1900–   ) 503
Proust, Marcel (1871–1922) 418, 512
Purchas, Samuel (*c.*1557–1626) 83
Puttenham, George (*c.*1529–91) 39,
51
Pym, Barbara (1913–80) 282, 515,
520

Rabelais, Francois (*c.*1494–1553) 84,
180, 191
Racine, Jean (1639–99) 142
Radcliffe, Ann (1764–1823) 209,
257, 265
Raine, Craig (1944–   ) 483, 487–8
Raleigh, Walter (*c.*1554–1618) 61, 82,
83, 90, 166
Ramsay, Allan (1686–1758) 204
Rattigan, Terence (1911–77) 453–4,
460
Raven, Simon (1927–   ) 512
Reed, Henry (1914–86) 471
Reeve, Clara (1729–1807) 201,
209–10, 255
Reid, Forrest (1875–1947) 108, 363,
442–3, 502

Reid, Thomas (1710–96) 162
Rendell, Ruth (also known as
Barbara Vine) (1930–   ) 518–19
Rhys, Jean (1894–1979) 516–17
Ricardo, David (1773–1823) 308
Richardson, Dorothy (1873–1957)
414, 435
Richardson, Samuel (1689–1761)
172, **175–7**, 178, 179, 186, 187,
191, 192, 211–12, 393
Rimbaud, Arthur (1854–91) 351
Robertson, Tom (T(homas)
W(illiam)) (1829–71) 340–1, 455
Rochester, John Wilmot, Earl of
(1647–80) 150–2, 173, 191
Roman de la Rose, Le 18
Rosenberg, Isaac (1890–1918) 357,
360, 366, 470
Rossetti, Dante Gabriel (1828–82)
333–4
Rossetti, William Michael
(1829–1919) 333
Rowe, Nicholas (1674–1718) 95
Rowley, William (*c.*1585–1626)
119–20
Rushdie, Salman (1947–   ) 525,
527–9, 534
Ruskin, John (1819–1900) 307–8

Sackville, Thomas (1536–1608) 70
Saki (Hector Hugh Munro)
(1870–1916) 397
Sand, George (Amandine-Aurore
Lucille Dupin) (1804–76) 265
Sapper (Herman Cyril McNeile)
(1888–1937) 399
Sartre, Jean-Paul (1905–80) 456
Sassoon, Siegfried (1886–1967) 357,
360
Sayers, Dorothy L(eigh)
(1893–1957) 399, 518
science fiction 303–4, 396–7, 400,
526, 538

Scott, Paul (1920–78) 526

Scott, Walter (1771–1832) 205, 217, 241, **260–5**, 266, 267, 272–3, 279, 280, 282, 284, 286, 289, 293, 296, 306, 319, 339, 379, 396, 480, 533

Seafarer, The 7–8, 10

Seneca, Lucius Annaeus (*c.*4BC–AD65) 69, 70, 95, 123

Sewell, Anna (1820–78) 305

Shadwell, Thomas (1640–92) 153

Shaffer, Peter (1926–) 465–6

Shakespeare, William (1564–1616) 3, 57, 61, 63–4, 65, 70, 71–2, 76, 80, 83–4, 85, 86, **89–104**, 105, 112, 113, 114, 116, 117, 119, 123, 126, 133, 135, 139–40, 142, 157, 173, 176, 180, 185, 191, 203, 232, 259, 264, 297, 298, 320, 325, 331, 337, 371, 384, 390, 420, 458, 461, 463; *see also Hamlet* 458, 461, 495–6, 524; *King Lear* 140, 337, 458, 463, 481; *Macbeth* 141; *Pericles* 117, 371; *Romeo and Juliet* 122; *The Tempest* 140, 298, 524

Shaw, George Bernard (1856–1950) 315, 341, 343, **382–4**, 411, 437, 451, 463, 464, 525

Shelley, Mary (1797–1851) 210–11, 255, 265–6

Shelley, Percy Bysshe (1792–1822) 135, 211, 219, 220, **239–43**, 250, 251, 252, 253, 255, 260, 265, 272, 281, 325, 334–5, 353

Sheridan, Richard Brinsley (1751–1816) 194–6

Shirley, James (1596–1666) 126

Sidney, Philip (1554–86) 61, 64–5, 101, 112, 199

Sillitoe, Alan (1928–) 504–5

Sinclair, May (1863–1946) 435, 515, 516, 522

Sir Gawain and the Green Knight 21, 27–8, 30–1, 50

Sir Orfeo 28, 30

Sisson, C(harles) H(ubert) (1914–) 479

Skelton, John (*c.*1460–1529) 49, 50–1, 65, 191

Smart, Christopher (1722–71) 109, 204

Smiles, Samuel (1812–1904) 283

Smith, Adam (1723–90) 162–3, 217, 267

Smith, Charlotte (1748–1806) 207–8

Smith, Joan (1953–) 518

Smith, Stevie (1902–71) 485–6

Smollett, Tobias (1721–71) 180, **189–92**, 204, 205, 274, 296

Snow, C(harles) P(ercy) (1905–80) 512

Sorley, Charles Hamilton (1895–1915) 362

Soutar, William (1898–1943) 380

Southey, Robert (1774–1843) 247–8

Spark, Muriel (1918–) 491, 505, 519–20

Spender, Stephen (1909–95) 376–7

Spenser, Edmund (*c.*1552–99) 61, **66–8**, 76–7, 135, 189, 325, 437

Spring 19

Steele, Richard (1672–1729) 159, 189, 194

Stephen, Leslie (1832–1904) 419

Stephens, James (1882–1950) 363

Sterne, Laurence (1713–68) 176, 185, **186–9**, 190, 246, 296, 318, 418

Stevenson, Anne (1933–) 485

Stevenson, Robert Louis (1850–94) 210, 266, 268, **305–7**, 395

Stewart, J(ohn) I(nnes) M(ackintosh) (also known as Michael Innes) (1906–94) 399

Stoker, Bram (1847–1912) 210, 266, 304

Stoppard, Tom (1937–) 461–2

Strauss, David Friedrich (1808–74) 281

stream of consciousness 252, 318, 350, 370, 393, **418–19**, 420, 423–5, 435

Suckling, John (1609–41) 109, 112

Sullivan, Arthur (1842–1900) 308

Summer is i-cumen in 19

Surrey, Henry Howard, Earl of (*c.*1517–47) 65

Surtees, R(obert) S(mith) (1805–64) 397

Swift, Graham (1949–) 531

Swift, Jonathan (1667–1745) 139, 152–3, 168, **172–4**, 181, 182–3, 185, 189, 191, 304–5, 437

Swinburne, Algernon Charles (1837–1909) 110, 334–5

Symons, Arthur (1865–1945) 351

Symons, Julian (1912–95) 519

Synge, J(ohn) M(illington) (1871–1909) 339, 349, 363, 385, 430, 437, 451

Taliesin (6th century?) 381

Tate, Nahum (1652–1715) 140

Tennant, Emma (1938–) 266

Tennyson, Alfred (1809–92) 107, 135, 278, **319–24**, 325, 328, 329, 330, 333, 334, 338, 339, 354–5, 357, 374, 518

Terence (Publius Terentius Afer) (2nd century BC) 69

Thackeray, William Makepeace (1811–63) 284, 287, 397, 511

Thomas, Dylan (1914–53) 237, 358, 381, **471–3**, 476, 487

Thomas, Edward (1878–1917) 362–3, 531

Thomas, Elizabeth (1675–1731) 200–1

Thomas, R(onald) S(tuart) (1913–) 381, 487, 539

Thomson, James (1700–48) 197–8, 207, 209, 238

Thomson, James (also known as B.V.) (1834–82) 332

Thoreau, H(enry) D(avid) (1817–62) 276–7

Tirebuck, W.E. (1854–1900) 301

Tolkien J(ohn) R(onald) R(euel) (1892–1973) 492

Tolstoy, Lev Nikolaevitch (1828–1910) 292

Tomlinson, Charles (1927–) 478–9

Torrington, Jeff (1935–) 339, 535

Tourneur, Cyril (*c.*1575–1626) 119

Traherne, Thomas (1637–74) 109–10

Tremain, Rose (1943–) 518

Tressell, Robert (Robert Noonan) (*c.*1870–1911) 301, 417

Trevor, William (William Trevor Cox) (1928–) 437, 517

Trollope, Anthony (1815–82) **285–8**, 289, 294, 295, 330, 396, 418

Trollope, F(rances) (1780–1863) 294

Tyndale, William (*c.*1495–1536) 86–8

Udall, Nicholas (1504–56) 70

Upward, Edward (1903–) 441

Urquhart, Thomas (1611–60) 180, 191

Vanbrugh, John (1664–1726) 145, 146–7

Vaughan, Henry (1621–95) 108–9, 110, 381

Vaughan, Thomas (1621–66) 109

Verlaine, Paul (1844–96) 351

Verne, Jules (1828–1905) 304

Vico, Giambattista (1668–1744) 428

Vine, Barbara *see* Rendell, Ruth

Virgil (Publius Vergilius Maro) (70–19 BC) 17, 66

Wace (12th century) 17
Wain, John (1925–94) 473, 504
Walpole, Horace (1717–97) 209, 265
Wanderer, The 8–9
Ward, Mrs Humphry (Mary Augusta) (1851–1920) 296
Warner, Rex (1905–86) 441
Waugh, Evelyn (1903–66) 397, 398, 433, **439–40**, 443, **493–4**, 499
Webster, John (c.1578–1632) 61, 117, 120–1, 122
Weldon, Fay (1933–) 522–3, 531
Wells, H(erbert) G(eorge) (1866–1946) 171, 266, 332, 396–7, 399–400, 420, 469, 504
Welsh, Irvine (1969–) 339, 534, 536–7
Wertenbaker, Timberlake (c.1950–) 467
Wesker, Arnold (1932–) 390, 455–6, 462
West, Rebecca (Cecily Isabel Fairfield) (1892–1983) 435–6, 522
Whitman, Walt (1819–92) 109
Wife's Lament, The 17
Wilde, Oscar (1854–1900) 210, 274, 284, 295, 298, 300, 302, 306, 307, 308, **309–10**, 315, 335–6, **341–2**, 343, 384, 393, 437, 451, 460, 532
Williams, Nigel (1948–) 531
Williams, Raymond (1921–88) 381
Wilson, A(ndrew) N. (1950–) 282
Wilson, Angus (1913–91) 503, 513, 517, 521
Wilson, Colin (1931–) 504
Wilson, Thomas (c.1525–81) 77
Winner and Waster 21, 25, 35, 69
Winterson, Jeanette (1959–) 520
Wisdom 48

Wodehouse, P(elham) G(renville) (1881–1975) 397–8
Wollstonecraft, Mary (1759–97) 254–5, 265
Wood, Mrs Henry (Ellen Price) (1814–87) 295
Woolf, Virginia (1882–1941) 168, 292, 293, 327, 349, 350, 393, 411, 414, **419–23**, 425, 434–5, 469, 489
Wordsworth, William (1770–1850) 78, 154, 197, 198, 203, 207, 208, 217, 219, 220, 221–2, 222–3, **226–9**, 230, 231, 232–4, 235, 237, 239, 240, 246, 247, 252, 253, 259, 260, 274, 319, 320, 327, 474, 475, 481
Wortley Montagu, Mary see Montagu, Lady Mary Wortley
Wright, Mehetabel (also known as Hetty Wright) (1677–1750) 201
Wright, Thomas (1810–77) 301
Wulf and Eadwacer 17
Wyatt, Thomas (1503–42) 65–6
Wycherley, William (1641–1715) 145–7
Wycliff, John (c.1330–84) 86, 87
Wynkyn, Jan van (also known as Wynkyn de Worde) (died 1535) 42, 49

Yeats, W(illiam) B(utler) (1865–1939) 300, 318, 349, 351, 363, **364–6**, 372–3, 378, 384, 428–9, 437, 450, 469, 471, 478, 481
Yonge, Charlotte (1823–1901) 305
Yorke, Margaret (1924–) 518–19
Yorkshire Tragedy, A 122
Young, Edward (1683–1765) 196

Zephaniah, Benjamin (1958–) 352, 488–9
Zola, Emile (1840–1902) 299, 341